Consumer Behavior and Managerial Decision Making

Consumer Behavior and Managerial Decision Making

SECOND EDITION

Frank R. Kardes

University of Cincinnati

Upper Saddle River, New Jersey 07458

To Perilou

Acquisitions Editor: Bruce Kaplan
Assistant Editor: Anthony Palmiotto
Media Project Manager: Michele Faranda
Marketing Manager: Annie Todd
Marketing Assistant: Elena Picinic
Managing Editor (Production): John Roberts
Production Editor: Renata Butera
Production Assistant: Keri Jean
Permissions Coordinator: Suzanne Grappi
Associate Director, Manufacturing: Vincent Scelta
Production Manager: Arnold Vila
Manufacturing Buyer: Diane Peirano
Design Manager: Patricia Smythe
Art Director: Kevin Kall
Cover Design: Michael J. Fruhbeis
Cover Illustration/Photo: Michael J. Fruhbeis
Manager, Print Production: Christina Mahon
Composition: Progressive Information Technologies
Full-Service Project Management: Progressive Publishing Alternatives
Printer/Binder: Courier

Library of Congress Cataloging-in-Publication Data

Kardes, Frank R.
  Consumer behavior and managerial decision making / Frank R. Kardes.—2nd ed.
    p. cm.
  Includes bibliographical references and index.
  ISBN 0-13-091602-1
  1. Consumer behavior. 2. Decision making. I. Title.
HF5415.3.K298 2001
658.8'342—dc21

2001 02 1949
CIP

Credits and acknowledgments borrowed from other sources and reproduced, with permission, in this textbook appear on appropriate page within text.

10 9 8 7 6 5 4 3 2 1
ISBN 0-13-091602-1

Brief Contents

Contents

SECTION III   MANAGERIAL DECISION MAKING   265

Preface

When people ask me what I do for a living, I tell them I'm a consumer psychologist and then I brace myself for a wide range of interesting reactions: Some people ask if I'm reading their minds, and others ask if I believe in mind control. When I respond that I don't believe in mind reading, mind control, ESP, or reincarnation, I half expect some people to say, "What's wrong with you? Don't you have any flaky beliefs?" Unfortunately, most people don't realize that consumer behavior can be studied scientifically, and many fail to appreciate how effectively science can be used to debunk myths. Scientific methods can be used to investigate the psychology of advertising, the psychology of consumer judgment, and decision making. Consumers are frequently unable to explain how an ad influenced them or why they made a particular purchase. Fortunately, scientific research can be used to uncover mental processes and influences that affect consumers with or without their knowledge. This is what I find most fascinating about scientific consumer research, and this is what this book is all about.

The scientific perspective is used throughout this book because research has shown that training in science (a) helps students to become critical thinkers (i.e., to not believe everything they read or hear), (b) helps students to improve their creative problem-solving skills, and (c) helps students to develop better decision-making skills (see Chapter 1). Critical thinking and strong problem-solving and decision-making skills are important to anyone who wants to be an effective manager in today's complex and extremely competitive marketplace. Firms need managers with strong critical thinking, problem-solving, and decision-making skills, and this book is designed to help students attain these important skills.

Consumer behavior is the study of people's reponses to products and services and the marketing of products and services. The focus on the consumer is the key contribution of marketing to business practice: other business functions (e.g., finance, accounting, production) ignore the consumer. However, managers who really understand their consumers develop higher quality products and services, promote their products and services more effectively, and devise marketing plans and strategies that foster sustainable competitive advantages for their firm.

This book is organized in three main sections. Section I explains how consumers acquire, remember, and use information about products and services. Section II focuses on persuasion and influence, and explains how to influence consumers more successfully through the effective use of advertising, promotion, and other marketing tools. Section III examines managerial decision making. This section helps students to apply the arsenal of marketing tools and principles available to them. It also explains common decision-making biases and errors that plague managers and offers tools and strategies for avoiding these pitfalls.

◆ NEW TO THE SECOND EDITION

The second edition has been updated with nearly 100 new references to help students keep abreast of the latest developments in scientifically grounded consumer research. This edition also features a new chapter on Online Consumer Behavior. This chapter explains how the Internet has changed the way consumers shop and the way products and services are marketed to consumers. In addition, the entire book has been updated significantly. Section I now opens with inportant new material on the key ways consumers differ from one another in terms of motives for buying and personality traits. These motives and traits are linked to current trends in the marketplace identified by executives from the DuPont Corporation. In addition, new material on really long-term memory has also been added to Section I. Section II opens with a new in-depth discussion of how to persuade consumers who are trying to avoid persuasion. Consumers recognize that advertisements are designed to influence their purchase decisions, and consumers often attempt to avoid, reduce, or correct for unwanted influences on their judgments and decisions. Group influence is also now discussed in much greater detail in Section II. Section III now includes important new material on group decision making. Managers often work together in groups (e.g., committee meetings) when attempting to solve problems faced by their firms. Group settings create the potential for a number of serious decision making biases and errors. Numerous other updates and improvements have been added throughout the second edition.

◆ CHAPTER PEDAGOGY

To help students understand and apply the concepts of consumer behavior to real companies and marketing situations, *Consumer Behavior and Managerial Decision Making* is filled with interesting examples, visuals, and exercises—including use of the Internet. The text not only discusses the principles and scientific research of consumer behavior but also demonstrates how companies and organizations use them every day. Here is a list of the key pedagogy in every chapter:

- **Chapter Outlines.** Chapter outlines list the major text headings to introduce students and instructors to concepts the chapter will cover.

- **Opening Vignettes.** Each chapter begins with a discussion of a real company, product, or situation to bring the subject of the chapter alive. For example, one opening vignette discusses the National Basketball Association's use of its athletes' global appeal to market its "brand" and products to worldwide audiences.

- **Introduction.** Each chapter introduction leads students from the vignette into the main subject of the chapter, serving as a bridge from the vignette's example to chapter contents.

- **Taking Issue Boxes.** The "Taking Issue" boxes use real companies or situations to discuss ethical issues in consumer behavior. Some of the issues explored in the book include the use of credit card logos to encourage consumer spending, new online stock trading, and Coca-Cola's agreement with Boys & Girls Clubs of America to sponsor tournaments and promote Coke products. Every chapter has a "Taking Issue" box to spur students to think about consumer behavior issues that surround them.

- **Making the Decision Boxes.** The "Making the Decision" boxes, which appear once or twice in each chapter, show how companies implement consumer behavior principles in their marketing and advertising campaigns or how consumer decisions affect companies. These boxes profile both solid and questionable company decisions. For example, one box discusses different companies' use of the Internet to enhance product demonstrations and provide additional consumer information, and another discusses Mercedes' decision to build a low-priced, basic car, which fights against its premium image in the marketplace.

- **Advertisements, Web Sites, Photos, and Illustrations.** Advertisements and Web site URLs appear throughout the text to show students how companies appeal to consumers. Many Web sites are included to demonstrate how marketers are using the Internet's global reach to tap new markets. Photographs of products discussed in the text supplement chapter discussions, and colorful graphs and charts summarize and help reinforce major text concepts.

- **Key Concepts and Glossary.** Key concepts are boldfaced in the chapter where they are defined. Boldfacing terms helps students locate and review important consumer behavior concepts. An end-of-book glossary compiles all terms and definitions presented in the text.

- **Chapter Summaries.** The summary at the end of each chapter provides a quick recap of the concepts discussed. Students can check their comprehension of the chapter by reviewing the summary.

- **Key Concepts List.** Following the chapter summary is a list of the key concepts presented in the chapter. A quick review of the list reinforces students' comprehension.

- **Discussion Questions.** Ten questions at the end of each chapter get students to think critically about what they have just read. The questions go beyond rote memory to help students apply the knowledge they have gained.

◆ SUPPLEMENTS

Teaching consumer behavior is an exciting and challenging task. To make the process of assimilating and preparing to teach the course easier, we have prepared a comprehensive collection of learning/teaching support materials. In tandem with the theme of this book, we decided to take a scientific approach to preparing the supplementary material and quizzed prospective professors on what supplements they actually value and in what form they would like to receive them. Our prospective early adopters responded very positively to receiving the teaching material in a less cumbersome form than the traditional paper format, either through the World Wide Web or packaged on a CD-ROM. We are thus among the first to provide instructor and student support material in an electronic format.

Our Instructor's Support Disk, prepared by David Houghton, includes instructor teaching notes and suggested answers to the end-of-chapter material, a set of test items, and a comprehensive selection of PowerPoint™ compatible electronic transparencies. A Web site that provides downloadable versions of the electronic transparencies and a *Consumer Behavior and Managerial Decision Making* home page is also available to both students and professors. The home page includes updates to the text, practice tests, and useful links to related sites. You can view this site at:

www.prenhall.com/Kardes

◆ ACKNOWLEDGMENTS

I am grateful to the following experts for their thoughtful comments, suggestions, and feedback they provided at various stages of the manuscript: Ronald J. Adams, University of North Florida; Subir Bandyopadhyay, McGill University; Richard H. Beltramini, Wayne State University; James R. Bettman, Duke University; Drew Boyd, Johnson & Johnson Corporation; Maria L. Cronley, Wright State University; Curtis P. Haugtvedt, Ohio State University; Paul M. Herr, University of Colorado; David C. Houghton, Northwest Nazarene College; Cynthia D. Huffman, University of Delaware; Vladimir Pashkevich, University of Cincinnati; Cornelia Pechmann, University of California–Irvine; John R. Rossiter, University of Wollongong; David W. Schumann, University of Tennessee; and Joel Steckel, New York University.

Pearson Education would like to thank Paul Herr, University of Colorado–Boulder; Carl Obermiller, Seattle University; Lois Bitner Olson, San Diego State University; Diane Phillips, Saint Joseph's University; Moses B. Altsech, Butler University; and Deborah Cowles, Virginia Commonwealth University.

◆ ABOUT THE AUTHOR

Frank R. Kardes is a Professor of Marketing at the University of Cincinnati and a former faculty member of the Sloan School of Management at MIT. His research focuses on a wide range of topics in consumer psychology and product management—including consumer judgment and inference processes, persuasion and advertising, the pioneering brand advantage, and judgment based on limited evidence. His research has appeared in many leading scientific journals, and he is frequently invited to present his research at leading universities throughout the world (including Wharton, INSEAD, Hong Kong University of Science and Technology, and the London Business School). He serves on the editorial boards of the *Journal of Consumer Research, Journal of Consumer Psychology, International Journal of Research in Marketing, International Quarterly Journal of Marketing,* and *Marketing Letters.* Dr. Kardes is a former Co-Editor of the *Journal of Consumer Psychology,* and *Advances in Consumer Research,* and is currently an Associate Editor of the *Journal of Consumer Research.* Dr. Kardes is a former President of the Society for Consumer Psychology and is a Fellow of the American Psychological Association, the American Psychological Society, the Society for Consumer Psychology, and the Society for Personality and Social Psychology.

The Scientific Study of Consumer Behavior

◆ AMAZON.COM

In July 1995, Jeff Bezos quit his job as an investment banker and founded the world's first electronic retail outlet, Amazon.com. His vision was not only to create the world's largest bookstore but to create an innovative new type of bookstore with unlimited shelf space. Amazon.com's Web site (www.amazon.com) states that Amazon.com is committed to consumer satisfaction and to the delivery of an educational and inspiring shopping experience. Amazon.com's commitment to consumer satisfaction enabled the firm to overstock products so these products could be delivered to consumers quickly even during holiday rushes when many retailers run out of stock and are unable to deliver. Amazon.com's emphasis on an inspiring shopping experience encouraged the firm to expand to music, video, DVD, electronics, tools, software, health and beauty aids, gourmet food and wine, toys, and even Pokémon cards. Today, only five years later, Amazon.com is the undisputed world leader in e-tailing (or electronic retailing), serving over 17 million consumers in over 160 countries.

Amazon.com is a tremendous success in terms of sales for many reasons. In terms of brand-name recognition, Amazon.com is 16 in the world for all firms and number one for e-tail firms (Bacheldor, 2000). The Web site is easy to navigate, the prices are clear, the graphics are minimal, and the Web site offers personal touches such as personal recommendations (based on purchase histories) for each individual user. If you happen to like science fiction books and movies, for example, a short list of science fiction books and movies will be recommended to you automatically each time you log on.

Amazon.com's major competitors, like Barnes and Noble (www.bn.com). have been attempting to design Web sites that are somewhat similar to Amazon.com's Web site.

Although Amazon.com is a success in terms of sales, many investors are disappointed with Amazon.com's performance in terms of profits. Not only has Amazon.com not turned a profit, Amazon.com is currently $900 million in the red, and the company is not expected to turn a profit until 2002 (Hof, Green, & Brady, 2000). Some critics believe that Amazon.com should have stuck to books, because expanding to music, video, electronics, and so on could lead to a diffuse image that many consumers find confusing. Some critics also believe that Amazon.com should not have spent $300 million on new distribution centers, overstocks, and customer service operators, but when Amazon.com delivered 99 percent of its orders on time during the holiday rush, it earned the loyalty of millions of customers, and repeat purchases from these customers make up 73 percent of Amazon.com's sales (Hof et al., 2000). Furthermore, Amazon.com's remarkably high level of brand-name recognition has enabled the firm to reduce its advertising costs (on average, it costs the firm only $19 to attract a new customer) and to encourage other e-tailers to advertise on Amazon.com's Web pages (other e-tailers have paid Amazon.com over $600 million for this service; Hof et al., 2000). In addition, the average lifetime value of an Amazon.com consumer has been estimated at $1,900 (Ververka, 2000), and $1,900 multiplied by 17 million consumers is $31.3 billion! The Amazon.com case nicely illustrates the importance of innovation, being the first firm to enter a new and exciting market (the pioneering advantage), brand-name recognition, investing in customer service, brand loyalty and repeat purchase, and partnering with other firms.

◆ **INTRODUCTION**

Will the Internet change the way consumers shop? Some industry experts believe that consumers change slowly and some believe that consumers change rapidly. According to Roger Deromedi, Kraft's executive vice president in charge of the famous cheese division, "Consumers talk more than they change. Americans don't change their habits that fast. It's like a glacier" (Ono, 1995). At the other extreme, Raymond Smith, the chairman and chief executive officer of Verizon, predicts that the Internet will receive widespread acceptance very rapidly. Smith told advertisers, "you can jump in early and help create this exciting new medium or you can let the world pass you by and find yourself operating the best darned buggy-whip business on Madison Avenue" (Goldman, 1995).

Today, it looks like Smith was a better prophet than Deromedi. As Table 1-1 indicates, consumers are spending billions of dollars while shopping on the Internet. However, consumers are not always quick to embrace new technologies: When television first appeared on the market (back in the black-and-white days), the vast majority of American consumers did not even consider buying a television set for many years. Moreover, some consumers like to try new products and services, whereas others are often the last on their block to try something new.

Predicting human behavior is a difficult and complicated enterprise, filled with uncertainties, risks, and surprises. Accurate predictions can yield vast fortunes, and inaccurate predictions can result in the loss of millions of dollars (see Fig. 1-2). How should we approach the problem of predicting consumer behavior in a complex and uncertain world? This textbook adopts the scientific approach toward analyzing and solving consumer marketing problems. The scientific approach is adopted throughout this textbook for three main reasons: (1) It is the best approach for helping people to develop a deep understanding of consumer behavior, (2) it is the only approach for dealing effectively with events that are influenced by probability or chance, and (3) extensive empirical evidence indicates that training in scientific thinking improves

TABLE 1-1 Consumer Spending on the Internet (1998)	
Category	*Millions of Dollars*
Travel	2,842
Computer hardware	1,887
Stocks (commissions only)	1,052
Computer software	762
Books	658
News and entertainment	437
Clothes	435
Electronics	430
Groceries	189
Music	116

Source: Adapted from Fiske, Grove, & John (2000).

For a century, Sears, Roebuck and Co. successfully met consumer needs through its catalog service. But recently it was forced by changes in consumer behavior to close the pages of its catalog forever.

Source: Courtesy of Sears, Roebuck and Co.

people's problem-solving and decision-making skills (Fong & Nisbett, 1991; Fong, Krantz, & Nisbett, 1986; Larrick, Morgan, & Nisbett, 1990; Larrick, Nisbett, & Morgan, 1993; Lehman, Lempert, & Nisbett, 1988; Lehman & Nisbett, 1990).

Unfortunately, many people prefer to rely on intuition or common sense rather than science. An intuition is a hunch or a guess. Usually, intuition involves a snap judgment made on the basis of little or no useful information. Of course, whenever a judgment is based on limited information, something important might be overlooked and costly mistakes may be made. For example, most people think that high quality is a good

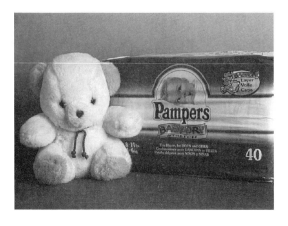

Mothers are more concerned about the benefits to their baby (comfort, dryness) than themselves (no cleaning), when deciding on diapers.

Source: © Mary Boucher.

thing. Common sense suggests that if you want people to like your product, all you have to do is make a high-quality product. At least, that's what the managers at Heinz thought when they introduced a new clam chowder made from the finest ingredients, including expensive, fresh, juicy, tender, high-quality clams. The product was a dismal failure. If the managers had done their homework and had conducted scientific research on consumer preferences, they would have learned that most consumers prefer tough, chewy, rubbery, low-quality clams in their clam chowder. You know the type: clams that seem to grow in your mouth as you chew and take a long time to eat. Make no mistake, I am not saying that quality is unimportant. However, managers' intuitions about quality do not always match consumers' preferences. Relying too heavily on common sense rather than on sound scientific research can be misleading and dangerous.

Even consumer marketing giants, like Procter & Gamble, fall into the intuition trap. P&G developed Pampers, the first disposable diaper. Disposable diapers are convenient and easy to use, and they save time. However, when these obvious benefits were emphasized in early ads and promotional campaigns, the product failed. Intuitions about obvious benefits proved to be dead-end hunches. Later, however, P&G conducted scientific research to gain insight into the problem and learned that mothers were more concerned about benefits to the baby than about benefits to themselves. This research led to a remarkable turnaround. New ads emphasized that Pampers kept baby drier and happier, and the product became a tremendous success. P&G learned the hard way that scientific research is the best protection against the intuition trap.

◆ WHAT IS CONSUMER BEHAVIOR?

Consumer behavior is the study of human responses to products, services, and the marketing of products and services. This topic is of considerable importance to marketing managers and marketing researchers because the focus on the consumer is the key contribution of marketing to business practice. Other business functions (e.g., finance, accounting, production) either neglect the consumer or overlook the consumer entirely. Organizations that lose sight of their customers cannot compete effectively against firms that stay close to their customers. Managers who really understand their customers develop better products and services, promote their products and services more effectively, and devise marketing plans and strategies that foster sustainable competitive advantages for their products and services. Furthermore, managers who know their customers can reach and satisfy them more efficiently. (See "Taking Issue, Supermarkets and Suppliers: Share and Share Alike?") Such managers are important assets to any organization and are rewarded accordingly.

CONSUMER RESPONSES

To understand consumers and why they make the choices they do, **consumer researchers** investigate a broad range of human responses, including affective (feelings), cognitive (thoughts), and behavioral (actions) responses. (See Fig. 1-1.) **Affective responses** are feelings and emotions we experience when we read about, hear about, think about, use, or dispose of products. **Cognitive responses** are beliefs, opinions, attitudes, and intentions pertaining to products and services. These responses can be either

SUPERMARKETS AND SUPPLIERS: SHARE AND SHARE ALIKE?

The scientific study of consumer behavior can be time-consuming and costly; thus, it stands to reason that organizations that have the common goal of serving the same customers would benefit by sharing the information they gather about those customers. Take supermarkets and their suppliers. If a large supermarket chain and a cereal manufacturer pooled their knowledge about consumers, profits for both would probably increase. The benefits of sharing—cutting research costs, putting information to use immediately—could be especially crucial when the demand for groceries is slack.

But retailers and manufacturers are slow to join forces; instead, they seem to undercut each other in the fight to grab consumer dollars. Manufacturers don't want to share consumer information—and subsequent plans for new products—with supermarkets because they are afraid that the supermarkets will use the information to develop their own products or, worse, pass the information along to competing manufacturers. Because a supermarket's primary aim is to sell products to consumers, not promote a manufacturer's interests, supermarket management sees nothing wrong with this practice.

In Great Britain, United Biscuits sells about $57 million of its Penguin chocolate biscuits per year. Recently, the manufacturer sued ASDA, a British supermarket chain, for putting its own brand of chocolate biscuit, called Puffin, on the shelves. Coca-Cola sued J. Sainsbury, another British supermarket chain, for offering its own brand of cola in a can that looked a bit too much like Coke.

But some "sharing" agreements have appeared to be successful, particularly if the manufacturer is extremely powerful. For instance, Procter & Gamble teamed up with local retailers in Great Britain to study consumer preferences and pare down its portfolio of soaps and detergents. Consumers had so many detergents to choose from—approximately 180—that they became confused by different brands. So Procter & Gamble reduced its offerings by about 20 percent, which helped detergent sales in all the stores increase by about 8 percent. When Procter & Gamble tried the same move in the United States, reducing its offerings by 13 percent, sales of Procter & Gamble detergents increased by 6 percent and profits by 22 percent.

As successful as these ventures sound, they may be damaging to smaller manufacturers if they go too far. Some supermarkets have already appointed leading manufacturers "category captains," allowing them a formal voice in how supermarket shelves are stocked. To smaller manufacturers, this seems a bit like the fox guarding the henhouse, and they are terrified that the fox will chase them out of business.

Information about consumers is a powerful tool in any industry; sharing it with the right recipients can benefit everyone, including consumers themselves. But using it as a weapon to drive others out of business may be less than ethical or just good marketing, depending on your point of view.

Source: "Categorical Imperatives," *The Economist,* May 17, 1997, p. 75.

evaluative or nonevaluative in nature, and the scope of these responses can be very specific (e.g., responses toward one particular attribute or one particular brand) or very broad (e.g., responses toward a general class of products). **Behavioral responses** include purchase decisions and consumption-related practices (i.e., actions involved in

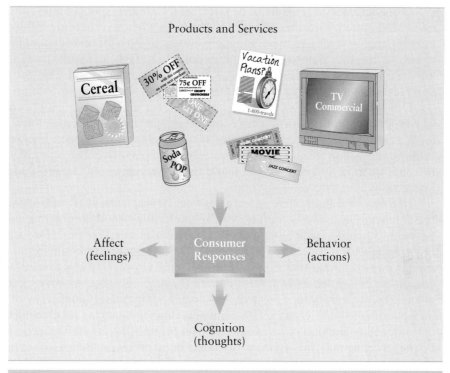

FIGURE 1-1

Consumer researchers continuously investigate a broad range of human responses, including affective, cognitive, and behavioral responses.

obtaining, using, and disposing of products or services). All of these responses are influenced by three major factors: person variables, situational variables, and person-by-situation interactions.

Person Variables

As the term *variable* implies, people vary and situations vary. No two people are exactly alike, and no two situations are exactly alike. People differ on many dimensions, such as intelligence, personality, interests, hobbies, opinions, and preferences. **Person variables** are dimensions that are internal to a specific individual.

Situational Variables

Situational variables are external, environmental variables that provide the context in which behaviors are performed. Marketing managers are interested in the influence of a wide variety of situational variables, such as the effects of various changes in the four P's of marketing: product, promotion, price, and place (distribution).

Person-by-Situation Interactions

Person variables and situational variables often jointly influence consumer behavior. An interaction between two variables means that the effects of one variable depend on the effects of another. For example, an advertising technique that is effective for one group of consumers is unlikely to be effective for another group. Some consumers are influenced more by ads that just present the facts, whereas others are influenced more by emotional appeals and hype. Some consumers weigh a lot of evidence about a lot of brands before they purchase a consumer durable, such as an appliance or an automobile, whereas other consumers make impulsive purchase decisions for consumer durables and nondurables (Venkatraman, Marlino, Kardes, & Sklar, 1990).

Different marketing strategies are required for different groups of consumers as well as for different products. Marketing techniques that are effective for selling automobiles are unlikely to be effective for selling toothpaste. Complex interactions such as those implied in these examples are extremely pervasive. The scientific method is the only method that enables the marketing manager to understand these complex interactions adequately.

In a recent collaborative research project between the DuPont Corporation and the Johnson Graduate School of Management at Cornell, interesting interactions between personal motives or drivers and situational macrotrends were examined (Isen, Aspinwall, O'Brien, & Fadem, 2000). Drivers are the determinants of what consumers want and what they do. For example, some key motivations that influence what consumers do are self-esteem maintenance (having a positive self-image), self-esteem enhancement (conveying a positive self-image to others), self-improvement (developing new knowledge and skills), belongingness (having satisfying relationships with others and feeling like part of a group), personal control (having an impact on others and on the environment), loss aversion (avoiding harm or loss, including loss of time, effort, health, or money), and enjoyment (seeking entertainment, variety, and positive affect). The importance of these motives or drivers differs from person to person. Some people are more concerned about their self-esteem or image than other people, some are more concerned about loss, and some are more fun-loving than others.

TABLE 1-2 Some Important Person Variables and Situational Variables

Person Variables (consumer drivers)	Situational Variables (macrotrends)	Some Implications of P × S Interactions
Self-esteem maintenance	Globalization	Transportation systems that preserve personal dignity
Self-esteem enhancement	Urbanization	Compact luxury products that impress others
Self-improvement	Cultural diversity	Improved educational products and services
Belongingness	Information flow, multimedia	Improved networking products and services
Personal control	Benefits–knowledge link	Faster and more powerful personal computers
Loss aversion	Gray market	Safe, convenient, easy-to-use products
Enjoyment	Personal responsibility for health and well-being	Healthy cookbooks and cooking appliances

Note: Person variables and situational variables jointly influence what consumers want and what firms should offer.

Some of the key macrotrends identified by DuPont managers include increasing globalization, urbanization, cultural diversity, information flow, greatly increased benefits for knowledgeable consumers, a large and growing group of older wealthy consumers (the gray market), and increased personal responsibility for health and well-being. Examining the intersection between drivers and macrotrends helps managers to identify new business opportunities (see Table 1-2). For example, examining the intersection between loss aversion and aging emphasizes the importance of developing safer and more comfortable transportation-related products. The intersection between personal control and personal responsibility for health and well-being emphasizes the importance of developing home medical products. The interaction among loss

To make sure your baby gets the right food at the right age, look for the right Gerber label.

What's in a label?
Fifty years of innovation assure you that Gerber has the right system for feeding your baby.

Gerber has a most knowledgeable staff of nutritionists dedicated to feeding babies. The Gerber Nutritional Guidelines help you make sure your baby gets the right food at the right age.

As baby's nutritional and developmental needs change, all you have to do is look for the right color label.

Blue label means Strained Foods for Infants.
Some babies are ready to begin Strained Foods at 4-6 months. Many earlier. When you and your health advisor decide your baby is ready for single ingredient foods, Gerber

has the largest variety. Of course, no single ingredient foods have added starch, salt, sugar, preservatives, or artificial flavors or colors. Offered along with breast milk or formula, Strained Foods provide nutrients essential for your baby's growth. Plus, spoonfeeding Strained Foods gives your baby new tastes, new textures and new stimulation. Once your baby has accepted single ingredient foods, strained combination foods can be included in the menu. For example, Gerber High Meat Dinners are an excellent source of protein and no one makes a strained dinner with more meat.

Red label means Textured Foods for Juniors.
When baby begins teething, add Gerber Junior Foods to

the menu. The tiny bits in most Junior Foods give baby practice chewing. They're made without added salt, preservatives, artificial flavors or colors.

Brown label means Chunky Foods for Toddlers.
When your toddler is able to self-feed, it's time for Gerber Chunky Foods.

Your baby is as unique as you are. So let the Gerber Nutritional Guidelines help you and your health advisor make the right choices for your baby.

 **Gerber**
Babies are our business...
and have been for over 60 years.
Gerber Products Company, Fremont, MI 49412

Marketing strategies need to be varied for different groups of consumers. An advertisement like this one for baby food will be more effective with consumers who have young children than those who do not.
Source: Courtesy of Gerber Products Company.

aversion, aging, and multimedia suggests that it may be useful to design "smart homes" with flat panel displays that enable consumers to view other rooms and operate appliances located in other rooms. Thinking about interactions between person variables and situational variables helps managers to develop innovative product concepts or ideas.

Person-by-situation interactions are also important for understanding persuasion and decision making. Research on age and susceptibility to persuasion supports the impressionable-years hypothesis (Krosnick & Alwin, 1989). This means that Generation X (young adults) and Generation Y (teenagers) consumers are much more susceptible to persuasion than are baby-boomer (middle-aged adults) and senior-citizen consumers. Baby boomers and seniors were equally resistant to persuasion. Consequently, depending on what types of products and services are offered, marketing managers should consider targeting a greater proportion of their advertising and promotion budgets to Generation X and Y consumers, relative to baby boomers and seniors.

◆ THE SCIENTIFIC METHOD

Before describing the application of the scientific method to the study of consumer behavior, it is useful to discuss the goals of science. The goals of scientists are to (1) describe, (2) predict, (3) control, and (4) explain phenomena. A **phenomenon** is an observable event. The four goals of marketing practitioners are to (1) describe, (2) predict, (3) control, and (4) explain consumer behavioral phenomena. Thus, the goals of scientists and of marketers are very similar, and there is a strong link between science and marketing practice. True, the scientist places special emphasis on explaining, whereas the marketing practitioner is concerned primarily with prediction and control. Nevertheless, the four goals are linked closely, and it is impossible to predict or control events without attaining at least a rudimentary understanding (explanation) of the phenomena involved. The **scientific method** helps researchers achieve the goals of science through the use of a set of formal rules.

Consider what happens when managers make risky decisions based upon limited or incomplete knowledge. RCA lost $500 million on the Videodisc, a product that could not record television programs (Power, Kerwin, Groover, & Alexander, 1993). Ford Motors lost $250 million on the Edsel, a gas-guzzling, overpowered tank of an automobile (Power et al., 1993). Procter & Gamble lost $200 million on Pringles potato chips, a snack food that intrigued consumers at first but later seemed too artificial (Dalrymple & Parsons, 1990). General Motors lost $200 million on the rotary engine (Urban & Hauser, 1992). DuPont lost about $100 million on Corfam, a synthetic leather that is less appealing than real leather (Power et al., 1993). (See Fig. 1-2.) Many firms cannot afford to absorb losses such as these. It is costly to make decisions based on hunches rather than on sound scientific research. If these firms had a better scientific understanding of their customers, these losses could have been avoided or at least reduced (Urban & Hauser, 1992; Urban & Star, 1991). Read about the challenges faced by marketers in "Making the Decision: The Variables of Vaccination."

Why, then, are so many managers reluctant to adopt the scientific perspective? Ask any manager (or any person, for that matter) how likely it is that a new product that sells very poorly during its first year will become the market leader by the end of its

The Intuition Trap

Product Developed via Intuition	Losses
RCA Videodisc	$500 million
Ford Edsel	$250 million
Procter & Gamble Pringles	$200 million
General Motors rotary engine	$200 million
DuPont Corfam	$100 million

FIGURE 1-2

Relying on intuition when developing new products can cost organizations millions of dollars.

second year. Most respond that this seems very unlikely. Ask another manager how likely it is that a new product that sells very poorly during its first year will be acquired by a much larger and more successful firm that redesigns the product, markets it more effectively, and turns it into the market leader by the end of its second year. Most managers respond that this scenario seems more likely than the first.

Logically, however, the first outcome (becoming the market leader) is more likely than the second (being acquired by another firm, being redesigned, being marketed more effectively, and then becoming the market leader). Four events occurring jointly is always less probable than one of these events occurring alone. This is because there are hundreds of ways a failing new product can turn around besides being acquired by another firm, being redesigned, and being marketed more effectively. Instead of the new firm, the company that originally designed the product may redesign it or develop a more effective marketing campaign. Consumer preferences may change and make the new product much more attractive. The competition may run into insurmountable legal problems, logistic problems, or other difficulties. Hence, becoming the market leader in an unspecified fashion will always be more likely than becoming the market leader through one particular sequence of events.

A specific sequence of events often seems more likely because people experience difficulty in thinking probabilistically, or in terms of probabilities (Kahneman, Slovic, & Tversky, 1982), and are especially ineffective at combining probabilities in their heads (Gavanski & Roskos-Ewoldson, 1991; Wyer, 1976). It is much easier to think in terms of sequences of events or scenarios than in terms of conjunctive probabilities. Although scenario thinking can be very seductive, it can lead to erroneous predictions (Dawes, 1988). The scenarios we construct seem so compelling that we cannot imagine how science could help us to produce better judgments and decisions. Moreover, scientific facts and figures are often so overwhelming and confusing that it is hard to imagine producing a story or scenario that could account for all the facts. Furthermore,

MAKING THE DECISION

THE VARIABLES OF VACCINATION

You may not even recall the last time you had a vaccination; perhaps you were a small child. But medical researchers at nonprofit organizations as well as biopharmaceutical companies have plans for you: As an adult, you will have more opportunities to face the needle. Research on vaccines against such illnesses as Lyme disease, cancer, and AIDS and even cocaine addiction is far more advanced than we may think. "We will see new vaccines for diseases that have not had vaccines as well as improvements to existing vaccines for all adults, including our aging population," predicts Anthony S. Fauci, executive director of the National Institute for Allergy and Infectious Diseases, a branch of the National Institutes of Health.

Indeed, industry experts maintain that vaccines are the fastest growing segment of the pharmaceutical industry. According to Frost and Sullivan, a New York marketing research firm, the global market for vaccines now stands at $4.1 billion per year, up from $1.6 billion in 1990. As the baby-boom generation ages, it may seem natural from a marketing standpoint—as well as a societal one—for this increase to take place. But plenty of variables face those involved in the development of these products.

The cost of research and production of vaccines is a major variable. Because of the high cost, small biopharmaceutical companies that focus on vaccine research and development have entered into alliances with nonprofit organizations and even other, larger commercial pharmaceutical manufacturers to bring products to the market. For instance, Aquila Biopharmaceuticals, which is working on a vaccine against Lyme disease, has teamed up with several organizations, including the National Institutes of Health and SmithKline Beecham. Research and production costs affect the price of each vaccine, which in turn may influence insurance coverage, which in turn may affect which consumers will be able to purchase inoculations.

The necessity of obtaining specific ingredients from far-flung locations may influence cost as well as availability. For example, Aquila Biopharmaceuticals extracts its proprietary ingredient Stimulon, used in the manufacture of a proposed malaria vaccine, from the bark of a tree found only in South America.

Consumer responses to the new vaccines are also an important factor. Some individuals may rush to obtain inoculations to feel more secure about their health, while others may decline them because of apathy or lack of trust in the product or the medical establishment. Some groups of people may be required by employers to receive certain vaccinations. Others may refuse inoculation because of religious beliefs.

Marketers involved with the new generation of vaccines must maintain a scientific approach toward these variables that is as rigorous as that of all the chemists, biologists, and geneticists whose laboratories are researching and developing these products. Clearly, the scientific method will be their best shot at success.

Source: Ronald Rosenberg, "Not Your Kid's Vaccine," *The Boston Globe,* September 10, 1997, pp. D1, D4.

researchers often use a very specific language (jargon), and the scenarios they construct are often abstract, complex, and difficult to understand. Finally, scientists can overlook important variables and draw inaccurate conclusions, so it seems dangerous to put too much stock in their predictions. For these reasons, many marketing managers prefer to make decisions on the basis of their own hunches and scenarios rather than on the basis of scientific research. Although sound scientific research cannot guarantee success, it can reduce (though not eliminate) uncertainty and improve the odds of success considerably.

CORRELATIONAL RELATIONSHIPS

Science involves applying the scientific method to increase understanding about the relationship between two (or more) variables. Two types of relationships are of special importance: **correlational relationships** and **causal relationships.** If two variables, such as amount of advertising and amount of sales, are correlated, then an observed change in one variable is accompanied by a corresponding change in the other variable (see Fig. 1-3). In other words, if the amount of advertising used changes (increases or decreases), sales should also change (increase or decrease). A positive correlation means that as one variable increases, the other also increases (e.g., as advertising increases, sales increase). In contrast, a negative correlation means that as one variable increases, the other decreases (e.g., as advertising decreases, sales increase). Zero correlation means that there is no systematic relationship between two variables. That is, a change in one variable is accompanied sometimes by an increase, sometimes by a decrease, and sometimes by no change in the other variable. Fortunately, in the case of advertising and sales we know that there is a positive correlation (Assmus, Farley, & Lehmann, 1984).

In everyday life, people try to learn about associations between variables. Unlike scientists, however, they do not try to measure or quantify the value of each variable. Instead, people rely on informal, casual observation in everyday life. Furthermore, in everyday thinking, a few observations are usually sufficient to convince us that there either is or is not a relationship between two variables. Scientists, on the other hand, like to create conditions that enable them to make many observations (sometimes hundreds or thousands of observations in a single study).

Furthermore, in everyday life, people often "see" relationships where none exist. This phenomenon is referred to as *illusory correlation*. When they expect to observe a relationship, people tend to focus on instances where both variables are present. The scientific establishment of correlation, however, requires the formal observation or recording of the number of instances in which A is present and B is present, the number of instances in which A is present and B is absent, the number of instances in which A is absent and B is present, and the number of instances in which A is absent and B is absent. All four of these cases are equally important. Unfortunately, in everyday life, people focus primarily on instances in which A is present and B is present. Absences are overlooked. For example, when attempting to assess the degree of relationship between advertising and sales, people tend to focus on cases (examples) involving high advertising and high sales. Cases involving high advertising and no sales, no advertising and high sales, and no advertising and no sales are easily neglected.

One additional point about correlation is important. Correlation is nondirectional. This means that even if we know that two variables are correlated, the direction of the relationship is still unknown. That is, A may influence B, B may influence A, or they may influence each other simultaneously. More concretely, advertising may influence sales, sales may influence advertising, or both variables may influence each other simultaneously. Correlation tells us nothing about the direction of the relationship.

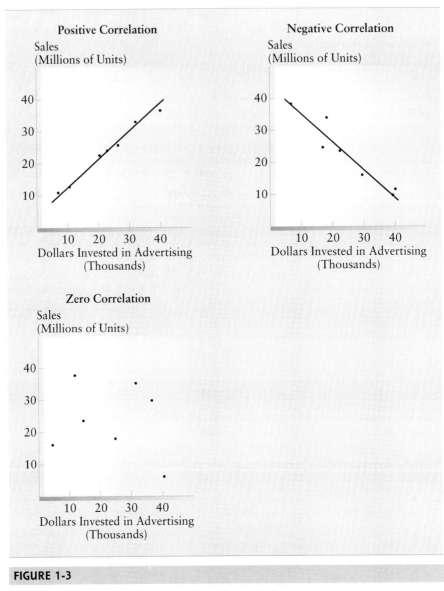

FIGURE 1-3

Graphs showing correlation between advertising and sales.

CAUSAL RELATIONSHIPS

In contrast, a causal relationship between two variables means that there is a correlation between two variables *and* that one variable influences the other, but not vice versa (see Fig. 1-4). The cause always precedes the effect. Hence, if there is a causal relationship between advertising and sales, and if advertising is the causal variable and sales is the effect, a change in advertising will produce a change in sales. However, a change in sales does not (directly) produce a change in advertising. Scientists call the antecedent, or

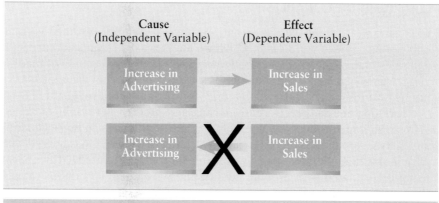

FIGURE 1-4

Causation implies that the independent variable influences the dependent variable, and not vice versa. Correlation is less informative because it is unclear which variable influences which.

causal, variable the **independent variable,** and they call the consequence, or effect, the **dependent variable** (because it is dependent on the independent variable).

Conducting an **experiment** is the best way to determine causality (Aronson, Ellsworth, Carlsmith, & Gonzales, 1990). A true experiment involves systematically manipulating the independent variable to assess its impact on the dependent variable. For example, advertising as an independent variable can be manipulated by showing one group of subjects (participants) an ad and showing another group no ad (the control group). Each subject must be randomly assigned to one of these two conditions. That is, on the basis of a coin toss (or some other random number generation procedure), each subject is assigned to the ad group or the control (no ad) group (e.g., heads = ad group, tails = no ad group). **Random assignment** of subjects to conditions ensures that individual differences among subjects (e.g., different personalities, different levels of knowledge about the advertised product, different beliefs and attitudes) do not influence the results. Randomization causes these differences to cancel out. If, on average, sales are greater in the ad group than in the no ad group, one can conclude that variations in advertising cause changes in sales. This simple experiment contains only two conditions (ad or no ad); most experiments contain more than two conditions. Learning occurs by making careful comparisons across conditions.

Unfortunately, in everyday thinking, people often assume that correlation implies causation. If they see that a change in one variable is often associated with a change in another, they tend to infer that one variable caused the change observed in the other. This inference is often premature. Unlike everyday reasoning, a sharp distinction between correlation and causation is made in scientific reasoning. Many variables are correlated, but not all correlational relationships are causal relationships. If there is a causal relationship between two variables, (1) the two variables must be correlated, (2) the cause must precede the effect, and (3) the effects of other variables must be controlled or ruled out.

CONFOUNDING VARIABLES

Two variables do not exist in isolation. A large number of other variables always impinge on any two variables in which we happen to be interested, such as advertising and sales. One of these other extraneous variables or some combination of extraneous variables may be responsible for an observed correlation between the two variables of interest. For example, firms with large advertising budgets also tend to have large product development budgets (i.e., advertising and product development are correlated). Firms with large product development budgets tend to design higher-quality products, and, maybe, product quality has a stronger influence on sales (compared with advertising). In this example, advertising would appear to be correlated to sales because advertising is correlated with product quality, and product quality drives sales. Of course, firms with large advertising budgets also tend to have a lot of power in the channel (i.e., they have much influence over distributors). Maybe power in the channel is the key variable, with respect to sales. Firms with large advertising budgets also tend to have large budgets for sales promotion, R&D (research and development), and market research. The list could go on and on. As the number of potential causal variables increases, uncertainty increases, and we can never be sure that our original two variables (advertising and sales, in this case) were the right ones on which to focus.

In everyday thinking, people tend to think of one plausible causal variable and then stop (Nisbett & Ross, 1980). Scientists, on the other hand, try to generate as complete a list of potential causes as possible (many more than one potential cause). They then conduct multiple experiments to rule out each plausible cause until only one remains (each experiment reduces uncertainty, but narrowing the field to one cause requires many years of programmatic research). This time-consuming, laborious process occurs rarely in everyday reasoning.

◆ THE BEHAVIORAL SCIENCES VERSUS THE PHYSICAL SCIENCES

Is marketing a science? If **science** is defined as the process of knowledge development based on a set of formal rules (i.e., the scientific method) and procedures for assigning numbers to empirical observations, testing for relationships between variables, determining causal order, and controlling for extraneous sources of variation by systematically ruling out alternative hypotheses, then the answer is a resounding yes. However, many marketing managers prefer to rely on hunches, intuition, and scenario thinking. Asserting that marketing is too complex to be reduced to a science, they claim that we will never be able to understand human beings the way physicists and chemists understand atoms, particles, and waves.

Most of the phenomena that physicists and chemists study are static and can be measured with a high degree of precision. For example, a rock weighs the same amount throughout the day, and day after day. Most of the phenomena studied by marketing researchers and other behavioral scientists (e.g., psychologists, sociologists) are dynamic and difficult to quantify precisely. For example, a consumer may rate a product as a 9 on a scale from 0 to 10 at one point in time, but this rating may change just a few hours later and is very likely to change days, weeks, or months later. The biggest difference between the behavioral and physical sciences is that behavioral scientists study relatively dynamic phenomena and physical scientists study relatively static phenomena.

Physicists and chemists, for example, think primarily about certain events, whereas social scientists are accustomed to thinking about probabilistic (chance) or uncertain events. Certain events are easier to measure, and most of the causal relationships investigated by physicists and chemists are both necessary and sufficient causes. This means that an effect is observed if and only if the cause is present. In contrast, uncertain events are difficult to measure, and most of the causal relationships investigated by social scientists are necessary or sufficient but rarely both necessary and sufficient. An effect must be preceded by a necessary cause, but sometimes the effect fails to occur even when the necessary cause is present (because other variables may inhibit the effect). A sufficient cause may produce an effect, but the effect is often observed even in the absence of a sufficient cause (because other causes may produce the effect).

REDUCTION OF UNCERTAINTY

The bad news is that causal relationships between variables are very difficult to ascertain when an effect is multiply determined (i.e., many different causes individually or in various combinations may produce the effect). Learning about causal relationships is also very difficult when measures are not perfectly reliable or stable. The good news, however, is that social scientists have learned how to live with uncertainty and, better yet, *how to reduce uncertainty*. This is an especially important and unique contribution of social scientists, because physical scientists are not accustomed to thinking about uncertain events and they do not know how to deal with uncertainty.

How is uncertainty reduced? (See Fig. 1-5.) First of all, multiple, converging measures are used to improve the reliability (stability) and validity (accuracy) of measures of consumer attitudes, beliefs, opinions, preferences, judgments, and dispositions. Although perfect reliability and validity is rarely attained, an adequate degree is commonly attained. This means that marketing researchers can often capture complex ideas with enough depth to permit the detection of systematic relationships between variables. Second, state-of-the-art statistical procedures are used to control for sampling error and for sources of variation produced by extraneous variables. Third, by

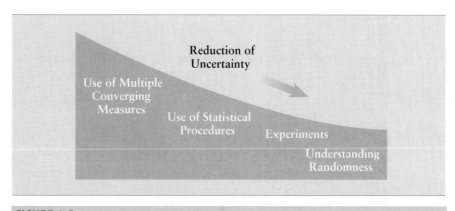

FIGURE 1-5

Marketers can take concrete steps to reduce uncertainty.

randomly assigning subjects to conditions in an experiment employing careful (i.e., unconfounded, nonoverlapping) manipulations of various situational variables, you can control for all sources of variation produced by extraneous person variables. Fourth, by being forced to deal with uncertainty, social scientists have attained a deeper understanding of the concept of randomness, or chance, than has ever before been possible (see Dawes, 1988; Gilovich, 1991; Kahneman et al., 1982).

Why is a clearer understanding of chance or uncertainty important to managers? Marketing managers must make difficult decisions under uncertain conditions on a daily basis. Consumer preference, the availability of supplies, competitive activity, and other market conditions are in a constant state of flux. (See "Making the Decision: Did Informix Put the Cart Before the Horse?") Making decisions under these conditions without an adequate understanding of the concept of uncertainty is like playing in Las Vegas casinos without any knowledge of the basic principles of probability. However, most people and most managers are remarkably naive about the laws of probability (Dawes, 1988; Gilovich, 1991; Kahneman et al., 1982). They see hot streaks when athletes are actually performing at chance levels (Gilovich, Vallone, & Tversky, 1985).

One way to deal with uncertainty in the way consumers will respond to a food product is to print nutrition facts on the label.

Source: Courtesy of Lipton.

DID INFORMIX PUT THE CART BEFORE THE HORSE?

In today's competitive, computer-driven world, it is easy for technology to speed way ahead of the marketplace. It is one thing to develop new technology and, with it, new products; it is quite another to ensure that there is a market for those new products. If people do not perceive a need for a new product, do not understand how to use it, and do not believe that the product offers value or reliability, they probably won't purchase it. Thus, no matter how innovative the product is, it is doomed to failure.

That is exactly what managers at Informix learned — the hard way. Informix designs databases that store and manipulate vast amounts of corporate data and make the resulting information available across computer networks. Determined to be a leader in the tech industry, Informix acquired Illustra Information Technologies — whose technology was even more advanced — and immediately focused on Illustra's technology, thrusting it into the marketplace. Illustra had developed the technology to deal with data that doesn't fit into standard columns or rows — for instance, illustrations and even videos. The idea was brilliant, and

Informix thought every corporation would want the new database, which was certain to make it a huge success.

As exciting as the new technology seemed, Informix failed to study scientifically how customers might respond to it. For instance, if marketers had used multiple, converging measures to improve the reliability and validity of measures of their customers' attitudes, beliefs, preferences, and judgments about the capabilities of a new database, they might have been able to reduce — or at least adapt to — the uncertainty surrounding the new technology in the marketplace. Instead, "Customers were left wondering, 'Is this a company making a standard database I can use, or is it in the stratosphere?'" observed Carl Olofson, an analyst for International Data Corp. In short, people were afraid of the new database and didn't buy it. During the first quarter of the following year, Informix posted a $140 million loss, which was more than its entire revenue for the quarter, stock plummeted, and sales representatives, engineers, and top management left the company.

Source: Erick Schonfeld, "Is Informix Toast?" *Fortune,* July 21, 1997, pp. 25–26.

They feel more confident when playing a lottery against a nervous-looking opponent, even though the opponent's appearance has no effect on the outcome (Langer, 1975). When a coin is tossed or a die is cast, they think a different outcome is due after observing a small streak involving a single outcome (e.g., five heads in a row, or five sixes in a row; this is known as the gambler's fallacy). They are insufficiently sensitive to regression effects (shifts toward the average). That is, extreme events (e.g., extremely high or extremely low sales) are usually followed by less extreme, intermediate events (e.g., average sales), but people tend to neglect this key statistical principle. These and many other biases are covered in greater detail in Chapter 14. Ways to overcome them are discussed in Chapter 15. For now, suffice it to say that people and managers experience difficulty in dealing with uncertain events.

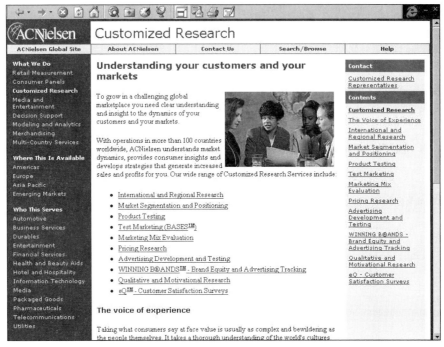

Companies like ACNielsen, which specializes in scientific research on consumer behavior, offer important information to managers in many industries. You can access Nielsen's Web site at http://acnielsen.com.

Source: Courtesy of ACNielsen.

BEHAVIORAL SCIENCE AND PROBABILITY

Behavioral scientists, however, are accustomed to thinking about uncertainty and are adept at reducing uncertainty. In fact, a recent study on the effects of graduate training in law, medicine, psychology, and chemistry shows that training in statistics and methodology significantly improves reasoning, judgment, and decision making under uncertainty (Lehman et al., 1988). All students, regardless of discipline, were given the same exam. This exam consisted of a set of statistics questions, a set of methodological questions, a set of logic problems, and a set of verbal reasoning problems. Most important, each set of problems contained a mix of scientific and everyday problems. The students performed similarly prior to receiving graduate training, regardless of discipline (law students exhibited a small advantage in verbal reasoning). However, after receiving just three years of graduate training, psychology and medical students outperformed law and chemistry students in statistical and methodological reasoning for both scientific and everyday problems. Psychology, medical, and law students also outperformed chemistry students in logical reasoning for both scientific and everyday problems. However, verbal reasoning (which is correlated to IQ) remained about the same for all four groups. Lehman et al. (1988) concluded:

It appears that the probabilistic sciences of psychology and medicine teach their students to apply statistical and methodological rules to both scientific and everyday-life problems, whereas the nonprobabilistic science of chemistry and the nonscientific discipline of law do not affect their students in these respects. (p. 438)

   . . . The luxury of not being confronted with messy problems that contain substantial uncertainty and a tangled web of causes means that chemistry does not teach some rules that are relevant to everyday life. (p. 441)

Hence, being confronted with probabilistic phenomena and being forced to learn how to think about and deal with uncertain events produces beneficial effects on thinking about and solving everyday problems. Uncertainty is a fact of life. Unfortunately, people and managers often fail to recognize random patterns of events and often overlook what and how much they do not know. They are too easily seduced by scenario thinking and too easily persuaded to follow their hunches and intuitions. Breaking these behavior patterns and adopting a more scientific perspective reduces uncertainty and improves decision making.

CHAPTER SUMMARY

Consumer behavior is defined as the study of human responses to products, services, and the marketing of products and services. The scientific perspective is emphasized throughout this textbook because this is the only useful perspective for thinking about probabilistic events and for improving decision making under uncertainty. The scientific approach is emphasized to provide you with three key benefits: (1) to help you acquire an in-depth, scientific understanding of consumer behavioral phenomena, or events, (2) to help you think more clearly about probabilistic events (i.e., events that are influenced by chance), and (3) to help you improve your managerial problem-solving and decision-making skills. Extensive research evidence indicates that training in scientific thinking improves students' problem-solving and decision-making skills (Fong & Nisbett, 1991; Fong et al., 1986; Larrick et al., 1990; Larrick et al., 1993; Lehman & Nisbett, 1990).

KEY CONCEPTS

- Consumer behavior
- Consumer researchers
- Affective responses
- Cognitive responses
- Behavioral responses
- Person variables

- Situational variables
- Person-by-situation interactions
- Phenomenon
- Scientific method
- Correlational relationships

- Causal relationships
- Independent variable
- Dependent variable
- Experiment
- Random assignment
- Science

DISCUSSION QUESTIONS

1. Why is the scientific approach the best approach to studying consumer behavior?
2. How might consumer researchers investigate the three different types of human responses to develop a new model of automobile?

3. In your own life, which do you use to make decisions: intuition or scientific method? Why? Does your decision-making method vary according to the type of decision you need to make? Why or why not?

4. Why do you think marketing managers and other executives are reluctant to use the scientific approach to studying consumer behavior?

5. Give an example of both a correlational relationship and a causal relationship that you observe in daily life. Explain how each example illustrates the relationship.

6. Why is randomization an important component to any scientific experiment that seeks to determine causality?

7. What is the major difference between the phenomena that physicists and chemists study and those that marketing researchers study?

8. If we think of marketing managers as social scientists, what kinds of uncertain events in consumer behavior might they have to face in trying to establish correlational or causal relationships?

9. Why is reducing uncertainty important to marketing managers?

10. Think of an instance in your own life when you followed a hunch to make a decision. Did the hunch turn out to be correct? Looking back, was there a random pattern of events surrounding the hunch? What information did you not have that might have reduced uncertainty and improved your decision making?

CHAPTER 2

Consumer Attention and Comprehension

◆ **BEN & JERRY'S HOMEMADE**

When two former hippies named Ben Cohen and Jerry Greenfield started an ice cream company in a renovated gas station in northern Vermont, they grabbed consumers' attention by doing everything in a novel, unconventional way. First, they publicized the fact that they were making their "super premium" ice cream with the purest, richest ingredients. To maintain high quality, they dealt only with certain local suppliers of milk and cream, which in turn fulfilled their social mission of supporting Vermont dairy farmers. Second, they embraced all kinds of social causes, such as donating pretax profits to charity and hiring homeless people for their workforce. Their popular ice cream flavor Rainforest Crunch is made with specially harvested nuts from tribal cooperatives in the Amazon, in a righteous effort to save the rainforests—and the tribes. Third, they were champions at unconventional, attention-getting promotional efforts—like making airdrops of ice cream at rock concerts and launching an essay contest in the hunt for a new CEO (applicants had to write a 100-word essay explaining why they'd make a good CEO and mail in a lid from their favorite Ben & Jerry's ice cream flavor). Finally, there were the flavor names themselves—Chunky Monkey, Cherry Garcia, Rainforest Crunch—that got people's attention.

But tastes and the marketplace changed, and Ben & Jerry's needed to assess those changes to appeal to its customers. Consumers began to worry more about cholesterol than social causes, meaning that Ben & Jerry's would probably have to come out with lower-fat products like sorbet or frozen yogurt. Competitors like Häagen-Dazs and Breyers began to eat away at Ben & Jerry's profits, forcing the company to opt for more conventional modes of promotion, like television and radio ads.

And those attention-getting methods that worked so well in the United States appeared to fall flat overseas, where Ben & Jerry's must make future inroads to survive. For instance, Häagen-Dazs is viewed by Europeans as a sophisticated luxury product; Ben & Jerry's just seems goofy. And while support of social causes is viewed by Americans as heroic, in Asia the idea is commonplace—and cheap. Further, although New Englanders trumpet Ben & Jerry's support of Vermont's dairy farmers, Californians could care less (and Europeans even less than Californians).

This is not to say that Ben & Jerry's will be melting away anytime soon; rather, it will be important for the company to find different ways to capture and hold the attention of consumers. As you read this chapter, consider ways that companies like Ben & Jerry's can use various stimuli to attract consumers to their products.

Source: "Raspberry Rebels," *The Economist,* September 6, 1997, pp. 61–62.

◆ INTRODUCTION

How do consumers acquire, remember, and use information and knowledge about products and services? Chapters 2 through 5 address this interesting and important question. Specifically, Chapter 2 examines attention and comprehension processes that enable consumers to obtain knowledge about products and services. Attention refers to bringing information into conscious awareness through perception (seeing, hearing, smelling, tasting, and feeling). Comprehension refers to the ability to learn the meaning of new information by relating it to old information stored in memory. Attention and comprehension are needed for memorization to occur. Chapter 3 examines memory processes that allow consumers to remember or retain product information. As we will see, memory is much more influential and important than most people realize because memory influences almost everything we think about and do, and sometimes we are unaware of these influences. Chapter 4 explains how consumers use product knowledge to form judgments, beliefs, and opinions. Chapter 5 describes the procedures and rules consumers use to make choices and decisions.

Managers need to understand consumer attention and comprehension to design better products and services and to market products and services more effectively. Why do some product packages seem to stick out on grocery store shelves, whereas others seem barely noticeable? Why do some television commercials grab the attention of consumers, whereas others are ignored? Why do some print ads prompt consumers to stop flipping through a magazine or newspaper, whereas others lead consumers to turn pages quickly? Consumers cannot attend to everything, so it is important to develop an understanding of what they do notice and absorb, as Ben & Jerry's Homemade has done and must continue to do.

◆ PRODUCT KNOWLEDGE ACQUIRED THROUGH FIRSTHAND EXPERIENCE

One way consumers learn about products and acquire product knowledge is through **product trial.** Product trial involves actually trying or using a product. Direct, firsthand experience with a product or service provides a great deal of rich and useful information about the characteristics and properties of a new product. For example, words alone cannot adequately describe how a new beverage or snack food tastes. Advertisers, salespersons, friends, and relatives often try to tell us how a new product tastes, but we have to try the product for ourselves to see exactly how it tastes. Similarly, hearing about a new movie is not the same as seeing it for ourselves. Hearing about the smooth ride and responsive handling of a new automobile is not the same as riding or driving the new car for ourselves. Direct, firsthand experience (i.e., product trial) is often more informative than indirect, secondhand experience (i.e., hearsay).

Of course, marketing managers recognize the importance of product trial and direct behavioral experience with a product. They often mail free samples of products to consumers so that consumers can try the products for themselves, rather than just hear about the products. New breakfast cereals, snacks, soaps, toothpastes, and other small packaged goods can be mailed directly to consumers relatively easily. Free samples of sausages and pizzas and other products that require some preparation can be given to consumers at grocery stores. Sales representatives often offer free samples of juices, soft drinks, and other beverages to consumers at grocery stores. Department stores that carry perfumes and colognes often provide "tester" bottles of perfumes and colognes so that customers can spray themselves to see how much they like the scent of these products.

PRODUCT TRIAL OF CONSUMER DURABLES

How can managers increase product trial of consumer durables, such as automobiles and personal computers? Clearly, products such as these are too costly to be given away as free samples. Should managers of consumer durables forget about product trial then? The answer is an emphatic NO! Product trial can be managed even for expensive consumer durables by encouraging potential customers to obtain direct behavioral experience with the durables by taking them out for a "test drive." Very few consumers are willing to buy an automobile without first taking it out for a test drive, which enables them to experience the smooth ride or responsive handling of a new car for themselves. Simply hearing about the car's features from a television commercial, print advertisement, or slick salesperson is not enough. In fact, the test-drive concept is so important to the marketing of consumer durables that it is now applied to other products besides automobiles. For example, many computer retailers encourage potential customers to take a personal computer home overnight for just such a test drive.

Product and Service Trials

In-Store Samples
- Foods and beverages
  (juices, pizzas, yogurt, ice cream)
- Perfume testers
- Cosmetic samples and makeovers

Mail Samples
- Snacks, cereals, and other foods
- Laundry detergent and other cleaners
- Personal-care products
  (toothpaste, razors, pain relievers)

Product Demonstrations for Durables
- Test drives for automobiles
- Software demonstrations in store or
  downloaded from the Internet
- Music CDs and audio systems
- Computers, vacuum cleaners, sewing
  machines

Service Samples and Demonstrations
- Free dry cleaning or laundry washing
- Housekeeping services
- Free manicures with haircuts
- Trial lawn care services
- Free carpet cleaning

FIGURE 2-1

Consumers gain direct knowledge about products and services through firsthand experience.

Direct, firsthand experience with a computer that is easy to use is more compelling than secondhand information simply stating that the computer is user friendly. Seeing is believing. Figure 2-1 summarizes the types of product trials currently available.

◆ **PRODUCT KNOWLEDGE ACQUIRED THROUGH SECONDHAND EXPERIENCE**

Although direct, firsthand experience is often more persuasive than indirect, second-hand experience, this does not imply that managers should ignore secondhand information. (See "Making the Decision: Show or Tell?") The mass media enables managers to reach a large number of potential customers very quickly and efficiently. Literally millions of consumers are exposed to commercials aired on television. Millions more are also exposed to radio ads that they listen to in their cars, at home, or at work, and millions of others are exposed to print advertisements in newspapers and magazines. Consumers acquire a great deal of information and knowledge about products through secondhand experience. Furthermore, secondhand information provided by advertising often leads consumers to try products that they would not have tried otherwise.

In addition to advertising, secondhand information is also provided by sales representatives, telemarketers, package labels, coupons, brochures, and point-of-purchase displays. Managers have a great deal of control over these sources. Other sources of secondhand information are less susceptible to managerial control and influence.

MAKING THE DECISION

SHOW OR TELL?

Samples, coupons, demonstrations, promotions, ads, TV commercials—you think you have seen them all and tried them all. Marketers know that the best way to get consumers to buy their products is to give consumers experience with the products—either firsthand through product trial or secondhand through ads, labels, sales representatives, and the like.

If you want to hear a song or two from one of Carly Simon's albums, you don't have to head to the nearest CD store and put on the headphones to find out if you like what you hear. Instead, if you have already bought her latest CD produced by Arista Records, *Film Noir,* pop the disk into your CD-ROM for a multimedia presentation that includes an interview with Simon, a video, and short takes from several of her other albums.

If you want to know what fashions, beauty trends, makeup products and colors best suit you, visit Cover Girl's Web site at http://www.covergirl.com for a complete, virtual makeover. The home page offers you choices ranging from makeup tips and trends, to information about Cover Girl models and photographers, to the company's annual volunteerism awards. If you want personal makeup recommendations, you can browse through the Cover Girl Color Match system, answering questions about your skin type, to find out what types of products are best for you. Of course, this procedure isn't the same as actually trying that new shade of lipstick, but it brings you much closer to identifying which products you will want to buy than looking at a print ad or television commercial.

Imagine that you want to remodel part of your house—the kitchen, for instance. Numerous companies and associations have Web sites that are chock full of information, pictures, videos, and even samples in the form of design plans. The National Association of the Remodeling Industry, at http://www.nari.org, has a special section called "Red Flags," which warns consumers about certain remodeling concerns, such as how to avoid choosing the wrong contractor, how to stay within budget, and how to avoid legal problems. Hometime, at http://www.hometime.com, offers photos of home renovations with lists of the products used. Homearts, at http://www.homearts.com, contains a compendium of home improvement articles that have appeared in Hearst publications. Finally, General Electric's appliance site, at http://www.ge.com/appliances/usa/index.htm, offers extensive descriptions of all its products, along with the opportunity to download detailed line drawings, measurements, and owners manuals.

Sources: Bart Ziegler, "Web Surfer's Guide to the Kitchen," *The Wall Street Journal,* July 25, 1997, p. B8; Cover Girl Web site, http://www.covergirl.com; Carly Simon, *Film Noir,* Arista Records, Inc.

These include articles appearing in consumer magazines that do not accept advertising or support from manufacturers (e.g., *Consumer Reports, Consumer Digest*); reports from government agencies; and word-of-mouth communications from acquaintances, friends, and relatives. Clearly, secondhand experience provides a great deal of information about products and services. Figure 2-2 lists company and more objective sources of information.

Secondhand Product and Service Information

Company-Provided Information
- Advertisements, commercials, and brochures
- Package labeling and instructions
- Company representatives (salespeople, telemarketers, service representatives)
- Point-of-purchase displays
- Internet sites (World Wide Web company sites)

Other Sources of Information
- Friends and relatives
- Professional and licensing organizations
- Consumer publications (*Consumer Reports, Consumer Digest*)
- Local, state, and federal governments (Chamber of Commerce, Better Business Bureau, Food and Drug Administration, Federal Trade Commission)
- Internet sites (*Consumer Reports* at www.consumer.org, *Journal of Consumer Psychology* at www.erlbaum.com/1022.html, *Colloquy* online newsletter at www.colloquy.org, federal government agencies' online sites)

FIGURE 2-2

Consumers gain valuable knowledge about products and services through information provided by companies and other sources.

◆ LIMITS OF ATTENTION

Consumers are exposed to so much first- and secondhand information that they could not possibly process or think about each and every product-related piece of data they encounter in their daily lives. If consumers had to think carefully about every ad, each package label, and every marketing communication they see or hear, there would be little time for anything else. In other words, consumers have **limits of attention;** they attend to a very small fraction of the marketing communications to which they are exposed and that is available in the marketplace.

Exactly how much information can people handle? According to Harvard psychologist George Miller (1956), people can attend to seven (plus or minus two) units, or pieces, of information at one time. A unit of information can be very small—such as a single number, letter, word, or idea—or very large—such as a string of numbers, letters, words, or ideas (Newell & Simon, 1972). The size of a unit depends on a person's level of knowledge or expertise: As knowledge increases, the size of a unit also increases (Newell & Simon, 1972). Consequently, compared with novices, experts attend to and think about larger units of information.

Because people can attend to only about seven units of information at a time, it is easy to overwhelm or overload consumers with too much information. For example, grocery stores may carry a dozen or more different brands of dishwashing detergents. Furthermore, dishwashing detergents are available in large (e.g., 32 ounces), medium (e.g., 16 ounces), and small (e.g., 8 ounces) containers. If 12 brands are available in three sizes, consumers are faced with 36 different alternatives from which to choose. To compare all possible pairs of these 36 alternatives, consumers would have to make over 1,200 comparisons (36!/(36 − 2)! = 1,260)! Most consumers are unwilling to put this much time and effort into choosing one brand of dishwashing detergent from a set of 36 alternatives.

Comparing 36 different brands of dishwashing detergent is easy, however, if information is presented in a manner that makes it easy to make comparisons. For example, a "summary sheet" is a list of alternatives with the best alternative presented at the top, the second best listed second, the third best third, and so on (Russo, 1977; Russo, Staelin, Nolan, Russell, & Metcalf, 1986). Figure 2-3 shows an example of a summary sheet. When a summary sheet with unit price information is provided for a set of dishwashing detergents, consumers make more intelligent purchase decisions and choose better buys for the money (Russo, 1977). When a summary sheet with added sugar

FIGURE 2-3 Summary Sheet

List of Unit Prices (Listed in Order of Increasing Price per Quart)

Par, 48 oz.	54¢	36.0¢ per Quart
Par, 32 oz.	38¢	38.0¢ per Quart
Sweetheart, 32 oz.	55¢	55.0¢ per Quart
Brocade, 48 oz.	85¢	56.7¢ per Quart
Sweetheart, 22 oz.	39¢	56.7¢ per Quart
Supurb, 32 oz.	59¢	59.0¢ per Quart
White Magic, 32 oz.	59¢	59.0¢ per Quart
Brocade, 32 oz.	63¢	63.0¢ per Quart
Brocade, 22 oz.	45¢	65.5¢ per Quart
Supurb, 22 oz.	45¢	65.5¢ per Quart
White Magic, 32 oz.	45¢	65.5¢ per Quart
Brocade, 12 oz.	27¢	72.0¢ per Quart
Supurb, 12 oz.	29¢	77.3¢ per Quart
Ivory, 32 oz.	80¢	80.0¢ per Quart
Dove, 22 oz.	56¢	81.5¢ per Quart
Ivory, 22 oz.	56¢	81.5¢ per Quart
Lux, 22 oz.	56¢	81.5¢ per Quart
Palmolive, 32 oz.	85¢	85.0¢ per Quart
Ivory, 12 oz.	32¢	85.3¢ per Quart
Palmolive, 22 oz.	60¢	87.3¢ per Quart
Palmolive, 12 oz.	34¢	90.7¢ per Quart

Source: From Russo (1977).

information is provided for a set of breakfast cereals, consumers make more intelligent decisions and choose healthier brands (Russo et al., 1986). Because consumers cannot attend to and think about a large amount of information at one time, presenting information in a way that reduces the time and effort involved in making brand comparisons helps consumers to make better decisions.

◆ ATTENTION INTENSITY

People have limited cognitive capacity and limited mental resources to devote to information processing, problem solving, and decision making. Consumers can attend to and think about only a relatively small amount of information at a time. However, **attention intensity,** or the amount of information people can attend to, can vary from five to nine units. One factor that influences the amount of information people can handle at a particular moment is prior knowledge or expertise (Alba & Hutchinson, 1987). People who are knowledgeable about a certain topic attend to and think about larger units or chunks of information. Knowledgeable people can also process more units. The ability to handle both more and larger chunks leads to a huge processing advantage (Newell & Simon, 1972). This processing advantage enables experts to solve problems more effectively and efficiently, compared with novices.

AROUSAL

Arousal is another factor that influences attention intensity (Kahneman, 1973). **Arousal** is defined as a state of wakefulness or alertness. When arousal is extremely low, people are asleep. When arousal is low, people are drowsy or nearly asleep. Moderate arousal is characterized by the typical or baseline level of wakefulness or alertness people experience during the normal course of a day. High arousal is produced by viewing exciting events, such as movies, concerts, basketball games, and football games (and, yes, even stimulating lectures). Consumption of caffeine products (e.g., coffee, tea, cola, Dr. Pepper, Mountain Dew) as well as exposure to loud noises, flashing lights, and unexpected events can also produce high levels of arousal. Extremely high arousal is produced by roller coaster rides, sports activities, and aerobic exercise.

An inverted-U-shaped relationship exists between arousal and attention intensity. That is, intensity is low when arousal is either low or high. When arousal is low, the amount of cognitive capacity and mental resources available for information processing is also low. It is difficult to attend to much information when we are tired, drowsy, or nearly asleep. Surprisingly, when arousal is high, cognitive capacity is low once again. When we are highly aroused, we are overstimulated, and overstimulation makes it difficult to attend to large amounts of information. When we are moderately aroused, however, we are alert but not so alert that we are overstimulated. Consequently, when arousal is moderate, cognitive capacity is greatest and we can attend to more information than when arousal is either low or high. (See Fig. 2-4.)

Consider the results of an interesting field experiment on attention and memory for television commercials aired during the Super Bowl (Pavelchak, Antil, & Munch, 1988). Fans from the two cities represented in the Super Bowl were highly aroused and

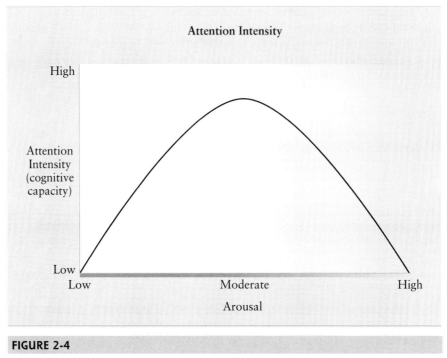

Attention Intensity

FIGURE 2-4

An inverted-U relationship exists between arousal and attention intensity.

overstimulated, and as a consequence, attention and memory for television commercials aired during the game was poor. By contrast, viewers from other cities across the country were only moderately aroused, and these viewers exhibited much better attention and memory for television commercials aired during the game. Attention and memory performance is poor when arousal is very high. Under moderate levels of arousal, attention and memory are at their best.

◆ SELECTIVE ATTENTION

The United States has over 1,200 television stations, nearly 10,000 radio stations, and about 12,000 newspapers and magazines (Pratkanis & Aronson, 1992). The typical American consumer watches 30 hours of television per week, and during this time he or she is exposed to over 700 television commercials (Pratkanis & Aronson, 1992). When the consumer is not watching television, he or she is exposed to over 700 radio and print ads per week (Pratkanis & Aronson, 1992). American firms spend over $45 billion a year on advertising and another $65 billion a year on promotions (coupons, sales, free samples, rebates, premiums, sweepstakes, sporting event sponsorships, etc.).

Obviously, consumers cannot attend to all product information to which they are exposed. **Cognitive capacity,** or the ability to attend to and think about information, is limited. Consumers attend to or focus on some, but not all, information. Consequently, managers need to figure out what guides selective attention, or the allocation of cognitive capacity. What leads consumers to focus on some marketing stimuli but ignore others? Why are only some ads interesting and attention-drawing? In grocery stores, why do we stop to examine some product packages but walk past others? In department stores, why do some product displays capture our attention while others fade into the woodwork? When driving, why do we notice some store signs and billboards but shut out others? What factors determine what we attend to and what we ignore?

VOLUNTARY AND INVOLUNTARY ATTENTION

According to Kahneman (1973), allocation of attention is influenced by both voluntary and involuntary factors. People voluntarily attend to information that is relevant to current plans, intentions, and goals. For example, when consumers plan to buy a new sound system, a new pair of shoes, or a new car, they selectively attend to information relevant to sound systems, shoes, or cars, respectively. However, involuntary influences on attention also exist. Some marketing stimuli are so attention-drawing that they are difficult to tune out, even when we try to ignore them. A clear understanding of these involuntary influences enables managers to design better products, develop better ads, and implement more effective marketing strategies.

Salient stimuli draw attention involuntarily (Greenwald & Leavitt, 1984; Nisbett & Ross, 1980). It is difficult to ignore salient stimuli. Some products, packages, and ads "stick out" because they are different and interesting. For example, Rolls Royces are very different from other types of automobiles, and as a consequence, they really stick out on the road. Pringles potato chips come in tall, cylindrical packages that are very different from typical cellophane potato chip packages. Consequently, Pringles potato chip packages are very noticeable on grocery store shelves. The early Energizer bunny battery commercials were very different from typical television commercials, and as a result, the bunny commercials tended to catch the eye of the consumer.

However, salience is context dependent. That is, stimuli that are salient in one context or situation may not be salient in another. (See "Making the Decision: Who's Getting Framed?") For example, a particular Rolls Royce automobile would not be very salient in the parking lot of an exclusive country club whose members all drive Rolls Royces. A particular can of Pringles potato chips would not be very salient on a shelf filled with similar cylindrical packages. A particular Energizer bunny commercial would not be very salient after consumers view hundreds of similar Energizer bunny commercials. Stimuli are salient only when they are very different from other stimuli. Unique or different stimuli are figural (focal) and everything else fades into the background. This is known as the **figure–ground principle of perception.** The salience of an ad is affected by its novelty and the use of unexpected stimuli. For example, one way the figure–ground principle can be used in advertising is by changing the camera angle: Instead of showing the advertised brand from an eye-level perspective, using an upward camera angle increases attention to the advertised brand and increases how much consumers think about the advertised brand (Meyers-Levy & Peracchio, 1992).

NOVELTY

A salient stimulus can differ from background stimuli in many ways. Novel, unusual, changing, moving, bright, intense, and complex stimuli are salient (Fiske & Taylor, 1991; Nisbett & Ross, 1980). Such stimuli "stick out," attract attention, capture our interest and have a strong influence on judgment and choice. Novel products, ads, and

It is difficult to ignore the salient stimuli in this ad — large type and bright, geometric computer-generated shapes.

Source: Courtesy of Hewlett-Packard Company.

The Pringles chips in a can are
different than traditional chips.
Source: © Mary Boucher.

marketing communications are salient and attention-drawing. They influence us
because they are different and therefore difficult to ignore. Novel products tend to
enjoy high sales initially. For example, several firms developed novel clear beverages.
Pepsi developed Crystal Pepsi (Lavinsky, 1993), Coca-Cola followed with Tab Clear
(Lavinsky, 1993), and the Miller Brewing Company developed a Miller Clear beer
(Lavinsky, 1993). Novel products, such as these, tend to sell well during their first year
(Lavinsky, 1993). Eventually, however, the novelty wears off and firms have to develop
new products all over again.

Advertisers constantly experiment with novel advertising executions. New characters, approaches, and scenarios are constantly being developed. For example, initially,
the Energizer bunny battery commercials were novel, amusing, and attention-drawing.
Moreover, advertisers were able to sustain the novelty for an extended period of time
by developing many different variations of the bunny theme (Haugtvedt, Schumann,
Schneider, & Warren, 1994; Schumann, Petty, & Clemons, 1990; Unnava & Burnkrant,
1991). One version of the ad showed the marching bunny interrupting a speech by a
famous football player who used to crunch quarterbacks but then crunched "Pigskin"
snacks, another version showed the bunny interrupting a scene with King Kong climbing a tall building, yet another showed the bunny escaping certain death from a laser
gun operated by an evil spy. The Energizer bunny's novelty would have worn out long
ago if numerous variations of the theme had not been employed. However, even with
varied advertising executions, the Energizer bunny's novelty eventually wore out.

Novel promotional campaigns are also attention-drawing and potentially effective.
For example, Sharples Jewelry in Chinook, Montana, guaranteed that if it snowed
more than three inches on New Year's Eve (which it did not), all customers who made
a purchase during the 1993 Christmas season would receive a full refund (Ortega,
1993). Sales rose from the usual $90,000 for the Christmas season to $135,000. Other
novel promotional schemes are also used by jewelers during the Christmas season. An
Arkansas jeweler mails videocassette catalogs to potential customers, an Iowa jeweler
feeds quarters into expired parking meters and leaves notes under windshield wipers
informing potential customers of their benefactor's actions, a Pennsylvania jeweler

MAKING THE DECISION

WHO'S GETTING FRAMED?

You have probably already noticed it: as you click from one Web site to another, certain advertisements stay in "frames" around the edge of your screen. Don't touch your dial—there is nothing wrong with your computer and nothing you can do about it. The practice is called "framing," and it is one of the new ways marketers are trying to get your attention. Both small and large companies are taking advantage of framing technology. Reader's Digest Association Inc. publishes *LookSmart,* a directory that imposes ads on all the sites to which it links. TotalNews Inc., a small firm based in Phoenix, offers consumers a "hot link" list of more than 1,100 new organizations and frames nearly all of them.

Not surprisingly, framing has both supporters and critics. "It's a completely parasitic Web site," says Bruce P. Keller, an attorney who represents several major media companies, about TotalNews. But Roman Godzich, creator of TotalNews, argues, "The whole point of the Internet is to be able to link to other sites."

"Everyone knows linking is one of the advantages of the Web," counters Keller, "but when one uses framing technology to make money off the backs of others . . . they've crossed the line." Indeed, the Internet has very little regulation, which allows creators of new technology to try just about anything they think

will work. "If you publish on the Web, you have to expect all kinds of weird things to happen to your content," observes Kevin Cooke, a programmer for the Mercury News site.

How does framing affect consumers? It has been getting consumer attention—at least for now. But the novelty is unlikely to last very long. Like junk mail and telemarketing calls, consumers may soon decide that framing is a nuisance and complain or just tune it out, perhaps even avoiding sites that they know will contain framing. Also, as novelty wears off, so does salience. One framed ad surrounded by half a dozen other framed ads is unlikely to stand out. Both of these factors may lead consumers to view framing as intrusive rather than helpful, which, in an age when more and more people are concerned about issues of privacy, may force framers to rethink their approach. While advertisers may love the access they have to consumers initially, consumers may rebuff the advertisers. "Our advertisers love it," claims Brian Cowley, head of advertising sales for *LookSmart.* "Our ads stay with [the user] when they're on web sites and give our advertisers more exposure." Exposure is good, but consumers may decide that framing, at the expense of their privacy as well as the Web sites they wish to visit, is too much of a good thing.

Source: Rebecca Quick, "Framing Muddies Issue of Content Ownership," *The Wall Street Journal,* January 30, 1997, p. B10.

mails tiny shovels that customers can use in a miniature gold mine displayed at the store (Ortega, 1993). Retailers such as these undoubtedly recognize the power of novelty.

Unusual, atypical, and unexpected stimuli are different by definition. Changing and moving stimuli are also different and salient. Spokespersons in television commercials typically move or walk while they talk because presentations delivered by stationary speakers are much less engaging. Moving signs, like the famous Las Vegas cowboy sign with the arm that moves up and down, are also more attention-drawing than stationary signs. Neon signs often have letters that light up one at a time and appear to

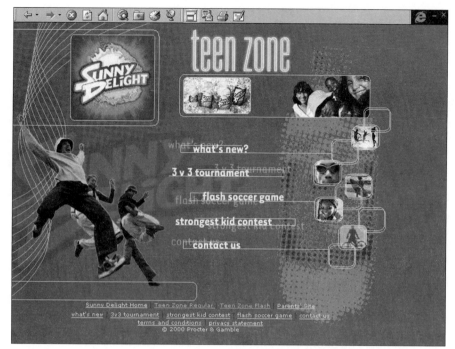

Sunny Delight's novel promotional campaign offers consumers the opportunity to play games and win prizes via the product's Web site (http://www.sunnyd.com).

Source: © The Procter & Gamble Company. Used with permission.

move. "Eat at Joe's" signs and other types of neon signs are also bright or intense, especially at night. Consumers attend to novel, unusual, atypical, unexpected, changing, moving, bright, and intense stimuli automatically and involuntarily. Such stimuli are difficult to ignore.

VIVIDNESS

Vivid stimuli also draw attention automatically and involuntarily (Kisielius & Sternthal, 1984, 1986; Nisbett & Ross, 1980; Taylor & Thompson, 1982). However, unlike salient stimuli, vivid stimuli are attention-drawing across contexts. Salience is context dependent (i.e., a salient stimulus differs in some way from other stimuli present in a given situation), and vividness is context independent (i.e., it does not matter what other stimuli are present in a given situation). Vivid stimuli are "(a) emotionally interesting, (b) concrete and imagery provoking, and (c) proximate in a sensory, temporal, or spatial way" (Nisbett & Ross, 1980, p. 45).

PERSONAL INTEREST

Of course, stimuli that are interesting to one person may not be interesting to another. For example, stamp collectors (like myself) find stamps incredibly fascinating. Stamp collectors like to spend hours studying their collections—examining watermarks, postmarks, and even perforations. I know one stamp collector who even dreams about

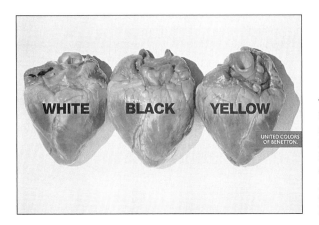

The vivid stimuli in this ad by United Colors of Benetton draw attention automatically and involuntarily, even though they have nothing to do with the company's product—clothing.

Source: Concept: O Toscani. Courtesy of United Colors of Benetton.

stamps and imagines seeing stamps when he looks at plaid shirts (the plaid squares turn into stamps). To this individual, stamps are very vivid and emotionally interesting. By contrast, people who are not stamp collectors (like my wife) find stamps hopelessly boring. When stamp collectors show their prized collections to non-stamp collectors, the non-stamp collectors feel like guests forced to watch slides of other people's children for hours on end.

Although both salient and vivid stimuli draw attention, what is salient in one situation may not be salient in another, and what is vivid to one person may not be vivid to another. That is, salient stimuli capture the attention of all of the people some of the time, whereas vivid stimuli grab the attention of some of the people all of the time. Perhaps the safest strategy is to develop marketing stimuli that are both salient and vivid.

Managers cannot make their products interesting to everyone, just like stamp collectors cannot make their stamps interesting to everyone. However, emotional interest is but one factor that influences the vividness of a product, ad, promotion, or package.

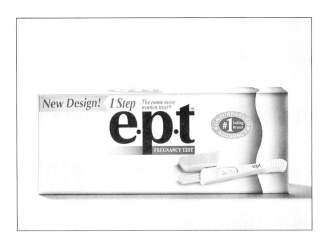

Consumers who pay attention to this ad will be primarily those who want to know if they are pregnant. Those without pregnancy concerns will probably ignore the ad.

Source: Courtesy of Warner-Lambert Company.

Vividness is also affected by **concreteness** and **proximity.** Concrete (specific) information is vivid and easy to visualize, whereas abstract (general) information is pallid and fuzzy. Concrete examples make it easier to learn abstract theories. For instance, one abstract theory suggests that ads that use catchy words are more effective; catchy words like *new, quick, easy, improved, now, suddenly, introducing,* and *amazing* can be quite persuasive (Pratkanis & Aronson, 1992).

CONCRETENESS

Concrete information is easy to picture, imagine, and think about and consequently is often very influential. Imagery-provoking stimuli, like pictures, are also easy to think about. Pictures are vivid, interesting, and influential (Childers & Houston, 1984; Houston, Childers, & Heckler, 1987; Mitchell, 1986), and, like the saying goes, a picture

Ads containing a lot of printed text tend to have less impact than those with concrete, vivid stimuli.

Source: Courtesy of Dux Interiors Inc., New York.

is worth a thousand words. Making a product attribute more concrete in an ad increases the amount of attention paid to the attribute and this increases the perceived importance of the attribute (MacKenzie, 1986). Advertising repetition also increases the amount of attention allocated to a focal attribute and this also increases the perceived importance of the attribute.

Face-to-face communications and meetings are often more vivid, interesting, and influential than boring written communications and memos. Herr, Kardes, and Kim (1991) investigated the effects of vivid (interesting) versus pallid (boring) messages on judgment by presenting subjects with a description of a new personal computer. The exact wording of the description was held constant. However, the description was presented either in a vivid face-to-face format (another student described the product to the subject in person) or in a pallid written format (the subject read a written description of the product). As Figure 2-5 shows, even though the words presented in each condition were exactly the same, the vivid, face-to-face, word-of-mouth message had a much stronger impact on subjects' evaluations of the described product. However, we also found that the vividness effect is weaker when subjects had a strong prior opinion about the described product. The vividness effect is also reduced when a lot of negative information is available. When a product is described by much negative information, strongly negative opinions are formed regardless of whether information is presented in a vivid or pallid manner.

FIGURE 2-5

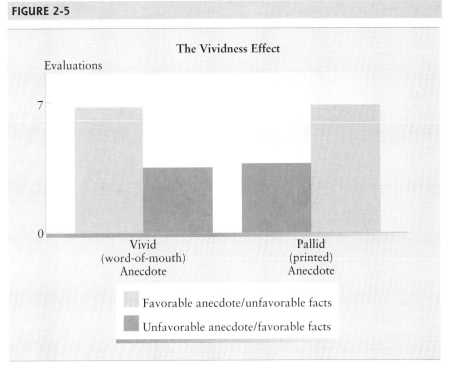

Although face-to-face and written messages are equally informative when the message is held constant, face-to-face messages are more vivid, interesting, and influential.

Source: Results of Herr, Kardes & Kim (1991), Experiment 1.

PROXIMITY

Information that is proximal, or close, to a consumer is more vivid and has more impact than information that is distant or not immediately relevant. Three different kinds of proximity are important: sensory, temporal, and spatial proximity. **Sensory proximity** refers to firsthand (proximal) versus secondhand (distant) information. Information that is perceived by our own eyes and ears is more vivid than information that is perceived and relayed by another person. Seeing for ourselves that a product works is more convincing than secondhand, hearsay evidence. **Temporal proximity** refers to how recently an event occurred. Events that occurred recently are much more vivid and attention-drawing compared with events that occurred a long time ago. We are more concerned about products that fell apart yesterday than about products that fell apart 10 years ago. Finally, **spatial proximity** refers to the location of events. Events that occur where we live now are much more vivid than events that occur overseas. Products that are available in our own neighborhood are more vivid and attention-drawing than products that are available only in foreign countries.

To summarize, there are many different ways to make information more vivid and attention-drawing. Vividness can be increased by making information more interesting, more concrete, or more proximal to the consumer. Proximity, or nearness, can be increased on many different dimensions—including the sensory, temporal, and spatial dimensions. Obviously, information that grabs our attention has a stronger influence on judgment and choice relative to information that is virtually ignored. However, less obviously, vivid information is less likely to have a strong impact on judgment and choice when the consumer's attentional system is not overburdened or overtaxed, when the consumer has a strong prior opinion of the target product, and when large amounts of negative information are available (Herr et al., 1991).

◆ COMPREHENSION

Effective marketing communications attract the attention of consumers and present information in a manner that allows consumers to comprehend or extract the meaning of these communications. Comprehension involves relating information presented in a message to information based on prior experience and stored in memory (Alba & Hutchinson, 1987). Gleaning meaning often involves forming interpretive inferences that fill in gaps and make incomplete information seem complete. For example, to understand the statements "Technics offers an integrated system" and "The turntable is high in quality," the consumer must realize that a turntable is one component of an integrated stereo sound system (Alba & Hutchinson, 1987). Consumers who are not knowledgeable about stereo systems may not realize this and may be unable to comprehend the message.

BELIEVABILITY

Remember those $1.99 X-ray glasses that were advertised in comic books? Do you believe the claim that these amazing glasses enable you to see right through things? Probably not, but when you were young, you probably did. Do you believe the claim that Listerine kills germs that cause colds? Many adults did. In fact, so many adults believed this false claim that the Federal Trade Commission (FTC) had to take action against Listerine (Armstrong, Gurol, & Russ, 1979). Why did this claim seem so believable? According to social psychologist Dan Gilbert, comprehension and belief are inseparable (Gilbert, 1991; Gilbert, Krull, & Malone, 1990; Gilbert, Tafarodi, & Malone, 1993). That is, initially we believe everything we see and hear. Unbelieving, or rejecting a false claim, comes later (maybe seconds later, but later nevertheless). In other words, believing is as easy and as automatic as comprehension. Unbelieving, however, requires more time and effort. To demonstrate this, Gilbert et al. (1990) asked subjects to learn a new language by studying statements presented on a computer monitor. After reading a statement, such as "a monishna is a star," subjects were told (or not told in some conditions) that the statement was either true or false. Furthermore, sometimes the true or false feedback was interrupted by a distracting tone-detection task (i.e., subjects were asked to perform multiple tasks at the same time). Later, all the statements were presented again and subjects were asked to indicate whether each statement was true or false. Because many statements were presented, subjects made a lot of errors. However, some types of errors were more common than others. Subjects were more likely to believe false statements were true than vice versa (i.e., that true statements were false). This is because believing is easier than unbelieving, believe it or not.

Naturally, we do not believe everything we hear, but the important point is that unbelieving or rejecting a false claim requires an additional step and extra effort than believing. However, when we are overloaded with too much information, when we have to make a judgment or decision quickly, or when we try to do too many things at once, we are less able to engage in the extra effort required for unbelieving and are more likely to believe claims that are not true (Gilbert et al., 1993). Of course, information overload, time pressure, and multiple task demands are facts of everyday life.

Distraction

Does Gilbert's analysis apply even to important decisions? Recent evidence indicates that it does (Gilbert et al., 1993). In this study, subjects read statements about two crime reports that crawled across the bottom of a television screen, just like an emergency weather bulletin, for instance. True statements were printed in black and false statements were printed in red. The false statements suggested that the first defendant was innocent and the second was guilty, or vice versa. Subjects were sometimes dis-

Consumers will sometimes believe almost anything because unbelieving takes time and energy.

Manufacturer of item is Ming Shing, Hong Kong.

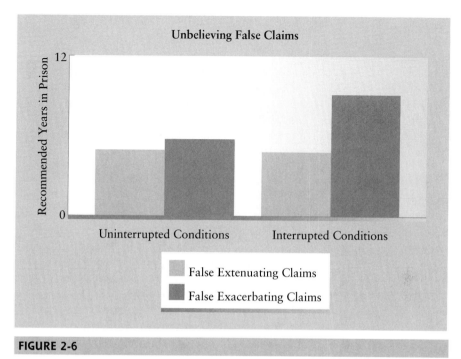

FIGURE 2-6

Distraction affects whether people believe false claims.
Source: Adapted from Gilbert, Tafarodi, & Malone (1993).

tracted by a second task they had to perform while reading the crime reports. This distraction greatly influenced subjects' judgments. On average, distracted subjects recommended 11.15 years in prison for the accused party when the false statements were exacerbating and only 5.83 years in prison when the false statements were extenuating. Hence, distracted subjects had a difficult time unbelieving false statements, even when true statements were printed in black and false statements were printed in red and subjects were aware of this fact (see Fig. 2-6). Of course, unbelieving false statements is even more difficult when the real-world mass media fails to print true statements in black and false statements in red.

Repetition

What happens when we are exposed to false statements over and over again, as in repetitive advertising? Recent evidence indicates that repetition exacerbates the tendency to believe what is not true (see Fig. 2-7). Hawkins and Hoch (1992) exposed subjects to a large number of true and false product claims—such as "Consumers are more satisfied with State Farm homeowner's insurance than with Allstate," "Prolonged use of Alka-Seltzer can lead to the formation of kidney stones," "Antihistamines have no effect on the common cold," and "Stone-ground flour retains more nutrients than conventional flour." Some of the statements were presented only once and some were presented twice. Half the subjects were asked to judge the validity of each statement, and half were asked to judge the comprehensibility of each statement. As expected, belief increased with repetition, especially when subjects were asked to judge compre-

Statement
Consumers are more satisfied with State Farm homeowner's insurance than with Allstate (true)
Red Lobster is the largest full-service dinner restaurant in the United States (true)
Weight Watchers is the worst-selling name-brand sweetener (true)
Prolonged use of Alka-Seltzer can lead to the formation of kidney stones (true)
Antihistamines have no effect on the common cold (true)
All nondietetic margarines contain the same amount of saturated fat (false)
Buffered aspirin tends to work more slowly than unbuffered aspirin (false)
Stone-ground flour retains more nutrients than conventional flour (false)
Rose hips vitamin C is better for the body than synthetic vitamin C (false)
The municipal water in Houston was rated higher on sensory qualities (e.g., taste, smell) than the municipal water in New York City (false)

FIGURE 2-7

Repetition exacerbates the tendency for people to believe claims that are not true.
Source: Hawkins & Hoch (1992).

hensibility. Repetition increases familiarity, which then increases believability. Familiar statements "ring a bell" and are often regarded as true. If we cannot remember whether a claim is true, we often assume that familiar claims are true. This assumption is easy to make. After all, why should we bother to familiarize ourselves with false information that clutters up memory? It seems more practical to try to learn and remember only what seems to be true. However, repetition makes everything (true or false) more memorable and believable.

◆ MISCOMPREHENSION (FAMOUS FEDERAL TRADE COMMISSION CASES)

Comprehension involves interpretation and inference formation. Inferences are beliefs or assumptions that "go beyond the information given" (Hastie, 1983; Kardes, 1993). **Pragmatic inferences** are everyday assumptions about claims that are literally true but figuratively false (Harris, 1977; Harris & Monaco, 1978). For example, the claim "Brand X pills may relieve pain" is literally true, because "may" means "maybe yes" or "maybe no." Figuratively, however, people tend to assume that "may" means "usually," because the word "may" is often used this way in everyday language. The FTC has no trouble taking legal action against literally false claims. However, dealing

BELIEVING THE GOOD HOUSEKEEPING SEAL

The Good Housekeeping seal is real: it is both a seal and a warranty. Since 1909, the seal has stood for consumer advocacy against false claims by advertisers. The seal is not just a stamp of approval for certain products; it is, in fact, a legal warranty. From 1909 to 1997, the warranty was good for a year; in 1997, Good Housekeeping extended the warranty to two years. The new warranty "gives the consumer an advantage over what they are getting [from the manufacturer]," notes publisher Patricia Haegele.

How does a product get the seal? Advertisers who want to participate in the program must buy at least one full-page ad in the magazine, at rates of $130,000 to $160,000. (Of course, this immediately disqualifies small companies with tiny ad budgets.) But before the ad is accepted and published, the Good Housekeeping Institute puts the advertiser's product through a rigorous review process, testing the item for quality. Once the product and ad are accepted, the seal is good for a year and then must be renewed. The Institute *does* turn down ads and products. "In the last couple of months alone we've turned down several hundred thousand dollars in advertising," notes Ellen Levine, editor-in-chief of the magazine. (And the magazine flatly rejects all cigarette and liquor advertising.)

Thus, the Good Housekeeping seal attracts consumers' attention, but it has become such a familiar symbol that consumers may doubt its meaning. "Ubiquity is exactly what they don't want," says Ari Paparo, a consultant for the market research firm Find/SVP. "They don't want the seal to just be there and have no significance—it's important for it to be meaningful, not just an accepted part of packaging." So, in conjunction with the new, extended warranty, Good Housekeeping is redesigning the seal for a new look.

The important thing, however, is for the institute to continue rigorous testing and review of both products and ads. This not only benefits consumers, it also benefits the magazine (by maintaining its reputation) and of course the advertisers who receive the seal. Is it ethical to require manufacturers to buy ads to receive the seal? And is the high price fair to small manufacturers who can't afford it? Supporters would probably argue that it's the cost of doing business; critics might doubt the validity of a seal that has, to some degree, been purchased. But so far, Good Housekeeping has set such high standards for the products it backs that consumers still are the winners—which, after all, is the point.

Sources: "In Which We Bash a Baby Seal," *Fortune,* September 8, 1997, pp. 36, 40; "Good Housekeeping to Boost Warranty on Advertised Products to Two Years," *The Wall Street Journal,* August 1, 1997, p. B12.

with claims that are literally true but that have false implications is much trickier. (See "Taking Issue: Believing the Good Housekeeping Seal.") Nevertheless, the FTC has enjoyed some success even with such difficult cases.

COMPARISON OMISSION

Using the word *may* in a misleading way is not the only way to induce pragmatic inferences. **Comparison omission** is another misleading procedure. For example, the claim "Brand X gasoline gives you greater mileage" is literally true because it gives you greater mileage compared with some substances (e.g., sugar water). However, comparison omission is potentially misleading because many consumers are likely to assume that Brand X gives you greater mileage than many other brands of gasoline, even though this is not stated. Other types of omissions are also potentially misleading. For example, the claim "50 doctors recommend Brand X" seems impressive initially. However, 50 doctors out of a sample of 1,000 seems considerably less impressive.

PIECEMEAL DATA

Piecemeal data can also be misleading. For example, "Brand X has more head room than a Mercedes, more leg room than a Cadillac, and more trunk space than a BMW" implies that Brand X is better than all these fine automobiles. Even if each individual statement is true, the overall impression made by the individual statements can be misleading. Juxtaposition of imperatives can also be misleading. For example, "Be popular! Brush with Ultra Brite!" implies that brushing with Ultra Brite will make you more popular, even though this is not stated explicitly. Similarly, negative questions like "Don't you want your child to be more successful in school? Try Brand X" implies that Brand X will make your child more successful in school, even though this is not stated.

AFFIRMATION OF THE CONSEQUENT

The claim "Women who look younger use Oil of Olay" is also misleading because of a common reasoning fallacy known as **affirmation of the consequent.** That is, statements of the form "if p, then q" are often misinterpreted as meaning "if q, then p." In this example, "Women who look younger use Oil of Olay" is misconstrued as "If women use Oil of Olay, then they will look younger." However, there are a lot of younger-looking women who do not use Oil of Olay, and there are a lot of older-looking women who use Oil of Olay. People frequently get their p's and q's mixed up (backwards), which results in erroneous conclusions.

Visual images can also have false implications. For example, one Milky Way commercial showed a glass of milk magically transform into a Milky Way bar, implying that this candy bar is as nutritional as a full glass of milk (Preston, 1977). The FTC took action against the makers of Milky Way and won this case. The FTC also won a case against Mattel, which aired an ad using extreme close-ups and camera angles that made toy cars appear much faster, and thus more appealing to children, than they were in reality. The FTC also won a case against an ad using piecemeal data: "Each glass of Carnation Instant Breakfast delivers as much protein as two eggs, as much mineral nourishment as two strips of crisp bacon, more energy than two slices of toast, and even Vitamin C." Although each individual statement was true, Carnation Instant Breakfast is not as nutritious as a balanced breakfast, which this description seems to resemble.

Ocean Spray aired a misleading ad stating that its cranberry juice has more food energy than orange or tomato juice (Preston, 1977). The problem here is that there is no universally accepted definition of *food energy*. Most consumers tend to interpret food energy in terms of nutritional value, even though Ocean Spray cranberry juice is just higher in calories than orange or tomato juice. Lysol "kills flu and other germs on surfaces" and Listerine "kills germs by the millions" imply that these products are of medical significance. The FTC won both cases and required Listerine to air **corrective advertising,** in which it was required to state that Listerine did not help prevent colds. Unfortunately, Gilbert's (1991) analysis and empirical evidence (Mazis & Adkinson,

1976; Mazursky & Schul, 1988; Schul & Mazursky, 1990; Wilkie, McNeill, & Mazis, 1984) suggests that corrective advertising is typically ineffective.

DEMONSTRATIONS

Demonstrations can also have misleading implications (Preston, 1977). For example, Colgate-Palmolive aired a television commercial in which a sandwich wrapped in a Baggie and a sandwich wrapped in a competing brand were dunked under water. The Baggie kept water out and the competing brand leaked, implying that Baggies keep food fresher even under ordinary circumstances. Black Flag showed a television commercial in which cockroaches were dumped into two separate containers, one filled with Black Flag insecticide and the other filled with a competing brand. Most of the bugs in the Black Flag container died, whereas most of the bugs in the other container did not. However, insects develop resistance to any insecticide to which they are frequently exposed (over several generations), and the makers of Black Flag bred these particular cockroaches to be resistant to the active ingredient of the competing brand but not their brand.

Campbell's Soup used an ad in which the meat, potatoes, and vegetables burst above the broth because marbles were placed in the bottom of the bowl (Preston, 1977). Grape-Nuts cereal aired an ad showing the famed naturalist Euell Gibbons eating wild plants and talking about the wholesome goodness of Grape-Nuts; the ad failed to warn viewers about the dangers of eating wild plants. Similarly, a Medi-Hair ad for a hair transplant process talked about the benefits of hair transplants without warning viewers about the dangers, which include discomfort, skin disease, and the possibility of permanent scarring. Finally, an ad for Vivarin pills, which are loaded with caffeine, stated, "All of a sudden Jim was coming home to a more exciting woman." The ad implies that Vivarin makes a person more attractive and improves one's personality, marriage, and sex life. Sound too good to be true?

What should we learn from these famous FTC cases? Most important, these cases reveal much about the thought processes of consumers. Everyday experience and common knowledge is used to facilitate comprehension and interpretation of ambiguous messages. Consequently, miscomprehension occurs when consumers are exposed to product claims that are literally true but figuratively false. Furthermore, most consumers do not have the training, time, or energy to think about the implications of every message carefully, and therefore consumer protection is warranted. Firms do not need to resort to misleading advertising practices to be successful. Advances in our understanding of consumer psychology make it possible to identify consumer needs more accurately, design products to meet these needs more effectively, and develop ads that truthfully and persuasively inform consumers about the benefits of well-designed brands.

CHAPTER SUMMARY ▪

Consumers must attend to product information before they can become knowledgeable about products. This chapter examined some of the most important features of human attention. Some information is acquired through direct, firsthand experience, while other information is acquired through indirect, secondhand experience.

However, people have a limited capacity to process information. Specifically, people can attend and think about only seven (plus or minus two) chunks of information at a time. We are easily overloaded with too much information. In fact, whenever we are exposed to more than nine chunks of information at one time, the attentional system is overloaded and some information will be ignored out of necessity.

Arousal, or alertness, has a strong impact on the amount of information that people can attend to. When arousal is low, people are sleepy or drowsy and it is very difficult for them to pay attention to product information. When arousal is high, people are overly excited and, again, it is difficult for them to attend to much information. Attentional performance is best when arousal is moderate. Even when attentional performance is good, however, consumers selectively attend to some information and ignore other information. Specifically, consumers selectively attend to salient and vivid information. Salient information differs from other information in a given context; and different is good. Vivid information is interesting, concrete, and proximal across situations.

Comprehension involves relating new information presented in the environment to old information stored in memory. New information is always interpreted in light of one's prior knowledge and experience. Surprisingly, recent research indicates that comprehension always involves believing. Consumers cannot understand a product claim without believing the claim is true. Unbelieving, or rejecting unacceptable claims, comes after comprehension. Believing is easier than unbelieving.

Pragmatic inferences are conclusions or assumptions about the meaning of product claims that are literally true but figuratively false. The FTC has taken legal action against many different types of misleading claims that prompt consumers to form pragmatic inferences—including claims that use the word *may* in a misleading way, comparison omission, incomplete data, piecemeal data, juxtaposition of imperatives, negative questions, and claims that encourage consumers to commit the common reasoning fallacy of affirmation of the consequent (reversing their p's and q's). Consumers need to be protected from misleading advertising.

KEY CONCEPTS ▪

- Product trial
- Limits of attention
- Attention intensity
- Arousal
- Cognitive capacity
- Salient stimuli

- Figure–ground principle of perception
- Vivid stimuli
- Concreteness
- Sensory proximity
- Temporal proximity

- Spatial proximity
- Pragmatic inferences
- Comparison omission
- Affirmation of the consequent
- Corrective advertising

DISCUSSION QUESTIONS ▪

1. What might be a unique way for marketers to use product trial for sporting equipment?
2. Do you think that superstores that specialize in one type of product—such as office supplies, athletic shoes, computers, televisions, and CD equipment—run the risk of overloading consumers with too much information? Why or why not? What steps might these stores take to avoid this problem?

3. Have you ever bought a particular product based on its packaging? Why? What were the salient stimuli on the package that attracted you to that product as opposed to another product?
4. As noted in this chapter, eventually the Energizer bunny's novelty wore out, and the effectiveness of the campaign became limited. As a marketer, what steps might you take to try to revitalize the campaign? How would you use novelty and vivid stimuli to try to attract consumers' attention?
5. Emotional interest plays a part in whether consumers pay attention to advertising for certain products. How might marketers for a line of diet food create interest in the product among consumers who are already thin?
6. How might an auto dealer use sensory and spatial proximity to get people interested in a new model of car?
7. Think of a time when you responded to an ad that was not believable by either buying the product or choosing another product instead. Why did you make the choice you did? How did the ad influence your choice?
8. How might an unethical marketer use distraction when designing a cereal box?
9. Think of advertising claims or slogans you have heard that, through repetition, have become familiar and believable to you. List as many as you can.
10. Do you believe that advertisers should be strictly regulated in the way they present information and that tactics such as comparison omission, use of piecemeal data, and affirmation of the consequent should be illegal? Why or why not?

CHAPTER 3

Consumer Memory

◆ 7-ELEVEN

The Slurpee is 7-Eleven's famous soft drink, just one item that the convenience store sells to customers on the go. But executives at Southland Corp., which owns and franchises 7-Eleven stores nationwide, want to change 7-Eleven's convenience-store image. In other words, they want consumers to think about—and remember—7-Eleven in a completely different way. After all, the sound of the word *Slurpee* doesn't exactly conjure up an upscale image.

Southland managers want consumers to forget the old memories of 7-Eleven as a cheap, quick-stop shop. Instead, they want people to think of 7-Eleven as a more upscale deli/restaurant that also offers convenience items. "All of this requires changing the perception of the customer [who is largely a blue-collar male] of what to expect from a convenience store," comments Southland chief executive Clark J. Matthews II. To do that, 7-Eleven is offering such delicacies as low-fat turkey breast on pita for $2.89 and a teriyaki rice bowl for $3.49. Southland executives are even hoping to offer dinner entrees in the near future.

But there are some real problems with the new menu. The food is prepared off-site at commissaries and bakeries, with 13 distribution centers delivering to the 2,500 stores. So far, quality seems to be lacking, falling somewhere between what you get from the hot dog machine and freshly prepared food, even at some of the fast-food chains. "The customer wants restaurant-quality food," explains Howard B. Stoeckel, head of marketing for Wawa Inc., a Philadelphia convenience-store chain that prepares its sandwiches daily on-site. 7-Eleven customer Jerry Ervin says he has recently switched to Wendy's.

The store's problems have been compounded by an onslaught of new competitors. Pharmacies, all-night supermarkets, and gas stations are all trying to capture convenience-store customers. For instance, Mobil Corp. has been planning new "On the Run" markets that sell food provided by Taco Bell and Blimpie.

For 7-Eleven to achieve success at its new venture, the store must succeed in changing consumers' memories about the store. Marketers must be able to create new associations in consumers' minds between 7-Eleven and positive images—of good food they enjoy eating and at prices they want to pay. Consumers must think of 7-Eleven as a better place to grab a sandwich than, say, Taco Bell or Wendy's. As you read this chapter, consider the importance of marketers creating memorable images—and positive ones, at that—for their products.

Source: Wendy Zeller and Emily Thornton, "How Classy Can 7-Eleven Get?" *Business Week,* September 1, 1997, pp. 74–75.

◆ INTRODUCTION

What happens after consumers attend to and comprehend information about products and services? What do consumers do with this information? Simply perceiving information is not enough. Consumers must also think about the information they perceive, as is evident by some of the challenges that 7-Eleven faces. Furthermore, purchase decisions may be made hours, days, weeks, or even months after product information is acquired. Hence, information must be retained, saved, or remembered for a potentially long period of time. The gap in time between information acquisition and information use must be bridged by some type of memory system.

This chapter shows that human memory comprises multiple memory systems, just as computer memory comprises multiple memory systems (see Fig. 3-1). Consider the manner in which your personal computer operates. Your computer can store a very large number of inactive files in its long-term memory. However, to work with a file,

FIGURE 3-1

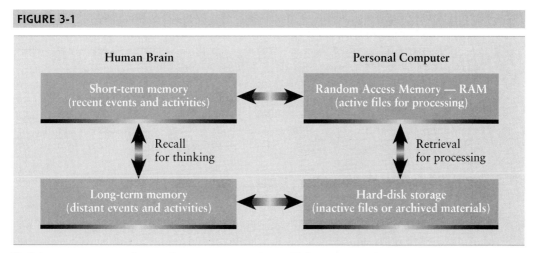

Both human memory and computer memory comprise multiple memory systems.

you must retrieve the file from long-term memory to make it an active file. To revise, edit, or add to a file, the file must be active in the computer's random access memory. Moreover, to execute a subroutine or to run a program, the file must be active. All computer operations and procedures must be performed on an active file.

Similarly, people can store a large number of inactive memory traces (or files) in long-term memory (Anderson, 1983; Atkinson & Shiffrin, 1968; Wyer & Srull, 1989). However, to work with information, or to think, relevant information must be retrieved from inactive long-term memory and brought into active short-term memory (Anderson, 1983; Atkinson & Shiffrin, 1968; Wyer & Srull, 1989). We are consciously aware of information held in short-term memory. **Conscious awareness** refers to information that is currently under active consideration. However, as Chapter 2 emphasized, attention is limited and we can consciously consider only seven (plus or minus two) units of information at a time. Consequently, short-term memory can hold only seven (plus or minus two) units of information at a time.

Although short-term memory has a limited capacity, many different types of cognitive operations, or thought processes, can be performed on information held in short-term memory. In fact, all thinking and reasoning processes are performed on information held in active short-term memory. By contrast, information held in inactive long-term memory is not under conscious consideration and, therefore, cannot be used in thinking and reasoning. What types of thinking and reasoning processes are performed by consumers? Thinking is involved in arithmetic computations, such as adding sales tax to the list price of a product or subtracting a discount from the list price of a product. Thinking is also involved in evaluating and rating products and in predicting, such as trying to predict how long a product will last or how much we will still like a product after using it for several years. Thinking is involved in problem solving, such as trying to figure out which particular tool is most appropriate for a home improvement chore or which particular beverage is most appropriate for a party involving a group of friends with widely diverging tastes and preferences. Thinking is also involved in decision making, such as choosing one particular product from a large set of alternative products or choosing one particular retail outlet from a large number of possibilities.

Before we can understand thinking, reasoning, problem solving, and decision making, however, we must understand memory. Basically, human memory is best conceptualized as an information processing system (see Fig. 3-2). Most information processing models (e.g., Anderson, 1983; Bettman, 1979; Sternthal & Craig, 1982; Wyer & Srull, 1989) extend and build upon the Atkinson and Shiffrin (1968) model. This model suggests that information is first perceived and transferred to the sensory register. Some of the information stored in the sensory register is transferred to short-term memory. The transfer of information from the sensory register to short-term memory is controlled by the attentional processes discussed in Chapter 2. Some of the information stored in short-term memory is transferred to long-term memory. The transfer of information from short-term memory to long-term memory is controlled by rehearsal and coding processes. **Rehearsal** involves repeating information over and over in your head. **Coding** involves relating information stored in short-term memory to information stored in long-term memory. Hence, coding involves moving some information from short-term memory to long-term memory and moving some information from long-term memory to short-term memory. The following section describes the properties and characteristics of short-term memory in greater detail.

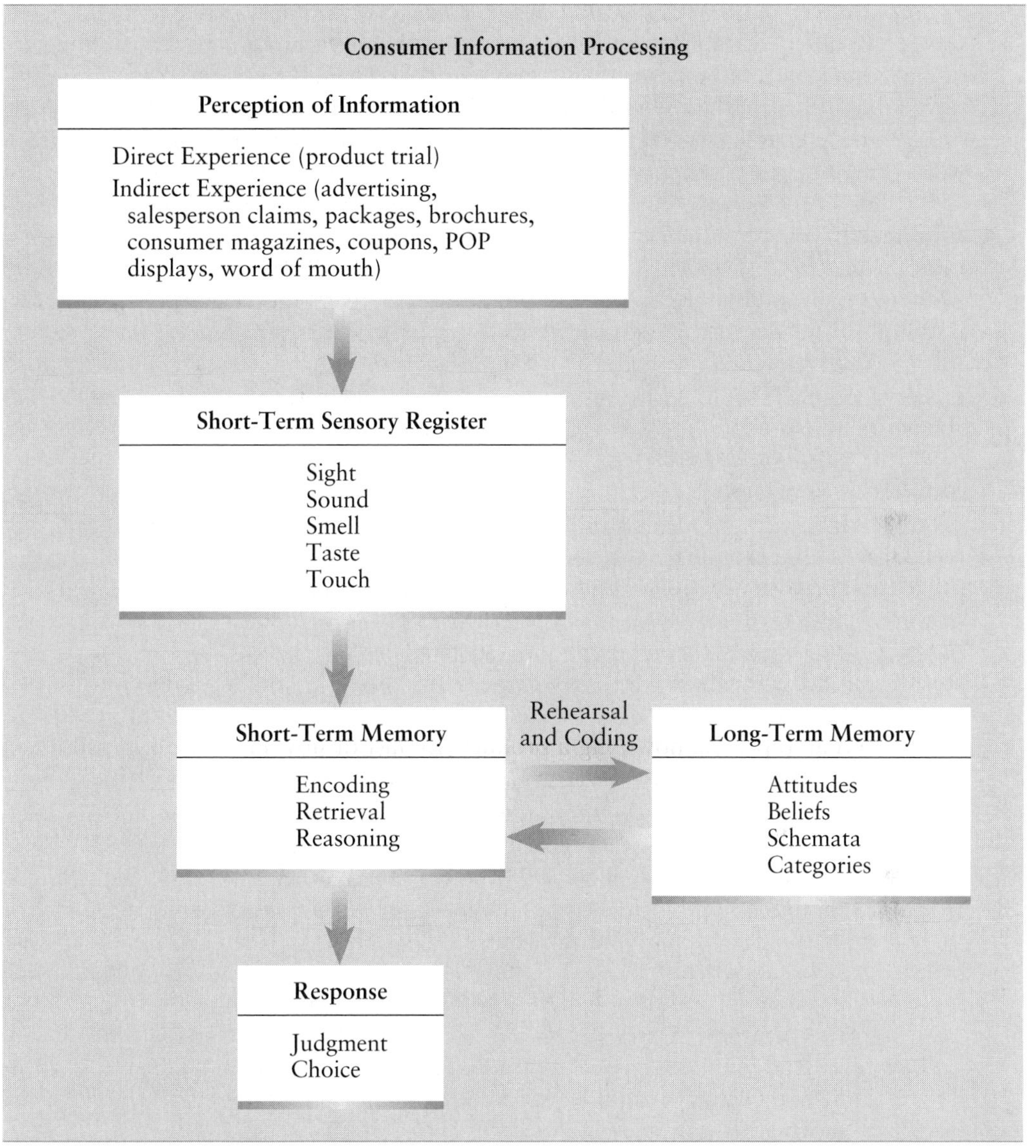

Consumer Information Processing

Perception of Information

Direct Experience (product trial)
Indirect Experience (advertising,
    salesperson claims, packages, brochures,
    consumer magazines, coupons, POP
    displays, word of mouth)

Short-Term Sensory Register

Sight
Sound
Smell
Taste
Touch

Short-Term Memory

Encoding
Retrieval
Reasoning

Rehearsal
and Coding

Long-Term Memory

Attitudes
Beliefs
Schemata
Categories

Response

Judgment
Choice

FIGURE 3-2

Human memory is best conceptualized as an information processing system.

◆ SHORT-TERM MEMORY

As the name "short term" suggests, information is held in **short-term memory** for a very brief period of time. In fact, a classic experiment conducted by Peterson and Peterson (1959) shows that information can be held in short-term memory for only 18 seconds. Subjects were shown sets of three nonsense syllables (i.e., words with no meaning) for three seconds and were asked to recall this information 0, 3, 9, 12, 15, or

18 seconds later. During this period of time, subjects were also asked to count backward by 3s from a number specified by the experimenter. Counting backward out loud distracts subjects and prevents them from rehearsing or repeating the target information in their heads. When subjects are unable to rehearse, information is retained for only 18 seconds or less. This study also shows that forgetting or information loss from short-term memory is due to rehearsal failure.

Miller's (1956) magic number—seven plus or minus two—suggests that short-term memory can hold an average of seven units, or chunks, of information, with a range from five to nine. Miller measured immediate memory-span performance by presenting a list of numbers, letters, or words and asking subjects to recall this information in its correct serial order immediately afterward. Most subjects recalled between five and nine items, with a mean of seven. Subsequent research has shown that regardless of whether these items are small (like individual numbers or letters) or large (like strings of numbers, letters, words, or ideas) about seven units are typically recalled (Newell & Simon, 1972). In fact, local phone numbers are only seven digits long because the scientists at Bell Labs are very familiar with Miller's magic number.

One of the most important differences between short-term and **long-term memory** is that short-term memory has a very small storage capacity, whereas long-term memory has a very large storage capacity. (See Fig. 3-3.) Another important difference between short-term and long-term memory is that information held in short-term memory is based on an acoustic (or sound-related) code, whereas information held in long-term memory is based on a semantic (or meaning-related) code. For example, Baddeley (1966a, 1966b) asked subjects to remember either a five-word list or a ten-word list. A five-word list is within the limits of short-term memory, whereas a ten-word list exceeds the limits of short-term memory. In both lists, all the words were acoustically related (like *bat, hat, cat*), semantically related (like *tiny, small, little*), or unrelated (like *bat, desk, tiny*). The results revealed that memory performance was poorest in acoustically related five-word list conditions and in semantically related ten-word list conditions. Acoustic confusion in five-word lists suggests an acoustic code for the contents of short-term memory, whereas semantic confusion in ten-word lists

FIGURE 3-3

Properties of Short-Term Memory and Long-Term Memory				
	Capacity	Duration	Information Loss	Coding
Short-Term Memory	seven plus or minus two	18 seconds	rehearsal failure	acoustic (sound related)
Long-Term Memory	unlimited	permanent	retrieval failure	semantic (meaning related)

Short-term memory and long-term memory have different properties.

suggests a semantic code for the contents of long-term memory. Hence, information is coded or represented differently depending on whether the information is stored in short-term memory or in long-term memory.

Additional evidence for the short-term versus long-term memory distinction is provided by the serial position curve (Glanzer & Cunitz, 1966; Kardes & Herr, 1990; Rundus, 1971). Recall accuracy for information presented in a long list varies systematically as a function of the position of an item in the list. Early items are recalled well (the primacy effect) and late items are recalled well (the recency effect). However, items in the middle of the list are remembered poorly. The primacy effect occurs because items at the beginning of a list are easy to rehearse and, consequently, much of this information is transferred to long-term memory. However, rehearsal of early items uses up cognitive capacity, and this leaves little capacity for rehearsing middle items. The recency effect occurs because late items are still in short-term memory when subjects perform the recall task. The primacy effect is a long-term memory phenomenon, and the recency effect is a short-term memory phenomenon.

All these short-term memory phenomena can be illustrated in a simple example. If a consumer needs to pick up a few items (i.e., seven plus or minus two items) at the grocery store, he or she should have no trouble holding this information in his or her head. If a consumer needs to pick up more items, however, the safest strategy would be to write up a grocery list. If a consumer needs to pick up several items but does not have time to write them down, he or she should concentrate on the items in the middle of the list because these items are easy to forget. Early items (primacy) and late items (recency) are easy to remember.

◆ **LONG-TERM MEMORY**

Unlike short-term memory, long-term memory has a very large storage capacity. Moreover, once information is **encoded,** or transferred into long-term memory, it remains there permanently (unless physical damage to the brain occurs). How do we know that storage in long-term memory is permanent? This seems surprising to us because forgetting occurs so quickly, but three types of evidence indicate that storage in long-term memory is permanent. First, brain surgery patients report that they can remember seemingly long-forgotten childhood memories when different portions of the brain are stimulated with electricity (Penfield, 1959). Although this finding is suggestive, it was impossible to verify the accuracy of these memories in this study. Second, Bahrick has published the results of many very long-term memory studies showing that people remember a surprisingly large amount of material from high school (e.g., classmates' names and faces, algebra, foreign languages) after a period of years, decades, and in one study, over 50 years (Bahrick, Bahrick, Bahrick, & Bahrick, 1993; Bahrick, Bahrick, & Wittinger, 1975; Bahrick & Hall, 1991; Bahrick, Hall, & Berger, 1996). Bahrick uses the term **permastore** to indicate that information remains in long-term memory permanently.

The best evidence for the permanence of information stored in long-term memory, however, comes from experiments using the now well-known savings and relearning method: Relearning something you forgot (e.g., high school algebra, Spanish, French, Latin) is easier than learning it the first time. In the classic savings and relearning experiment (Nelson, 1971), subjects learned 20 pairs of numbers and words (e.g.,

43–dog). Two weeks later, subjects were unable to recall 25 percent of this material. In the relearning condition, subjects learned the same old 20 number–word pairs again. In the control condition, subjects learned new words with old numbers for all forgotten pairs (e.g., the original 43–dog was changed to 43–house). There should be no difference in memory performance across these two conditions if forgotten information is lost forever. In contrast, the results showed that memory performance was far superior in the relearning condition than in the control condition. Nelson (1978) later replicated these results with a recognition memory test instead of a recall memory test. Savings and relearning studies show that forgotten information is still stored in memory somewhere.

If information is stored in long-term memory permanently, why does forgetting occur? Forgetting is not due to information loss or decay. Instead, forgetting occurs because we cannot find the information that we are trying to find during memory search. For example, students often realize that they know an answer to a difficult exam question even when they are unable to retrieve the answer during the exam. Sometimes searching through memory seems like searching for a needle in a haystack. The more information that is stored in memory, the more difficult it is to locate one specific piece of information. The larger the haystack, the more difficult it is to find the pin. Information is especially difficult to locate in memory if you do not understand the material (comprehension improves memory performance) or if the material was encoded into memory in a disorganized or haphazard way (organization improves memory performance). It is very difficult to find a particular piece of information in disorganized filing cabinets. Similarly, it is very difficult to find a particular piece of information in disorganized memory bins. Students and managers who understand how memory operates are able to develop better strategies for studying and for improving memory performance. Moreover, understanding human memory is important for developing better strategies for dealing with managerial problems associated with forgetful consumers.

In the sections that follow, I discuss three key principles of long-term memory: the **organization principle** (organization facilitates memory performance), the **encoding–specificity principle** (contextual or background cues present during learning and during retrieval influence memory performance), and the **association principle** (pieces of information stored in long-term memory are connected to other related pieces of information).

THE ORGANIZATION PRINCIPLE OF LONG-TERM MEMORY

"The notes went sour because the bag was ripped." This sentence seems confusing and incomprehensible because the individual words appear to be unrelated. Imagine how difficult it would be to memorize a large number of incomprehensible sentences such as this one. This is exactly what Bransford and Johnson (1972) asked subjects to do. Not surprisingly, memory performance was poor. However, some subjects were given a word that made each sentence comprehensible. For example, "Bagpipe: the notes went sour because the bag was ripped." Now it is easy to see how the words are related. If the bag of a bagpipe was ripped, the musical notes would go sour, or sound awful. Subjects who understood the sentences exhibited excellent memory performance.

SUBARU'S OUTBACK IMAGE

Lately, Subaru seems to be doing everything right. The introduction of the Outback (a station wagon with sport utility features) was met with cheers from both auto reviewers and consumers. Both camps like that the Outback handles like a car instead of a top-heavy sport utility vehicle that critics claim are prone to rollovers. But they also like the fact that the Outback has Subaru's famous, high-quality, all-wheel drive and sits a few inches higher from the ground than does a traditional station wagon or sedan.

The Outback was so popular that, less than two years later, Subaru set its new Forester on the road. The Forester's boxy body looks more like a sport utility vehicle, but it still handles like a car, with a low center of gravity (ground clearance is only 7.5 inches). The Forester is also quite a bit smaller than, say, a Ford Explorer or even a Nissan Pathfinder. But the tires can take so much bounce that even the worst roads ride fairly smoothly. The price? Both the Outback and the Forester range anywhere from $2,000 to $10,000 less than the average large sport utility vehicle.

How does Subaru get consumers to remember their new cars—and buy them? Subaru has maintained a consistently organized image for its new autos—rugged, outdoorsy, sporty, youthful, stylish. Every ad and commercial skillfully ties concepts together. TV commercials show the cars easily handling streambeds, dirt roads, steep hills, and the like. Print ads show the cars parked in attractive wilderness locations, such as above a rocky beach. Sometimes a mountain bike is strapped to the back of the car; sometimes a young couple, dressed in hiking or biking clothes, stands outside the car, taking in the view. Ads also show features that reflect the outdoor lifestyle, such as storage areas that are just the right size to hold fishing rods and soft drinks. Even the model names—Outback and Forester—evoke images of the outdoors. Drivers in the ads are always rugged and outdoorsy themselves, so consumers will remember an image they want to emulate. Thus, consumers associate the cars with everything from adventure to sexiness.

Of course, people who buy the Outback and Forester do not need to be outdoor types at all—they just need to think they are, or at least be attracted to the image. The fact that they can buy the image from Subaru for considerably less money than they can from other auto manufacturers adds to the perceived value of the car. Subaru is banking on it.

Sources: Greg Anderson, "Off the Beaten Path," *Edmund's Automobile Buyer's Guides,* Summer 1997, downloaded from Edmund's Web site; Subaru sales brochures for Forester and Outback model autos.

Organization is the process of grouping or chunking individual pieces of information into larger units on the basis of a specific relationship between the pieces. If the pieces are in some way related, they can be grouped together, and memory for the individual pieces will be greatly improved. (See "Making the Decision: Subaru's Outback Image.") If, on the other hand, the pieces are unrelated, they cannot be grouped together, and memory performance will be poor.

Consider another example. Bower, Clark, Lesgold, and Winzenz (1969) presented a list of minerals (such as gold, slate, copper, sapphire, lead, limestone) to subjects. (See Fig. 3-4.) Later, subjects were asked to recall as many minerals from the list as possible. Most subjects could recall only a few items (15 percent, on average). However, another

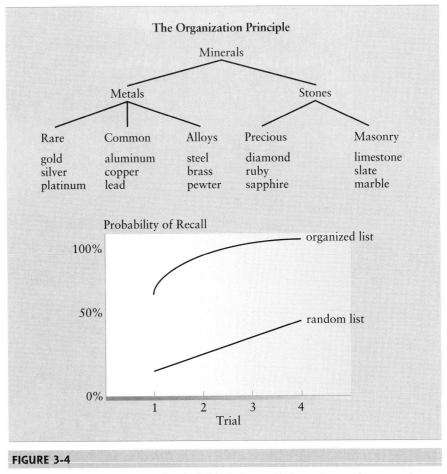

FIGURE 3-4

Memory performance is better when individual pieces of information can be grouped together.

Source: Adapted from Bower, Clark, Lesgold & Winzenz (1969).

group of subjects received the same list presented in an organized framework: The rare metals were presented together (e.g., gold, silver, platinum), the common metals were presented together (e.g., aluminum, copper, lead), the precious stones were presented together (e.g., diamond, ruby, sapphire), the masonry stones were presented together (e.g., limestone, slate, marble), and so on. Subjects who received the organized list could recall most of the items (70 percent, on average). Moreover, after receiving the list four times, subjects in the random list condition recalled about half the items, whereas subjects in the organized list condition recalled nearly all the items. Because subjects were randomly assigned to conditions, the results cannot be attributed to individual differences between subjects (i.e., subjects in one condition did not have more powerful memories than subjects in the other condition). Moreover, because all subjects were asked to recall the exact same information (i.e., the items on the lists were the same, only the format varied), the results cannot be attributed to differences in the memorizability of the individual items.

Together, these studies demonstrate the critical importance of organization. If individual pieces of information (like words in a sentence or items in a list) can be related together and organized in some fashion, memory performance will be greatly enhanced. By contrast, random words, items, and ideas are incomprehensible and difficult to remember. The implications of the organization principle of long-term memory for business students are very clear: If your notes are neat and well organized and if you understand the relationships between the topics covered in a course, memory performance (and exam performance) will be enhanced. On the other hand, if your notes

When pieces of information—like these photos of wild animals—are related, memory of the information is greatly improved.

Source: Courtesy of DuPont.

are disorganized and if you do not understand the material, memory performance (and exam performance) will be poor.

The organization principle also has straightforward implications for managerial decision making. If you want your consumers to remember information presented in an advertisement, information must be presented in an organized manner. If you want your sales representatives to remember a set of tactics you want them to use in the field, the tactics must be described and explained in an organized fashion. If you are a retailer, you want to group similar products together (e.g., all breakfast cereals should be located in the same aisle, all soft drinks should be located in the same aisle), and dissimilar products should not be grouped together (e.g., toilet bowl cleansers should not be located near gourmet foods for people). Furthermore, retailers do not like to move a product category to a new aisle because consumers become frustrated when they remember that a particular product used to be in aisle 3 but is now in another aisle. Organized displays enable consumers to find the items they need quickly and easily.

THE ENCODING-SPECIFICITY PRINCIPLE OF LONG-TERM MEMORY

Long-term memory is context dependent. That is, contextual cues or background cues have a surprisingly powerful influence on memory performance. When people encode or learn information they wish to remember, irrelevant background information tends to be encoded along with the relevant information. According to the encoding-specificity principle of long-term memory, memory performance is better when the contextual cues present during encoding and during retrieval are the same (as opposed to different).

In a dramatic demonstration of this principle, Godden and Baddeley (1975) asked scuba diver subjects to learn a list of words in either a wet context (20 feet under water) or a dry context (above water). (See Fig. 3-5.) Needless to say, underwater environments are very different from above-water environments. Later, memory performance was tested either under water or above water. The results indicated that memory performance was much better when the encoding and retrieval environments were the same (i.e., both under water or both above water) than when the encoding and retrieval environments were different (i.e., one under water and one above water). Of course, it is not necessary to vary people's environments in such a dramatic fashion. Memory performance is better whenever encoding and retrieval environments are the same (versus different).

Measuring Memory Performance

Before discussing another demonstration of the encoding-specificity principle, we should discuss different ways of measuring memory performance. As you know, exams measure memory performance, but there are many different types of exam questions. Multiple-choice questions are **recognition** questions, because they involve detecting one correct answer from a set of four (or more) possibilities. This is the easiest type of memory test. Fill-in-the-blank questions are **cued recall** questions, because a cue or clue is given and you must supply the rest. For example, your professor might provide the cue "encoding-specificity principle" and you would be asked to provide the definition. A cued recall test is more difficult than a recognition test because cued recall involves two steps—retrieving answers from memory and deciding if an answer is correct—whereas recognition involves one step—deciding if an answer is correct. Finally,

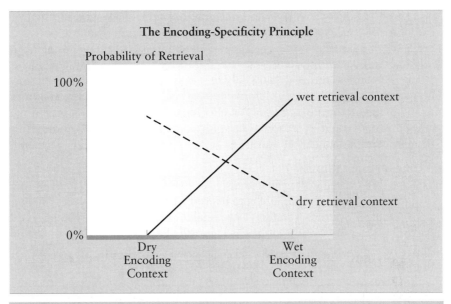

FIGURE 3-5

Memory performance is better when contextual cues present during encoding and retrieval are the same.

Source: Adapted from Godden & Baddeley (1975).

essay questions are **free recall** tests because no cues are given and all information must be retrieved by the student. This is the most difficult type of memory test.

Even though recognition is easier than cued recall, context effects are so powerful that it is possible to make a cued recall test easier than a recognition test. In an important experiment (Watkins & Tulving, 1975), subjects received pairs of words such as "train–black" and were asked to memorize the second word ("black" in this case). The first word was merely the context word. Later, subjects received either a recognition test or a cued recall test. The recognition test involved giving subjects a word related to a memory word, asking subjects to generate four related words, and then asking subjects to recognize which of the four related words was a memory word. For example, in response to the word *white* subjects should generate *black* and three additional words. Next, they should recognize that *black* was a memory word. The cued recall test involved giving subjects a context word, such as *train,* and seeing if they could retrieve *black.* The results indicated that memory performance was better for cued recall than for recognition because context words were present during encoding and retrieval for the cued recall task. Context words were present only during encoding for the recognition task.

According to the encoding-specificity principle, memory performance is enhanced when study and test conditions are similar. Hence, you should study in a quiet room filled with other people (e.g., the library) and you should take an exam in a quiet room filled with other people (i.e., the classroom). If you drink coffee while studying, you should drink coffee while taking an exam. Note that lectures and exams are usually given in the very same classroom. Even this simple similarity improves memory. In fact, you should even try to sit in the same seat during lectures and during exams. To the extent that noise levels, lighting, seating, and other seemingly minor background conditions match during encoding and retrieval, memory performance will be enhanced. On the other hand, when the study context differs from the exam context, memory performance decreases. Hence, if you study in a noisy dormitory, memory performance will be poor in a quiet classroom. If you study while consuming mass quantities of coffee, memory performance will be poor in a caffeine-free environment (Eich, 1980). Even if emotional moods differ between the study context and the exam context, memory performance is reduced (Eich, 1989).

Business Applications

The encoding-specificity principle also has many important business applications. For example, several years ago, Life cereal aired a popular television commercial featuring "Little Mikey." Mikey's brothers were reluctant to try this new cereal, so they thought they should get Mikey to try it first because "he'll try anything." When the brothers saw that Mikey really liked Life cereal, they began gobbling it up also. However, most consumers visit the grocery store days or weeks after viewing a television commercial and a lot of forgetting can take place over this period of time. To help consumers remember the Little Mikey ad, Life placed Little Mikey's picture on the box of Life cereal. Hence, during encoding, consumers viewed a television ad featuring Little Mikey. Later, during retrieval, consumers encountered packages of cereal with Little Mikey's picture. This tactic improves memory for information conveyed in an ad (Keller, 1987).

Similarly, each year as Halloween approaches, Coors beer used to air a television commercial featuring the famous horror movie hostess Elvira, Mistress of the Dark. Later, while shopping for groceries, consumers encountered a life-size cardboard point-of-purchase display of Elvira. Again, featuring Elvira in a television ad and in a point-of-purchase display enhances memory for previously encoded information. The strategic application of the encoding-specificity principle helps to bridge the gap in time between watching television commercials and shopping for groceries.

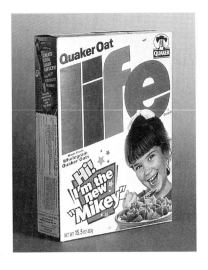

The marketers of Life cereals are continuing the "Little Mikey" commercial theme with a "I'm the New Mikey" campaign.
Source: © Mary Boucher.

THE ASSOCIATION PRINCIPLE OF LONG-TERM MEMORY

According to the association principle of long-term memory, each concept, idea, or piece of information stored in memory is represented as a **node** and each node or idea is connected to other nodes by links referred to as **associations** (Anderson, 1983, 1993). Together, all the nodes and all the associations between nodes form a complex **associative network,** in which all pieces of general knowledge are interrelated with other pieces. Ideas that are closely related are connected directly by a single association. Ideas that are less closely related are connected by a series of associations between many related concepts. (See "Making the Decision: From Yo-Yos to Zippos, Memory Serves.")

For example, consider the concept Lite beer from Miller. Whenever we think of Lite beer, the first thing that pops into our heads is "tastes great" and "less filling." These are key features of Lite beer that are emphasized in advertising. If we thought a bit longer about the concept "Lite beer," other less closely related ideas would occur to us. For example, we know that beer contains alcohol and that beer is made from hops. If we thought about the concept still longer, even less-related ideas might emerge, such as beer is a beverage. Hence, in our associative network for Lite beer from Miller, there is a direct association between "Lite" and "tastes great." There is also an association between "beer" and "alcohol." Furthermore, there is an association between "alcohol" and "beverage." Note that there is no direct association between "alcohol" and "Lite." Instead, "alcohol" is linked to "beer" and "beer" is linked to "Lite." Furthermore, "beverage" is even more remotely related to "Lite," and, consequently, instead of a single association between "beverage" and "Lite," there is a string of associations.

Experimental investigations of the associative network structure of long-term memory employ **response-time methods,** in which statements or propositions are presented one at a time on a computer monitor and subjects press a "True" button or a "False" button as quickly as possible (Anderson, 1983, 1993; Collins & Loftus, 1975; Collins & Quillian, 1969; Herr, Farquhar, & Fazio, 1996). Usually, half of the propositions are true and half are false. If we presented propositions about Lite beer in this experiment, very fast response times would be observed for the proposition "Lite beer tastes great." Slower response times would be observed for "Lite beer contains alcohol." Still slower response times would be observed for "Lite beer is a beverage." Relative response times, or response time differences between propositions containing closely related versus distantly related ideas enable researchers to make inferences about the precise nature of the structure of an associative network in long-term memory.

Merely thinking about two concepts at the same time is sufficient for forming an association in memory between two concepts. Thinking about the two concepts frequently or carefully increases the strength of the association between the two concepts. As the strength of an association between two concepts increases, response speed increases. Specifically, when one concept is activated from memory (or comes to mind), the other concept is activated quickly and automatically (or the other concept comes to mind, too). Response speed also increases as the distance between two concepts decreases (distance is determined by the number of nodes between two concepts; note that if there is a direct association between two concepts, there are zero nodes between the two concepts). The associative network model explains two phenomena that have important implications for marketing theory and practice: the priming effect and associative interference.

MAKING THE DECISION

FROM YO-YOS TO ZIPPOS, MEMORY SERVES

Remember the yo-yo that rolled down the string, bounced a few times, and went still? You rewound it by hand, tried again, and got the same results. Or maybe you were a yo-yo whiz, flipping your wrist over, sending the yo-yo whirring toward the ground, then jerking the string gently at just the right second for the disk to come climbing back to your hand.

Yo-yos are back with a vengeance, along with other products, like Zippo lighters, that we associate with bygone times. Some consumers are old enough to remember previous crazes for these products; others are experiencing them for the first time. Marketers want to capture the attention of both age groups, in the United States as well as abroad. They can do so by making all kinds of associations with their products, both new and old. Yo-yos can easily be associated with childhood, with play, with simple toys; for consumers overseas in countries like Japan and Australia, American-made yo-yos can be associated positively with America itself. Yo-yo industry leader Duncan Toys reports that sales have increased 30 percent in a single year; waiting lists have reached the 200 mark in San Francisco; over one million Duncan yo-yos sold in Japan in just two months.

Zippo lighters are another case in point. Sixty-five-year-old Zippo Manufacturing had just about burned itself out, mostly because of the product's negative association with cigarette smoking. But a completely new association between two previously unrelated concepts began to emerge during the 1990s: Zippo lighters and collectibles. Zippos appeared at flea markets and were snapped up quicker than one could "flick a Bic [lighter, that is]." Why?

"They are pieces of our history," explains Judith Sanders, a cofounder of On the Lighter Side, one of seven collectors clubs now operating worldwide. Every Zippo made since the company's founding has an individual code stamped on it, enhancing the item's collectibility. And more than one million designs have adorned Zippo lighters, including Elvis, the Three Stooges, U.S. presidents, the Daytona 500, and the Civil War. Zippos also come with camouflage and scrimshaw patterns. All this variety gives Zippo collectors plenty to collect, and Zippo collectors are crazed: A 1933 brushed-chrome first-edition Zippo can easily sell for $5,000 (a new one sells for $12.95).

Not content to rely on the collectibles market, Zippo marketers are hard at work forging new associations between Zippo and activities other than smoking. Calling it "the other-use campaign," marketers plan new ads featuring Zippos used for lighting birthday candles and campfires. "We want to plant the image that you don't have to be a smoker to carry a lighter," notes vice president James Baldo. "You have matches in the house and you don't smoke. Why not a Zippo?"

Will the yo-yo/Zippo surge last? "History shows it's a craze—and that it won't continue," admits Mike Burke, marketing coordinator for Duncan Toys. That's probably true for the yo-yos, whose aficionados could easily move on to hula hoops or 3-D glasses. And Zippo collectors could shift to Barbies or Beanie Babies. But if Zippo marketers can successfully plant in consumers' minds the association between a Zippo lighter and positive activities, the company may be lighting its own birthday candles for many years to come.

Sources: Susan Q. Stranahan, "Zippo Makes a Comeback," *Fortune,* September 8, 1997, pp. 40, 44; Herb Greenberg, "Around the World: Yo-Yo Shortages," *Fortune,* June 23, 1997, p. 40.

THE PRIMING EFFECT

Retrieving product information from memory begins with the activation of a node. **Activation** refers to the transfer of information from inactive long-term memory to active short-term memory. However, once one node is activated, other closely related nodes are activated also. Simply put, activation spreads. Anderson (1983) describes spreading activation using his famous irrigation ditch example: Each node is analogous to a pool of water that is connected to other pools via a system of ditches. When one pool is filled with water, water spills out to other nearby pools that are connected by ditches. The more water poured into a pool, the farther the spillage spreads. Eventually, however, one runs out of water and the spreading ceases.

In their classic demonstration of spreading activation, Meyer and Schvaneveldt (1971) exposed subjects to pairs of items presented on a computer monitor. Subjects were told to press a button labeled "Yes" if both items were real words (like "nurse" and "butter"), and they were told to press a button labeled "No" if one or both items were nonwords (like "plame" and "reab"). The results revealed that reponse times were faster when the items were related (like "bread" and "butter") as opposed to unrelated (like "nurse" and "butter"). This is because "bread" and "butter" are strongly associated in memory, and activating "bread" leads to the automatic activation

Advertisements prompt consumers to learn associations quickly, such as the association between milk and health and attractiveness. Repetition strengthens the association to the point where milk will prime health and beauty. That is, thinking about milk will lead consumers to think automatically about the benefits of drinking milk, namely, health and beauty.

Source: Courtesy of the National Fluid Milk Processor Promotion Board and Bozell Worldwide, Inc.

of "butter" (and other concepts closely related to "bread"). Hence, "bread" primes or facilitates the activation of "butter" and other closely related concepts.

Activated concepts can also influence the interpretation of ambiguous evidence. Information is ambiguous if it has many meanings. For example, the statement "Ocean Spray has more food energy than other breakfast drinks" is ambiguous because "food energy" has many different possible meanings. The statement could be interpreted either favorably (e.g., Ocean Spray is more nutritious) or unfavorably (e.g., Ocean Spray is higher in calories). A favorable interpretation is likely to be formed when nutrition-related concepts have been activated, whereas an unfavorable interpretation is likely to be construed when calorie-related concepts have been activated (Higgins, 1996; Higgins & King, 1981; Wyer & Srull, 1989). Concepts that are currently active and accessible (on top of the head) color the interpretation of ambiguous information. Currently active concepts prime or facilitate the activation of closely related concepts.

Merely thinking about a concept activates that concept. Once a concept has been activated, it influences how we think about other topics. Even subtle exposure to concepts can influence how we think about other issues. For example, Herr (1989) led subjects to think about extremely inexpensive automobiles by giving them a word puzzle consisting of a 20-by-20 matrix of letters. (See Table 3-1.) The names of extremely inexpensive automobiles—like the Chevy Chevette, Ford Pinto, and Ford Fiesta—were embedded in the matrix. Subjects were asked to find the hidden names and circle them. This simple task resulted in the activation of the concept of several extremely inexpensive automobiles. Another group of subjects received a similar word puzzle containing the names of moderately inexpensive automobiles—like the Chevy Citation, Ford Escort, and Plymouth Horizon. A third group received a puzzle containing the names of moderately expensive automobiles—like the Pontiac Grand Prix, Olds Cutlass, and Mazda RX-7. Finally, a fourth group received a puzzle containing the names of extremely expensive automobiles—like the Mercedes-Benz, Porsche, and Ferrari. Hence, depending on which puzzle subjects received, the concept of either extremely

TABLE 3-1

	Price Categories				
	Extremely Inexpensive	*Moderately Inexpensive*	*Moderate*	*Moderately Expensive*	*Extremely Expensive*
Ratings	Chevette	Citation	Ford Grenada	Pontiac Grand Prix	Mercedes-Benz
	V.W. Beetle	Tercel	Buick Skyhawk	Mazda RX-7	Rolls Royce
	Ford Pinto	Ford Escort	Ford Mustang	Olds Cutlass	Ferrari
	Ford Fiesta	Plymouth Horizon	Honda Accord	Thunderbird	Porsche
Mean[a]	2.87	4.19	5.22	6.80	9.69
S.D.[b]	1.30	1.41	1.29	1.08	0.54

[a]Higher scores indicate greater perceived expense on a 0–10 scale.
[b]Averaged standard deviations in each grouping.
Priming a particular price catagory changes the way people think about the price of a car.
Data source: Priming stimuli used by Herr (1989).

Would moderately inexpensive and moderately expensive priming change your perception about the price of this BMW?
Source: © Dick Morton.

inexpensive, moderately inexpensive, moderately expensive, or extremely expensive automobiles was activated.

After completing the puzzle, subjects were dismissed. As they were leaving, a second experimenter asked subjects to participate in a second ostensibly unrelated study. Subjects were asked to examine two automobile ads and indicate how expensive they thought each car would be on a scale from 0 (extremely inexpensive) to 10 (extremely expensive). Although price was not mentioned, both ads featured cars that were actually moderately priced (neither expensive nor inexpensive for a car). In one ad, the make and model was specified (either a Chevrolet Celebrity or a Buick Skyhawk), whereas in the other ad, make and model information was omitted. Hence, subjects were asked to rate an unambiguous target car and an ambiguous target car. The results revealed that the previous puzzle task had a surprising influence on subsequent judgments.

In part two of the study, subjects were asked to rate an ambiguous (i.e., hypothetical) or unambiguous (i.e., real) target automobile. Subjects who completed the puzzle containing moderately or extremely expensive automobiles rated the ambiguous target automobile as expensive also. Subjects who completed the puzzle containing moderately or extremely inexpensive automobiles rated the ambiguous target automobile as inexpensive also. Hence, when the target was ambiguous, assimilation effects were observed: The target was perceived as similar in price to the automobiles presented earlier in the puzzles.

The results were very different when the target automobile was unambiguous. In this case, the target was rated as inexpensive when the primed automobiles were expensive, and the target was rated as expensive when the primed automobiles were inexpensive. When the target was unambiguous, contrast effects were observed: The target stimulus was perceived as dissimilar to the primed stimuli. Even though subjects believed that part one (completing the puzzles containing the priming stimuli) and part two (rating the target automobile for expensiveness) were unrelated, what occurred during part one (which puzzle they received) had a powerful influence on their ratings in part two. Priming produced assimilation effects when the target was ambiguous and contrast effects when the target was unambiguous.

The **priming effect** is very common. The mass media is constantly exposing us to topics and issues that we do not normally think about. Books, newspapers, magazines, radio, and television activate concepts that influence how we interpret, rate, and judge subsequently considered but related concepts and issues. After watching the evening news, fires, tornados, and violent crimes seem much more likely (Fischhoff, Lichtenstein, Slovic, Derby, & Keeney, 1981). After watching television programs featuring glamorous stars, our spouses and significant others seem less attractive and less adequate (because perceived differences are exaggerated; Kenrick & Gutierres, 1980). Judgment often involves comparing a target stimulus with some comparison stimulus, and different comparison stimuli are primed or activated in different situations. (See Figure 3-6.) When the target and the primed concept are similar, perceived similarities are exaggerated if the target is ambiguous. When the target is unambiguous or when the primed concept is extreme or unusual, perceived differences are exaggerated. Moreover, most people are generally unaware of the subtle influence of primed stimuli. When questioned directly about the possible influence of recently activated material, most people deny that they were influenced at all (Herr, 1986, 1989; Herr, Sherman, & Fazio, 1983).

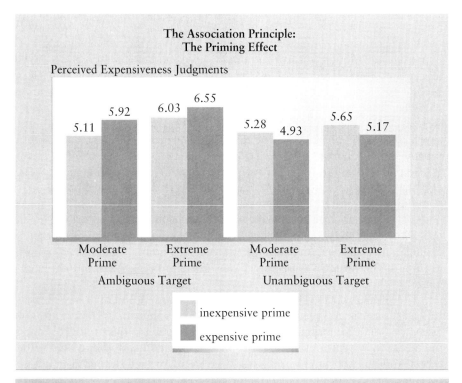

**The Association Principle:
The Priming Effect**

Perceived Expensiveness Judgments

FIGURE 3-6

Priming can lead to either assimilation or contrast depending on the relation between the priming stimulus and the target stimulus.

Source: Adapted from Herr (1989), Experiment 1. Note that assimilation effects were observed when the target was ambiguous, and contrast effects were observed when the target was unambiguous. In Experiment 2, both types of effects were reduced when participants were unknowledgeable about automobiles.

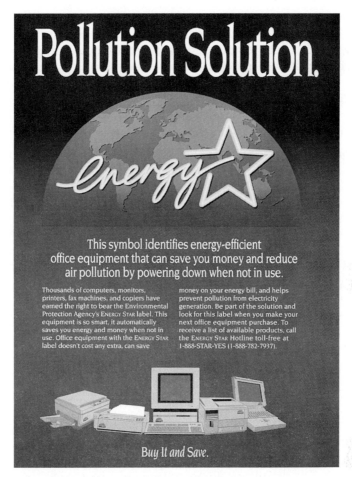

Reinforcing the association between energy efficiency and reducing pollution can encourage consumers to adopt a more pro-environmental attitude.

Source: Public Service Announcement Developed by U.S. EPS ENERGY STAR® Program.

ASSOCIATIVE INTERFERENCE

Although it takes more time for activation to spread as the number of nodes in a network path increases, it also takes longer for activation to spread across some nodes than others. Specifically, some nodes are linked directly to many other related nodes or concepts, whereas other nodes are linked to few other related nodes or concepts. The rate at which activation spreads across a particular node increases as the number of related concepts linked to that node increases. This phenomenon is known as **associative interference.** Basically, complex, embellished associative networks lead activation to spread in many different directions at once, and this uses up activation. On the other hand, simple, impoverished associative networks channel activation through just a few associative paths. It takes time to find (activate) a particular node in a rich, elaborate associative network. The bigger the associative network, the longer it takes to find a particular node. Understanding associative interference is useful for dealing with difficult and tricky business problems, such as marketplace rumors and media clutter.

COMBATING MARKETPLACE RUMORS

Companies regularly combat marketplace rumors. (See "Taking Issue, Strikes: Who's In and Who's Out?") Several years ago, McDonald's franchises in the Chicago area were faced with a very difficult business problem. A rumor that McDonald's uses worms in their hamburger meat was spreading like wildfire (Tybout, Calder, & Sternthal, 1981). (See Fig. 3-7.) Not surprisingly, sales plummeted. However, most consumers did not actually believe the rumor. How can a rumor that no one believes still hurt sales? The answer to this question should be clear by now. Hearing the rumor led consumers to form an associative link in memory between "McDonald's" and "worms." Consequently, every time consumers thought about McDonald's, they also thought about worms (a priming effect). Thinking about worms is not very appetizing, even if you do not believe the rumor.

McDonald's dealt with this problem by arguing that the rumor was not true. Signs were posted in McDonald's fast-food restaurants stating that McDonald's used only 100 percent FDA-approved ground beef in its hamburgers. The signs also stated that worm meat is actually more expensive than beef, implying that it makes no sense whatsoever to use worm meat in hamburgers. However, the signs had no effect on sales. Most consumers did not believe the rumor, so denial was futile.

FIGURE 3-7

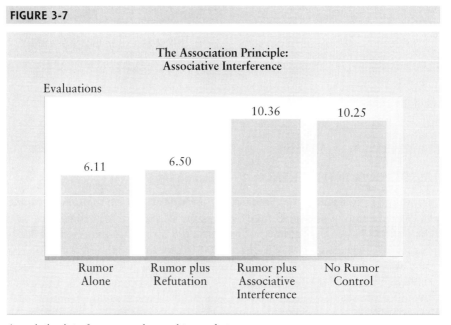

Associative interference can be used to combat rumors.

Source: Adapted from Tybout, Calder, & Sternthal (1981).

STRIKES: WHO'S IN AND WHO'S OUT?

No one would argue that strikes are not diffi-cult for everyone—workers who must stay home without pay, replacement workers who must endure crossing the picket line and try to do a job they may not be trained for, and cus-tomers who are unable to obtain the striking organization's goods or services. At no time was this more evident than during the recent, month-long UPS strike, the first one in the company's history. Families of workers suffered financial hardship, at least one manager who was forced to drive a truck without proper training died in an accident, and small busi-nesses that relied on UPS to ship its packages to consumers teetered on the brink of disaster.

The strike also changed the way con-sumers thought about UPS. Mass media played a large part in changing the associations con-sumers made about "the tightest ship in the shipping business." Shots of altercations between striking workers and management or police, interviews with frustrated customers, sound bites of arguments between manage-ment and union officials all contributed to a new view of UPS.

UPS's competitors—most notably, Federal Express Corp. and the U.S. Postal Service—capitalized on the change, hoping to create new memories in consumers' minds. Both made a huge effort to woo customers, although small businesses were rarely able to meet their shipping requirements through the postal service because the agency at first would accept only four packages per day from each walk-in customer. Still, the postal service enjoyed a 70 percent increase in volume for its express service during the strike. "We did see this as an opportunity for customers for whom we thought we could provide good value," admits Nicholas Barranca, vice president of operations support for the U.S. Postal Service. For instance, postal service representatives wrote, called, and even visited some companies, such as Replacements Ltd. (a china and flat-ware mail-order company), immediately before the strike. Replacements was impressed. "They're doing a good job here, and we'll respond by doing some business with them," said Scott Fleming, vice president of operations for Replacements.

Once the strike was over, UPS began the huge job of reestablishing its reliable image in people's minds. Executives appointed a "Customer Win-Back Task Force" at its Atlanta headquarters to come up with ways to regain customers' confidence. In addition to contact-ing clients, they sent candy and cookies to clients' secretaries in an effort to establish an association between UPS and a pleasant expe-rience. But the comeback was not easy. "The reality is [our customers] are not all coming back," lamented James P. Kelly, chairman and chief executive of UPS.

In addition to fighting an uphill battle with business customers, individual consumers now had a completely different view of UPS from the one they had before the strike. Because of the media slant, many people sympathized with the workers and were horrified at the images of traffic accidents involving managers who drove UPS trucks. Could the company re-create posi-tive memories in people's minds? Perhaps the best way to start was to put its drivers, the best emissaries UPS has, back to work.

Source: Anna Wilde Mathews and Nikhil Deogun, "After the Strike: Piles of Parcels, Business Woes," *The Wall Street Journal,* August 20, 1997, pp. B1, B12.

How, then, does a manager deal with this problem? One solution is to induce consumers to think about other things besides worms. Tybout et al. (1981) accomplished this by administering a survey about McDonald's containing questions about many different aspects of McDonald's restaurants. Questions about french fries, milkshakes, friendliness of service, cleanliness, convenience, and many other dimensions of McDonald's restaurants were included in the survey. While completing this survey, associations in memory between "McDonald's" and many other concepts were strengthened. Later, those who completed the survey were less likely to think about worms and more likely to express favorable overall evaluations toward McDonald's. Essentially, the survey increased the

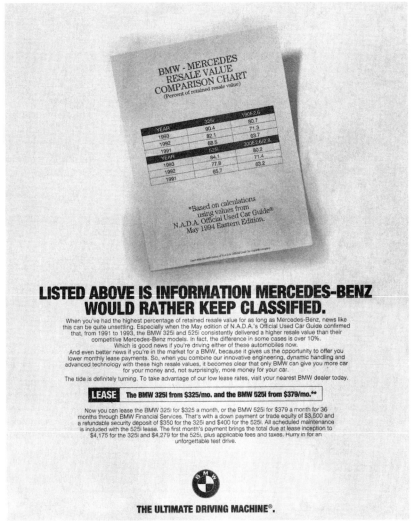

This ad essentially starts a rumor that Mercedes-Benz is dishonest about the resale values of its cars.

Source: © 1994 BMW of North America, Inc. Used with permission. The BMW name and logo are registered trademarks.

McDonald's wants happy meals,
not worms.
Source: © Mary Boucher.

richness and complexity of consumers' associative networks for McDonald's. As the number of associations linked to the "McDonald's" node increased, the likelihood that consumers will think about worms when they think about McDonald's decreased because of associative interference. The worm association can be buried in an embellished associative network, just as a needle can be buried in a haystack.

COMBATING MEDIA CLUTTER

The nation's oldest advertising agency, N. W. Ayer, Inc., was in a slump. Ayer's U.S. revenues dropped from $892 million in 1990 to $781 million in 1993 (Landner, 1994). During this period, Ayer lost several key accounts, including a $150 million account with AT&T ("Reach out and touch someone"), a $55 million account with Sterling Drug (Bayer Aspirin), and a $45 million account with JCPenney (Landner, 1994). For the first time in its 125-year history, Ayer hired a CEO from outside the company. Ayer believed it needed a fresh new perspective and fresh new ideas and was willing to spend an estimated $1 million a year for a new leader.

Saatchi & Saatchi, another leading advertising agency, was also in a slump. During the period 1990–1993, Saatchi & Saatchi lost an $80 million account with Helene Curtis, a $30 million account with Brown & Williamson (Kool cigarettes), and a $25 million account with Chrysler's Jeep/Eagle Division (Dwyer, Landner, Melcher, &Weber, 1994). Saatchi & Saatchi also believed it needed fresh new ideas, so it hired several new top executives from Great Britain.

One key problem faced by Ayer, Saatchi & Saatchi, and other leading ad agencies is **media clutter,** or consumer exposure to large amounts of mass-media advertising. As consumers are exposed to more and more ads, attention decreases (Webb, 1979; Webb & Ray, 1979) and memory performance decreases (Bagozzi & Silk, 1983; Baumgardner, Leippe, Ronis, & Greenwald, 1983; Burke & Srull, 1988). Attention decreases because of boredom and fatigue, and memory performance decreases because of associative interference. It is important to emphasize that it is not just the passage of time that leads consumers to forget advertised information: Forgetting is due to retrieval failure caused by associative interference. Over an eight-hour period, people forget more when they are awake (and therefore are likely to be exposed to other information) than when they are asleep (Jenkins & Dallenbach, 1924). This is known as **retroactive associative interference** because subsequently considered information interferes with memory for information learned earlier. The opposite type of associative interference has also been demonstrated: **Proactive associative interference** occurs when information learned earlier interferes with memory for information learned later. Both types of associative interference involve memory search through a large associative network, which is analogous to searching through hundreds of computer files to find one particular file.

In an important study of competitive advertising interference, Burke and Srull (1988) exposed consumers to three target ads: a Bolens B7100DT lawn and garden tractor ad, a Fujitsu Ten car stereo ad, and a Eureka Space II tent ad. After seeing these print ads, subjects examined several additional ads (retroactive associative interference). The additional ads were either for products in other product categories (i.e., not tractors, not car stereos, and not tents), for different brands in the same product categories (i.e., other tractors, other car stereos, and other tents), or for different ads for the same target products. These three experimental conditions were referred to as the varied product context, same product context, and same brand context, respectively. The results revealed that memory performance decreased as the similarity between the contextual information and the target information increased. This is because similar information is likely to be stored in the same associative network, whereas different information tends to be stored in different associative networks. Moreover, the results showed that these effects were not driven simply by confusion between information in one ad for information in another.

In a second experiment, Burke and Srull (1988) presented the context ads before (rather than after) presenting the target ads (proactive associative interference). Again, memory performance decreased as the degree of similarity between the context and target ads increased. Finally, in a third experiment, Burke and Srull (1988) manipulated the number of times they presented a target ad (once, twice, or three times) as well as context. In the high competitive advertising interference context, ads for directly competing brands were presented before and after the target ad (to permit proactive and retroactive associative interference). In the moderate competitive advertising interference context, an ad for a directly competing brand was presented after the target ad (to permit retroactive associative interference). In the low interference condition, a varied product context was used. Again, the results demonstrated that memory performance decreased as competitive advertising interference increased. Moreover, this decrease in memory performance was reduced by repetitive advertising in low, but not moderate, or high interference conditions. Hence, ad repetition can be used to combat media clutter when competitive advertising is low but not when competition is intense. Decreasing the degree of similarity between your ads and competitors' ads may also help to combat media clutter. Novelty and fresh new ideas are extremely important.

It is also important to recognize that associative interference is a two-edged sword. Competitors' ads interfere with memory for your ads. However, your ads also interfere with memory for competitors' ads. Advertising serves many functions: Ads inform and influence consumer judgments concerning your brands, but they also interfere with memory for information presented in competitors' ads.

◆   IMPLICIT MEMORY

In the mid 1950s, thousands of people flocked to see the popular movie *Picnic* in a New Jersey movie theater. Unbeknownst to them, the messages "Eat Popcorn" and "Drink Coke" were flashed on the screen at 1/3,000 of a second during the show. Although no one could detect the messages, advertiser James Vicary claimed that these messages increased popcorn sales by 58 percent and increased Coke sales by 18 percent (Pratkanis & Aronson, 1992). These **subliminal** messages were so subtle that people were unaware that they had been presented at all. Is it possible to influence people by attacking the subconscious with subliminal messages? Many attempts to reproduce Vicary's findings in controlled laboratory settings have failed (Moore, 1982), leading Vicary to finally admit that he made up his results to try to save his failing advertising business (Weir, 1984). Nevertheless, the possibility of subconscious mind control continues to intrigue and frighten most people, mainly because most people do not understand how the subconscious operates (Pratkanis & Aronson, 1992; Pratkanis & Greenwald, 1989).

The best way to understand the subconscious is by drawing a distinction between memory as an object versus memory as a tool (Jacoby, 1991; Jacoby, Kelley, & Dywan, 1989; Jacoby, Woloshyn, & Kelley, 1989). When people consciously try to retrieve information from long-term memory to perform an **explicit memory** task—such as a recognition, cued recall, or free recall task—memory serves as an object of attention. That is, people are aware that they are focusing on and consulting memory. However, memory is also often used as a tool for making judgments and decisions. When we use memory as a tool to perform an **implicit memory** task, we are not aware that we are using memory, and we do not realize that we are being influenced by prior experiences and memories.

Because memory can have both automatic and controlled influences on judgment, Jacoby et al. (1989) developed the **method of opposition** to separate these influences. **Automatic influences** occur without intention or awareness. **Controlled influences** occur with intention and awareness. The method of opposition involves pitting these two types of influences against each other. For example, immediately after reading a list of names of people, like "Sebastian Weisdorf," the names seem more familiar and the automatic influence of memory leads subjects to confuse familiarity for fame (famous names seem familiar, and familiar names seem famous). However, if subjects are told that none of the names on the list are famous, the controlled influence of memory leads subjects to judge the names as nonfamous. Hence, the automatic and controlled influences of memory have opposite effects on judgment.

After subjects read the first list of names, they received a second list with some old names (i.e., names that were on the first list) and some new names (i.e., names that were not on the first list). Subjects were asked to judge the fame of each name. However, half of the subjects judged fame while performing another distracting task at the same time (the divided attention condition) and half judged fame with no distraction (the full attention condition). It was reasoned that dividing attention should prevent subjects from thinking carefully about the judgment task, and this should cause the automatic influence of memory on judgment to dominate. In contrast, when subjects are permitted to deliberate about a judgment task, the controlled influence should prevail. As Figure 3-8 indicates, this is exactly the pattern of results that was observed. "Sebastian Weisdorf" and the other old names became famous overnight

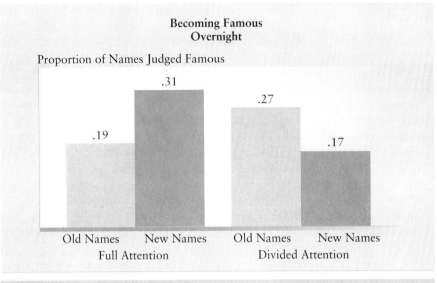

FIGURE 3-8

Familiarity is confused for fame when attention is divided, but not when attention is not divided.

Source: Adapted from Jacoby, Woloshyn, & Kelley (1989).

when attention was divided. Conversely, old names seemed less famous than new names when attention was not divided.

Basically, subjects confused fame with familiarity because they did not know where the feelings of familiarity came from. Familiar things seem famous, valid or true, and controllable, except when feelings of familiarity are influenced by irrelevant events and we are aware of this influence. When we are unaware of where a feeling or belief comes from, we are experiencing **source amnesia.** This makes us susceptible to source confusion and incorrect inferences or conclusions. Returning to the "Eat Popcorn" and "Drink Coke" subliminal messages, it is interesting that *if* a moviegoer received this message (which is impossible at 1/3,000-of-a-second exposure) and *if* he or she assumed that the subconscious was the source of the message (rather than realizing that the movie screen was the source of the message), this approach might work (of course, these are very big "ifs"). It is also interesting that people are unaware of the source of many different feelings and beliefs. For example, most people have heard of subliminal advertising but are unaware of where they heard about it. Ironically, this particular instance of source amnesia leads many to assume that subliminal advertising is more effective than it actually is!

CHAPTER SUMMARY ■

Human memory is best conceptualized as a multiple memory system. A large amount of inactive information is stored in long-term memory. Using information involves activating it by retrieving information from inactive long-term memory and bringing it into active short-term memory. Consumers are consciously aware of the contents of short-term memory, and they can perform a large number of cognitive operations on these contents (e.g., thinking, reasoning, judging, and deciding). However, consumers have a limited capacity to process information and can hold only seven (plus or minus two) chunks of information in short-term memory at a time.

The three key principles of long-term memory are the organization principle, the encoding-specificity principle, and the association principle. According to the organization principle, comprehending and grouping related information together enhances memory performance. According to the encoding-specificity principle, memory is context dependent. Memory performance is best when the encoding (learning) context and the retrieval (test) context are similar. The association principle emphasizes that concepts or ideas are represented in memory as nodes and that related nodes are linked together in an associative network. This principle explains several important memory phenomena, including spreading activation, priming, proactive associative interference, and retroactive associative interference.

Consumers are aware that they are using memory when they focus on memory as an object to perform explicit memory tasks, such as recognition (e.g., a multiple-choice test), cued recall (e.g., a fill-in-the-blank test), and free recall (e.g., an essay test). Consumers are unaware of memory when they use it as a tool for performing an implicit memory task. Prior experiences influence feelings of familiarity, which then influence a wide variety of judgments, including judgments of fame, validity, and controllability. Memory is involved in virtually all cognitive tasks, and memory enables us to perform these tasks more efficiently.

KEY CONCEPTS

- Conscious awareness
- Rehearsal
- Coding
- Short-term memory
- Long-term memory
- Encoded
- Permastore
- Organization principle
- Encoding-specificity principle
- Association principle
- Organization

- Recognition
- Cued recall
- Free recall
- Node
- Associations
- Associative network
- Response-time methods
- Activation
- Priming effect
- Associative interference
- Media clutter

- Retroactive associative interference
- Proactive associative interference
- Subliminal
- Explicit memory
- Implicit memory
- Method of opposition
- Automatic influences
- Controlled influences
- Source amnesia

DISCUSSION QUESTIONS

1. What is the main cause of information loss from short-term memory? How might marketers use this knowledge to help consumers transfer information about products from short-term to long-term memory?
2. As a marketer, if you wanted consumers to remember a list of features about the new model of cordless phone your company was getting ready to launch, where would you place the most important features in your list? Why?

3. In your career as a student, have you performed best on recognition, cued-recall, or free-recall tests? Why do you think that is?

4. Based on what you have learned about long-term memory in this chapter, what techniques might you use to study for an exam more effectively?

5. Besides the examples described in the chapter—of Little Mikey and Elvira—describe one or two other examples of the encoding-specificity principle as you have seen it used in advertising.

6. Choose a product such as the Ford Explorer, Taco Bell tacos, Nike shoes, Tylenol, or the like and create your own associative network for it. At the center of a blank sheet of paper, write the name of your product. Nearby, write your first association to the product and draw a line between the two. Then write your next association, linking the second and third, and so forth, until your paper is full. See how far afield the associations go.

7. How can marketers use the priming effect to their advantage?

8. Recently, when it was discovered that a large supplier of hamburger meat to various restaurants around the United States had shipped tons of contaminated beef, consumers everywhere were afraid to eat hamburger. The timing was especially bad for restaurants and supermarkets because the scare took place during the summer—the season when Americans are most likely to be grilling and ordering hamburgers frequently. If you were the owner or franchiser of a restaurant whose most popular food items included various types of hamburgers, what steps might you have taken to combat marketplace rumors about the meat you served?

9. In the previous chapter, you learned that the FTC's policy of corrective advertising isn't necessarily effective. What implications might associative interference have for the FTC?

10. Consider a task you know how to complete without "thinking"—brushing your teeth, backing the car out of the garage, walking from your dorm room to class. Your task is an example of implicit memory. Write down all the steps your brain actually has to remember in order to complete the task.

CHAPTER 4 Consumer Judgment

◆ STAR WARS

A whole new generation of video viewers is glued to their sets: They are watching the rerelease of the original *Star Wars* trilogy, cheering Luke Skywalker and booing Darth Vader. George Lucas, creator of the films, is banking on 20 years of consumer judgments to pass from one generation to the next—he is banking on the baby-boom generation to revisit the films and the baby boomers' children to discover them for the first time.

Lucas isn't just releasing videos. He is also negotiating with current license holders Hasbro and Galoob Toys, along with Mattel, for such game and toy tie-ins as plastic figures of the *Star Wars* heroes and villains, board games, and CD-ROMs. Not content to rest on the laurels of past *Star Wars* success, Lucas released a new trilogy of related films—prequels to the *Star Wars* story that take viewers back as far as Darth Vader's childhood, before the character became a villain.

Future success of all these ventures will be based on the judgment of consumers—their beliefs about the *Star Wars* movies, their attitudes toward the characters, and their preferences for *Star Wars* products over other products. Marketers connected with the various *Star Wars* projects are well aware of this, and they are banking on the likelihood that consumers who have had favorable experiences with *Star Wars* products in the past will predict favorable experiences in the future—and make purchases accordingly. "[Star Wars tie-ins] have demonstrated the ability to sell well in the absence of an event, such as a movie every year," notes Sean McGowan, a toy analyst at Gerard Klauer Mattison. *Star Wars* toy sales reached $500 million in one recent year, signaling that consumers are still ready and willing to purchase a piece of the *Star Wars* mystique.

This means that Lucasfilm Ltd. (George Lucas's company) can command huge royalties and licensing fees from toymakers, who in turn seem willing to pay up front for the chance to cash in later on favorable consumer judgments. (Mattel offered $1 billion for licensing privileges.) Galoob expects to make $150 million in a single year on *Star Wars* toys (under its current license), nearly half its total annual sales. Hasbro, a larger company than Galoob, expects to earn $350 million in *Star Wars* revenues. Clearly, each company hopes that the force of consumer judgments will be with it. As you read this chapter, consider the profound effects that different types of consumer judgments have on the success of goods and services.

Source: Lisa Bannon and Joseph Pereira, "Toy Makers Offer the Moon for New *Star Wars* Licenses," *The Wall Street Journal,* August 19, 1997, pp. B1, B10.

◆ INTRODUCTION

People are likely to form many different judgments while viewing commercials and evaluating products and services. A judgment refers to the location of a target object or issue on a cognitive continuum (Wyer, 1974; Wyer & Carlston, 1979; Wyer & Srull, 1989). Some cognitive continua are nonevaluative, such as the concepts "safe," "gentle," or "effective." Nonevaluative judgments are referred to as **beliefs.** Consumers hold many beliefs. For example, many consumers believe that Bufferin is safe, gentle, and effective. Products differ in how safe, gentle, and effective they are perceived to be (i.e., these are continuous dimensions), and the makers of Bufferin want consumers to believe that Bufferin is very safe (as opposed to somewhat safe or not safe), very gentle, and very effective. Beliefs are important because they often serve as building blocks for more complex judgments, such as **attitudes** (evaluative judgments) and **preferences** (evaluative judgments involving more than one product). George Lucas, creator of *Star Wars,* has been able to capitalize on consumers' preference for his movies.

Some cognitive continua are evaluative, such as "good," "bad," "favorable," and "unfavorable." Like nonevaluative dimensions, evaluative dimensions are continuous in nature. This means that consumers may have very unfavorable, unfavorable, somewhat unfavorable, neutral, somewhat favorable, favorable, or very favorable attitudes toward an object or issue. Attitudes are important because they often exert a strong influence on purchase decisions. (See "Making the Decision: The British Are Coming.") If you have a very favorable attitude toward a particular product, you are more likely to buy the product.

This chapter discusses the different types of judgments consumers form. Some are nonevaluative, and others are evaluative. Some are abstract or general, and others are

MAKING THE DECISION

THE BRITISH ARE COMING

When Americans think of international cuisine, they don't usually think of British cooking. Instead, they are apt to conjure up Parisian, northern Italian, Thai, or Japanese delights. Many of us think of British food as bland—boiled meat, overcooked vegetables, lots and lots of potatoes. Sir Terence Conran, Britain's famous restaurant and style tycoon (owner of the Conran's home furnishing stores that were so popular in the 1980s), wants to change the beliefs and attitudes Americans hold about British food. He thinks that if he can do that, the American restaurant market will be a gold mine.

Conran isn't starting small or easy. He has chosen one of the toughest restaurant markets to crack: New York. He is planning a huge complex consisting of several restaurants adjacent to a 35,000-square-foot home furnishing shop to be built under Manhattan's Queensboro Bridge on a deserted site called Bridgemarket. Not much exists there right now, and the location may seem odd to some people. "It's a dead street," says Chris Katrakazis, owner of the Sutton Place Coffee shop, which lies a block away from the site. "The only traffic is bridge traffic." Perhaps therein lies the difference between Conran and a coffee shop owner: Conran sees the bridge, sees traffic driving across the bridge, and then sees that traffic stopping at his Bridgemarket complex.

Conran plans to use some of the same tactics that have made his restaurants successful in Britain—large scale, variety in food, excellent service, and attention to every detail. At Quagliano's in London, he serves rabbit with spiced aubergine and coriander; at Mezzo, the 700-seat dining room overlooks the massive, gleaming kitchen in which chefs perform like actors. Conran's menus include Asian, Mediterranean, and French cuisine—a far cry from meat pie.

When confronted by skeptics, Sir Terence replies, "Yes, [New York] is competitive, but with all modesty, we think we can bring something in terms of style of operation that we have here." His style of operation feeds 35,000 to 40,000 Londoners a week. What would make New Yorkers change their beliefs and attitudes about British food? "It will have to be unique—not a regular restaurant," observes Freddie Ramallo, owner of the Tapas Lounge and Eros restaurant on First Avenue in Manhattan. "A regular restaurant will die," Antoine Bouterin, owner of the restaurant bearing his own name, concurs. Bouterin adds, "New York is a city that likes new things. A new thing in New York is always a good thing." Thus, Conran could capitalize on New Yorkers' favorable attitude toward new things, at least initially. If he serves them well, his Bridgemarket could actually become a preferred place to dine.

Source: Robert Frank and Lisa Shuchman, "A British Foodie Tries to Tempt Manhattanites," _The Wall Street Journal,_ August 22, 1997, pp. B1, B2.

concrete or specific. A clearer understanding of the different types of judgments consumers form and the major factors that influence these judgments will help managers to make more informed decisions about strategies designed to influence consumer beliefs, attitudes, and other types of judgments. The chapter closes with a discussion about the relationship between judgments and purchase decisions.

The type of consumer beliefs marketers are most interested in are beliefs about product attributes and benefits (**consequences of attributes**). All products have attributes, or features, that are of concern to consumers. (See Fig. 4-1.) For example, when it comes to aspirin, people worry about attributes such as safeness, gentleness, effectiveness, and speed of relief. Automobiles have attributes such as braking, handling, air conditioning, and miles per gallon. In fact, many automobile manufacturers administer surveys with questions on over 100 different product attributes. Beliefs about braking, for example, can be measured on a scale from 0 (poor braking) to 10 (excellent braking). Similar scales can be developed for any attribute (i.e., specific physical feature) or benefit (i.e., abstract consequence, such as quality, reliability, safety, or prestige) and for any product or brand. Belief scales are continuous, because belief dimensions in people's heads are also continuous. Presumably, when a consumer circles a 7 on a 0–10 scale, the 7 position corresponds to a similar location on an unobservable continuous dimension in the consumer's head. It should also be noted that a belief implies a perceived relationship between two concepts or ideas (Bem, 1970). For example, the belief that Bufferin is effective implies a relationship between the concept "Bufferin" and the concept "effective."

Successful marketers pay a lot of attention to consumer beliefs. Beliefs influence what people do and fail to do. For example, Procter & Gamble's (P&G) Ivory soap has dominated the soap market for over 100 years (Aaker, 1991). Ironically, part of the

FIGURE 4-1

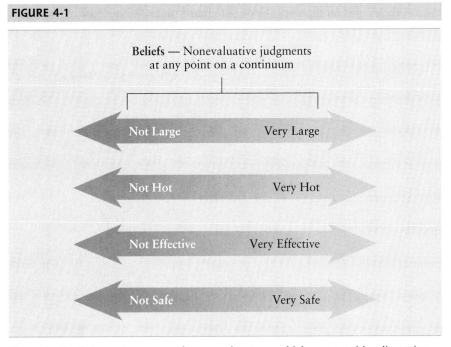

Beliefs — Nonevaluative judgments
at any point on a continuum

Not Large   Very Large

Not Hot   Very Hot

Not Effective   Very Effective

Not Safe   Very Safe

Nonevaluative judgments can range from very low to very high on a cognitive dimension.

reason for Ivory soap's success is that when the product was first introduced in 1879 it floated in water because of a design flaw. P&G's early advertising emphasized that it floated because it was 99 and 7/8% pure. The soap was also pure white and much gentler than rival yellow and brown soaps that irritated skin and stained clothing. Ivory soap was so superior to competing brands that it served as the market leader (i.e., had more market share than any other brand) for well over 100 years. Then, suddenly, in 1991, something remarkable happened. Lever Brothers introduced Lever 2000 soap for "all 2000 body parts," and Lever Brothers is now cleaning up. In 1991, Lever 2000 achieved $113 million in sales, and the Lever soaps (Lever 2000, Dove, Caress, Shield, Lux, and Lifebuoy) achieved a 31.5 percent market share, whereas P&G's soaps' (Ivory, Zest, Coast, Safeguard, and Camay) market share dropped to 30.5 percent (Reitman, 1992). Of course, even a very small percentage drop is significant in a $1.6 billion market, such as the soap market—1 percent of $1.6 billion is $16 million.

One of the keys to Lever 2000's success is that it is an "all-in-one" brand for all family members. Now families can buy one brand for everyone, instead of the usual two or three or more brands. *The Wall Street Journal* (Reitman, 1992) interviewed consumer Mary Beth Hageman of Havertown, Pennsylvania, who says, "It's the one soap we can all use." She likes Lever 2000 even though her skin is dry. Her husband likes it even though his skin is oily, and it is even gentle enough for their six-year-old son. Mary Beth Hageman also likes its light fragrance and says that "a lot of soaps smell the way men are supposed to smell. Who wants to go around smelling like a pine tree?" These beliefs have had a strong impact on Mary Beth Hageman, who buys Lever 2000 even though it is more expensive than the brands she once purchased.

Of course, P&G is reacting quickly to the Lever Brothers challenge. P&G made several changes on the package of Safeguard that were designed to change consumers' beliefs. The Safeguard package used to say "deodorant soap," but it now says "antibacterial deodorant soap." The Safeguard package also says "mild enough for the whole family." Interestingly, the Safeguard soap formula has not changed. Only the package has changed. Where purchase decisions and other consumer behaviors are concerned, subjective beliefs and perceptions are more important than objective facts and formulas.

TYPES OF BELIEFS

There are three major types of beliefs: **descriptive beliefs, informational beliefs,** and **inferential beliefs** (Fishbein & Ajzen, 1975). Descriptive beliefs are based on direct, firsthand experience with a product (e.g., what we see and hear with our own eyes and ears). Informational beliefs are based on indirect, secondhand information (e.g., information we obtain from other people in interpersonal or mass-media communications). Descriptive beliefs are often stronger than informational beliefs because we often trust what we see and hear with our own eyes and ears more than we trust what we hear from other people. Inferential beliefs are beliefs that go beyond the information given or the information that is available from firsthand or secondhand sources (Hastie, 1983; Kardes, 1993).

Inferences about missing information can be made on the basis of correlated presented information (Ford & Smith, 1987; Huber & McCann, 1982; Johnson & Levin,

This ad attempts to influence consumers' overall attitudes by influencing specific beliefs. Favorable beliefs about strength and easier cleaning contribute to favorable attitudes toward Mr. Clean.

Source: © The Procter & Gamble Company. Used with permission.

1985; Kardes & Sanbonmatsu, 1993; Meyer, 1981; Ross & Creyer, 1992). For example, when the price of a product is known and quality is unknown, consumers often use price to infer quality. Because consumers believe that price and quality are positively correlated, high price implies high quality and low price implies low quality (you get what you pay for).

Evaluation-based inferences are beliefs about specific unknown attributes based on overall impressions (Beckwith & Lehmann, 1975; Eagly, Ashmore, Makhijani, & Longo, 1990; Sanbonmatsu, Kardes, & Sansone, 1991). For example, if a consumer's overall impression of a particular brand of camera is very favorable, the consumer may assume that the camera has a high-quality close-up lens even if the consumer received no information about this particular feature.

Prior knowledge about product categories can also serve as a basis for inferences (Sujan, 1985; Sujan & Dekleva, 1988). Categories often imply default values. For example, consumers know that cars have four wheels, brakes, a rearview mirror, and so on. Consequently, consumers do not need to be told that a new car has four wheels, brakes, and a rearview mirror. Consumers can safely assume that these features are givens.

Inferences can also be based on schemas, or organized knowledge structures based on prior experience (Hastie, 1983; Kardes, 1988, 1993; Kardes, Kim, & Lim, 1994).

Knowledge structures provide a basis for logical reasoning, as when consumers infer that if Brand A is better then Brand B, and if Brand B is better than Brand C, then Brand A must be better than Brand C. Knowledge-based logical reasoning also allows consumers to infer links between attributes and benefits. For example, consumers who know a lot about compact-disc players know that brands with an audible scanner (an attribute) are easy to use (a benefit) because audible scanners allow users to find specific passages quickly and easily.

◆ EVALUATIVE JUDGMENT (ATTITUDE)

An attitude is an evaluative judgment (Eagly & Chaiken, 1993; Fazio, 1990; Fishbein & Ajzen, 1975; Petty & Cacioppo, 1981). An evaluative judgment has two main components: direction (e.g., good or bad, positive or negative) and extremity (e.g., slightly good, somewhat good, fairly good, very good, extremely good). (See Fig. 4-2.) Of course, an evaluation is always made with respect to some target object or issue. The object can be general (e.g., soft drinks, homes, financial services) or specific (e.g., Coca-Cola, Drees homes, Allstate insurance). Furthermore, the object can be a physical object (like a consumer product) or an abstract issue (such as a political platform or an economic theory).

People can form attitudes toward any object or issue. Moreover, attitudes can be based on many different types of information. As explained in Chapter 3, information does not refer merely to facts and figures. Instead, information refers to any stimulus

FIGURE 4-2

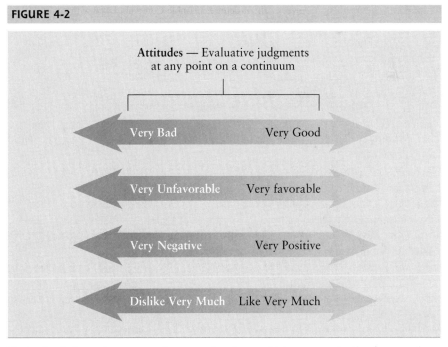

Evaluative judgments can range from very low to very high on an evaluative (e.g., good or bad) dimension.

or cue that is psychologically meaningful or influential. For example, beliefs can be viewed as information that has direct implications for attitudes, and, indeed, beliefs often serve as building blocks for attitudes (Fishbein & Ajzen, 1975; Zanna & Rempel, 1988). Consider the case of Dr. Marten's shoes. Consumers who are familiar with this brand are likely to have beliefs about several attributes or benefits of this brand, such as comfort, long-lastingness, and style. Consumers who believe that Dr. Marten's shoes are comfortable, long-lasting, and stylish are likely to form favorable overall evaluations or attitudes toward Dr. Marten's shoes. That is, beliefs about specific aspects or features of a brand may be combined into a global, overall evaluation of a brand.

Before we can study beliefs and attitudes, we must first be able to measure or describe beliefs and attitudes. Table 4-1 provides a summary of several commonly

---

TABLE 4-1 **Judgment Scales**

Belief Scales

Semantic Differential Scale (Bipolar Adjective Scale)

Dr. Marten's shoes are:

Uncomfortable ____ : ____ : ____ : ____ : ____ : ____ : ____	Comfortable
Expensive ____ : ____ : ____ : ____ : ____ : ____ : ____	Inexpensive
Unfashionable ____ : ____ : ____ : ____ : ____ : ____ : ____	Fashionable

Likert Scale (Agree–Disagree Scale)

Dr. Marten's shoes provide excellent arch support.	SA	A	N	D	SD
Dr. Marten's shoes absorb unpleasant foot odor.	SA	A	N	D	SD
Dr. Marten's shoes are long-lasting.	SA	A	N	D	SD

Guttman Scale (Rank-Ordered Statements):

Dr. Marten's shoes are somewhat stylish.	Agree	Disagree
Dr. Marten's shoes are stylish.	Agree	Disagree
Dr. Marten's shoes are very stylish	Agree	Disagree

Attitude Scales

Semantic Differential Scale (Bipolar Adjective Scale):

Dr. Marten's shoes are:

Bad ____ : ____ : ____ : ____ : ____ : ____ : ____	Good
Unfavorable ____ : ____ : ____ : ____ : ____ : ____ : ____	Favorable
Unlikeable ____ : ____ : ____ : ____ : ____ : ____ : ____	Likeable

Likert Scale (Agree–Disagree Scale)

Overall, Dr. Marten's shoes are very desirable.	SA	A	N	D	SD
My overall impression of Dr. Marten's shoes is favorable.	SA	A	N	D	SD
Overall, I like Dr. Marten's shoes very much.	SA	A	N	D	SD

Guttman Scale (Rank-Ordered Statements):

Dr. Marten's shoes are somewhat good.	Agree	Disagree
Dr. Marten's shoes are good.	Agree	Disagree
Dr. Marten's shoes are very good.	Agree	Disagree

used judgment scales, or rating scales, for measuring beliefs and attitudes. These types of scales are often included in consumer surveys, political polls, and other types of paper-and-pencil questionnaires for assessing beliefs (opinions) and attitudes (evaluations). Semantic differential scales (also known as bipolar adjective scales) have endpoints labeled by adjectives with opposite meanings. For example, the opposite of comfortable is uncomfortable. The more comfortable the shoe is perceived to be, the more subjects' check marks should approach the far right end of the scale. Conversely, the less comfortable the shoe is perceived to be, the more subjects' check marks should approach the far left end of the scale. Similar ratings are performed for expensive/inexpensive and fashionable/unfashionable.

Beliefs can also be measured using Likert scales, or agree–disagree scales. Subjects should indicate the extent to which they agree or disagree with each statement presented in a questionnaire by circling either SA (strongly agree), A (agree), N (neither agree nor disagree), D (disagree), or SD (strongly disagree). Again, belief scales can be constructed for many different attributes or benefits (e.g., arch support, foot odor asbsorption, long-lastingness).

Guttman scales consist of a series of rank-ordered statements, and subjects are asked to indicate whether they agree or disagree with each statement. The statements are usually fairly neutral at first (e.g., somewhat stylish), and they gradually become more (e.g., stylish) and more (e.g., very stylish) extreme. Note that if a consumer endorses an extreme position (e.g., very stylish), he or she should also agree with less extreme positions (e.g., stylish, somewhat stylish).

Attitudes can also be measured using semantic differential scales, Likert scales, and Guttman scales. Note, however, that belief scales focus on specific attributes (e.g., comfort) and specific benefits (e.g., long-lasting), whereas attitude scales are general and evaluative (e.g., "Overall, I like Dr. Marten's shoes very much"). Returning to the idea that specific beliefs often serve as building blocks for general attitudes, several quantitative models describe precisely how beliefs are combined or integrated into overall evaluations or attitudes. A brief discussion of two such models, the Theory of Reasoned Action and the Information Integration Theory, follows, focusing exclusively on the implications of these models for understanding how beliefs are combined to form attitudes. The implications of these models for understanding belief change and attitude change are discussed in Chapter 8.

Are you familiar with Doc Marten's shoes? What is your attitude?

Source: © Dick Morton.

THE THEORY OF REASONED ACTION

Fishbein and Ajzen's (1975) **Theory of Reasoned Action** suggests that beliefs are combined additively to form attitudes. The greater the number of favorable beliefs one holds, the more favorable one's attitude. Specifically, the Fishbein model states that

$$A_o = \Sigma b_i e_i,$$

where A_o is the attitude toward the object (the object can be a product, a service, an issue, an action, or an event), b_i is the belief about attribute i (measured in terms of the likelihood that o has i), and e_i is the evaluation of i. Of course, consumers do not think about every attribute or benefit associated with an attitude object: They think about only **salient beliefs,** or important, attention-drawing beliefs (Ajzen & Fishbein, 1980; Sheppard, Hartwick, & Warshaw, 1988). Typically, consumers think about only seven (plus or minus two) salient beliefs, consistent with Miller's magic number reflecting limited information processing capacity. Fishbein and Ajzen's (1975) equation specifies that beliefs and evaluations are multiplied and that each product arrived at by multiplying b times e is added. For example, suppose a consumer believes, on a scale from -3 to $+3$, that Dr. Marten's shoes are comfortable ($+2$), fairly expensive ($+1$), and very fashionable ($+3$). Further, suppose that comfort is evaluated $+1$ (comfort is positive), expensive is evaluated -2 (spending a lot of money on shoes is negative), and fashion is evaluated $+3$. As Table 4-2 indicates, multiplying each b times e and adding these products results in an overall attitude of $+9$. Computing attitudes from beliefs requires simple multiplication and addition. In industry, the Theory of Reasoned Action is used to predict attitudes from beliefs and to diagnose problem attributes.

The Fishbein model is a simple additive model: As the number of favorable beliefs increases, the overall attitude increases in favorableness. The Fishbein model was extended into the Theory of Reasoned Action when subjective norms (or rules) were added to the model by Fishbein and Ajzen (1975). The Theory of Reasoned Action

---

TABLE 4-2   Combining Beliefs to Form Attitudes

Theory of Reasoned Action

Attribute	Belief (b_i)		Evaluation (e_i)		$b_i e_i$
Comfortable	+2	×	+1	=	+2
Expensive	+1	×	−2	=	−2
Fashionable	+3	×	+3	=	+9
					+9

Information Integration Theory

Attribute	Weight (w_i)		Scale Value (s_i)		$w_i s_i$
Comfortable	.2	×	+1	=	+.2
Expensive	.2	×	−2	=	−.4
Fashionable	.6	×	+3	=	+1.8
					+1.6

suggests that behavior is purposeful and intention-driven. The Theory of Reasoned Action also suggests that intentions are influenced by attitudes (which are influenced by beliefs) and by subjective norms, which are influenced by normative beliefs (or beliefs about what other people will think of you after you perform a behavior) multiplied by the motivation to comply (or how concerned you are about what other people think of you). Research has shown that the attitude component of the model becomes more important when consumers think in terms of actions (or how to reach one's goals or end states) and that the subjective norm component of the model becomes more important when consumers think in terms of end states (Bagozzi, Baumgartner, & Yi, 1992). The Fishbein model has also been extended by adding perceived control, or the ability to plan behaviors deliberately (Ajzen & Madden, 1986), and the process of trying (Bagozzi & Warshaw, 1990) to the model.

INFORMATION INTEGRATION THEORY

Anderson's (1981, 1982) **Information Integration Theory** offers a more general variation of the Theory of Reasoned Action. It is more general because it does not assume that beliefs are combined additively. Sometimes, beliefs are combined using a subtraction rule (e.g., for some types of preference judgments; Shanteau & Anderson, 1969), and sometimes beliefs are combined using a multiplication rule (e.g., some types of probability judgments; Anderson & Shanteau, 1970). For most consumer goods and services, however, beliefs are combined using an averaging rule to form attitudes (Anderson, 1981, 1982; Troutman & Shanteau, 1976). The weighted-average model for determining how beliefs are combined into attitudes is expressed as

$$A_o = \Sigma w_i s_i$$

where

$$\Sigma w_i = 1$$

Again, A_o refers to the attitude toward the object, s_i refers to the scale value for attribute i (s_i is conceptually similar to and measured the same way as e_i in the Theory of Reasoned Action), and w_i refers to the weight, or importance, of each attribute. Unlike b_i, which is measured directly by asking consumers to complete belief scales, w_i is estimated indirectly by using statistical tests (such as the analysis of variance or multiple regression) to determine the extent to which each s_i influenced A_o. These statistical tests constrain w_i to sum to unity (1), which changes an adding model into an averaging model. This is an important distinction because an adding model suggests that "more is better" and that simply adding additional positive features to a product will result in more favorable consumer attitudes. By contrast, an averaging model suggests that "less is better," because a small number of very favorable features considered alone results in more favorable attitudes than the same very favorable features plus many slightly favorable features considered together. For many consumer goods and services, the weighted-average model outperforms the additive model (Anderson, 1981, 1982; Lynch, 1985; Troutman & Shanteau, 1976).

For example, Table 4-2 shows that, on a scale from -3 to $+3$, Dr. Marten's shoes were rated as a $+1$ for comfort, a -2 for expensive, and a $+3$ for fashionable. Regressing consumers' overall evaluations (mean = $+1.6$) onto scale values yielded beta weights (a statistical measure of importance) of .2, .2, and .6, respectively. Note that the weights always sum to 1. Multiplying each *w* times *s* and adding these products results in an overall attitude of +1.6. In this example, overall attitude ratings and attribute ratings were used to statistically estimate attribute importance weights.

ZANNA AND REMPEL'S (1988) MODEL

Although many attitudes are based on beliefs, this is not true for all attitudes. According to **Zanna and Rempel's (1988) Model,** attitudes can be formed on the basis of beliefs (cognitions), affect (i.e., feelings, moods, and emotions), behaviors (actions), or some combination of beliefs, affect, and behaviors. For example, many people have very favorable attitudes toward Dairy Queen hot fudge sundaes because eating hot fudge sundaes makes people feel good, and positive moods and feelings result in positive evaluations or attitudes. Note that beliefs about how fattening and unhealthy hot fudge sundaes are have little impact on attitudes toward hot fudge sundaes. In this particular case, affect is a more important determinant of attitudes than is belief.

In other cases, behaviors have a powerful influence on attitudes. For example, after buying a new car (a behavior), most consumers' attitudes toward the new car become even more favorable. Interestingly, Zanna and Rempel (1988) emphasize that not only are attitudes influenced by belief, affect, and behavior, attitudes also influence belief, affect, and behavior. Positive attitudes lead consumers to focus on positive beliefs, positive feelings, and positive behaviors (e.g., approach behaviors such as buying or using the attitude object). Negative attitudes lead consumers to dwell on negative beliefs, negative feelings, and negative behaviors (e.g., avoidance behaviors such as not buying or not using the attitude object). Hence, there is a **reciprocal relationship** between attitudes and bases of attitudes. Attitudes influence and are influenced by belief, affect, and behavior.

◆ PREFERENCE JUDGMENT

In contrast to attitudes, which are evaluative judgments toward one object, preferences are evaluative judgments concerning two or more objects. Preferences always involve making comparisons between objects. Sometimes attitudes serve as building blocks for preferences, and sometimes preferences are based on comparisons of attributes or features of two or more products. For example, consumers may form preferences

Sometimes cold weather can temper favorable attitudes about hot fudge sundaes.
Source: © Dick Morton.

concerning soft drinks by comparing their attitudes toward Coca-Cola and Pepsi Cola. If consumers have more favorable attitudes toward Coca-Cola than toward Pepsi Cola, they should prefer Coca-Cola. Note that consumers may have very favorable attitudes toward both products, but if their attitudes are more favorable toward Coca-Cola, they should prefer Coca-Cola. Preferences formed on the basis of consumers' overall attitudes toward two or more products are known as **attitude-based preferences.**

However, preferences are not always based on attitudes. Sometimes preferences are based on comparisons of specific attributes or features of two or more products. For example, if a consumer is unfamiliar with different brands of house paints, he or she is unlikely to have previously formed attitudes toward different brands, so instead of considering attitudes toward different brands, the consumer may simply compare the different brands on one or more attributes or dimensions. For example, if the consumer is concerned primarily with cost, he or she may compare prices and form a preference favoring the brand with the lowest price. Preferences formed on the basis of comparing one or more attributes of two or more brands are known as **attribute-based preferences.**

HOW ARE PREFERENCES DETERMINED?

What determines whether consumers' preferences will be attitude-based versus attribute-based? The earlier examples suggest one important determinant: to form attitude-based preferences consumers must have previously formed attitudes toward each relevant alternative stored in long-term memory. If attitudes are unavailable, preferences cannot be based on attitudes. Another important determinant is suggested by research conducted by Sanbonmatsu, Kardes, and Gibson (1991). In this study, the researchers manipulated information processing goals and the evaluative implications of the unique attributes of two products. By unique attributes is meant attributes that are included in the description of one product but omitted from the description of the other product (Tversky, 1977). Both products also had several shared attributes, or attributes that were identical for both products. To make it easy to tell whether unique or shared attributes had a stronger impact on preferences, the researchers constructed product descriptions in which the unique versus shared attributes always had opposite evaluative implications. For example, if the unique attributes were favorable, the shared attributes were unfavorable for both products. Conversely, if the unique attributes were unfavorable, the shared attributes were favorable for both products.

The results showed that shared attributes had little influence on preference judgments. Moreover, the results showed that the unique attributes of the product described second had a greater impact on preferences, relative to the unique attributes of the product described first. This asymmetry is known as the **direction-of-comparison effect.** That is, the order in which two products are considered has a surprisingly strong influence on preference judgments. (See Fig. 4-3.) Because attribute comparisons cannot be performed until the attributes of the product described second have been encountered, and because recently encountered attributes are more accessible from memory than attributes encountered earlier (even just a few minutes earlier), the attributes of the second product are more prominent and influential. These prominent

MCI Math?

20% = 6%

20% = The discount on calls to MCI customers in your Friends & Family calling circle.

6% = The average discount that shows up on your MCI Friends & Family Basic bill.

Huh? MCI advertises a 20% discount off your long distance calls, as long as you call other MCI users who are also in your calling circle. Well, truth is, when the bill comes, the average discount MCI Friends & Family Basic callers really see is only about 6%.* Not 20%.

Because about two-thirds of their calls aren't to MCI users on their calling circle list. They're to other people, maybe even other MCI customers, and they don't count.

And if people are in your circle and then leave MCI—for their

own reasons—then your calls to these people don't count any more. Although MCI allows calling circles of up to 20 people, most people really call only 1 or 2 people in their circle.

So that discount that started out with a big number can turn out a lot smaller when you check the math for yourself. In fact, 2 out of 3 Friends & Family users on Basic will save more with AT&T *True USA*℠ Savings.

So if MCI Math doesn't add up for you, please read the other page, and you'll see...

AT&T wants consumers to develop a more favorable attitude (preference) toward its service than toward MCI's service.

Source: Copyright AT&T. Illustrations © Bonnie Timmons.

attributes also set the agenda for the comparison process. Specifically, the attributes of the second product are compared with the attributes of the first. This comparison process makes it readily apparent that the shared attributes are not very informative because neither alternative has a differential advantage on these attributes. However, the unique attributes of the second brand are highlighted because these attributes are missing for the first brand, and consequently the unique attributes of the focal brand have a strong impact on preference judgments. If the unique attributes of the focal brand are favorable, the focal brand is preferred. If the unique attributes of the focal brand are unfavorable, the other alternative is preferred. Interestingly, this pattern is observed even when the unique features of each brand are equivalent in terms of favorableness and importance. This indicates that the unique features of the nonfocal (first) brand are neglected almost entirely.

Another important finding from this study is that the direction-of-comparison effect is observed only when consumers perform attribute-based comparisons. The effect goes away when consumers perform attitude-based comparisons. This important point was demonstrated by manipulating consumers' processing goals. Half the consumers were told to try to memorize the product information, and this led them to

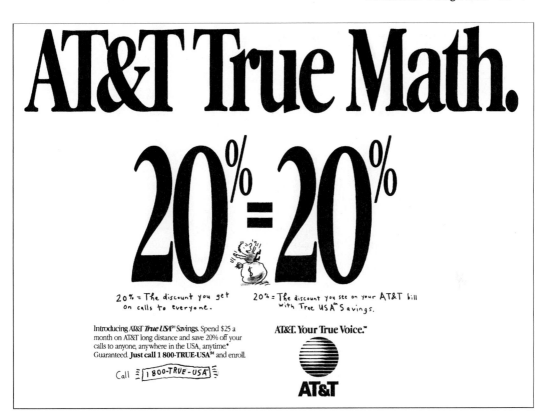

focus on attributes and perform attribute-based comparisons. The remaining consumers were told to form an overall impression toward each alternative, and this led them to focus on attitudes and perform attitude-based comparisons. The results show that the direction-of-comparison effect is eliminated when consumers form attitude-based preferences. To truly understand a psychological phenomenon, one must know

FIGURE 4-3

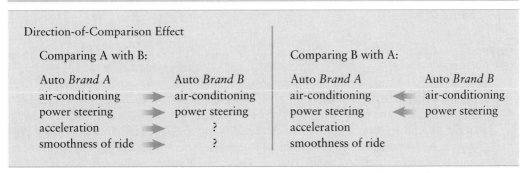

Direction-of-Comparison Effect

Comparing A with B:

Auto *Brand A*		Auto *Brand B*
air-conditioning	⟶	air-conditioning
power steering	⟶	power steering
acceleration	⟶	?
smoothness of ride	⟶	?

Comparing B with A:

Auto *Brand A*		Auto *Brand B*
air-conditioning	⟵	air-conditioning
power steering	⟵	power steering
acceleration		
smoothness of ride		

The order in which two products are considered has a strong influence on preference judgments.

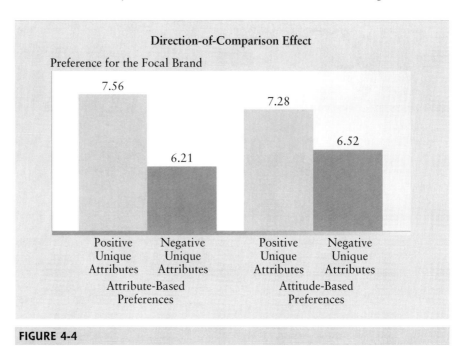

FIGURE 4-4

The direction-of-comparison effect has limiting conditions.
Source: Adapted from Sanbonmatsu, Kardes, & Gibson (1991).

when the effect is likely to be observed and when the effect is unlikely to be observed. The Sanbonmatsu et al. (1991) experiment specifies several important boundary, or limiting conditions of the direction-of-comparison effect. (See Fig. 4-4.)

Follow-up research has shown that a personality variable, the need for cognition, also influences how likely consumers are to form attribute-based rather than attitude-based preferences (Mantel & Kardes, 1999). The need for cognition personality scale measures the degree to which people enjoy thinking. The more consumers enjoy thinking, the more likely they are to be able to recall and use specific attribute information when forming preferences, and consequently, the more likely they are to exhibit the direction-of-comparison effect. This finding is interesting because it helps us to understand the role of personality and individual differences in preference formation and because it shows that greater thought and effort can actually lead to more bias in some situations!

◆ SATISFACTION JUDGMENT

Satisfaction involves comparing a chosen product with a rejected product. (See "Taking Issue: When Customers 'Can't Get No Satisfaction.'") The chosen product is the product the consumer actually purchased. The rejected product is a product that was considered for purchase but was not chosen. If the chosen product seems superior to the rejected product, the consumer will be satisfied. However, if the chosen product seems inferior to the rejected alternative, the consumer will experience dissatisfaction or regret ("Gee, I wish I bought the other brand"). Satisfaction is important because it

WHEN CUSTOMERS "CAN'T GET NO SATISFACTION"

Over and over, marketers claim that customer satisfaction is their main goal; after all, a satisfied customer will return to stay at the hotel, eat at the restaurant, buy clothes, stock up on groceries. Right? Not necessarily. Sometimes, satisfied customers don't return, for a variety of reasons. Perhaps the location of the store or restaurant is a factor; it might not be convenient for frequent visits. Perhaps satisfaction is a matter of degree rather than an absolute. Xerox did a study, eventually published in the *Harvard Business Review,* revealing that if customer satisfaction is ranked on a 1-to-5 scale, from completely dissatisfied to completely satisfied, the 4s will be *six times* more likely to defect to another product or service than the 5s.

Consumers are also more likely to express dissatisfaction today than they were in the past. This can cause havoc in settings such as the restaurant business, where customers now routinely return meals to kitchens. "Consumers aren't going to accept hot food that's cold and cold food that's hot," observes Ron Paul, president of Technomic Inc., a Chicago restaurant-consulting firm. "They're less tolerant of problems." The effects on the bottom line can be disastrous. "You're throwing [a meal] away and you're making a new one, and that definitely doubles your food cost," notes Ron Trimberger, owner of TrimB's in Appleton, Wisconsin. The added time it takes to make a new meal also disrupts the balance of timing in the kitchen, potentially causing more dissatisfaction among other customers.

What can marketers do to obtain satisfied, repeat customers? Unfortunately, some companies have taken a heavy-handed approach, neutralizing competition through patents, pushing for certain regulations (such as airport landing rights and broadcast licenses), creating mergers that could be construed as conflicts of interest (such as doctors who own portions of medical testing firms), and the like. In cases like these, consumers are captives: They can't choose between airlines because only one airline flies to a certain airport; they can't choose the hospital they want to use because their doctor is affiliated with only a certain one or their insurance company recognizes only one; they can't choose between cable companies because only one is available in their area. While these circumstances create repeat customers, marketers can hardly credit themselves with creating satisfied, loyal customers. Indeed, if regulations or other environmental conditions change, these marketers can bet that their customers will defect in a snap.

Marketers would do better to develop loyalty through satisfaction in every detail, with every contact between the marketer and the customer. Scott Timmins, senior vice president at The Forum Corp., a consulting and training firm in Boston, sums it up simply: "The question is, What's our brand of customer delight—what are we known for, what do customers expect us to deliver reliably, where's our wow?" Maybe it's quality, maybe it's price, maybe it's customer service, maybe it's simple courtesy on the part of the restaurant wait staff or the grocery store clerk. More likely, the leap from customer satisfaction to customer loyalty comes not from just one component but from the sum of many parts—the whole experience with a product or service.

Sources: Thomas A. Steward, "A Satisfied Customer Isn't Enough," *Fortune,* July 21, 1997, pp. 112–113; Elizabeth Seay, "Diners Today Send Their Entrees, Not Compliments, Back to the Chef," *The Wall Street Journal,* August 8, 1997, p. B3A.

influences repeat purchase. If a consumer is satisfied with a product, he or she will continue to buy the product. Dissatisfaction is important because it influences complaining behavior (which may influence many other consumers) and decreases the likelihood of repeat purchase.

Because satisfaction involves comparison processes (i.e., comparing a chosen product with a rejected or nonchosen product), you should not be surprised to learn that direction of comparison influences satisfaction judgment as well as preference judgment. That is, different judgments may be formed depending on whether the consumer compares the chosen brand with a rejected brand or a rejected brand with the chosen brand. To test this hypothesis (or prediction), Houston, Sherman, and Baker (1991) presented descriptions of two products to consumers. The descriptions contained either good unique attributes and bad shared attributes, or bad unique attributes and good shared attributes. The descriptions were the same as those used by Sanbonmatsu et al. (1991), and like Sanbonmatsu et al. (1991), Houston et al. (1991) found that most consumers chose the product described second (the focal product) when the unique attributes were good, and most consumers chose the product described first (the nonfocal product) when the unique attributes were bad. However, after consumers indicated their choices, they performed a 15-minute distraction task and then received the description of the chosen product or the rejected product once again. Consumers indicated how satisfied they were with their prior choice on a scale from 1 (very unhappy) to 12 (very happy). They also indicated the extent to which they wanted to change or keep their choice on a scale from 1 (strongly prefer to change the choice) to 12 (strongly prefer to keep the choice). For those who received the description of the chosen product, consumers were more satisfied when the unique attributes were good. Conversely, for those who received the description of the rejected product, satisfaction was greater when the unique attributes were bad. Again, it is important to emphasize that this asymmetry in judgment occurred even though pretesting ensured that the two products were actually equally good or equally bad. The direction-of-comparison effect stems from greater attention to the unique attributes of the product described second (as opposed to first).

EXPECTANCY DISCONFIRMATION MODEL

Of course, many other factors beside direction of comparison also influence satisfaction judgments (Oliver, 1980, 1981; Oliver & Desarbo, 1988). Oliver's (1980, 1981) **expectancy disconfirmation model** suggests that consumers form expectations about product performance before they purchase a product. After they buy a product, they compare the product's actual performance with the level of performance that was expected prior to purchase. If actual performance is better than expected, consumers are satisfied with the product. If actual performance is worse than expected, consumers are dissatisfied with the product. Note that consumers' prior expectancies are confirmed if actual product performance is exactly what was expected. Consumers' prior expectancies are disconfirmed if actual product performance is better or worse than expected.

Expectancies and disconfirmation both influence satisfaction. Generally, as expectancies increase, satisfaction decreases, because most products cannot meet consumers' highest expectations. As disconfirmation increases, satisfaction increases if the disconfirmation was positive (the product performed better than expected), and dissatisfaction increases if the disconfirmation was negative (the product performed worse than expected). The expectancy disconfirmation model suggests that consumers will be dissatisfied with excellent products if consumers' expectations exceeded actual product performance. Conversely, consumers will be satisfied with poor products if consumers' expectations fell below the actual level of performance. Hence, that which exists in the mind of the consumer (i.e., expectations) is as important as that which exists in reality (i.e., actual product performance).

Another factor that has an important impact on satisfaction judgments is consumers' **attributions,** or causal inferences concerning why a product performed worse than expected (Folkes, 1984; Oliver & DeSarbo, 1988; Weiner et al., 1971). A product will perform worse than expected for one of two main reasons: The user may have used the product inappropriately (this is an internal attribution because the fault lies within the person), or the product was designed poorly (this is an external attribution because the fault lies outside the person). Although negative disconfirmation leads to dissatisfaction, even greater dissatisfaction will be experienced if the consumer forms an external (as opposed to an internal) attribution. Reasons or explanations for product failure have a powerful influence on judgments of satisfaction/dissatisfaction.

◆ PREDICTION AND INTENTION JUDGMENT

Predictions about future events influence many other types of judgments, including expectancies, attributions, and intentions. Good consumer decision making requires accurate probability or likelihood judgments about a wide variety of events, such as accurate predictions about future product performance (Will the product do what I need it to do?), accurate predictions about when a product requires replacement (Should I buy a new car or should I continue to pay expensive repair bills?), accurate predictions about investments (Should I invest mainly in stocks, bonds, or mutual funds? Which particular stocks, bonds, or mutual funds should I invest in?), accurate predictions about the behaviors of others (Will my spouse like this gift? Will this salesperson try to trick me?), and accurate predictions about one's own future behaviors (Will I still like this color or this model five years from now?).

Although the ability to predict future events accurately is very important, the research evidence suggests that people are not very good at this type of judgment task. In fact, people often form impossible judgments. For example, one of my doctoral students and I recently provided information about eight business machine companies and asked undergraduate business majors to estimate next year's market shares for each of the eight firms (Houghton & Kardes, 1998). In some conditions, market share estimates summed to over 200 percent. This is, of course, impossible because actual market shares must sum to 100 percent or less. However, overestimation is common when people think about the extent to which information supports one prediction and fail to think about the extent to which the same information supports other possibilities (Sanbonmatsu, Posavac, & Stasney, 1997). Focusing on only one event at a time leads to serious errors in prediction. However, it is difficult to think about several possibilities at the same time.

TABLE 4-3	Number of Airline Passengers Bumped (1997)	
Airline	Voluntary Bumping	Involuntary Bumping
TWA	31,862	2,930
Continental	66,945	360
Southwest	72,142	12,074
US Air	85,232	4,662
United	110,754	3,792
American	215,003	4,596
Delta	259,413	15,297

Data source: Adapted from Fiske, Grove, and John (2000).

Consumer satisfaction is even more important for intangible services than it is for tangible products. After paying for an airline ticket, how satisfied would you be if you lost your seat? How should the major airlines deal with the thousands of passengers who lose their seats?

HEURISTICS

Another reason why prediction is so difficult is because people can often predict things without knowing how they arrived at the prediction. This is because people often use **heuristics,** or cognitive shortcuts, to generate predictions, and heuristics are used with little mental effort and awareness. Predictions are sometimes based on similarity, or **representativeness** (Kahneman, Slovic, & Tversky, 1982; Sherman & Corty, 1984; Tversky & Kahneman, 1974). For example, if a new product reminds us of an old brand we really liked, we tend to predict that the new product will perform well, too. However, if we focus on an irrelevant similarity (e.g., the packages for the new product and the old brand are the same shade of green), the prediction will not be very accurate. The danger of using shortcuts is that something important might be overlooked (many other things beside color influence product quality). However, heuristic thinking and mental shortcuts usually involve basing judgments on only one piece of information.

The **availability** heuristic involves forming predictions based on the ease with which instances can be retrieved from memory (Kahneman et al., 1982; Sherman & Corty, 1984; Tversky & Kahneman, 1974). If many high-quality Sony products can be recalled from memory, people will predict that a new Sony product will also be high in quality. If few high-quality Chrysler products can be recalled from memory, people will predict that a new Chrysler will be low in quality. However, as Chapter 3 mentions, memory is influenced by many factors. Some of these factors may relate to predictive accuracy, but many clearly do not. For example, people overestimate the likelihood of uncommon but highly publicized events and underestimate the likelihood of common but less publicized events. For example, people are accustomed to seeing fires, earthquakes, and other disasters on the evening news, and as a result, people reliably overestimate the likelihood of these events. Conversely, people rarely hear about heart attacks, diabetes, and other illnesses on the news, and consequently, people underestimate these events.

The **anchoring and adjustment** heuristic involves forming an initial judgment or first impression (an anchor) and then shifting (adjusting) this judgment upward or downward depending on the implications of imagined possibilities (Kahneman et al., 1982; Sherman & Corty, 1984; Tversky & Kahneman, 1974). For example, an advertisement might claim that a brand is 100 percent effective, in which case consumers might predict that the brand works 100 percent of the time. However, upon thinking about this prediction, consumers might suspect that the advertiser has exaggerated. If so, the predictive judgment should be adjusted downward, perhaps from 100 percent to 90 percent. Typically, however, the adjustment is insufficient. That is, people often adjust a little (e.g., down to 90 percent) when they should adjust a lot (e.g., down to 50 percent).

Predictions are often based on other predictions. For example, many firms administer surveys designed to measure consumers' purchase intentions or predictions about whether they will buy a new product. Market share estimates are often based on these predictions. However, recent research indicates that merely measuring intentions changes behavior (Morwitz, Johnson, & Schmittlein, 1993). Merely measuring intent once increases the likelihood that consumers will buy the product. Repeated measurement results in polarization: If initial intentions are high, subsequent purchase rates increase; if initial intentions are low, subsequent purchase rates decrease. Measuring predictions changes predictions. Moreover, measuring predictions changes behavior in a way that leads initial predictions to come true (Sherman, 1980).

◆ JUDGMENT AND BEHAVIOR

Until 1969, most marketing researchers assumed that judgment influences purchase behavior. It seemed obvious that if consumers have a favorable attitude toward a product, they will buy it. If consumers have an unfavorable attitude toward a product, they will not buy it. There is just one problem with this obvious idea: It is not true! Wicker (1969) summarized the results of over 30 studies examining the relationship between attitudes and behaviors and found that, generally, attitudes are only weakly related to behaviors. He was so shocked and dismayed by the results of his analysis that he advised researchers to abandon the attitude concept entirely.

Fortunately, Wicker's (1969) famous paper had the opposite effect: Instead of bringing research on attitudes to a halt, research activity and intensity increased dramatically. Scientists were curious about when and why attitudes fail to predict behavior. What could be responsible for such a counterintuitive finding? We now know the answer is threefold: (1) Behavior is multiply determined (many variables influence behavior, not just attitudes), (2) individuals are very different from each other (some people are more consistent than others), and (3) strong attitudes influence behavior but weak attitudes do not.

NORMS

Evaluative and other types of judgments represent only one determinant of behavior. Social norms, personal norms, and other constraints also have an important influence on behavior. **Norms** are rules that dictate what actions are appropriate or inappropriate. Social norms are unwritten rules adopted by a group of people. Sometimes norms and attitudes conflict; when this happens, norms usually win (Schofield, 1975). For example, a person might have a very favorable attitude toward fur coats but be afraid to buy one because she is concerned about what her friends and neighbors would think. Another person might hate vegetables but eat them anyway because of social pressures to eat more vegetables and eat less red meat. Social norms dictate what is "PC" (politically correct), and these rules often have a strong impact on behavior.

Personal norms are adopted as codes of conduct by specific individuals rather than by social groups. For example, a person who has a favorable attitude toward cigarettes or alcohol may nevertheless fail to buy these products because of a New Year's resolution or a personal commitment to quit for health reasons. Many people have very favorable attitudes toward BMWs, condominiums in Hawaii, and Dom Perignon. Of course, not everyone who likes these products will actually buy them. Conversely, most people have very negative attitudes toward going to the dentist's or doctor's office, but they do it anyway for obvious reasons.

Social norms and personal norms can be viewed as constraints, or rules that prevent us from doing certain things in particular situations. Of course, some situations are

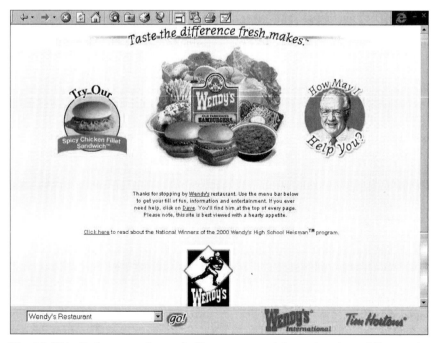

Wendy's Web site (www.wendys.com) offers consumers information about different subjects that represent social and personal norms, from nutrition to adoption.

Source: Courtesy of Wendy's International, Inc.

more constraining than others. For example, the unwritten rules concerning what to do and what not to do are very clear in many routine situations, such as the office (e.g., wear business attire), grocery stores (e.g., do not cut ahead in line), restaurants (e.g., pay at the end of the meal), courtrooms (e.g., behave in an orderly manner), classrooms (e.g., do not sleep), and church (e.g., do not sleep, eat, drink, smoke, or tell rude jokes even if you have favorable attitudes toward each of these activities). Other situations are less constraining. For example, usually in the privacy of your own home it is alright to sleep, eat, drink, smoke, and tell jokes.

INDIVIDUAL DIFFERENCES AND PERSONALITY PROCESSES

Individual differences and personality processes also influence the extent to which attitudes guide behavior. For example, high self-monitors, or individuals who are sensitive and responsive to social cues (Snyder, 1974), behave like social chameleons and constantly change and adapt their behaviors to meet the requirements of a particular situation. By contrast, low self-monitors, or individuals who are sensitive and responsive to internal cues (such as moods, feelings, beliefs, and opinions), behave consistently in line with their attitudes across situations (Becherer & Richard, 1978; Snyder, 1982). Moreover, individuals with an external locus of control believe their outcomes are controlled by luck, fate, or more powerful others (Rotter, 1966). Consequently, their behaviors seem to vary almost randomly across situations. Individuals with an internal locus of control, however, believe that they are masters of their own destinies and are more likely to behave in accordance with their attitudes (Sherman, 1973). Many other personality variables also influence the relationship between attitudes and behavior (Zanna, Higgins, & Herman, 1982).

PROPERTIES OF ATTITUDES

Finally, properties of attitudes themselves influence the degree to which attitudes guide behavior. Simply put, strong attitudes guide behavior, whereas weak attitudes do not. Although there are many different ways to measure attitude strength (Petty & Krosnick, 1995), the approach that has received the greatest amount of research attention and support is Fazio's (1986, 1989, 1990, 1995) response-latency approach for assessing attitude accessibility, or the speed with which attitudes can be retrieved from long-term memory. (See Fig. 4-5.) This approach involves seating research participants in front of a personal computer monitor that displays the names of various attitude objects (e.g., products, brands, names of social or political issues or ideas). Participants are asked to press a key labeled "Good" or a key labeled "Bad" as quickly and as accurately as possible in response to each object. Participants usually respond very quickly (in about a second or less). However, participants typically respond about a half second faster toward objects associated with strong accessible attitudes than toward objects associated with weak inaccessible attitudes. Although this difference seems small, it is highly predictive of the extent to which attitudes influence subsequent behavior.

When are consumers likely to form strong accessible attitudes? Research has shown that effortful thinking and deliberation leads to strong attitudes and that snap judgments lead to weak attitudes (Fazio, 1989, 1995). Furthermore, many variables determine when consumers put a lot of thought and effort into attitude formation and

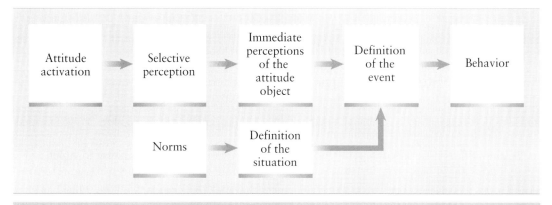

FIGURE 4-5

Fazio's model suggests that attitudes influence behavior through a relatively effortless process.

when they form quick impressions. Consumers often engage in greater levels of thought and effort when the attitude is based on direct experience as opposed to indirect experience. For example, consumers form stronger attitudes when they directly experience a new snack food by eating it than when they simply read about the new product while viewing an ad (Smith & Swinyard, 1983).

THE MODE MODEL

Merely demonstrating that accessible attitudes influence behavior is not enough. Recently, Fazio (1990) developed a theory that explains how and why accessible attitudes influence behavior. He calls this theory the **MODE model** because **M**otivation and **O**pportunity are key **DE**terminants of the manner in which attitudes guide behavior. Motivation is high when a behavior is personally relevant and consequential. Opportunity is high when people have the time and ability to think carefully and to deliberate. When motivation and opportunity are high, people carefully consider the pros and cons of a particular course of action, form a behavioral intention, and behave intentionally and deliberately (Fishbein & Ajzen, 1975). (See Fig. 4-6.) However, when either motivation or opportunity are low, accessible attitudes are activated or retrieved automatically when people are exposed to the attitude object (Fazio, Sanbonmatsu, Powell, & Kardes, 1986), and attitudes "color" what we see through a selective perception process (Fazio, Powell, & Herr, 1983). That is, favorable attitudes lead people to focus on positive aspects of a product and neglect negative aspects; conversely, unfavorable attitudes lead people to focus on negative aspects of a product and neglect positive ones. When positive dimensions are highlighted, approach behaviors are likely (e.g., consumers are likely to say nice things about a product, consider buying it, or actually buy it). When negative dimensions are accentuated, avoidance behaviors are likely (e.g., consumers are likely to distance themselves from the product, complain about it, not consider it, and not buy it). This sequence (attitude activation, selective

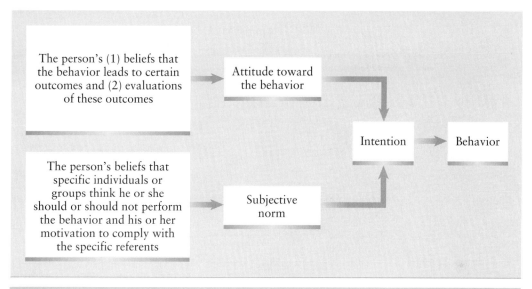

FIGURE 4-6

The Theory of Reasoned Action suggests that attitudes influence behavior through an effortful process.

perception, approach/avoidance) often occurs in the absence of awareness or intention: People often fail to recognize that their attitudes are influencing them in this manner. Finally, the MODE model emphasizes that norms can override attitudes, regardless of whether a spontaneous (low awareness, low effort, unintentional) attitude-to-behavior process was activated or a deliberate (high awareness, high effort, intentional) attitude-to-behavior process was initiated.

Fazio, Powell, and Williams (1989) measured consumers' attitudes toward ten different snacks (e.g., a Snickers bar, a Mounds bar, Sun Maid raisins, Dentyne gum, Cracker Jacks, Dr. Pepper) and asked them to choose 5. The 10 products were displayed in two rows of 5. Consumers who had favorable and accessible attitudes toward some of these products selected their favorite products among the set of 10 quickly and easily. Consumers who did not have accessible attitudes toward any of the 10 products, however, selected mainly the products that were prominently displayed in the front

Which snack is more appealing?
Source: © Mary Boucher.

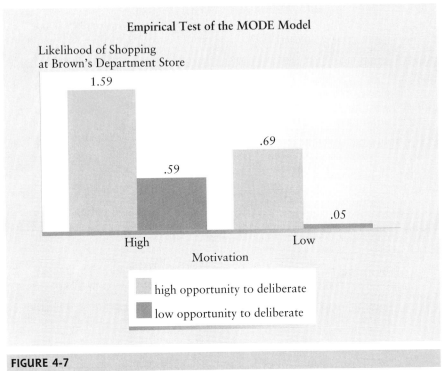

FIGURE 4-7

The MODE model helps researchers to predict when consumers are likely to use general impressions versus specific details when making a decision.

Source: Adapted from Sanbonmatsu & Fazio (1990).

row. Hence, the manner in which products are displayed has a strong influence on consumers with inaccessible attitudes but little effect on consumers with accessible attitudes. Similarly, the location of a brand on a grocery shelf (an eye-level location is best) may have a stronger influence on consumers with relatively inaccessible attitudes.

The MODE model also has important implications for store choice. Sanbonmatsu and Fazio (1990) presented descriptions of two department stores: Smith's and Brown's. (See Fig. 4-7.) Most of Smith's departments (e.g., clothing, jewelry) were described very positively, and subjects formed very favorable attitudes toward Smith's. Most of Brown's departments were described negatively, and subjects formed unfavorable attitudes toward Brown's. After subjects formed attitudes toward Smith's and Brown's, they were asked to decide which store they should visit to shop for a camera. If subjects simply used their attitudes to make this decision, they would choose Smith's. However, if they attempted to recall the detailed information they received earlier, they would choose Brown's because Brown's camera department was described much more positively than Smith's camera department. According to the MODE model, consumers should think carefully and try to recall detailed information only when motivation and opportunity to deliberate are high. Consistent with this hypothesis, most subjects chose Brown's only when motivation was high (i.e., they were told they would have to explain their decisions) and opportunity was high (i.e., no time limits were imposed). Otherwise, most subjects chose Smith's because when motivation is low (i.e., they were not told they would have to explain their decisions) or opportunity is low (i.e., they were given only 15 seconds to make a decision), consumers make quick and easy attitude-based decisions.

CHAPTER SUMMARY ▪

Human judgment involves locating one's position on an issue on a cognitive continuum. A cognitive continuum can be nonevaluative (e.g., extremely safe to extremely unsafe) or evaluative (e.g., extremely good to extremely bad). Nonevaluative judgments are referred to as beliefs, and evaluative judgments are referred to as attitudes. Preferences are evaluative judgments concerning two or more objects.

Comparison processes are used in forming preferences: Sometimes attitudes toward two or more objects are compared (attitude-based preferences), and sometimes attributes of two or more objects are compared (attribute-based preferences). Comparison processes are also involved in satisfaction judgments: Actual outcomes are compared with expected outcomes.

Predictions and likelihood judgments are often based on cognitive heuristics, or shortcuts. The representativeness heuristic involves using similarity as a basis for judgment. The availability heuristic involves using memory (ease of retrieval) as a basis for judgment. The anchoring and adjustment heuristic involves forming an initial judgment and then shifting this judgment upward or downward depending on the implications of imagined possibilities. Each of these heuristics simplifies and reduces the amount of cognitive effort required to perform a judgment task.

Finally, judgments are important because they influence other judgments and behaviors. Nonevaluative judgments (beliefs) often influence evaluative judgments (attitudes), which often influence purchase decisions (behaviors). However, attitudes do not always influence behaviors. The extent to which attitudes influence behaviors depends on situational variables (e.g., norms), personal variables (e.g., self-monitoring, locus of control), and attitudinal variables (e.g., attitude accessibility). Fazio's MODE model emphasizes that attitudes can influence behaviors either spontaneously or deliberately, and degree of deliberation depends on motivation and opportunity to think carefully about a purchase decision. When motivation and opportunity are high, careful deliberation is likely. When either is low, less effortful, spontaneous processes are likely.

KEY CONCEPTS ▪

- Beliefs
- Attitudes
- Preferences
- Consequences of attributes
- Descriptive beliefs
- Informational beliefs
- Inferential beliefs
- Theory of Reasoned Action
- Salient beliefs
- Information Integration Theory

- Zanna and Rempel's (1988) Model
- Reciprocal relationship
- Attitude-based preferences
- Attribute-based preferences
- Direction-of-comparison effect
- Satisfaction
- Expectancy disconfirmation model

- Attributions
- Heuristics
- Representativeness
- Availability
- Anchoring and adjustment
- Norms
- MODE model

DISCUSSION QUESTIONS ▪

1. Select one of the following products—Big Mac, Ford Explorer, Crest toothpaste, Tide laundry detergent, Ben & Jerry's ice cream, Apple computer—and list your own beliefs and attitudes about the product. Have marketers been successful in causing you to have a positive attitude toward the product? Why or why not?

2. How might marketers for Ivory soap change their advertising so that consumers develop beliefs about Ivory that could make it the top-selling soap again?

3. What are the similarities and differences between the Theory of Reasoned Action and Information Integration Theory?

4. Consumers who have an overall positive attitude toward MCI might choose MCI over AT&T for its long-distance service, even though the ad on pages 92–93 claims that AT&T has the attribute of a lower price. What further steps might AT&T marketers take to change consumers' preferences in favor of their product?

5. If you were a marketer for Trek mountain bikes, how might you use the direction-of-comparison effect to your advantage in creating a television commercial for your product?

6. If you worked for a resort that vacationers were likely to visit about once a year, how would you use satisfaction judgment to get customers to return?

7. How do representativeness and the availability heuristic influence the way consumers make predictions about products?

8. Describe an instance from your own experience in which social norms conflicted with your own attitude. What behavior did you adopt? Why?

9. How do properties of attitudes influence the degree to which attitudes guide behavior? What are the implications of this for marketers?

10. If a new shopping mall had space for two major department stores, how might marketers for each of the two stores use the MODE model to draw customers?

CHAPTER 5

Consumer Choice

◆ BENJAMIN MOORE, RALPH LAUREN, AND MARTHA STEWART

One weekend, you decide to paint your dorm room or apartment. You go to the paint store, where you are barraged by color. You wander through the aisles, picking up paint chips bearing numbers—302 yellow, 1052 taupe, 456 green. You flip through brochures of color and discover names like Silk Suede, Lipstick Lacquer, Kentucky Bluegrass. Suddenly, you are overwhelmed with the number of choices surrounding you. How can you possibly decide?

Benjamin Moore has been in the paint business for a long time. Ralph Lauren and Martha Stewart, on the other hand, are designers who want your life to have a total look made of their products. All three companies want you to buy their paint. Like other aspects of home decorating, paint has gone high style, and consumers apparently like the idea. They are willing to pay $20 for a gallon of specially mixed Benjamin Moore paint from the Historical Color Collection, $40 for Ralph Lauren specialty finishes such as River Rock (a textured finish that is supposed to look like water-worn rocks), and $75 a gallon for one of Martha Stewart's premium paints (manufactured by the Dutch company Schreuder Paint).

Who buys designer paints? Women, say marketers and retailers. "Ralph Lauren would not have happened if people thought the buyer was male," comments Ellen

Singer, director of marketing at Benjamin Moore. "Women choose the color more." John Lahey, president of Fine Paints of Europe Inc. (which sells Martha Stewart paints at its Vermont store), concurs. "Women appear to be very good shoppers. They're more aware of the price–value relationship than men are, at least in regards to the home."

What factors influence consumers' choices? "If I find a superior product, I will at least give it a chance," notes Helen Demarco, a consumer who spent $2,000 on Martha Stewart paint and is very satisfied with it. "It's always a pleasure to look at the colors when you're finished using them." Although the paint is expensive, Gay Schonbrunn, another consumer who bought the Martha Stewart paint, believes that, "in the long run, I probably saved money [because] you get more wall covering" with the Martha Stewart paint. Mundi Smithers agrees. She "doesn't even want to think about [the price], but it's absolutely worth it . . . the quality of the paint is amazing. No matter what color you use, it looks great."

While competitors and some professional painters scoff at the designer labels' claims to better quality, Lahey disagrees. He says that the Martha Stewart paint is based on an eight-pigment proprietary mix of certain ingredients that cannot be duplicated by competitors. "What cannot be achieved by a knockoff is the complexity of the color and the interaction of the pigments," he declares. Consumers seem to be sold on the idea.

In a thriving capitalist economy, consumers are confronted by choices every day. As you read this chapter, consider how important it is for marketers to understand how consumers make their choices—such as what colors of paint are available, what they believe or know about the paint's quality, what their attitude toward decorating is, and how much they think they should spend. Then decide what kind of paint *you* would buy.

Sources: Barbara Martinez, "Expensive Coverups: Designer Paints Find Their Market," *The Wall Street Journal,* August 8, 1997, p. B8; Benjamin Moore Paints, "Historical Color Collection, 1996."

◆ INTRODUCTION

Consumer choice involves selecting one product from a set of possibilities. Unlike judgment, which is continuous, choice is discrete (noncontinuous): Consumers either buy the product or they do not—there are no in betweens. Sometimes, choice is based on judgment—if consumers have a favorable attitude toward a product, they are more likely to choose it. However, at other times, choice is attribute-based (e.g., I'll buy the least expensive brand). Understanding consumer choice involves understanding three key issues: what products or brands are considered for purchase, what information is used to detect differences among considered alternatives, and how this information is used.

◆ THE CONSIDERATION SET

How many different products and which particular products are considered when consumers need to make a purchase decision? Although dozens of different brands are available for most product categories, consumers tend to consider a fairly small number of brands when making purchase decisions. (See Fig. 5-1.) A **consideration set** is the group of products a consumer considers in making a purchase decision. Consideration set size typically ranges from one (brand-loyal consumers consider only one brand) to

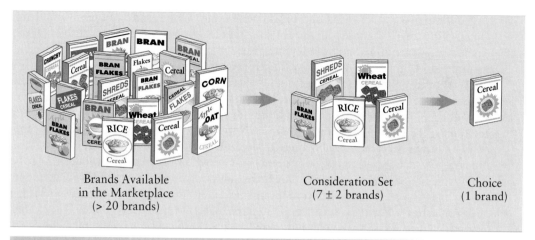

Brands Available
in the Marketplace
(> 20 brands)

Consideration Set
(7 ± 2 brands)

Choice
(1 brand)

FIGURE 5-1

Consumers rarely consider more than nine brands before making a buying choice.

about nine. Only rarely do consumers consider more than nine brands, because of limited information processing capacity (Miller's magic number, seven plus or minus two; see Chapter 3). Because consumers consider so few brands, marketing managers have to be creative to get consumers to consider their brands rather than competitors' offerings. One way to get consumers to consider your brand is by drawing attention to the brand using the attention and perception principles discussed in Chapter 2 (salient, vivid, and personally relevant information is attention-drawing). The memory principles discussed in Chapter 3 (recently, frequently, or extensively considered product information is memorable) also influence what particular brands consumers focus on when deciding which brands should be considered. Using attention and memory principles to build brand awareness is crucial for success. Brand awareness is even more important than brand attitude as a determinant of brand choice, because without brand awareness, the brand will not even be considered (Nedungadi, 1990; Percy & Rossiter, 1992).

PART-LIST CUING

Consumers' consideration sets are likely to vary over time, depending on how many and which particular brands happen to be salient, vivid, or accessible from memory at the time the purchase decision is rendered. This dynamic aspect of consideration set formation raises some interesting issues for marketing strategy. For example, a product manager can increase the likelihood with which his or her brand is chosen by developing tactics designed to reduce the size of the consideration set, provided that his or her brand remains in the consideration set (Alba & Chattopadhyay, 1985, 1986). One way to reduce the size of the consideration set is through **part-list cuing:** presenting the names of some brands when consumers are trying to recall as many brands as possible, which reduces the number of brands retrieved. For instance, Alba and Chattopadhyay (1985) asked subjects to memorize the names of 25 brands of shampoo. Later, when subjects were asked to recall the brands, Alba and Chattopadhyay mentioned the names of 0, 5, or 15 brands from the original list of 25 brands. Recall was best when the experimenter mentioned no brand names during the retrieval task. Recall decreased as the number of brands mentioned by the experimenter increased. (See Fig. 5-2.)

Why does the part-list cuing effect occur? That is, why does reminding subjects about some of the brands from the original list decrease memory performance? Rundus (1973) suggests that the probability of retrieving a particular brand name is a function of the strength of the association between that brand and the product category (e.g., shampoos in the Alba and Chattopadhyay study) divided by the sum of the strength of the associations between each individual brand and the product category. Rundus (1973) also hypothesizes that retrieval involves sampling with replacement. That is, the retrieval process has a random component (much like randomly drawing a card from a deck of cards), and after an item is drawn, it is replaced (shuffled back into the deck). This allows for the possibility of drawing the same item repeatedly. The more a particular item is sampled, the greater the strength of the association between the item and the category. This leads to extensive repeated sampling of the same item, and sampling discontinues when the same item is sampled x times. The value of x depends on how important the task is and how hard people try to retrieve as many items as possible. Typically, however, the same item is retrieved over and over again, and people stop searching memory for more items prematurely.

FIGURE 5-2

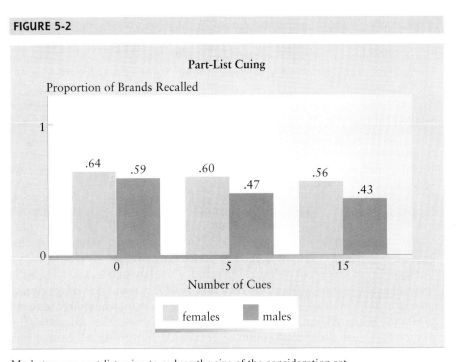

Marketers use part-list cuing to reduce the size of the consideration set.

Source: Adapted from Alba & Chattopadhyay (1985). Note that the part-list cuing effect is less pronounced for females because females are generally more knowledgeable about shampoos, and their knowledge structures contain more subcategories.

When some brands are mentioned during memory search, the mentioned brands are retrieved repeatedly, and each time they are retrieved the likelihood of retrieving them again increases. When the same brand is retrieved over and over again x number of times, consumers erroneously assume they have made a thorough memory search, and the retrieval process is terminated. Consistent with Rundus's (1973) model, Alba and Chattopadhyay (1985) demonstrated that the part-list cuing effect is reduced when consumers are very knowledgeable about a product category and they have formed several subcategories. This is because the set of brands mentioned by the experimenter during the retrieval process is unlikely to include examples from each subcategory if consumers are knowledgeable and familiar with several different subcategories. Moreover, consistent with Rundus's (1973) model, Alba and Chattopadhyay (1986) have shown that increasing the salience of one brand increases the magnitude and duration of the part-list cuing effect. Specifically, Alba and Chattopadhyay (1986) instructed subjects to think about Nyquil for one minute before trying to recall as many cold remedies as possible. This simple instruction increased the strength of the association between Nyquil and the product category (cold remedies) so much that subjects retrieved Nyquil repeatedly and were unable to recall other brands. Similarly, heavy promotion and advertising for one brand can increase the memorability of this brand and decrease memory for other brands. Hence, one way managers can influence consumers' consideration sets is by increasing the accessibility of some brands, which thereby reduces the accessibility of others.

THE ATTRACTION EFFECT

Another way managers can influence consumers' consideration sets is by adding a new brand to a product line. For example, Williams-Sonoma, a premium food preparation retailer, offered a home bread bakery priced at $275. Initially, sales were satisfactory but not particularly remarkable. However, Williams-Sonoma later offered a second home bread bakery that was much larger and much more expensive than the first brand. Although this new brand did not sell very well, adding this new alternative to the product line almost doubled the sales of the original brand! This is known as the **attraction effect,** because compared with a similar but inferior decoy product, the original brand seems much more attractive (Huber, Payne, & Puto, 1982; Huber & Puto, 1983; Lehmann & Pan, 1994; Pan & Lehmann, 1993; Simonson, 1989, 1993; Simonson & Tversky, 1992). Decoy brands do not sell very well themselves, but they increase sales of another brand on the product line.

The addition of a high-end product can spur sales of the lower-priced product.
Source: © Mary Boucher.

In an experimental investigation of the attraction effect, subjects were given a choice between a Cross pen and $6 in cash (Simonson & Tversky, 1992). Only 36 percent of the subjects chose the Cross pen. Another group of subjects was given a choice among a Cross pen, a decoy pen (i.e., a similar but less attractive pen), and $6. Forty-six percent of these subjects chose the Cross pen. A decoy product makes a target product seem much more attractive, resulting in an increased probability of choice. This effect has been demonstrated across a wide variety of target products.

THE TRADE-OFF CONTRAST EFFECT

Rather than simply comparing one product with another, consumers sometimes compare attribute trade-offs across products. For example, when considering the purchase of a new personal computer, consumers need to decide how to resolve a trade-off between price and kilobyte memory. A higher price means more memory, but there is a limit to how much you can afford to spend. Which would you choose—a $1,000 personal computer with 640K, or a $1,200 personal computer with 960K? This decision involves a trade-off of $200 for an additional 320K. This decision is difficult for most people, but it becomes much easier when a third alternative is added to the consideration set: a $1,300 personal computer with 960K (which involves a tradeoff of $300 for

FIGURE 5-3

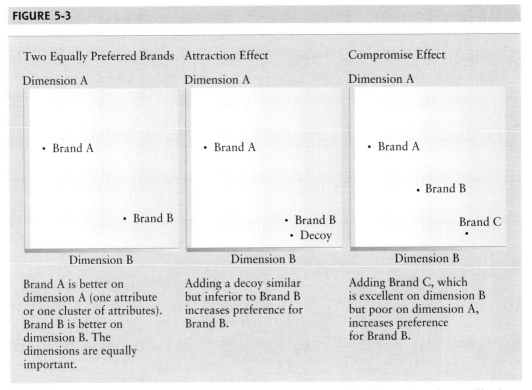

Marketers may use the attraction effect or the compromise effect to make their own brands seem like the best choice.

an additional 320K). This encourages a greater percentage of people to choose the $1,200 personal computer with 960K. This effect is known as the **trade-off contrast effect,** which is similar to the attraction effect except that trade-offs (as opposed to single attributes) are compared across brands (Simonson & Tversky, 1992).

THE COMPROMISE EFFECT

Another way to increase the probability of brand choice is to "play the middle against both ends." Intermediate brands, or compromise brands, seem like safe bets to many consumers. For example, consumers may initially have a hard time choosing between a low-priced camera and a moderately priced camera. However, adding a third camera, a high-priced camera, to the consideration set makes the camera with the intermediate price seem like a reasonable compromise. This phenomenon is known as the **compromise effect** (Simonson, 1989; Simonson & Tversky, 1992). Brands that are intermediate in terms of price, quality, number of "bells and whistles," or virtually any dimension are frequently chosen, and they are chosen even more frequently when consumers are required to justify their decisions to others (e.g., spouses, bosses, friends, or peers). It is often easier to justify choosing intermediate brands rather than extremes, and many brands can be made to appear like compromise alternatives simply by adding extreme brands (e.g., very high or very low brands) to the consideration set. (See Fig. 5-3.)

◆ STIMULUS-BASED VERSUS MEMORY-BASED CHOICE

After the consideration set has been determined, consumers need to focus on differences between considered brands. Some brands have features or options (i.e., bells and whistles) other brands lack, and these options help consumers detect differences between brands. In fact, focusing on differences is so important that consumers are willing to use any attributes, even trivial ones, to discriminate between brands that are otherwise quite similar (Brown & Carpenter, 2000; Carpenter, Glazer, & Nakamoto, 1994; Simonson, Carmon, & O'Curry, 1994). Typically, however, consumers focus on important differences; unimportant differences are considered only when important ones do not exist.

In **stimulus-based choice,** all relevant brand and attribute information is directly observable (Lynch & Srull, 1982), as when consumers visit a grocery store to buy cereal and all seven brands they wish to consider are available on the shelves. It is relatively easy to detect differences among brands in this case because direct comparison is possible. For example, if one was concerned about differences in sugar content, one can easily examine the sugar content of each of the seven brands by reading this information on the product packages. All the information the consumer needs is directly available on the product packages in this particular situation.

Sometimes, however, choice is **memory-based.** In this situation, none of the information the consumer needs is directly available, and comparisons among brands must be performed by retrieving relevant information from memory (Lynch & Srull, 1982). For example, when sitting at home trying to decide which restaurant to go to for dinner, names of restaurants, type of food served, quality of service, and other relevant information must be retrieved from memory.

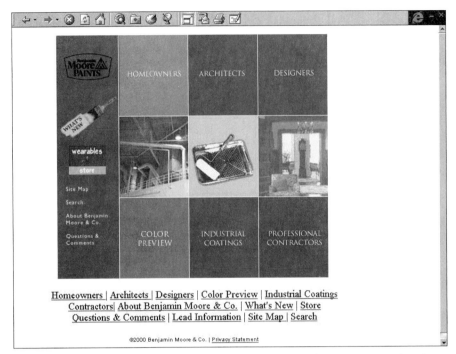

The Benjamin Moore Web site, at www.benjaminmoore.com, helps consumers make stimulus-based choices by providing brand and attribute information. By accessing the site, consumers can compare product information against competing product information.

Source: Courtesy of Benjamin Moore and Co.

MIXED CHOICE

Mixed choice is the most common type of choice scenario (Alba, Hutchinson, & Lynch, 1991). Mixed choice has elements of both stimulus-based and memory-based choice: Some relevant information is directly observable and some information must be retrieved from memory. For example, when shopping for an automobile, a consumer may visit one dealership and then visit another. While examining automobiles at the second dealership, where the considered alternatives are directly observable (stimulus brands), the consumer may try to recall alternatives from the first dealership (memory brands). When comparing stimulus brands with memory brands, stimulus brands typically enjoy a choice advantage because consumers may recognize that they have forgotten many important details about the memory brands (Biehal & Chakravarti, 1983). Consequently, a stimulus brand may be chosen over a memory brand even when the memory brand is actually superior. This stimulus-brand advantage effect may stem in part from consumers recognizing that relevant information has been forgotten (Sanbonmatsu, Kardes, & Sansone, 1991). This realization increases uncertainty about the quality of the memory brand, resulting in a decreased probability of choosing this brand.

Alba, Marmorstein, and Chattopadhyay (1993) expanded on Biehal and Chakravarti's (1983) stimulus-brand advantage effect by exploring the limits of this phenomenon. Although consumers usually prefer a stimulus brand over a memory brand, in some special circumstances the memory brand is preferred. Specifically, Alba and his colleagues predicted that the memory brand would be preferred more over time when it is described as having a large number of favorable features, because consumers are likely to remember that the memory brand is good on many dimensions even if they cannot remember any specific details (Alba & Marmorstein, 1987). Alba and his colleagues also predicted that the memory brand would be preferred more over time if "puffery," or exaggerated claims (e.g., stating that the brand is the best when it is really only slightly above average), was presented, because exaggerations can be both memorable and persuasive. These hypotheses were supported by the results of three experiments.

In Experiment 1, subjects received descriptions of either a strong or a weak memory brand. The strong memory brand performed extremely well on important dimensions (e.g., a television set with excellent resolution, a good warranty, and good audio capability), but no additional dimensions were mentioned. The weak-memory brand performed poorly on important dimensions but well on many less important dimensions (e.g., the television set had an earphone jack and many other bells and whistles). After reading a description of the strong or the weak memory brand, subjects received a description of an average-stimulus brand (e.g., a television set that was objectively better than the weak memory brand but not as good as the strong memory brand). In addition, the stimulus brand was presented either immediately after the memory brand or two days later. In no-delay conditions, the strong-memory brand was preferred over the weak-memory brand. However, after a two-day delay, the weak-memory brand was preferred over the strong-memory brand. Over time, it is easy to remember that the weak brand had a large number of positive features and hard to remember details (e.g., many of the positive features, like an earphone jack, were relatively unimportant). Moreover, the results of Experiment 3 showed that this effect was amplified when subjects were asked to justify their choices. In fact, while justifying their choices, most subjects told the experimenter that the weak memory brand had a greater number of positive features than the stimulus brand.

Experiment 2 showed that puffery can also reverse the stimulus-brand advantage over time. Subjects received an ad for a memory brand claiming that the PQ-70 camera was used by serious photographers and was carefully engineered (puffery). Some technical details were also specified. The ad also claimed that the camera was easy to use (more puffery), and this claim was weakly supported by accompanying details (e.g., a padded shoulder strap). By contrast, the ad for the stimulus brand contained only technical information and no puffery. Careful reading of the ads reveals that the stimulus brand is better than the memory brand in terms of both technical sophistication and ease of use. In no-delay conditions, where it is easy to compare the two brands, the stimulus brand was strongly preferred. However, when the stimulus brand was presented seven days after presentation of the memory brand, the memory brand was strongly preferred. This is because subjects could remember puffery but not specific details. Memory fades over time, and as a consequence preferences may change dramatically over time as well.

When consumers choose a product to purchase, their decision strategy is based either on a comparison of their previously formed attitudes toward the considered alternatives (**attitude-based choice**) or on a comparison of specific attributes or features offered by the considered alternatives (**attribute-based choice**). Attitudes (overall evaluations) toward each of the various brands are compared only if they exist (i.e., consumers have previously formed attitudes toward each brand) and if they are accessible (retrievable) from memory. If the brands are new and consumers have not yet formed attitudes toward the brands, attitudes cannot be used as a basis of comparison. If the brands are old but infrequently used, attitudes may exist but these attitudes are likely to be weak and inaccessible. Weak attitudes are unlikely to be used as a basis of comparison. Similar arguments can be made for attributes. If consumers cannot remember the attributes of the considered brands, attributes are unlikely to be used as a basis of comparison (Alba et al., 1991; Biehal & Chakravarti, 1982, 1983, 1986).

THE ACCESSIBILITY–DIAGNOSTICITY MODEL

The **accessibility–diagnosticity model** (Feldman & Lynch, 1988) provides a useful framework for understanding what information is likely to be used in consumer choice. Marketers need to know what information consumers are likely to use because this information should be emphasized in promotion and advertising, product packages, and other sources of product information. Conversely, information that is not likely to be used by consumers should not be presented in promotion and advertising, packages, and other sources. The accessibility–diagnosticity model suggests that choice depends on the accessibility of an input (i.e., an input is a piece of information), the accessibility of alternative inputs, and the diagnosticity (or perceived relevance) of the inputs. Accessibility depends on the recency and frequency with which an input is used and on the extent to which consumers think about and elaborate on an input. Diagnosticity depends on the knowledgeability of the consumer (e.g., knowledgeable consumers know what information is important) and on the structure of the choice environment.

What are the attributes of this TV set?

Source: © Mary Boucher.

For example, if all considered brands are the same price, price is irrelevant (nondiagnostic) and should be ignored. On the other hand, if the considered brands differ markedly in price, price is relevant (diagnostic) and useful for making decisions.

In a complicated but important experiment investigating the utility of the accessibility–diagnosticity model, Lynch, Marmorstein, and Weigold (1988) presented attribute information about three color television target brands (Sanyo, Philco, and Sharp). Next, the accessibility of this information was manipulated by asking subjects to perform a simple unrelated task (low interference conditions) or to perform a complex task that made it difficult to remember the attribute information for the three target brands (high interference conditions). Next, subjects were asked either to

FIGURE 5-4

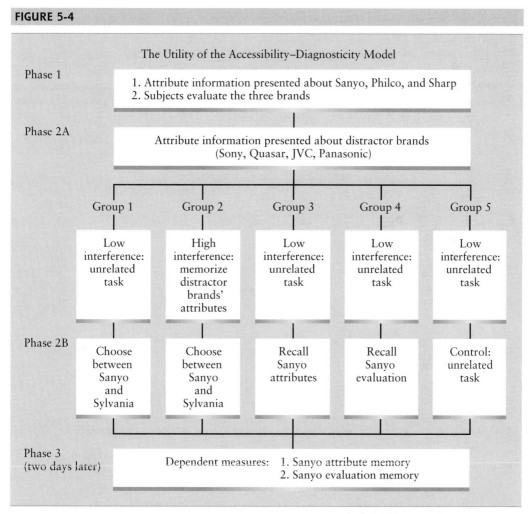

The accessibility–diagnosticity model suggests that choice depends on the accessibility of an input as well as alternatives and the diagnosticity of the inputs.

Source: Adapted from Lynch et al. (1988).

choose between a target memory brand (Sanyo) and a stimulus brand (Sylvania), to recall Sanyo attributes, to recall their overall evaluations of Sanyo, or to perform a simple unrelated task. Finally, two days later, subjects were asked to recall attributes and evaluations of Sanyo. (See Fig. 5-4.)

Prior research has shown that recalling attributes at one point in time makes it easier to recall these same attributes at a later point in time (the hypermnesia effect; Lichtenstein & Srull, 1985). In other words, practice helps. The key question, however, is what happens when subjects are asked to choose between a memory brand and a stimulus brand at one point in time and then asked to recall the attributes of the memory brand at a later point in time? A strong recall performance suggests a practice effect (i.e., to perform the choice task, subjects spontaneously recalled attributes even though they were not asked to do so), whereas a weak recall performance suggests the absence of practice (i.e., no attempt to recall attributes was made until subjects were asked to do so). The results revealed that subjects who performed a choice task exhibited a strong recall performance—as strong as those subjects who were asked to perform the recall task twice. However, this finding was observed only in low interference conditions. In high interference conditions, choice task subjects recalled far fewer attributes than control subjects who performed the recall task twice. The overall pattern of results suggests that attributes are recalled spontaneously (without explicit prompting) during choice when these attributes are accessible from memory but not when they are inaccessible. (See Figs. 5-5 and 5-6.)

FIGURE 5-5

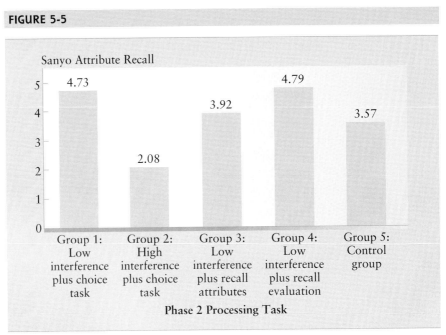

Subjects had high Sanyo attribute recall when they performed a choice task with low interference, recalled attributes with low interference, or recalled evaluation with low interference.

Source: Adapted from Lynch et al. (1988).

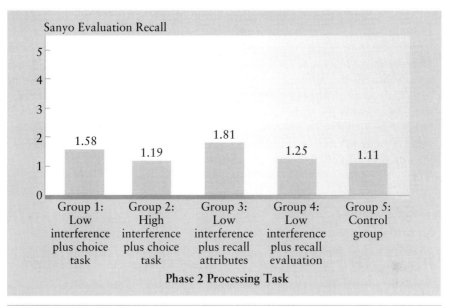

FIGURE 5-6

Subjects had high Sanyo evaluation recall when they performed a choice task with low interference or recalled attributes with low interference.

Source: Adapted from Lynch et al. (1988).

FIGURE 5-7

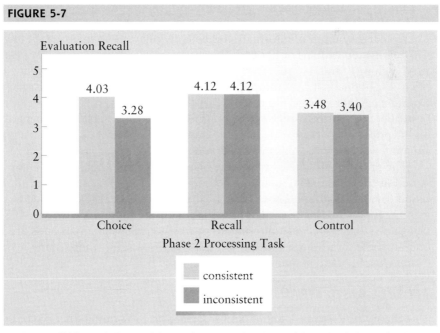

Both accessibility and diagnosticity are important for determining what information is likely to be used in consumer choice.

Source: Adapted from Lynch et al. (1988).

In a second experiment, another group of subjects received attribute information about several different brands from several different product categories. Subjects rated each brand in terms of "quality without considering price" and "value for the money." Diagnosticity (relevance) is high if both ratings are consistent (e.g., high quality and a good value for the money), and diagnosticity is low if the two ratings are inconsistent (e.g., high on one dimension but low on the other). The results revealed that these evaluations were likely to be used as choice inputs only when they were diagnostic. Otherwise, attributes were used instead of evaluations (attitudes). Hence, both accessibility (memorability) and diagnosticity (relevance) are important for determining what information is likely to be used in consumer choice. (See Fig. 5-7.)

◆ CHOICE HEURISTICS

Sometimes consumers are unwilling or unable to use complex and effortful decision strategies. They sometimes prefer to make quick-and-dirty easy decisions that do not require a lot of thought or effort. To do this, consumers use choice heuristics, or mental shortcuts (Kahneman, Slovic, & Tversky, 1982). Heuristics enable consumers to make decisions quickly and easily. Of course, with any quick-and-dirty approach, one uses minimal information and risks overlooking something important and making a bad decision. For example, one commonly used choice heuristic is the price–quality heuristic by which consumers assume that a high price indicates high quality (and low price signals low quality). Rather than carefully evaluating all relevant information to determine the true quality of a product, a consumer may simply purchase the most expensive brand and assume that it is the best brand. This approach simplifies decision making because it involves the use of only one piece of information, price, in a situation where a large amount of information is actually relevant. In many cases, the consumer will be satisfied with his or her choice (extremely expensive low-quality brands do not survive long), and consequently the consumer is likely to continue using the price–quality heuristic on future purchase occasions. However, even casual perusal of *Consumer Reports* magazine reveals that the most expensive brand is not always the best (there is a lot of variation across product categories). Hence, relying too heavily on the price–quality heuristic may result in the purchase of an expensive product in a situation where a less expensive brand is actually better.

The price–quality heuristic is only one type of choice heuristic—many others are stored in the consumers' arsenal of mental shortcuts. Heuristics are either attitude-based (overall evaluation-based) or attribute-based (specific). Attitude-based strategies involve comparing overall impressions of different brands. Attribute-based heuristics involve either **between-alternative processing,** where many brands are compared one attribute at a time, or **within-alternative processing,** where many attributes are examined one brand at a time.

ATTITUDE-BASED STRATEGIES

The Theory of Reasoned Action and Information Integration Theory (both discussed in Chapter 4) suggest two types of attitude-based choice strategies. According to the Theory of Reasoned Action, an overall attitude toward a brand is formed by assessing beliefs (b) and evaluations (e) for each relevant attribute, multiplying b times e for each attribute i, and adding this information ($A_o = \Sigma b_i e_i$). According to Information Integration Theory, an overall attitude toward a brand is formed by multiplying weights (w) by scales values (s) of each relevant attribute and integrating this information using a quantitative rule—typically, an averaging rule for most consumer products ($A_o = \Sigma w_i s_i$, where $\Sigma w_i = 1$). These two strategies are not heuristics because they involve effortful processing of all relevant information. Both strategies are **compensatory strategies,** which means that good attributes can compensate for bad attributes, and both strategies suggest that the brand associated with the most favorable attitude is chosen.

The Attitude Heuristic

Heuristics require relatively little effort to apply and are typically based on relatively little information. When consumers already hold attitudes toward all brands in a consideration set, it is unnecessary to form attitudes toward each brand using adding (Theory of Reasoned Action) or averaging (Information Integration Theory) rules. In this case, consumers may simply select the brand associated with the most favorable previously formed attitude—the **attitude heuristic** (Pratkanis & Greenwald, 1989; see also Wright, 1975). Attitudes greatly simplify decision making: It is easy to choose the brand one likes best and to ignore information about other brands.

One important variant of the attitude heuristic is the brand-name attitude heuristic (Maheswaran, Mackie, & Chaiken, 1992; Simonson, 1992). Having a highly favorable attitude toward brand names like Sony, Disney, or Starbucks makes decision making easy: Consumers often choose highly favorable brands without extensive information gathering, thinking, and deliberating. Consumers are especially likely to make quick-and-easy choices using the brand-name heuristic when involvement is low (Maheswaran et al., 1992) or when they are highly concerned about the possibility of making a very bad decision (Simonson, 1992).

The Frequency of Good and Bad Features Heuristic

Another attitude-based strategy involves forming a very simple attitude toward each considered alternative by counting the number of good features, counting the number of bad features, and choosing the brand with the largest number of good features and

When consumers use the brand name heuristic, a strong brand name like Sony increases the probability of choosing a Sony brand.

smallest number of bad features (Alba & Marmorstein, 1987). This **frequency of good and bad features heuristic** is easy to apply because counting is easy. Moreover, relatively little information is used because consumers applying this heuristic need not worry about how important each attribute is (instead, all attributes are treated as equally important or are equally weighted) or about difficult trade-offs between attributes. For instance, if you want a satisfactory product for the lowest price possible, you need to determine how much you are willing to pay and what lowest level of quality you are willing to accept. Trade-offs between price and quality are often difficult to make, and consumers are sometimes motivated to use a simple choice heuristic to avoid thinking about trade-offs.

ATTRIBUTE-BASED STRATEGIES

When consumers do not already have attitudes toward all considered brands and when they are unmotivated or unable to form attitudes toward these brands, attribute-based strategies are used. Between-alternative attribute-based heuristics involve comparing multiple brands one attribute (such as price) at a time. There are several types of between-alternative attribute-based heuristics, including the lexicographic heuristic, the lexicographic semiorder heuristic, the elimination-by-aspects heuristic, the additive-difference heuristic, and the majority of confirming dimensions heuristic. Heuristic strategies are **noncompensatory** because a high score on one attribute cannot compensate for a low score on another attribute. That is, each attribute is considered in isolation, and trade-offs between attributes are not considered. Ignoring trade-offs greatly simplifies decision making but also increases the probability of a poor decision (e.g., the best brand overall might actually perform very poorly on one or two relatively unimportant attributes).

The Lexicographic Heuristic

The **lexicographic heuristic** involves choosing the best brand on the basis of its most important attribute (Payne, Bettman, & Johnson, 1993). For example, if a consumer decides that price is the most important attribute, he or she will choose the brand with the best price. Hence, the price–quality heuristic is one type of lexicographic heuristic. If a consumer assumes that the brand with the highest quality is the brand with the highest price, the consumer can choose the highest-priced brand quickly and easily. However, some consumers are not concerned mainly about quality and just want to buy the least-expensive brand. Here, too, the consumer can choose the lowest-priced brand quickly and easily. The lexicographic heuristic is used in both cases because only one attribute, price, is used. In the case of ties (i.e., two or more brands with the exact same price), the consumer uses the second most important attribute as a tiebreaker. If ties remain, the third most important attribute is used as a tiebreaker, and so on, until one brand remains.

Of course, price is not the most important attribute for all consumers in all product categories. Anytime a consumer focuses on one most important attribute, whatever that attribute is, the consumer is using the lexicographic heuristic. For example, if a consumer is concerned about eating too much sugar, he or she may apply the lexicographic heuristic by buying the brand of cereal with the lowest sugar content. If a consumer is worried about safety, he or she may apply the lexicographic heuristic by buying the automobile with the best reputation for safety.

The Lexicographic Semiorder Heuristic

The **lexicographic semiorder heuristic** is similar to the lexicographic heuristic except that close values are treated like ties (Tversky, 1969). For example, if two brands differ in price by only three dollars, this is interpreted as a tie and the brands are compared on the next most important attribute, ease of use. If two brands differ in ease of use by only four points, this is interpreted as a tie, and the comparison process must continue. This heuristic is interesting because it may lead to violations of transitivity. Transitivity implies that if Brand A is preferred to Brand B, and if Brand B is preferred to Brand C, then A should also be preferred to C. However, suppose a consumer deems price to be the most important attribute and ease of use to be the second most important, and assume that the consumer is considering three brands of drip coffeemakers:

Mr. Coffee Accel PR12A	$27	90 rating on ease of use
Mr. Coffee Accel PR16	$25	85 rating on ease of use
Mr. Coffee BL110	$22	80 rating on ease of use

In this case, the Accel PR12A is preferred to the Accel PR16 because they are tied on price but the PR12A is easier to use. The Accel PR16 is preferred to the BL110 because they are tied on price but the Accel PR16 is more user-friendly. However, the BL110 is preferred to the PR12A because the BL110 is significantly less expensive and the consumer was more concerned about price than about ease of use.

The Elimination-by-Aspects Heuristic

The **elimination-by-aspects heuristic** involves comparing alternatives on an attribute selected probabilistically (the more important the attribute, the more likely it is that this attribute will be selected) and eliminating or rejecting alternatives that do not meet a minimum cutoff point on this attribute (Tversky, 1972). The process is iterative (repetitive): Attributes are selected and unsatisfactory alternatives are eliminated until only one brand remains. As with the other heuristics, consumers are likely to make a choice quickly and easily without examining all relevant information.

The Additive-Difference Heuristic

The **additive-difference heuristic** involves computing the difference between the values of each attribute of two brands, weighting the differences by attribute importance, and then summing the weighted differences to obtain an overall score (Tversky, 1969). More formally,

$$P = \Sigma w_i(A_i - B_i)$$

where P = preference, w_i = importance weight for attribute i, A_i = value of attribute i for alternative A, and B_i = value of attribute i for alternative B. A positive overall score indicates a preference for Brand A, a negative overall score indicates a preference for Brand B, and an overall score of zero reflects an equal preference between the two brands.

The Majority of Confirming Dimensions Heuristic

The **majority of confirming dimensions heuristic** (Russo & Dosher, 1983) is a simpler variation of the additive-difference heuristic. The values of each attribute of two brands are compared, and the brand with the greatest number of superior attributes is chosen. This heuristic is easier to use because it uses less information than the additive-difference heuristic. Specifically, unlike the additive-difference heuristic, the majority of confirming dimensions heuristic does not distinguish between slightly better attributes and much better attributes—both types of attributes are superior attributes. However, like the additive-difference heuristic, the majority of confirming dimensions heuristic is easiest to use when only two brands are considered but can be used when more than two brands are considered, provided that pairwise comparisons (i.e., comparisons between two alternatives at a time) are performed.

To reiterate, between-alternative processing involves comparing many brands one attribute at a time, whereas within-alternative processing involves examining many attributes one brand at a time. The attribute-based heuristics discussed so far involve between-alternative processing. Next, we turn to within-alternative attribute-based heuristics, which include the conjunctive heuristic and the disjunctive heuristic. Like the between-alternative attribute-based heuristics discussed earlier, the conjunctive and disjunctive heuristics simplify decision making by reducing the amount of information that is considered and by ignoring trade-offs between dimensions (i.e., the conjunctive and disjunctive heuristics are noncompensatory choice strategies). Unlike between-alternative attribute-based heuristics, within-alternative attribute-based heuristics sometimes enable consumers to make a choice by considering only one brand—if the first brand considered is satisfactory, it is selected without considering any other alternatives. This greatly simplifies information processing and decision making.

The Conjunctive Heuristic

The **conjunctive heuristic** involves setting a minimum acceptable cutoff level for each attribute and selecting the first alternative that meets the minimum standard for all attributes (Einhorn, 1970). If the first brand considered meets these standards, it is deemed satisfactory and is selected without further consideration of any other alternative. This approach is conjunctive because all relevant attributes are considered together—one bad attribute can eliminate an alternative. By contrast, a disjunctive approach involves focusing on one attribute considered separately from the other attributes—one good attribute can save an alternative. Specifically, the **disjunctive heuristic** involves setting an acceptable standard (usually higher than a minimum standard) for each attribute and choosing the first alternative that meets this standard on one attribute (Einhorn, 1970). The conjunctive and disjunctive heuristics are elimination strategies because any alternative that does not meet a particular standard is eliminated.

Phased Strategies

Phased strategies involve the use of more than one choice strategy. For example, one commonly used phased strategy is to first eliminate clearly unsatisfactory alternatives using a noncompensatory heuristic approach and then examine the remaining alternatives much more carefully using a compensatory nonheuristic approach (i.e., the Theory of Reasoned Action's additive rule or Information Integration Theory's weighted-average rule). Hence, phased strategies combine the best qualities of several different approaches—a simple heuristic is used to reduce the number of considered alternatives to a smaller, more manageable number (e.g., two or three brands) quickly and easily, and a more complex and accurate compensatory rule is used to choose among the two or three best alternatives by weighing all relevant information concerning these brands (Payne, 1976; Payne, Bettman, & Johnson, 1992, 1993).

◆ **DETERMINANTS OF CHOICE STRATEGY**

Processing goals, processing load, and contextual variables jointly determine what approach (or set of approaches) will be used in a given situation (Payne et al., 1992, 1993).

PROCESSING GOALS

Processing goals are influenced by variables such as involvement and accountability. Involvement refers to the personal relevance or importance of a decision (Celsi & Olson, 1988; Greenwald & Leavitt, 1984; MacInnis & Park, 1991; Petty, Cacioppo, & Schumann, 1983; Ratneshwar & Chaiken, 1991; Zaichowsky, 1985), and accountability refers to a requirement to justify or explain one's decisions to others (Simonson, 1989; Tetlock, 1991). (See "Taking Issue: Is International Callback Fair Play?") Both goals increase one's motivation to make good decisions, even if a lot of time and effort is required. As involvement or accountability increases, processing effort increases and consumers become more likely to use effortful compensatory choice strategies and less likely to use simple choice heuristics.

The perceived risks associated with a bad decision also motivate consumers to apply effortful choice strategies and avoid using simple heuristics that may lead to negative outcomes (Kruglanski, 1989; Peter & Tarpey, 1975). Perceived risks include financial risks (as price increases, concern about bad decisions increases), physical risks (as physical danger increases [e.g., with lawnmowers, drugs], concern about bad decisions increases), and social risks (as the potential for embarrassment increases, concern about bad decisions increases). When people are concerned about making decisions that could turn out badly, they are more likely to think long and hard (systematic processing) and less likely to use quick-and-dirty shortcuts (heuristic processing).

PROCESSING LOAD

Processing load refers to the amount of limited cognitive capacity (or limited mental resources; see Chapter 2) needed for information processing. Processing load increases as decision difficulty increases. Many variables influence decision difficulty, including the number of brands considered (as the number of brands increases, decision difficulty increases), the number of attributes considered (as the number of attributes increases, decision difficulty increases), and time pressure (as time pressure increases, decision difficulty increases). As decision difficulty increases, consumers become more likely to use simplifying choice heuristics to make the choice task more manageable (Payne et al., 1992, 1993).

CONTEXTUAL VARIABLES

Contextual variables also influence choice strategy. Information about products can be presented in many different ways, and the manner in which information is presented influences how this information is processed. For example, a brand-based format in which each brand is described separately (across several attributes) encourages

➤ New integrated control panel

➤ New driver's door remote keyless entry system

➤ Improved steel safety cell construction

➤ New AM/FM stereo with premium speakers

➤ Standard dual air bags*

➤ New 2.0L 4-cylinder SPI engine with 25% more power

*Always wear your safety belt. MSRP '97 Escort & '97 Escort LX with PEP 317A. Title, tax extra.

For more info: 1-800-286-1153 or http://www.ford.com

BUILT

IT'S PRICED REALLY NICE AND IT'S BUILT OH-SO WELL.

Smart

Most consumers have high involvement and accountability in the decision to purchase a car. This ad reassures them that they are making a "smart" decision.

Source: Courtesy of Ford Motor Company.

IS INTERNATIONAL CALLBACK FAIR PLAY?

If you were going to make a choice between cheaper phone rates and more expensive ones, you would probably choose the cheaper ones, assuming that the quality of both services was equal. If you were running a business whose livelihood depended on cheap phone rates, you would probably make the same choice, especially if you were being held accountable by others for the decision.

That is the simple part of this story. Now things get a little more complicated, a little more murky. Consumers in the United States enjoy some of the cheapest long-distance phone rates in the world; callers in other countries may pay as much as 600 percent more. The United States has a highly competitive market, with a larger consideration set than other countries do, a higher volume of calls, and sophisticated technology that now costs less. The sophisticated technology includes callback systems, which even in their most primitive form allow a caller outside the United States to call a U.S.-based callback service operator, wait two rings and hang up, then receive an automatic "callback" at a cheaper rate. Callers can use this same procedure to call just about anywhere in the world, connecting two points outside the United States. For instance, a marketer in London can dial an American callback switch and have the callback service complete a call to Tokyo at a much cheaper rate than if the marketer dialed Tokyo direct.

It's legal, but even those who make the practice a regular part of their business don't want to call attention to it. "We're not violating any laws," claims one operations manager for a European petrochemical company that uses IDT Corp.'s callback service, "but we'd rather not call attention to what we're doing." A spokesperson for an industrial parts supplier in Zimbabwe concurs. "Yes, callback has saved us a considerable sum of money, especially with calls to Australia, which is a major market for us. And, no, we don't care to comment further."

Accountability—the need to justify purchases to others—may play a crucial part in the practice of choosing international callback as a way to keep business expenses under control, particularly in an age when competition has reached global proportions. Callback systems give even small companies and individual entrepreneurs a better chance at entering the global market.

Managers at larger companies are increasingly pressured to find ways to make purchases as cost-effective as possible. The manager of the European petrochemical company, who is actually stationed at a plant in Indonesia, uses the inexpensive callback rates not only to boost business but to boost employee morale; the system allows displaced employees to call home more frequently. "We can give them the same call allowance [as they would have in Europe] and they can spend twice as much time talking with their friends and family," he explains.

Still, government agencies and others frown on the practice and are attempting to disconnect overseas callback arrangements. According to one expert in the industry, Alan Sandler, vice president of Justice Technology Corp. (a callback provider based in California), the opponents to callback arrangements can lower long-distance rates in their own countries, giving callers more choices based on price; they can declare the practice illegal and prohibit callback services from advertising publicly; or they can try to use technology to block the systems from actually working.

Is international callback fair play, or is it the product of a free market? Does it provide businesses with a fair chance, or does it throw competition for phone rates out of balance? Perhaps if some users did not have to justify their expenses to others, the practice would not be as widespread; but then again, maybe the lure of the low price would be too hard to resist.

Source: Lenny Liebmann, "The Siren Song of Callback Services," *International Business,* March 1997, pp. 37–38.

within-alternative processing (Biehal & Chakravarti, 1982, 1983, 1986). By contrast, an attribute-based format in which each attribute is presented separately (across several brands) increases the likelihood of between-alternative processing. Hence, comparisons by brand or by attribute are determined by the manner in which information is presented. Brand-based formats increase the ease and likelihood of applying within-alternative heuristics, such as the conjunctive and disjunctive heuristics. Attribute-based formats encourage the use of between-alternative heuristics, such as the lexicographic, elimination-by-aspects, and additive-difference heuristics (or other related heuristics).

Other types of contextual variables are also important. For example, the same product can often be described in many different ways. Almost any object can be described in either positive or negative terms. Consumers are more likely to buy ground beef described as 75 percent lean as opposed to 25 percent fat, even though both descriptions refer to the exact same product (Levin & Gaeth, 1988)—a product that is 75 percent lean is also, by definition, 25 percent fat. This phenomenon is known as the **framing effect,** because how a product is framed, or described, influences how people think about the product (Tversky & Kahneman, 1981, 1986). (See "Making the Decision: Using the Framing Effect: Rogaine.") People think very differently when they focus on positives than when they focus on negatives. They spend money much more freely when price differentials are referred to as "cash discounts" rather than "credit card surcharges" (Thaler, 1980, 1985) or "volume discounts" rather than "single-item surcharges."

Although Shakespeare said, "A rose by any other name would smell as sweet," this is not true in marketing. Names, frames, and descriptions produce powerful effects on choice. Which product would you rather buy: "salmon" or "horse tuna"? Both names refer to the same thing! Salmon used to be called horse tuna, which sold very poorly. Simply changing the name to salmon led to a tremendous marketing success. (To learn more, please continue reading this deluxe, premium, limited-edition textbook.)

Another interesting type of context effect occurs when information that appeals to a very small market segment is used in mass marketing. For example, Pillsbury offered a brownie cake mix with a collector's plate premium that could be purchased at a drastically reduced price with proof of purchase. Although a small group of consumers was interested in the collector's plate, it was not for everybody. In fact, most consumers were more likely to buy the cake mix when the collector's plate was not mentioned (Simonson, Carmon, & O'Curry, 1994). Simply mentioning the unwanted premium provided consumers with a surprisingly strong reason for not buying the cake mix, even though consumers could have easily ignored the irrelevant information about the collector's plate. Rather than ignoring irrelevant information, however, consumers used this information as a reason for not buying the product (e.g., "I don't want the plate, so I won't buy the cake mix"). Similar effects have been observed with irrelevant options (e.g., an option to buy a golf umbrella when you buy Fuji 35mm film) and irrelevant features (e.g., a watch that can display East and West Coast time zones). Consumers have become so accustomed to rejecting products with unwanted features that any unwanted feature, even irrelevant features that do not affect the value of a product, provides a surprisingly powerful reason for rejection (Simonson et al., 1994; Simonson, Nowlis, & Simonson, 1993).

USING THE FRAMING EFFECT: ROGAINE

The only people who care whether Rogaine, the hair-growing formula manufactured by Pharmacia & Upjohn, really regrows hair are people who have suffered hair loss—and the people at Pharmacia & Upjohn. But the case of Rogaine is one worth examining, as consumers and as potential marketers.

Rogaine initially was sold only through prescription. When it received approval from the FDA to become an over-the-counter item, the product's sales reached heady heights as balding men rushed to try Rogaine without the inconvenience and expense of a trip to the doctor. Then they flagged, dropping more than 57 percent (from $162.3 million to less than $100 million) during the second year as an over-the-counter product. Why? For one thing, the consideration set increased: Competitors entered the market, selling their products at about half the price of Rogaine (which sells for about $28 for a month's supply). Consumers had more brands to choose from, at competitive prices. Because Rogaine was not on the shelves for very long before competitors joined it, many consumers did not have the chance to form strong attitudes toward the product and could easily have shifted to attribute-based choices.

But equally important is the issue of whether Rogaine really works. "Everyone knows what Rogaine is. People have tried it, or know someone who has, and the perception is that it's been marginally effective at best," notes Hemant K. Shah, a health care analyst at HKS & Co. Rogaine advertising doesn't present the picture this way. Instead, it emphasizes the positive results, using the framing effect to state that 26 percent of men who use the product get "excellent" results. Of course, this means that 74 percent do not. Pharmacia & Upjohn marketers further note that an additional 19 percent of consumers who have tried the product got "moderate" results, but this means that more than half did not.

Pharmacia & Upjohn is not giving up. The manufacturer has been developing a new product for women and is almost ready to launch Rogaine Extra-Strength for Men, which, it claims, will grow as much as 46 percent more hair than the current Rogaine. But consumers may ask: 46 percent more than what? And the new Rogaine will still require consumers to rub the liquid into their scalps twice a day and deal with uncomfortable side effects such as dry, itchy scalps. The pharmaceutical giant Merck, however, is working on a prescription pill for hair growth.

Still, about 40 million men in the United States suffer from hair loss. If Pharmacia & Upjohn can get them to develop an attitude that hair loss is bad—and that hair regrowth, particularly through the use of Rogaine, is good—the manufacturer still stands to make a profit. One way the company is trying to do this is by offering a promotion of buy one, get one free—encouraging men to give the product a try, with the opportunity to stick with it long enough to see results, without having to buy more. But in the long run, no matter how marketers describe the product, and no matter how much of it they offer consumers for free, if Rogaine is going to stay ahead, it will have to cover the heads of consumers.

Source: Yumiko Ono, "Pharmacia Sets Broad Assault for Rogaine," *The Wall Street Journal,* August 4, 1997, p. B5.

CHAPTER SUMMARY ▪

Consumer choice involves selecting one product from a set of possibilities. The set of possibilities that are considered, or the consideration set, may vary in size (number of alternatives) or content (which specific alternatives) across purchase occasions. The consideration set may be stimulus-based (e.g., the set of brands directly in front of you at a grocery store), memory-based (e.g., the set of brands you think about when you are not inside a retail outlet), or mixed (e.g., some brands are physically present and some are retrieved from memory). A particular brand may seem attractive or unattractive, depending on whether inferior or superior brands, respectively, are included in the consideration set. Compromise brands are frequently chosen when difficult trade-offs are required for choice. Choosing among brands involves detecting dissimilarities or differences among alternatives. These differences may be general (overall judgment-based choice) or specific (attribute-based choice). Heuristics, or mental shortcuts, are often used to simplify decision making, but whether heuristics are used and which heuristics are used depends on processing goals (e.g., is the consumer trying to select the best brand or just a satisfactory brand?), processing load (e.g., does the consumer have the cognitive resources needed to achieve a particular goal?), and a wide variety of contextual variables (e.g., information presentation format, framing, presence or absence of irrelevant information).

A clearer understanding of the key factors that guide consumer choice helps managers to design more effective marketing programs and gain competitive advantage. Getting your brand into consumers' consideration sets requires an understanding of salience, vividness, and memory accessibility effects. Effective consumer consideration-set management requires an understanding of part-list cuing, attraction, trade-off contrast, and compromise effects. Knowing what to emphasize (e.g., attributes that are important to a target market) and what not to emphasize (e.g., attributes that are irrelevant to a target market) requires an understanding of consumer choice strategies and the key variables that influence these strategies.

KEY CONCEPTS ▪

- Consumer choice
- Consideration set
- Part-list cuing
- Attraction effect
- Trade-off contrast effect
- Compromise effect
- Stimulus-based choice
- Memory-based choice
- Mixed choice
- Attitude-based choice
- Attribute-based choice
- Accessibility–diagnosticity model

- Between-alternative processing
- Within-alternative processing
- Compensatory strategies
- Attitude heuristic
- Frequency of good and bad features heuristic
- Noncompensatory strategies
- Lexicographic heuristic
- Lexicographic semiorder heuristic

- Elimination-by-aspects heuristic
- Additive-difference heuristic
- Majority of confirming dimensions heuristic
- Conjunctive heuristic
- Disjunctive heuristic
- Phased strategies
- Processing goals
- Processing load
- Contextual variables
- Framing effect

DISCUSSION QUESTIONS ▪

1. Why does the part-list cuing effect occur?
2. Think of an instance from your own experience when you used either the trade-off contrast effect or the compromise effect in making a purchase decision. Explain how you arrived at the decision. Was the purchase large enough for accountability to be a factor? Why or why not?
3. How might marketers for grocery products use nutrition information on packaging to enhance the chances of consumers' making stimulus-based choices in favor of their products?
4. Do you think the use of puffery in advertising is an effective tactic? Why or why not?
5. In what general instances are consumers more likely to make attitude-based choices? In what instances are they more likely to make attribute-based choices?
6. According to the accessibility–diagnosticity model, on what three factors is consumer choice based?
7. In general, when are consumers likely to use a heuristic for a purchase decision? When are they unlikely to do so? Provide some examples.
8. As a marketer for a brand of laundry detergent, how might you wade through all the different heuristics that consumers could use to make their purchase decisions? How might you use some of the heuristics to your advantage?
9. What are the two main variables that influence processing goals? Name some examples of purchases for which processing goals would be important for most consumers.
10. Imagine that you are the marketer for a new type of popcorn snack food. Briefly outline an ad for the new snack, using contextual variables (including the framing effect, if you find it appropriate).

PERSUASION AND INFLUENCE

CHAPTER

6

The Message-Learning Approach to Persuasion

◆ JANE

Jane: It's not only the medium and the message, it's also the source. *Jane* is the name of a new magazine (the medium) for young adult women. It's also the name of the new magazine's editor, Jane Pratt (the source of the message). Jane's message to young women is that straight talk is OK.

Jane Pratt is only in her thirties, but she is already a veteran of publishing. She was hired in her early twenties by an Australian publishing firm, John Fairfax Ltd., to edit a sharp new magazine called *Sassy*, which was designed to compete with the more demure *Seventeen. Sassy* was, in a word, sassy. Pratt dared to tackle subjects such as contraception and homosexuality. She wanted teen readers to trust her and the magazine to deal honestly with topics that concerned them. Unfortunately, although Pratt developed a following, she scared off religious groups and conservative advertisers like Revlon, Maybelline, and Noxell, who were afraid that conservative consumers would associate their products with controversial topics. Eventually, *Sassy* folded its pages for good.

Now Walt Disney Co. wants to take another chance on Pratt. Although Disney tends to avoid controversy, its Fairchild Publications unit is convinced that the time is right for *Jane*. Fairchild's chairman and editorial director, Patrick McCarthy, believes that Jane Pratt is the right person to connect with young consumers. She's young, smart, and attractive. Young readers seem to relate to her. McCarthy is also realistic about what Pratt will—and will not—be allowed to do. "This company isn't going to produce a magazine that will embarrass us," he insists. "*Jane* will be provocative and exciting . . . in a sophisticated way."

Disney/Fairchild is making sure that *Jane*—and Jane—receive as much good publicity as possible. Pratt has made appearances on "Good Morning America" and even the ABC soap drama "All My Children." Fairchild is backing the magazine with $5 million for advertising and promotion—and that doesn't include hefty start-up costs. Initial advertisers include Nike and Revlon (back for another try, after defecting from *Sassy*).

Jane's topics will include the usual beauty, fashion, films, music, food, and fiction, as well as some in-depth features on topics of concern to young readers. Each *Jane* cover will feature a celebrity. All this sounds like other magazines targeted for young women. But Pratt says that *Jane* will be different in its "mix of subjects, tone, and attitude. There is room for a magazine that really talks to young women in a way that I hear them talk." Pratt and Disney/Fairchild hope that young women consumers hear the message. As you read this chapter, consider the complex interplay among the marketer's message, the source of the message, the medium that delivers the message, and the recipient of the message.

Source: Patrick M. Reilly, "Disney Millions Give Jane a Splashy Newsstand Debut," *The Wall Street Journal,* August 21, 1997, pp. B1, B12.

◆ INTRODUCTION

One of the earliest systematic, scientific approaches to the study of **persuasion** (an active attempt to change belief and attitude) was the **message-learning approach,** which was initially developed by a famous group of Yale University psychologists (Hovland, Janis, & Kelley, 1953). The leader of the group, Professor Carl Hovland, was also famous for the World War II propaganda materials (e.g., the *Why We Fight* film shown to army recruits) he developed for the U.S. government (Hovland, Lumsdaine, & Sheffield, 1949). Hovland and his colleagues suggested that effective persuasive communications (i.e., advertisements, point-of-purchase displays, salesperson claims, telemarketing messages, propaganda films and leaflets, or any message designed to persuade) are attention-drawing, comprehensible, convincing, and memorable. Hence, there are four basic stages involved in the processing of any persuasive communication: attention, comprehension, yielding (i.e., finding the message convincing and compelling), and retention (memory). These four psychological processes are influenced by four key independent variables: source variables (who says the message), message variables (what is said), recipient variables (who receives the message), and medium variables (e.g., television, radio, magazine, or newspaper media). The message-learning approach is also known as the "who says what to whom" (and with what effect?) approach.

◆ EXPOSURE CONTROL

It seems obvious that consumers must attend to and comprehend a persuasive message before the message can influence them. It also seems obvious that consumers cannot attend to and comprehend every message they encounter. Less obvious, however, is the finding that consumers try to avoid attending to advertisements (Wilson, Gilbert, & Wheatley, 1998) even though most consumers believe that advertising does not affect them personally (Wilson & Brekke, 1994).

Rather than watching a televised speech by a disliked politician or a televised ad for a disliked product, consumers can simply change the channel. Instead of reading an article or a book that advocates a position opposite to what they believe personally, consumers can easily refrain from reading the article or the book. Avoiding unwanted messages is known as **exposure control** (Wilson et al., 1998). In an important study on exposure control, subjects were asked to imagine that they would see several different types of persuasive messages about some political candidates running for mayor (Wilson et al., 1998). For each type of message, subjects were asked to indicate how much they would want to be influenced by the message, and they were also asked to rate how much they thought they and someone else would actually be influenced by the message. One type of message was a television ad that described positive aspects of a candidate without mentioning any of the candidate's positions on the issues. Another type of message was a flier that had a picture of a candidate with no information. Another type of message was a subliminal message about a candidate embedded in a television program. Another type of message was a newspaper article that wrongly accused a candidate of stealing funds. The results revealed that for each of these messages, the wanted influence was much lower than the perceived actual influence. Moreover, subjects thought they were personally less likely to be influenced by these messages than other people, except for subliminal messages, which were perceived to be equally and moderately influential for everyone. (See Fig. 6-1.)

In a follow-up experiment, subjects received the same four different types of messages and were asked to check one of five different boxes for each message: (1) They want to receive the message to help them make up their minds, (2) they want to receive the message even though it would not influence them, (3) they do not want to receive the message because it might bias their judgments, (4) they do not want to receive the message because it would be bothersome or a waste of time, or (5) they do not care whether or not they receive the message (Wilson et al., 1998). For the television ad, 0 percent of the subjects indicated that they wanted to see it because it would provide useful information! The remaining four boxes were checked by about 25 percent of the subjects. Similar results were found for the flier, except that a small percentage (less than 10 percent) wanted to see the flier and a small percentage thought that the flyer would bias their judgments. By contrast, a high percentage of subjects did not want to receive the subliminal message or the newspaper article with a false claim because they thought these messages would bias their judgments in an unfair manner. (See Fig. 6-2.)

Given that most people do not want to be exposed to advertisements, what should advertisers do? One possibility is to design ads that are salient or vivid, because such ads are difficult to ignore (see Chapter 2). Another possibility is to design ads that are

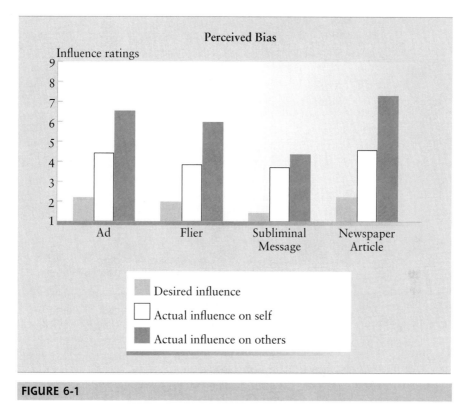

FIGURE 6-1

Desired versus actual influences on the self versus others of biased messages.
Source: Adapted from Wilson, Gilbert, & Wheatley (1998).

pleasant or humorous or that put consumers in a good mood. Such messages are unthreatening and they encourage consumers to let their guard down. For example, examine the leaflet that tells the American soldier to "give yourself a break and think about the good old days." (See poster, "Maneuvers the Easy Way.") The soldier in the leaflet is shown happily daydreaming about a frosty mug of beer while standing in the hot sun. The leaflet also appears to be helpful: A maneuver can either be rough or easy, and instead of complaining about bad food it is better to simply think about the good old days. If you were an American soldier, would you be willing to read this leaflet, and would you allow this leaflet to influence you? Now let me add one more detail: The leaflet is actually Nazi propaganda designed to decrease the morale of American soldiers!

What lessons can advertisers learn from this leaflet? First, if the source of the message is unlikable or untrustworthy (like the Nazis), hide or disguise the source. American soldiers were extremely unlikely to realize that the leaflet came from the Nazis. If they had known, they would have avoided the message or they would have avoided influence from the message by reminding themselves that the message is a

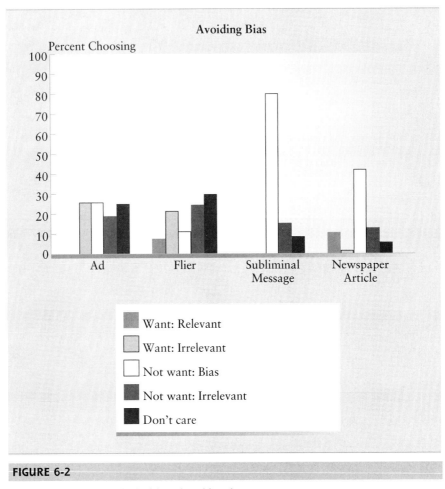

FIGURE 6-2

Preferences for how to deal with various biased messages.

Source: Adapted from Wilson, Gilbert, & Wheatley (1998).

dirty trick. Second, the message should be pleasant and unthreatening so that recipients will let their guard down. A large number of studies have shown that pleasant ads are more persuasive compared to neutral or unpleasant ads (Batra & Stayman, 1990; Brown, Homer, & Inman, 1998; MacKenzie, Lutz, & Belch, 1986; Mitchell & Olson, 1981). The typical explanation for this finding is that some of the positive feelings created by the ad transfer to the advertised brand (this classical conditioning process is described in greater detail in Chapter 8). However, the research of Wilson et al. (1998) suggests an important alternative explanation: Exposure control may be less likely for pleasant ads! Future research should test this possibility. Finally, rather than telling American soldiers what to believe, the Nazi leaflet tries to influence their beliefs subtly by using the contrast effect: Compared to the good old days, the present seems even more unbearable (the contrast effect is described in greater detail in Chapter 7). Overcoming exposure control and resistance to persuasion is the first step toward the creation of effective advertising.

Source: From Zimbardo, Ebbesen, & Maslach (1977). Copyright by Pearson Education. Reprinted with permission.

◆ SOURCE FACTORS

The source, or originator, of a message has a large impact on how a message is received. The most effective sources tend to be expert, trustworthy, or attractive communicators. For example, in one classic study of source trustworthiness or credibility (Hovland & Weiss, 1951), subjects read a persuasive message about the utility of atomic submarines. Although all subjects read the exact same message, half were told the message was written by the famous American physicist Robert Oppenheimer of the University of Chicago, and the remaining half were told the message came from the Russian newspaper *Pravda*. Subjects were randomly assigned to the high-credibility (Oppenheimer) or low-credibility (*Pravda*) conditions. Even though the message was held constant (i.e., all subjects read the exact same message), greater persuasion occurred in the high-source-credibility condition.

CREDIBILITY

The reputation of the source is one factor that influences source credibility. (See "Taking Issue: How Reputations Are Won and Lost.") Another factor is whether the message is consistent or inconsistent with the source's vested interests. For example, a criminal who argues that the justice system is too lenient is very persuasive even though criminals are usually untrustworthy (Walster, Aronson, & Abrahams, 1966). Similarly, a student who argues that a class is too easy and that more reading materials and more difficult exams are needed is also very persuasive. Any time a source argues against his or her own best interests, perceived trustworthiness and persuasion increase. This principle has also been applied in advertising by using a spokesperson who provides reasons for not buying the advertised product (Pechmann, 1992; Smith & Hunt, 1978; Swinyard, 1981). This increases the credibility of the spokesperson. After admitting that the product has some deficiencies on some relatively unimportant attributes, however, the spokesperson then continues by extolling the virtues of the product on other, more important, attributes. Hence, **two-sided messages** (messages containing both pros and cons) enhance source credibility because some information goes against the source's vested interests. This increases persuasion because credible sources who claim that the product is superior on several important dimensions can be very effective.

ATTRACTIVENESS

Attractive sources can also be very persuasive. Attractiveness is influenced by physical appearance, similarity to recipients (e.g., in terms of personal backgrounds, beliefs, or attitudes), and presentational style. Advertisers purposefully attempt to select physically attractive spokespersons and models to endorse their products. Advertisers also tend to use communicators similar to members of the intended audience because people like others similar to themselves. For example, products for teenagers (e.g., pimple medications) are frequently endorsed by teenagers. Products for retired persons (e.g., medical insurance supplements) are often endorsed by elderly people. Presentational styles also have an influence. Effective communicators look to the audience (Hemsley & Doob, 1978), speak rapidly and fluently (Miller, Maruyama, Beaber, & Valone, 1976), and avoid using hesitations and hedges like "um," "well," "kinda," "I guess," and "you know" (Lind & O'Barr, 1979).

Although source factors are usually important, they are more important in some situations than others. When the source is highlighted or likely to draw much attention, source factors are especially important (Andreoli & Worchel, 1978; Chaiken & Eagly, 1983; Pallak, 1983; Pallak, Murroni, & Koch, 1983). On the other hand, when the source is hidden or unlikely to draw attention, source factors are less important. Hence, the medium makes a difference: Source factors are more important for television ads than for radio or print (magazine or newspaper) ads. Putting a spotlight on the source, placing the source up on a pedestal, or highlighting the source by making the source different from others present in an ad (e.g., the only female in a room filled with males) can also be effective. Any variable that increases the salience of a source also increases the importance of source factors.

HOW REPUTATIONS ARE WON AND LOST

When the American Medical Association talks, people usually listen. The nonprofit organization, made up of 300,000 of the nation's physicians, is generally viewed as an unbiased authority on medical practices. Ideally, the AMA should be a reliable source of opinion and information about medicine, medical practice, policy, and so forth. That is why, when it was revealed that the AMA had entered into an agreement with Sunbeam Corp., concern reverberated among the country's physicians.

According to the Sunbeam deal, the AMA had agreed to put its seal of approval exclusively on various Sunbeam home health products in exchange for millions of dollars in royalty payments. But, unlike the Good Housekeeping Institute, which thoroughly tests every product that applies for the seal before it gives the product the Good Housekeeping seal, the AMA had no plans for testing the Sunbeam products. Thus, consumers would be buying Sunbeam products based on a message from a source that they believed to be credible—when in fact the source knew nothing about the quality of the products at all. This might be considered less than ethical if the products included such items as laundry detergent or facial tissues, but some thought it would be downright dangerous in the case of home health products.

The Sunbeam deal isn't the only commercial venture the AMA has embarked on. For years, to raise funds, the organization engaged in everything from publishing to real estate (even now, about two-thirds of its $200 million annual budget comes from such ventures). Recently, however, the AMA has explored the idea of potential partnerships with such firms as Procter & Gamble, Hoffmann-LaRoche, and Minnesota Mining and Manufacturing Co. The AMA has a business development committee that explores, develops, and oversees its fund-raising ventures.

Almost as soon as it was announced, the Sunbeam deal was struck down by the AMA board. In the furor that followed, it was unclear how much members of the board knew, and when. Member physicians who didn't know much about the AMA's commercial activities were upset. Even a former chairman of the AMA board expressed concern: "The board and the staff have to be much more forthright about what business relationships are planned or are under development," noted Dr. Raymond Scaletar. "We need to know—in what direction is this organization heading?"

Unfortunately, after the AMA backed away from the agreement, Sunbeam decided to sue the organization for $20 million (or force it to go through with the deal), causing the AMA to potentially lose even more. Ironically, even if the AMA eventually put its seal of approval on the Sunbeam products, the message contained by the approval would be worthless to consumers. Who will take seriously a claim that was forced by a $20 million lawsuit? So, both Sunbeam and the AMA would lose some of their credibility.

The Sunbeam–AMA scandal teaches us the importance of reputation when it comes to credibility—how hard it is won and how easily it is lost.

Source: Judith Graham, "Sunbeam Deal May Cost Jobs at AMA," *Chicago Tribune,* September 17, 1997, pp. 1, 16.

Many different types of messages are used by advertisers and other persuasion professionals (e.g., politicians and lawyers). Persuasive communications may be simple or complex, one-sided or two-sided, or rational or emotional. Moreover, the effectiveness of a particular type of message often depends on the effects of other factors, such as source, recipient, and medium factors. For example, factual messages are likely to be more persuasive when they are delivered by an expert (such as a famous scientist) as opposed to a person who is below average in intelligence (such as Jim Carrey's character from the movie *Dumb and Dumber*). This example suggests an interaction between source expertise (knowledgeable or unknowledgeable) and type of message (factual or nonfactual). Recall from Chapter 1 that an interaction involves the effects of one independent variable dependent on the effects of another independent variable. Some independent variables work jointly to produce an effect on a dependent variable. For this reason, it is crucial to study the effects of several variables at the same time, rather than examining the effects of one variable considered in isolation.

MESSAGE COMPLEXITY

Some messages are very simple and contain only a conclusion or a bottom line, such as "Buy Brand X." Other messages are more complex—in addition to presenting the conclusion "Buy Brand X," several supporting arguments or reasons for buying Brand X are offered as well. Which type of message is more effective? It depends. Message complexity interacts with message source. This was demonstrated in an experiment in which subjects were randomly assigned to simple or complex message conditions (Norman, 1976). In simple message conditions, subjects read only a conclusion (e.g., "Buy Brand X"). In complex message conditions, subjects read the conclusion plus six supporting arguments for believing the conclusion. In addition, subjects were randomly assigned to source conditions. In expert source conditions, subjects were told that the message was written by an expert. In attractive source conditions, subjects were told that the message was written by a smiling, physically attractive person (a picture was shown). Moreover, a **factorial design** was used. This means that all levels of each independent variable were crossed with or combined with all levels of each other independent variable. For example, a 2 (simple or complex message) $\times$ 2 (expert or attractive source) factorial design produces four ($2 \times 2 = 4$) conditions: a simple message/expert source condition, a simple message/attractive source condition, a complex message/expert source condition, and a complex message/attractive source condition. The results revealed that for a simple message, an attractive source is more persuasive than an expert source. However, the opposite is true for a complex message, for which an expert source is more persuasive than an attractive source. (See Fig. 6-3.)

Message complexity is also influenced by comprehensibility, or by how easy or difficult it is to understand the message (Eagly, 1974). In this study, subjects listened to a message containing a conclusion and several supporting arguments. However, the manner in which this information was presented was varied. In the high comprehensibility condition, the message was easy to process because the arguments flowed logically and sequentially. In the medium comprehensibility condition, subjects heard the

IBM uses a complex message—a conclusion and several supporting reasons—to persuade consumers to buy the ThinkPad.
Source: Courtesy of IBM Corp.

same message, but the sentences were cut in half and put back together in a random order, so the message was harder to follow. In the low comprehensibility condition, subjects heard the same message, but the words were randomized, which made the message nearly impossible to follow. The results showed that as comprehensibility decreased, persuasion decreased and subjects' ability to recall message arguments also decreased.

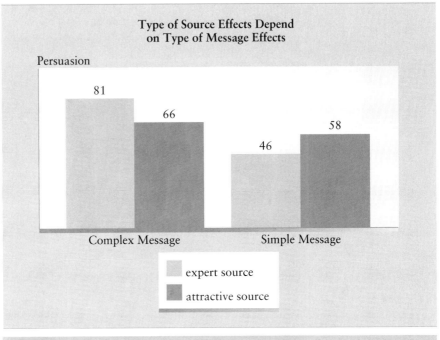

FIGURE 6-3

Message complexity interacts with the message source to determine effectiveness.

Source: Adapted from Norman (1976). An expert source is more effective when the message is complex, but an attractive source is more effective when the message is simple.

ONE-SIDED VERSUS TWO-SIDED MESSAGES

A **one-sided message** is a biased, lopsided message that contains only supporting arguments, or arguments consistent with the conclusion (e.g., "Buy Brand X"). A two-sided message is a more even-handed message that provides both pros and cons, or supporting arguments (arguments consistent with the conclusion) and counter-arguments (arguments inconsistent with the conclusion). Of course, advertisers want consumers to believe the conclusion ("Buy Brand X"), so it is important to use weak counterarguments (e.g., on unimportant attributes, Brand X is no better than other brands) or counterarguments that are refuted or attacked by additional arguments or information.

Which is more effective, a one-sided or a two-sided message? Again, it depends. Specifically, type of message (one-sided or two-sided) interacts with the initial opinions of the intended audience or target market and with the knowledgeability of the target audience. That is, type of message interacts with recipient factors. If consumers already like the product and purchase it frequently, one-sided messages are more effective (Hovland et al., 1949; Lumsdaine & Janis, 1953). On the other hand, if the brand is unattractive or unfamiliar to consumers, two-sided messages are generally more effective.

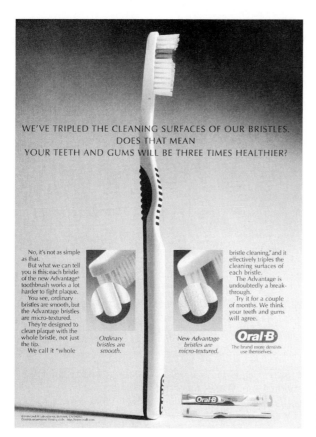

WE'VE TRIPLED THE CLEANING SURFACES OF OUR BRISTLES.
DOES THAT MEAN
YOUR TEETH AND GUMS WILL BE THREE TIMES HEALTHIER?

No, it's not as simple as that.
But what we can tell you is this: each bristle of the new Advantage® toothbrush works a lot harder to fight plaque.
You see, ordinary bristles are smooth, but the Advantage bristles are micro-textured. They're designed to clean plaque with the whole bristle, not just the tip.
We call it "whole

Ordinary bristles are smooth.

New Advantage bristles are micro-textured.

bristle cleaning," and it effectively triples the cleaning surfaces of each bristle.
The Advantage is undoubtedly a break-through.
Try it for a couple of months. We think your teeth and gums will agree.

Oral-B
The brand more dentists use themselves.

Oral-B presents a two-sided message in this toothbrush ad.
Source: Courtesy of Oral-B Laboratories.

Knowledge levels about the product category are also important. Unknowledgeable consumers are influenced more by one-sided messages because they do not have the knowledge base needed to generate their own counterarguments and because they are less likely to think about other brands (Faison, 1961). Knowledgeable consumers, on the other hand, are more likely to recognize that one-sided communications are biased and unfair, and this realization may prompt them to form their own counterarguments or consider other alternatives.

RATIONAL VERSUS EMOTIONAL APPEALS

Messages may appeal either to the intellect or to the heart. **Rational appeals** contain factual details that are useful for generating an informed opinion. For example, a car ad may contain a lot of technical details that are very important to consumers who are highly knowledgeable about automobiles. By contrast, **emotional appeals** tug at our heartstrings and encourage us to act on our feelings rather than our heads. For example, a television ad showing sick, starving children from a remote corner of the globe encourages us to donate money to a charitable organization by appealing to feelings like guilt and sorrow. Another type of emotional appeal is a **fear appeal,** which scares us into action (e.g., buy Brand X life insurance now because tomorrow may be too late).

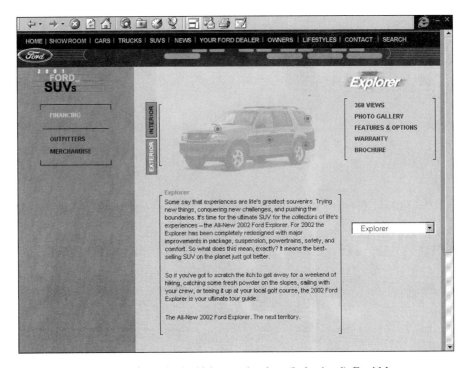

At its Explorer Web site (www.fordvehicles.com/explorer/index.html), Ford Motor
Company presents both an emotional appeal to our sense of adventure and factual details
(see continuation on p. 147) about its Explorer models that are useful for generating an
informed opinion.

Source: Courtesy of Ford Motor Company.

Which type of approach is more effective, the rational or the emotional approach?
By now, you should realize that this is a bad question. A better question is: When are
rational appeals likely to be effective and when are emotional appeals likely to be
effective? Type of appeal interacts with recipient factors. Specifically, recipients who
are high in need for cognition (Cacioppo & Petty, 1982; Cacioppo, Petty, & Kao, 1984),
or who enjoy thinking and effortful intellectual pursuits (e.g., chess, bridge, puzzles),
are more heavily influenced by rational appeals (Venkatraman et al., 1990).
Conversely, recipients who are low in need for cognition, or who do not enjoy effortful
cognitive exercises and who think carefully only when necessary (need for cognition is
a preference and is not strongly correlated with intelligence), are influenced more by
emotional appeals. (See Fig. 6-4.)

The effectiveness of a particular appeal also depends on the function of an attitude, or the purpose that an attitude serves (attitude functions are discussed in greater
detail in Chapter 8). For example, some attitudes summarize large amounts of information and help us to better understand complex topics and issues (i.e., the knowledge
function). Rational appeals are useful for changing attitudes of this nature. Other attitudes help us to feel safe and comfortable even when we think about threatening
issues. For example, cigarette smokers do not like to think about lung cancer, heart disease, or other dangers associated with smoking, and consequently they tend to form

Model	2-door Sport	4-door XLT	4-door Eddie Bauer	Limited
Package	934A	945A	946A	943A
Key Features	P235/75R/15SL OWL all-terrain tires Luggage rack Cloth sport buckets with 6-way power driver's seat and power driver/passenger lumbar support 5-speed automatic overdrive Luxury Group: high-series console, front overhead console (includes reading lamps, electronic compass and outside temperature readout), Electronics Group (includes 2 keyless remote transmitters, keypad, anti-theft, autolock/relock and puddle lamps on outside rearview mirrors), fog lamps Floor mats and cargo cover	AM/FM stereo/single CD radio and clock Luggage rack Cloth sport buckets with 6-way power driver's seat and power driver/passenger lumbar support 5-speed automatic overdrive Luxury Group: high-series console, front overhead console (includes reading lamps, electronic compass and outside temperature readout), Electronics Group (includes 2 keyless remote transmitters, keypad, anti-theft, autolock/relock and puddle lamps on outside rearview mirrors), fog lamps Floor mats and cargo cover	Sport buckets with leather seating surfaces, 6-way power driver's seat and power driver/passenger lumbar support Color-keyed running boards Luxury Group: high-series console, front overhead console (includes reading lamps, electronic compass and outside temperature readout), Electronics Group (includes 2 keyless remote transmitters, keypad, anti-theft, autolock/relock and puddle lamps on outside rearview mirrors), fog lamps Premium Group: electronic automatic temperature control, message center, two-spoke steering wheel with auxiliary controls, MACH™ Audio System (includes cassette/CD/clock, subwoofer, amplifier, digital signal processor and power antenna)	Unique Limited 15" luxury aluminum wheel Color-keyed running boards Automatic day/night mirror and automatic headlamps Power 6-way luxury buckets with leather seating surfaces, 3-position driver's memory and power lumbar support Premium Group: electronic automatic temperature control, message center, two-spoke steering wheel with auxiliary controls, MACH™ Audio System (includes cassette/CD/clock, subwoofer, amplifier, digital signal processor and power antenna) Luxury Group: high-series console, front overhead console (includes reading lamps, electronic compass and outside temperature readout), Electronics Group (includes 2 keyless remote transmitters, keypad, anti-theft, autolock/relock and puddle lamps on outside rearview mirrors), fog lamps
Engines	4.0-liter OHC V6	4.0-liter OHC V6	4.0-liter SOHC V6 5-speed automatic	4.0-liter SOHC V6 5-speed automatic
Safety	Second Generation depowered dual front airbags	Second Generation depowered dual front airbags	Second Generation depowered dual front airbags	Second Generation depowered dual front airbags

(Continued)

attitudes that serve an ego-defensive (or self-protective) function. They may convince themselves that the dangers have been overstated or that these dangers happen only to other people. These beliefs are not rational and not susceptible to rational appeals. The best way to fight fear is with fear: Fear-based attitudes should be attacked by fear appeals.

Protection Motivation Theory

Protection motivation theory (Maddux & Rogers, 1983) suggests that three key variables jointly influence the effectiveness of fear appeals: likelihood of danger, coping effectiveness, and self-efficacy (self-effectiveness or ability to cope). Smokers were

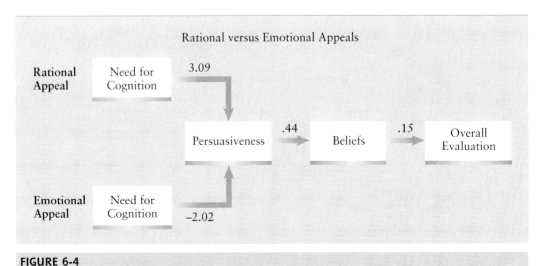

FIGURE 6-4

The type of appeal used in a message interacts with recipient factors.

Source: Adapted from Venkatraman et al. (1990). Note that persuasiveness *increases* with need for cognition for rational appeals and *decreases* with need for cognition for emotional appeals.

exposed to a persuasive communication that contained information about the likelihood of contracting cancer (either higher or lower than indicated by earlier research), coping effectiveness (quitting will either lower the probability of danger or not), and self-efficacy (quitting is either easy using some new techniques or not). Hence, this experiment used a 2 (high or low likelihood) × 2 (high or low coping effectiveness) by 2 (high or low self-efficacy) factorial design, with eight conditions (2 × 2 × 2 = 8). A significant three-way interaction was found: The effects of any single variable depended on the effects of the other two. The fear appeal (stop smoking or else) was most effective when the likelihood of danger was high, provided that either coping effectiveness or self-efficacy was also high. When coping effectiveness and self-efficacy were both low, subjects gave up and did not even try to quit (if I'm going to get cancer anyway, why bother trying?). Fear appeals were completely ineffective when people felt helpless. Fear appeals were also ineffective when the likelihood of danger was low (why worry about it?), except when coping effectiveness and self-efficacy were both high. Here recipients adopted a precaution strategy, because even though the probability of danger was low, quitting was easy and effective, so why risk even a low probability of danger? (See Fig. 6-5.)

Of course, fear appeals are used in many other cases besides antismoking campaigns. Fear appeals are used to sell many different kinds of insurance (e.g., life, medical, car, and home insurance) as well as antitheft devices for cars (e.g., The Club, the Viper system) and homes (e.g., the Honeywell home-security system). Fear appeals are also used in many political advertisements concerning the dangers of pollution, nuclear power, foreign competitors, higher taxes, and political opponents. Fear appeals seem especially appealing for health- and welfare-related issues.

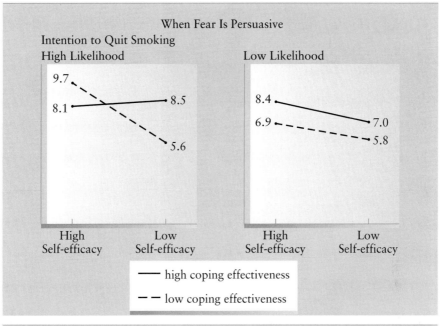

FIGURE 6-5

Likelihood of danger, coping effectiveness, and self-efficacy jointly influence the effectiveness of fear appeals.

Source: Adapted from Maddux & Rogers (1983).

ORDER OF PRESENTATION

Should your best arguments be presented first in a persuasive communication, or should you present this information at the end of the message? In a lengthy print ad, for example, should you present the most important information first to put your best foot forward, or should you save the best for last? Research on order of presentation effects in persuasion indicates that early information tends to receive a lot of attention and that fatigue or boredom may result in decreasing attention to subsequent information as message length increases (Jones & Goethals, 1971; Kruglanski & Freund, 1983; Miller & Campbell, 1959). However, information presented at the end of a message tends to be more memorable because this information was most recently activated. Hence, early (primacy effect) or late (recency effect) information tends to have more impact than information buried in the middle of a lengthy message. The primacy effect is strongest when late information is processed immediately after processing early information, whereas the recency effect is strongest when there is a time delay between the presentation of early and late information. Both order effects are reduced, however, when the message is brief or when recipients are motivated to carefully process all relevant information (Haugtvedt & Wegener, 1994; Kruglanski & Freund, 1983).

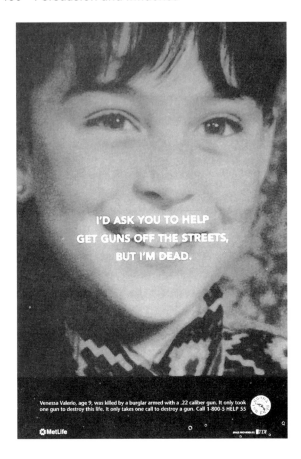

I'D ASK YOU TO HELP GET GUNS OFF THE STREETS, BUT I'M DEAD.

Venessa Valerio, age 9, was killed by a burglar armed with a .22 caliber gun. It only took one gun to destroy this life. It only takes one call to destroy a gun. Call 1-800-S HELP SS

MetLife

This ad uses both emotion (sadness) and fear (that one's child, friend, sibling, etc. may be killed) to argue for gun control.

Source: Courtesy of Andrew Morris.

THE SLEEPER EFFECT

Sometimes a message becomes more persuasive over time. This phenomenon, known as the **sleeper effect,** occurs as the result of a complex interaction between message factors, source factors, and time (Cook, Gruder, Hennigan, & Flay, 1979; Hannah & Sternthal, 1984; Hovland et al., 1949; Kelman & Hovland, 1953; Mazursky & Schul, 1988; Pratkanis, Greenwald, Leippe, & Baumgardner, 1988). The sleeper effect is most likely to occur when a credible message is presented by a noncredible source. Initially, little or no persuasion occurs because the message is discounted or its impact is weakened to make allowances for an unknowledgeable or untrustworthy source. Over time, however, the message and the source may become dissociated (or separated) because of poorer memory for the source than for the message. If so, the persuasive effect of the message will increase over time, while the qualifying effect of the source will decrease over time. For example, if you read a believable article in the *National Enquirer,* you might not believe the article at first because it's hard to believe anything published by the *National Enquirer* (e.g., Elvis was abducted by space aliens). Over time, however, you might remember the gist of the article but forget that you read it in the *National Enquirer.* In this case, persuasion will increase over time.

Similarly, a television ad may make some extreme and remarkable claims about the merits of a particular brand. Initially, these claims may be discounted because we all know that advertising is meant to persuade and that advertisers will say almost anything to get us to buy their products (Friestad & Wright, 1994, 1995). Over time, however, the gist of the message may be retained but the source of the message (a potentially biased advertisement) may be forgotten. If so, the sleeper effect is likely to be observed. Hence, an ad may be totally ineffective intially but quite effective later in time.

◆ RECIPIENT FACTORS

Are some types of people easier to manipulate than others? Earlier in this chapter, I discussed one type of recipient by message interaction: Individuals high in need for cognition are more heavily influenced by rational appeals, whereas individuals low in need for cognition are more heavily influenced by emotional appeals. Furthermore, individuals whose attitudes serve a knowledge function are more readily influenced by rational appeals, whereas individuals whose attitudes serve an ego-defensive (self-protective) function are more easily influenced by fear appeals. Early research on recipient factors suggested that women are more susceptible to persuasion than men, but here, too, recipient factors interact with message factors: Women are easier to influence when a persuasive message concerns male-oriented topics, whereas men are easier to influence when a persuasive message focuses on female-oriented topics (Tesser & Leone, 1977; discussed in greater detail in Chapter 9).

McGuire's (1968, 1972, 1976) theory of personality and persuasion is still, today, the richest and most elegant theoretical framework available for explaining the effects of recipient factors on persuasion. McGuire's theory is composed of three key principles: the mediational principle, the combinatory principle, and the situational-weighting principle. The mediational principle suggests that a series of psychological processes mediate or underly persuasion: perception, comprehension, agreement, retention, retrieval, and decision making. Although recipient factors may influence each of these processes, McGuire's theory of personality and persuasion focuses primarily on two stages: reception (perception plus comprehension) and yielding (agreement).

The combinatory principle suggests that personality is related to the two mediators (reception and yielding) in opposite ways. That is, a personality trait or characteristic that increases reception also decreases yielding. Consequently, attitude change (AC) is a function of a multiplicative relationship between reception (R) and yielding (Y): $AC = R \times Y$. This is an inverted-U-shaped function, with the greatest attitude change occurring at an intermediate level of a personality trait. For example, intelligence (IQ) is one important personality trait that should be related to persuasion. When intelligence is very low, reception is very low because the individual has a hard time understanding persuasive messages (e.g., Forrest Gump). Conversely, yielding is very high because such an individual tends to be quite gullible. On a scale from 0 (very low) to 10 (very high), then, $AC = R \times Y = 0 \times 10 = 0$. As intelligence increases, however, reception increases and yielding decreases. When intelligence is very high, reception is very high because the individual is smart enough to understand almost anything (e.g., Albert Einstein), but yielding is very low because only the most thorough and rigorous evidence will influence such an individual. Hence, $AC = R \times Y = 10 \times 0 = 0$. Therefore, at both extremes (very low or very high intelligence) little persuasion occurs, but for different reasons. At the very low end of the continuum, little persuasion occurs because of a reception problem. At the very high end, little persuasion occurs because of a yielding problem.

At intermediate levels of intelligence, however, reception is intermediate and yielding is intermediate. Hence, AC = R × Y = 5 × 5 = 25. That is, for recipients of average intelligence, reception is average and yielding is average. These individuals are most susceptible to persuasion because there is neither a reception problem nor a yielding problem. Thus, McGuire's theory of personality and persuasion provides a relatively simple explanation of the complex relationships between intelligence and persuasion. However, the theory goes far beyond intelligence: It suggests that the combinatory principle applies to *all* personality traits! That is, any given personality trait (and psychologists have studied hundreds of traits) influences reception and yielding in opposite ways. So far, this bold and powerful theoretical statement has been tested on two traits—intelligence (Eagly & Warren, 1976; Rhodes & Wood, 1992) and self-esteem (Nisbett & Gordon, 1967; Rhodes & Wood, 1992; Zellner, 1970)—and the results are generally positive. (See Fig. 6-6.) Many other personality traits (and combinations of traits) await empirical testing.

It should be emphasized that the combinatory principle is good news for advertisers. This principle suggests that people who are average, on any personality

FIGURE 6-6

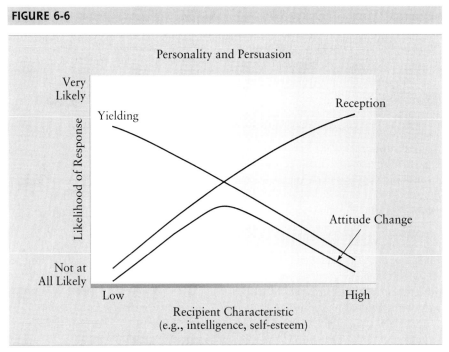

McGuire's theory of personality and persuasion suggests that the combinatory principle applies to all personality traits.

Source: Adapted from Petty & Cacioppo (1981).

SATURDAY NIGHT AD FEVER

Marketers love their recipients to be a captive audience. But consumers who receive telemarketing calls at dinnertime can always hang up, television watchers can change channels or head for the kitchen to fix a snack during a commercial, junk mail often finds its way to the trash barrel unopened. So how, short of tying them there, can marketers get consumers to stay in their seats and listen to or watch messages about products?

Go to the movies. Recently, marketers have discovered the potential power of commercials screened before the features at movie theaters. The idea itself isn't new; concessions have been flashing shots of happy snackers for years, and, of course, movie production companies offer viewers previews of upcoming films. But now, companies like General Motors Corp. and Sears are creating commercials for movie theaters. General Motors Corp. used movie theater ads to help launch its new Intrigue; Sears tried putting its Canyon River Blues (jeans) on the big screen. John H. Costello, senior vice president for marketing at Sears, says that results were so good that the company is thinking about running another movie ad. (Sears enjoyed a bonus—in some cases, the movie theaters that ran the jeans commercial were located in the same malls as the Sears stores themselves. So captive movie audiences had to walk only a few feet to pick up a pair of jeans.)

Marketers are excited not only by reaching people in their theater seats but also by the people themselves. Moviegoers are generally young, under 25. They can afford the $6 to $10 it costs to buy a movie ticket, and they are usually willing to spring for a bag of popcorn and a soda. In other words, they have some disposable income. They are at the movies to have fun, and once they've paid for a ticket, they are not likely to leave.

We might wonder how the consumers are receiving these new commercials. Will they grow annoyed and then increasingly bored with the idea? Will they stay home? When on-screen ads first appeared (actually, a decade ago), audiences booed them. But during this new surge, viewers seem more apt to shrug than hiss. One couple who went to a movie in Chicago gave a lukewarm response to a Levi's ad. "I'd seen it on TV, so I knew it was an ad," said the husband. "It's OK with me." He didn't say that he was going to rush straight to the Levi's store for a new pair of jeans.

Not everyone is wild about on-screen commercials. Movie studios are afraid that the ads will detract from the features that consumers have paid to see. Both Walt Disney Co. and Warner Brothers refuse to allow theaters to show commercials preceding their films and have even threatened to pull their films from theaters that don't abide by their rules. They have not said how they plan to enforce the rules, and so far, no one has shown data that demonstrate the ads are either detrimental or beneficial to movie ticket sales. So the fate of on-screen commercials remains to be seen. In the end, of course, consumers will decide.

Source: Ellen Neuborne and De'Ann Weimer, "Saturday Night at the Ads," *Business Week,* September 15, 1997, pp. 63–64.

dimension, are most susceptible to persuasion and influence. This is good news because most people, by definition, are average, and average people are easy to influence. Moreover, fairly average people are fairly easy to influence. Weird, atypical people are difficult to influence, but advertisers are less concerned about this group because it is composed of the tail ends of the distribution (personality traits are normally distributed across the population, with the bulk of the distribution occurring in and near the middle).

The **situational-weighting principle** suggests that reception and yielding are not always equally important. In some situations, reception is more important, whereas in other situations, yielding is more important. (See "Making the Decision: Saturday Night Ad Fever.") For example, for very simple persuasive messages, reception is easy and there will be little variation in reception. That is, people at all levels of a personality trait should find the message easy to understand. In this situation, yielding will be much more important than reception because reception problems should be rare. At the other extreme, it is theoretically possible to construct the ultimate persuasive message — a message that any reasonable person would find compelling. For such a message, reception is a problem because the message is likely to be difficult to comprehend, but yielding is not a problem because if people could understand the message, they would find it convincing. In this case, reception will be much more important than yielding because yielding problems should be uncommon. Of course, these are extreme examples, and most persuasive messages are neither perfectly understandable nor perfectly convincing. However, as reception difficulties decrease, yielding becomes more important. As yielding difficulties decrease, reception becomes more important.

◆ MEDIUM FACTORS

Which medium is most persuasive: audiovisual (television), audio (radio), or written (print media)? Naturally, the answer is that this factor interacts with other factors. (See "Making the Decision: Fruit Label Sticks to a New Medium.") Chaiken and Eagly (1976) conducted an experiment in which message complexity was manipulated by using short sentences and simple vocabulary in simple message conditions and long sentences and sophisticated vocabulary in complex message conditions. Message complexity (simple or complex) was crossed with type of medium (audiovisual, audio, or written) in a 2×3 factorial design. Greater persuasion occurred in simple than in complex message conditions when either the audiovisual or audio modality was used. Conversely, greater persuasion occurred in complex than in simple message conditions when the written modality was used. Moreover, when the message was complex, greater persuasion occurred with the written format because written information can be processed at one's own pace and repetitively, if desired. When the message was simple, persuasion was greatest when the message was presented via videotape, intermediate when the message was presented on audiotape, and low when the message was presented in written format. Hence, consistent with McGuire's situational-weighting principle, reception is more important for complex messages and yielding is more important for simple messages.

FRUIT LABEL STICKS TO A NEW MEDIUM

You've seen television commercials, read newspaper and magazine ads, sped by billboards, surfed through Internet ads. But have you ever plucked an apple from the bin at the supermarket only to find yet another commercial staring at you from the skin of the fruit? If The Fruit Label Co. has its way, you will have this experience soon.

Fruit Label teams up with advertisers to produce millions of mini-ads on stickers that go on individual pieces of fruit. One of its first attempts at a blockbuster was a tiny sticker featuring Jim Carrey to promote the video release of the Universal Pictures film *Liar, Liar,* which stars Carrey. Twelve million Granny Smith and Fuji apples received the stickers. "We are talking millions and millions of mini-billboards," says an enthusiastic Brian Fox, the ad executive who came up with the idea for fruit as the new advertising medium and established The Fruit Label Co. Fruit Label stuck more labels on apples, coinciding with the video release of *The Lost World: Jurassic Park.*

The idea isn't as crazy as it may sound. Television commercials are extremely expensive—they can cost nearly half a million dollars for 30 seconds during popular prime-time shows. Fruit-label advertising, on the other hand, costs less than one penny per piece of fruit. Consumers also tend to get bored or even annoyed at television commercials, turning them off or walking away. With a fruit-label ad, they need to pay attention—at least for the few seconds it takes to peel off the sticker before they wash the fruit. They may even laugh (and children love to peel stickers). "This is interactive because you have to peel it off," notes Fox. "People have to look at ten pieces of fruit before they pick one, so we get multiple impressions." And, since the message is simple—"Watch this movie" or "Buy this product"—it can be delivered easily via a little sticker.

Of course, Fruit Label doesn't plan to stop with stickers for one or two movies. Fox and his partner, Irv Weinhaus, are already negotiating with a number of companies to stick the right label with the right kind of fruit. For instance, an iced-tea maker could advertise on lemons, an ice cream maker could advertise on bananas, and so forth.

Source: Lisa Bannon, "Commercial Appeal: Jim Carrey Is Coming to a Fruit Bin Near You," *The Wall Street Journal,* August 21, 1997, p. B1.

Chaiken and Eagly (1983) conducted a follow-up experiment in which message modality (audiovisual, audio, written) and source attractiveness (likable or unlikable) were manipulated. They hypothesized that source attractiveness would be more important when broadcast media (audiovisual or audio) were used than when print media (written) were used. This is because the communicator should be more salient and influential when he or she is seen or heard. When broadcast media were used, subjects agreed with the communicator more when he was likable and disagreed with the communicator more when he was dislikable. When print media were used, however, communicator likability had no effect on persuasion. (See Fig. 6-7.) This is because people are more likely to focus on the message and less likely to focus on the communicator when the communicator is not salient.

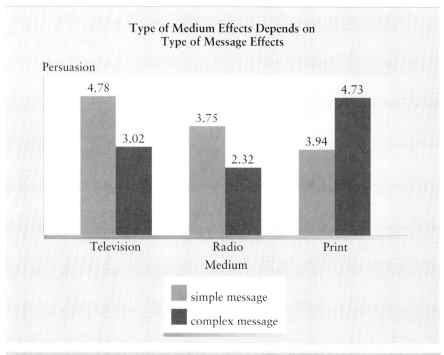

FIGURE 6-7

Medium factors interact with other factors, such as message complexity.

Source: Adapted from Chaiken & Eagly (1983). Television and radio are more effective for simple messages, but print media are more effective for complex messages.

CHAPTER SUMMARY ▪

The message-learning approach, or the "who says what to whom" approach, focuses on the effects of source factors (who), message factors (what), recipient factors (whom), and medium factors (television, radio, or print media) on reception (attention and comprehension), yielding (agreement), and persuasion (belief and attitude change). These factors interact with each other in complex ways. An interaction involves the effects of one factor dependent on the effects of other factors considered at the same time.

Source factors include important variables such as communicator credibility, trustworthiness, and attractiveness. Message factors include important variables such as message complexity, one-sided versus two-sided messages, rational versus emotional appeals, order of presentation effects (primacy and recency effects), and the sleeper effect (messages that produce greater persuasion over time). Recipient factors include all personality traits and characteristics, such as intelligence, self-esteem, need for cognition, gender, and so on. McGuire's theory of personality and persuasion suggests that persuasion is mediated by reception and yielding (the mediational principle), a personality variable is related to reception and yielding in opposite ways (the combinatory principle), and the relative importance of reception versus yielding depends on situational variables such as message complexity and message convincingness (the situational-weighting principle). Medium factors include mode of presentation, such as audiovisual (television), audio (radio), and written (print) formats.

One useful feature of the message-learning approach is that it helps us to identify important variables that should be considered in any "complete" theory of persuasion. It also provides a useful framework for thinking about persuasion in general and for thinking about interactions among source, message, recipient, and medium factors. The message-learning approach provides a useful first step toward understanding persuasion and provides a useful framework for thinking about other theories of persuasion. A topic as complex as persuasion can never be captured completely by a single theory. It is both necessary and desirable to have many theories of persuasion, where each theory focuses on a different dimension and reflects a different aspect of the complex processes involved in belief and attitude change.

KEY CONCEPTS ▪

- Persuasion
- Message-learning approach
- Exposure control
- Two-sided messages
- Factorial design
- One-sided message

- Rational appeals
- Emotional appeals
- Fear appeals
- Protection motivation theory
- Sleeper effect

- McGuire's theory of personality and persuasion
- Combinatory principle
- Situational-weighting principle

DISCUSSION QUESTIONS ▪

1. According to the message-learning approach, what are the four stages involved in the processing of persuasive communication?
2. If you were creating a public service announcement for television to discourage people from smoking, which of the following people would you choose as a source to deliver the announcement? Why?
   a. Brad Pitt
   b. C. Everett Koop
   c. Nancy Reagan
3. When you watch local or national news on television, which programs and broadcasters do you find the most credible? Why?
4. Should an automobile dealer use a one-sided or two-sided message? Why?
5. As a marketer, how might you use an emotional appeal to persuade consumers to buy your brand of computer?
6. Volvo ads have historically used fear appeals—reenactments of car crashes—to illustrate how safe its cars are compared with other cars. Do you think this use of the fear appeal is effective? Why or why not?
7. Would a fear appeal used in advertising for earthquake insurance be more effective in New England or southern California? Why?
8. What is the sleeper effect? When is it most likely to occur?
9. Name and describe briefly the three key principles underlying McGuire's Theory of Personality and Persuasion.
10. What type of medium would you use to advertise a cellular phone? Why?

Cognitive Approaches to Persuasion

◆ Theories of Comparative Judgment
　　Adaptation Level Theory
　　Social Judgment Theory
　　Perspective Theory
　　Influencing Consumers' Reference Points
◆ Attribution Theories
　　Self-Perception Theory
　　Kelley's Attribution Theory: 1. Covariation Principles
　　Kelley's Attribution Theory: 2. Causal Schemata

Two entrepreneurs—one an artsy type and another a computer type—want to reach software-news readers everywhere. Doug Green, a business journalist and aspiring novelist, and Richard Anders, a founding member of the Massachusetts Interactive Media Council and author of CD-ROM guidebooks, have teamed up to form Software Publications Inc. Both Green and Anders have already founded and sold other successful businesses. Now they want to combine the old world of publishing with the new world of the Internet. Software Publications Inc. publishes three monthly controlled-circulation papers—in New York, Chicago, and Boston—that cover the local software industry and feature online advertising, including online job ads.

Of course, other publications cover the software industry. But Green and Anders need to persuade two camps of consumers—advertisers and readers—that their software-news publications are the best. To do that, they need to set their publications apart from competing publications so that when advertisers and potential subscribers compare different publications, Software Publications comes out on top. One way to do that is to offer expanded electronic job ads. When users access the paper's Chicago Web site (the Boston and New York Web sites are under construction), not only do they get job ads in the computer industry, they also have access to synopses of the companies themselves that are advertising job openings. The synopses include information on the number of employees in a given firm, the type of software the company develops, and even newspaper articles that have been written about the company. Thus, Software Publications helps job hunters do their homework about the companies at which they may be applying for jobs. In addition, at the Chicago site, users can find directories of intellectual property attorneys and computer-oriented recruiting firms. No other software-news publication does this.

In fact, Michael Oliveri, the current publisher of *Mass. High Tech,* the first publication that Green founded and later sold, admits, "I wouldn't see [Green] as any more of a competitor to *Mass. High Tech* than any other publication, and any more than the *Boston Business Journal* is. I see him as focusing on a small component of what we focus on."

Josh Bernoff, a senior analyst for the Forrester Research Group, observes, "[Richard Anders] is pretty wired into what's going on in the local community. So I don't think you're going to see the same old rehashed press releases that are typical of this type of organization."

As you read this chapter, observe how important it is for marketers to find ways to set their products and services apart from those of competitors. They can do this by understanding and influencing the way consumers think about, compare, and judge products and services.

Source: Tom Duffy, "Setting Their Sites on a Software-News Empire," *The Boston Globe,* October 15, 1997, pp. E1, E4.

◆ INTRODUCTION

When consumers say that a particular product is good or bad, large or small, hot or cold, or expensive or inexpensive, they do so with some comparison product in mind. Thus, marketers like Doug Green and Richard Anders of Software Publications Inc. need to find ways to make consumers compare their products favorably. Most products are good or bad in a relative sense. That is, a product seems good when it is compared with a product that is not as good. Similarly, a product seems bad when it is compared with a product that is not as bad. Judgment is relative: How good or how bad a product seems depends on one's point of view or point of comparison. For example, a Ford Taurus seems good when it is compared with a Yugo. However, a Ford Taurus seems bad when it is compared with a BMW. Absolute judgments (e.g., judgments of a product as good or bad regardless of the point of comparison) are rare. Of course, the **principle of relative judgment** has important implications for persuasion: If you want consumers to believe your product is of high quality, you have to get them to compare your product with one that is lower in quality.

Another important cognitive principle is involved in **attributional judgments,** or causal inferences (e.g., assumptions about why someone behaved as he or she did). For example, when Shaquille O'Neil says in his television commercial that Pepsi is good, the effectiveness of the commercial depends on consumers' assumptions about why Shaq endorsed Pepsi. Greater persuasion should occur if consumers assume he endorsed Pepsi because he likes the product than if consumers assume he endorsed Pepsi simply because he was paid millions to do so. Causal attributions, or "why" judgments, have an important influence on the effectiveness of an advertisement. Consequently, it is important to understand the key factors that influence causal attributions.

◆ THEORIES OF COMPARATIVE JUDGMENT

The key theories of relative (comparative) judgments are adaptation level theory, social judgment theory, and perspective theory. The key theories of attributional judgments are self-perception theory, Kelley's covariation principles, and Kelley's causal schemata. Both types of judgments are cognitive in the sense that thinking and reasoning processes are involved. Relative judgments involve comparative thinking and reasoning. Attributional judgments involve causal reasoning and detective work to answer "why" questions (why does the advertising spokesperson claim to like the advertised product?).

ADAPTATION LEVEL THEORY

According to **adaptation level theory,** the same product can seem either good or bad depending on what it is compared with. The **point of comparison** is also known as a *reference point, anchor,* or *standard of comparison.* What determines one's point of comparison? One determinant is the context or background in which an object is judged. When a target object is judged in the context of several extremely attractive stimuli, the target object seems less attractive. When a target object is judged in the context of several extremely unattractive stimuli, the target object seems more attractive. In both cases, judgments of the target object shift away from the judgment context. (See Fig. 7-1.) This type of context effect is known as the **contrast effect** because judgments of the target object contrast or shift away from the reference point.

Contrast Effect

This phenomenon is important because people tend to underestimate the impact of contextual or background factors on judgment (see Chapter 2). People do not spend a lot of time thinking about the context or background in which a product is judged. Although people tend to be somewhat unaware of the influence of contextual variables, these variables exert a surprisingly powerful influence on judgment. Contextual variables influence what we buy, why we buy, and how satisfied we are with what we buy.

A clever salesperson can trick us into spending more than we initially intended to spend. In many situations, people are unwilling to buy an expensive accessory or option. However, a salesperson can make an expensive accessory or option seem less expensive by influencing our point of reference. For example, after buying a $300 business suit, a $30 tie seems cheap. That is, in the context of a $300 expenditure, an additional $30 expenditure seems trivial. Hence, a clever salesperson will try to sell an expensive item first, and then try to sell several less expensive add-ons. Normally, we may be very reluctant to spend $30 on a tie or a fashion accessory, but after making a major purchase, an additional small purchase seems inconsequential. Similarly, after agreeing to spend $20,000 on a new automobile, spending an additional $1,000 on a new car stereo system seems like a very small expenditure. So, the order in which the items are presented is crucial—salespeople try to sell the high-ticket item first and then suggest accessories, options, and add-ons.

The context or background in which an object is judged can influence judgments or ratings of virtually any object. For example, in the search for a perfect 10, Kenrick and Gutierres (1980) asked male college students to rate the attractiveness of a female

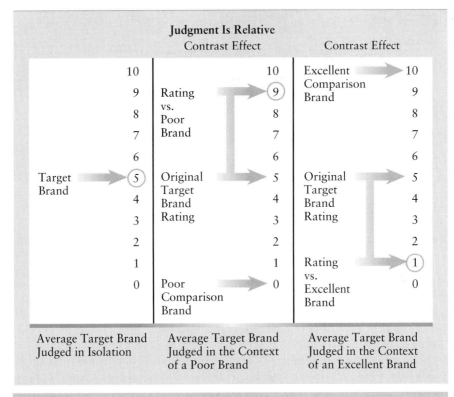

FIGURE 7-1

One way to change judgments is to change the reference point. Judgments of a target product shift away from extreme reference points.

college student shown in a photograph. Subjects rated the attractiveness of the target on a scale from 0 to 10. However, before they rated the female student, the male subjects watched a one-hour videotaped television show. Half the subjects were randomly assigned to the "Charlie's Angels" condition, where they watched an episode of "Charlie's Angels," a series featuring three very attractive actresses. The remaining subjects participated in a control condition in which they watched a boring nature documentary. A contrast effect was found: The target was rated as much less attractive in the "Charlie's Angels" condition than in the control condition. The mass media provides a context or background that influences how we rate persons, products, and virtually any object.

How satisfied are you with life in general? How you answer this question depends on what contextual stimuli come to mind while answering the question. In a fascinating but disturbing study, Brickman, Coates, and Janoff-Bulman (1978) asked subjects to rate the pleasantness of several typical, ordinary, everyday life experiences, such as watching television, eating breakfast, listening to a funny joke, and so on. Before rating these events, half the subjects happened to win over $50,000 in a state lottery, and the remaining subjects (nonwinners) served as control subjects. A contrast effect was observed: Ordinary, everyday life events seemed much less pleasant after winning the

If one of these tickets is a big winner, will the owner's life be less pleasant?

Source: © Mary Boucher.

lottery. This is because winning the lottery changes our perceptions of what is typical or normal, and these perceptions provide a context or background for judging target events. Brickman et al. (1978) concluded that people are running on a hedonic treadmill: The more we get, the more we want, and the process never stops. Everything we experience influences our point of view or reference point for judgment. Consequently, we can never truly be satisfied: We just want more.

Adaptation Level

You can probably think of many more examples of contrast effects. Contrast effects are very common in everyday life. Now, however, we need to turn to a more formal explanation of why we experience contrast effects. According to adaptation level theory (Helson, 1959), all objects can be arranged in a meaningful order. Objects differ on many dimensions—such as bad/good, small/large, cold/hot, and so on, to list a few—and all objects can be rank ordered from very bad to very good, very small to very large, very cold to very hot, and so on. Moreover, all dimensions of judgment have a psychological neutral point, and this point is called the adaptation level (hence, adaptation level theory). The **adaptation level** is a weighted geometric average* of all stimuli a person takes into account while making a judgment. In other words, it is the average point, or neutral point. Hence, when a consumer thinks about expensive stimuli (such as expensive suits or automobiles), his or her adaptation level, or neutral point, goes up. When an accessory or add-on is compared with this temporarily elevated neutral point, it seems much less expensive than it would seem otherwise. Over time, however, the neutral point shifts back down to its baseline, or typical, position, and the consumer may later wonder what possessed him or her to pay so much for an unnecessary accessory or add-on.

---

* The most commonly used average or mean is the simple arithmetic mean:

$$M = \sum \frac{x_i}{N}$$

where each scale value x is divided by N, or the number of xs, and summed over the individual observations i.

The geometric mean:

$$M_G = (x_1 x_2 \ldots x_N)^{1/N}$$

is the product of all the x_i values with the Nth root taken. The geometric mean is less influenced by extreme x_i values, relative to the simple arithmetic mean.

Similarly, seeing attractive actresses or actors on television raises one's adaptation level for an average or normal level of attractiveness, and most people seem less attractive when compared with this unusually high standard. Eventually, however, the adaptation level shifts back to its typical position, and the contrast effect goes away. After winning the lottery, people adapt to, or become accustomed to, wealth and luxury, and ordinary events that used to seem pleasurable seem much less pleasurable. Conversely, debilitating accidents and illnesses lower one's adaptation level, making previously ordinary events seem much less ordinary. We constantly adapt to what we experience, and our adaptation level exerts a powerful influence on how we judge objects and events.

SOCIAL JUDGMENT THEORY

The contrast effect is only one type of context effect. Unfortunately, adaptation level theory can explain only the contrast effect—a different theory is needed to explain other types of context effects. You should already be familiar with another important type of context effect: the Herr (1989) study on priming price (discussed in Chapter 3), which examined two different context effects—the contrast effect and the assimilation effect. A contrast effect is a shift in judgment *away from* a reference point, whereas an **assimilation effect** is a shift in judgment *toward* a reference point. (See "Taking Issue: Public Schools—and Retailers—Take the Uniform Approach.") For example, in the Herr (1989) experiment, the inferred price of an unfamiliar automobile shifted away from the primed reference price when the two prices seemed very different (contrast) but shifted toward the primed reference price when the two prices seemed very similar (assimilation). Hence, contrast and assimilation effects reduce "shades of gray" and result in exaggerated judgments—different stimuli seem even more different, and similar stimuli seem even more similar than they really are.

Contrast and Assimilation Effects

Social judgment theory explains contrast and assimilation effects by suggesting that the adaptation level is not the only type of reference point people use (Sherif, Sherif, & Nebergall, 1965; Sherif & Hovland, 1961). In some cases, one's own attitude is used as a reference point or filter through which target objects and issues are perceived and judged. Of course, one's own attitude will be used as a reference point only when a previously formed attitude exists and is stored in memory and when the attitude is accessible (easily retrievable from memory) and important to the individual (Fazio, 1986, 1989, 1990). Political attitudes, for example, are often accessible and important to an individual. In a classic study of contrast and assimilation effects in judgments of presidential candidates in the 1968 election, Granberg and Brent (1974) asked Hubert Humphrey supporters (i.e., voters who had strong and favorable attitudes toward Humphrey) to judge the candidates' positions toward the Vietnam War, the most important issue of the election. Granberg and Brent (1974) found that subjects' own attitudes toward the Vietnam War had a powerful influence on their judgments of the candidates. (See Fig. 7-2.) Humphrey supporters who were personally against the war perceived George Wallace to be very prowar. However, Humphrey supporters who were prowar perceived Wallace to be much less prowar. In other words, contrast effects were found: Judgments of Wallace's position shifted away from the subject's own position. Although contrast effects were found in judgments of Wallace's position,

PUBLIC SCHOOLS — AND RETAILERS — TAKE THE UNIFORM APPROACH

In many communities around the United States, back-to-school shopping no longer involves the purchase of baggy chinos and high-top sneakers. Flared jeans, miniskirts, y-necklaces, and crop tops aren't on the shopping list, either. True, these items are very much in style, and kids will be wearing plenty of them on weekends. But they won't be wearing them to school; instead, they will be wearing uniforms specified by their school districts. Parents and students still shop, but they shop for certain items—skirts, blouses, sweaters, tailored khakis, and the like—designated by the schools.

Once considered the domain of private and parochial schools, uniforms are now appearing, in greater and greater numbers, in public schools. Adults and students have varying attitudes about the requirement. Surprisingly, many students like the idea. "It makes getting dressed in the morning a lot easier," explains Zalencia Dorrough, an 11-year-old student in Dallas. "It also looks a lot more sophisticated and a lot cooler than normal clothes." But some students aren't happy. "Now we have to wear the same old stuff that everybody else is wearing," complains 10-year-old Jessica Rios, also of Dallas. But Jessica—and other students like her—plan to jazz up their uniforms with tights and "chunky" shoes. In a sense, they are justifying their own purchasing behavior (even though they have no control over it) by personalizing the uniform.

Teachers and administrators are hoping that uniform requirements will cut down on competition among youngsters when it comes to clothing, blurring class distinctions and, in extreme cases, bringing down the number of muggings and robberies related to clothing and jewelry. Adult attitudes about uniforms may have even more specific social and political roots—the idea was endorsed by President Clinton during a State of the Union address, so Democrats or other Clinton supporters may also support the uniform idea, while Republicans and other Clinton critics may chafe against it.

Retailers who are involved in the new uniform boom love it. Now that school districts in at least 20 states have school uniform requirements, stores and catalog merchants are seizing the opportunity in a variety of ways. JCPenney, Sears, Macy's, Target Stores, Kids 'R' Us, and even Wal-Mart have gotten into the uniform act. JCPenney sells school uniforms both in its stores and a new catalog called "Class Favorites." "It's really been a nice complement to our back-to-school sales," observes Carol Brady, a Penney merchandise manager. After conducting research on the market possibilities, Lands' End, the clothing catalog giant in Wisconsin, decided to take the leap; 8 percent of all public schools already require uniforms, and another 15 percent are likely to follow. Lands' End has launched a school uniform grouping of clothes that includes its tailored chinos, oxford shirts, navy blazers, and the like. "When almost one in four students could be wearing uniforms, that's big business," notes Michael Grasee, director of school uniforms at Lands' End.

Consumers (students and their parents) are likely to experience either a contrast effect or an assimilation effect in their attitudes toward uniforms; some have already shifted either toward or away from the idea. While they may not have a choice in whether to purchase uniforms, students can express their attitudes in the way they wear the clothes, just as the two young students from Dallas plan to. Either way, uniforms represent a new boom in school clothing—and money in the bank for retailers.

Source: Stephanie Anderson Forest, "Dressed to Drill," *Business Week,* September 8, 1997, p. 40.

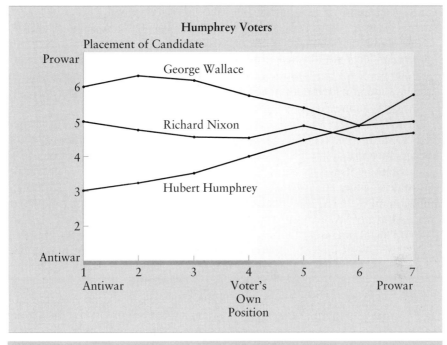

FIGURE 7-2

Assimilation and contrast in Humphrey voters' perceptions of Hubert Humphrey and George Wallace in the 1968 election.

Source: Adapted from D. Granberg and E. E. Brent (1974). Dove-hawk placements in the 1968 election: Application of social judgment and balance theories. *Journal of Personality and Social Psychology, 29,* 687–695. Copyright 1974 by the American Psychological Association. Reprinted with permission.

assimilation effects were found in judgments of Humphrey's position: Antiwar Humphrey supporters perceived Humphrey as antiwar, whereas prowar Humphrey supporters perceived Humphrey as much less antiwar. Subjects who supported Humphrey perceived Wallace's views as very different from their own (and also quite unacceptable), and they perceived Humphrey's views as very similar to their own. Moreover, although large shifts in judgment were found for Wallace and Humphrey, no shifts in judgment were found for Richard Nixon, because Nixon's speeches were much less ambiguous compared with Wallace's and Humphrey's. As ambiguity decreases, there is less room for shifts in judgment to occur (Herr, 1986, 1989; Herr, Sherman, & Fazio, 1983).

Social Judgment Theory and Persuasion

To be useful as a theory of persuasion, however, social judgment theory must specify how different a target of judgment has to be from the reference point to result in contrast and how similar a target of judgment has to be to the reference point to result in assimilation. Social judgment theory achieves this through the **method of ordered alternatives.** This method involves constructing a series of statements ranging from very positive to very negative. For example, a very positive, or pro, position might be that all packages (plastic, glass, or cardboard) should be recycled. A very negative, or anti, position might be that nothing should be recycled. Moreover, a series of statements between these two extremes should be constructed. Subjects are then asked to circle statements they find acceptable. These statements form the **latitude of acceptance.** Subjects are also asked to check the statements they find unacceptable. These statements form the **latitude of rejection.** The remaining unmarked statements form the **latitude of noncommitment** (subjects have no opinion one way or the other).

Social judgment theory predicts an inverted-U-shaped relation between persuasion and the extent to which the position advocated in a persuasive communication differs from the recipient's initial position (see Fig. 7-3). Statements within the latitude of acceptance are assimilated, resulting in little change from the initial attitudinal position. Statements within the latitude of rejection are contrasted, again, resulting in little attitude change. The greatest attitude change occurs in the middle, in the latitude of noncommitment. Arguments in this region are different from recipients' current attitudes but not so different that they are automatically rejected (Bochner & Insko, 1966). Social judgment theory also predicts that as **involvement**—the perceived relevance or importance of an issue—increases, the latitude of acceptance decreases and the latitude of rejection increases. Furthermore, as source credibility decreases, the latitude of acceptance decreases and the latitude of rejection increases (Bochner & Insko, 1966). Hence, the range of positions that are considered acceptable or unacceptable varies depending on involvement and source credibility. As the latitude of rejection increases, people become more closed-minded and persuasion becomes more difficult.

FIGURE 7-3

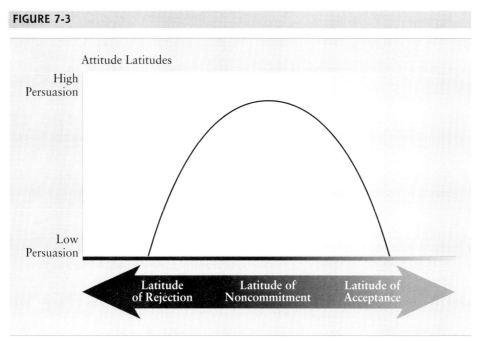

Social judgment theory predicts an inverted-U-shaped relation between message extremity and persuasion with the greatest level of persuasion occurring in the latitude of noncommitment.

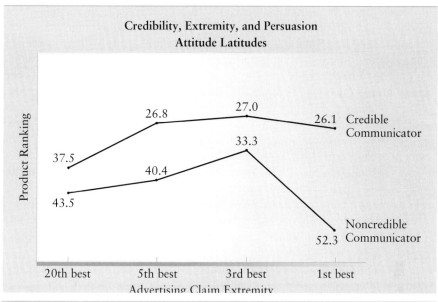

Credibility, Extremity, and Persuasion
Attitude Latitudes

FIGURE 7-4

Goldberg and Hartwick (1990) found an inverted-U-shaped relation between advertising claim extremity and persuasion.

Source: Adapted from Goldberg & Hartwick (1990).

Consistent with the implications of social judgment theory, Goldberg and Hartwick (1990) found an inverted-U-shaped relation between advertising claim extremity and persuasion. (See Fig. 7-4.) Extremity was manipulated by stating that the advertised product was either the 20th best, 5th best, 3rd best, or 1st best out of 100 products tested. Little persuasion occurred at the extremes (20th best or 1st best), and the greatest level of persuasion occurred in the middle (5th or 3rd best). Moreover, this pattern was more pronounced when the advertiser had low credibility (a relatively unsuccessful new firm) than when the advertiser had high credibility (a successful, experienced firm). This is because the "first best" claim was in the latitude of rejection for the low- but not the high-credibility firm. Claiming that the product is the best is effective only when such a claim is made by a reputable firm.

PERSPECTIVE THEORY

According to **perspective theory,** another reference point that has been shown to influence attitudinal judgments of objects and issues is one's interpretation of the endpoints of a rating scale. Consumers are often asked to evaluate products on a rating scale ranging from 0 (very bad) to 10 (very good). For example, when rating cars, some people may assume that a 0 refers to "below-average" cars like the Ford Escort. Others may assume that a 0 refers to "extremely bad" cars like the Yugo. Similarly, some consumers may assume that a 10 refers to "above-average" cars like the Cadillac. Others may assume that a 10 refers to "extremely good" cars like the Rolls-Royce. The manner in which consumers interpret the endpoints of a rating scale has an important influence on their ratings. Compared with a Ford Escort, an average car seems fairly good (an assimilation effect); compared with a Yugo, an average car seems very good (a contrast effect). Similarly, compared with a Cadillac, an average car seems fairly bad (an assimilation effect); compared with a Rolls-Royce, an average car seems very bad (a contrast effect). Scale interpretation effects are also referred to as **response language effects** (Wyer, 1974; Wyer & Carlston, 1979; Wyer & Srull, 1989) or **measurement effects** (Feldman & Lynch, 1988; Schumann & Presser, 1981). These effects refer to a shift in judgment due to the way people interpret rating (measurement) scales.

Perspective theory suggests that a shift in judgment may be due to a change in the way people interpret a judgment scale or to a change in the judgment itself (Ostrom & Upshaw, 1968; Upshaw, 1978). The former type of change is a measurement effect that occurs only when people use rating scales in experiments and surveys. The latter type of change is a shift in the cognitive representation of the underlying judgment that is stored in memory. This is an important distinction because only the latter type of change is likely to influence actual purchase decisions (Chakravarti & Lynch, 1983; Lynch, Chakravarti, & Mitra, 1991).

Mathematically, the relations among ratings, interpretations of scale endpoints, and cognitive representations of judgments can be expressed as follows:

$$R = f\left(\frac{J - L}{U - L}\right)$$

where R refers to a rating on a scale, J refers to the "true" underlying judgment, U refers to the interpretation of the upper endpoint, and L refers to the interpretation of the lower endpoint (Ostrom & Upshaw, 1968). This equation suggests that ratings are influenced by three factors: the underlying judgment, the interpretation of the upper endpoint, and the interpretation of the lower endpoint. Changes in any one or combination of these three factors result in changes in ratings. Hence, a shift in ratings does not always imply a shift in the cognitive representation of an underlying judgment.

As mentioned at the beginning of the section on perspective theory, contrast effects occur when an endpoint is interpreted more extremely. On a rating scale from 0 to 10, an average car is rated a 5, and the mental image also corresponds to a 5. Even if the mental representation of this average car does not change, the rating will shift to a higher scale value if the lower endpoint is interpreted more extremely (e.g., Yugo). Again, even if the cognitive representation does not change, the rating will shift to a lower scale value if the higher endpoint is interpreted more extremely (e.g., Rolls-Royce). These are both contrast effects because the ratings shift away from the more

Where do you rate this Lincoln Town Car on a scale of 0 to 10?
Source: © Dick Morton.

extreme endpoint. Assimilation effects occur if the number of scale points is increased, even if the cognitive representation and the interpretation of the upper and lower endpoints do not change. For example, increasing the scale from 0 through 10 to 0 through 15 may result in a rating shift from 5 to 10. This is because the rating shifts toward the nearest endpoint when the scale range increases, but the interpretation of the endpoints remains the same.

Lynch et al. (1991) developed a useful test for determining whether shifts in ratings stem from response language effects or from changes in underlying judgments. They asked subjects to rate each brand in a set of eight target brands and each brand in a set of eight context brands. The target brands were typical, average subcompact cars described in terms of gas mileage, warranties, acceleration, and price. The context brands were better on gas mileage, much better on gas mileage, or worse in terms of price. Contrast effects were found: The target brands were rated as less desirable when the context brands were superior in terms of gas mileage or more desirable when the context brands were inferior in terms of price. Although individual ratings shifted as a function of context, overall preferences remained the same. That is, the eight target brands were ranked from 1 (best) to 8 (worst) on the basis of the ratings, and correlations between ranks and gas mileage and between ranks and price were computed. The rank-order correlations did not differ as a function of the context manipulations, suggesting that the observed contrast effects resulted from changes in the way subjects expressed their judgments of the individual products, rather than from changes in their underlying judgments. Moreover, in a follow-up study, subjects knowledgeable about cars exhibited measurement-induced contrast effects, whereas unknowledgeable subjects exhibited equally powerful contrast effects, reflecting true attitude change (i.e., shifts in underlying judgments).

INFLUENCING CONSUMERS' REFERENCE POINTS

Judgments are influenced by reference points, but many different reference points are available to consumers. (See Fig. 7-5.) Sometimes, the adaptation level serves as the reference point, and products are judged in relation to this particular point of reference (adaptation level theory). At other times, one's own attitude serves as the reference point, and the attitude is used as a standard of comparison (social judgment

FIGURE 7-5

Theories of Relative Judgment

Theory	Reference Point	Phenomena Explained
Adaptation Level Theory	Adaptation level	Contrast effect
Social Judgment Theory	One's own attitude	Contrast effect Assimilation effect
Perspective Theory	Scale end points	Contrast effect Assimilation effect

Judgments are influenced by many different reference points.

theory). A scale endpoint may also serve as a reference point or anchor (perspective theory). Both adaptation level theory and social judgment theory suggest that shifts in ratings correspond to shifts in cognitive representations of judgments. However, perspective theory suggests that shifts in ratings may or may not correspond to shifts in cognitive representations. Ratings are influenced by cognitive representations and by the way scale endpoints are interpreted.

Which Reference Point Is Used?

What determines which reference point people use in a particular situation? **Norm theory** suggests that salient or accessible stimuli or categories (i.e., sets of stimuli) are recruited to serve as a norm or reference point (Kahneman & Miller, 1986). As discussed in Chapter 2, salient stimuli are stimuli that "stick out" and draw attention because they differ from other stimuli present in a particular context. Hence, in some circumstances, a single stimulus may be used as a reference point for judging a target. For example, comparative advertising draws attention to two brands: the advertised brand and a competitor's brand. The advertised brand seems high in quality if the competitor's brand is similar but inferior (a contrast effect). In this case, a single salient brand is used as the reference point. However, in other circumstances, a range of brands may be averaged to form a neutral point or adaptation level. Brands that are accessible from memory because of recent activation (the brand was encountered or thought about recently), frequent activation (the brand was encountered or thought about repeatedly), or elaborative processing (effortful and meaningful thinking about the brand) have a powerful influence on the adaptation level. Similarly, accessible attitudes are likely to serve as reference points for judgment, whereas inaccessible attitudes are not. Finally, scale endpoints are likely to serve as important reference points when interpretations of the endpoints change during the course of a study but not when interpretations remain the same.

In an interesting study on the influence of accessible reference points on the interpretation of ambiguous advertisements, subjects examined ads for two different personal computers (Yi, 1990). The target ad stated that the advertised brand had a large number of features. Having a large number of features can be either good or bad, depending on whether one is more concerned about versatility or ease of use. Before reading the target ad, subjects viewed a context ad that manipulated the accessibility of "versatility" or "ease of use." The versatility ad emphasized the importance of being able to perform many different functions ("I didn't know it could do that"), whereas the user-friendly ad highlighted the importance of having a computer that is very easy to use (children were shown using this brand). As predicted, more favorable attitudes toward the target brand were formed after viewing an ad for a versatile brand than after viewing an ad for a user-friendly brand. Hence, judgments of the target brand were assimilated toward either the versatile product reference point or the user-friendly product reference point.

The country in which a product is manufactured (country of origin) can also serve as an important reference point. Many American consumers have stereotypes about products produced in different countries. For example, many assume that the best electronic products (e.g., PCs, TVs, VCRs) are made in Japan and Germany, whereas the Philippines and Mexico have a poor reputation in the electronic products category. Note that, in this case, the reference point is a category, or group of products, rather than a single product. Research shows that country of origin is used as a reference point when this information is learned some time before learning additional details about the product (Hong & Wyer, 1990). Assimilation effects were found: Ratings of individual attributes and overall judgments shifted toward the reference point. That is, more favorable judgments were formed when subjects were told the product was made in Japan or Germany than when subjects were told the product was made in the Philippines or Mexico. However, when country of origin was presented at the same time as the attribute information (rather than one day before), country of origin did not serve as a reference point. Instead, country of origin influenced judgments by encouraging greater scrutiny and thinking about the product (Hong & Wyer, 1989, 1990).

In comparative advertising, a product seems better when it is compared with an inferior brand. The same product seems worse when it is compared with a superior brand. However, comparative advertising has multiple effects, and, in some instances, reference point effects may be overshadowed by other effects. For example, comparative advertising increases the perceived similarity of two brands (Johnson, 1986; Pechmann & Ratneshwar, 1991; Pechmann & Stewart, 1990, 1991). Consequently, comparative advertising can help a weak brand that is compared with a strong brand by making the weak brand seem similar to but less expensive than (as is usually the case) the strong brand. Comparative advertising can also hurt a strong brand by providing free advertising for a weak comparison brand.

◆ ATTRIBUTION THEORIES

In addition to comparisons, consumers may also be affected by other types of cognitions, such as attributions, or assumptions about the causes of a particular behavior. Attribution theories look at questions of why something happens. The attribution theories examined here are self-perception theory, Kelley's covariation principles, and Kelley's causal schemata.

SELF-PERCEPTION THEORY

Beliefs and attitudes are not always strong and accessible from memory. According to **self-perception theory,** when beliefs and attitudes are relatively inaccessible, people form inferences about their beliefs and attitudes on the basis of their behavior and the context in which the behavior occurs (Bem, 1965, 1972). That is, self-perceptions of our own behavior provide insights about our beliefs and attitudes, the same insights available to other people observing our behavior. For example, when compact-disc players were first introduced to the marketplace, we might have been unsure about which brand to buy and may have selected one brand fairly haphazardly. Later, we may infer we bought the brand because we liked it. Anytime we purchase a product or service on the basis of little or no information, we might later assume we bought it because we liked it. In a way, this is backwards thinking—usually, we like a product, so we buy it. However, for unfamiliar products (e.g., totally new products, products we know little about) and services (e.g., our first doctor, lawyer, accountant), we may first make a purchase and later infer liking it (Tybout & Scott, 1983).

The Overjustification Effect

Marketers want consumers to believe that they bought a product because it is a high-quality product. However, when there are too many reasons (or justifications) for buying a product, one reason (e.g., quality) seems weak. For example, if a consumer buys a product for just one reason—quality—the consumer realizes that quality drove the decision. However, if a consumer buys a product for many reasons—quality, low price, and convenience—the role of quality becomes less clear—maybe price was more important, or maybe convenience was more important. This is known as the **overjustification effect** (Lepper, Greene, & Nisbett, 1973). Many reasons or justifications undermine or weaken the perceived significance of a particular cause.

Implications for Price Promotion

Marketers often use coupons, prizes, and other promotions to reward consumers for buying their products. However, the overjustification effect suggests that there are hidden costs to rewards: A price reduction provides another reason for buying a product besides quality, and consequently, a price reduction can weaken the influence of product quality (Dodson, Tybout, & Sternthal, 1978; Scott & Yalch, 1980). (See "Making the Decision: Best Buys Aren't Always Best.") For example, a field study conducted with the cooperation of Chicago-area grocery stores showed, not surprisingly, that coupons (from magazines, newspapers, inserts, direct mail, etc.) and cents-off deals (temporary

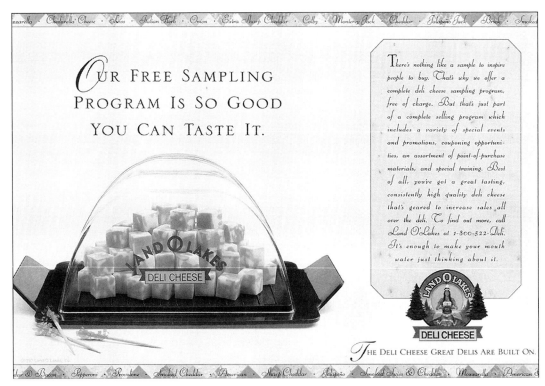

Trying free samples can alter consumers' self-perceptions and attitudes.
Source: © 1993 Land O'Lakes Inc.

MAKING THE DECISION

BEST BUYS AREN'T ALWAYS BEST

Setting low prices is a good way to get consumers to buy products, isn't it? Not necessarily. Sometimes, low prices can backfire, damaging an entire industry. That is what happened in the music world when Jeff Abrams, a former executive at the huge electronics chain Best Buy, decided the best way to get customers into his stores was to offer the best price on CDs. While other retailers were charging $14 to $17 for CDs, Best Buy began offering them at $9.98 for some of the hot new releases and a dollar or two more for other titles. Abrams's idea was to entice customers into Best Buy stores with low CD prices, then direct them to other low-priced electronics items, such as VCRs and stereos. Best Buy stores stocked their discount-CD sections with 60,000 titles at prices no one else could beat. Abrams thought that by doing this he would create customer loyalty. "We decided early on that the purpose of music was to create a customer for life," he recalls.

Things didn't work out that way. Instead, a price war ensued, nearly draining the record business of life. "The whole nature of the business changed overnight," recalls Jerry Goldress, CEO of the California Wherehouse Entertainment chain. Circuit City was the only discounter that could match Best Buy's prices. In the meantime, traditional retailers, who couldn't keep up, began to file for bankruptcy. When Wherehouse Entertainment, which oper-

ated 345 stores, went under, the record labels finally began to take notice, with PolyGram taking the first steps toward correction by instituting its MAP (minimum advertised price) policy. Since music retailers can return unsold CDs and cassettes to producers, and since so many retailers filed for bankruptcy owing record companies money, the music industry itself began to falter financially. When Musicland, the nation's largest music retailer, began to falter, the record labels bolstered it by extending credit deadlines.

At Best Buy, for the most part consumers bought the discount CDs and went home without purchasing the big-ticket electronics items. The company's revenues grew, but margins diminished and net earnings dropped from $58 million in one year to $1.7 million two years later. Jeff Abrams left the company to form a retail consultancy, and Best Buy decided to cut back on its CD inventory, from 60,000 titles per store to about 40,000. "There was a portion of our inventory that was not productive enough to warrant continued stocking of it," comments Gary Arnold, current head of Best Buy's music division.

So price discounts didn't create loyal customers. Instead, they created havoc in an entire industry. It may take a while for music producers and retailers to recover. Meanwhile, consumers will pocket the change.

Source: Tim Carvell, "These Prices Really Are Insane," *Fortune,* August 4, 1997, pp. 109–116.

price deals presented on a product package) increase brand switching (Dodson et al., 1978). (See Fig. 7-6.) That is, consumers who bought Brand A the last time they went shopping switched to Brand B when a price promotion was offered for Brand B. Hence, price promotions helped in the short run. Surprisingly, however, the researchers found that price promotions hurt in the long run. When consumers bought Brand A at the regular price on one purchase occasion, then bought Brand A again when given a price deal on the next purchase occasion, they switched to a different brand when the price deal was no longer available for Brand A on the following purchase occasion.

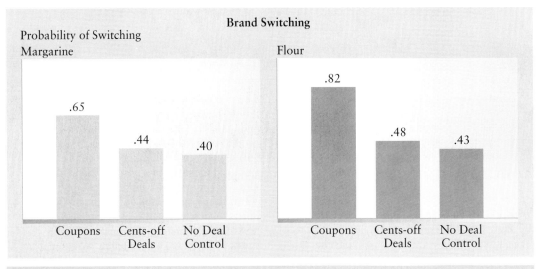

FIGURE 7-6

Price promotion increases brand switching.

This pattern was found for both frequently (margarine) and infrequently (flour) purchased goods, suggesting that, in the long run, price promotions reduce brand loyalty. (See Fig. 7-7.)

KELLEY'S ATTRIBUTION THEORY: 1. COVARIATION PRINCIPLES

The most influential and widely used theory of how people attribute causality to observed behaviors is **Kelley's** (1967, 1971, 1973) **attribution theory**. (See Fig. 7-8.)

FIGURE 7-7

Price promotion decreases brand loyalty.

Source: Adapted from Dodson, Tybout, & Sternthal (1978).

Kelley's Covariation Principles			
Distinctiveness	Consistency	Consensus	Type of Attribution
High (e.g., different from other brands)	High (e.g., works all the time)	High (e.g., most consumers like it)	Product attribution
High	Low (e.g., works sometimes)	Low (e.g., some consumers like it)	Situation attribution
Low (e.g., similar to other brands)	High	Low	Person attribution
High	High	Low	Person by product attribution

FIGURE 7-8

According to Kelley's covariation principles, causes and effects should covary; that is, a change in the cause should result in a change in the effect.

Causes and effects should covary—that is, a change in one should be accompanied by a change in the other. When the cause is present, the effect should occur. When the cause is absent, the effect should not occur. Three main types of causes should be considered: The product, the situation, or the person may cause someone to buy a product. To determine which cause is responsible for an observed behavior, three main types of information are needed: distinctiveness (e.g., to what extent does the behavior generalize across products?), consistency (e.g., to what extent does the behavior generalize across situations?), and consensus (e.g., to what extent does the behavior generalize across people?) information.

If a consumer buys only Brand X, distinctiveness is high—Brand X is different from all the rest. If a consumer buys many different brands, distinctiveness is low. If a consumer buys Brand X all the time, regardless of the situation, consistency is high. If a consumer buys Brand X only sometimes, consistency is low. If many different people buy Brand X, consensus is high. If few people buy Brand X, consensus is low. Patterns of information determine whether people are likely to form a product, situation, or person attribution (Mizerski, Golden, & Kernan, 1979; Orvis, Cunningham, & Kelley, 1975; Sparkman & Locander, 1980).

With respect to their products, marketers want consumers to assume high distinctiveness, high consistency, and high consensus (high-high-high). This information pattern fosters a product attribution: People buy the product because there is something special about it (e.g., high quality). Hence, advertising claims often emphasize high distinctiveness (the advertised brand is different from all the others), high consistency (the advertised brand is useful in many different situations), and high consensus (everyone likes the advertised brand).

Other patterns foster other types of attributions. High distinctiveness, low consistency, and low consensus suggest a situation attribution. That is, something unusual about the situation (a fluke) caused the person to buy the product. For example, Brand X may have been offered at a ridiculously low price, and in this unusual situation, anyone would buy the product. Or perhaps Brand X was the only brand carried by a particular store and there was no time available for shopping around. Other unusual circumstances also suggest a situation attribution. Sometimes marketers want consumers to make a situation attribution (Folkes, 1984, 1988; Folkes & Kotsos, 1986). For example, when a product breaks or when service is lousy, marketers want consumers to attribute the problem to unusual circumstances. Managers may tell the consumer that their product was the only defective one in the bunch. Restaurant managers may tell dissatisfied customers that the service was bad that evening because the chef or the waiter was new.

Finally, low distinctiveness, high consistency, and low consensus suggest a person attribution: Something unusual about the person caused him or her to buy the product. For example, a Covina, California, company (How Can It Be So Sour Co.) manufactures novelty products, like SNOT (Super Nauseating Obnoxious Treat) candy. The package for this product is a plastic nose with a hole at the bottom. If you knew someone who preferred this candy to other more conventional confections, and if this person ate it all the time (at home, at school, in the car), you would probably make a person attribution: Something unusual about the person is causing him or her to behave this way. Maybe the person has a weird sense of humor, or maybe the person likes practical jokes. Marketers generally do not want consumers to form person attributions because in such cases low generalization across different market segments is implied.

KELLEY'S ATTRIBUTION THEORY: 2. CAUSAL SCHEMATA

Sometimes consumers do not have the luxury of observing patterns of covariation over time. Sometimes they must form attributions on the basis of relatively little information observed at only one point in time. Under these circumstances, consumers apply **causal schemata,** or **causal expectations** based on prior knowledge and experience. When observed information supports or confirms consumer expectations, the information is relatively uninformative. For example, consumers expect advertisers to say that their product is the best (Friestad & Wright, 1994, 1995). Consequently, when consumers see an ad claiming that the advertised product is the best, they view the ad as biased. Biased information is discounted or disbelieved. The **discounting principle** is one type of causal schemata: Expected information is viewed with skepticism because there are many reasons or causes for expected events to occur. As the number of possible causes or reasons increases, the perceived causal role of a particular cause is discounted or reduced because some other cause may have been primarily responsible for the event. For example, an advertiser may claim his or her product to be the best because of **reporting bias:** The advertiser may lie (or not report what he or she really believes) to trick consumers into buying his or her brand. Another possibility is **knowledge bias:** The advertiser might not be aware of (or knowledgeable about) better brands. Advertisements that convey expected or unsurprising information are often perceived as biased (Wood & Eagly, 1981).

The Effect of Unexpected Information

One way to reduce perceived bias and increase persuasion is to present unexpected information. For example, admitting that an advertised product has some negative features reduces perceived bias and increases the perceived factualness of an ad (Wood & Eagly, 1981). Of course, presenting only negative information would lead to negative

Lemon.

This Volkswagen missed the boat.

The chrome strip on the glove compartment is blemished and must be replaced. Chances are you wouldn't have noticed it; Inspector Kurt Kroner did.

There are 3,389 men at our Wolfsburg factory with only one job: to inspect Volkswagens at each stage of production. 13000 Volkswagens are produced daily; there are more inspectors than cars.1

Every shock absorber is tested (spot checking won't do), every windshield is scanned. VWs have been rejected for surface scratches barely visible to the eye.

Final inspection is really something! VW inspectors run each car off the line onto the Funktionsprüfstand (car test stand), tote up 189 check points, gun ahead to the automatic brake stand, and say "no" to one VW out of fifty.

This preoccupation with detail means the VW lasts longer and requires less maintenance, by and large, than other cars. (It also means a used VW depreciates less than any other car.)

We pluck the lemons; you get the plums.

Presenting unexpected information can reduce perceived bias.

Source: Courtesy of DDB Needham Worldwide.

evaluations of the advertised brand. However, presenting unfavorable information about some relatively unimportant attributes and presenting favorable information about other, more important attributes makes an ad seem more factual, and this increases the influence of the favorable attributes on overall evaluations (Etgar & Goodwin, 1982; Pechmann, 1992; Smith & Hunt, 1978). Two-sided ads (i.e., ads presenting both unfavorable and favorable information) are particularly effective when the unfavorable attributes are expected to be negatively correlated with other attributes (Pechmann 1992). For example, an ad stating that a particular brand of ice cream is high in calories is emphasizing a negative feature (high calories) that is negatively correlated with a positive feature (rich flavor). In this case, the negative feature makes the advertiser seem honest, and the positive feature compensates for the negative feature. Consumers expect a negative correlation between calories and flavor, and when it comes to ice cream, most consumers are more concerned about flavor.

Unexpected or surprising information is highly informative (Jones & Davis, 1965; Kelley, 1971, 1973) and thought provoking (Hastie, 1984). Unexpected or unusual behaviors tell a lot about the internal dispositions, traits, and characteristics of an individual. For example, salespeople are expected to be talkative, gregarious, and extroverted. If you happened to interact with a shy, introverted salesperson, however, you would infer that this person must really be shy and introverted. There are powerful situational constraints that require salespeople to be extroverted. To overcome these constraints to exhibit shyness, a salesperson must be exceptionally shy. This is an example of the **augmentation principle:** When there are strong situational forces that should prevent an event from occurring but the event occurs anyway, the cause of the event must be exceptionally powerful. The perceived cause of an event is augmented or strengthened if the event occurs despite obstacles.

To summarize, when there are many different reasons for expecting an event to occur, the perceived strength of a cause is discounted or weakened. However, when there are many different reasons for expecting an event not to occur, the perceived strength of a cause is augmented or strengthened. Marketers often use the discounting principle to cast doubt on the reason why a product broke or failed to perform adequately. Rather than letting consumers infer the product failed because of low quality, marketers often highlight other possible causes for product failure (e.g., maybe the product was not used properly by the consumer, or maybe the product had a rare defect). Marketers often use the augmentation principle to influence attributions for product success. For example, Timex watches take a licking but keep on ticking. Timex commercials show Timex watches getting buried under a pile of dirt unloaded by a dump truck or withstanding other unusual punishments and continuing to function properly. The augmentation principle suggests that if Timex watches perform successfully under these conditions, they must be exceptionally high in quality. Similarly, Bic pen commercials show Bic pens being taped on to the heels of Flamenco dancers and getting pounded into the ground over and over, but they still work. Cheer laundry detergent commercials show clothes getting soaked with mud, dirt, grease, and other substances, and even under these conditions the clothes come out spotless. In each of these cases, the augmentation principle increases the perceived strength of a focal cause (i.e., quality).

CHAPTER SUMMARY ■

The principle of relative (or comparative) judgment suggests that a product seems good when it is compared with a product that is not as good, and a product seems bad when it is compared with a product that is not as bad. Contrast effects occur when judgments of a target shift away from a dissimilar reference point. Assimilation effects occur when judgments of a target shift toward a similar reference point. Several different reference points are possible, including the psychological neutral point (adaptation level theory), the consumer's prior attitudes or expectations (social judgment theory), or the consumer's interpretation of the endpoints of a rating scale (perspective theory).

Attribution theories explain how causal inferences are formed. Why does an advertising spokesperson endorse a particular product? The answer has important implications for persuasion: Greater persuasion occurs if consumers infer that the endorser likes the product or that the product is high in quality. Little persuasion occurs if consumers infer that powerful situational constraints caused the endorsement (e.g., maybe the endorser does not like the product, but he or she said they did because they were paid millions to do so). Self-perception theory suggests that people use their own behaviors and the context in which the behaviors occur to make attributions about their personal attitudes, traits, and dispositions. These attributions have important implications for inferences about why consumers bought a product. Kelley's covariation principles suggest that patterns of distinctiveness, consistency, and consensus information determine whether people will make product, situation, or person attributions. Kelley's causal schemata suggest that prior expectations influence causal judgments. When many possible causes are present, people expect a target event to occur, and the subsequent occurrence of the event provides little information about which cause was responsible for the event (the discounting principle). Conversely, when many obstacles are present, people do not expect a target event to occur, and the subsequent occurrence of the event suggests that a particularly powerful causal force was present (the augmentation principle). The discounting principle and the augmentation principle are important for managing consumers' attributions for product failure and product success.

KEY CONCEPTS ■

- Principle of relative judgment
- Attributional judgments
- Adaptation level theory
- Point of comparison
- Contrast effect
- Adaptation level
- Assimilation effect
- Social judgment theory

- Method of ordered alternatives
- Latitude of acceptance
- Latitude of rejection
- Latitude of noncommitment
- Involvement
- Perspective theory
- Response language effects
- Measurement effects

- Norm theory
- Self-perception theory
- Overjustification effect
- Kelley's attribution theory
- Kelley's causal schemata
- Discounting principle
- Reporting bias
- Knowledge bias
- Augmentation principle

DISCUSSION QUESTIONS ■

1. If a group of consumers was asked to judge a restaurant meal of a hamburger with french fries and cole slaw, how would they probably judge it compared with (1) a peanut butter sandwich with potato chips or (2) filet mignon with baked potato and fresh salad? Which type of context effect does this judgment illustrate?
2. Have you ever been talked into spending more than you originally intended when you entered a store? How did this happen? How did you justify your purchase?
3. How does social judgment theory explain the contrast and assimilation effects?

4. According to perspective theory, if a group of consumers who were rating seafood restaurants assumed that a "10" meant Boston or Seattle restaurants, how might they rate seafood restaurants in Cincinnati or Kansas City? If they were then asked to rate the best seafood restaurant in Kansas City against a fast-food place, how might they rate the seafood restaurant?

5. Wendy's often compares itself with other hamburger restaurants; McDonalds, on the other hand, rarely uses this strategy. What is the logic behind the two strategies?

6. What steps might a manufacturer of golf clubs take to prevent overjustification from hurting its brand?

7. Manufacturers often hire celebrity spokespeople to promote their products. What implications does Kelley's attribution theory have for this practice?

8. How does the discounting principle work?

9. How might an advertiser engage in reporting bias or knowledge bias?

10. Doug Green and Richard Anders claim that they have come up with a way for users of their electronic job ads site to find out more about the companies at which they may want to apply for jobs and that this will distinguish their site from competitors' sites. How does this illustrate the contrast effect?

8 Affective and Motivational Approaches to Persuasion

◆ **SQUIRREL BRAND CO.**

Question: What alternative rock band, with its blend of jazz, ragtime, and bayou swing, was named after an obscure brand of candy? Answer: The Squirrel Nut Zippers. Several years ago, a group of musicians from North Carolina was trying to come up with a name for their newly formed band. Jim Mathus, lead singer and songwriter, came up with the candy name during a brainstorming session. He'd eaten Squirrel Brand candy since he was a boy and made an association between the treat and his music. So he called Bill Colwill, vice president of Squirrel Brand Co. in Massachusetts and asked if his band could use the name. Colwill was a little leery at first. "You have groups out there that use lyrics that you'd rather not have your name associated with," recalls Colwill. "But we listened to their tape, and as far as bands today are concerned, it's good healthy music." So permission was granted.

Much of marketing is about associations that consumers make—emotions, memories, experiences, opinions, smells, sounds, and so forth—with products. The best marketers are those who can foster the right associations for the most people to persuade people to buy the marketers' products. In the case of Squirrel Brand Co. and the Squirrel Nut Zippers, the association seems to have worked.

In four years, the Squirrel Nut Zippers had sold nearly a million albums. Their disc, "Hot," is nearly platinum, and some of the more prestigious radio stations began to play the band's music regularly. The Squirrel Nut Zippers headed up the top-40 charts. Meantime, Squirrel Brand Nut Zipper candies, which have been manufactured since 1926, enjoyed new popularity. "Where the band has helped us make some solid gains is with the generation that we had lost," notes Paul Graham, the confectioner's marketing director. "Most of the people who have called me who are interested in Squirrel Brand are much older than I am. [Graham is in his early thirties.] What's cool is that when the band comes to town, I get people my age and younger than me turned on to the Squirrel Brand, and that's our next generation of customers. My immediate concern when I came to Squirrel Brand was that our customer base was dying of old age." Indeed, the older generation calls the company and expresses surprise that the candy is still available.

People who liked the band also liked the candy, and vice versa, perhaps because the two work so well together. "The culture of Squirrel Brand and the band are completely compatible," notes Graham. "They like to listen to scratchy old 78s, and are definitely a scratchy old 78." Young and old, when people listened to the band, they remembered the candy; when they ate the candy, they remembered the band. The combination spelled sweet success for both.

As you read this chapter, consider all the ways that marketers use associations to promote positive evaluations of products.

Source: Christopher Muther, "A Bittersweet Deal," *The Boston Globe,* October 14, 1997, pp. D1, D14.

◆ INTRODUCTION

Automobile ads on television often show sleek, shiny cars driving by breathtaking scenery. Cuddly puppies and cute kittens frolic in ads for pet food and many other products unrelated to pets. Attractive models and celebrities tell us what products they use, and carefully selected popular music fills the television airwaves. Seinfeld gets into all kinds of silly predicaments and gets out of them by using the "Card." Jay Leno cracks jokes and tells us to eat Tostitos, "crunch all you want, we'll make more." Another television ad states that "friends don't let friends drink and drive" while showing scenes of disturbing traffic accidents. What do these ads have in common? All of them are designed to evoke feelings, or affective responses, from viewers. Often, positive feelings are emphasized, such as those associated with beautiful landscapes, playful pets, laughter, popular music, and likable people. Sometimes negative feelings are emphasized, such as those used by fear appeals in ads imploring us not to drink and drive, smoke, or eat foods high in cholesterol.

Affective responses are surprisingly powerful, as you can see in the opening vignette about Squirrel Brand Co. and the Squirrel Nut Zippers. Even very simple mood-altering events, such as finding small change in a phone booth or receiving a small gift (e.g., gum or candy), can dramatically influence the way we think and behave (Isen, 1984, 1987; Isen, Daubman, & Nowicki, 1987; Kahn & Isen, 1993). Positive affect encourages us to be more helpful, more creative, and more willing to try new things and leads us to reminisce about positive events in our lives. Moreover, affect is a

A LOT OF TIRES COST LESS THAN A MICHELIN. THAT'S BECAUSE THEY SHOULD.

To everyone out there looking to save a few dollars on a set of tires, let's not mince words. You buy cheap, you get cheap.

There may be a lot of tires out there that cost less than a Michelin. The only question is, what do you have to give up if you buy one?

Do they handle like a Michelin? Do they last like a Michelin? Are they as reliable as a Michelin? Then ask yourself this:

Do you really want to find out?

At Michelin, we make only one kind of tire. The very best we know how. Because the way we see it, the last place a compromise belongs is on your car.

As a matter of fact, we're so obsessed with quality we make the steel cables that go into our steel-belted radials.

We even make many of the machines that make and test Michelin tires.

And our quality control checks are so exhaustive that they even include x-rays.

These and hundreds of other details, big and small (details that may seem inconsequential to others), make sure that when you put a set of Michelin tires on your car, you get all the mileage Michelin is famous for.

True, there may be cheaper tires. But if they don't last like a Michelin, are they really less expensive?

So the next time someone tries to save you a few dollars on a tire, tell him this: It's not how much you pay that counts. It's what you get for your money.

And then *he'll* know that *you* know that there's only one reason a tire costs less than a Michelin.

It deserves to.

MICHELIN
BECAUSE SO MUCH IS RIDING ON YOUR TIRES.

Ads often appeal to emotions. Here, Michelin puts a baby in one of its tires to draw attention to its quality and safety.

Source: Courtesy of DDB Needham Worldwide.

powerful motivator: Positive affect encourages us to think about and do things that maintain positive affect; negative affect encourages us to think about and do things that reduce or eliminate negative affect.

◆ AFFECTIVE APPROACHES

CLASSICAL CONDITIONING

Classical conditioning involves forming an association between two objects or stimuli. One object, the **unconditioned stimulus,** should be familiar and should elicit (or automatically produce) an affective response, called the **unconditioned response.** For example, food causes people (and animals, like Pavlov's dogs) to salivate. Food is an unconditioned stimulus and salivation is an unconditioned response. In **classical conditioning** (or Pavlovian conditioning), the unconditioned stimulus is paired with a novel **conditioned stimulus.** For best results, the conditioned stimulus should immediately precede the unconditioned stimulus, and the conditioned and unconditioned stimulus should be paired repeatedly. When an association between the unconditioned stimulus and the conditioned stimulus is learned, the conditioned stimulus presented alone will elicit a **conditioned response** that is very similar to (but somewhat weaker than) the original unconditioned response. For example, Pavlov paired food with a bell, and after repeated pairings, the bell alone produced salivation.

Attitudes can also be conditioned through repeated pairing of an attitude object with an unconditioned stimulus. For example, repeated pairing of a target word with electric shock changes people's attitudes toward the target word (Staats, Staats, & Crawford, 1962; Zanna, Kiesler, & Pilkonis, 1970). Electric shock produces negative affect, and pairing a word with electric shock results in more negative attitudes toward the word. This occurs even when attitudes are measured in a seemingly unrelated second experiment (Zanna et al., 1970), when the target word is presented in an unattended channel in a shadowing task (a shadowing task involves asking subjects to wear headphones and to attend to one ear while ignoring the other; Corteen & Wood, 1972), and even when the conditioned stimulus is presented subliminally, or below the level of conscious awareness (Krosnick, Betz, Jussim, & Lynn, 1992).

Higher-order conditioning involves pairing an unconditioned stimulus with a conditioned stimulus until an association is learned and then pairing the old conditioned stimulus with a new conditioned stimulus. For example, new music is often paired with positive unconditioned stimuli, such as fun parties and good food and drink. Eventually, positive attitudes are formed toward the music. The music is then paired with a new conditioned stimulus, such as a new product in an advertisement, and the advertisement is shown repeatedly (Gorn, 1982). Eventually, positive attitudes are formed toward the advertised product. Likable music, attractive scenery, or virtually any positive stimulus can be paired with a product. When an association between the positive stimulus and the product is learned, favorable attitudes toward the product result (Bierley, McSweeney, & Vannieuwkerk, 1985; Kim, Allen, & Kardes, 1996; McSweeney & Bierley, 1984; Shimp, Stuart, & Engle, 1991; Stuart, Shimp, & Engle, 1987). (See Fig. 8-1.)

Many ads use sex appeal to sell. Sexy models draw attention to an ad and generate positive affect. In one study on the effects of sex in advertising, male subjects viewed an ad featuring a sexy female model caressing a new car (Smith & Engle, 1968). In the control condition, subjects viewed the exact same ad without the female model. The mere presence of the model led subjects to rate the advertised car as faster, more appealing, more expensive looking, and better designed. Moreover, when asked later, subjects refused to believe that the presence or absence of the female model could have influenced their judgments of the automobile in any way.

Advertisers like to use classical conditioning principles because conditioning occurs almost automatically and effortlessly, and conditioning occurs even when consumers are unaware of the influence of carefully selected advertising stimuli. However, advertisers often fail to apply classical conditioning procedures properly, because of a lack of understanding of classical conditioning principles (McSweeney & Bierley, 1984). Timing is critical. Stronger conditioning occurs when the conditioned stimulus is presented before the unconditioned stimulus (**forward** conditioning) as opposed to after (**backward** conditioning). As the table in the bottom half of Figure 8-1 indicates, there are several different types of forward conditioning procedures (Mackintosh, 1974). **Simultaneous conditioning** involves presenting the conditioned and unconditioned stimuli at exactly the same time. **Delayed conditioning** involves presenting

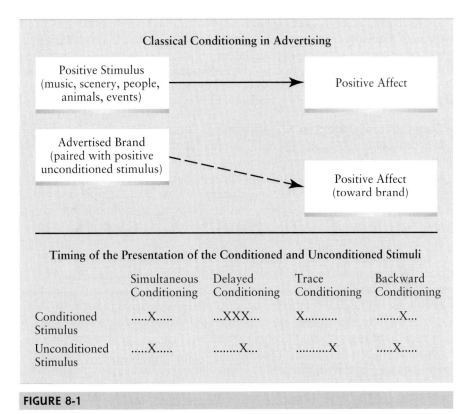

FIGURE 8-1

When used correctly, classical conditioning can have a major impact on the success of advertising.

Source: Gorn (1982), Mackintosh (1974).

the conditioned stimulus before and during the presentation of the unconditioned stimulus. **Trace conditioning** involves presenting the conditioned stimulus first and presenting the unconditioned stimulus after a brief period of time has elapsed. **Backward conditioning** involves presenting the conditioned stimulus after the presentation of the unconditioned stimulus. Extensive research has shown that delayed conditioning leads to the strongest conditioning, followed by simultaneous conditioning, which is followed by trace conditioning (Mackintosh, 1974). Backward conditioning leads to the weakest conditioning and sometimes leads to no conditioning.

Unfortunately, backward conditioning is very common in advertising practice. Many ads present pleasant music, scenery, pretty faces, and so on first, followed by the advertised brand. Many ads also allow too much time to elapse between the presentation of the conditioned and the unconditioned stimulus. Furthermore, many ads use unconditioned stimuli that are ineffective because they were previously encountered alone without pairing (the **unconditioned stimulus pre-exposure effect**) or because they were previously paired with other conditioned stimuli (**blocking**). Both the unconditioned stimulus pre-exposure effect and blocking suggest that highly familiar unconditioned stimuli are ineffective. Highly familiar conditioned stimuli are also ineffective because of **latent inhibition:** A conditioned stimulus loses its effectiveness through prior presentation alone. Considered together, the unconditioned stimulus pre-exposure effect, blocking, and latent inhibition suggest that classical conditioning is much more effective for new products than for old, familiar brands. Recent empirical evidence supports this hypothesis (Cacioppo, Marshall-Goodell, Tassinary, & Petty, 1992).

Classical Conditioning in Nonadvertising Contexts

Classical conditioning is important in nonadvertising contexts as well. In an intriguing series of studies, Feinberg (1986) investigated how the mere presence of credit-card-related stimuli (i.e., credit-card insignias, symbols, and logos) influence the psychology of spending. Classical-conditioning principles have led to strong associations between credit cards and the benefits of spending and weak associations between credit cards and the costs of spending. This is because the benefits of credit-card usage are immediate: After purchasing a product or service, it is ours to use and enjoy. The costs come much later in the form of a monthly bill. The **temporal contiguity** principle of classical conditioning states that stronger associations are learned when events occur close together in time as opposed to far apart in time. Consequently, credit cards should encourage spending because the benefits are stronger, psychologically, than the costs.

Consistent with this analysis, Feinberg (1986) found that consumers leave larger tips when paying with credit cards rather than cash. In a follow-up study, he found that consumers are willing to pay more for mail-order catalog items when credit-card logos are present (as opposed to absent). This finding is particularly remarkable given that the credit-card logos just happened to be present: No attention was drawn to them and no explanation for their presence was provided. Moreover, in a follow-up response-time study, Feinberg (1986) found that consumers reached the decision to spend faster given the mere presence of credit-card logos. In a final study, Feinberg (1986) found that college students donated more cash to charity (the United Way) when the request to donate was made in a room containing credit-card logos. (See Table 8-1.) The mere presence of credit-card-related stimuli induces consumers to spend faster and spend

Do credit-card logos in store windows lead you to use credit cards?

Source: © Mary Boucher.

Studies show that the mere presence of a credit-card logo entices consumers to spend more.

Source: © 1998 Visa International Service Association. All rights reserved.

TABLE 8-1 The Price Is Right

Product	Price Estimates		Decision Times (seconds)	
	Credit Cards Absent	Credit Cards Present	Credit Cards Absent	Credit Cards Present
Toaster	$ 21.50	$ 67.33	21.41	11.46
Black-and-white TV	$ 67.00	$136.92	23.94	13.11
Lamp	$ 34.42	$ 47.17	20.51	9.33
Digital clock	$ 18.08	$ 31.25	20.77	11.90
Pocket camera	$ 29.58	$ 52.67	18.99	9.49
Home stereo system	$157.42	$191.17	23.96	11.35
Dress	$ 25.42	$ 49.42	21.01	11.77
Mixer	$ 17.75	$ 36.25	15.46	7.95
Tent	$ 7.58	$ 28.42	14.90	8.60
Saw	$ 33.42	$ 67.33	20.61	8.35
Chess set	$ 8.67	$ 25.75	14.21	12.53
Cassette tape recorder	$ 26.50	$ 42.75	15.04	14.62

Through classical conditioning, consumers may leave larger tips or spend more when credit-card symbols are present.

Data source: Adapted from Feinberg (1986).

more, even when they pay using cash instead of credit cards. Of course, the practical implications are obvious: Retailers and direct marketers should display credit-card insignias, symbols, and logos prominently in menus, on point-of-purchase displays, and in catalogs and other promotional materials. (See "Taking Issue: Is MasterCard Smart Money?")

COLOR AND AFFECT

Another subtle variable that can influence consumers' affective responses is the color used in ads, packages, and other marketing stimuli. Color has three properties: hue (or pigment, such as blue, red, and yellow, or the three primary colors), chroma (or saturation, intensity, or amount of pigment), and value (or lightness; low values are dark and high values are light). A recent advertising experiment manipulated hue, chroma, and value and found that red was more stimulating than blue (Gorn, Chattopadhyay, Yi, & Dahl, 1997). The results also showed that feelings of excitement increased as chroma increased or as value decreased. Similarly, more favorable attitudes toward the target ad were formed as chroma increased or as value decreased.

THE MERE EXPOSURE EFFECT

The mere presence of credit-card-related stimuli that just happen to be lying around (almost accidentally) has surprisingly powerful effects on affective responses and spending. The mere presence of other stimuli also has surprisingly powerful effects on affect and behavior. Research on the **mere exposure effect** has shown that mere exposure to a neutral stimulus increases liking for that stimulus (Zajonc, 1968). (See Fig. 8-2.) Moreover, repeated exposure increases liking even more, but the effect tends to level off with high levels of repetition (10 to 20 stimulus presentations), perhaps because of boredom. We often hear new tunes on the radio that we do not really care for much, initially. After hearing a new song several times, however, the song often begins to "grow on you" and you begin to like it more. Many foods (e.g., sushi) and beverages (e.g., tomato juice) that may be new to us, initially, become more familiar and likable with repeated exposure (Zajonc & Markus, 1982, 1985). Many things grow on us and become more familiar and likable with repeated exposure.

The mere exposure effect has been found for a wide range of stimuli, including nonsense syllables, meaningful words, polygons, people, and foods (Saegert, Swap, & Zajonc, 1973; Zajonc, 1968; Zajonc, Crandall, Kail, & Swap, 1974; Zajonc, Markus, & Wilson, 1974). Moreover, the mere exposure effect has been found even when stimuli are presented subliminally, below the level of conscious awareness (Kunst-Wilson & Zajonc, 1980; Zajonc, 1980). Several boundary conditions, or limiting conditions, for the phenomenon have also been found. The mere exposure effect is most pronounced for neutral stimuli, but it has also been observed for likable stimuli (Bornstein, 1989). Likable stimuli become even more likable with repeated exposure. By contrast, dislikable stimuli become even more dislikable with repeated exposure. If you really dislike spinach, sushi, or tomato juice the first time you try them, repeated exposure often increases disliking. Moreover, the mere exposure effect is less pronounced with simple (versus complex) stimuli, long (versus brief) exposures, and shorter (versus longer) delays between exposures and when many different stimuli (versus the same stimulus presented over and over) are presented (Bornstein, 1989).

IS MASTERCARD SMART MONEY?

Studies show that the mere presence of credit-card logos makes people spend more money, more readily. Of course, credit-card companies are delighted by these findings. MasterCard has launched all kinds of campaigns designed to capitalize on the phenomenon; for instance, one commercial, set in a supermarket, promotes MasterCard as "smart money." Consumers are encouraged to charge their daily and weekly grocery purchases at participating supermarkets on MasterCard instead of paying cash or writing checks. Why? They will probably buy more, and some consumers will carry balances with finance charges accruing.

An even more recent campaign leads with the slogan "There Are Some Things Money Can't Buy . . . For Everything Else, There's MasterCard." In an emotional appeal, one of these ads shows a father and son at a baseball game, ringing up charges for items like tickets, hot dogs, and souvenirs (those things can be bought with MasterCard). The one thing that can't be bought with MasterCard, of course, is the father's joy at spending an afternoon at a ballgame with his son. "We're very excited about the direction in which this new campaign is taking our brand and are convinced that the advertising will communicate the attributes of MasterCard in a way that is unique and meaningful to consumers," notes Nick Utton, senior vice president of U.S. marketing for MasterCard International, in a press release. "This advertising is rooted in our equity and creates a strong emotional bond with consumers. Extensive consumer research gives us

confidence that it has all of the qualities that make for a successful, enduring campaign." Not coincidentally, the first set of these commercials aired during the 1997 World Series; at the same time, MasterCard announced a multiyear sponsorship agreement with the Major League Baseball organization.

MasterCard also wants students on its list of customers, creating a MasterQuad site as part of its Web site on the Internet. MasterQuad offers information on establishing credit, budgeting, school financial aid, and so forth. The site also offers an opportunity to apply for a MasterCard, deals on entertainment and travel, and a survey for students to fill out.

In addition to its credit cards, MasterCard International now markets debit cards under the MasterMoney name. Debit cards look like credit cards but work like ATM cards: Money is deducted from a customer's account automatically when a clerk or customer runs it through a special machine. Debit cards have exploded in popularity; consumers like the convenience, the security of not having to carry cash, and the fact that it is impossible to spend more money than they have. But that logo is still an encouragement to spend.

No one doubts that credit-card companies have a right to use their logos to sell their products, but it's a good idea for consumers to have as clear an understanding of their own behavior as marketers do. That way, when they use their "smart money," they will be smart shoppers, as well.

Sources: Stephen E. Frank, "MasterCard Says It Puts $50 Limit on Debit-Card Loss," *The Wall Street Journal,* July 31, 1997, p. B5; press releases from MasterCard Web site (www.mastercard.com), "MasterCard Launches New U.S. Advertising Campaign" and "MasterCard Signs as an Official Sponsor of Major League Baseball"; and MasterQuad site from MasterCard Web site (accessed October 1997).

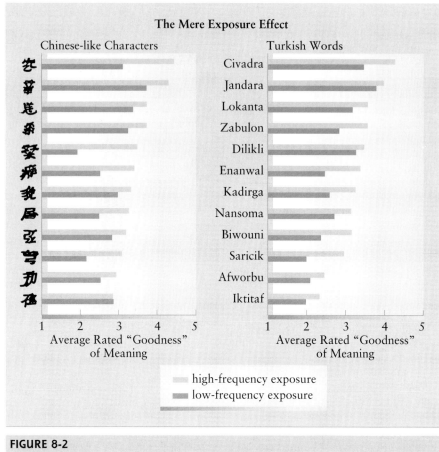

FIGURE 8-2

Mere exposure to a neutral stimulus increases liking for that stimulus.

Source: R.B. Zajonc, *Journal of Personality and Social Psychology,* Monographs Supplement, Part 2, 1968, pp. 1–27. Copyright 1968 by the American Psychological Association. Adapted with permission.

If repeated exposure increases liking, repeated exposure to a product in repetitive advertising should be very effective. Again, however, the mere exposure effect and the effect of repetitive advertising should be strongest when the stimulus is neutral (e.g., a new product), interesting, and when you do not overdo it with overly long exposures or too many repetitions. Excessive repetition can even decrease liking, because of advertising wearout and boredom (Calder & Sternthal, 1980; Zajonc et al., 1974). Repetition may initially increase liking and eventually decrease liking (because of overrepetition), consistent with Berlyne's (1970, 1971) two-factor theory of optimal arousal: Repetition produces **positive habituation** (i.e., familiarity and uncertainty reduction) and boredom. Initially, the effects of positive habituation overwhelm the effects of boredom. With continued repetition, however, the effects of boredom may eventually overwhelm the effects of positive habituation.

ZILLMANN'S THEORY OF EMOTION

Affective experiences are intensified when they are accompanied by physiological arousal or excitation of the sympathetic nervous system. Moreover, arousal or excitation produced by one stimulus can transfer and intensify excitation produced by another stimulus. **Emotion** is defined as intense affect (i.e., affect plus arousal), and arousal that combines and transfers from one stimulus to another is referred to as **excitation transfer** (Zillmann, 1978). **Zillmann's theory of emotion** rests on four key principles of emotion: Arousal is nonspecific with respect to emotion (i.e., arousal intensifies both positive and negative emotions), people are insensitive to small changes in arousal, people often look for a single cause for their arousal (even when there are actually multiple causes), and physiological arousal dissipates at a slower rate than perceived arousal. These principles suggest that there is a narrow window in which arousal can transfer from one stimulus to the next, thereby intensifying the emotional experience attributed to the second stimulus. Initially, little transfer occurs because a single salient stimulus is perceived to be the cause of the arousal. After a period of time, arousal decreases so much that there is no arousal to be transferred. After a moderate period of time (depending on the intensity of the arousing stimulus), however, excitation transfer is likely to occur.

Zillmann (1978) applied his theory primarily to mass-media effects. (See Fig. 8-3.) For example, an exciting sporting event or action movie is likely to produce arousal

FIGURE 8-3

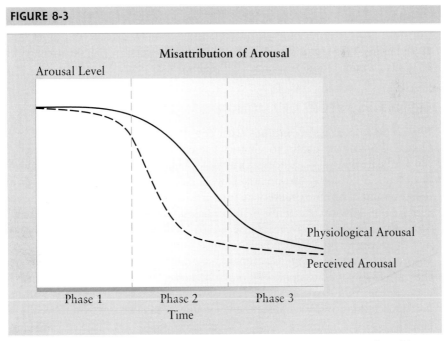

According to Zillmann's excitation transfer theory, we may confuse one emotion with another. Note the gap in phase 2. When we think we are less aroused than we actually are, misattribution of arousal can occur.

that may transfer to an advertisement embedded in the program. Ads aired during the Super Bowl and other exciting events may benefit from this excitation transfer: The advertised product may seem even more exciting during an exciting television program, provided that the timing is right. Similarly, college-age men often like to take their dates to exciting horror films and sporting events, hoping that emotions such as fear and joy may transfer into romantic attraction. In fact, some evidence for this type of transfer exists: Emotions are often difficult to interpret by themselves, and people often use contextual cues to interpret their emotional reactions (Schacter & Singer, 1962; Sinclair, Hoffman, Mark, Martin, & Pickering, 1994). Hence, whether one feels joy, sorrow, fear, disgust, and so on depends on one's cognitive interpretation of an arousing event, because physiological cues by themselves are weak and difficult to interpret. This makes it easy to confuse one type of emotion for another. In fact, in a classic field study, an attractive female experimenter interviewed male subjects as they crossed either a scary, rickety old bridge or a sturdy concrete bridge on the way to campus (Dutton & Aron, 1974). During the interview on the rickety bridge, fear transferred to romantic attraction, and subjects on the rickety bridge were much more likely to later telephone the experimenter "to learn more about the results of the study."

Excitation transfer has important implications for explaining how arousal produced by one event may spill over and combine with arousal produced by another event. These implications are especially important for understanding the effects of mass media (e.g., sex and violence on television). Perhaps the most interesting aspect of this theory is that it appears that nearly any emotion can be confused for another: Fear can transfer to romantic attraction (Dutton & Aron, 1974), sexual arousal can transfer to aggression (Zillmann, 1971), disgust can transfer to humor (Cantor, Bryant, & Zillmann, 1974), and arousal due to physical exertion (e.g., exercise) can intensify virtually any emotional response (Zillmann, 1978).

MANDLER'S THEORY OF EMOTION

Physiological arousal combines with cognitive interpretation to produce emotion. Hence, it would be useful to identify the causes of physiological arousal. Of course, physical exertion (e.g., exercise) produces physiological arousal. Mandler (1982, 1984) has identified other determinants as well. According to **Mandler's theory of emotion, discrepancies,** or unexpected events, are arousal-producing. Discrepancies often require our immediate attention, so it is a good thing that discrepancies wake us up and increase arousal. Moreover, arousal increases as discrepancy increases. Small discrepancies produce pleasant arousal, because they are interesting and stimulating (small surprises are good). Large discrepancies, however, produce negative arousal because they are highly inconsistent with our **schemas** (prior knowledge structures) that drive expectations that drive behavior (large surprises are bad). That is, we often act on the basis of schemas, and large discrepancies suggest that what we think we know or expect is wrong.

Interruptions also produce arousal. When we are watching television or studying for an exam, interruptions from a noisy roommate or neighbor are arousal-producing. As the importance of the task increases (studying for an exam is more important than watching television), the amount of arousal produced by an interruption increases.

Interruptions that prevent us from achieving a desired goal produce negative arousal. Interruptions that help us to achieve a desired goal (e.g., a roommate or neighbor who interrupts because he or she wants to help us study) produce positive arousal.

Consistent with the implications of Mandler's discrepancy/interruption theory of emotion, Meyers-Levy and Tybout (1989) found that brands that are moderately different from other brands in a product category produce positive arousal and are evaluated more positively than brands that are typical of a product category. (See Fig. 8-4.) For example, most soft drinks are high in preservatives and artificial ingredients. However, new all-natural soft drinks (e.g., Corr's, Slice, Clearly Canadian) taste different and interesting and are evaluated positively in blind taste tests. Conversely, most fruit juices are all natural, and, consequently, a fruit juice that is high in preservatives tastes different and interesting, and this results in favorable evaluations in blind taste tests. This study has important implications for new product development: Designing a new product that is virtually the same as all the other brands in a category produces no excitement and results in mediocre evaluations. New features or moderate discrepancies must be introduced to generate excitement and positive evaluation. Large discrepancies, however, produce negative evaluations (Meyers-Levy & Tybout, 1989) or encourage recategorization (Stayman, Alden, & Smith, 1992).

FIGURE 8-4

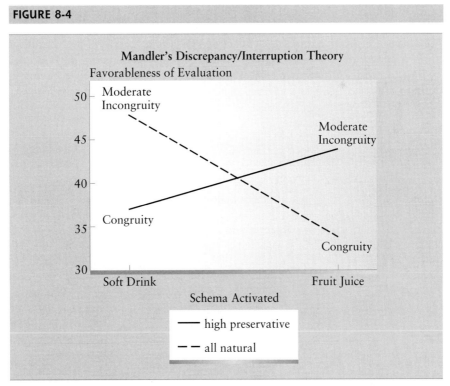

Brands that are only moderately different from other brands in a product category are evaluated more positively than typical brands.

Source: Adapted from Meyers-Levy & Tybout (1989).

◆ MOTIVATIONAL APPROACHES

One way to get people to change their beliefs and attitudes is to make people *want* to change their beliefs and attitudes. Persuasion attempts that are too obvious, however, may backfire, so subtle motivational or goal-relevant techniques are needed. The major subtle motivational techniques focus on the **consistency principle:** People like consistency and dislike inconsistency. In fact, people dislike inconsistency so much that they are often willing to change their beliefs and attitudes to make inconsistencies seem more consistent. However, there are many different types of inconsistencies, and each theory focuses on a different type of inconsistency.

BALANCE THEORY

Heider's (1958) **balance theory** focuses on perceived relationships among elements (or stimuli) in a triad (or set of three elements). (See Fig. 8-5.) The three elements are *p*, or the person who receives the persuasive message; *o*, or another person (friend, enemy, celebrity) known to *p*; and *x*, or a stimulus such as a product, service, issue, or topic. Balance exists if all three relations among elements are positive (e.g., *p* likes *o*, *o* likes *x*, and *p* likes *x*) or if two relations are negative and one is positive. Balanced triads are learned more readily, are more memorable, and are rated as more pleasant, consistent, and stable (Insko, 1981, 1984). People like balanced triads. However, people do not like imbalanced triads, or triads in which all three relations among elements are negative (e.g., *p* dislikes *o*, *o* dislikes *x*, and *p* dislikes *x*) or in which two relations are positive and one is negative (i.e., the opposite of the conditions that foster balance). Imbalanced triads produce unpleasant tension, and people are motivated to reduce this tension by changing one (or more) of the perceived relations within the *p-o-x* triad.

FIGURE 8-5

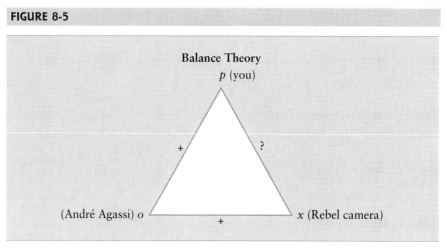

If you like André Agassi and if André Agassi likes the Rebel camera, then you experience a subtle pressure to like the Rebel to achieve balance.

Source: From Petty & Cacioppo (1981).

WELCOME TO VIRGINIA—

A STATE OF EXTRAORDINARY NATURAL BEAUTY AND RICH HERITAGE

Virginia's appeals today are as broad and diverse as its geography and as abundant as its nearly four centuries of history. Stretching from the Atlantic Ocean to the Blue Ridge and Allegheny mountains, Virginia is a mixture of exciting cities, thrilling theme parks, historic homes and villages and as much recreational activity as you'd care to squeeze into your stay.

History comes alive throughout Virginia. Visitors to the commonwealth find much to enjoy. Experience the lives of those who founded the first permanent English settlement in the New World. Tour birthplaces and homes of seven of the eight Virginia-born U.S. presidents. Discover numerous Revolutionary and Civil War battlefields and sites on Virginia's soil.

The longest stretch of the Appalachian Trail runs along the western bend of Virginia. Barrier islands off the Eastern Shore offer some of the East Coast's most exciting saltwater fishing. The warm, sandy beaches of Hampton Roads and Tidewater and the stately elegance of James River plantations are close enough for a single day's visit. Giant limestone caverns extend under the serene Shenandoah Valley, and scenic highways like the 105-mile Skyline Drive and the 217-mile Virginia

portion of the Blue Ridge Parkway allow travelers to take in scenic vistas.

Visitors enjoy a full range of recreational activities including camping, hiking, bicycling, skiing and golfing at its four-season resorts and at Virginia's more than 50 regional, state and national parks. Nearly 3,000 miles of freshwater streams, rivers and lakes, and more than 1,200 miles of tidal shoreline afford water activities galore.

Located mid-way between New York and Miami, the commonwealth boasts well-maintained major highways and scenic byways, service at 12 commercial airports-including Washington Dulles International and Washington National airports -

and at 57 general aviation airports, and Amtrak rail service connecting Virginia cities to commuter and long-distance travel routes.

Virginia is for lovers of mountains and beaches, history and culture, theme parks and natural wonders, vibrant cities and postcard-perfect towns. Your first visit here might be as a visitor, but you will undoubtedly return as a lingering traveler.

VIRGINIA IS FOR LO♥ERS

According to balance theory, if vacationers want to be lovers and Virginia is the place for lovers, vacationers should travel to Virginia.

Source: Courtesy of Virginia Tourism Corporation.

For instance, if *p* is you, *o* is Popeye, and *x* is spinach, imbalance exists if you like Popeye (*p* likes *o*), Popeye likes spinach (*o* likes *x*), and you dislike spinach (*p* dislikes *x*). This triad becomes balanced, however, if you change your attitude toward spinach (you like spinach) or, less preferably, if you change your attitude toward Popeye (you dislike Popeye). Another way to resolve the imbalance is through denial: Popeye does not really like spinach. He just says he does so kids will eat it. Finally, imbalance can be resolved through differentiation: You like Popeye the entertainer (the cartoon hero), but you do not like Popeye the preacher (eat your spinach).

This type of analysis can be applied to almost any set of three elements. For example, cigarette smoker, *p*, likes cigarettes, *o*, which cause cancer, *x*. Of course, the person dislikes cancer (*p* dislikes *x*). The person can resolve the imbalance through attitude change (e.g., disliking cigarettes and quitting), denial (e.g., cigarettes do not really cause cancer), or differentiation (e.g., the person likes the way cigarettes make him feel now but does not like the long-term side effects; research on classical conditioning shows that short-term benefits are more impactful than long-term costs). Finally, many ads feature a likable celebrity, *o*, endorsing a new product, *x*. If you the viewer, *p*, likes *o*, and if *o* likes *x*, subtle pressure toward consistency induces you to form a favorable attitude toward *x* so that the triad will be balanced.

COGNITIVE DISSONANCE THEORY

According to **cognitive dissonance theory,** another type of consistency consumers strive for is **consonance,** or consistency between a target behavior and a target attitude (Festinger, 1957). **Dissonance,** or behavior–attitude inconsistency, produces an unpleasant tension referred to as **dissonance arousal.** When it occurs, people are motivated to reduce dissonance arousal by changing their attitude to make it consistent with the behavior that was performed. A shift in attitude that increases behavior–attitude consistency is known as the **dissonance effect.** After attitude change occurs, people can convince themselves that the behavior that was performed was the correct behavior. Hence, the dissonance effect often involves **effort justification,** or attempts to rationalize the initially troublesome behavior.

In the classic dissonance-effect experiment, Festinger and Carlsmith (1959) asked subjects to perform a senseless and boring task: They were asked to turn a series of pegs on a cardboard pegboard one quarter of a turn. (See Fig. 8-6.) After turning each peg, they were asked to return to the beginning and turn each peg one quarter of a turn once again. This continued for about a half-hour. In the control condition, subjects were asked to rate the task, and, not surprisingly, they rated the task as very boring. In the high-dissonance condition, each subject was asked to tell the next subject that the task was "exciting and fun," and they received insufficient justification (only one dollar) for performing the behavior of telling the next subject that the task was exciting and fun. This produced dissonance arousal because saying the task was exciting and fun when they knew it was not is inconsistent and 1 dollar is a small incentive for lying. But these subjects convinced themselves that they did not lie! Their ratings of the task were very favorable after performing the behavior of saying the task was exciting and fun! Finally, in the high-justification condition, subjects received 20 dollars for telling the next subject that the task was exciting and fun. Because 20 dollars was a large incentive, subjects' attitudes toward the task remained negative despite the fact that

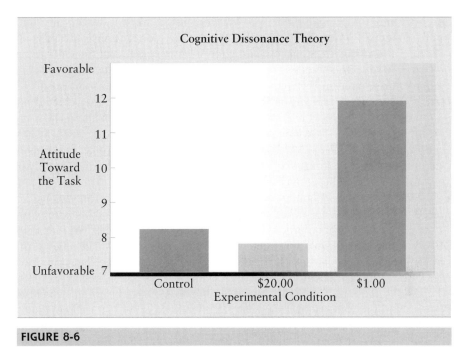

FIGURE 8-6

Performing attitude-inconsistent behaviors with minimal inducement produces attitude changes.

Source: Adapted from Festinger & Carlsmith (1959).

they told the next subject it was exciting and fun. Small incentives and minimal justification are needed to produce dissonance effects.

Decision Making and Dissonance

Making almost any type of decision can also set the stage for dissonance effects. For example, suppose a consumer made a bad decision by buying a mediocre product. This produces dissonance arousal because the behavior of making a bad decision is inconsistent with the belief that "I usually make good decisions." Postdecisional dissonance is especially likely when the decision (a) is important, (b) involves giving up positive features of a rejected alternative or accepting negative features of a chosen alternative, or (c) involves alternatives that are dissimilar in terms of specific features but similar in terms of overall desirability. Postdecisional dissonance can be reduced by adopting one of four possible strategies: revoking the decision, increasing the perceived attractiveness of the chosen alternative (sweet lemons), decreasing the perceived attractiveness of the rejected alternative (sour grapes), or increasing the perceived similarity of the alternatives.

In a classic study of postdecisional dissonance, Brehm (1956) asked subjects to rate the attractiveness of several products, including a stopwatch, a silk screen print, a portable radio, and a fluorescent lamp. Subjects were also told that, at the end of the study, they would receive one of these products as a gift. In the high-dissonance condition, subjects were asked to choose between two products they rated as nearly equal in desirability. In the low-dissonance condition, subjects were asked to choose between a product they rated highly and a product they rated much lower. In the control condition, subjects did not make a choice (the experimenter chose the gift) and, consequently, there was no decision and therefore no postdecisional dissonance. After receiving their gift, subjects were asked to rate all the products again. Large shifts in judgment occurred in the high-dissonance condition: The chosen product was rated much higher after the decision than before the decision, and the rejected product was rated much lower after the decision than before the decision. Small shifts in judgment occurred in the low-dissonance condition: The chosen product was rated somewhat higher after the decision (versus before), and the rejected product was rated somewhat lower after the decision (versus before). In the control condition, virtually no shifts in judgment occurred before versus after receiving the gift.

Similar shifts in judgment have been observed in other settings as well. For example, gamblers at a racetrack are more confident that they picked the winning horse after placing a bet than before (Knox & Inkster, 1968; Younger, Walker, & Arrowood, 1977). Moreover, gamblers rate themselves as luckier after placing a bet than before. Making a decision changes the way people think about the decision. Performing a behavior changes the way people think about the behavior. (See Fig. 8-7.)

Finally, it should be emphasized that inconsistencies between behaviors and attitudes do not always produce dissonance effects. (See Fig. 8-8.) Dissonance effects do not occur when the consequences of attitude-discrepant behaviors are inconsequential or nonaversive (Cooper & Fazio, 1984). Dissonance effects do not occur when large incentives are present, or when people are forced to do something they do not want to do. Finally, dissonance effects do not occur when dissonance arousal is misattributed to

FIGURE 8-7

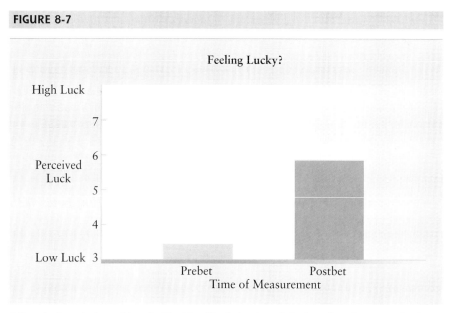

After placing a bet, gamblers feel luckier. The behavior of placing a bet changes attitudes toward gambling.

Data source: Younger, Walker, & Arrowood, 1977.

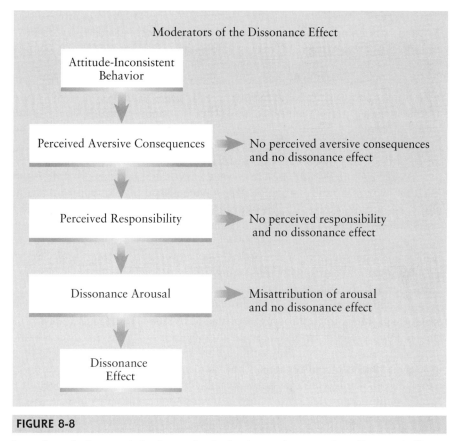

Moderators of the Dissonance Effect

Attitude-Inconsistent
Behavior

Perceived Aversive Consequences → No perceived aversive consequences
and no dissonance effect

Perceived Responsibility → No perceived responsibility
and no dissonance effect

Dissonance Arousal → Misattribution of arousal
and no dissonance effect

Dissonance
Effect

FIGURE 8-8

Inconsistencies between behaviors and attitudes do not always produce dissonance effects.

some source other than behavior–attitude inconsistency. As Zillmann's (1978) theory suggests, interpreting arousal is difficult, and arousal often transfers from one source to another. Misattribution of arousal to another source, such as a (placebo) pill that subjects believed would cause tension (Zanna & Cooper, 1974) or placement inside a small room that subjects believed would cause tension (Fazio, Zanna, & Cooper, 1977), eliminates the dissonance effect.

IMPRESSION MANAGEMENT THEORY

Several different theories can explain the dissonance effect. Cognitive dissonance theory suggests that the dissonance effect stems from attitude change occurring to reduce unpleasant dissonance arousal caused by behavior–attitude inconsistency. Self-perception theory (discussed in Chapter 7) suggests that the dissonance effect occurs when people infer attitudes from behavior (e.g., "If I did it I must like it"). **Impression management theory** suggests that people are motivated to give the appearance that their behaviors and attitudes are consistent (Tedeschi, Schlenker, & Bonoma, 1971). Self-perception theory offers a cold, cognitive perspective, and consequently, self-perception theory cannot explain how misattribution of arousal reduces the dissonance effect (Fazio et al., 1977; Zanna & Cooper, 1974). Cognitive dissonance theory and impression management theory are both motivational theories, but they focus on different motivations. According to cognitive dissonance theory, people are motivated to reduce dissonance arousal by increasing behavior–attitude consistency. According to impression management theory, people are motivated to convey a favorable impression to others by displaying behavior–attitude consistency. Hence, cognitive dissonance theory emphasizes actual behavior–attitude consistency, whereas impression management theory emphasizes apparent behavior–attitude consistency. It is important to appear consistent to others because inconsistent people (e.g., people who say one thing but do the opposite) seem flaky and wishy-washy.

People are often motivated to convey a favorable impression of themselves to others. One way to do this is to appear to have consistent behaviors and attitudes (other impression management techniques, including ingratiation and control of indirect associations, will be discussed in Chapter 10). Hence, when behaviors and attitudes are inconsistent, pretending to change one's attitudes in a direction in line with behaviors will make a person appear consistent. Maybe subjects in the one-dollar condition of the Festinger and Carlsmith (1959) study really thought the task was boring and awful. However, by pretending to have favorable attitudes toward the task by circling high numbers on the rating scale, subjects can appear to be consistent. Some evidence consistent with this interpretation was provided by Gaes, Kalle, and Tedeschi (1978), who showed that subjects are less likely to change their attitudes in a direction more consistent with behaviors when they believe they are hooked up to a machine that can monitor their physiological responses and determine their true underlying attitudes. No machine can actually do this, but what subjects believe is what is important, and clever experimenters can trick people into believing that the bogus pipeline machine can do this (Gaes et al., 1978; Jones & Sigall, 1971; Quigley-Fernandez & Tedeschi, 1978).

Most robust phenomena, like the dissonance effect, have multiple causes. The dissonance effect is influenced by many psychological processes. For important attitudes, inconsistent behaviors are likely to be personally upsetting, and cognitive dissonance theory can explain the dissonance effect quite well. For unimportant attitudes and for topics for which people hold no attitudes (most people do not have attitudes about everything), observable behaviors provide clues about unobservable internal states, and self-perception theory can explain the dissonance effect quite well. Finally, when people are especially concerned about what other people will think of them, impression management theory can explain the dissonance effect quite well. Each theory has a different area of application.

ATTITUDE FUNCTIONS

Why do people have attitudes? Are attitudes useful? What psychological functions do attitudes serve? The answers to these questions have surprisingly important implications for persuasion. (See "Making the Decision: Halloween's New Hype.") Actually, attitudes have many different functions (Katz, 1960; Smith, Bruner, & White, 1956). Some attitudes summarize large amounts of information and simplify the world so we can make decisions quicker and easier (the knowledge function). Some attitudes express our traits, characteristics, and preferences to others so they will know how to interact with us more effectively (the value expression function). Some attitudes

HALLOWEEN'S NEW HYPE

You remember the dark Halloween nights of your childhood? Clad in costume and face paint, dragging a trick-or-treat bag laden with sweets across neighborhood lawns, shrieking when you ran into unrecognizable friends? They're back. Halloween, which languished for a number of years as a nonholiday because of trick-or-treat scares, is now a booming business, second only to Christmas in sales of candy, greeting cards, costumes, party items, and even gifts. Halloween has become a $2.5 billion annual industry. "We started planning for Halloween in December," notes Sal Perisano, chairman and cofounder of The Big Party, a 49-store party-goods chain in the Boston area. "It's our endgame."

How have marketers managed to resuscitate a dying holiday? Somehow, they have persuaded consumers that Halloween is worth spending their money on. One way they did this was to get adults involved. By changing people's beliefs that Halloween was just for children, marketers changed attitudes about celebrating Halloween. Commercial haunted houses, haunted hayrides, and adult costume parties sprang into being. Spookyworld, a monthlong theme park in Massachusetts that features all kinds of grisly attractions, employs 472 people and draws 150,000 customers each year. While Spookyworld does admit children,

others, like Barrett's Haunted Mansion, discourage it. "We don't even recommend it for young children," says the mansion's director, Mary Barrett.

Marketers also appeal to consumers' emotions about Halloween—in particular, nostalgia for baby boomers. William Evans, a grandfather who decorates his lawn with scarecrows, artfully carved jack o'lanterns, and a witch's cauldron, admits, "I really think I do this for me." Others spend hundreds of dollars for that nostalgic feeling. One man wears $550 orange contact lenses to make his Dracula costume appear more realistic. He also inserts $50 fangs to give his get-up more bite. "I could bite through your arm and I wouldn't dent these things," he boasts. Elaborate rubber masks, sold everywhere from party stores to television's QVC, can run as high as $75 to $100.

Of course, in all their efforts, marketers can rely on people's response to Halloween as a stimulus. When consumers see Halloween products, all kinds of thoughts, memories, emotions, and attitudes are evoked. And while almost everyone is familiar with Halloween, it seems that the mystique of the holiday never wears off. So the bounties of Halloween are plentiful for marketers—a little creepy perhaps, but these days, ghoulishness sells.

Source: Nathan Cobb, "Tricks Now Adults' Treat," *The Boston Globe,* October 17, 1997, pp. A1, A37.

bolster our self-esteem and help us to feel better about ourselves (the ego defense function). Some attitudes help us to gain immediate rewards and avoid immediate punishments (the utilitarian function). Once again, we will see that the consistency principle is of fundamental importance: To be effective, a persuasion technique must be consistent with the underlying function of an attitude (see Table 8-2).

The Knowledge Function and Factual Appeals

Many attitudes serve a **knowledge function** by summarizing a large amount of complex or ambiguous information to provide people with an organized, meaningful, and stable view of the world. Attitudes serving this function help people to make decisions

TABLE 8-2   Attitude Function Theory

Attitude Function	Approach	Avoid	Approach Based Advertising	Avoidance Based Advertising
Knowledge	Certainty	Uncertainty	Factual appeals Quality appeals Logical arguments	Mystery ads Confusing ads Surprise
Value Expression	Indirect positive associations	Indirect negative associations	Image appeals Celebrities	Unattractive users of competing brands
Ego Defense	Desirable future outcomes	Undesirable future outcomes	Authority figures Experts	Fear appeals
Adjustment	Pleasure	Pain	Immediate benefits	Immediate costs

Persuasion is enhanced when the persuasion strategy matches the function of the attitude held by consumers.
Source: Adapted from Kardes & Cronley 2000b.

quickly and easily without having to refer to the detailed attribute information that was originally used as an information base for forming these attitudes (Kardes, 1986; Lingle & Ostrom, 1981). For example, if you are knowledgeable about personal computers, your attitude toward Macintosh personal computers is based on large amounts of technical details about the features and uses of Macintosh computers. Rather than thinking about hundreds of features and uses when deciding whether to buy a Macintosh computer, it is much easier to retrieve a single overall evaluation. If your overall impression of Macintosh computers is very favorable, you are more likely to buy one. Knowledge-based attitudes are often useful decision aids.

Attitudes that serve a knowledge function are likely to be activated or retrieved from memory when we encounter ambiguous or uncertain situations. The knowledge function helps us to deal with ambiguity and uncertainty more effectively. Attitudes

What is your opinion of the technical features of this Apple Macintosh computer?
Source: © Mary Boucher.

based on large amounts of prior knowledge and experience help us to interpret ambiguous information and fill in missing details to help make ambiguous information make sense. The best way to influence attitudes serving the knowledge function is by using factual appeals, meaningful information, and meaningful frameworks. **Factual appeals** provide meaningful information about the specific features and uses of products. However, facts are useful only for knowledge-based attitudes. Again, consistency is the key: Factual appeals are useful for influencing knowledge-based attitudes but not for influencing attitudes serving one of the other three functions.

The Value Expression Function and Impression Management

Some attitudes help us to communicate our traits, preferences, and interests to others. Attitudes serving the **value expression function** help us to manage or control the impressions others form of us. People are often concerned about what other people think of them, and our attitudes often have a large impact on the impressions we convey to others. Some products are "image" products, and attitudes toward image products serve a value expression or impression management function. For example, favorable attitudes toward Dom Perignon champagne, Chateau Mouton-Rothschild bordeaux, Remy Martin cognac, S.T. Dupont lighters, Piaget watches, Armani suits, and Mercedes-Benz automobiles reflect sophisticated and expensive tastes. People often buy these products to impress others. Attitudes toward American-made products also serve a value expression function: Some people are proud to be American and wish to support their country by buying American-made products. Attitudes toward clothes and clothing accessories also frequently serve a value expression function: Conservative clothes reflect conservative attitudes and lifestyles; wild or daring clothes reflect fun-loving attitudes and lifestyles; sweatshirts, T-shirts, and baseball caps with logos, insignias, or names of organizations (e.g., universities, football or baseball teams, etc.) reflect favorable attitudes toward these organizations.

Value-expressive attitudes are activated by salient cues associated with values. For example, seeing an American flag displayed on a product label may encourage some people to buy American-made products. Seeing our friends wear clothing displaying the name of our university may encourage us to wear similar clothing. Publicly used products (e.g., clothes, cars) that are conspicuous or attention-drawing are often associated with attitudes serving a value expression function. The most effective way to influence attitudes serving this function is to use image-oriented appeals. For example, people who idolize Michael Jordan or want to be like him are more likely to buy products endorsed by him. Actors, supermodels, rock stars, and athletes are often used in advertising to influence value-expressive attitudes. Names of famous celebrities are often placed on products (e.g., Jack Nicklaus golf clubs, André Agassi tennis rackets) to influence value-expressive attitudes. Image-oriented appeals are effective for value-expressive attitudes but ineffective for attitudes serving other functions.

The Ego Defense Function, Fear Appeals, and Wishful Thinking

Some attitudes serve a self-protective or **ego-defensive function.** Attitudes serving this function help people to deal with frustration, emotional conflict, and threats to ego, or self-esteem. Ego-defensive attitudes involve the use of Freudian defense mechanisms, such as denial (refusing to believe what one does not want to believe), repression (forgetting things we do not want to think about), and projection (seeing our flaws and weaknesses in others). For example, negative attitudes and stereotypes toward other

Insurance ads influence ego-defensive attitudes by helping consumers to feel protected.

Source: National Flood Insurance Program administered by FEMA.

groups of people help us to feel better about ourselves. **Wishful thinking,** or believing that good things are likely to happen to us and bad things are not, also reassures and calms us when we are worried about threatening events like crime, disease, pollution, and poverty. Attitudes toward protection devices, such as security systems for homes and automobiles, guns, insurance policies, retirement policies, condoms, medicines, and other health-related products and activities (e.g., diet and exercise) often serve an ego-defensive function.

Ego-defensive attitudes are activated when people feel threatened or frustrated. Freud suggested that threats and frustrations build up inside people and that these tensions must be released in some manner. Some release mechanisms are socially acceptable (e.g., competing with others, watching violent movies and sporting events) and some are not (e.g., lashing out or attacking others). The most effective way to influence ego-defensive attitudes is by using fear appeals or by using persuasive messages delivered by an authority figure (e.g., a political or religious leader or an expert, such as a doctor, lawyer, professor, executive, etc.). Fear appeals and authority figures are useful for changing ego-defensive attitudes but not for changing attitudes serving other functions.

The Utilitarian Function and Operant Conditioning

Some attitudes serve a **utilitarian,** or an instrumental (a means to an end), **function.** For example, children are often rewarded for expressing opinions similar to those of their parents, and children are often punished for expressing opinions dissimilar to those of their parents. Attitudes associated with reward are reinforced. Attitudes associated with punishment are weakened. Earlier in this chapter, I discussed persuasion tactics based on classical (or Pavlovian) conditioning. Attitudes can also be influenced through **operant** (or instrumental, or Skinnerian) **conditioning** (Insko, 1965; Insko & Butzine, 1967; Insko & Cialdini, 1969). One key difference between classical versus operant conditioning is that the stimulus precedes the response in classical conditioning (S-R), whereas the response precedes the stimulus in operant conditioning (R-S). Also, learning occurs relatively spontaneously with classical conditioning, whereas learning through operant conditioning requires greater effort and intention.

Both **positive reinforcement** (the presence of reward) and **negative reinforcement** (the absence of punishment) strengthen or increase the probability of a target response. Punishment weakens the probability of a target response. The absence of reward also weakens a response. Learning occurs faster through **continuous reinforcement** (i.e., a reward is given each and every time the response occurs), but **partial reinforcement** (i.e., a reward is given only some of the time the response occurs) causes learning to persist longer after reinforcement is discontinued. Rewards used in marketing contexts include coupons, trading stamps, frequent-user bonuses (e.g., frequent-flyer miles), rebates, and prizes given to consumers who purchase your product. Consumers who do not purchase your product or service provide no desired response for you to reinforce, but you can encourage nonusers to consider your product through **shaping,** or reinforcing successive approximations of the desired response. For example, you may first reward nonusers to visit the mall by offering a fashion show, live music, or some form of entertainment at the mall. Next, you might encourage nonusers to enter your store by offering a door prize. Next, you might reward nonusers to open a charge account at your store by offering a discount on items purchased in your store with new store charge cards. Finally, when the desired response occurs (i.e., product purchase), you can reinforce this response by offering frequent-user bonus points for each purchase.

Again, the key principle of **attitude function theory** is that, to be effective, a persuasion strategy must match the attitude function (Katz, 1960; Smith et al., 1956). Factual and rational appeals are useful only for knowledge-based attitudes. Social-image-oriented appeals are useful only for value-expressive attitudes. Fear appeals and authority figures are useful only for ego-defensive attitudes. Reward and punishment are useful only for utilitarian attitudes. Recent research on attitude functions shows that different types of people hold attitudes serving different attitude functions (Snyder & DeBono, 1985). (See Fig. 8-9.) Specifically, high self-monitoring individuals are highly concerned about their image (Snyder, 1974, 1979), and consequently, image-oriented advertising should be very effective for this group of individuals. Conversely, low self-monitoring individuals are less concerned about image and more concerned about utility or quality, and consequently, quality-oriented advertising should be effective for this group. Snyder and DeBono (1985) showed subjects image-oriented and quality-oriented ads for several products (Canadian Club whiskey, Barclay cigarettes, Irish Mocha Mint coffee). For example, the image-oriented whiskey ad showed a whiskey bottle on top of a set of house blueprints, and the caption stated: "You're not just moving in, you're moving up." The image-oriented cigarette ad showed a handsome gentleman about to light a cigarette while looking at an attractive female companion through a mirror (with her hand resting gently on his shoulder), and the caption stated: "You can see the difference." The image-oriented coffee ad showed a smiling

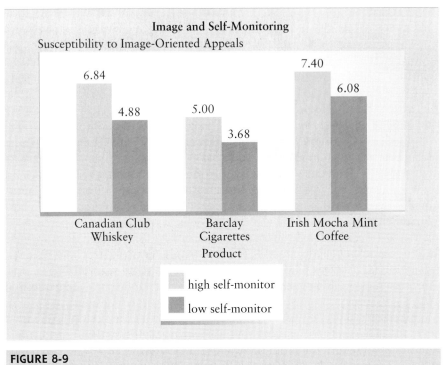

FIGURE 8-9

High self-monitors are more susceptible to image-oriented appeals.
Source: Adapted from Snyder and DeBono (1985).

couple relaxing in a romantic, candlelit room, and the caption stated: "Make a chilly night become a cozy evening with Irish Mocha Mint." For each product, the quality-oriented ad was identical to the corresponding image-oriented ad except the captions emphasized taste and flavor, rather than appearance. The results indicated that high self-monitors rated the image-oriented ads as more persuasive, whereas low self-monitors rated the quality-oriented ads as more persuasive.

Attitudes toward different product categories also tend to be associated with different attitude functions (Shavitt, 1990). (See Fig. 8-10.) Consumers tend to form utilitarian attitudes toward air-conditioners because this product keeps people cool and comfortable (reward) rather than hot and uncomfortable (punishment). This product does not really have many other uses, and most people do not really care about what an air-conditioner looks like. Attitudes toward coffee are also utilitarian to the extent that people are concerned about flavor and waking up. By contrast, attitudes toward greeting cards and perfumes serve a value-expressive function because people are trying to make a favorable impression on others with these products. Consequently, utilitarian (quality-oriented) ads are more effective for products like air-conditioners and coffee, whereas image-oriented ads are more effective for products like greeting cards and perfumes (the results were weaker for perfumes because perfumes serve many functions; e.g., to please oneself and others).

Consistency between attitude function and persuasion is an extremely important principle. Inconsistency results in little or no persuasion. For example, facts, figures, and

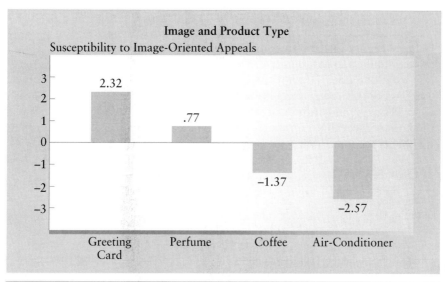

FIGURE 8-10

Image-oriented appeals are more effective for products associated with value-expressive attitudes.

Source: Adapted from Shavitt (1990).

appeals to reason are useless for changing political or religious attitudes. This is because political and religious attitudes serve a mixture of value-expressive and ego-defensive functions. Hence, change requires appeals to important values made by respected political and religious leaders. Fear also works (e.g., vote for me or the country will go to ruin; support my church or face eternal damnation). However, values, fear, and authority figures are less useful for changing knowledge-based attitudes. Moreover, facts, figures, values, fear, and authority are useless for changing utilitarian attitudes (e.g., I like it because it tastes good; I like it because it works properly). Designing effective persuasive communications requires a careful analysis of attitude functions.

CHAPTER SUMMARY ■

Affective approaches to persuasion involve the use of feelings and emotions to influence consumers' attitudes toward products and services. Attitudinal conditioning requires the careful pairing of unconditioned and conditioned stimuli. Advertisers carefully select unconditioned stimuli that they want consumers to associate with advertised products. Classical conditioning produces response generalization: Conditioned affective responses resemble unconditioned affective responses. Mere exposure to a novel stimulus (e.g., a new product) increases familiarity and liking (affect), and repeated exposure increases familiarity and liking even more (to a point). Zillmann's theory of emotion explains how emotional responses produced by one stimulus may be transferred to another through misattribution of arousal. Mandler's theory of emotion explains the causes of emotion (discrepancies and interruptions) and explains processes that influence the direction (positive or negative) and magnitude (intensity) of emotional experience.

Motivational theories of persuasion emphasize the role of consistency in attitude change. People are motivated to approach consistency and avoid inconsistency. Balance theory focuses on consistent relations between elements in a *p-o-x* (person-other-stimulus) triad. Cognitive dissonance theory stresses consistency between behavior (what one does) and attitude (what one thinks). Impression management theory emphasizes the importance of the appearance of behavior–attitude consistency, even when behavior and attitude are actually inconsistent. Attitude function theory explains the knowledge, value expression, ego defense, and utilitarian functions of attitudes and highlights the importance of consistency between function and strategy.

KEY CONCEPTS

- Unconditioned stimulus
- Unconditioned response
- Classical conditioning
- Conditioned stimulus
- Conditioned response
- Higher-order conditioning
- Forward conditioning
- Backward conditioning
- Simultaneous conditioning
- Delayed conditioning
- Trace conditioning
- Unconditioned stimulus pre-exposure effect
- Blocking
- Latent inhibition
- Temporal contiguity
- Mere exposure effect

- Positive habituation
- Emotion
- Excitation transfer
- Zillmann's theory of emotion
- Mandler's theory of emotion
- Discrepancies
- Schemas
- Consistency principle
- Heider's balance theory
- Cognitive dissonance theory
- Consonance
- Dissonance
- Dissonance arousal
- Dissonance effect

- Effort justification
- Impression management theory
- Knowledge function
- Factual appeals
- Value expression function
- Ego-defensive function
- Wishful thinking
- Utilitarian function
- Operant conditioning
- Positive reinforcement
- Negative reinforcement
- Continuous reinforcement
- Partial reinforcement
- Shaping
- Attitude function theory

DISCUSSION QUESTIONS

1. Think of an incident in which an advertisement evoked an affective response in you that was either positive or negative and led you to make a decision—say, to purchase or not purchase an item, to donate or not donate money to a cause, or the like. Describe the ad, the response it evoked in you, and the action you took. Share your experience with the class.
2. Why do advertisers like to use classical conditioning principles in their advertising?
3. According to the temporal contiguity principle, why might a shopper buy more items from a toy catalog when using a credit card than he or she might buy in a toy store, using cash?
4. Suppose a clothing designer wants to introduce a new line of casual wear made of a new, synthetic fabric no one has ever heard of. How might the designer use the mere exposure effect to get people to try the clothes?
5. Think of a time when you experienced positive habituation to an ad. Describe the ad, your initial reaction to it, and your later response to it after having seen it many times. Do you still remember the exact brand that the ad was promoting or just the ad itself?

6. On what four key principles of emotion is Zillmann's theory of emotion based?
7. How might marketers for a new brand of all-natural breakfast cereal use Mandler's theory of emotion to create an ad for the cereal?
8. Imagine that a couple buys a new sofa for their family room, then finds another sofa later at a second store that fits their decor and budget better than the first sofa does. In what ways might they reduce their postdecisional dissonance?
9. Note several characteristics about yourself that you want to convey to others in their overall impression of you. Now list the products that you own (or want to buy) that fit your value expression. Then list some products you own that contradict the image you want to convey. How do you reconcile any dissonance this creates? Share your findings with the class.
10. How might marketers for a chain of resorts like Club Med use partial reinforcement to get vacationers to stay at their resorts?

Self-Persuasion Principles

- ◆ Philosophies of the Leading Ad Agencies
    - Facts versus Emotions
    - Soft Sell versus Hard Sell
- ◆ The Elaboration Likelihood Model
    - Central versus Peripheral Routes to Persuasion
- ◆ Role Playing
- ◆ Attitude Polarization
- ◆ Indirect Persuasion
    - The Syllogistic Inference Rule

◆ McDONALD'S

Let's face it: McDonald's is middle-aged. Now over 40 years old, the fast-food giant needs a few nips and tucks—in its food, its image, its pricing, its advertising. Several recent marketing campaigns fell flat. The Arche Deluxe line, higher-priced burgers and other sandwiches aimed at adults, fell flat. Campaign 55, meant to echo McDonald's pricing during its first year of operation, was far too confusing to consumers. And some ads, such as one featuring Ronald McDonald sitting in a bar chatting with women, never aired. What can Big Mac do to rejuvenate its image and persuade consumers to bite?

After a top-management shakeup, McDonald's also decided to change advertising agencies. Leo Burnett, a large, Chicago-based agency, had the McDonald's account for 15 years. Most recently, the agency had tried to reverse its own history of aggressive, price-driven ad campaigns, but to no avail. McDonald's executives decided to return to DDB Needham, whose chairman and chief executive officer, Keith Reinhard, wrote the famous "Two All Beef Patties . . ." jingle years ago; the agency also produced "You Deserve a Break Today."

Why is the change in advertising agencies important? Ads, and the methods of persuasion underlying them, affect the way people view products and ultimately the decision whether to make a purchase. So the philosophy of an agency—for instance, whether to try to persuade consumers with a direct, hard sell or a more subtle, soft sell—makes a huge difference in how messages are created and delivered.

It looks like McDonald's executives want to return their focus to the food itself and the dining experience, with price being a lesser concern. "There's no question we can move a lot of customers through our doors when we lower the price," notes Brad

Ball, senior vice president in charge of domestic marketing. "But customer after customer says price is not the No. 1 driver. McDonald's happens to be in the restaurant business, but the experience you have with the food goes way beyond what it is you're eating." Indeed, one of McDonald's most successful promotions ever—the Teenie Beanie Babies promotion with Happy Meals—was discontinued abruptly when it became apparent that adults were buying the Happy Meals in huge numbers to horde the Teenie Beanie Babies. Scores of Happy Meals were tossed in the trash instead of eaten.

So McDonald's is going back to its old agency in an effort to recapture its old connection with consumers. Burnett will still handle some of the business, including work in 21 foreign countries. In addition, Big Mac makers admit that they must take a hard look at the food as well as changes in consumers' tastes. John W. Weiss, an analyst with Montgomery Securities, writes, "McDonald's sluggish sales trends in the U.S. derive largely from problems other than price: changes in consumer preferences, the absence of truly distinctive products, [and] the relatively bland taste of most of the chain's products." Even McDonald's CFO, Michael Conley, concedes that "the competition has caught up." Serving up good food is McDonald's job. Persuading consumers to think about McDonald's in a positive way is DDB Needham's job. What have they come up with so far? Reinhard has been prepared for the call back to service ever since he lost the account over a decade ago. The new slogan is "Did somebody say McDonald's?" Somebody did, indeed.

As you read this chapter, consider how the different philosophies of advertising agencies influence how messages are created and delivered and how consumers ultimately think about products.

Sources: Sally Goll Beatty and Richard Gibson, "In Latest Flip-Flop, McDonald's Orders Up New Agency," *The Wall Street Journal,* July 30, 1997, pp. B1, B2; Lori Calabro, "Mac Attack," *CFO,* September 1997, pp. 54–60.

◆ INTRODUCTION

Whenever we watch a television commercial about a brand belonging to a product class that we never use, we either ignore the message or we listen to it without thinking much about it. However, when we watch a television commercial about a brand belonging to a product category that is important and interesting to us personally, our reactions are very different. We are less likely to just ignore the message, and we are also less likely to listen to it without thinking. Furthermore, we are likely to think about points somewhat different from but related to the points the advertiser is trying to make. In fact, these related points often seem more important than the points raised by the advertiser. To the extent that this is true, our attitudes will be influenced more by our personal reactions to a message than by the message itself.

This is not to say, however, that the message has no impact—quite the contrary. If the message can lead us to think more extensively about a brand, and if these thoughts have primarily favorable implications for evaluating the brand, the ad can be very effective. To create an ad that can do all this, however, we have to understand how advertising induces consumers to think more extensively about a brand. We also need to identify the key factors that determine the evaluative implications of message-induced thoughts. This topic is critical because more extensive thinking about a topic can lead to either more favorable or less favorable brand attitudes.

Chapter 9 explores the major approaches toward understanding self-persuasion. It begins with a discussion of the philosophies of the leading ad agencies begun in the opening vignette about McDonald's. Many of these philosophies are inconsistent and even contradictory. Fortunately, the elaboration likelihood model of persuasion helps to resolve these inconsistencies and contradictions. Research on the elaboration likelihood model shows that our own personal reactions to a persuasive message are more important than the message itself. Consistent with the elaboration likelihood model, several studies also show that active role playing leads people to think more extensively about a topic or an issue. Active thinking also leads people to form more extreme opinions. Actively thinking about and forming our own conclusions also results in greater persuasion, compared with merely reading other people's conclusions.

◆ PHILOSOPHIES OF THE LEADING AD AGENCIES

All ad agencies live by a set of assumptions or working hypotheses about how advertising affects consumers' attitudes toward the advertised brand. This is not surprising, but what is surprising is the lack of consensus among the leading ad agencies about how advertising works. In fact, in many cases, the assumptions of different agencies are not just inconsistent, they are contradictory. How can two contradictory assumptions both be right?

FACTS VERSUS EMOTIONS

Consider the philosophies of Ogilvy & Mather. Initially, David Ogilvy, a well-known advertiser, believed that it was important to use celebrities to endorse products in television commercials. After spending several years in the business, he now believes that celebrities are completely ineffective. However, other agencies still believe that celebrities are worth every penny spent to compensate them for product endorsement.

Ogilvy & Mather also operates under the assumption that the typical American consumer is intelligent. Therefore, ads should just present the facts and allow the consumer to make his or her own purchase decisions. Because of this assumption, Ogilvy & Mather uses primarily informational appeals and presents facts to inform the consumer. For example, the ad agency's famous American Express ads present detailed information about the benefits of using the American Express card. In contrast, the Leo Burnett agency assumes that the typical American consumer is not capable of understanding complex facts. Burnett avoids factual, informational appeals. Instead, Burnett sometimes entertains consumers with cartoon characters, such as *Tony the Tiger*™, Charlie the Tuna, and the Keebler Elves.

Ogilvy & Mather believes that the typical television viewer is rational and, therefore, content is more important than form (what you say is more important than how you say it). Burnett uses a lot of flair and drama (e.g., "Fly the friendly skies of United"), whereas Ogilvy & Mather uses a lot of facts (e.g., "Come to Shell for answers"). Which philosophy is correct? Both agencies have many powerful and

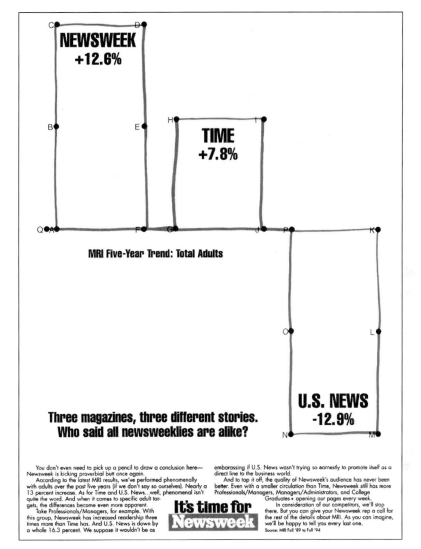

Some ads present the facts and allow consumers to make their own decisions.
Source: © 1994 of Newsweek, Inc. Reprinted with permission.

important clients. Both agencies create ads that produce sales. Could they both be right?

SOFT SELL VERSUS HARD SELL

Ogilvy & Mather and Burnett agree about one thing. They both believe that a subtle, soft-sell approach is more effective than a forceful, hard-sell approach. Maybe this is the key aspect that makes an ad effective. Maybe the issues upon which they disagree (informational versus emotional appeals, serious ads versus animation and humor,

Leo Burnett relies on ads with flair, drama, and characters like Morris the Cat and the Pillsbury Doughboy.
Sources: 9-Lives®Plus™ Cat Food; Courtesy of The Pillsbury Company.

content versus form) are unimportant. However, this seems very unlikely. Furthermore, another leading ad agency, Ted Bates, uses the hard-sell approach with great success. Bates likes forceful, irritating, obnoxious ads that are difficult to ignore. Bates likes fear appeals that emphasize the aversive consequences—like cavities, bad breath, unpopularity, headache pain, and so on—of not using a particular brand. It likes to drill simple points into the heads of consumers by repeating these points over and over within each ad exposure (e.g., "How do you spell relief? . . . R-O-L-A-I-D-S") and by using very high levels of advertising repetition.

In contrast to the Bates approach, Doyle, Dane, and Bernbach (DD&B) downplays the role of belaboring simple points and using high levels of advertising repetition. Instead, DD&B emphasizes the use of creative ads that "stand out" even in cluttered media environments. The effective use of humor and hyperbole (exaggeration) results in ads that are attention-drawing and entertaining and that generate positive feelings and emotions in consumers. For example, the famous DD&B Tourister luggage ad shows an ape bellhop throwing luggage into walls and jumping on top of suitcases. Although hotels don't really use apes for bellhops (this is a good example of

SELLING HARD: THE TABLOIDS WON'T GO SOFT

Tabloid newspapers are perhaps the quintessential example of the hard sell. The headlines are sensational. The photos are weird, grisly, and revealing. The stories are, well, not exactly credible. But they are surviving, even in the wake of Princess Diana's tragic death in a car accident in Paris, for which not only the general public but other sectors of the press actually blamed the tabloids. They are surviving because the hard sell works. People who buy the tabloids like the hard sell. "If it were to become chronic and [the tabloids] kept holding to a higher and higher standard . . . it would be negative," explains Kevin M. Kuzio, a fixed-income analyst with KDP Investment Advisors in Montpelier, Vermont. "At retail, people are willing to pay [for shocking photographs and headlines]. It appears to be what they want."

Consumers seem to take only a peripheral route to persuasion when buying publications like the *National Enquirer*, the *Globe*, the *Star*, and the *National Examiner*. They make the decision while standing in the supermarket checkout line, where the tabloids are displayed. They don't cost much—typically, much less than glossy magazines—so it is not a decision that requires high involvement. They buy the paper with the most intriguing headline or photo.

"The crowd that buys these tabloids will pay for the latest story," says Kuzio. "It's an impulse purchase, not a moral decision." Daniel Schwartz, editorial director of the *Globe* and the *National Examiner*, confirms this. He says, "It pays to have a big story. It's exclusives that sell newspapers." Schwartz claims that exclusive stories about Frank Gifford's personal life and JonBenet Ramsey's murder increased circulation of his papers by 14 percent.

Although advertisers exert some control over the editorial content of other types of newspapers and magazines because those publications rely on revenue from advertising, the American tabloids typically get only about 9 percent of their revenues from ads. (British tabloids draw about 20 percent, but that still is not enough to influence content.) So they don't have to worry about scaring off advertisers by printing things that may be considered in questionable taste. Instead, they just raise the price when necessary—and people keep buying the papers.

Tabloid publishers claim that they are just giving people what they want, and the only way to do that is with a hard sell. In circumstances like this, it might be wise to consider whether what works is really the best approach after all.

Source: Elizabeth Lesly and Julia Flynn, "How Awful. How Could They? I'll Take One," *Business Week,* September 15, 1997, p. 42.

hyperbole), most consumers believe that bellhops are rough with luggage. Tourister luggage, however, is so sturdy that it can withstand extremely rough treatment. DD&B argues that really creative ads, such as the Tourister ads, do not require high levels of advertising repetition to be effective. This idea is extremely attractive to clients because it helps them to manage high media costs by using lower levels of advertising repetition.

Which ad agency is right? Is the typical American consumer intelligent or unintelligent? Are factual appeals or emotional appeals more effective? Is the soft-sell approach superior to the hard-sell approach? Is humor distracting, or does it draw attention to an advertised brand? Are high levels of advertising repetition always needed? The answer to all of these questions is "it depends." (See "Taking Issue: Selling Hard: The Tabloids Won't Go Soft.") The effects of advertising are extremely complex, and no single hypothesis or philosophy can capture all the intricacies of advertising and persuasion. No single approach will be effective for all consumers and all products under all situations. The best way to understand advertising is to adopt a contingency perspective. That is, the effectiveness of a given advertising approach depends on (or is contingent upon) individual differences and situational variables present at the time of ad exposure. One especially useful contingency theory is the **elaboration likelihood model** of persuasion (Petty & Cacioppo, 1981, 1986). This model helps us to predict when celebrity spokespersons are likely to be effective versus ineffective. It also helps us to identify the conditions that favor the use of factual versus emotional appeals. In addition, it helps us to predict the reactions a consumer is likely to have to virtually any ad execution. Furthermore, the model is built on a foundation of years of sound scientific research. For these reasons, the elaboration likelihood model has become one of the most influential theoretical models in advertising.

◆ THE ELABORATION LIKELIHOOD MODEL

As the name *elaboration likelihood* implies, consumers are sometimes likely to elaborate upon the information conveyed in an ad, while at other times, little thought occurs. The average American consumer is exposed to 300 to 600 ads per day (Britt, Adams, & Miller, 1972), and the typical consumer does not have the time or energy to think carefully about the attitudinal implications of each and every ad encountered. If the ad is particularly interesting or if the ad pertains to a product that is personally relevant to a consumer, the consumer may think carefully about the information presented in the ad. Conversely, if the ad is uninteresting or irrelevant, little attention or thought is likely to be directed toward the ad. Marketers like Mike Veeck in "Making the Decision: Mike Veeck Plays Hardball" need to come up with ways to capture attention.

CENTRAL VERSUS PERIPHERAL ROUTES TO PERSUASION

The elaboration likelihood model emphasizes that there is more than one path to persuasion. (See Fig. 9-1.) When an ad is interesting and relevant and when the consumer has the time and knowledge required to think about the ad, consumers are likely to follow the **central route to persuasion.** The term *central* refers to the idea that people will focus on the most central, or important, information provided when forming an attitude or opinion. Central information usually consists of strong arguments or reasons that support or justify holding a particular attitude or opinion. This route to persuasion requires a lot of thinking, or cognitive effort. Those following this route focus on **elaboration,** or the process of using reasons and justification, rather than on less important details.

In contrast, the **peripheral route to persuasion** involves relatively little thought or effort. When people do not have the time or inclination to think carefully about an ad,

MAKING THE DECISION

MIKE VEECK PLAYS HARDBALL

Most people outside of the St. Paul, Minnesota, area probably have never heard of the St. Paul Saints. They are a professional baseball team, but they play for the Independent Northern League. They aren't a major league farm team; they have no major league affiliation at all. They may not be in the big leagues, but they are a big deal—at least to their owner, Mike Veeck, and 6,000 fans who fill the stadium for nearly every game.

People who attend Saints games love baseball—some might even call this type of baseball game the real thing. They also love the marketing antics that Mike Veeck pulls to get their attention, to draw them in and keep them coming back. During the middle of one game, Hamlet, the live pig who serves as the team's mascot, trots onto the field to deliver a fresh baseball to the umpire. In the bleachers, a Roman Catholic nun administers backrubs at $7 for 10 minutes to fans with stiff backs (presumably from sitting in the bleachers). At the seventh-inning stretch, reporters in the press box toss bags of peanuts to kids. At other games, kids have participated in harmless graffiti contests and a few lucky fans have won dinners at an Italian restaurant.

Mike Veeck has a simple philosophy: "Fun is good." In fact, his philosophy is plastered to his office wall. Effective marketing, asserts Veeck, is "the culmination of twenty-five different little things. The sum is definitely greater than the parts." Wacky is fun, and fun is good.

But does Veeck have any boundaries? "I don't do things I consider to be in poor taste," he states. "I try not to cross over ethnic and gender lines. Tasteless, to me, are wet T-shirt contests. That being said, nothing is too crazy."

In a way, Veeck has a great marketing niche. His fans love baseball. They know at least something about the game. They also love their team. Their decision to purchase a ticket doesn't require high involvement—a peripheral route to persuasion is all that is necessary. And how can anyone be against fun? So tossing a few fun, whimsical, memorable promotions onto the field can be only positive (even if Veeck gets some bad press, which he has).

Does Veeck's approach work? If a full stadium is any indication, then the answer is yes. In fact, the Saints' 6,329-seat Midway Stadium sold out 41 of 43 games in one recent year, even though the team had a mediocre 45–40 record that year. The team sells 2,200 season tickets and even carries a waiting list of more than 1,200 people who want season tickets. Total revenue from the year just mentioned topped $1 million.

So Saints fans keep coming back for more baseball. By now they have developed a favorable attitude toward the experience, regardless of how well the team is actually doing. Does it matter that Saints fans will never get to follow their team to the World Series? Apparently not. They have everything they need right at home, at Midway Stadium.

Source: Erika Rasmussen, "Baseball's Wild Card," *Sales & Marketing Management,* August 1997, pp. 30–32.

they can still form an opinion toward the advertised brand on the basis of peripheral cues. Peripheral or background cues include such factors as source attractiveness (e.g., a popular celebrity versus an average, unknown person), source expertise (e.g., a Stanford professor versus a grade school teacher), background music that creates a pleasant mood, cute babies or animals that generate positive feelings, and so on. These

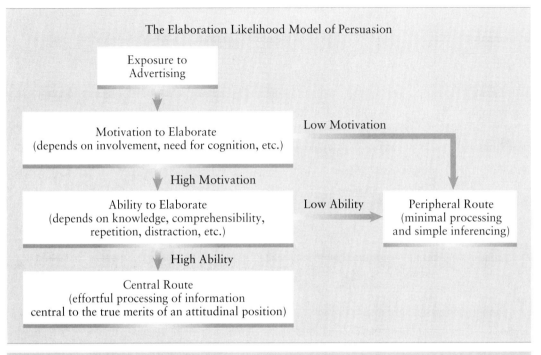

The Elaboration Likelihood Model of Persuasion

FIGURE 9-1

The elaboration likelihood model of persuasion emphasizes that there is more than one path to persuasion.

contextual cues are very superficial, compared with the facts and logical arguments used when consumers follow the central route to persuasion. However, peripheral cues are useful for forming opinions quickly and easily.

What determines whether consumers follow the central versus the peripheral route to persuasion? Consumers follow the central route when they are motivated and able to elaborate upon a persuasive message. (See Fig. 9-2.) People are more motivated to elaborate when a message is relevant to them personally. Issue involvement is high when a message pertains to a topic that is interesting or relevant to consumers. Consumers are likely to follow the effortful central route to persuasion when issue involvement is high. Conversely, issue involvement is low when a message is uninteresting or irrelevant. Consumers are likely to follow the less effortful peripheral route to persuasion when issue involvement is low.

Although consumers must be motivated to elaborate to follow the central route to persuasion, they may be motivated to elaborate but unable to do so. For example, a poorly designed television commercial may convey so much information so quickly that most consumers are unable to comprehend the message (Moore, Hausknecht, & Thamodaran, 1986). In this case, consumers will be unlikely to elaborate even if they are motivated to do so. Similarly, distractions (e.g., background noise from busy streets or from companions, children, pets, etc.) can prevent people from elaborating upon a persuasive message even when they are motivated to do so (Petty, Wells, & Brock,

Determinants of the Route to Persuasion
and Attitude Strength

Motivation

		High	Low
Ability	High	Central Route (strong attitudes)	Peripheral Route (weak attitudes)
	Low	Peripheral Route (weak attitudes)	Peripheral Route (weak attitudes)

FIGURE 9-2

When motivation and ability to elaborate are high, consumers follow the central route and form strong attitudes. When motivation or ability to elaborate is low, consumers follow the peripheral route and form weak attitudes.

1976). Ad repetition also affects the ability to elaborate (Cacioppo & Petty, 1985). It is difficult to elaborate on an ad seen only once or a few times. It is also difficult to elaborate in arousing situations, because high levels of physiological arousal reduce the amount of information consumers can attend to simultaneously (Sanbonmatsu & Kardes, 1988). Any factor that decreases the ability to elaborate upon a persuasive message will induce consumers to follow the peripheral route to persuasion even if they are motivated to elaborate. Consumers follow the central route to persuasion when motivation and ability is high. If motivation or ability or both are low, consumers follow the peripheral route to persuasion.

It is important for advertisers to predict when consumers are likely to follow the central route and when consumers are likely to follow the peripheral route because consumers use different types of information when they follow different routes to persuasion. Message strength (e.g., convincingness, compellingness, and quality of the message arguments) is the most important variable when consumers follow the central route. Conversely, peripheral cues (e.g., source attractiveness, background stimuli, message length, product popularity cues) are important when consumers follow the peripheral route. Moreover, effortful central-route processing encourages consumers to form strong brand attitudes that are persistent, resistant to counterpersuasion, and have a powerful influence on behavior (Haugtvedt & Petty, 1992; Haugtvedt, Schumann, Schneider, & Warren, 1994; Haugtvedt & Wegener, 1994; Krishnan & Smith, 1998). By contrast, less effortful peripheral route processing often results in weak attitudes (see Fig. 9-3).

Types of Elaboration

When consumers are both motivated and able to elaborate, elaboration likelihood is high, and consumers are likely to follow the central route to persuasion. Under these conditions, what type of elaborations are consumers likely to generate? Four major

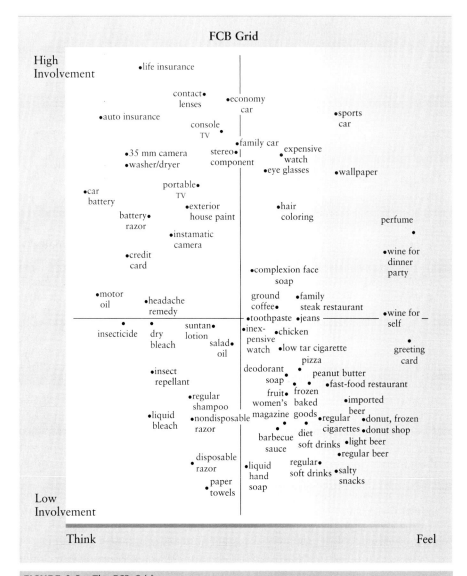

FIGURE 9-3 The FCB Grid

The Foote, Cone, and Belding (FCB) ad agency extended the elaboration likelihood model by sorting products into high or low involvement and think or feel categories. Rossiter et al. (1991) extended this model by emphasizing that brand awareness must precede brand attitude formation.

Source: Rossiter et al. (1991).

types of elaborations have been identified: **source derogations, counterarguments, support arguments,** and **curiosity statements** (Petty & Cacioppo, 1981, 1986). If a consumer dislikes the source delivering the persuasive message, the consumer is likely to think of reasons for not believing the source. When many different source derogations, or reasons for not believing the source, are generated, little persuasion is likely to occur even if the arguments presented by the source are reasonable and compelling. Another type of elaboration is a counterargument. Counterarguments are reasons for not believing a message regardless of who delivers the message. If large portions of a message are inconsistent with a consumer's beliefs and opinions, the consumer is likely to think of reasons for disregarding the entire message, and again, little persuasion will occur. Conversely, support arguments are reasons for believing a message regardless of who delivers it. If large portions of a message are consistent with the consumer's prior knowledge and experience, the consumer is likely to think of reasons for accepting the entire message. The message itself is perceived as compelling and convincing, and consumers may think of additional reasons for believing the message. Finally, some elaborations are merely curiosity statements, or thoughts that are only tangentially related to the main points of a message. When the elaborations or message-related thoughts are consistent with a message, persuasion is likely to occur. When elaborations or message-related thoughts are inconsistent with a message, little persuasion is likely to occur.

Involvement

Petty and Cacioppo and others have conducted many studies that support the elaboration likelihood model. In one typical study (Petty, Cacioppo, & Schumann, 1983), involvement (personal relevance) was manipulated by telling subjects that they were about to see a magazine ad for a new disposable razor that would soon be available (high involvement) or unavailable (low involvement). The people endorsing the product in the ad were either celebrities or noncelebrities. The text consisted of strong arguments (e.g., "the razor is scientifically designed") or weak arguments (e.g., "the razor is designed with the bathroom in mind"). The ad was identical in all other respects: Only endorser status and argument strength was varied. (See Fig. 9-4.)

As predicted, in high-involvement conditions, subjects formed more favorable attitudes toward the advertised brand when they were exposed to strong as opposed to weak arguments. Whether a celebrity endorsed the product had no effect on brand attitudes when involvement was high. In contrast, when involvement was low, much more

What communication strategy should Gillette use with the introduction of its Sensor razor?
Source: © Mary Boucher.

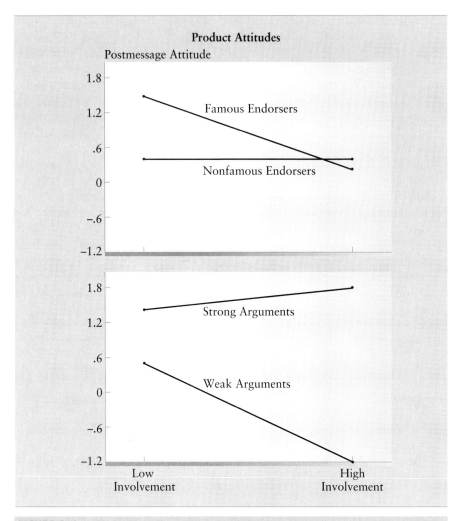

FIGURE 9-4

When involvement is high, consumers follow the central route and are influenced by argument strength. When involvement is low, consumers follow the peripheral route and are influenced by endorser status.

Source: Adapted from Petty, Cacioppo, and Schumann (1983).

favorable attitudes toward the advertised brand were formed when the endorser was a celebrity as opposed to a noncelebrity. Hence, when involvement is high, consumers are likely to follow the central route to persuasion and message strength is critical. Conversely, when involvement is low, consumers are likely to follow the peripheral route to persuasion and are influenced by superficial cues such as endorser status. Furthermore, many other types of superficial cues—such as communicator attractiveness, communicator likability, communicator expertise, the sheer number of arguments presented (irrespective of argument strength), number of communicators, audience reactions, consensus information, mood (e.g., Alba & Marmorstein, 1987; Axsom, Yates, & Chaiken, 1987; Batra & Ray, 1986; Chaiken, 1980; Chaiken, Liberman, & Eagly, 1989; DeBono & Harnish, 1988; Miniard, Sirdeshmukh, & Innis, 1992; Norman, 1976; Petty & Cacioppo, 1981, 1986; Ratneshwar & Chaiken, 1991; Sanbonmatsu & Kardes, 1988; Yalch & Elmore-Yalch, 1984), and other related cues—have been found to produce similar effects on attitudes when consumers follow the peripheral route to persuasion.

◆ ROLE PLAYING

Early research on self-persuasion demonstrated that attitude change is greater when people actively present their own arguments than when they passively listen to the arguments of others (Janis & King, 1954; King & Janis, 1956). In these studies, subjects were given an outline of arguments that could be used to prepare a speech to persuade others. Attitudes about the topic of the speech were measured before and after the speech was delivered. By comparing subjects' prespeech attitudes with the postspeech attitudes, the investigator could assess the persuasive impact of the speech. The results indicated that greater persuasion occurred when subjects gave a speech rather than listened to one. Furthermore, the results revealed that although subjects used the arguments listed in the outline when they gave their speech, they also improvised many of their own arguments that were not included in the original list. These improvisations had a dramatic effect on subjects' postspeech attitudes.

Actively presenting a message has other important effects on persuasion as well. Presenting a message is a fairly demanding task, and most people think about the message carefully before they deliver it. In fact, when examining information for possible use in a speech, people tend to engage in biased scanning of information (Janis & Gilmore, 1965). Specifically, they tend to focus on information that strongly supports the advocated position and they tend to neglect less important and less supportive information. Although this process is reasonable for accomplishing the task at hand, it has implications that go beyond the act of giving a speech. After the speech has been delivered, highly supportive evidence continues to influence the opinions of the speaker, whereas less supportive evidence tends to be forgotten.

Of course, active presenting and passive listening also have different effects on memory and on attitude persistence. Several weeks after the speech was delivered, those who gave the speech continued to hold extreme attitudinal positions, whereas persuasion decreased for those who passively listened to the speech (Watts, 1967). Hence, improvisations tend to take on a life of their own.

◆ ATTITUDE POLARIZATION

Often, when we think about one of our favorite products, the more we think about it the more we like it. Similarly, when we think about one of our least favorite products (such as a car that turned out to be a real lemon), the more we think about it the less we like it. Simply thinking about an object can make our opinion of the object more extreme.

How does merely thinking about an object change our opinion of it? To answer this question, we need to consider what goes on in the minds of consumers when they think about a liked or disliked product. First of all, prior opinions tend to guide the thought process. Specifically, if you have an initially favorable attitude toward a product, you are likely to consider primarily the positive aspects of the product when you think about it. Conversely, if you have an initially unfavorable opinion, you are likely to think primarily about the product's negative aspects. Information that is inconsistent with the initial opinion tends to be overlooked, discounted, or perhaps even distorted (Tesser, 1978). Second, thinking often involves forming inferences about unknown aspects of an object to fill gaps in knowledge. For example, even if you do not know much about the mechanics of automobiles, you are likely to assume that your car has a fine driveshaft if you like your car. If you dislike your car, you are likely to assume it has a terrible driveshaft. The combination of focusing on known information that is consistent with an attitude and forming attitude-consistent inferences about unknown information provides a great deal of support for a particular attitudinal position. Thinking about all this supportive evidence (and neglecting nonsupportive evidence) increases the extremity of an attitude.

In the classic study of the polarizing effects of mere thought (the **mere thought effect**), subjects were asked to view a film showing either a series of football tackles or a series of new clothing fashions (Tesser & Leone, 1977). Not surprisingly, the majority of male subjects were more knowledgeable about football than about fashion, whereas the majority of female subjects were more knowledgeable about fashion than about football. The attitudinal effects of one additional variable was also examined: Half the subjects were distracted while they viewed the film, and half were not. It was reasoned that subjects would be able to think more extensively about the information presented in the film if they were not distracted. The results revealed that for those subjects who viewed the football film, more extreme evaluations were formed by nondistracted males than by subjects in the remaining conditions. For instance, distracted males did not think much about the tackles because they were distracted, and females did not think much about the tackles because they were unknowledgeable about football. For

Could you be distracted from concentrating on the Super Bowl?

Source: © Mary Boucher.

those subjects who watched the fashion film, more extreme evaluations were formed by nondistracted females than by subjects in the remaining conditions. Distracted females did not exhibit the mere thought effect because they were distracted. Similarly, males did not think much about the new fashions because they were unknowledgeable about fashion.

Hence, if people are given time to think about a topic, and if they are sufficiently knowledgeable about the topic, favorable attitudes become more favorable and unfavorable attitudes become more unfavorable. Subsequent research has shown that the mere thought effect is more likely when people are committed to their attitudes (Tesser & Millar, 1989). People do not like to think much about trivial topics, and the mere thought effect does not occur when people do not think. The mere thought effect is also more likely when a person's knowledge structure is undifferentiated. That is, a person who knows a lot about one dimension or one aspect of a topic is more susceptible to the mere thought effect than someone who knows a lot about several different, unrelated dimensions (Chaiken & Yates, 1985; Judd & Lusk, 1984; Millar & Tesser, 1986).

◆ INDIRECT PERSUASION

The elaboration likelihood model highlights the important idea that consumers' reactions to a message are more important than the message itself (Greenwald, 1968; Petty & Cacioppo, 1986). **Indirect persuasion** extends this idea by purposely omitting portions of a message and subtly inducing consumers to draw inferences about this omitted information. The less information presented in a message, the more room there is for inferential activity. Effective indirect persuasion requires knowledge about what portions of an ad to delete, what inferences most consumers are likely to form, and

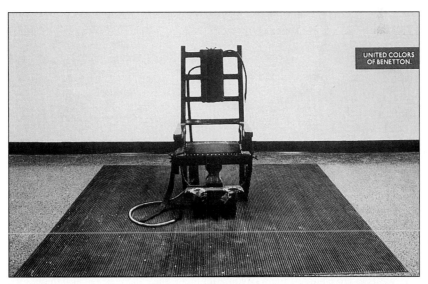

Many consumers would understandably fail to draw any conclusion about Benetton's products from this ad.

Source: Concept: O. Toscani. Courtesy of United Colors of Benetton.

how to subtly motivate consumers to draw these inferences to "lead them down the garden path."

What portions of an ad should be deleted to apply indirect persuasion most effectively? Most ads present information in the form of pictures or words designed to support one or more key points or conclusions. Typically, print ads try to convey a greater number of key points, relative to television ads, because consumers can process information at their own pace and have greater opportunity to elaborate (Chaiken & Eagly, 1976, 1983). When these key points or conclusions are omitted from an ad, however, consumers have an opportunity to infer these conclusions themselves. Because consumers trust themselves more than they trust advertisers, they should have stronger beliefs in their own conclusions than in conclusions provided by advertisers. Stronger beliefs should then lead to stronger attitudes. This is the key benefit of indirect persuasion. This technique is not without risk, however, because consumers may not always infer the conclusions advertisers want them to infer.

Fortunately, extensive research on consumer inference processes has made it possible to predict what inferences consumers are likely to form in many different situations (Kardes, 1988, 1993; Sawyer, 1988; Sawyer & Howard, 1991; Stayman & Kardes, 1992). An **inference** is a conclusion derived from available information on the basis of a rule that associates the information to the conclusion in a subjectively logical fashion

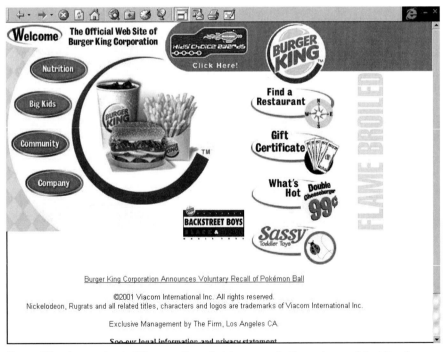

Burger King boasts that its Whopper® sandwiches come in three sizes and that it only wants to serve burgers the way you want them. Since the message also implies that people prefer their burgers this way, we infer that people will prefer Burger King's burgers.

Source: Burger King Corporation is the exclusive licensee of the registered Burger King, Whopper, and Bun Halves Log trademarks.

This ad makes its conclusions explicit.
Source: Courtesy of Rayovac Corp.

(Hastie, 1983; Kardes, 1993). If an advertiser understands consumers' subjective rules for linking conclusions and data, the advertiser can predict the conclusions consumers are likely to infer on the basis of a given set of information.

THE SYLLOGISTIC INFERENCE RULE

For example, one inference rule commonly used by consumers is the **syllogistic infer-ence rule** (Wyer, 1974; Wyer & Carlston, 1979; Wyer & Srull, 1989). Syllogisms have the following form: if A implies B, and if B implies C, then A implies C. For example, Burger King recently aired a television ad with arguments presented in the form of a syllogism. The first premise stated, "People prefer their hamburgers at home flame-broiled" (if A, then B). The second premise stated, "Now if McDonald's and Wendy's fry their hamburgers and Burger King flame-broils theirs" (if B, then C), "where do you think people should go for a hamburger?" No answer was provided to this question in the ad. Instead, the advertiser decided to let consumers draw their own conclusion. People who believe the premises and who reason syllogistically will draw the conclusion that people should go to Burger King (A implies C).

Of course, conclusion omission is not always effective. In fact, early research on the topic suggested that messages are more persuasive when conclusions are presented explicitly as opposed to omitted (Fine, 1957; Hovland & Mandell, 1952). Conclusions stated explicitly in a message are known as **explicit conclusions;** conclusions that are implied by the message arguments but that are not stated explicitly are known as **implicit conclusions.** Recent research suggests that explicit conclusions are more effective when consumers are unlikely to draw their own conclusions, whereas implicit conclusions are more effective when consumers are likely to infer the conclusions the advertiser intended them to draw (Kardes, 1988; Sawyer & Howard, 1991; Stayman & Kardes, 1992). (See Fig. 9-5.)

In one experiment (Kardes, 1988), subjects were exposed to mock print ads containing information about a fictitious compact-disc player, the CT-2000. (See Fig. 9-6.) The ad contained three different sets of arguments implying three different conclusions about the benefits of the advertised brand. For example, the first set of arguments stated that the CT-2000 had a motorized drawer and that inserting a disc is easy when the CD player has a motorized drawer. These arguments syllogistically imply the conclusion that inserting a disc is easy with the CT-2000. The second set of arguments

FIGURE 9-5

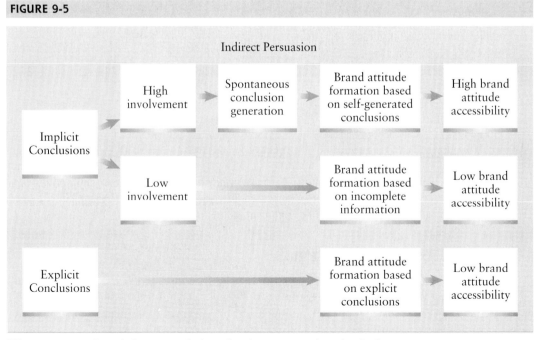

When consumers draw their own conclusions, they form stronger brand attitudes.

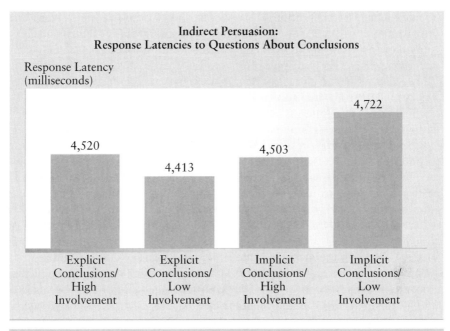

FIGURE 9-6

Response latencies are faster when consumers retrieve old conclusions from memory than when they form new conclusions.

Source: Adapted from Kardes (1988).

syllogistically implied the conclusion that the advertised brand filters out sampling frequency distortions at less cost, and the third set implied the conclusion that the advertised brand reduces more distortion from surface irregularities than most brands. Either all three conclusions were stated explicitly in the text (explicit conclusions) or all three were omitted (implicit conclusions).

The ad also contained a manipulation (low or high involvement) designed to influence elaboration likelihood. In the low-involvement condition, the ad began with an uninformative, uninteresting boldface headline that simply said "Compact-Disc Players." In the high-involvement condition, the ad contained an informative, thought-provoking, and, therefore, inference-provoking opener. Specifically, the headline stated that "You Will Own a Compact-Disc Player Sooner than You Think." This portion of the headline was intended to increase the personal relevance of the ad. The headline also stated that "Some CD Players Are Very Bad and Some Are Very Good." Both statements were designed to induce subjects to think about the information presented in the ad more carefully. People are more likely to think carefully about several sets of message arguments when the message is personally relevant and when brands are perceived to vary in quality (when quality is about the same for all brands, any brand will be satisfactory).

The results revealed that subjects were likely to infer their own conclusions and form very favorable brand attitudes when involvement was high and when conclusions were omitted from the text of the ad. Favorable brand attitudes were also formed in explicit conclusion conditions. However, stronger brand attitudes were formed when involvement was high and conclusions were omitted than when conclusions were presented explicitly. Attitude strength or accessibility refers to the speed with which subjects can retrieve their attitudes from memory. Accessible attitudes are strong because they exert a strong impact on purchase behavior; inaccessible attitudes are weak because they have almost no influence on purchase behavior (Berger & Mitchell, 1989; Fazio, Powell, & Williams, 1989). Hence, it is important to design ads that lead consumers to form strong brand attitudes as well as favorable brand attitudes.

Indirect persuasion offers several important advantages over more commonly used persuasion techniques. Because consumers are encouraged to draw their own conclusions and persuade themselves, counterargumentation is reduced (why argue with yourself?). Furthermore, hard-sell approaches, in which consumers are told what they should believe, run the risk of inducing psychological reactance and boomerang effects (Brehm, 1966; Clee & Wicklund, 1980). That is, when a message is too direct and forceful, consumers often decide to believe the opposite to reassert their freedom to believe whatever they want to believe. With indirect persuasion, however, the message is stated in a subtle, soft-sell manner, and the risk of inducing psychological reactance is reduced greatly. Moreover, information that subjects infer themselves is often more memorable (Moore, Reardon, & Durso, 1986; Tyler, Hertel, McCallum, & Ellis, 1979) and often held with greater confidence (Levin, Johnson, & Chapman, 1987), relative to information that is simply read from a message. Finally, attitudes formed on the basis of

FIGURE 9-7

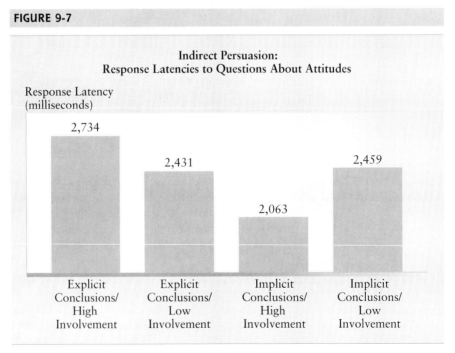

Indirect Persuasion:
Response Latencies to Questions About Attitudes

Response Latency
(milliseconds)

2,734	2,431	2,063	2,459
Explicit Conclusions/ High Involvement	Explicit Conclusions/ Low Involvement	Implicit Conclusions/ High Involvement	Implicit Conclusions/ Low Involvement

Response latencies are faster when consumers form attitudes based on spontaneously generated conclusions.

Source: Adapted from Kardes (1988).

MAKING THE DECISION

SOFT SELL BY MAIL ORDER

The average American household receives 100 catalogs every year, though only 54 percent of the households actually read the catalogs, according to the Direct Marketing Association. So each catalog competes feverishly for consumers' attention. Some use a hard-sell approach. But others, like Abercrombie & Fitch, Louis Boston, Lands' End, and even Neiman Marcus, have tried a soft-sell approach by turning their catalogs into magazines—or magalogs, as people in the industry term them.

Abercrombie & Fitch publishes its "A&F Quarterly," a 130-page publication edited by magazine publishing editor Tyler Brule. "A&F Quarterly" contains a lot more than clothes, although the company is known for its cargo pants, baseball caps, and big sweaters. The magalog includes tips on how to be really cool (buy a Vespa scooter, drink Belgian Chimay beer, use a Nokia Personal Communicator) and how to choose the best type of dog as a pet (go to the humane society). In short, "A&F Quarterly" is selling a lifestyle—and by the way, the clothes to go with it. "['A&F Quarterly'] sells the Abercrombie lifestyle," explains the company's president, Michael Jeffries. "It will attract more people to the stores."

For a number of years, Lands' End catalogs have featured articles and stories by well-known writers. One holiday issue, more than 250 pages long, included writing by Garrison Keillor, Charles Kuralt, and Jacquelyn Mitchard. Lands' End also jazzes up its pages with profiles of craftspeople as well as articles describing how some of its more exclusive products (such as cashmere sweaters) come to

market (starting, of course, with the sheep in Kashmir).

Clothier Louis Boston publishes a semiannual magalog called "Louie," which features articles on "The Origins of Style" and "Refined Comfort Food." Louis Boston clothes are in there, with fine-print descriptions—almost as an afterthought, as if to say to readers, "by the way, we offer clothes as well." The idea is to exert subtle, indirect pressure to visit Louis Boston stores.

In all three of these cases, consumers are encouraged to come to their own conclusions about the products, but it is no accident that the products are presented in a certain way. If consumers want to project a certain image and live a certain lifestyle, they can do so by buying the clothes. Marketers believe that by using indirect persuasion they are actually more apt to attract and keep consumers' attention. Steven Kornajcik, senior vice president of creative services for Neiman Marcus, which also produces a "Book" that it mails to charge-card customers, observes that his customers "have a very high taste level, and the psychographics are right: they are also proven shoppers. The customer is picking up the 'Book' and holding onto it—not like every other catalog that they look at and throw in the trash."

Not everyone in the industry agrees that this approach, which they believe clutters up the pages of catalogs with irrelevant material, works. Richard Grunsten, of GSP Marketing Services Inc. (a Chicago agency that designs and produces catalogs), warns, "It's never worked—ever. But there is always someone who wants to try again." And again, and again, if our stuffed-full mailboxes are any indication.

Sources: Laura Bird, "Beyond Mail Order: Catalogs Now Sell Image, Advice," *The Wall Street Journal,* July 29, 1997, pp. B1, B5; Lands' End catalog, November 1997.

self-generated inferences are more accessible than attitudes formed through a less effortful process (Kardes, 1988, 1993; Stayman & Kardes, 1992). (See Fig. 9-7.) Accessible attitudes exert a strong influence on actual purchase decisions and are resistant to counterpersuasion (Fazio, 1986, 1989; Fazio et al., 1989). (See "Making the Decision: Soft Sell by Mail Order.")

The need for cognition, or the preference to engage in effortful thinking (even when it is not necessary to do so), produces effects similar to those of involvement. When need for cognition or involvement is high, consumers think extensively and elaboratively about a persuasive message. When need for cognition or involvement is low, consumers think briefly and form quick impressions. Consequently, consumers are more likely to draw their own conclusions when conclusions are missing from an ad when the need for cognition or involvement is high (Stayman & Kardes, 1992). However, self-generated conclusions do not always influence brand attitudes. Low self-monitoring individuals, or individuals who are sensitive to internal cues (such as their personal beliefs and opinions) but not to external cues (such as the beliefs and opinions of other people), are likely to use their own conclusions when forming attitudes. High self-monitoring individuals, or individuals who are sensitive to external but not to internal cues, are unlikely to use their own conclusions. Consequently, in response to ads using implicit conclusions, the strongest and most accessible brand attitudes are formed by consumers who are both high in need for cognition (and therefore likely to generate their own conclusions) and low in self-monitoring (and therefore likely to use their own conclusions).

Well-constructed syllogisms provide strong reasons for buying a particular product. Multiple sets of syllogisms can be even more compelling than a single syllogism. How should multiple sets of syllogisms be organized or structured? A horizontal argument structure is used when multiple sets of syllogisms imply the same conclusion independently. That is, completely different arguments are used to support the same conclusion. A vertical argument structure is used when the conclusion of the first syllogism serves as the first premise of the next syllogism, the conclusion of the second syllogism serves as the first premise of the third syllogism, and so on. However, interdependent sets of arguments result in a house of cards: When doubt is cast on one argument, then the entire structure collapses. Recent research shows that brand attitudes are stronger and more resistant to counterpersuasion when they are based on a horizontal as opposed to a vertical argument structure (Kardes, Cronley, Pontes, & Houghton, in press).

CHAPTER SUMMARY ▪

People are good at influencing themselves. They know what kind of arguments they find compelling, and they know their likes and dislikes better than anyone else. Furthermore, their personal, private reactions to a persuasive message are more important than the contents of the message itself. As psychological theories of self-persuasion become more precise and sophisticated, marketers will become more effective at helping people to influence themselves.

Persuasion is a very complex topic. In fact, it is so complex that the leading ad agencies disagree on most issues. Some agencies emphasize facts and others emphasize feelings. Some agencies try to create pleasant ads and others design obnoxious, irritating ads. Some agencies prefer to use celebrity endorsers and other agencies prefer not to. Much of this confusion has been reduced by the elaboration likelihood model of persuasion. We now know that consumers who are motivated and able to elaborate on a message are likely to follow the central route to persuasion. Consumers following this route are especially sensitive and responsive to factual information and logical arguments. In contrast, consumers who are unmotivated or unable to elaborate are likely to follow the peripheral route to persuasion. Consumers following this route are responsive to superficial cues, such as spokesperson expertise or attractiveness, message length, and brand name or reputation.

Early work on role playing shows that increasing consumer involvement in a message and encouraging consumers to actively deliver a persuasive message results in greater persuasion than asking them to passively read the same message. Tesser's theory of attitude polarization emphasizes that the more one thinks about an issue, the more extreme one's opinions become. Thinking about an issue generally results in a more coherent and consistent knowledge structure about the issue and an increase in the number of consistent beliefs that are formed.

Indirect persuasion involves omitting the main conclusions of a message and inducing consumers to think about and form their own conclusions. This technique offers several advantages over more traditional techniques: Counterargumentation is minimized, psychological reactance is avoided, self-generated information is credible and memorable, and inference-based brand attitudes are more accessible than attitudes based on less effortful cognitive mechanisms.

KEY CONCEPTS ■

- Elaboration likelihood model
- Central route to persuasion
- Elaboration
- Peripheral route to persuasion

- Source derogations
- Counterarguments
- Support arguments
- Curiosity statements
- Mere thought effect
- Indirect persuasion

- Inference
- Syllogistic inference rule
- Explicit conclusions
- Implicit conclusions

DISCUSSIONS QUESTIONS ■

1. Why do you think Tony the Tiger was such a successful character in Kellogg's advertising campaign for Frosted Flakes? Name some other characters—and their products—that have attracted and kept your attention.
2. In what ways does the elaboration likelihood model help marketers?
3. Would a consumer be more likely to follow a central route or a peripheral route to persuasion when deciding what type of personal computer to buy? Why?
4. Explain how a marketer might use your answer to question 3 to construct an effective ad for a personal computer.
5. What are the four major types of elaborations?
6. Which would be more effective for an ad for a diamond engagement ring: one that presented several strong arguments for purchasing the ring or one that presented no arguments at all? Why?

7. Are people more apt to change their attitudes by delivering a message or listening to one? What implications might this have for a marketing promotion at a resort in which current guests receive a discount on future stays if they recruit a certain number of new customers?
8. Under what circumstances is the mere thought effect most powerful?
9. What three conditions does effective indirect persuasion require?
10. What advantages might the indirect persuasion approach have in a commercial for a weight loss program?

Social Influence Principles

◆ THE NBA

The National Basketball Association doesn't just govern a game in which athletes pound up and down a court, slam dunking an orange ball through a hoop as many times as they can. The NBA governs a global marketing effort that involves everything from entertainment to licensed products to joint ventures with high-scoring companies like McDonald's, Reebok, and Coca-Cola. The NBA is also about image—represented by players as diverse as Michael Jordan and Dennis Rodman.

The whole world likes Michael Jordan. In fact, a survey of 28,000 teenagers in 45 countries by Darcy Masius Benton & Bowles, a worldwide marketing agency, revealed that Michael Jordan was the world's favorite athlete, way ahead of everyone else in every other sport. Having a player like Jordan was a gold mine for the NBA—fans all around the world want to associate with him in some way, whether by watching games or buying official caps and T-shirts. "Jordan is on the scale of [soccer player] Pele," says

Georges Eddy, an NBA broadcaster in France. "To me, there was Pele, there was Jordan, and that's it."

Worldwide appeal to consumers is crucial to the NBA's future. The organization sells out most of its games in the United States, and its licensing revenues here are flattening because the market is mature. "That's why we're moving internationally," explains NBA commissioner David Stern.

Basketball is already an international sport—pro and amateur leagues have been playing for years in Europe and Asia—so people already understand the game, in many languages. People like to associate with others who are similar to them. To help boost familiarity even further, the NBA relies on players from abroad. Furthermore the NBA actually gives away its programming in China, where 250 million TV households watch *NBA Action* and a game of the week. Stern thinks the free programming is worth the expense if he can win the loyalty of two billion Chinese fans.

Commissioner Stern recognizes the incredible power of television to make an impact on consumers worldwide. Even in such countries as Mongolia, Namibia, and Kuwait, where revenues are tiny compared with revenues from European and South American countries, Stern figures that he is ahead of the game. Namibia pays about $22,500 for a season's broadcast rights, whereas France and Mexico pay around $1 million. "That's the beauty of television. Other brands have to buy their way on through advertising. Our core product is a two-hour commercial that someone pays us to run."

In marketing, popularity begets popularity—people like to support winning teams, winning sports, winning products. It makes them feel like part of a group, as if they are winners, too. They associate not only directly by attending games but also indirectly by buying licensed products such as sweatshirts and athletic shoes. NBA fans can even show their association by drinking Sprite, a Coca-Cola product. Coke has put NBA and team logos on Sprite soft drinks sold in 30 countries. Indirect associations influence social perceptions and social power.

Source: Marc Gunther, "They All Want to Be Like Mike," *Fortune,* July 21, 1997, pp. 51–53.

◆ INTRODUCTION

Salespersons, fund-raisers, politicians, con artists, friends, and associates use a wide variety of influence techniques designed to get you to say "yes," as does the NBA. The wording of their requests is crucial—requests worded one way are very effective, whereas the same requests worded just a little bit differently fail. Timing is also crucial—there is a narrow window of opportunity in which people are susceptible to requests they would normally prefer to decline. Professor Robert Cialdini (1993) has conducted many pioneering scientific investigations of behavioral compliance techniques and has uncovered many principles and secrets that most influence agents wish would remain shrouded in mystery. This chapter discusses these secrets and summarizes scientific evidence bearing on the effectiveness of seven key principles of influence (automaticity, commitment and consistency, reciprocity, scarcity, social validation, liking, and authority). Knowledge of these principles allows you to be more effective in influencing others. On the flip side of the same coin, knowledge of these principles permits you to stay on your guard against others who are trying to influence you.

◆ THE AUTOMATICITY PRINCIPLE

According to Cialdini (1993), the **automaticity principle** is the cornerstone of all influence techniques. Sometimes people use simple heuristics or shortcuts for processing requests. Heuristics enable people to make quick and easy decisions almost automatically. When people behave automatically (Schneider & Shiffrin, 1977; Shiffrin & Schneider, 1977), or "mindlessly" (i.e., with little conscious effort; Langer, 1978, 1989), they are susceptible to a wide variety of influence techniques. When salespersons or other agents of influence are knowledgeable about the heuristics targets use when processing requests, and when targets behave automatically or mindlessly, heuristic-based requests are likely to be quite successful. This chapter discusses these heuristics.

DIFFERENT TYPES OF HEURISTICS

Before discussing these heuristics, however, it would be useful to specify the distinctions among prediction heuristics (i.e., representativeness, availability, simulation, anchoring, and adjustment; see Chapter 4), persuasion heuristics (e.g., experts are usually correct, length implies strength, etc.; see Chapter 9), and influence heuristics. All heuristics are shortcuts that simplify cognitive tasks, but different heuristics are needed for different tasks. **Prediction heuristics** influence likelihood judgments, **persuasion heuristics** influence beliefs and attitudes, and **influence heuristics** influence behavior. However, people do not always use heuristics. They are most likely to use heuristics when they are unmotivated (e.g., because of low involvement or lack of interest in a topic) or unable (e.g., because of low levels of knowledge, high time pressure, high distraction, or the effects of other variables that limit information processing) to think carefully and effortfully about an issue (Chaiken, Liberman, & Eagly, 1989; Langer, 1978, 1989; Petty & Cacioppo, 1986; Schneider & Shiffrin, 1977; Shiffrin & Schneider, 1977). The amount of cognitive effort involved in information processing varies on a continuum ranging from very low (automatic, peripheral, heuristic, or mindless information processing) to very high (controlled, central, systematic, or mindful information processing). The lower the effort, the more likely people are to engage in simple heuristic thinking.

The Because Heuristic

Harvard psychologist Ellen Langer (1978, 1989) claims that people spend a large proportion of a typical day in a mindless state. Habitual, routine behaviors are performed over and over with relatively little conscious thought. Moreover, we have neither the time nor the resources needed to think carefully about every idea that comes our way. People are selective. Some topics receive careful attention; others are processed mindlessly or heuristically. For example, suppose that you are about to use the Xerox machine in the school library and another student approaches you and says, "Excuse me, I have five pages. May I use the Xerox machine?" Such a small request requires little thought, and many people say "yes" without really thinking about it. In fact, this is precisely what happened in the control condition of a classic field study on mindlessness conducted by Langer, Blank, and Chanowitz (1978). (See Fig. 10-1.) The wording of the request varied slightly across the different experimental conditions, however. Langer reasoned that people are more likely to comply with a request if you give them a reason for complying—the **because heuristic.** The word *because* implies a reason for

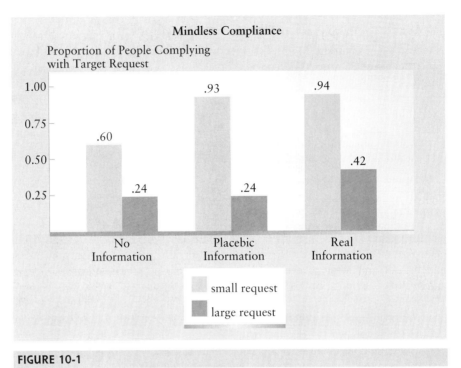

FIGURE 10-1

Even placebic information is effective when people mindlessly comply with a small request.
Source: Adapted from Langer, Blank, & Chanowitz (1978).

complying, so maybe including the word *because* in the request will increase compliance rates. In fact, changing the request to "Excuse me, I have five pages. May I use the Xerox machine because I'm in a rush" greatly increased compliance rates. In the most interesting condition, however, the word *because* was used with no real reason: "Excuse me, I have five pages. May I use the Xerox machine because I have to make copies?" This condition was called the *placebic information condition* because no real information was provided. Subjects received only a request and a nonsensical reason. However, if people process this small request mindlessly and use the because heuristic, merely hearing the magic word *because* may be sufficient to produce compliance. This is exactly what happened: Compliance rates increased from 60 percent in the control condition to 93 percent in the placebic information condition. In fact, compliance rates in the placebic information (93 percent) and real information (94 percent) conditions were statistically equivalent.

This is not the whole story, however. In some conditions, the request was large: "Excuse me, I have 25 pages. May I use the Xerox machine?" Theoretically, large requests should encourage mindful thinking, which should reduce the likelihood of using the because heuristic. Consistent with this prediction, compliance rates for large requests were quite low in control and placebic information conditions—much lower than in the real information condition. Subsequent research has shown that bad excuses (e.g., "Because I don't want to wait") also result in low compliance rates (Folkes, 1985), perhaps because bad excuses increase mindfulness (Langer, Blank, & Chanowitz, 1985).

MAKING THE DECISION

WHO WANTS A CHEAP MERCEDES?

Mercedes wants to launch a bargain-basement version of itself. It's called the Smart Car, and it is so small and goofy looking that it makes the VW Beetle look like, well, a Mercedes. The Smart Car venture originally started as a deal between Volkswagen and SMH, the Swiss watchmaker known for its trendy, inexpensive watch line, the Swatch. But when Volkswagen changed leadership, the car company's incoming chairman, Ferdinand Piech, withdrew from the project. He didn't think that cheap, fashionable cars were synonymous with cheap, fashionable watches.

So Mercedes (with significant help from its parent company, Daimler-Benz) entered the picture. Mercedes is currently in the middle of an effort to transform itself into a full-range car manufacturer (as opposed to a luxury-car maker). The company acquired Micro Compact Cars (MCC), the business unit out of which the Smart Car was to drive. The cars will now come from a new MCC factory in France, and Mercedes is arranging for lease financing and a special network of dealers to sell and lease the cars to consumers. MCC claims that it plans to sell 200,000 cars a year, making a profit within five or six years.

That's an ambitious goal. For one thing, the car is so small that Mercedes is offering free use of its midsized cars to lease customers during the holidays, when they need the space for luggage and passengers. For another, Smart Car has to pit itself against its main competitor, Volkswagen. Why would consumers want to buy the two-door Smart Car for $8,800 when for the same money they could buy the four-door VW Lupo?

Then there is the price–quality relationship that many consumers believe in: If the car is inexpensive, it can't be very good. Perhaps this heuristic will be modified by the Mercedes name, which has always been synonymous with quality. But the Smart Car may be the first of the new Mercedes cars to fall victim to Mercedes' own luxury reputation — will consumers want the less expensive Mercedes line, even if Mercedes swears that these cars are of the same quality as its luxury vehicles? If so, how will Mercedes justify continuing to charge premium prices for its top-line cars? Thus, success of the Smart Car — despite its name and price tag — is by no means a sure thing. Consumers may just walk away saying, "Who wants a cheap Mercedes, anyway?"

Source: "Not So Smart," *The Economist,* September 6, 1997, p. 63.

The Price–Quality Heuristic

Another commonly used heuristic is the **price–quality heuristic.** Quality-hungry consumers frequently assume that high-price items are also high in quality. (See "Making the Decision: Who Wants a Cheap Mercedes?") Although this heuristic is true in many cases (e.g., Rolls-Royces are actually high-quality automobiles), consumers typically overestimate the strength of the relationship between price and quality (Lichtenstein & Burton, 1989). Merely expecting to see a strong relationship between price and quality leads consumers to focus on instances confirming their expectation and to neglect instances inconsistent with their expectation (Broniarczyk & Alba, 1994a, 1994b). Consumers are especially likely to use the price–quality heuristic when quality is ambiguous or difficult to judge (Hoch & Deighton, 1989).

Note that both the because heuristic and the price–quality heuristic involve the use of minimal information. Both heuristics involve the use of only one cue, or only one piece of information. The single cue needed for the because heuristic is the magic word *because*. The single cue needed for the price–quality heuristic is the price of the product. This is the nature of heuristic thinking: Only one cue is used, and other potentially more relevant pieces of information are neglected. Of course, the actual quality of a reason for a favor depends on many other things besides the use of the word *because*. Similarly, the actual quality of a product depends on many other things besides price. Quick-and-dirty heuristic thinking leads people to overlook these other things. Effective influence agents know this, and they also know what buttons (i.e., heuristics) to push. Resisting their influence involves avoiding heuristic thinking.

◆ THE COMMITMENT AND CONSISTENCY PRINCIPLE

Consistency pressures are surprisingly powerful. People are expected to exhibit beliefs, attitudes, and behaviors that are coherent and that seem to go together, and inconsistencies are often interpreted as personality flaws or even, in extreme cases, symptoms of mental illness (Dawes, 1994). This principle is known as the **commitment and consistency principle.** When people notice an apparent inconsistency in their belief system, they often change one or more beliefs to make the system more consistent (see Chapter 8). When people notice a behavior–attitude inconsistency, they often change the attitude to make it more consistent with the behavior (see Chapter 8). Similarly, once people say "yes" to a request or offer, they are likely to continue to say "yes" to subsequent requests or offers. After complying with an initial small request, people are more likely to comply with a subsequent large request (the foot-in-the-door technique). After saying "yes" to a deal, people are more likely to stick to their initial commitment even if the deal changes (the low-ball effect).

THE FOOT-IN-THE-DOOR TECHNIQUE

First make a small request and then follow up with a larger request. This is the **foot-in-the-door technique.** Many telemarketers use this technique: First they ask for a small favor and then they follow up with a sales pitch. For example, some unscrupulous telemarketers pretend to be survey researchers, and they ask you to answer a few brief questions over the phone. If you comply with their small request and answer the questions, you are more likely to continue to be helpful by buying whatever it is they are trying to sell. If you knew from the beginning, however, that they were just trying to sell you something, you would have been much more resistant to the sales pitch.

Similarly, many fund-raisers know that past donors are likely to continue to donate, and they may donate even more this year. Many salespeople know that customers who have purchased small orders previously are likely to continue to buy, and they may purchase even larger orders this year. "Start small and build" foot-in-the-door tactics are surprisingly simple and effective (Cialdini, 1993).

In a classic field experiment, Freedman and Fraser (1966) went door-to-door and asked California residents to post a large, ugly sign in their front lawns saying "Drive Carefully." Not surprisingly, in the request-only control condition, only 17 percent said "yes." However, the results were very different when this large request was preceded

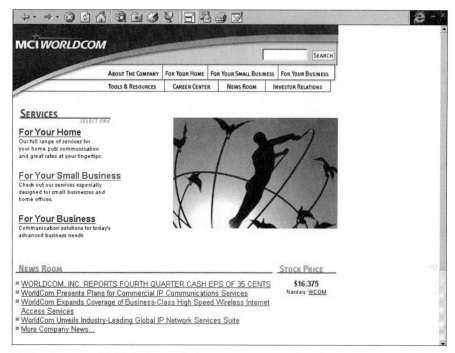

MCI makes several initial offers on its home page (www.mci.com) to get consumers to sign up for its phone services.

Source: Courtesy of MCI Telecommunications Corporation.

by a small initial request. When people were first asked to post a small "Be a Safe Driver" sign, 76 percent later agreed to post the large "Drive Carefully" sign. Moreover, nearly half the people agreed to post the large sign after first agreeing to post a small sign dealing with a different issue ("Keep California Beautiful") or after first agreeing to sign a petition pertaining to a similar (driving safety) or dissimilar (keep California beautiful) issue. (See Fig. 10-2.) These results are even more surprising when one considers that the large request was made nearly two weeks after the small request and that the requests were made by two different people. The most widely accepted psychological explanation for the foot-in-the-door technique is based on self-perception theory (Bem, 1972), which suggests that complying with a small request leads people to label themselves as helpful good citizens or as reasonable people, and this increases the likelihood of continuing compliance (DeJong, 1979; Reingen & Kernan, 1977, 1979).

THE LOW-BALL TECHNIQUE

Used-car salespersons (and other types of salespersons) often try to get an initial commitment from their customers and then change the deal. First the salesperson offers customers a very attractive deal. They say "yes," fill out a bunch of forms, and convince themselves it is a good deal by thinking of many reasons why it is such a good deal. Once this happens, the hook is set. Then the deal changes. The customer learns that the car is actually more expensive than they originally thought. Maybe the salesperson

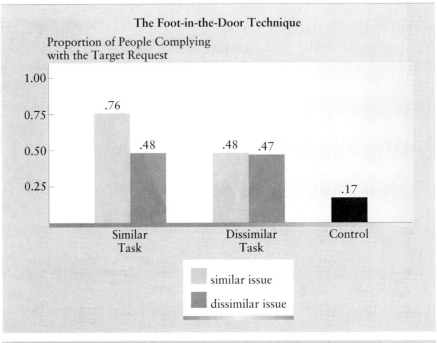

FIGURE 10-2

People are more apt to comply with a large request when they have already complied with a smaller request.

Source: Adapted from Freedman & Fraser (1966).

forgot to add the cost of an expensive option, or maybe the salesperson's boss did not approve the sale (it's easy to come up with lame excuses; try it yourself!). However, because the hook had already been set, many customers go through with the deal even though the deal was no longer attractive. When a deal changes, people should rethink the deal, but surprisingly few do. This is the **low-ball technique.**

Cialdini (1993) first learned about the low-ball technique while pretending to be a sales trainee at a Chevrolet dealership. After learning about the technique, he returned to his laboratory at Arizona State University and conducted a series of controlled experiments (Cialdini, Cacioppo, Bassett, & Miller, 1978). In the first experiment, students were approached on their way to class and were asked if they would be willing to participate in an experiment. Most said "yes." Then the deal changed. After saying yes, subjects were told that the experiment would begin at 7 A.M. Saturday morning. Although most students do not like to participate in studies conducted at 7 A.M. Saturday morning, nearly every student who said "yes" to the initial request actually showed up on time for the experiment! By contrast, students in the control condition were told up front that the study would be conducted at 7 A.M. Saturday morning before they were asked to participate. Very few students said "yes," and even fewer showed up at the lab. (See Fig. 10-3.)

In a follow-up experiment, Cialdini et al. (1978) compared the low-ball technique with the foot-in-the-door technique. Both techniques involve obtaining initial compliance in the hopes of obtaining future compliance through mindless consistency.

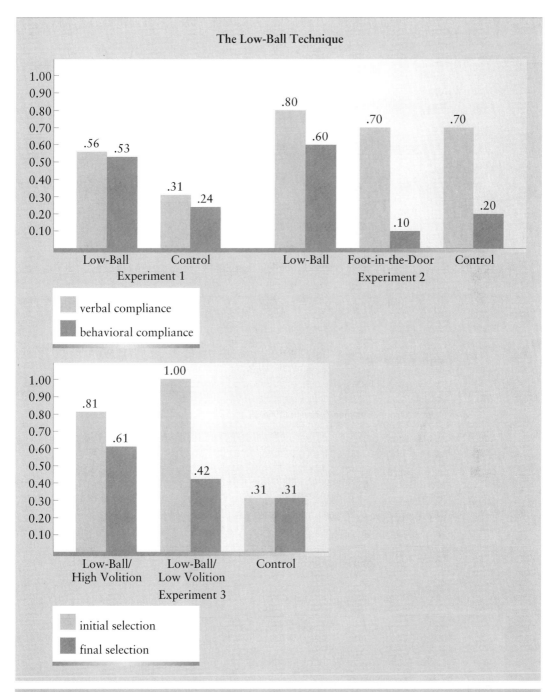

FIGURE 10-3

People are more likely to comply with an unattractive request when they have already agreed to a previous, attractive request.

Source: From Cialdini, Cacioppo, Bassett, & Miller (1978).

However, with the low-ball technique, after the initial commitment is obtained, the deal changes so that the factors leading to the initial commitment are nullified. With the foot-in-the-door technique, the deal does not change; instead, two separate requests/deals are made. Cialdini's assistant went door-to-door through the dormitories asking students to display United Way posters on their dorm windows and doors. In the low-ball condition, subjects were first asked if they would be willing to help. Most said "yes." After obtaining the crucial "yes," subjects were told that they would need to go downstairs to the dormitory desk to get the posters. In the foot-in-the-door condition, subjects were first asked to display a window poster that was given to them (the small request) and then asked to go downstairs to get the door poster (the large request). In the control condition, subjects were told up front that they would need to go downstairs to collect the posters before they could display them. The results indicated that the vast majority of subjects participating in the low-ball condition collected and displayed the posters, whereas very few subjects gathered the posters in the foot-in-the-door or control conditions. Hence, the low-ball technique is more powerful than the foot-in-the-door technique.

Commitment Theory

In a third experiment, Cialdini et al. (1978) tested four theories about why the low-ball technique works so well. One theory suggests that behavior (i.e., saying "yes") is more salient than the context in which the behavior occurred (i.e., the initial deal), and consequently, the initial "yes" has a larger effect on subsequent behavior than the initial context. This **salience hypothesis** suggests that people will stick to initial commitments even if they had no choice about the initial commitment and were later given a choice. Self-perception theory and cognitive dissonance theory both suggest that people's attitudes toward a requested task may change after they agree to perform the requested task. However, this change occurs for different reasons: Self-perception theory suggests that saying "yes" leads people to infer that the task is worthwhile, whereas cognitive dissonance theory suggests that saying "yes" leads people to change their attitude to convince themselves that they did the right thing. Finally, **commitment theory** (Kiesler, 1971) suggests that the purpose of commitment is to impart resistance to change and that commitment to a decision makes the decision less changeable.

To test these four explanations for the low-ball technique, subjects were shown two lengthy questionnaires and were asked to fill out one of the two questionnaires. In the low-ball/free-choice condition, subjects were told they could choose either questionnaire but that they would receive two credits for questionnaire A and only one credit

A student chooses to fill out a questionnaire during a study of the low-ball technique.
Source: © Mary Boucher.

for questionnaire B. Most chose questionnaire A, and afterward they were told that the experimenter made a mistake and that questionnaire A was worth only one credit (it was worth two last semester). They were then given the opportunity to choose again. Most subjects stuck to their initial commitment even though the deal had changed. In the low-ball/no-choice condition, subjects were told that they had to complete questionnaire A (no choice) and that A was worth two credits. Next, they were told that A was worth only one credit, so now they could freely choose either questionnaire. Finally, in the control condition, subjects were simply asked to choose either questionnaire. The results revealed that the low-ball technique was greatly reduced in the no-choice condition. Hence, the salience hypothesis cannot account for the observed pattern of results. Moreover, subjects indicated their attitudes toward each questionnaire before and after saying "yes." No attitude change occurred, ruling out the self-perception and cognitive dissonance explanations. The only explanation consistent with the entire pattern of results was the commitment hypothesis. Hence, the low-ball technique is clearly a technique based on commitment and consistency.

It is important to recognize that car salespersons and tricky experimenters are not the only ones who use the low-ball technique. People low-ball people every day. Any time someone asks, "Would you do me a favor?" you run the risk of being low-balled. The correct answer to this question is, "It depends, tell me what the favor is *first.*"

◆ THE RECIPROCITY PRINCIPLE

According to the **reciprocity principle,** when someone does you a favor, you feel obliged to return the favor. This is not only a rule of social etiquette (sociologists have shown that the rule applies to all human societies; Gouldner, 1960), it is also a surprisingly powerful influence principle. (See "Taking Issue: Coke's Money: It's the Real Thing.") The problem is that people can often be easily tricked into giving much larger favors than they received (Cialdini, 1993). Hare Krishnas and members of other religious groups often give people small gifts—such as flowers, books, or pamphlets—and then ask for a charitable donation in return. After accepting a small gift, people have a surprisingly difficult time refusing to donate. Similarly, salespersons often give small gifts of free samples of food in supermarkets. After accepting a free sample, consumers are more likely to purchase the item. Amway salespersons go door-to-door and offer free "test drives" of their products. For example, the BUG consists of a bag of Amway products (such as furniture polish, window cleaner, detergent, shampoo, deodorizers, pesticides, etc.). Amway salespersons leave the BUG with clients for a few days and ask them to try the products for free. Of course, after accepting the BUG bait, people are more likely to purchase one or two items from the Amway representative.

THE DOOR-IN-THE-FACE TECHNIQUE

Invoking the reciprocity principle does not always involve free gifts, free samples, or free test drives. More subtle favors are also used. For example, following up a large unreasonable request with a smaller, more reasonable request is a concession that usually begets larger concessions. This multiple request technique, however, is quite different from the multiple request technique discussed earlier. The foot-in-the-door technique involves a small request followed by a large request. The **door-in-the-face technique** involves the opposite: a large request followed by a small request. When

COKE'S MONEY: IT'S THE REAL THING

Money talks. It can buy influence, favors, a philanthropic image. Is there anything inherently wrong with this? Not necessarily, but it is a part of the reciprocity principle that may deserve a closer look.

At Boys & Girls Clubs all over the United States, Pepsi is out and Coke is in. As part of a $60 million agreement between Coca-Cola and the Boys & Girls Clubs of America (a nationwide network of nearly 2,000 nonprofit youth groups), Coke vending machines expel soft drinks in club centers, Coke scoreboards keep track of club basketball games, and kids log on to the Internet via Coke-purchased PCs. In addition, Coca-Cola has pumped $8 million in cash into clubs across the country and is paying for such educational programs as after-school reading sessions. Over the next decade, Boys & Girls Clubs will receive a cut of some of Coke's promotional campaigns; Coke will sponsor fund-raisers at local clubs, such as basketball and golf tournaments. Coke will market club-branded T-shirts and caps, and the clubs will get generous cuts from those on-site vending machines.

There is a term for this new type of charitable giving: strategic philanthropy. Strategic philanthropy isn't just a tax write-off for the donor; it is tied directly to business goals, aiming for positive financial results. "Partnerships like this don't come through the donation window, but through the marketing door," observes Richard Goings, chairman of the Boys & Girls Clubs of America National Board of Governors.

How do companies like Coke get financial results if they are giving so much away? Strategic philanthropy is a two-sided (reciprocal) arrangement. In exchange for the infusion of cash, products, and sponsorships, Boys & Girls Clubs open their doors to Coke, giving Coke access to millions of American preteens. Club youth will appear at Coke promotions, and clubs will help Coke win accounts at donor companies. But youngsters will not sell Coke products directly.

The line between support and sales is blurry in an arrangement like this. Thomas M. McKenna, national executive director of Big Brothers/Big Sisters of America, a similar group, says, "We'd be inclined to draw the line if we were asked to drum up support for a particular product." But nonprofit organizations cannot afford to ignore the trend toward strategic philanthropy, especially as traditional corporate giving is declining. Boys & Girls Clubs now has a professionalized marketing group, with account managers who handle branding and promotion alliances with not only Coca-Cola but also Nike, Taco Bell, and Major League Baseball. Other corporate–nonprofit partnerships include American Express and Share Our Strength (an antihunger organization) and Home Depot and Habitat for Humanity.

Do these partnerships compromise the social mission of nonprofit organizations? In some cases, they might. In others, they might not. As in all reciprocal relationships, both sides hope to give a little and get a lot.

Source: Nicole Harris, "Things Go Better with Coke's Money," *Business Week,* September 15, 1997.

influence agents make a large request that is rejected, they often follow up with a smaller, more reasonable request. When someone tries to be reasonable with you, you feel compelled to be more reasonable in return. However, many salespersons know full well that the first unreasonable request will be rejected and that this will increase the likelihood of obtaining compliance with the second, more reasonable request. For example, many television and stereo salespersons try to sell customers three-year service coverage plans. Most customers reject these expensive coverage plans. After the expensive plans are rejected, many salespersons offer a much less expensive one-year plan. Customers are much more likely to accept the one-year plan after rejecting the more expensive three-year plan.

Cialdini et al. (1975) conducted a series of field experiments designed to test the effectiveness of the door-in-the-face technique (rejection, then moderation). (See Fig. 10-4.) Arizona State University students were approached on their way to class and were asked to work for two years as nonpaid volunteers for the Juvenile Detention Center. Not surprisingly, 100 percent said "no." Next they were asked to volunteer to take a group of juveniles to the zoo for two hours, and 50 percent said "yes." In the control condition, students were simply asked to volunteer to take a group of juveniles to the zoo for two hours, and only 17 percent said "yes." Hence, the door-in-the-face technique is quite effective. Moreover, the technique involves more than a simple contrast effect (the small request seems even smaller when compared with the large request) because only 25 percent agreed to take the juveniles to the zoo when subjects heard the large and the small requests and were asked to choose one.

In a follow-up study, students were asked to serve as nonpaid volunteers for a group of low-income children (not juvenile delinquents). After this request was rejected, the door-in-the-face subjects were asked to take a group of low-income children to the zoo for two hours. In the control condition, subjects received only the second request. Again, the door-in-the-face technique proved effective. This study also included a two-requestor condition, in which one individual made the initial large request and a different individual made the second, more reasonable, request. Consistent with the implications of the reciprocity principle, the two-requestor approach was ineffective. A concession occurs only when the same individual makes both requests.

A third experiment tested the possibility that multiple requests may run down the target person's resistance. Perhaps sheer persistence on the part of the influence agent is more important than conveying the appearance of reasonableness and a willingness to offer a concession. In the door-in-the-face condition, subjects were first asked to serve as nonpaid volunteers for two years and subsequently asked to serve as nonpaid volunteers for two hours. This technique was much more effective than the second, request-only, control approach. In the small multiple-request condition, subjects were first asked to take a group of children to the museum for two hours and were next asked to take a group of children to the zoo for two hours. The small multiple-request approach was no more effective than the target-request-only approach. Overall, the results of the three field experiments suggest that the door-in-the-face technique is an effective reciprocity-based influence technique. The illusion of reasonableness and concession is more important than simple contrast or sheer persistence on the part of the agent of influence.

In a study directly comparing the door-in-the-face and foot-in-the-door techniques, target-request-only control subjects were asked to distribute 15 traffic safety pamphlets to their neighbors (Cann, Sherman, & Elkes, 1975). (See Fig. 10-5.) Half said "yes" and half said "no." In the door-in-the-face condition, this target request was preceded by a very large unreasonable request: Would you keep a record of traffic flow at a busy intersection for two hours? In the foot-in-the-door condition, the target request

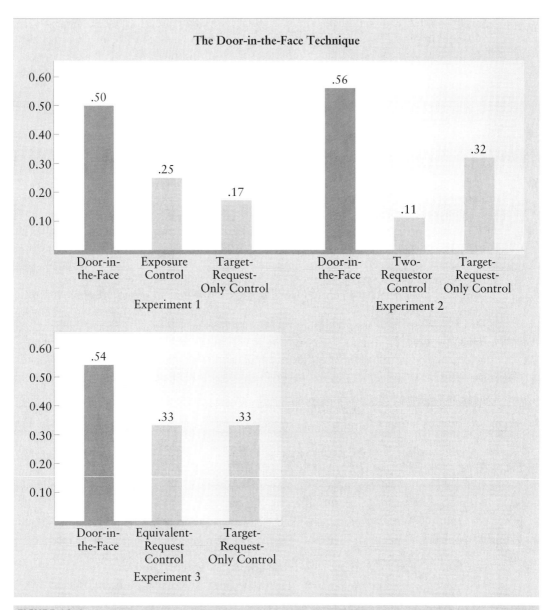

FIGURE 10-4

People are likely to comply with a small request after they have rejected a large request.
Source: From Cialdini, Cacioppo, Bassett, & Miller (1978).

was preceded by a very small request: Would you answer a few short questions about driving safety? In multiple-request conditions, the target request immediately followed the initial request (no-delay conditions) or the target request followed the initial request by seven to ten days (delay conditions). Consistent with the reciprocity explanation of the door-in-the-face technique, the rejection-then-moderation approach was

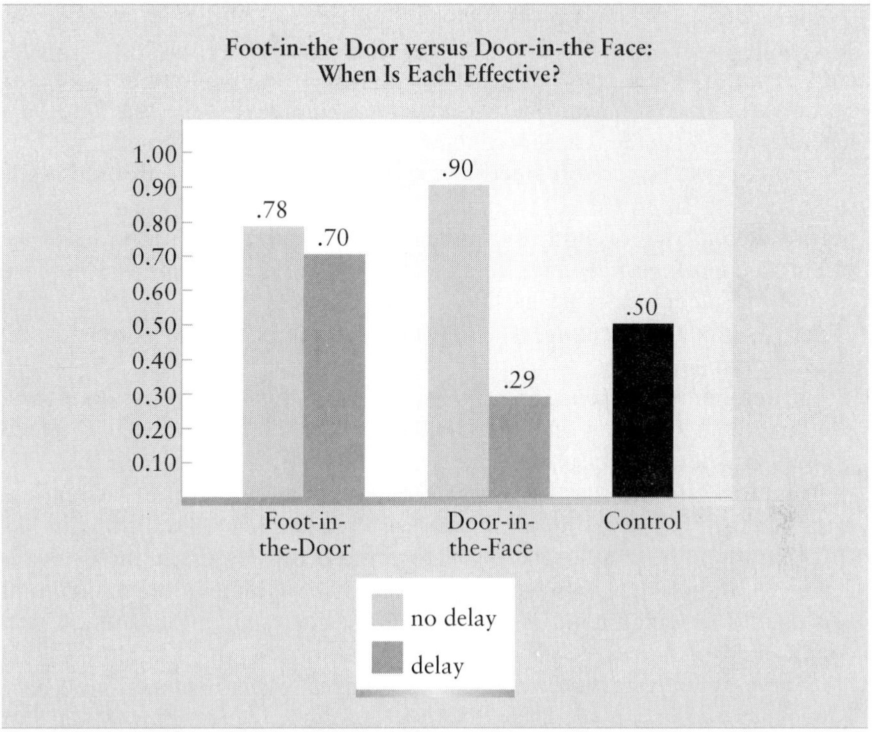

Foot-in-the Door versus Door-in-the Face:
When Is Each Effective?

FIGURE 10-5

The rejection-then-moderation approach is effective in no-delay conditions.
Source: From Cann, Sherman, & Elkes (1975).

effective only in no-delay conditions. The illusion of concession is shattered after a period of several days. Consistent with the self-perception explanation of the foot-in-the-door technique, the start-small-and-build approach was equally effective in no-delay and delay conditions. Labeling oneself as helpful and compliant has long-lasting consequences. Hence, the two multiple-request techniques are driven by quite different psychological processes.

THE THAT'S-NOT-ALL TECHNIQUE

The Popeil Pocket Fisherman, the Ginzu knife, the blue-light special, and holiday sales are all examples of the **that's-not-all technique.** Each of these examples involves a deal that is changed into an even better deal before the consumer has a chance to respond (e.g., "But wait, with this set of Ginzu knives you also get a free pair of scissors and a free steamer basket"). The that's-not-all technique invokes the norm (rule) of reciprocity: The salesperson appears to try to offer a good deal, so the customer feels forced to try to be reasonable. Burger (1986) conducted a series of field experiments to test the effectiveness and mediation (underlying causes) of the that's-not-all technique. In the first experiment, that's-not-all subjects were offered a cupcake for 75 cents at a bake sale and the deal was sweetened (literally) by adding two free cookies. In the control condition, subjects were told up front that for 75 cents they got a cupcake and two cookies. Even though the deal was identical across the two conditions, the sales presentation had a large impact: 73 percent accepted the deal in the that's-not-all condition, whereas only 40 percent accepted the deal in the control condition.

Similar results were obtained by reducing the price. In the that's-not-all condition, subjects were first offered a cupcake for $1 and the price was reduced to 75 cents before the customer could respond. In the control condition, subjects were simply offered a cupcake for 75 cents. In a follow-up study, the salesperson reduced the price from $1 to 75 cents because he said he wanted to leave soon. This approach was more effective than a price change due to a mistake (e.g., "I'm new here and I made a mistake about the price").

In another price-reduction experiment, two salespersons went door-to-door selling candles. In the that's-not-all/negotiation condition, the candles were offered for $3, the second salesperson whispered something to the first salesperson, and the price was reduced to $2. In the that's-not-all/accident condition, the price change was due to a mistake (i.e., "These are the $2 candles; we already sold all the $3 candles"). In the control condition, the candles were simply offered for $2. Again, the deal was identical across the three conditions. Nevertheless, sales were high in the that's-not-all/negotiation condition, medium in the that's-not-all/accident condition, and low in the control condition.

The next experiment tested a simple contrast-effect explanation of the that's-not-all technique (75 cents seems especially inexpensive compared with $1). Subjects were asked to imagine that the experimenters were selling cupcakes for either $1 or 75 cents. Next they were asked to forget for a moment how much was charged and to indicate a fair price for the product. Mean fair prices did not differ across the $1 versus 75-cent conditions, contrary to the contrast-effect explanation.

Another follow-up experiment compared the that's-not-all technique with a price change labeled simply as a bargain. In the that's-not-all condition, $1.25 cupcakes were reduced to $1 after two salespersons whispered to each other. In the bargain condition, the cupcakes were offered for $1 and customers were told that the cupcakes were sold earlier for $1.25. In the control condition, the cupcakes were simply offered for $1. Again, the that's-not-all technique was effective, whereas the bargain condition was no more effective than the control condition.

In the final experiment, the that's-not-all technique was compared with the door-in-the-face technique. In the that's-not-all condition, the price of the cupcakes was reduced from $1.25 to $1 after the two salespersons conferred with each other. In the door-in-the-face condition, the cupcakes were offered for $1.25. If customers rejected this offer, the price was reduced to $1. In the control condition, the cupcakes were offered for $1. Sales were highest in the that's-not-all condition, next highest in the door-in-the-face condition, and lowest in the control condition. Together, this series of seven experiments suggests that the that's-not-all technique is robust and is best explained by the reciprocity principle of compliance.

Cialdini (1993) argues that all compliance techniques are more effective when consumers are in a mindless, couch potato state. This hypothesis appears to be correct for the that's-not-all technique. In an interesting field experiment, passersby on a college campus were asked to buy a small (inexpensive) or a large (expensive) box of chocolates from the Psychology Club (Pollack, Smith, Knowles, & Bruce, 1998). In the control conditions, the small box sold for $1 and the large box sold for $5. In placebic information conditions, the price changed (from $1.25 to $1 or from $6.25 to $5) because the first salesperson quoted the wrong price and uninformative information was given: "This candy is made of chocolate and sold in this box." In real information conditions, the price changed because the first salesperson quoted the wrong price and informative information was provided: "These Sweet Shop chocolates are fudge hand-dipped in chocolate with pecans. Also, Sweet Shop has been in the business over 20 years." In small-box conditions, the that's-not-all technique dramatically increased sales in placebic and in real-information conditions. In large-box conditions, the that's-not-all technique was ineffective. Hence, the that's-not-all technique is only effective when consumers are relatively mindless, because the request is small (e.g., buy an inexpensive, small box of chocolates). Furthermore, when consumers are in a mindless state, placebic and real information are equally effective.

THE MULTIPLE-DEESCALATING-REQUESTS TECHNIQUE

The door-in-the-face technique involves two requests: a large request followed by a small request. The **multiple-deescalating-requests technique** involves more than two requests. This approach was examined in the context of a university fund-raising drive in which telemarketers initially requested $1,000 donations (Comer, Kardes, & Sullivan, 1992). If this request was rejected, it was followed by a request for $750. If this request was rejected, it was followed by a request for $500, and so on. This approach yielded greater compliance rates and amounts compared with a request-only control condition. Moreover, this technique was more effective than presenting statistical information about typical donation levels and ranges. Statistical-information conditions were no more effective than the control condition, consistent with the automaticity principle and with research on the neglect of statistical information in noncompliance settings.

THE EVEN-A-PENNY TECHNIQUE

Influence agents can appear to be reasonable and induce clients to be reasonable through a wide variety of reciprocity-based tactics: free gifts, concessions, or multiple concessions. Another way to appear to be reasonable is to make extremely small requests. This approach is known as the **even-a-penny technique,** and it involves the legitimization of paltry contributions (a penny, a dollar, or any extremely small amount of money). Interestingly, this approach has been shown to be effective in increasing compliance rates without decreasing the average amount donated by contributing individuals in fund-raising efforts for the American Cancer Society (Cialdini & Shroeder, 1976), the American Heart Association (Reingen, 1978), and the Reyes Syndrome Foundation (Brockner, Guzzi, Kane, Levine, & Shaplen, 1984). Moreover, this reciprocity-based technique appears to be equally effective in face-to-face and telemarketing contexts (Brockner et al., 1984).

According to the **scarcity principle,** since valuable objects are rare or scarce, scarce objects are assumed to be valuable. Furthermore, to assert their unique individuality and identity, consumers often want what others cannot have. (See "Making the Decision: Watching the Watch Market.") Clever firms can influence perceptions of scarcity by limiting production (e.g., manufacturers of many upscale products, such as Rolls-Royce automobiles, purposely limit production; however, sometimes production is limited accidentally, as in the case of Cabbage Patch dolls), limiting distribution (e.g., manufacturers of many upscale products, such as Armani business suits, do not allow

MAKING THE DECISION

WATCHING THE WATCH MARKET

Luxury watches are in; but even if you can afford one, the one you want may be hard to get. We aren't talking Timex, not Rolex (which is no longer chic), not Omega, Movado, Tag Heuer (excellent watches, but not handmade), not even Baume & Mercier, Concord, or Ebel (even though they contain precious stones that nudge their prices into five figures). No, these watches are the elite of the elite; their names are Jaeger LeCoultre, Vacheron Constantin, Audemars Piquet, Patek Philippe. To be sure, they are made exquisitely, by hand. "Nobody makes watches like Patek," claims one jeweler. "You want my advice?" asks another. "If you want jewelry, look at Bulgari or Cartier. For a watch, Patek." The price—$7,000 for a starter Patek—and you have to wind it yourself. If you want one with a perpetual calendar, it can run you $43,000.

If you can get one, that is. Many of these watches are manufactured in limited editions, which makes them even more attractive to those who can afford them, thus invoking the scarcity principle of influence. This drives the price even higher. A 1989 limited-edition Patek that was originally priced at $9,150 sold for $26,000 at auction less than ten years later.

What do you get for your money? Some models have built-in chronographs for timing such events as the Kentucky Derby or an Olympic 100-yard dash (not to mention your child's three-legged race at field day). They also display the day, date, year (with leap years accounted for), and, in case you're interested, the phases of the moon. Of course, most notations (such as abbreviations for the months) are in a foreign language—French, for instance. So you need to learn how to read them. The price for the model just described can hover around $250,000, which could buy you a nice house in most parts of the country.

Marketers of these watches pitch them as investments, which they are, if you put them in the same category as, say, one-of-a-kind jewelry pieces, fine art, or even antiques. Scarcity makes those pieces more attractive, too. Hank Edelman, the head of Patek Philippe of America, bought his own Patek used. "It's plain and simple, a model from the '50s. I'm going to give it to one of my kids." Like an antique or work of art, the luxury watch becomes an heirloom. Who knows? If your trusty Timex suddenly becomes hard to come by, maybe it will become an heirloom, as well—if it keeps ticking long enough.

Source: Deborah Weisgall, "Buying Time," *Fortune,* September 8, 1997, p. 192.

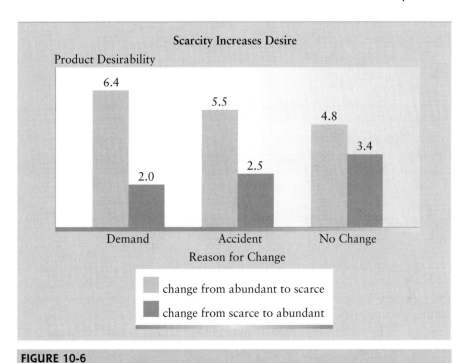

FIGURE 10-6

People want scarce objects even when the objects are not perceived as higher in quality.
Source: Adapted from Worchel et al. (1975).

distribution of their products at discount retail outlets, such as Wal-Mart and Kmart), or through advertising emphasizing scarcity (e.g., limited-time offer, going fast, limited availability). The DeBeers Company has been tremendously successful in influencing perceptions of the scarcity of diamonds. Diamonds are not as rare as most people think (they are used extensively in industrial settings), and, in the not-so-old old days, diamond engagement rings were not automatically and mindlessly exchanged. Government attempts to limit the availability of a product through prohibition or censorship often backfire because consumers often end up wanting the product even more (Worchel & Arnold, 1973; Worchel, Arnold, & Baker, 1975). During Prohibition in the United States, alcoholic beverages became more scarce and more desirable, and consumers were willing to go to great lengths to obtain these products. More recently, bans on marijuana and Cuban cigars have fueled the flames of desire.

Research on the effects of scarcity has also shown that reducing availability increases desirability. Even as simple a manipulation as the presence of many (ten) versus few (two) chocolate chip cookies in a glass jar exerts a surprisingly powerful effect on the desirability of a product (Worchel, Lee, & Adewole, 1975). Subjects wanted more cookies (in a taste-test setting) when there were only two (versus ten) cookies in the jar. This effect was more pronounced when product availability changed because of an accident (i.e., the second experimenter said he accidentally grabbed the wrong jar and then switched jars). The effect was even more pronounced when product availability changed because of demand (i.e., the second experimenter said he needed more cookies because his subjects ate most of his cookies). (See Fig. 10-6.) Interestingly, these scarcity effects occurred even though subjects' taste ratings did not differ across conditions. People want scarce objects even when such objects are not perceived as higher in quality.

◆ THE SOCIAL VALIDATION PRINCIPLE

Thousands of satisfied customers cannot be wrong—a product is famous or the fastest-growing or the largest-selling product around. McDonald's advertises that it has sold over one billion hamburgers. Public broadcasting stations, charity telethons, and insurance salespersons love to show long lists of names of individuals who have been involved in their causes in the past. Televised fund-raising drives show dozens of telephones in the background ringing off the hook. Billy Graham has thousands of supporters who wait for his instructions on when and where to meet to give the impression of a spontaneous mass outpouring when he arrives in a new city (Altheide & Johnson, 1977). Church ushers, bartenders, and street musicians salt their tip jars to give the impression that many people leave tips. Nightclub ushers limit the number of people allowed into the club so that long lines will form outside the door to suggest that the club is extremely popular. Canned laugh tracks on television make sitcoms seem funnier (even though most people claim not to like canned laughter) because they give the impression that many people are laughing (Nosanchuk & Lightstone, 1974).

What do all these examples have in common? They are all applications of the **social validation,** or "proof in numbers," **principle.** The perceived validity (or correctness) of an idea increases as the number of people supporting the idea increases. The opinions of other people can be extremely informative, especially under conditions of ambiguity or uncertainty (Festinger, 1954; Kruglanski & Mayseless, 1987, 1990). Moreover, the effects of peer pressure, conformity (Asch, 1948), and social modeling (i.e., observing another individual perform a specific behavior; Bandura, Grusec, & Menlove, 1967; Bandura & Menlove, 1968) can be surprisingly powerful.

Presenting a list of names of supporters or donors to target individuals is known as the list technique. Research on the list technique has shown that the technique is surprisingly effective. In a door-to-door fund-raising campaign for the American Heart Association, half the target individuals were shown a long list of names of previous donors before a donation was requested, and half received only a request for a donation (Reingen, 1982). Forty-three percent donated in the list-technique condition, whereas only 25 percent donated in the request-only control condition.

Classic research on bystander intervention has shown that people are less likely to help a person in need as the number of other people present and not helping increases (Latane & Darley, 1968; Latane & Rodin, 1969). One reason for bystander nonintervention is pluralistic ignorance, or the assumption that the person in need does not really need help because no one else seems alarmed or concerned. Of course, the other people are also looking around and seeing that no one seems alarmed or concerned. Diffusion of responsibility (why doesn't someone else help?) also reduces the likelihood of helping when many people are present. Because of pluralistic ignorance and the diffusion of responsibility, it is unsurprising that 38 witnesses can passively watch a young woman being stabbed to death over a half-hour period in the streets of New York City (the famous Kitty Genovese case; see Rosenthal, 1964).

As shown by its Web site (www.earthshare.org), Earth Share hopes the pressure of conformity to the politically correct idea of environmentalism will encourage people to donate to its organization.

Source: Courtesy of Earth Share/Environmental Federation of America.

NORMATIVE VERSUS INFORMATIONAL INFLUENCE

In a classic article, Deutsch and Gerard (1955) developed an important distinction between **normative influence** or the "influence to conform with the positive expectations of another" and **informational influence** or the "influence to accept information obtained from another as evidence about reality" (p. 629). Normative influence can be surprisingly powerful because people receive rewards from others (e.g., social approval, acceptance, liking) when they behave in a socially appropriate manner (i.e., in a manner consistent with others' positive expectations), and they receive punishments from others (e.g., disapproval, rejection, disliking) when they behave inappropriately. Informational influence can also be powerful, but for different reasons. Social comparison theory suggests that informational influence is important when consumers are motivated to hold valid beliefs and attitudes (Festinger, 1954). Other people can be an important source of information about the validity of our opinions, but some types of people are more influential than others. Friends, peers, and people similar to us are particularly influential when we are forming new beliefs and attitudes (Kruglanski & Mayseless, 1987, 1990). For example, when forming an opinion about a new skateboard, tattoo, or body-piercing, members of Generation Y are more interested in the opinions of other members of Generation Y than in the opinions of their parents. By contrast, the opinions of dissimilar people are more important when we are attempting to judge the validity of previously formed beliefs and attitudes. For example, if we already know that we like a particular brand of personal computer, it could be useful to find out if people dissimilar to us also like the computer. If everyone likes the computer, it must be a superior product.

Kelman (1961) expanded on Deutsch and Gerard's (1955) ideas by distinguishing between two kinds of normative influence—**compliance** and **identification**—and by drawing an important distinction between public (or superficial) and private (or genuine) influence. Compliance occurs when people feel coerced to hold a certain opinion or behave in a certain way. Parents and supervisors reward us for correct behavior and punish us for incorrect behavior. This encourages us to behave in line with their expectations publicly even if we privately disagree. Compliance is related to the utilitarian function of attitudes (see Chapter 8). Identification occurs when people agree with someone that they like. Holding beliefs similar to those we like enhances our self-esteem. Such beliefs are held privately as well as publicly and are similar to beliefs serving the value-expressive function of attitudes. Finally, **internalization** occurs when we agree with another person because his or her opinions seem valid or correct because they are consistent with our personal values. Internalized beliefs are held privately as well as publicly, and internalization is related to informational influence and to the knowledge function of attitudes.

The distinction between public and private influence is important for understanding **reference group** influence on the purchase of publicly consumed versus privately consumed products (Bearden & Etzel, 1982). A reference group is a group whose beliefs, attitudes, values, and norms are used as standards for appropriate thinking and behavior by an individual. Members of a particular group often wear similar clothing, fashion accessories, and hairstyles. Purchase decisions for publicly consumed products, such as these, are influenced heavily by reference groups. Many groups value conformity, and consequently, many group members are highly similar in terms of appearance, interests, and actions. Conformity pressures can be sufficiently powerful to encourage underage drinking and illegal drug use by individuals who would normally never consider such actions (Rose, Bearden, & Teel, 1992). Group members are more likely to differ, however, in terms of their private lifestyles and the types of products they purchase for private use at home. In general, informational influence is more important for publicly consumed products and informational influence is more important for privately consumed products.

INDIVIDUAL DIFFERENCES IN SUSCEPTIBILITY TO CONFORMITY

All consumers are not equally susceptible to conformity pressures. Some consumers are more susceptible to normative influence, and others are more susceptible to informational influence (Bearden, Netemeyer, & Teel, 1989). In addition, high self-monitoring individuals—who are highly sensitive and responsive to social cues—are more susceptible to normative influence than are low self-monitoring individuals (Beardan & Rose, 1990). Individuals who are members of collectivist (versus individualistic) cultures are also more susceptible to normative influence (Han & Shavitt, 1994). Even within a culture, individuals with a strong collectivist orientation are more susceptible to normative influence (Cialdini, Wosinska, Barrett, Butner, & Gornik-Durose, 1999).

The most important difference across different cultures is in terms of their individualistic versus collectivistic orientation (Han & Shavitt, 1994; Markus & Kitayama, 1991). Members of individualistic cultures define themselves as independent from groups and focus on personal goals, whereas members of collectivistic cultures define themselves in terms of group membership and focus on group goals. In general, Western cultures (e.g., North America, Western Europe) are individualistic and Eastern cultures (e.g., Japan, China, Korea) are collectivistic (this distinction is discussed in greater detail in Chapter 12). However, even within a specific culture, individuals differ in terms of their individualistic versus collectivistic orientations (Cialdini et al., 1999). In fact, recent research indicates that individual differences in terms of individualism/collectivism are more important than cultural differences in terms of individualism/collectivism (Cialdini et al., 1999).

Cialdini and his colleagues (1999) investigated the effectiveness of social-validation-based versus commitment/consistency-based techniques for influencing consumers in the United States (an individualistic culture) and Poland (a collectivistic culture). Individual differences in individualistic/collectivistic orientation were also measured using a personality scale. Subjects were asked to imagine that they had been approached by a representative from the Coca-Cola Company who wished to ask them some questions about Coca-Cola. In social-validation conditions, subjects were told that all (or half or none) of their classmates had agreed to participate. In commitment/consistency conditions, subjects were told that in the past their classmates had always (or never) complied with survey requests. The results showed that the social-validation procedure was more influential for collectivistic subjects, whereas the commitment/consistency procedure was more effective for individualistic subjects. Moreover, the individualistic/collectivistic personal orientation of the subjects had a much stronger impact than the individualistic/collectivistic cultural background of the subjects.

◆ THE LIKING PRINCIPLE

The **liking principle** is surprisingly simple: Successful salespeople recognize that liking is power. The more people like you, the more power you have over them. Joe Girard, the famous Chevrolet salesman, won the title of "Number One Car Salesman" 12 years in a row and enjoyed a salary of over $200,000 per year while doing so (Cialdini, 1993). Girard is also listed as the world's greatest car salesman in the *Guinness Book of World Records.* How does he do it? He claims people like him because he's a nice guy and he always offers customers a fair price. He also sends a greeting card every month to every one of his 13,000-plus customers. The message inside the card is always the same, "I like you," and nothing else. Consumers prefer to say "yes" to someone they know and like.

FACTORS IN THE LIKING PRINCIPLE

What factors influence how much we like another person? One factor was discussed in Chapter 8: the mere exposure effect. Repeated exposure to a stimulus, such as a person stimulus, increases familiarity and liking (Zajonc, 1968). Hence, people tend to like familiar people better than strangers. Tupperware parties can be tremendously successful because the participants tend to be close friends, and salespeople try to help their clients get to know them better. Another important factor is physical attractiveness. Research on the halo effect shows that people tend to assume that attractive people are also kind, honest, intelligent, persuasive, sociable, and likable (Eagly, Ashmore, Makhijani, & Longo, 1990). That is, people overgeneralize: One positive trait (physical attractiveness) seems to imply the presence of many other positive traits. Successful salespeople pay close attention to the latest fashions and try to appear as attractive as possible. Successful politicians do, also—physically attractive politicians receive over twice as many votes as their less attractive counterparts (Efran & Patterson, 1976).

Similarity

Similarity is another important factor (Byrne, 1971). We like those who are similar to us, including those who are similar to us in terms of appearance, attitudes, opinions, lifestyles, traits, or social or educational backgrounds. Of course, the opposite is also true: We dislike those who are dissimilar to us (Rosenbaum, 1986), and this finding has important implications for understanding stereotyping and prejudice. Even seemingly trivial similarities can be surprisingly influential. Salespeople often try to find out what hobbies their clients have, and when they meet with a client they pretend to enjoy the same hobbies (e.g., Do you golf? What a coincidence, so do I!). Many sales training programs instruct trainees to "mirror" the client's body posture, mood, and verbal style (LaFrance, 1985; Locke & Horowitz, 1990; Woodside & Davenport, 1974).

Impression Management

Impression management strategies also influence perceived likability (Schlenker, 1980). Three main tactics are commonly used: ingratiation (brown nosing), indirect positive associations, and indirect negative dissociations. We like those who like us, and flattery often enhances a person's likability even when we realize we are being ingratiated (Jones & Wortman, 1973). Remembering a client's name (Howard, Gengler, & Jain, 1995) or asking a client how he or she is doing (Howard, 1990) can increase compliance. Even Joe Girard's transparent greeting cards with the simple message "I like you" can be surprisingly effective. However, ingratiation can backfire if the ingratiator goes too far (the ingratiator's dilemma; Jones & Wortman, 1973).

Indirect Association

Creating indirect associations to favorably evaluated stimuli (such as one's favorite cities, universities, sports teams, and so on) can also increase perceived likability. When their team wins, people often wear T-shirts, sweatshirts, baseball caps, and so on with their team's logo. Cialdini et al. (1976) call this basking in reflected glory. Fans do not have anything directly to do with the performance of a team, but a victory feels like a personal victory, and a loss feels like a personal loss (Hirt, Zillmann, Erickson, & Kennedy, 1992). Even indirect associations with a winning team, such as indirect

New York Ranger fans in 1994, Northwestern Wildcat fans in 1995, and Michigan Wolverine fans in 1998 all wore their colors proudly.
Source: © Mary Boucher.

associations created by wearing or drinking from something that bears the team's logo, can enhance likability. If the team loses, however, people seem to distance themselves or dissociate themselves from the team; some fans wear bags over their heads, and apparel, mugs, and cups with the team's logo become less visible.

Good News

Similarly, people like to tell other people good news, because some of the positive feelings created by the good news rub off on the communicator. Conversely, people are reluctant to communicate bad news, because the bad mood created by bad news tends to be indirectly associated with the bearer of the bad news. The tendency to keep mum about unpleasant messages (the MUM effect; Tesser & Rosen, 1975) is more pronounced when future contact with the message recipient is anticipated, because of greater concern about the impression one conveys (Kardes & Kimble, 1984). Ancient Persian kings used to kill the messenger when the messenger brought bad news, and many modern television viewers send hate mail to meteorologists who report the coming of bad weather (Cialdini, 1993). What we say, what we wear, and what we use have surprisingly strong effects on the impressions others form of us.

◆ THE AUTHORITY PRINCIPLE

According to the **authority principle,** authority figures use titles, clothes (e.g., uniforms, business suits), and expensive possessions that convey status (e.g., BMWs, condominiums) to impress and influence others. Disobeying authority figures can have obvious aversive consequences. But how far will people go when following the orders of authority figures? Yale University professor Stanley Milgram (1963) attempted to answer this question in one of the most influential and controversial studies in the annals of experimental psychology. (See Fig. 10-7.) Subjects were asked to play the role of a "teacher" who read questions to another person labeled the "learner." Each time the learner gave a wrong answer, the teacher was instructed to administer an electric shock to the learner. Subjects were told that the purpose of this study was to investigate the effects of punishment on learning. However, subjects were also told to administer increasingly intense electric shocks for each wrong answer. An impressive array of shock switches with very clear labels (i.e., slight shock, strong shock, intense shock, danger: severe shock, and maximum [450 volts]) was positioned directly in front of the subject. As shock intensity increased, the learner screamed louder and louder and eventually begged to be released from the experiment. However, any time the teacher hesitated, an authority figure in a white laboratory coat told the teacher that he must continue.

These experimental procedures were described to a group of 39 psychiatrists who were asked to predict how many subjects would "go all the way" and use the maximum 450-volt switch. The psychiatrists predicted that only one person in a thousand would pull the maximum-volt switch. By contrast, the results revealed that 65 percent of the subjects actually pulled this switch! Fortunately, the learner was an actor and no real electric shock was actually delivered. Milgram himself was shocked by the results. He originally intended to conduct a follow-up experiment in Germany to test the hypothesis that Germans are more blindly obedient to authority than Americans. He never carried out this investigation. Instead, he concluded that all people are surprisingly

The authority principle in advertising has been around for a long time.

obedient to authority, and his published article ended with the warning that what happened in Nazi Germany could happen anywhere. Since 1963, Milgram's experiment has been replicated in Germany, Holland, Spain, Italy, Australia, and Jordan with virtually identical results (Meeus & Raaijmakers, 1986).

◆ THE CONFUSION PRINCIPLE

If you can't dazzle them with your brilliance, baffle them with your BS. Is their any truth to this old adage? Can confusing people make them more susceptible to influence under some circumstances? Although this tactic does not fit neatly into Cialdini's (1993) framework, recent research indicates that confusion can increase susceptibility to influence (Davis & Knowles, 1999). Door-to-door salespersons asked consumers to buy a box of Christmas cards to support a local center for developmentally delayed children and adults. In the control condition, consumers were simply told that the price of the box of cards was $3. In the confusion condition, consumers were told that the

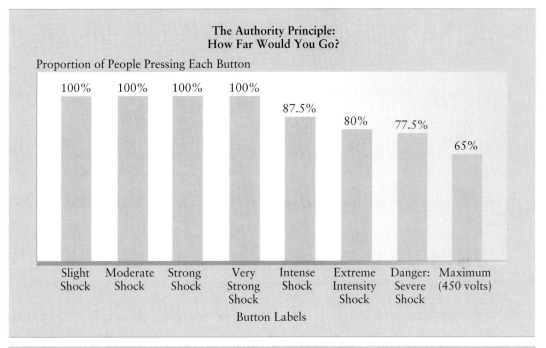

FIGURE 10-7

People will go to surprising extremes to obey authority figures.
Source: From Milgram (1963).

Lee Iaccoca, former chairman of Chrysler Corporation, was considered an authority on his company's automobiles, so his advertisements were very persuasive.
Source: Courtesy of Chrysler Corporation.

price was "300 pennies . . . that's $3." In the disrupt-then-reframe condition, consumers were first confused and then the confusing statement was stated differently. Specifically, consumers were told that the price was "300 pennies . . . that's $3. It's a bargain." The results revealed that twice as many consumers purchased the box of cards in the disrupt-then-reframe condition than in the control or confusion conditions. Hence, confusion by itself was ineffective, but confusion followed by reframing was remarkably effective.

Why is the disrupt-then-reframe technique effective? The famous clinical psychologist Milton Erickson believed that many of his clients both wanted and resisted hypnotic induction. Erickson believed that the hypnotist had to reduce resistance using the confusion technique (including strange speech patterns, strange movements, and interruptions [e.g., starting a handshake and then stopping]). Erickson believed that confusions distracted the conscious mind, reduced resistance to hypnosis, and increased suggestibility.

An alternative explanation is offered by action identification theory (Vallacher & Wegner, 1987). Any behavior can be described on a continuum ranging from low levels pertaining to specific motor movements to high levels pertaining to higher-order plans and goals. For example, reading a textbook can be described at a low level—such as reading a bunch of words—or at a high level—such as acquiring knowledge that will help me to achieve my career goals. High-level interpretations of our own behaviors do not change readily. However, low-level interpretations are susceptible to reinterpretation. Confusions disrupt high-level interpretations and force people to focus on low-level, concrete details, and this increases susceptibility to influence.

Kardes and Cronley (2000b) offer another explanation that Davis and Knowles (1999) failed to consider. Confusion may increase the need for closure, or the preference to complete a cognitive task quickly (Kruglanski & Webster, 1996). When the need for closure is high, people are likely to use any easy-to-use information, even tangentially relevant information, that helps them to complete a judgment task quickly. The reframing offered by the salesperson helps consumers make a decision quickly and attain closure. The need-for-closure interpretation of Davis and Knowles's (1999) results suggests that the reframing should be easy to understand and should be offered immediately after the disruption. More research is needed on this interesting new technique to understand the roles of resistance to suggestion, action identification, and the need for closure in disruption then reframing.

CHAPTER SUMMARY ▪

People are susceptible to a wide variety of influence tactics. Consumers are most susceptible to these tactics when humming along mindlessly on automatic pilot without carefully analyzing reasons for compliance (the automaticity principle). Commitment-and-consistency–based tactics, such as the foot-in-the-door technique and the low-ball technique, exploit the tendency of consumers to choose courses of action consistent with past commitments and past courses. Reciprocity-based techniques—such as the door-in-the-face, that's-not-all, multiple-deescalating-requests, and even-a-penny approaches—capitalize on the tendency of consumers to return a favor when they receive a favor (even if they did not want to receive the favor). The scarcity principle of influence suggests that since valuable objects are rare, rare objects are assumed to be valuable. Limited-time offers, limited distribution, and limited availability can be surprisingly effective. The social validation (proof in numbers) principle suggests that the perceived validity of an idea increases as the number of people supporting the idea increases. Large numbers (hundreds, thousands, or millions of satisfied customers) can be very persuasive. Likability is also a weapon of influence, and consequently, many firms hire physically attractive salespersons and instruct them to use similarity and impression management (ingratiation, indirect positive associations, indirect negative dissociations) to increase liking, power, and influence. Finally, most people are more obedient to authority than they realize. Authority figures (e.g., doctors, lawyers, teachers, executives, politicians) can be surprisingly persuasive and influential. Understanding these principles helps people to influence others and helps people to avoid being influenced by others.

KEY CONCEPTS ■

- Automaticity principle
- Prediction heuristics
- Persuasion heuristics
- Influence heuristics
- Because heuristic
- Price–quality heuristic
- Commitment and consistency principle
- Foot-in-the-door technique
- Low-ball technique

- Salience hypothesis
- Commitment theory
- Reciprocity principle
- Door-in-the-face technique
- That's-not-all technique
- Multiple-deescalating-requests technique
- Even-a-penny technique
- Scarcity principle
- Social validation principle

- Normative influence
- Informational influence
- Compliance
- Identification
- Internalization
- Reference group
- Liking principle
- Authority principle
- Confusion principle

DISCUSSION QUESTIONS ■

1. Describe one or two instances in which you have used social influence techniques to get your friends to do something you wanted them to do. Which techniques did you use?

2. Why should consumers be wary of the price–quality heuristic? Give an example of a type of product for which people often rely on the price–quality heuristic to make a purchase decision.

3. How might nonprofit organizations make use of the foot-in-the-door technique?

4. What four theories potentially explain why the low-ball technique works so well? Which theory is correct?

5. In what cases do you think the reciprocity principle is effective? Why?

6. In some ways, the scarcity principle and the social validation principle seem like opposites. How can both principles be effective, and when is each principle likely to be effective?

7. Describe an instance in which you bought a product, made a donation, dined at a restaurant, or joined a volunteer group because you found the person(s) representing the product or organization likable. What characteristics did the person have that led you to the decision?

8. Name any items you own as a result of a favorable indirect association, such as a university sweatshirt or a baseball cap with a team logo. How do you feel when you wear or use these items?

9. Name some specific ways you have observed salespeople using the authority principle.

10. Has a salesperson ever talked you into buying a product that you did not really want? What technique did the salesperson use? How did you justify the purchase afterward?

CHAPTER 11

Online Consumer Behavior

- ◆ The Age of Interactivity
- ◆ Information Search in Bricks-and-Mortar versus Electronic Retail Environments
- ◆ Effects of Reduced Search Costs on Sensitivity to Price and Quality
- ◆ Interactive Decision Aids and Electronic Satisfaction

◆ DELL COMPUTER

With online sales of over $10 million per day, Dell Computer (www.dell.com) is an excellent example of an e-commerce success. The Dell Direct Model has enabled Dell to customize and distribute products very efficiently and at relatively low cost (Rangan & Bell, 1998). When Dell receives an order online, the configuration details are broken down into a list of parts needed to build a custom-built computer. First, the requested hardware options are installed at state-of-the-art factories. Next, the requested software options are loaded. Finally, the system is tested and packaged with peripherals like a mouse, a mouse pad, a keyboard, and manuals. Remarkably, the order receipt to shipping process takes only about 36 hours!

Dell also developed over 200 customer-specific Web pages, called Dell Premier Pages, that provide different amounts of information to different categories of customers. Bigger customers get more information, more customized service, and better volume-based price deals. For example, all customers have access to product information, order information, list prices, investor relations, and technical support. Gold customers (i.e., customers with Dell purchases exceeding $5 million) also get newsletters, order history information, custom links, and even greater technical support (e.g., support team phone numbers, pager numbers, e-mail addresses). Platinum customers (i.e., customers with Dell purchases exceeding $10 million) also get their own home pages and even greater and more personalized technical support. In addition, platinum customers are encouraged to participate in online interactions with Dell product designers to help Dell develop products and services that will meet their specific needs more effectively. Platinum customers are treated more like business partners than like clients. Other online firms could learn a lot from Dell.

Source: V. K. Rangan and M. Bell, "Case Study: Dell Online," *Journal of Interactive Marketing,* 12, pp. 63–86.

Dell (www.Dell.com) makes it easy for consumers to custom order.

◆ INTRODUCTION

As the Dell Computer example illustrates, the Internet is changing the way firms do business. Manufacturers can now produce custom-made products and services more quickly and efficiently. Interactive shopping environments are also enabling manufacturers and retailers to learn more about how to satisfy consumers' individual tastes and preferences more effectively. Consumers are learning that they can obtain custom-made products and services at a reasonable price. Moreover, the number of choices and the amount of information available about these alternatives is increasing at a staggering pace. The information explosion is both a benefit and a curse for consumers: As the number of choice options increases, the potential for better decisions and more satisfying choices exists. However, too much information can be confusing and overwhelming to consumers. Interactive decision aids, or "smart agents" or "bots" (see www.botspot.com) can help consumers use the vast amounts of information available on the Web more intelligently.

Although manufacturers and retailers seem to appreciate the benefits of interactivity, they also fear the problem of "cost transparency" (Sinha, 2000). The Web makes it easy for consumers to compare prices and determine if a given price is fair or unfair. Manufacturers and retailers believe that comparing prices on the Web will make consumers more price sensitive, and this could erode profits dramatically. Understandably, most firms do not want to fight a price war on the Web.

It is important to recognize that interactivity and the ease with which comparison shopping can be performed will have a powerful influence on consumer behavior.

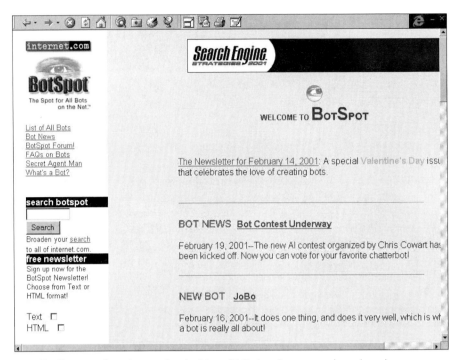

www.BotSpot.com is an interactive decision aid that makes comparison shopping easy.

However, it is also important to recognize that most of the principles explained in Chapters 1–10 also apply to the Web. Salience and vividness effects clearly apply to banner ads and other types of Web advertising. Consumers will be forced to use judgment and choice heuristics to simplify decision making on the Web. Source, message, and audience effects have a strong influence on persuasion on the Web. Affective and cognitive theories of persuasion will continue to explain how advertising tactics influence consumer judgment, and all of Cialdini's (1993) influence principles can be found on the Web. While keeping these basic principles in mind, let us now proceed to examine the effects of interactivity and comparison shopping in greater depth.

◆ THE AGE OF INTERACTIVITY

The degree of interactivity present in an exchange relationship varies on a continuum ranging from a one-way communication from a firm to a customer to a two-way communication involving extremely detailed information between a firm and a customer (Alba et al., 1997; Hoffman & Novak, 1996). High-quality two-way communication involves fast response times between intercommunications and high levels of response contingency. This means that one party's response depends heavily on the other party's response, and this helps both parties to get the information they need when they need it.

The highest level of interactivity occurs in face-to-face communications: One party tells the other what is wanted and the other party responds, and the negotiation continues until an agreement is reached or until one party terminates the negotiation process. A relatively high level of interactivity occurs on many Web sites: The customer and the retailer communicate back and forth until an agreement is made or until the customer leaves the site. Moreover, the retailer keeps an electronic record of the individual customer's purchase history, and this may enable the retailer to better serve the individual customer in future transactions. However, the two parties do not see each other face-to-face (yet), and responses are not always immediate. Some Web sites are less interactive because they require the customer to inquire about shipping and handling or place an order over the telephone. Traditional mass-media advertising is not interactive at all: The advertiser provides a one-way communication to the television, radio, newspaper, or magazine audience, and the audience either accepts or rejects the information.

High levels of interactivity enable retailers to provide exactly the type of information about products, services, and pricing that the individual customer wishes to receive. High levels of interactivity also encourage customers to provide exactly the type of information about themselves that retailers want—including credit card numbers, e-mail addresses, shipping addresses, personal preferences, and purchase histories. Retailers also try to make repeat purchase easy: With the click of a button customers can tell retailers to ship the requested items to the usual address and to bill the usual credit card. Shopping becomes quick and easy. Customers can shop from home for products offered by retailers in their hometown, in other cities, and even in other countries (e.g., gourmet food and wine from France). No waiting in lines, no endless searching for parking spots, no airports, and no typical travel-related frustrations and hassles.

In addition to making shopping easy, the Web makes shopping fun, at least for some consumers. People are having the most fun when they are in a state of "flow" (Csikszentmihalyi, 1990). Flow is experienced when people perform an activity skillfully and effortlessly, and with little or no thought. During a "hot streak," professional athletes and weekend warriors typically describe themselves as being in a state of flow: Home runs, touchdowns, baskets, and birdies just come naturally and effortlessly. Similarly, when consumers navigate through a well-designed Web site, they obtain the information they want exactly when they want it and shopping becomes effortless and virtually automatic. Consumers have fun on the Web when their state of flow is high due to high levels of skill and control, high levels of attention and arousal, and high levels of interactivity (Novak, Hoffman, & Yung, 2000).

Research on the psychology of happiness and optimism indicates that people are happiest when they are proactive and engaged rather than passive or alienated (Ryan & Deci, 2000). Self-determination theory suggests that intrinsic motivation—or the desire to engage in an activity for its own sake rather than for an extrinsic reward, such as money—is maximized when autonomy, belongingness, and competence (or the ABCs of self-determination) are maximized. Autonomy means that the person has the resources needed to achieve a desired goal without aid from others. Belongingness means that the person feels like part of a valued group. Competence means that the person has the knowledge and skills necessary to reach a desired goal. Retailers should design Web pages with these principles in mind: Retailers should make sure that the customer has the resources (e.g., wealth, maturity, knowledge) needed to make and enjoy the purchase (autonomy), the retailer should strive for a high-quality and trustworthy image and make the customer feel like part of the retailer's family of valued customers (belongingness), and the Web page should provide neither too much nor too little information and should be easy to navigate (competence).

◆ INFORMATION SEARCH IN BRICKS-AND-MORTAR VERSUS ELECTRONIC RETAIL ENVIRONMENTS

Comparing products and prices across bricks-and-mortar stores requires considerable time and effort on the part of consumers. Consumers are not always willing or able to visit many different stores and consider many different brands on many different attributes (see Chapter 5). Information processing constraints often encourage consumers to consider a relatively small number of stores, brands, and attributes. However, the amount of product information consumers seek is influenced by several factors, such as the possible consequences of the purchase decision (Beatty & Smith, 1987) or the degree of uncertainty consumers experience regarding the purchase decision (Urbany, Dickson, & Wilkie, 1989).

The more consequential the purchase decision, the more time and effort consumers are willing to expend to search for information that they believe will lead to a good decision (Beatty & Smith, 1987). Consequentiality increases as involvement or as risk increases. Involvement refers to the perceived relevance or importance of the purchase decision. Risk refers to the probability of undesirable consequences following a poor purchase decision. Generally, involvement increases as perceived risk increases. For example, involvement is higher for expensive product categories because such categories carry considerable financial risk. No one likes to pay thousands of dollars for an automobile to discover later that the car one bought is a lemon. Therefore, it makes sense to gather a lot of information about many dealers, brands, and attributes before making a decision that one may need to live with for many years. Similarly, some product categories are associated with considerable social risk (e.g., it is socially embarrassing to buy publicly consumed products, such as clothes, that others perceive as ugly, nerdy, or uncool) or physical risk (e.g., some products can be physically dangerous, such as lawn mowers or pharmaceuticals). As any type of perceived risk increases, consumers typically search for more information before making a purchase decision.

How knowledgeable consumers are about a product category can also influence the amount of product information that is gathered (Beatty & Smith, 1987; Johnson & Russo, 1984). Knowledge varies across consumers and across product categories: Consumers who are knowledgeable in one domain may be unknowledgeable in another. Unknowledgeable consumers or novices generally search for little information because they do not fully understand the evaluative implications of the available evidence. Knowledgeable consumers or experts also generally search for little information because they are often highly certain that they already possess the information needed to make an intelligent decision, and therefore, it is unnecessary to search for more information to reduce uncertainty. Moderately knowledgeable consumers frequently search for a relatively large amount of information because they recognize that they may not have as much information as they need to make a good decision.

Search costs are high in most brick-and-mortar retail environments. It takes planning, time, physical energy, and mental energy to visit many different stores and compare many different brands on many different attributes. As a result, consumers often search for relatively little information, even in a single store. For example, Dickson and Sawyer (1990) found that the typical grocery shopper spends only 12 seconds per decision while shopping, and many shoppers (41 percent) reported that they did not even bother to check the price of the products they purchased. Comparing the prices of many different brands takes time and energy, even when the brands are located right next to each other on the same shelf.

By contrast, search costs are much lower on the Web. With the click of a button, consumers can scan the prices and features of hundreds of products quickly and easily by using an interactive decision aid that lists brands by price with the least expensive brand listed first (e.g., www.bizrate.com, www.botspot.com, www.bottomdollar.com, www.mysimon.com, www.pricescan.com). When it is easy to compare the prices for a product offered by many different online retailers, cost transparency increases (Sinha, 2000). That is, a seller's costs become more obvious to buyers, and buyers can use this information to determine if a price is fair. Manufacturers and retailers are concerned about cost transparency because it decreases their ability to charge high prices and earn high margins. For example, when MCI and Sprint first started charging much lower rates for long-distance phone calls, many consumers switched and AT&T was eventually forced to reduce its rates.

Cost transparency also turns brands into commodities, and this reduces brand loyalty. For example, online stock trading companies (e.g., Ameritrade, E-trade, National Discount Brokers, MyDiscountBroker, Datek) provide nearly the same products and services as traditional brokers (e.g., Merrill Lynch, A.G. Edwards) for much lower fees. If a product or service is perceived as pretty much the same no matter who offers it, why not buy the least expensive option? The opposite of commoditization is branding or product differentiation, and as commoditization increases brand loyalty decreases. Brand loyalty can also deteriorate if consumers believe that firms enjoy healthy profit margins even when a sales promotion or price discount is offered. For example, Procter

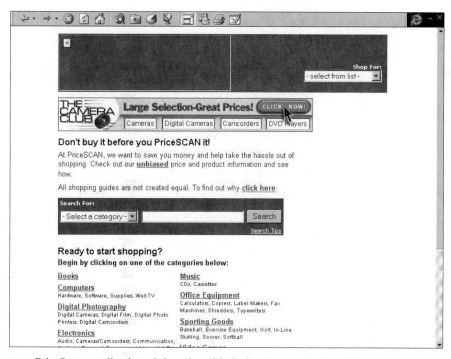

www.PriceScan.com lists brands by price with the least expensive brand first.

TAKING ISSUE

IS E*TRADE FOR EVERYONE?

E*Trade Group, a company that owns a rapidly growing online brokerage firm, wants to be your broker; more to the point, E*Trade wants you to be your own broker. The company wants to convince you and millions of other consumers who have access to the Internet that you can do your own investing, with a minimum of help—from E*Trade, of course. "Someday, we'll all invest this way," predicts one of E*Trade's ads. E*Trade hopes so.

E*Trade positions itself in two important ways. First, it does so by user. That user, says E*Trade, should be the average citizen who knows how to operate a computer (and, of course, who has at least a little discretionary income to invest). New E*Trade commercials are appearing in time slots surrounding such upper-middle-class TV shows as *Seinfeld, Friends,* and *60 Minutes.* "We are looking for reach," says Sheri Baron, president of Gotham Inc., the New York ad agency that is producing the ads. In other words, they want to reach everyone from college kids to baby boomers to senior citizens.

E*Trade also positions itself by price. Because E*Trade customers participate in their own trading online, commissions are lower than traditional trading commissions. E*Trade commissions typically range from $14.95 to $19.95 for up to 5,000 shares, then a penny a share thereafter. "Low commissions. Leave your kids more to fight over," says one newspaper ad. In a television commercial, a well-dressed couple walks toward an upscale house. "Your invest-ments helped pay for this dream house," intones the voiceover. "Unfortunately, it belongs to your broker."

E*Trade doesn't want to be seen as a fly-by-night operation but rather as a pioneer. "We're in a unique position of being the category killer and the category builder," boasts president and CEO, Christos M. Cotsakos. "People don't want to trust their financial transactions to bargain basement institutions." Instead, claims Cotsakos, they want low prices from a brand-name brokerage like E*Trade.

Is E*Trade for everyone? E*Trade thinks so, claiming that it is attracting 700 new accounts per day, totaling up to $13 million in new deposits daily. E*Trade is ahead of other discount brokers such as Charles Schwab and mutual fund giant Fidelity, but those organizations are involved in a greater variety of businesses. So far, E*Trade hasn't really hurt these companies; however, Mark Wolfenberger, a Deutsche Morgan Grenfell analyst, predicts that "as they start to hurt these bigger names, it's going to become a much more competitive battle."

The fact remains that consumers who use services like E*Trade should be educated about what they are doing—they are, after all, playing with their own money. The lure of easy trading should not lull consumers into believing that they are making inconsequential purchases such as picking up a few things at the grocery store. Perhaps E*Trade should stand for everyone, as long as they are educated consumers.

Source: Deborah Lohse, "E*Trade Bids to Be a Household Name," *The Wall Street Journal,* September 5, 1997, p. B6.

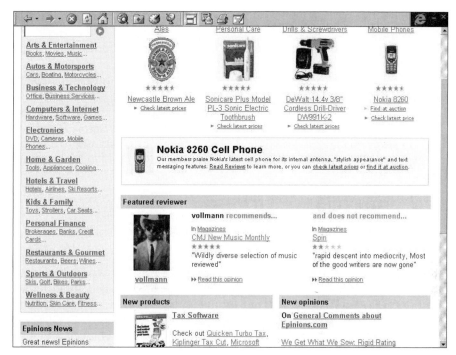

www.epinions.com provides the opinions of many different consumers who have purchased various products and services.

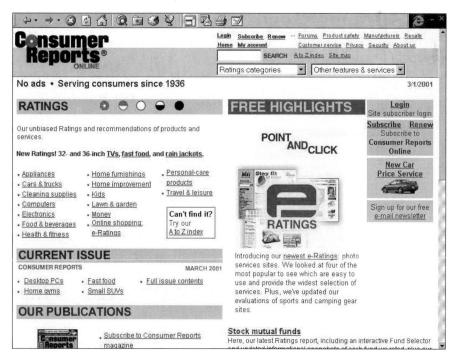

www.consumerreports.org provides unbiased ratings and recomendations for many different products and services.

& Gamble relied heavily on sales promotions in the 1980s and early 1990s, and consumers inferred that P&G was still making a profit. When P&G changed its policy in the mid-1990s to "efficient promotion" (or no sales promotion), consumers switched to less expensive private labels.

Of course, price information is not the only type of information available on the Internet. The Web also offers a vast amount of information about product quality and reliability. Sites like www.epinions.com and www.consumerreports.org provide product reviews and ratings from other consumers for thousands of different products. The latter site also provides product ratings from a panel of experts. The Web is dramatically reducing search costs for product quality information as well as for price information.

◆ EFFECTS OF REDUCED SEARCH COSTS ON SENSITIVITY TO PRICE AND QUALITY

Reducing search costs for price information increases price sensitivity, whereas reducing search costs for quality information decreases price sensitivity (Alba et al., 1997; Lynch & Ariely, 2000). However, many large retailers are so concerned about reducing search costs for price information that they try to block smart agents from accessing their Web sites (Bounds, 1999). This is a potentially ineffective strategy because trying to prevent smart agents from reducing search costs for price information will also prevent smart agents from reducing search costs for quality information. Furthermore, as consumers become more reliant on smart agents, retailers that shun smart agents will become less likely to be included in consumers' consideration sets.

Research on traditional non-Internet advertising effects has shown that price advertising—or advertising that compares the advertised brand's low price to competitors' high prices—increases price sensitivity (Popkowski-Leszczyc & Rao, 1990). However, differentiating advertising—or advertising that compares the advertised brand's superior features to competitors' inferior features—decreases price sensitivity and also decreases the number of brands consumers include in their consideration sets (Mitra & Lynch, 1995, 1996).

Recent research has shown that similar effects are found for Internet advertising (Lynch & Ariely, 2000). These researchers experimentally manipulated the manner in which information was presented on Web pages similar to those of www.wine.com. Specifically, price comparability (high or low), quality comparability (high or low) and store comparability (high or low) were manipulated independently, and graduate students and university staff were randomly assigned to conditions. When price comparability was high, price information was provided on the first page along with the list of available wines and a tool was available for listing the wines by price. When price comparability was low, the sorting tool was unavailable and price information was not provided on the first page. Instead, consumers had to click on the brand name to obtain price information for a specific brand. When quality comparability was high, wines could be sorted by the type of grape (e.g., chardonnay, cabernet sauvignon) and detailed descriptive information was provided (e.g., complexity, acidity, body, dryness). When quality comparability was low, wines could not be sorted by category and the descriptive information was not provided on the first page. Instead, consumers had to click on the brand name to obtain quality information for a specific brand.

www.wine.com makes price and quality comparison shopping easy.

When electronic store comparability was high, a split screen was used so that consumers could compare the offerings of two electronic stores (Dionysus and Jubilee) on the same screen. When store comparability was low, consumers could visit only one electronic store at a time. Consumers made eight shopping trips and some of the wines were offered on a price discount on half of these trips. They were told that one of the eight trips would be selected randomly and they would be asked to use their own money to pay for the wines they selected. After completing the eight shopping trips, consumers participated in a wine-tasting session and their direct-experience-based preferences were assessed.

The number of wines (Q = quantity) purchases at the regular (Q_{regular}) and discount (Q_{discount}) prices was recorded for each participant. The proportional price change (P = price) was also computed (this value was held constant at 15 percent in this experiment). These measures permitted the calculation of price elasticity using the following equation:

$$\text{Price elasticity} = \frac{(Q_{\text{discount}} - Q_{\text{regular}})}{(Q_{\text{discount}} + Q_{\text{regular}})/2} \left/ \frac{(P_{\text{discount}} - P_{\text{regular}})}{(P_{\text{discount}} + P_{\text{regular}})/2} \right.$$

As price sensitivity increases, the number of wines purchased at the discount price increases and the number of wines purchased at the regular price decreases. Price sensitivity and price elasticity increases as the quantity-purchased difference increases and as the price difference decreases. Consequently, a negative value for price elasticity indicates that consumers are price sensitive and they purchase more bottles at a discount than at the regular price (while controlling for the size of the discount).

The results showed that price sensitivity was lower when quality usability was high than when quality usability was low, as predicted. When it is easy to compare products in terms of quality, price does not have a strong influence on the quantity purchased. Furthermore, the results revealed an important unique/common brands by store comparability interaction: For unique brands (i.e., brands offered by one store but not the other), store comparability had no effect on price sensitivity. However, for common brands (i.e., brands offered by both stores), price sensitivity increased as store comparability increased. Product differentiation is a retailer's best defense against price sensitivity.

The results also showed that consumers enjoyed navigating through the Web site most when all three search costs were low (i.e., low price search costs, low quality search costs, and low store search costs). Furthermore, consumers made better and more satisfying decisions when all three search costs were low. These results suggest that retailers should cooperate with smart agents and should strive to reduce all three types of search costs because this should lead to the highest repeat purchase rates. This implication is surprising, because many retailers believe that they should make it difficult rather than easy for consumers to comparison shop.

FIGURE 11-1

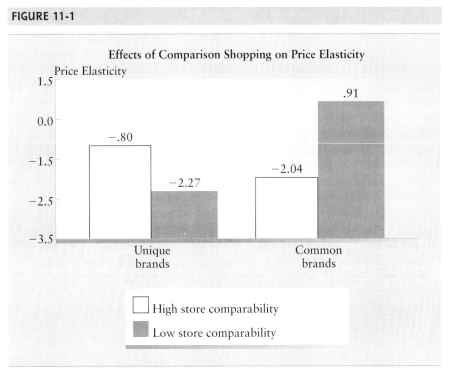

Store comparability had no effect on price elasticity for unique brands, but for common brands, price elasticity decreased dramatically as store comparability decreased. Less negative numbers indicate less price elasticity.

Source: Adapted from Lynch & Ariely, 2000.

Reducing search costs can benefit the manufacturer as well as the consumer and the retailer. Lynch and Ariely (2000) analyzed the percent of unique brands purchased when store comparability was high versus low and found that consumers purchased a larger percentage of unique brands when store comparability was high (74 percent) as opposed to low (64 percent). Consequently, manufacturers of innovative, distinctive brands should strive to reduce consumers' search costs and should consider increasing the perceived uniqueness of their offerings through private labels (e.g., using the retailer's name for the product's brand name), branded variants (e.g., using different model numbers with different retailers), and partnering with a single retailer (e.g., many automobile manufacturers sell to exclusive dealerships). (See Figure 11-1.)

◆ INTERACTIVE DECISION AIDS AND ELECTRONIC SATISFACTION

Consumers are limited information processors and are only able to think about a relatively small set of brands and a small set of attributes at any given time (Chapter 2). One way consumers deal with this cognitive limitation is to simplify decision making by using a phased choice strategy: The available brands are screened quickly and unsatisfactory brands are eliminated from the consideration set in the first stage; the remaining brands are compared and evaluated more carefully in the second stage (Chapter 5). Haubl and Trifts (2000) distinguish between two different types of interactive decision aids (or smart agents or bots) that are designed to facilitate screening (or eliminating alternatives in the first stage) or evaluating (or rating alternatives in the second stage) brands. A **recommendation agent** is an interactive decision aid that helps consumers to screen alternatives using personal preference-related information provided by consumers. Amazon.com uses a simple type of recommendation agent that provides personal recommendations based on consumers' prior purchase histories. A **comparison matrix** is an interactive decision aid that helps consumers to evaluate alternatives by providing a brand-by-attribute matrix that makes it easier for consumers to compare brands. *Consumer Reports* (www.consumerreports.org) uses a simple brand-by-attribute matrix with brand columns and attribute rows (see also www.compare.net).

Participants examined Web pages for backpacking tents and compact stereo systems. Information about a large number of fictitious brands and real attributes could be examined by clicking on the appropriate links. Participants were randomly assigned to recommendation agent or comparison matrix conditions. The recommendation agent used participants' personal attribute importance ratings to screen out alternatives that performed poorly. The comparison matrix allowed participants to save selected brand and attribute information on a single page (rather than trying to remember information presented on several different pages). Consideration set size (the number of brands considered seriously for purchase), consideration set quality (the percent of clearly superior brands included in the consideration set), and decision quality were measured. Three interesting measures of decision quality were used: whether or not a clearly superior brand was chosen, whether or not the participant changed his or her mind and switched to a different brand when given the opportunity to do so, and the participant's degree of confidence in the decision.

THE WEB GETS REEL

Imagine being able to shop on the Web without feeling like a techno geek. Some marketers want you to feel like a real person, and they want to serve you like a real person. They know that if you feel comfortable, they can learn more about your preferences as a consumer and provide better service. Reel Inc. is one company that is well on its way to accomplishing this.

Reel was created by Stuart Skorman, who used to own a chain of video stores in Vermont before he sold it to Blockbuster for $4 million. Skorman's stores were known for their personal service, and he wanted to duplicate this on the Internet. So he started Reel Inc., with a Web site at www.reel.com, which recommends movies for free, based on customers' preferences. At his video stores, Skorman "trained our sales staff not to give a yes-or-no answer when a customer held up a film and asked whether it was good. They were instructed to find out more about the customer's tastes first." Reel Inc. does this electronically, and it costs the company much less than the same procedure did in the video stores. "A person can come onto my Web site and spend five hours learning all she can about movies and not buy a single thing, and it doesn't cost me anything," explains Skorman. "In the real world, you'd be out of business pretty quickly if you had salespeople spending five hours with customers."

One of the most important aspects of Reel is that the company isn't selling anything yet.

Instead, Skorman is concentrating on gathering information about his customers in a systematic way, so that he can make the accurate predictions he needs to build a successful business. Meanwhile, he is also developing an online store supported by a physical store that will serve as a warehouse. Using the information that he collects from the site, Skorman plans to market certain titles directly to customers online, accompanied by personal messages. "We're not trying to make the quick sell," Skorman says. "What we're after is the repeat customer and repeat sales. The idea is that you'll want to come back to us because we're being so good and honest about helping you. The more you come, the better chance we have of selling." Once the Web "store" is set up, Skorman plans to ship packages of three movie rentals directly to customers for $12.95 a week, including return postage.

Based on what he has already learned about his customers, Skorman feels that Reel's niche will be in locating older, hard-to-find movies for his customers. But he's looking a lot further down the information superhighway than that, to when consumers will be able to download movies directly from the Web. When that happens, he believes he'll have a billion-dollar business. Skorman is an unusual manager who can afford this kind of confidence; it is backed by the reliable, valid information he gathers from his own customers.

Source: David Carnoy, "Holy Data!" *Success,* May 1997, pp. 45–48.

The results indicated that both types of interactive decision aids reduce decision effort and increase decision quality. Specifically, consideration set size decreased and consideration set quality increased when interactive decision aids were used as opposed to not used. Moreover, both types of interactive decision agents tended to improve decision quality, but these results were somewhat stronger for recommendation agents than for comparison matrices. These results suggest that interactive decision aids available on the Web reduce search costs and help consumers to make better and more satisfying purchase decisions.

It is important to emphasize that decision quality depends on the quality of the information that is used to make a decision. Some types of attributes are more useful and informative than others. Consumer researchers often distinguish between three different types of attributes: search attributes, experience attributes, and credence attributes (Darby & Karni, 1973; Wright & Lynch, 1995). **Search attributes** are attributes that enable consumers to evaluate the quality of a brand before they buy it. Price and brand name are good examples of search attributes because consumers believe that they can predict product quality very accurately based on these attributes. **Experience attributes** enable consumers to evaluate the quality of a product only after purchase and use. Sensory attributes pertaining to the taste, smell, and feel of products are good examples of experience attributes. **Credence attributes** are attributes that can be evaluated only after extended use. Reliability and durability are good examples of credence attributes.

It is easy to present information about search attributes in bricks-and-mortar stores and in electronic stores. However, for experience attributes, bricks-and-mortar stores appear to have an advantage over electronic stores. In a bricks-and-mortar store, consumers can touch and feel the material used in clothing products and they can smell the delicious aromas of gourmet foods. How can these experiences be simulated in online environments? Currently, most interactive decision aids tend to focus primarily on a search attribute that is easy to use as a point of comparison across brands: price.

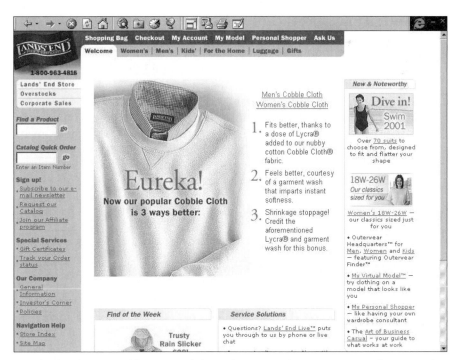

www.landsend.com provides sensory information to permit consumers to evaluate experience and credence attributes.

However, some online retailers are beginning to provide more detailed and higher quality information about products on the Web. For example, Lands' End (www. landsend.com) provides detailed information about experience and credence attributes by showing color pictures of their clothing products and by providing detailed information about stitching, construction, and the specific materials that were used. Moreover, as consumers become more experienced users of information provided on the Web, they will learn how to predict product quality from attributes other than price and brand name. Experience attributes, and perhaps even credence attributes, can be transformed into search attributes by knowledgeable consumers who know how these attributes correlate with product quality (Wright & Lynch, 1995). For knowledgeable consumers, the Web may become an even more powerful tool than it is today.

CHAPTER SUMMARY

The Internet provides vast amounts of product information that can be accessed with the click of a button. Compared to traditional bricks-and-mortar stores, electronic stores have the advantages of high levels of interactivity and low search costs. High levels of interactivity involve two-way communication, fast response times between inter-communications, and high levels of response contingency. High levels of response contingency are observed when the questions and answers of one party depend on the questions and answers of the other. Interactivity helps both parties, the retailer and the consumer, get the information they need when they need it.

Comparing prices and features of products offered by different bricks-and-mortar stores is time-consuming and difficult. Many consumers are unwilling to rearrange their schedule to visit many different stores to find the single best product that best meets their needs. Instead, many consumers settle for the first satisfactory product that they encounter. In sharp contrast to the amount of time and effort needed to compare brands across bricks-and-mortar stores, comparison shopping is quick and easy on the Web. With the click of a button, consumers can quickly access almost any type of product information that they want. Interactive decision aids available on the Internet reduce search costs for price, search costs for quality, and search costs for retail outlets. Reduced search costs decrease decision effort and lead to higher quality and more satisfying purchase decisions.

KEY CONCEPTS

- Bots
- Comparison matrix
- Credence attributes
- Experience attributes
- Flow

- Interactivity
- Intrinsic motivation
- Interactive decision aids
- Price elasticity
- Recommendation agent

- Search attributes
- Search costs
- Self-determination theory
- Smart agents

DISCUSSION QUESTIONS ■

1. How will interactivity change the way consumers acquire, remember, and use information about products and services?
2. What variables influence search costs and search patterns in bricks-and-mortar stores?
3. What variables influence search costs and search patterns on the Internet?
4. What are the effects of reduced search costs on the Internet on consumer decision making?
5. What types of products have you purchased on the Internet?
6. How did you decide what brands to purchase when you shopped on the Internet?
7. Explain the relationships among price sensitivity, price elasticity, and quality sensitivity?
8. From a retailer's perspective, what are the advantages of having unlimited shelf space?
9. From a manufacturer's perspective, what are the advantages of having extensive product lines?
10. What future trends are likely to shape the way consumers use the Internet to shop?

CHAPTER 12

Segmentation and International Marketing

◆ **VOLVO**

You probably don't think of a Volvo as a sporty car. Its boxy shape, storage capacity, and advertisements that focus on safety and durability make you think of kids, dogs, and groceries. Until now, Volvo has wanted you to think of its autos that way. The Volvo has been aimed at a certain segment of the automobile market: upper-middle-class families. (The Volvo station wagon carries a slightly heftier price tag than, say, a Ford Taurus or Toyota Corolla.) In fact, Leif Johansson, Volvo's CEO, fits the prototypical image of the traditional Volvo customer: He is in his mid-forties, has five children, and likes to spend his leisure time sailing and sport hunting (he says he's never actually killed an animal).

But Johansson and Volvo are now racing after a new segment of the car market — consumers who buy sports cars and other luxury cars. They want the Mercedes-Benz, BMW, and Lexus customers. Volvo has already rolled out a new, two-door coupe called the C70. Although the golden retriever and groceries won't fit too well in the new car, Volvo does claim that back-seat passengers will have plenty of leg room. The price tag — $40,000 — puts the C70 in direct competition with the Mercedes CLK (the

282

convertible version will sell for $45,000). Volvo hopes that by introducing the C70 and other luxury models, it can increase its sales to 500,000 cars per year, up from its current 385,000.

Pursuing a new segment can increase sales volume, but it can also be risky because a new strategy can damage a brand's traditional image. Should Volvo pursue a new segment? If so, which segment?

Source: Alex Taylor III, "Too Slow for the Fast Lane?," *Fortune,* July 21, 1997, pp. 68–72.

◆ INTRODUCTION

Segmentation is a "divide and conquer" strategy. Effective segmentation involves dividing a market into subcategories and pursuing different strategies for each subcategory. There are many different ways to segment a market. One way is to divide groups of consumers into subgroups of consumers, as Volvo does. Another way is to divide groups of products into subgroups of products. Yet another way is to divide groups of situations into subgroups of situations. The best way to segment a market depends on the structure of the market. This chapter discusses the issues of when and how much to segment. It also discusses the many different bases of segmentation. The chapter closes with a discussion of a useful procedure for analyzing the structure of a market.

◆ SEGMENTATION VERSUS AGGREGATION STRATEGIES

Segmentation is a multiproduct strategy: Different products are developed for different subcategories. For example, Coca-Cola markets Coke Classic, Cherry Coke, and Diet Coke to different subgroups of consumers. **Aggregation** is the opposite of segmentation: Instead of dividing up a market, a single product is offered to an entire market. For example, just a few decades ago, Coca-Cola offered only one product — Coca-Cola (now referred to as Coke Classic) — to everyone: There was no Cherry Coke, Diet Coke, or other varieties of Coke. An aggregation strategy is a "one size fits all" strategy. Differences among different groups of consumers are ignored and a single product is offered for everyone.

Coke and Diet Coke are just two of the Coca-Cola varieties available.
Source: © Mary Boucher.

When should a firm pursue a segmentation strategy and when should a firm pursue an aggregation strategy? The best answer depends on three main considerations: consumer preference heterogeneity (or variability), the majority fallacy, and the sales–costs trade-off. Each of these considerations is discussed next.

◆ CONSUMER PREFERENCE HETEROGENEITY

Perhaps the most important reason for segmenting is **consumer preference heterogeneity,** or variability in consumer preference. Tastes and preferences differ among people. Some people prefer hot and spicy food, whereas others prefer bland food. Some people are highly concerned about the appearance of a product, whereas others are more concerned about functionality. As preference heterogeneity increases, the case for segmentation increases in strength. Moreover, the greater the variability, the larger the number of profitable segments present in a market.

Of course, preferences are not always highly variable. Some preferences are shared by large groups of people. Universal preferences frequently involve a "more is better" rule. For example, more value (i.e., quality for the money) is better than less value. More miles per gallon is better than fewer miles per gallon. Bigger is better for some product categories (e.g., homes, televisions, yachts), and smaller is better for others (e.g., laptop computers). Some product categories are composed of relatively homogeneous (nonvariable) brands (e.g., commodities, laundry detergents, dishwashing liquids). In these cases, segmentation may not be a viable strategy. A firm should instead consider an aggregation strategy.

◆ THE MAJORITY FALLACY

When consumers' preferences are variable, it is important to analyze how preferences are distributed among consumers. A **normal distribution,** or bell-shaped curve, is typical for many different types of heterogeneous preferences. That is, the largest group of consumers often has preferences located in the middle of a distribution, and very small groups tend to be positioned at the very low and very high ends of a distribution. (See Fig. 12-1.) For example, the vast majority of consumers prefers foods that are average (not too high, not too low) in terms of spiciness. However, a small segment of consumers prefers bland, tasteless food. In addition, a small segment prefers extremely spicy food loaded with jalapeño, Tabasco, green chili, and habañero peppers (habañero peppers are about 100 times hotter than jalapeño peppers). Similarly, a very large segment of consumers prefers desserts that are average in terms of sweetness, and smaller segments prefer desserts that are just barely sweet (e.g., cheesecakes) or that are off the scale in terms of sweetness (e.g., donuts with a vanilla cream filling, a.k.a. Crisco and sugar). Similarly, the largest segment of consumers prefers automobiles that are average in terms of colorfulness (e.g., basic colors), and smaller segments prefer extremely drab (e.g., gray) or extremely bright (e.g., shocking pink, glow-in-the-dark aquamarine) colors. Many different preferences are normally distributed.

A normal distribution implies that the greatest number of consumers, or the largest consumer segment, is located in the middle of the distribution. Hence, many firms decide to pursue this segment, because market size is positively related to

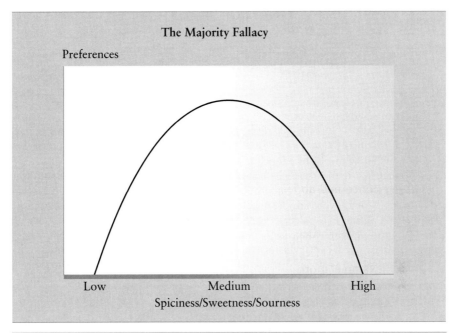

The Majority Fallacy

Preferences

Low   Medium   High

Spiciness/Sweetness/Sourness

FIGURE 12-1

Most preferences are normally distributed, and the largest segment is usually the middle segment. However, competition is usually greatest for this segment.

profitability. (See "Making the Decision: Chinese Readers Love *Readers*.") Focusing exclusively on this large "average" segment, however, and neglecting smaller, less typical, segments is known as the **majority fallacy.** Pursuing the majority is a fallacy because the largest segment is not always the most profitable segment. The reason for this is that many firms pursue the largest segment, and, consequently, competition tends to be most intense for the majority segment. Smaller segments can actually be more profitable than larger segments when there is much less competition for smaller than for larger segments. For example, Ragu spaghetti sauce and many other spaghetti sauces are average in terms of spiciness. Although most consumers prefer spaghetti sauces that are not too bland and not too spicy, the competition for this segment is intense. Hunt's Prima Salsa is a fairly spicy spaghetti sauce that appeals to a much smaller market segment. Although this segment is small, it is quite profitable because there is little competition for this segment. Hence, it is important to consider both the size of a segment and the level of competition for the segment.

The middle of a distribution tends to be unprofitable when heavy competition is centered in this location. The middle is also problematic when the distribution is bimodal as opposed to normal. For example, hot tea should be fairly hot, and ice tea should be fairly cold. Lukewarm tea is positioned in the middle of the distribution, but lukewarm tea is unlikely to appeal to either hot tea drinkers or ice tea drinkers.

CHINESE READERS LOVE "READERS"

In 1981, Chinese intellectual and entrepreneur Hu Yaquan launched a magazine that he called *Reader's Digest,* which was filled with articles by foreign journalists as well as "classics" in translation, including pieces by French author Guy de Maupassant and Charles Dickens. The magazine also had a humor section, profiles of famous scientists, and even a selection of cartoons. But the Chinese *Reader's Digest* was decidedly more highbrow than its American namesake. "Back then everyone in my high school and the first few years of college read it," recalls Sun Huixia, who grew up in western China. "It was something that was passed around and really opened our eyes." Hu's *Reader's Digest* was a crucial publication after the totalitarianism of the Cultural Revolution, when all ideas were suppressed. Within the first year of publication, Hu's magazine was selling 100,000 copies annually.

But during the early 1990s, the American *Reader's Digest* got fed up with its imitator and threatened to sue Mr. Hu. So Hu changed the name to *Readers* and, in a different political climate, also changed the focus to a more middlebrow chronicle of daily life in China, appealing to average Chinese citizens rather than students and intellectuals.

Readers now emphasizes Chinese authors and more topical subjects, although it handles potentially sensitive issues gently. Writers do not criticize the Chinese Communist Party, but they do cover current events. For instance, one article that covered a movie theater fire that killed almost 100 children highlighted the heroic efforts of teachers and emphasized the need for better fire safety regulations in public places. Each issue of *Readers* has some familiar departments—People, Humorous Anecdotes, Between Two Generations, Essays, and Letters to the Editor.

The change has been a huge success. Four million copies are sold each month, making *Readers* the undisputed best-selling magazine in China. "I pick it up every month," says Wang Hong, a traffic policeman who works in Inner Mongolia. "It's got these punchy short articles describing foreign countries that I love to read." Zhu Hong, a migrant laborer who now works as a furniture saleswoman in Beijing, explains, "I don't have time for reading books, so *Readers* gives me a general introduction to what's going on in the world. I want to raise my level of knowledge." And at 35 cents per issue, the magazine is still affordable to the average Chinese worker.

Readers of the original edition, who represent a distinctly different segment of the magazine market, have drifted away from the new *Readers.* "[The new] *Readers* is too bourgeois for me," comments Beijing artist An Weidong. "It's such a healthy magazine with lots of happy endings." And competition is on the rise, as naturally occurs when products try to serve the greatest number of consumers in a market. One competitor, *Family,* has only 100,000 fewer subscribers than *Readers* does. But *Readers* has taken hold and appears to have a loyal following among the Chinese middle class, much like its counterpart in the United States. Happy endings is an age-old formula that seems to work.

Source: Ian Johnson, "Reader's Digest Knockoff Wins 4 Million Chinese Fans," *The Wall Street Journal,* August 1, 1997, pp. B1, B3.

◆ THE SALES–COSTS TRADE-OFF

How many segments should firms pursue? Many firms pursue many different segments with many different products. For example, as discussed earlier, Coca-Cola has a product line consisting of many different brands (e.g., Coke Classic, New Coke, Cherry Coke, Diet Coke, caffeine-free Diet Coke), each of which is designed to appeal to a different market segment. As the number of products added to a product line increases, sales will increase because the odds that consumers will find a brand on the product line that is just right for them will increase. Hence, at one extreme, a firm can offer one product for everyone (an aggregation strategy); at the other extreme, a firm can offer a custom-made product for each customer, in which case there are as many segments as there are customers. Of course, custom-made products are very expensive to make, and not all customers are willing to pay the high price necessary for a custom-made product even if they prefer this product. Instead, many customers settle for a mass-produced product that fits their needs fairly closely. Hence, as segmentation increases, sales increase because a firm's offerings align more closely to consumers' preferences. However, as segmentation increases, costs increase because a multiproduct strategy costs more to implement than a one-product strategy. This is the **sales–costs trade-off.** (See Fig. 12-2.)

Why are multiproduct product line strategies expensive and difficult to implement? Manufacturing costs increase as the number of products offered increases because different types of equipment, different skills, and different resources are needed to manufacture different products. As the number of products offered increases, economies of scale decrease. Furthermore, marketing costs increase as product line breadth increases. It is more expensive to develop several different

FIGURE 12-2

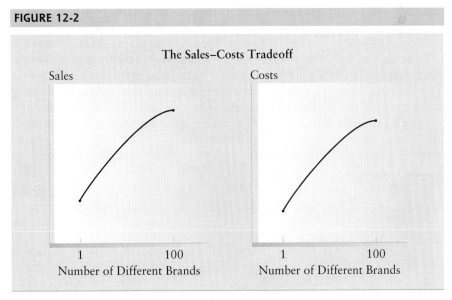

As segmentation increases, so do sales and costs.

advertisements for several different products than it is to develop a single promotion and advertising strategy for a single product. There are also several less obvious marketing costs associated with multiproduct strategies. Shelf space is limited and retailers may be unwilling to carry many different varieties of a product. When Coca-Cola introduced New Coke, Burger King switched from Coke to Pepsi because it did not want to carry both New Coke and Coke Classic in its fountains.

CANNIBALIZATION

Cannibalization represents another hidden cost. Different brands on the same product line are often so similar that they compete among themselves. For example, many consumers who typically drink Miller beer also drink Miller Lite; Miller competes against itself. Similarly, Buick, Pontiac, and Oldsmobile compete against each other—therefore, General Motors competes against itself. At one time, Quaker State offered 1,500 different brands of motor oil. Quaker State cut its product line in half and profits increased dramatically because cannibalization and other types of costs decreased. What is the ideal number of brands a firm should offer in a product line? There should be enough offerings to allow the firm to compete effectively in the major market segments but not so many that costs erode profits.

Sometimes, however, it is possible to control costs by sharing costs across offerings on a product line. Sharing costs across offerings allows a firm to develop a more extensive product line and pursue a greater number of segments. Manufacturing costs are reduced when several products on a product line share the same components. For example, the Buick Somerset, the Buick Skylark, the Pontiac GrandAm, and the Oldsmobile Calais share the same engine, drivetrain, and chassis; only minor trim differences exist among these brands. Marketing costs are reduced when several products in a product line share the same advertising. For example, Coca-Cola airs some ads that promote all Coca-Cola brands, rather than create several different ads for several different brands.

Another way to control costs is to target segments that are easy to reach, in the sense that they are localized or isolated in some way from nonusers. For example, manufacturers of sailing equipment can focus their promotion and advertising efforts on their target segment by advertising in specialty magazines, such as *Sail, Yachting,* and *Cruising World.* This is much less expensive and much more efficient than advertising on prime-time television—many prime-time viewers do not own boats, and

The *Wine Spectator* is a good vehicle for reaching an affluent market segment.
Source: © Mary Boucher.

Which magazines, newspapers, and television shows is the owner of the BMW with the "BIMER" plates likely to read and watch?

Source: © Dick Morton.

advertising dollars spent on sailing equipment would be wasted on nonowners. Similarly, manufacturers of luxury products (such as gourmet foods and wines, DuPont lighters, Piaget watches, Mercedes-Benz automobiles, etc.) can reach their target segment relatively inexpensively and efficiently by advertising in specialty magazines, such as *Cigar Aficionado* and *Wine Spectator.* In addition to specialty magazines, trade magazines offer yet another medium for reaching target segments. Direct marketing is another useful approach for controlling marketing costs and reaching very specific target markets.

Controlling costs can reduce the problems caused by cannibalization. In addition, cannibalization can be tolerated if the total revenue increases sufficiently. Total revenue (or sales from all products) = total variable costs (or the costs that increase as the number of units produced increases; e.g., supply and labor costs) + total fixed costs (e.g., costs that do not vary as the number of units produced increases; e.g., plant and equipment costs, annual budgets). If the unit contribution increases when a new product is added to the product line, cannibalization may be acceptable: Unit contribution = unit selling price − unit variable cost. Break-even analysis and contribution analysis should also be performed to make sure that adding new products to a product line helps a firm to meet its profit goals.

$$\text{Unit break-even} = \frac{\text{Total fixed costs}}{\text{Unit selling price} - \text{Unit variable costs}}$$

$$\frac{\text{Unit volume needed}}{\text{to reach profit goal}} = \frac{\text{Total fixed costs} + \text{Profit goal}}{\text{Unit contribution}}$$

◆ BASES OF SEGMENTATION

Analyzing consumer preference heterogeneity and sales–costs trade-offs is useful for determining whether and how much to segment, but it does not tell you how to segment. There are many different ways to segment a market, and several different approaches should always be considered. Consumers differ on many dimensions, and each of these dimensions suggests a potentially useful basis for dividing up a market. (See Fig. 12-3.) **Geographic segmentation** involves segmenting on the basis of cultural differences among consumers living in different cities, states, regions (e.g., north or south), or countries. **Demographic segmentation** involves segmenting on the basis of

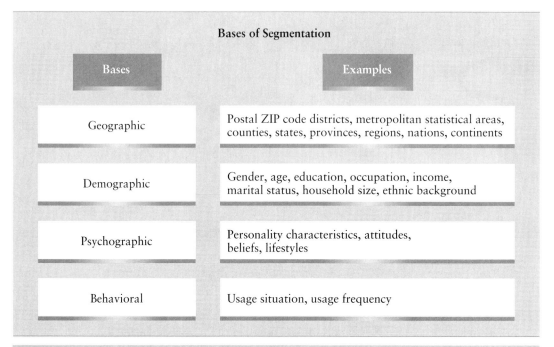

FIGURE 12-3

Segmentation can be made on geographic, demographic, psychographic, and behavioral bases.

gender, age, education, occupation, income, marital status, household size, or ethnic background. **Psychographic segmentation** involves segmenting on the basis of personality characteristics, attitudes, beliefs, or lifestyles. **Behavioral segmentation** involves segmenting on the basis of usage situation (e.g., breakfast only, weekends only, special occasions only) or usage frequency (e.g., nonusers, light users, medium users, heavy users).

GEOGRAPHIC BASES

Boundaries defined by postal ZIP code districts, metropolitan statistical areas, counties, states, provinces, regions, nations, and continents often provide useful bases for segmentation. These boundaries are particularly useful when consumers within a particular area share similar tastes and preferences. For example, Campbell's markets a spicy nacho cheese soup in Texas and California, where people tend to like relatively spicy food (e.g., Tex-Mex and Cal-Mex). Heinz sells more Home Style Gravy in the northeastern United States than in other parts of the country (Semenik & Bamossy, 1993). Rather than committing the majority fallacy, Gottschalks' clothing store chain targets relatively small rural markets to avoid competing with Gap and The Limited (Semenik & Bamossy, 1993).

Geographic boundaries are also useful overseas. Heineken markets a nonalcoholic beer in several countries in the Middle East, where the sale of alcohol is forbidden

SnackWell's products are generally targeted for women who enjoy sweets but who also believe they should be conscious of their weight and health.

Source: © Nabisco, Inc. Used with permission.

(Semenik & Bamossy, 1993). Light beer sells very poorly in countries like Germany, England, Ireland, and Mexico, where most consumers prefer heavier beers. Spicy foods sell poorly in countries in cold, northern climes, where relatively bland foods are preferred. By contrast, bland foods sell poorly in warm, southern countries, where spicy foods are preferred. Even within a particular country, bland foods are preferred in colder regions and spicy foods are preferred in warmer regions (e.g., northern vs. southern United States, India, etc.). Another important geographic consideration is that about 75 percent of the world's goods and services are consumed by 25 percent of the world's population. The G7 countries (the countries with the seven highest gross domestic product levels—Canada, France, Germany, Italy, Japan, the United Kingdom, and the United States) control 75 percent of the world's wealth (Semenik & Bamossy, 1993). Australia, New Zealand, Switzerland, Norway, Sweden, Denmark, and Finland are also highly industrialized. South Korea, Singapore, Hong Kong, and Taiwan are newly industrialized countries that are enjoying tremendous economic growth; consequently, these countries offer important opportunities for global marketing development.

Cultural differences also exist across geographic boundaries. Individualism/collectivism is the most important cross-cultural difference (Han & Shavitt, 1994). Individualists focus on personal goals, whereas collectivists focus on group goals (See Table 12-1 and Table 12-2). Although there are some obvious and important differences between individualistic versus collectivistic cultures, it is important to recognize that many of these differences are quantitative rather than qualitative. For example, Cialdini's (1993) weapons of influence are generally effective in individualistic and collectivistic cultures, but some influence techniques are more effective in the West and some are more effective in the East (Cialdini et al., 1999). It is important to remember that there are important similarities in terms of basic attention, memory, judgment, and choice processes across cultures. The theory of reasoned

TABLE 12-1 Differences between Individualistic versus Collectivistic Cultures

Variable	Individualistic Culture	Collectivistic Culture
Self-definition	Independent from group	Dependent on group
Self-perceptions	Stable (I am always the same person)	Variable (I am many different people depending on who I am with)
Self-esteem	Self-enhancement	Group enhancement
Role of others	Social comparison	Self-definition
Goals	Uniqueness	Belongingness
	Express oneself	Occupy one's proper place
	Be direct (say what's on your mind)	Be indirect (read other's mind)
	Self-promotion	Group promotion

Members of individualistic cultures focus on themselves, and members of collectivistic cultures focus on others.

Data source: Adapted from Markus & Kitayama, 1991.

action (Bagozzi, Wong, Abe, & Bergami, 2000), the accessibility–diagnosticity model (Aaker, 2000), and the elaboration likelihood model (Aaker & Maheswaran, 1997) generalize quite well to collectivistic cultures. In addition, individual differences in the individualistic/collectivistic orientation are more important than cultural differences (Cialdini et al., 1999).

TABLE 12-2 Language Translation Problems

English	Translation / Interpretation
Chevrolet Nova	Nova = "no go" (Spanish)
Got Milk?	"Are you lactating?" (Spanish) "Do you have the resources needed to provide for your family?" (Japanese)
Coors: Turn it loose	Suffer from diarrhea (Spanish)
Clairol: Mist Stick curling iron	"Manure stick curling iron" (German)
Perdue: It takes a strong man to make a tender chicken	"It takes an aroused man to make a chicken affectionate" (Spanish)
Pepsi: Come alive with the Pepsi Generation	"Pepsi brings your ancestors back from the grave" (Chinese)
Coca-Cola	Pronounced ke-kou-ke-la, meaning "bite the wax tadpole" (Chinese)
Gerber: Picture of a Caucasian baby on the baby food jar	African companies use pictures instead of words to describe the contents of jars because of illiteracy problems

Cross-cultural differences raise many interesting challenges.

DEMOGRAPHIC BASES

Demographic segmentation involves segmenting a market on the basis of gender, age, education, occupation, income, marital status, household size, or ethnic background. Measuring these variables using application forms, questionnaires, or surveys is relatively quick, easy, and inexpensive. These qualities have made demographic segmentation a particularly popular basis for segmenting a market. Also, not surprisingly, buying patterns and spending habits vary dramatically as a function of many different demographic variables. Males and females, for example, prefer different brands of clothes, different brands of cologne or perfume, and different brands of shampoo and other types of health and beauty products. Gap offers three different styles of jeans for males and four different styles of jeans for females. Historically, handguns were made primarily for male customers; Smith & Wesson's LadySmith line of handguns (for women), however, now accounts for 18 percent of the company's total sales volume (Zinn, 1991).

Age represents another important demographic variable. Teens and young adults, for example, prefer sweet products; consequently, sweet products such as Pepsi, New Coke, and Cherry Coke sell well among the young generation. The baby boomer segment represents another large and attractive segment because it consists of highly educated, high-income individuals. Although baby boomers used to be concerned primarily with prestige, most baby boomers are now middle-aged parents and their concerns

An ad targeted for women.
Source: Courtesy of Lever Brothers Company.

have changed. Consequently, BMW, Liz Claiborne, and other manufacturers of upscale products now run ads that emphasize safety and value rather than status or prestige. Another segment that will receive much attention from marketers over the next 30 years is the over-55, or "gray," segment. Because people are living longer and healthier lives, this segment is expected to grow by over 50 percent (from about 21 percent of the total population in 1990 to about 31 percent of the total population in 2020; Urban & Star, 1991). Moreover, this segment enjoys an active lifestyle, and members of this segment appreciate products that are marketed just for them (e.g., the Richard Simmons Silver Foxes exercise video for people over 55).

PSYCHOGRAPHIC BASES

Psychographic segmentation involves segmenting a market on the basis of personality characteristics, attitudes, beliefs, or lifestyles. Consumers differ on many different personality traits (e.g., need for cognition, self-monitoring, locus of control, need for closure, need for evaluation, etc.), and different consumers hold vastly different beliefs and attitudes. Lifestyles are measured by asking consumers questions about activities (e.g., type of employment, vacation preferences), interests (e.g., hobbies), and opinions (e.g., political, religious, and social beliefs; Kahle, Beatty, & Homer, 1986).

One widely used psychographic technique is the **VALS 2™** (Values and Life Styles—Version 2; Riche, 1989). SRI International conducted two national surveys in which 2,500 consumers were asked to agree or disagree with each of 43 statements pertaining to a wide range of values and lifestyles. Some of the statements focused on resources (e.g., income, intelligence, health, energy) and some focused on orientation. (See Fig. 12-4.) *Principle-oriented consumers* act on the basis of their own personal beliefs and attitudes (similar to low self-monitors). *Status-oriented consumers* are

FIGURE 12-4

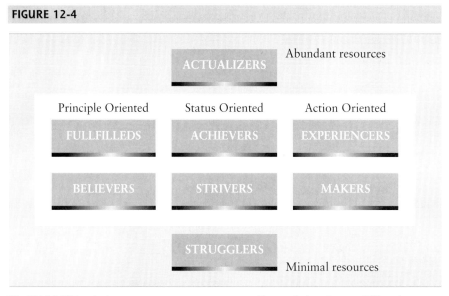

The VALS 2™ technique segments consumers according to their values and lifestyles.
Source: Adapted from VALS 2™ Eight American Lifestyles.

primarily concerned with the beliefs and attitudes of others (similar to high self-monitors). *Action-oriented consumers* are physically and socially active. Based on their responses to these statements, consumers are assigned to one of eight groups, or segments. *Actualizers* have the greatest incomes and resources, and this group has achieved a balance among the three orientations. At the other end of the spectrum, *Strugglers* have the lowest incomes and resources and are more concerned about survival than about the three orientations. Strugglers tend to be older and more brand loyal than the other groups. *Fulfilleds* are high- and *Believers* are low-income, principle-oriented consumers. *Achievers* and *Strivers* try to impress others, but Achievers have more of the resources necessary to achieve this goal. *Experiencers* and *Makers* have extremely active lifestyles, but Experiencers have greater resources. Experiencers tend to be relatively young and highly interested in new products and services.

As one would expect, principle-oriented consumers prefer brands that provide quality and value. Status-oriented consumers favor products with prestigious brand names. Action-oriented consumers are sensation seekers who like products associated with a wide range of activities, such as skiing, scuba diving, parachuting, tennis, golf, and so on. Within each of these three categories, consumers with greater resources tend to purchase more expensive brands.

BEHAVIORAL BASES

Behavioral segmentation involves segmenting a market on the basis of the usage situation, or usage frequency. (See "Taking Issue: Business Travelers Don't Love Disney.") Examples of different usage situations include different times of the day (morning, afternoon, evening), different times of the year (spring, summer, autumn, winter), and different events or occasions (e.g., for everyday use or only for special occasions). People prefer different foods and beverages during different parts of the day. Cereal, toast, and orange juice are for breakfast; sandwiches and soft drinks are for lunch; and larger entrees and alcoholic beverages (e.g., beer, wine) are for dinnertime usage. Different seasons call for the use of different types of products. Warm and heavy coats and wool sweaters are used in the winter, whereas cool and light T-shirts and shorts are used in the summer. Finally, inexpensive products tend to be used every day, whereas expensive products tend to be used on special occasions. People frequently drink inexpensive brands of beer and wine for regular consumption, but they serve premium beers and wines for special get-togethers and special occasions such as birthdays, weddings, anniversaries, and so on. Again, different situations call for the use of different types of products.

Usage frequency also serves as an important basis for segmentation. It is a sound strategy to treat nonusers (i.e., people who have never tried the product), light users (i.e., people who occasionally use the product), and heavy users (i.e., people who frequently use the product) differently. Nonusers may be unaware of the product category or unaware of the benefits of the product. Consequently, advertising targeted toward nonusers should emphasize attentional principles and should be designed to increase awareness and to educate the consumer about the specific benefits of the product. Light users, on the other hand, are already aware of the product and some benefits. Advertising targeted toward this group should emphasize belief- and attitude-change principles and should attempt to increase the importance of familiar benefits,

Burn the cookbooks. Make it up as you go along.

There is something about the look of stainless steel that compels you to create, to experiment, to discover the chef inside you. Now you can have that professional look, uniquely accented with white or black. And it's very affordable: standard suite of refrigerator, range and dishwasher accented with black costs less than $4000.* They're also available with exclusive features: the range has a separate warming drawer

below the large self-cleaning oven. The refrigerator has an ice and water filter to remove impurities. And the dishwasher's wash system can handle even a dinner party's worth of dishes without prerinsing. The Frigidaire Gallery Professional Series™ freestanding and built-in appliances. You will not simply leave this kitchen; you will emerge triumphant. Call 1-800-FRIGIDAIRE or http://www.frigidaire.com

FRIGIDAIRE GALLERY PROFESSIONAL SERIES   THE LOOK OF BETTER PERFORMANCE   ▦ FRIGIDAIRE

This Frigidaire kitchen ad will appeal to action-oriented consumers who may be achievers.

Source: Courtesy of Frigidaire Home Products.

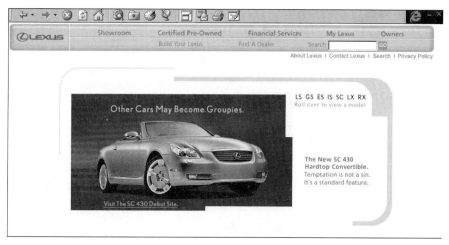

This Lexus Web site (www.lexus.com) will appeal to status-oriented actualizers.
Source: 2001 Lexus Web Site Home Page.

educate the consumer about other less familiar benefits, or position a brand more effectively with respect to competitors' brands. Advertising targeted toward heavy users should employ a maintenance strategy. That is, heavy users already know about and like the product. Therefore, advertising targeted toward this group should emphasize memory principles and should serve primarily as a reminder or as a tool for increasing the accessibility of a brand and its benefits from memory. Very different advertising strategies are required for different groups of consumers.

Frequency Marketing
Many firms are now practicing **frequency marketing** principles. Frequency marketing involves targeting heavy users (i.e., a firm's best customers) and offering them special benefits and privileges. Airlines were among the first to adopt frequency marketing principles. Frequent-flyer programs are essentially frequency marketing programs. The more a customer flies, the more frequent-flyer miles the customer accumulates. Frequent-flyer miles can then be used to purchase free flights or free upgrades from coach to first class. Many hotels also use frequency marketing principles. Customers earn points each time they spend a night at a particular hotel chain, and these points can be accumulated and applied toward free rooms or free upgrades. Some fast-food chains also use frequency marketing. Each time a customer buys a sandwich at Subway or Sub Station II, a card is punched, and when a certain number of punches is attained, the customer gets a free sandwich. Some bookstores, movie theaters, and department stores have also adopted frequency marketing principles. The more purchases the customer makes, the more points the customer accumulates toward special prizes or benefits.

Frequent users also tend to be **brand loyal.** That is, they tend to purchase one brand repeatedly and tend to view competing brands as poor substitutes to their preferred brand. Lighter users tend to be brand switchers. However, they tend to switch for different reasons. **Variety seekers** switch purposefully because they get tired of the

BUSINESS TRAVELERS DON'T LOVE DISNEY

It's almost un-American to say you don't love Mickey Mouse, or Pluto, Donald, and Daisy for that matter. But that is just how some business travelers feel. Thinking that they are going to spend an enjoyable few days in Orlando while actually getting some business done, they book their hotels and come ready and willing to work. What they find is what they don't want: lots of children, distracting events and hotel decor, loud restaurants, lack of convenient transportation, and a communications network not set up for their needs. One attorney who attended the American Bar Association's annual conference found Mickey Mouse phones in her hotel room that could not accommodate her laptop. "It was silly," she comments.

We might ask, what did they expect? The Magic Kingdom, after all, is supposed to be magic—leave the business at home. Disney targeted its original theme park for families with young children. Over the years, it has expanded to further segment this market as well as accommodate other market segments. For instance, families can now choose from a wide range of hotels, villas, and even trailer parks in which to stay. In recent years, Disney has run commercials aimed at couples, touting the Magic Kingdom as a great place for honeymoons, anniversaries, and other romantic getaways—kind of a wholesome Club Med.

In an attempt to cast an even wider net over consumers, both the city of Orlando and Disney have gone fishing for business travelers. Orlando has invested over $400 million to triple the size of its convention center and $800 million to expand the airport. Las Vegas is now the only city in the United States with more hotel rooms than Orlando. William Peeper, chief executive officer of the Orlando/Orange County Convention and Visitors Bureau, boasts, "We're booking some of the largest conventions in the United States."

Disney World officials say that they make every effort to separate business guests from tourists. And they claim that businesses and organizations have responded. "The conventions have really taken advantage of the Disney magic," claims George Aguel, a Disney vice president. Conventions held in Orlando typically have a high attendance rate. But complaints abound. Air-conditioning in some hotel rooms won't go on unless all doors and balcony windows are locked (for childproofing), all-you-can-eat buffets aren't the best place for business lunches, and noise curfews don't go into effect until 11 P.M. Overall, there's a culture clash between vacationers and conventioneers.

What would be the best way to handle a market that has two segments with such diverse needs? Is there room for only one? Not necessarily. Perhaps Orlando and Disney could work harder to offer hotels and restaurants that cater exclusively to their business customers—with necessary communications links, quiet dining rooms, and the like. And perhaps organizations planning conventions and conferences in Orlando should be realistic—business travelers want to have some fun, too. Why else would they choose a spot like this for a convention? They must want to enjoy at least a bit of the magic.

Indeed, business travelers are still headed to Orlando in droves. William Peepers can cite a number of organizations that have booked conventions in his city for the coming year, including one that has 50,000 members. Disney has opened its new Coronado Springs Resort, a 1,967-room extravaganza that combines a five-story Mayan pyramid with a pool and a water slide, not to mention the largest hotel ballroom in the country—and 95,000 square feet of conference space. It's hard to tell whether the hotel is intended for work or play. Maybe if they leave out those Mickey phones, everyone will be happy.

Source: Nancy Keates, "Orlando's Fun Is Lost on Business-Minded," *The Wall Street Journal*, September 5, 1997, pp. B1, B10.

same brand all the time and like to try many different brands. **Market stimulus switchers** also switch purposely because they tend to buy the least expensive brand, the brand for which they have a coupon, or the brand that happens to be advertised the most heavily at the time of purchase. **Random switchers** seem to switch brands for no apparent reason. Perhaps they confuse product packages (e.g., store brands and name brands often have similar packaging in terms of color and design), or perhaps they were in a hurry and simply grabbed the first brand they saw. Different marketing programs are needed for different types of switchers. New and improved versions of a product and new varieties (e.g., flavors, colors) of a product may appeal to variety seekers. Heavy promotion and advertising should be effective in influencing market stimulus switchers. Similar packaging and prominent locations (e.g., eye-level shelves, end-of-aisle displays, shelves located next to the cashier) should influence random switchers and impulsive buyers.

This AT&T ad is targeted to market stimulus switchers.
Source: Copyright AT&T.

◆ THE CUSTOMER × PRODUCT × USAGE SITUATION MATRIX

Effective market segmentation requires knowledge of the structure of a market. One way to define market structure is in terms of variability. Markets vary on three key dimensions: customers, products, and product usage situations. (See Fig. 12-5.) One way to assess the degree of variability across these three dimensions is to analyze consumer judgments of the appropriateness of a particular product for a particular situation and to subject these judgments to a statistical technique known as the analysis of variance (Srivastava, Alpert, & Shocker, 1984). Srivastava et al. showed subjects a matrix of 24

FIGURE 12-5

Customer × Product × Usage Situation Matrix

Structure	Implications
Customer	Preference heterogeneity exists. Find a customer segment that currently is not served adequately.
Product	Brand heterogeneity exists. Design a new type of product.
Usage Situation	Usage situation heterogeneity exists. Develop a new usage situation.
Customer × Product Interaction	Different groups of customers are loyal to different brands.
Customer × Usage Situation Interaction	Different groups of customers use the product in different usage situations.
Product × Usage Situation Interaction	Different brands are used in different usage situations.
Customer × Product × Usage Situation Interaction	Different groups of customers use different brands in different usage situations.

Markets vary on three main dimensions: customers, products, and product usage situations.

different products and 12 different usage situations and asked them to judge the appropriateness of each product for each usage situation on a four-point likelihood-of-use judgment scale. An analysis of variance performed on these judgments reveals the structure of the market by indicating which factors and what combination of factors significantly influence these judgments.

Some markets have very simple structures consisting of only one or a few main effects. Main effects indicate that a factor's influence is independent of the other factors. For example, if a specific product market is characterized by a customer main effect without any other significant effects, this means that customer preferences are heterogeneous (highly variable), and, therefore, it makes sense to segment on the basis of preference differences between large consumer segments. However, different markets have different structures. Some markets are best characterized by a product main effect. This means that a large number of brands differs markedly in quality. That is, the variability is localized in brands rather than in customers. Finally, a usage situation main effect means that the product category has many different uses.

Not surprisingly, most markets are more complex. Frequently, there are important interactions among the three factors. An interaction means that the effects of one factor depend on the effects of another (as discussed in Chapter 1). For example, a customer × product interaction means that different groups of customers prefer different brands across usage situations. The soft drink market has this type of structure: A large group of customers drinks Coke and another large group of customers drinks Pepsi, and these preferences appear to be quite stable across usage situations. Another possible structure is a customer × usage situation interaction: One large group of customers uses the product in one situation (e.g., for breakfast), whereas another large group of customers uses the product in a different situation (e.g., for dinner). A product × usage situation interaction indicates that consumers use one type of product in one usage situation and another type of product in a different usage situation. For example, Urban, Johnson, and Hauser (1984) hypothesized that the coffee market is characterized by a product × usage situation interaction: Perhaps most consumers prefer to drink coffee with caffeine (one type of product) in the morning to wake up, whereas decaffeinated coffee might be preferred after dinner to avoid staying up too late. Urban et al.'s data failed to support this type of structure. Instead they found that one large consumer segment prefers coffee with caffeine across usage situations (e.g., mornings, afternoons, and evenings), whereas another large consumer segment always prefers decaffeinated coffee. Hence, the actual structure of the coffee market is a customer × product interaction.

Finally, the most complex type of market structure is a customer × product × usage situation triple interaction. This means that different groups of customers prefer different brands for different usage situations. For example, one large group of customers prefers inexpensive American beers for typical everyday use and prefers imports for special occasions. Another large group prefers inexpensive American beers across usage situations, and yet another large group prefers imports across usage situations. Market structure analysis tells us which factors have an important influence on consumer preferences. Only important factors should be considered when developing a segmentation strategy.

CHAPTER SUMMARY ▪

Effective segmentation involves dividing a market into subcategories and pursuing different marketing strategies for each subcategory. The decision of whether and how much to segment depends on three key considerations: consumer preference heterogeneity (variability), the majority fallacy, and the sales–costs trade-off. Segmentation strategy increases in importance as consumer preference variability increases and as competition among firms intensifies. The number of segments that will be profitable depends on the sales–costs trade-off, because sales and costs both increase as segmentation increases. As the number of segments targeted increases, a firm will reach a point where the costs of further segmentation will outweigh the benefits. In addition to deciding whether and how much to segment, managers must also decide the best way to segment. Geographic segmentation involves segmenting on the basis of geographic areas, such as different cities, states, regions, or countries. Demographic segmentation involves segmenting on the basis of gender, age, education, occupation, income, marital status, household size, or ethnic background. Psychographic segmentation involves segmenting on the basis of personality characteristics, attitudes, beliefs, or lifestyles. Behavioral segmentation involves segmenting on the basis of usage situation, or usage frequency. Market structure analysis informs managers about the relative importance of customer preferences, product differences, and usage situations in forming an effective segmentation strategy.

KEY CONCEPTS ▪

- Segmentation
- Aggregation
- Consumer preference heterogeneity
- Normal distribution
- Majority fallacy
- Sales–costs trade-off

- Cannibalization
- Geographic segmentation
- Demographic segmentation
- Psychographic segmentation
- Behavioral segmentation
- VALS 2™

- Frequency marketing
- Brand loyal
- Variety seekers
- Market stimulus switchers
- Random switchers

DISCUSSION QUESTIONS ▪

1. Name several universal preferences among consumers.
2. According to the majority fallacy, why might an entrepreneur decide to open a sweet shop to sell gourmet specialty chocolates without worrying about competing against Hershey's?
3. What are some of the costs associated with segmentation?
4. Name and describe briefly the four main dimensions that marketers use for segmentation.
5. In what ways might segmenting by ZIP code be useful to marketers?
6. Perform a demographic analysis of yourself as a consumer. Then note some products you own that fit your analysis and some that fall outside it. How do you explain the purchases that fall outside your demographic profile?

7. According to the VALS 2™ technique, what type of consumer would probably buy a big-screen television? What type of consumer would take a hot-air balloon ride? Why?

8. How might SnackWell's marketers use usage situation to actually broaden the product's segment?

9. Describe an instance in which, as a consumer, you have made use of frequency marketing to gain greater value. (An example might be renting 10 videos at one video store to get the 11th video free.)

10. What might be the variables involved in a customer × product × usage situation matrix for the ice cream market?

CHAPTER 13

New Product Development

◆ GATEWAY VERSUS DELL

New products from the computer world arrive daily. In fact, it seems to many consumers that as soon as they have bought a computer and learned how to use it, it becomes obsolete. As difficult as this phenomenon seems for consumers, staying ahead of the competition technologically is a matter of survival for hardware and software manufacturers. And staying ahead is a matter of having the best new products, either for existing markets or for new markets.

Marketers for computer companies will try anything to distinguish themselves from the competition. Ted Waitt, founder and CEO of Gateway, the company that first popularized custom-built, mail-order computers for consumers, talks about his company's competition with Dell Computer. "The separation between the two of us will become more apparent over the next two years," he vows. (Ironically, Gateway's unique image has been apparent to consumers for more than a decade, from its beginnings in a barn to the cow motif it has been known for ever since. Consumers are more likely to confuse Gateway with Ben & Jerry's than with other computer companies.) Gateway and Dell have been locked in competition for home PC users for several years, but even so, both companies have grown at twice the industry rate because they developed a way to customize computers and sell them directly to consumers at a good price.

Now Gateway is going after Dell's other customers: corporate buyers. Gateway has developed a new line of desktop personal computers designed for businesses and has agreed to buy Advanced Logic Research, which makes server computers used by businesses. "Guess Who's No. 1," boasts a Gateway ad, which quotes a trade journal survey that discovered Gateway's business computers were less expensive to purchase and operate than those of Dell, Compaq, IBM, and others.

Naturally, Dell is not sitting still. Launching a new product of its own, the company has decided to make the leap into high-end computer workstations, which it is selling at prices below its competitors. Already successful at selling servers at low prices, Dell is trying to do the same with workstations. Dell plans to market the new workstations to engineers who work in computer-aided design, software developers, and large financial institutions.

As you read this chapter, consider the different ways marketers can identify opportunities for growth by developing new products and make them successful by using different strategies to position them in new or existing markets.

Sources: Evan Ramstad, "Gateway, in a Shift, Seeks Business Buyers for Its PCs," *The Wall Street Journal,* July 29, 1997, p. B4; "Dell Computer to Sell Workstations at Prices Below Competitors'," *The Wall Street Journal,* July 28, 1997; Melanie Warner, "Gateway to Wealth," *Fortune,* September 8, 1997, p. 80.

◆ INTRODUCTION

Firms like Gateway and Dell Computer must continually develop new products to compete effectively in today's complex and rapidly changing marketplace. Consumers are constantly looking for fresh new ideas that make life better and easier. On average, new products generate about 25 percent of a firm's sales (Wind, Mahajan, & Bayless, 1990). However, the new product failure rate is also relatively high, about 35 percent across industries (Urban & Hauser, 1993). Consequently, firms need to decide whether they should be proactive or reactive. Proactive firms aggressively develop many new products and try to be first in the race to the market. Reactive firms wait to see what new products other firms offer and then develop their own copycat brands. Firms also need to develop effective **positioning strategies** for their brands. Positioning refers to consumer perceptions of a target brand relative to competing brands. Positioning influences and is influenced by all elements of the marketing mix (the four Ps: product, promotion, price, and place). In addition to describing positioning strategies, this chapter discusses new developments in consumer-driven engineering, a research-based technology that enables firms to position their brands more effectively.

◆ PROACTIVE VERSUS REACTIVE STRATEGIES

Ford Motor Company introduced the automobile to consumers and dominated the automobile market for decades. This proactive strategy was very profitable. However, Ford also aggressively promoted the Edsel in the 1950s and lost over $250 million. This particular proactive strategy was not at all profitable. Other firms prefer to play a reactive "wait and see" game, letting other firms take the risks associated with developing a totally new product. P&G observed that Colgate toothpaste was such a tremendous success that it decided to develop its own brand of toothpaste in the 1950s—Crest

How should marketers at P&G react to Colgate's "Tartar Control Whitening" new product introduction?

Source: © Mary Boucher.

toothpaste. Crest dominated the toothpaste market for decades, and, in 1980, it held 33 percent of the $1 billion toothpaste market and outsold Colgate two to one. This reactive strategy was remarkably successful. Crest was not the first toothpaste, but for decades most consumers viewed Crest to be the best toothpaste. In 1985, P&G observed that Colgate developed new gels, pumps, and tartar control brands. Consequently, P&G developed its own gels, pumps, and tartar control varieties of Crest. However, Crest's market share dropped, and Colgate's share skyrocketed to 28 percent. This particular reactive strategy was unsuccessful. There are no guarantees of

FIGURE 13-1

Opportunities Matrix

	New Products	Existing Products
New Markets	Diversification	Market Development
Existing Markets	Product Development	Market Penetration

	New Products	Existing Products
New Markets	Deodorant, Detergent, Carpet Cleaner	New Uses (deodorize refrigerators, freezers, sinks; clean batteries)
Existing Markets	Larger-sized box	Coupons

Growth opportunities can be assessed with an opportunities matrix. The bottom matrix shows examples of how to use the opportunities matrix to identify new opportunities for baking soda.

Source: From Ansoff (1957).

Campbell's has diversified not only by developing different soup products but also by offering a variety of products for different markets.

Source: Courtesy of Campbell Soup Company.

success—sometimes proactive strategies are successful and sometimes they are not; sometimes reactive strategies are successful and sometimes they are not.

When are proactive strategies likely to be successful, and when are reactive strategies likely to be successful? This is a much better question than the "which is better" question. Five factors should be considered in deciding when to use reactive and when to use proactive strategies: growth opportunities, protection for innovation, market size and margin, competition, and position in the channel of distribution. Growth opportunities are assessed through the use of the Ansoff (1957) opportunities matrix. (See Fig. 13-1.) This is a 2 × 2 matrix with two types of products (new or existing) and two types of markets (new or existing). Proactive strategies are appropriate for new high-growth markets that are responsive to new product innovations. Developing new products for new markets is known as **diversification.** One example of diversification is Arm & Hammer's strategy to develop new laundry detergents and deodorants in 1977: Its total sales increased from $22 million to $99 million. Proactively developing new uses for baking soda was an extremely successful strategy. Other types of products do not have many new uses, and firms are forced to focus on existing products or markets. A **market penetration** strategy involves using heavy promotion and advertising to increase sales of existing products in existing markets. A **product development** strategy involves building on a firm's unique strengths and developing new products for existing markets. This usually involves variations on a theme, such as new flavors for an already successful beverage or food product. A **market development** strategy involves

When to Use Proactive versus Reactive Strategies

	Proactive	Reactive
Market Growth	High	Low
Protection for Innovation	Strong	Weak
Market Size and Margin	Large	Small
Competition	High	Low
Channel Position	Strong	Weak

FIGURE 13-2

The best choice for positioning strategy depends on several factors.

introducing existing products to new markets. This often involves taking your products overseas. For example, McDonald's and Coca-Cola have been tremendously successful in introducing their products to Europe and Asia.

Protection for innovation is another key factor. For example, Polaroid's products were well protected by patents and, for many years, it was illegal for other firms to copy Polaroid's products. Coca-Cola protected itself by keeping its formula a secret. This prevented other firms from copying Coca-Cola. If a firm anticipates high levels of protection through patents, secret formulas, or other types of secrets, a proactive strategy makes sense. Otherwise, a firm may be forced to rely on reactive strategies.

The first firm to enter a large market is likely to benefit from economies of scale, learning curves, and fast returns on investment. These benefits are often unavailable from small markets. Hence, proactive strategies should be used in large markets, and reactive strategies should be used in small markets. Large firms have greater resources for developing and protecting their brands, relative to small firms. Large firms are also able to absorb short-term losses to put small firms out of business. Large firms also have greater power in the channel and are often able to encourage cooperation among channel members; small firms rarely have this luxury. Consequently, proactive strategies can be very effective for large firms, whereas reactive strategies tend to be safer and more appropriate for small firms. (See Fig. 13-2.).

◆ THE PIONEERING ADVANTAGE

Pioneering brands, or the first brands to enter a new market, often enjoy a long-term consumer preference advantage over follower brands. This preference advantage is known as the **pioneering advantage,** and it has been observed in a wide variety of

Ivory Soap was a pioneer 100 years ago; today, the brand is still
popular.

Source: © The Procter & Gamble Company. Used with permission.

consumer markets. It has also been observed in growing markets, mature markets, markets with low brand-switching costs, and even in markets with high brand-switching costs (Gurumurthy & Urban, 1992; Robinson & Fornell, 1985; Urban, Carter, Gaskin, & Mucha, 1986). In short, the phenomenon is remarkably robust and pervasive. Moreover, the phenomenon has very important managerial implications because it suggests that speed is of the essence and all firms should try to get their products to the market as soon as possible.

Rather than blindly accepting these implications, however, the scientific perspective suggests that we should analyze the phenomenon carefully. Why does the pioneering advantage occur? What psychological phenomena, if any, contribute to the pioneering advantage? The answers to these questions are very important because they determine whether firms should speed up their new product development and launching processes. There exist three possibilities. First, there may be an inherent advantage associated with being first to market. Perhaps the first brand benefits from consumer psychological processes that do not occur for later entrants. Second, there may be an enabling advantage. That is, being first may enable firms to pursue strategies that cannot be pursued for later entrants. For example, the first brand can be effectively positioned and advertised in many different ways, whereas the number of effective positioning strategies and advertising strategies available for later entrants decreases as competition increases. Third, the pioneering advantage may be a spurious (or false) effect. Maybe most pioneering brands are developed by large, powerful firms with vast resources. Perhaps being first has no effect, but being first may be correlated with firms having large promotion and advertising budgets and far-reaching power in the channel of distribution.

THREE HYPOTHESES ABOUT PIONEERING

The **inherent advantage hypothesis** suggests that merely being first, per se, is sufficient to create an advantage. That is, a brand will be more successful if it is first as opposed to not first. Moreover, faster is better: A brand should be more successful if it is a pioneer as opposed to an early follower or if it is an early follower as opposed to a late follower. The **enabling advantage hypothesis** suggests that being first is good but not enough. Being first helps only if the brand is positioned and advertised effectively. There are greater strategic opportunities for pioneering brands than for later entrants. This is because, for novel product categories, the consumer's perceptual space is blank and the pioneering firm is free to position the brand anywhere (perceptual maps will be discussed in greater detail later in this chapter). Degrees of freedom are used up as more followers enter the market because early brands preempt later brands. Finally, the **spurious effect hypothesis** suggests that speed is irrelevant. If pioneering is correlated with firm size and resources, it is possible that firm size and resources, not pioneering, drive success (this is a good example of the third variable problem discussed in Chapter 1). (See Fig. 13-3.)

Set-Size Effect

My research (Kardes & Gurumurthy, 1992; Kardes, Gurumurthy, Chandrashekaran, & Dornoff, 1993) and research conducted by Carpenter and Nakamoto (1989) suggest that there is an inherent advantage to being first to the market. (See Fig. 13-4.) The pioneering brand is novel and interesting, and, consequently, consumers tend to pay much more attention to the pioneering brand than to redundant, less interesting, copycat

FIGURE 13-3

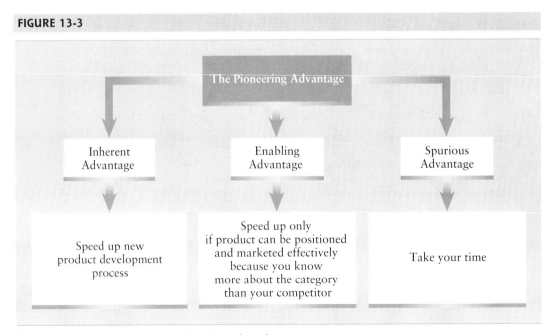

Three alternative hypotheses about the pioneering advantage.

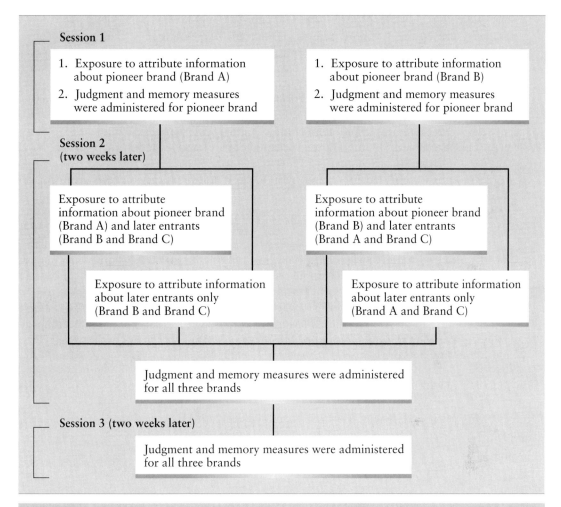

Session 1

1. Exposure to attribute information about pioneer brand (Brand A)
2. Judgment and memory measures were administered for pioneer brand

1. Exposure to attribute information about pioneer brand (Brand B)
2. Judgment and memory measures were administered for pioneer brand

Session 2 (two weeks later)

Exposure to attribute information about pioneer brand (Brand A) and later entrants (Brand B and Brand C)

Exposure to attribute information about pioneer brand (Brand B) and later entrants (Brand A and Brand C)

Exposure to attribute information about later entrants only (Brand B and Brand C)

Exposure to attribute information about later entrants only (Brand A and Brand C)

Judgment and memory measures were administered for all three brands

Session 3 (two weeks later)

Judgment and memory measures were administered for all three brands

FIGURE 13-4

Some research suggests that there is an inherent advantage to simply being first to the market.

Source: F. R. Kardes & Gurumurthy, K. (1992). Order-of-entry effects on consumer memory and judgment: An information integration perspective. *Journal of Marketing Research, 29,* 343–357. Reprinted with permission of the American Marketing Association.

brands. As a consequence, consumers learn more and remember more about the pioneering brand, and this creates an internal set-size effect. The **set-size effect** refers to the tendency to form more extreme and confident judgments as the amount of information available for judgment increases, even when the favorableness of the individual pieces of information is controlled (Anderson, 1981, 1982). That is, the sheer amount of information available for judgment has an important influence on judgment. Typically, set size is manipulated externally by varying the amount of information presented for different brands (e.g., two positive attributes for Brand A and four positive attributes for Brand B). However, Kardes and Gurumurthy (1992) manipulated set size inter-nally by presenting seven attributes for each of three brands (A, B, and C) and by demonstrating that consumers learn more about the first brand (the pioneer) than about later brands. It did not even matter which brand was presented first. When Brand A was presented first, subjects learned more about A. When Brand B was pre-sented first, subjects learned more about B. The second and third brands were pre-sented one week after the first brand was presented. An internal set-size effect was observed: More favorable and more confident judgments were formed toward the pio-neer because subjects learned more about the pioneer and more information is better than less information. (See Fig. 13-5.)

   Not surprisingly, because more favorable and confident judgments were formed toward the first brand, the first brand was preferred to the second and third brands (the pioneering advantage). More surprisingly, this preference advantage occurred even though the third brand was superior to the first brand! Why was the pioneer pre-ferred to a superior follower? The results showed that subjects paid very little attention to the third brand, and consequently, they never learned that the third brand was supe-rior. A superior follower brand can fail if it seems like an uninteresting copycat brand and consumers fail to attend to it. Kardes and Gurumurthy (1992) also conducted a follow-up experiment that showed that the pioneering advantage disappears when the three brands are presented simultaneously as opposed to sequentially. This is because subjects learned the same amount of information about each of the brands when the three brands were presented at the same time, and consequently, the internal set-size effect was eliminated.

FIGURE 13-5

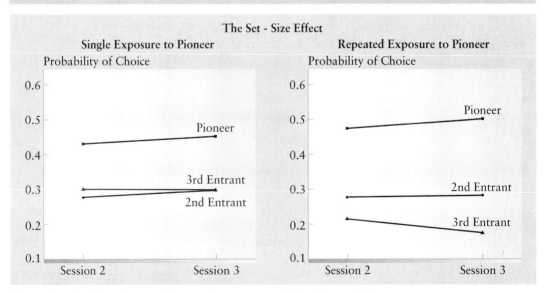

Pioneer brands enjoy a large preference advantage, especially with repeated exposure.

Source: Kardes, F. R. & K. Gurumurthy (1992). Order-of-entry effects on consumer memory and judgment: An infor-mation integration perspective. *Journal of Marketing Research, 29,* 343–357. Reprinted with permission of the American Marketing Association.

Consideration Set Processes

In another follow-up study, Kardes et al. (1993) showed that the internal set-size effect is not the only psychological mechanism responsible for the pioneering advantage. Other mechanisms also contribute. Kardes et al. presented brand names for 18 brands of good-tasting, low-calorie chocolate bars (a fictitious new product category). Only brand names were presented. Because no attribute information was presented, subjects learned virtually nothing about the brands, and therefore, set-size effects were unlikely to occur. Nevertheless, most subjects preferred the first brand that was presented, regardless of whether the first brand was called Topnut, Delight, or Escape. One week after the first brand was presented, 6 new brands were presented. One week after these brands were presented, 11 additional followers were presented. Subjects were asked to indicate how much they liked each brand name and to make inferences about the qualities of each brand based upon the name. One week after the final set of brands was presented, subjects were asked to recall as many brand names as possible, to indicate which brands they were considering trying, and to choose one brand. The results revealed that subjects were more likely to remember, consider, and choose the pioneer brand. Again, subjects preferred the pioneer over a superior follower (pretests showed that Indulge was the most preferred brand name in the set).

Preference Ideal Point-Formation Processes and Direction of Comparison

Carpenter and Nakamoto (1989) identified yet another psychological process that leads to an inherent preference advantage for the pioneer. Consumers are often unfamiliar with really new product categories, and consequently their preferences are often ambiguous. That is, consumers do not yet know what they want. When initial preferences are ambiguous, the combination of features and benefits associated with the pioneering brand seems especially useful, so much so that the pioneer actually sets the ideal point for the category! In addition, a direction-of-comparison effect is observed: Consumers compare follower brands with the pioneer (but not vice versa), and consequently, the pioneer seems unique and special while followers seem like pale imitations of the pioneer. This is because the pioneer sets the agenda for the comparison process (the direction-of-comparison effect is discussed in greater detail in Chapter 4).

In sum, at least four different psychological phenomena appear to contribute to the pioneering advantage: the set-size effect (Kardes & Gurumurthy, 1992), consideration set processes (Kardes et al., 1993), preference ideal point-formation processes (Carpenter & Nakamoto, 1989), and the direction-of-comparison effect (Carpenter & Nakamoto, 1989). Nevertheless, some researchers suggest that the pioneering advantage may be spurious. The most well-known and influential study implying that the pioneering advantage may be a marketing myth was conducted by Golder and Tellis (1993). These researchers argued that many of the studies designed to determine the magnitude of the pioneering advantage used large databases (i.e., PIMS and ASSESSOR databases) that failed to include pioneering brands that failed: Only relatively successful brands were included in the databases. Excluding failures may result in overestimation of the magnitude of the pioneering advantage. Golder and Tellis (1993) obtained historical data from several media sources that included product failures and found that prior research overestimated the average market share of pioneering brands. However, Golder and Tellis (1993) failed to obtain data for nonpioneering brands. If the failure rates were equally high for pioneering brands and nonpioneering brands, there would be no overestimation. Future research should examine this possibility. Until this issue is resolved, most of the research conducted on the pioneering advantage so far suggests that there is an inherent advantage to being the first to the market, and this advantage provides a strong argument for the use of proactive product development strategies.

◆ OPPORTUNITY IDENTIFICATION

Not all markets are equally attractive, and markets that are attractive to one firm may not be attractive to another. Most successful firms have unique strengths and skills, and it is a good idea to focus on markets where those particular strengths and skills will prove to be useful. When choosing a particular market to focus upon, managers should list as many potentially attractive markets as possible and evaluate each market systematically. Each market should be evaluated on the same set of criteria, and the criteria should be applied consistently. What criteria are typically important? Sales potential, penetration, scale, input, reward, and risk are market characteristics relevant to most firms (Urban & Hauser, 1993). **Sales potential** refers to the potential size of a market in dollar sales. This criterion is important because it is usually easier to obtain a share of a growing market than to take shares away from competitors in a stagnant market. **Penetration** refers to the vulnerability of competitors. Competitors with poorly designed or obsolete products are vulnerable to new products that offer new benefits that consumers find attractive. **Scale** refers to cumulative sales volume. *Economies of scale* refers to the tendency of unit costs to decrease as the number of units produced increases. For example, for many consumer goods, the costs incurred for producing a single unit of a product are lower when 1 million units are produced than when 1,000 units are produced. This is because firms that produce large amounts of a good frequently benefit from volume discounts from suppliers and often learn how to produce and market the product more efficiently. Economies of scale are not always large, however. In many service industries, for example, unit costs do not decrease appreciably as scale increases.

   Input refers to the costs of entering and penetrating a new market. These costs include product development, promotion, advertising, and distribution costs. Although many firms find low market-entry costs attractive, large market-entry costs can be attractive to large firms that can enter a market more easily than smaller competitors. This is because entry costs can serve as a barrier to competitors. **Reward** refers to expected profits or return on investment. Small firms typically require a fast return on investment, whereas large firms can usually afford to wait. Finally, **risk** refers to uncertainty due to instability in the availability of supplies, rapidly changing consumer preferences, or changes in the legal environment.

   The relative importance of each of these criteria varies from firm to firm. Firm size and resources are strongly related to importance considerations. Managers should evaluate the importance of each criterion by allocating 100 points across the six criteria. More points indicate greater importance, but the ratings must sum to 100. This type of rating system is called a **constant sum scale.** Managers should also evaluate the attractiveness of each market on each criterion on a scale ranging from −2 (very unattractive) to +2 (very attractive). Multiplying importance ratings by attractiveness ratings yields an overall evaluative rating for each market. The market with the highest overall rating wins. This approach combines managerial judgment (i.e., the ratings are based on managerial judgment) and a quantitative model (i.e., overall rating = Σia, where i refers to importance ratings and a refers to attractiveness ratings) that improves decision making by helping managers to be more systematic and consistent in their thinking.

◆ POSITIONING STRATEGIES

Positioning refers to consumers' relative perceptions of a particular brand. A brand is typically not perceived or judged in isolation. It is judged relative to other brands. A particular brand seems expensive, inexpensive, large, small, ordinary, or extraordinary depending on what brand or set of brands with which it is compared. All marketing variables and activities influence positioning. Consider the marketing mix variables or the four Ps (product, price, promotion, and place). Product variables such as the design of the product and the product's components or ingredients influence how the product is perceived compared with competitors' offerings. Products perceived as high-quality products have a superior design and superior components or ingredients compared with competitors' products. Price also influences relative perceptions. Relatively expensive products are commonly perceived to be higher in quality relative to less expensive products. Promotion and advertising tell consumers what is special or unique about a particular brand, and this strongly influences relative perceptions. The place of distribution is also important. Upscale products are sold only at upscale retail outlets.

All marketing variables affect positioning, and positioning affects all marketing variables. If you believe that a particular brand manufactured by your firm is higher in quality than other brands, you need to ensure that (a) only high-quality components/ingredients are used, (b) a high price tag is used, (c) promotion and advertising emphasize quality, and (d) only upscale retail outlets are used. In other words, all marketing activities must be consistent with and well coordinated with the positioning strategy. Any inconsistency is potentially dangerous. For example, Armani does not allow Wal-Mart or Kmart to carry its line of high-quality men's suits because this inconsistency would undermine Armani's positioning strategy. For that matter, neither Wal-Mart nor Kmart would want to carry Armani suits because this would be inconsistent with their image as low-cost retail outlets. Such inconsistencies tend to confuse consumers.

The key to effective positioning is differentiation. Within a target market segment, how is your brand perceived as different from other brands? Ideally, your brand is different on dimensions (or bundles of attributes/benefits) that are important to consumers, and, ideally, consumers are sensitive to and responsive to these differences. However, dimensions that managers think are important to consumers are not always actually important to consumers. Marketing research is necessary to determine the importance of the various dimensions to consumers.

POSITIONING PIONEERING BRANDS

Brands frequently differ in many ways. One important way brands differ is in terms of order of entry into a market. The pioneering brand is the first brand to enter and define a market, and all other brands are mere copycats or followers. Of course, many

Malaysia Airlines positions itself as being the most popular airline originating in Southeast Asia.

Source: Courtesy of Malaysia Airlines.

You can't find these products at Kmart.

Source: © Dick Morton.

pioneering brands emphasize this important difference in their advertising (Ries & Trout, 1981). The classic example is Coca-Cola advertising in which Coca-Cola is described as "the real thing," implying that everything else is a pale imitation. Advertising stating that "Coke is it" implies the same thing. Coca-Cola invented the cola category, and much of its advertising stresses this important point. Similarly, advertising for many pioneering brands argues that "we invented the product," implying that we know more about the product category than anyone else. This message can be seen in ads for pioneering products such as Xerox photocopiers, Polaroid instant cameras, and even Zippo disposable cigarette lighters. Pioneering brands frequently serve as the standard against which all other brands are compared, and this important point is often made in comparative advertising for pioneers.

POSITIONING BY ATTRIBUTES/BENEFITS

Products are often bundles of attributes that provide problem-solving benefits to consumers. Differentiation is the key to successful positioning, and one way to guarantee that a new product offering will be different is by "doing the opposite" (Ries & Trout, 1981). For instance, in the mid-1950s, U.S. automakers were designing larger, longer, lower, and more streamlined cars. Volkswagen did the opposite: The Beetle was small, short, squat, and ugly, and the company promoted this strikingly different automobile with its highly successful "Think Small" campaign. The Volkswagen Beetle was also much less expensive to own and operate compared with the large, heavy U.S. brands.

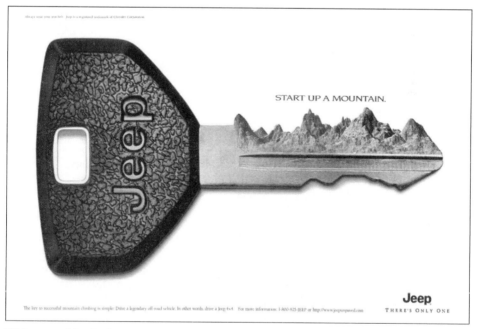

With competition in the sport utility vehicle market heating up from new entrants, Jeep positions itself as the pioneering brand with its slogan "Jeep—There's Only One."

Source: Printed with permission from Jeep Marketing, Chrysler Corp.

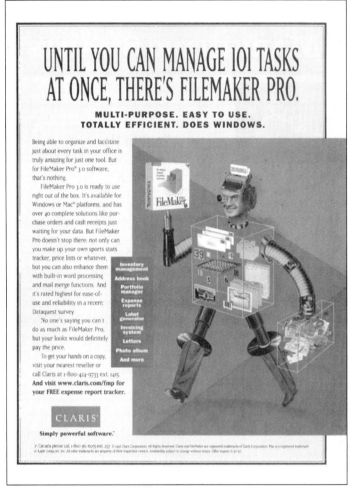

In this ad, Claris shows the many attributes of its FileMaker Pro 3.0 software: inventory management, address book, portfolio management, expense reports, label generator, invoicing systems, letters, photo album, and more. Plus, it does "Windows."

Source: Courtesy of FileMaker, Inc. (Claris).

Another classic example of doing the opposite is the famous 7-Up uncola campaign. The opposite of a cola is an uncola. A cola is opaque, sweet, and strong in aftertaste. By contrast, the uncola is clear, not too sweet, and has no aftertaste. Television advertising for 7-Up used a highly successful comparative advertising campaign in which dried-up, shriveled, dead "cola nuts" (cocoa beans, actually) were compared with juicy, colorful, lively "uncola nuts" (fresh lemons and limes). The company also created uncola drinking glasses, which were upside down (i.e., opposite) Coca-Cola hourglass drinking glasses. The uncola campaign successfully enabled 7-Up to enter consumers' consideration sets for soft drinks, and this resulted in a 20 percent increase in sales per year during the late 1960s. Prior to this campaign, consumers did not think of 7-Up when they bought soft drinks. 7-Up was used mainly as a mixer and headache remedy (it was promoted "for home and hospital use" when it was introduced in 1929)—a tiny market compared with the large and still growing soft drink market of the 1960s and 1970s.

Turning disadvantages into advantages is another useful positioning strategy. Avis is number two, so "we try harder." Many Americans like and sympathize with the underdog, and Avis was able to capitalize on these emotions. "With a name like Smuckers, it has to be good." Smuckers wants customers to believe that it puts all its time and energy into obtaining high-quality ingredients for its syrups and jams and has no time or energy left to worry about the name.

Many firms attempt to develop a **core benefit proposition,** or a single attribute/benefit that differentiates their brand from competitors' offerings. A single benefit is short and sweet: It is easy to remember and it sharply differentiates a product from competing brands. Volvo emphasizes the single benefit of safety, even though it may have other benefits as well. Volvo's main competitor, BMW, emphasizes performance (the "ultimate driving machine"). Volvo and BMW are direct competitors because both firms target the yuppie market and therefore, both firms have to emphasize different core benefit propositions. Bounty paper towels are the "quicker picker uppers," whereas Viva paper towels "keep on working." Crest toothpaste fights cavities, whereas Aim tastes good so kids brush longer. Emphasize a single benefit. Keep it short and sweet. This can be a very effective positioning strategy.

POSITIONING BY PRICE

What should a manager do if it is not possible or feasible to emphasize a single core benefit proposition? What if a product differs from others in many complex ways that are not easy to communicate to consumers? One possibility is to differentiate the product in terms of price. The price of a product is a simple variable that all consumers understand. Moreover, most consumers routinely pay a great deal of attention to the price of a product, so price differences are easy for consumers to detect. This makes it easy to differentiate a product in terms of price. The manager sets the price of the product, and it is easy to select a price that is much higher or much lower than that of the other brands.

Upscale retail stores—like Nieman Marcus, Bloomingdales, and Saks Fifth Avenue—typically sell only high-priced products. Consequently, the products carried by these stores and the stores themselves are perceived by consumers as very different

Are you more likely to rent from Avis because they try harder?

Source: © Dick Morton.

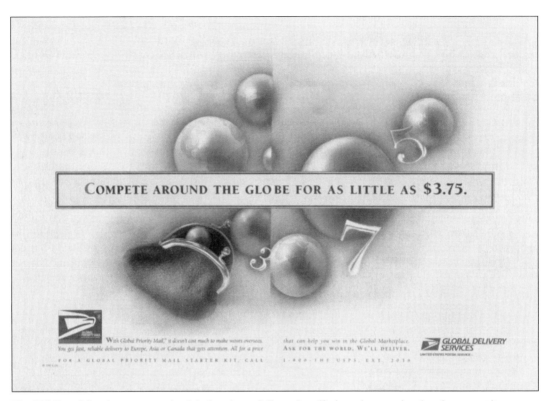

The U.S. Postal Service competes in global package delivery by offering a lower price than its competitors.
Source: United States Postal Service.

from other products and stores. Moreover, consumers' assumptions about the relationship between price and quality encourage them to use the price–quality heuristic, which results in the inference that high price signals high quality. Quality, of course, is a complex multidimensional variable, and it is easier to communicate price differences rather than quality differences to consumers.

Many luxury upscale products are advertised as very expensive in luxury magazines such as *Wine Spectator* and *Cigar Aficionado.* S. T. Dupont lighters cost $1,500 and down. Joy is the "costliest perfume in the world." Piaget makes extremely expensive watches. Interestingly, positioning by price used to be reserved for complex luxury products but is now used for simple mundane products such as Whitney's Yogurt, Orville Redenbacher's Gourmet Popping Corn, Eukanuba dog food, and Sheba gourmet cat food. Positioning by price affords managers of all types of products a positioning strategy that clearly differentiates their brands on a variable that is very important and noticeable to consumers.

Pricing your product lower than competitors' brands is another way of differentiating your product in terms of price. This strategy is commonly used by many store brands—such as Kmart brands, Kroger brands, Safeway brands, and others. This strategy can be very effective because store brands are often promoted as being the same as name brands but lower in price. Moreover, price differences can be highlighted easily by placing store brands directly next to name brands on the retailer's shelves.

POSITIONING BY USER

Sometimes it is useful to position by the user or the consumer (Aaker & Shansby, 1982). With this positioning strategy, promotion and advertising focuses on the type of person who uses the product. For example, the *Wall Street Journal* advertising often shows rich, successful executives reading the *Wall Street Journal,* implying that the *Wall Street Journal* is for rich, successful executives (and for people who want to be rich, successful executives). Advertising for many upscale products often depicts suave, sophisticated people using the product, suggesting that the product is only for suave, sophisticated people.

Positioning by user links positioning with segmentation. (See "Making the Decision: Peddling for Profit.") This strategy can be used to expand one's market by targeting larger and more profitable segments. For example, Johnson & Johnson's baby shampoo used to be promoted as just for babies. However, the population growth rate in the United States is currently nearly zero, so Johnson & Johnson created advertising saying that its baby shampoo is now for adults. Moreover, it is mild and gentle enough to be used every day. Similarly, milk is not just for children anymore, and advertising for milk often shows adults drinking and enjoying the product.

Lipton tea and Oldsmobiles are not just for older people now, and advertising for these products shows young adults enjoying these products. Miller High Life, the champagne of beers, was originally targeted for yuppies. However, this segment is relatively small and most yuppies prefer wine to beer and do not drink much beer even when they do drink beer. Miller's repositioning for blue-collar workers was highly effective. Its ads showed construction workers, railroad workers, and other blue-collar workers working hard and at the end of a hard day, "And Now It's Miller Time!" The blue-collar segment is much larger than the white-collar segment, and, best of all, blue-collar workers are heavy users of the product. Similarly, Marlboro cigarettes were originally targeted for women. However, very few women smoked in the 1950s and those who did smoked very little. The rugged Marlboro man helped reposition the cigarettes for men, and Marlboro became the market leader.

POSITIONING BY USAGE SITUATION

Another useful positioning strategy is to position by usage situation (Aaker & Shansby, 1982). Advertising that builds a strong association between a particular brand and a particular usage situation leads consumers to think of that brand whenever the particular usage situation arises. For example, Campbell's soup was originally positioned for use at lunchtime, and to bolster this association, radio advertising for Campbell's soup was aired during the noon hour. For consumers who formed a strong association between Campbell's soup and lunchtime, merely seeing the clock strike noon was sufficient to make them hungry for soup.

Similarly, AT&T's "reach out and touch someone" campaign encouraged consumers to form a strong association between the telephone and keeping in touch with long-distance friends and relatives. Instead of writing faraway friends and relatives, consumers started using the telephone more frequently.

The "Michelob is for weekends" campaign was designed to induce consumers to form a strong association between Michelob beer and weekends. Once this association is in place in memory, at the end of the week consumers start thinking about Michelob.

MAKING THE DECISION

PEDDLING FOR PROFIT

The process of developing products may be viewed by some as the quest for the better mousetrap. This is certainly true in the case of the electric bicycle—which, believe it or not, already is available under several brand names. ZAP Power Systems is one, Charger Bicycles (a joint venture between GT Bicycles and AeroVironment Inc.) is another, and Electric Bicycles is still another. An electric bicycle is a pedal-powered bicycle with an auxiliary, battery-powered motor that riders can kick in for help getting up hills.

Sound like the ideal cross between a bike and a motorcycle? This is actually part of the positioning problem that marketers of the electric bike face: People who want to pedal buy bicycles; people who want a free ride buy a motor scooter or motorcycle. Thus, it has been difficult initially to position the electric bike by user or usage situation. "If a cyclist uses a bike for exercise, the purpose is defeated by a motor," explains Richard A. Newman, owner of the Toga Bike Shop in New York.

But consumers themselves seem to be carving out at least one niche for the new-fangled bike. Senior citizens who have tried it seem to love it. Carol Noel, a retired child-care provider in her mid-sixties, says that asthma had always prevented her from riding bicycles. She bought a ZAP Power Systems electric bike, and now she rides it 15 to 20 miles a day in her Florida community. Noel pedals as far as she can comfortably, but when she needs a rest, she activates the motor. "If I get tired, I just press a little yellow button and the bike goes like a motorcycle," she says. "I go up the hills lickety-split." William Lahm, a retired teacher from upstate New York, started cycling at age 69 when he discovered that an electric bike could help him up steep hills.

Other users have appeared. Central & Southwest Corp., a Dallas utility, recently bought 50 electric bikes and donated them to local police. "This puts a face on police in their communities," says a utility spokesman. "It gets them out of the patrol car." It also puts a face on a new electrical product. New York City's Transportation Department has bought twelve electric bikes for use by parking-control agents. The electric bikes help the agents get around faster, thereby issuing more tickets. "If you increase mobility, you increase productivity," notes Christopher R. Lynn, New York's transportation commissioner.

Marketers are also turning their attention to commuters. In an effort to foster interest in bicycle commuting, Charger Bicycles is offering a volume discount on its bicycles to a San Bernardino, California, program that is trying to encourage bicycle commuting. People who do not otherwise ride bikes for recreation might be willing to try commuting by bike if they have the help of a motor. Of course, bicycle commuting is very practical only in areas of the country (like California) where the weather is good most of the time.

If the electric bicycle seems too good to be true, it does have its drawbacks. One is the battery has to be recharged every 15 or 20 miles (although the bike can always be pedaled home without the motor); another is the hefty price tag, which can run between $900 and $1,500. Finally, the bikes themselves are heavy, a drawback in an industry that strives to produce lighter and lighter products.

Still, the electric bike is testimony that the entrepreneurial spirit is alive and well as we approach the new millennium. It's a simple, low-tech product that may very well catch on. It doesn't require a computer, a telecommunications network, or use of the Internet. And it sounds like a lot of fun.

Source: Jeffrey A. Tannenbaum, "The Ups and Downs of Peddling Electric Bikes," *The Wall Street Journal,* July 28, 1997, pp. B1, B2.

On its Web site (www.reebok.com), Reebok positions its products both by user and by usage situation.

Source: Courtesy of Reebok International Ltd.

Gatorade is positioned as good for replacing bodily fluids lost during vigorous exercise and during participation in various sporting activities. When these situations arise, Gatorade quickly enters consumers' consideration sets. Arm & Hammer baking soda is positioned as good for deodorizing. Hence, the product can be used for deodorizing refrigerators, freezers, sinks, carpets, and even mouths (e.g., toothpastes and mouthwashes with baking soda).

Of course, it is important for managers to pick the right usage situation for their product. Ideally, the usage situation helps to differentiate the brand from competitors' offerings, and it is one that consumers encounter frequently. When consumers form a strong association in memory between a brand and a particular usage situation, the brand comes to mind whenever the situation arises.

REPOSITIONING THE COMPETITION

One of the most famous examples of repositioning the competition or changing consumers' perceptions of a competing product was used by Tylenol (Ries & Trout, 1981). Tylenol radio ads stated that, "for the millions who should not take aspirin, if your stomach is easily upset, or if you have an ulcer, or if you suffer from asthma, allergies, or iron-deficiency anemia, it would make sense to check with your doctor before you take aspirin. Aspirin can irritate the stomach lining, trigger asthmatic or allergic reactions, cause small amounts of hidden gastrointestinal bleeding. Fortunately, there is Tylenol."

Some things scratch. Some don't.

You don't have to hurt your surfaces to get them really clean.
Because Soft Scrub® with Bleach gently lifts out stains.
It's the safe way to scrub.

The Clorox Company reposi-
tions the competition for cleaning products by contrasting its
cleanser, Soft Scrub, against
other abrasive cleaners—represented by sandpaper in the ad.
Source: Courtesy of The Clorox
Company.

Repositioning the competition changes the way consumers think about the competition. People usually think of aspirin as a health aid, but Tylenol's ad stated that
aspirin can be harmful to your health. Political advertising also uses repositioning the
competition strategies frequently, but in politics, this is known as mudslinging. Making
the competition look bad makes your product look good.

Royal Doulton china changed consumers' perception of Lenox china by informing
consumers that Lenox is made in Pomona, New Jersey, and Royal Doulton is made in
Stoke on Trent, England. Lenox sounds British but is not. Royal Doulton china is real
British china. Moreover, New Jersey conjures up negative images of factories, black
smoke, and pollution for many American consumers. Similarly, Stolichnaya changed
consumers' perceptions of competing vodkas with ads that stated that "Most American
vodkas seem Russian. Samovar: Made in Schenley, Pennsylvania. Smirnoff: Made in
Hartford, Connecticut. Wolfschmidt: Made in Lawrenceburg, Indiana. Stolichnaya is
different. It is Russian. Made in Leningrad, Russia."

Borden's Wise potato chips was the market leader, but P&G's Pringles took a lot
of share away from Wise when Pringles were first introduced. In fact, Pringles captured
18 percent of the potato chip market in its first year. Borden countered with a television ad emphasizing the ingredients of the two products. Wise potato chips are made

from potato chips and vegetable oil. Pringle's potato chips are made from dehydrated potatoes, mono- and diglycerides, ascorbic acid, and butylated hydroxy-anisole. Wise potato chips are made from natural ingredients, whereas Pringle's potato chips are made mostly from chemicals. The uniform shape and size of Pringle's potato chips and the cylindrical packages they came in reinforced the idea of artificiality that quickly ended Pringle's initial success.

Scope mouthwash used repositioning to combat the competition very effectively. Scope's television ad stated that Listerine gives you "medicine breath" and that Scope gives you "fresh minty breath." Moreover, Scope's repositioning the competition campaign was well timed with Listerine's campaign stating that Listerine gives you "the taste you hate, twice a day."

In summary, there are many different positioning strategies. The best depends on the characteristics of your product, the characteristics of your competitors' products, and the type of associations you want consumers to form about your brand. If your brand is the pioneer, you should emphasize this in your promotion and advertising campaigns. If your brand is markedly different from competitors' products on a single easy-to-communicate and important attribute/benefit, a single core benefit proposition should be advertised. If your brand is highly similar to competitors' offerings or difficult to differentiate, you may be able to differentiate your brand anyway by price, user, or usage situation. If competing brands have weaknesses a manager can exploit, repositioning the competition can be very effective.

◆ CONSUMER-DRIVEN ENGINEERING

Quality design requires in-depth knowledge of consumers' preferences and the ability for different business functions (e.g., marketing, research and development, engineering, production) to work together effectively and synergistically to satisfy consumers' preferences. Preference analysis begins with the "voice of the customer," in which consumers indicate their preferences and attribute importance weights in focus groups, interviews, and surveys (Urban & Hauser, 1993). Focus groups and interviews help researchers to describe product attributes in consumers' own words for subsequent use in surveys for measuring consumers' attribute ratings for several different brands. Attribute ratings can then be subjected to a statistical technique known as **factor analysis,** which is used to construct **perceptual maps.** Factor analysis is a correlation-based technique that reduces a large set of attributes to a smaller and more manageable number of underlying factors. For example, specific ratings of how easily a car door opens and closes and how well it keeps out water and noise load onto a single factor that could be labeled "overall door quality." This enables the researcher to reduce a large number of ratings to one factor (i.e., overall door quality).

CONSTRUCTING A PERCEPTUAL MAP

When two or more factors exist, a perceptual map can be constructed. Two factors can be easily graphed as X- and Y-axes, and the location of the different brands in a product category can be plotted on these axes. Similar brands are plotted close together, and dissimilar brands are plotted far apart (many computer programs are available for doing this). Hence, one thing a perceptual map tells us is who our direct competitors are (i.e., brands plotted near our brand) and who we should be less concerned about (i.e., brands plotted far away from our brand). Another thing a perceptual map tells us is where the gaps are. Typically, a perceptual map has several different subsections where many brands are grouped close together. A perceptual map also has blank spaces that may reflect potential opportunities (i.e., look for a gap and fill it). Blank spaces should be analyzed carefully because they may reflect (a) true opportunities (i.e., gaps) where competition is scarce, (b) combinations of attributes that are technologically infeasible, or (c) combinations of attributes that consumers do not want. (See Fig. 13-6.)

Ideal Vectors

Ideal vectors can also be plotted on perceptual maps. Ideal vectors show how important different combinations of attributes are to consumers. Ideal vectors are constructed through another correlation-based technique, **multiple regression,** in which the relationships between specific attributes ratings and overall product evaluations are determined statistically (many computer programs are available for doing this). The stronger the correlation between an attribute and the overall evaluation, the more important the attribute. Attributes can also be grouped together (based on factor analysis) to determine the relative importance of groups of attributes. For a perceptual map with two axes (things become much more complicated with more than two axes, but you can always analyze multiple sets of two axes),

$$P(y) = b_1 X_1 + b_2 X_2$$

where $P(y)$ = consumer preference for Brand y; b_1 and b_2 = importance weights for factors 1 and 2, respectively; and X_1 and X_2 = Brand y's location on factors 1 and 2, respectively. Importance weights are determined statistically, and the ratio of the

FIGURE 13-6

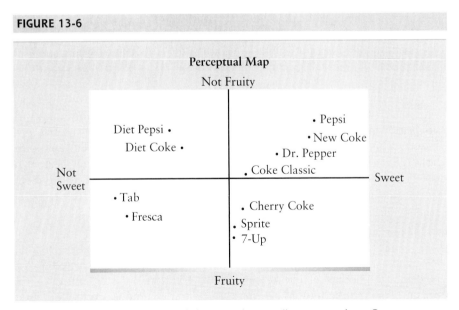

On a perceptual map, brands located close together are direct competitors. Open spaces (gaps) are potential opportunities.

weights (i.e., b_1/b_2) gives the slope of the ideal vector. If the importance weights are equal, the ratio is 1 and the angle of the ideal vector is 45 degrees. As one factor increases in importance, the ideal vector moves closer to that factor's axis. Ideal vectors can be analyzed across all consumers or analyzed separately for different consumer segments.

Quality Function Deployment

Today's statistical packages make it easy to analyze consumers' preferences. Analyzing preferences helps managers to design better products. Perceptual maps and ideal vectors are important tools for analyzing positioning strategies and for helping managers to make difficult trade-offs between attributes (or groups of attributes). Managers need to make difficult trade-offs whenever two attributes (or groups of attributes) are negatively correlated (or inversely related). For instance, returning to our example of car doors, we know that consumers want car doors that open and close easily and that keep out water and noise. However, it is technologically impossible to build a door that is perfect on all four of these attributes (easy to open, easy to close, keep out water, keep out noise). To make a door easy to open, engineers add insulation to the door, but this makes the door hard to close (i.e., there is a negative correlation between ease of opening and ease of closing). However, the picture becomes more complicated because there is a positive correlation between ease of opening and keeping out water and keeping out noise (i.e., adding insulation reduces water and noise leakage). So how much insulation should engineers put into a car door? The answer should be obvious by now: Ideal vectors tell managers how to trade off one attribute (or group of attributes) against another. Moreover, recent developments in **quality function deployment**—or techniques for assessing the relationship between consumers' attribute ratings and engineering variables (e.g., technical specs such as energy to close door, check force on level ground, check force on 10-degree slope, etc.)—enable different business functions (e.g., marketing, research and development, engineering, production) to work together more effectively. This is very important because marketers know about consumer attribute ratings and preferences, but do not know anything about energies, forces, and other engineering variables.

PREFERENCE ANALYSIS

What happens when firms carefully analyze consumer preferences and work hard to facilitate intercommunication among the business functions? In these cases, well-designed new products are developed—such as the Apple PowerBook, the Gillette Sensor razor, Reebok's Pump athletic shoe, Motorola's MicroTac cellular phone, and Chrysler's LH cars (Nussbaum, 1993). These products are either already billion-dollar sellers or well on their way to becoming billion-dollar sellers.

The first portable computers were just small desktop computers that could not be used the way consumers wanted to use them. Consumers wanted computers they could use on airplanes, commuter rails, taxis, and at home. The PowerBook's TrackBall pointer and palm rest enabled consumers to use this computer in such places, and the product became an instant success. Not only is the product easy to use the way consumers wanted to use it, but the features that make it easy to use also make it look distinctive, and this helps differentiate the product from other products.

Building strong relationships with other firms can also enhance design quality. For example, Reebok teamed up with a consulting firm, Design Continuum, to develop a new way to compete against Nike. The consulting firm had been doing some work on an inflatable splint for hospitals, and this technology became the basis for the Pump athletic shoe. Who says medical technology and sporting equipment have nothing to do with each other?

Gillette's market research showed that consumers want razors that are solid, not disposable, and easy to use, and that provide a close shave, fit in the hand comfortably, and fit easily on bathroom shelves. Gillette developed a new laser technology to build the twin-floating-head cartridge and developed a high-tech-looking, metal-based, gray handle to match the high-tech cartridge. The Sensor quickly became the market leader. The product was such a success that the same laser technology was subsequently used to build the Sensor for Women, which also became the market leader in its category.

Motorola learned that it is really difficult to get the different business functions to work together. Even within engineering, design engineers wanted a cellular phone with a thin casing to keep the product pocket-sized, and materials and supply engineers wanted a product with a thick casing for strength. Small size was important because consumers wanted a product that would fit in their pockets, and strength was important because market research with prototypes showed that consumers were constantly dropping cellular phones. Motorola pushed GE and other partner firms to develop a thinner and stronger plastic, which they were able to do. The result: a plastic that was strong enough to allow consumers to drop the MicroTac cellular phone repeatedly, without scratching or otherwise damaging it.

Chrysler's LH cars feature a new cab-forward design that offers several benefits: It is easy to get into the car, it is easy to get out of the car, visibility is excellent, and the rear seats have surprisingly large amounts of leg room. The cab-forward design also gives the car a distinctive appearance that helps to differentiate the product from competitors' automobiles.

Another extremely well-designed product is Hewlett-Packard's Deskjet Portable Printer (Nussbaum, 1993). While watching the giant robot that shot death rays from a narrow slit across its round helmet in the 1951 sci-fi classic *The Day the Earth Stood*

The Motorola cellular phone was a very successful product introduction.
Source: © Mary Boucher.

Still (Klaatu barada nikto!), HP's designer thought of a clever way of embedding indicator lights in round buttons: Place a thin strip of clear plastic across the middle of the button! This feature allowed the designer to keep the controls compact and easy to use. The printer was also designed so that the sheet feeder did not take up much space—an important feature for a portable printer. (Ideas for new products can come from strange places, even from classic movies!)

CHAPTER SUMMARY

All firms need new products to survive. New products can be developed proactively (before the competition) or reactively (after the competition), depending on market size, firm size and resources, protection from imitation, and power in the channel. Proactive new product development enables firms to capitalize on the pioneering advantage (a long-term consumer preference advantage for the first brand to enter a market over follower brands). Being first captures a lot of attention, generates a lot of excitement, and provides an important distinction for differentiating a brand from competitors' products. Differentiation is the key to successful product positioning, and there are many ways to differentiate a brand—including positioning by attributes/benefits, positioning by price, positioning by user, positioning by usage situation, and repositioning the competition (mudslinging). Consumer-driven engineering helps managers to give consumers the new products they want—first by analyzing consumer preferences carefully and second by organizing the firm so that the different business functions (e.g., marketing, research and development, engineering, production) work together effectively and synergistically to satisfy consumer preferences.

KEY CONCEPTS

- Positioning strategies
- Diversification
- Market penetration
- Product development
- Market development
- Pioneering advantage
- Inherent advantage hypothesis
- Enabling advantage hypothesis

- Spurious effect hypothesis
- Set-size effect
- Sales potential
- Penetration
- Scale
- Input
- Reward
- Risk
- Constant sum scale
- Positioning

- Core benefit proposition
- Factor analysis
- Perceptual maps
- Ideal vectors
- Multiple regression
- Quality function deployment

DISCUSSION QUESTIONS

1. What five factors should marketers consider when deciding whether to use proactive or reactive strategies in developing products?
2. Name and describe briefly four proactive strategies.
3. McDonald's has had a pioneering advantage for many years. Since competition from organizations like Burger King and Wendy's has siphoned off some of McDonald's customers, how might McDonald's use diversification, product development, or market development to ensure the continuation of its advantage? (Hint: If you have a specific idea for a new product or a new market, describe it.)

4. Why might the pioneering advantage be even stronger for services than it is for physical products? Give at least one example.

5. When is it useful to position by attributes/benefits and when is it dangerous to do so?

6. Nieman Marcus, Bloomingdales, and Saks Fifth Avenue are known for selling high-priced products. Do you think that a strategy of offering some products at more moderate prices would help increase these stores' market share? Why or why not?

7. How might a product like Tropicana orange juice be repositioned by user and usage situation to increase its market size?

8. If you were a marketer for a new, premium brand of ice cream, how would you reposition Ben & Jerry's?

9. What important information can a perceptual map provide for marketers and product designers?

10. Consumer-driven engineering is usually discussed in the context of consumer durables (such as automobiles and washing machines) and high-tech products (such as computers and cell phones). How might consumer-driven engineering be applied to a common, nondurable household product such as a toothbrush or a container of milk?

CHAPTER 14

Product Management

◆ FERRARI

The Ferrari brand stands alone. It is never compared with another automobile, only to other wannabe products that marketers want to associate with it (for instance, "This is the Ferrari of washing machines" or "This is the Ferrari of lawnmowers"). We never hear, "This car is like a Ferrari," because there are no other cars like the Ferrari.

The Ferrari is now 50 years old. How does the company, particularly chairman Luca di Montezemolo, keep its brand so young? By making new models—very limited, very expensive, very fast. The Ferrari factory builds about a dozen cars a day, or a little over 3,000 per year. So, even if you can afford one, you may not be able to get one when you want it. Can you afford it? The price tag hovers around $204,000 for the newest model, the 550 Maranello (named after the Italian village where the cars are manufactured). How fast can you cruise? The new 550 packs 490 horsepower, making it "quicker than the Testarossa" (Ferrari's previous speed demon), according to Montezemolo. In other words, faster than most legal speed limits.

Quality is an important part of the strength of Ferrari's brand. "We're a low-volume, high R&D operation," explains Montezemolo. Ferrari workers take their time when crafting their masterpieces. Speed is not the buzzword in the factory.

But it is the buzzword at the Ferrari driving school, where new owners learn how to pamper their sensitive vehicles, maneuvering them around a real race track. The school isn't free (it costs $5,000, including hotel and meals) but if you can afford a Ferrari, you can afford the school. Meeting other Ferrari customers (some of whom may own several models) makes new owners feel like they are part of an exclusive club, thus strengthening their conviction that they have bought the best car in the world.

As you read this chapter, note the different strategies marketers use to manage their brands, whether they are trying to maintain their position as market leaders or trying to move their products up the ladder to the top.

Source: Sue Zesiger, "Ferrarissima!" *Fortune,* May 12, 1997, pp. 194–195.

◆ INTRODUCTION

The previous chapter discussed the new product development process, a process that focuses mainly on ideas rather than physical objects. Chapter 14 describes what happens after an idea is transformed into a tangible object. First, the product manager must generate an **entry strategy:** How should the product be introduced to the marketplace? Provided that the introduction is successful, the product manager must then focus on the growth stage. As competition intensifies, sales eventually level off and the product enters the maturity stage. Finally, the product enters the decline stage as sales fall when the product is replaced by a new innovation. Each stage is accompanied by a different set of managerial challenges that must be met.

Chapter 14 also discusses the value of a brand name. For example, the Ferrari name is much more valuable than the Hyundai name. Consumers often make strong inferences on the basis of the brand name and the reputation of the manufacturer. In addition, this chapter discusses product line management because managers in today's complex marketplace need to develop synchronized strategies for a family of products rather than concentrating on only one brand. Finally, this chapter discusses different strategies for managing top-selling brands versus struggling brands. Managers of top-selling brands want to stay on top, whereas managers of struggling brands want to survive. Different strategies are required for different managerial objectives and goals.

◆ ENTRY STRATEGY AND INNOVATION DIFFUSION

Different new products diffuse, or spread across the marketplace, at different rates. When black-and-white televisions were first introduced, for example, the diffusion process was relatively slow. Radio still provided a popular form of entertainment, and the benefits of television were not readily apparent to all consumers. Several decades later, however, consumers were quick to adopt color television; this new product innovation diffused like wildfire. Why? The **diffusion of innovation** is influenced by several factors (Rogers, 1983). For instance, the diffusion rate increases as the magnitude of the advantage of the new product innovation over previous products increases. Most consumers were satisfied with radio, and the relative advantage of black-and-white television was not immediately apparent to many consumers. By contrast, the relative advantage of color television over black-and-white television was obvious. Hence, color television diffused at a much faster rate than black-and-white television.

The diffusion of Kodak's innovative product was so complete that almost every household now has at least one camera.

The new product's compatibility with consumers' beliefs, opinions, and lifestyles also influences the rate of diffusion. Black-and-white television diffused very slowly among upper-middle-class and wealthy consumers because a passive medium is incompatible with an active lifestyle. That is, wealthy consumers prefer to actively travel and do the things shown on television rather than passively assume the role of a couch potato. Product complexity or user unfriendliness also influence diffusion rates. Black-and-white television was such a novel innovation that many consumers may have been unsure about whether they could adjust the antenna and the picture adequately. Moreover, products consumed privately in one's own home diffuse less rapidly than publicly consumed products.

Perceived risk also influences the rate of diffusion. As risk increases, the diffusion rate decreases. Many different types of risk are important, including financial risk (black-and-white televisions were very expensive when they were first introduced), social risk (embarrassment), and physical risk (risk of physical harm). Financial risk is often correlated with another important factor: trialability. People are often willing to take a chance with inexpensive products (try it to see if you like it; if you do not, then throw it out). Expensive products like televisions, however, are not amenable to such experimentation. Fortunately, marketers have come up with a creative solution to the trialability problem—namely, the test drive. Consumers can test drive a car to see if they like it before committing to an expensive purchase. Many personal computer retailers also let consumers take a computer home for a day to test drive it to see if they like it. The test-drive approach can be applied to any new product innovation to increase trialability and to increase the rate of diffusion.

The typical diffusion curve is often S-shaped: the percent of potential adopters is very low initially because it takes time for marketing programs (i.e., promotion and advertising) to create awareness and stimulate trial. Once this is accomplished, the percent of potential adopters often increases dramatically because of a word-of-mouth snowballing effect. That is, consumers often tell other consumers about their exciting new purchases and this increases the rate of adoption to a much greater extent than would be possible if the decision to adopt was made on an individual case-by-case basis. Eventually, the market becomes saturated and competition with another new product innovation takes place. (See Fig. 14-1.)

RAPID TAKEOFF STRATEGY

Although the diffusion curve typically retains its S-shape, it can be influenced by four basic entry strategies. The **rapid takeoff strategy** involves identifying innovator consumers and concentrating all of one's marketing activities on these individuals. Innovators are usually venturesome, open-minded, and sensation seeking (Rogers, 1983). They are unusually willing to try new things. Innovators also tend to be highly educated and upwardly mobile. Furthermore, innovators tend to seek product information from specialty magazines and to be heavy users of a product category. For example, the first consumers to adopt color television tended to be heavy users of black-and-white television. The first consumers to adopt compact-disc players tended to be heavy users of stereo systems. The characteristics and behavioral tendencies of innovators help product managers to identify these individuals for direct marketing

FIGURE 14-1

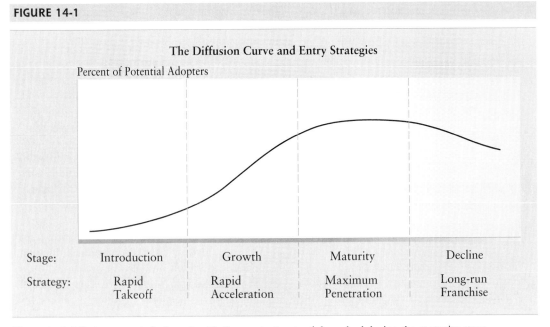

The typical diffusion curve is S-shaped, with the greatest potential reached during the maturity stage.

tactics. The rapid takeoff strategy influences the introduction stage of the diffusion curve, and this helps product managers of small firms to impress and gain the acceptance of retailers and other members of the channel of distribution.

RAPID ACCELERATION STRATEGY

The **rapid acceleration strategy** influences the growth stage of the diffusion curve. This strategy involves the heavy use of the mass media (e.g., heavy promotion and advertising on television and radio, and in newspapers) to influence early adopters and the early majority (rather than first adopters or innovators). This strategy makes sense only if your firm is relatively large and well known and, consequently, you anticipate little trouble gaining acceptance from other channel members. The rapid acceleration strategy is especially important and useful if the product is expected to have a relatively short product life cycle due to intense competition and rapidly changing technology. Essentially, the rapid acceleration strategy is designed to beat the competition by gaining widespread consumer adoption before it is too late.

MAXIMUM PENETRATION AND LONG-RUN FRANCHISE STRATEGIES

The **maximum penetration strategy** influences the maturity stage of the diffusion curve. This strategy involves attaining a long-term market leadership position through highly effective positioning, pricing, and protection from imitation. Usually only the largest and most powerful firms (e.g., Procter & Gamble, Sony, Kodak, Coca-Cola) can pursue this strategy. It makes sense only if a relatively lengthy product life cycle is anticipated and if competitors can be fended off with top-secret parts and ingredients, patent protection, high costs of entry, or other entry barriers. Finally, the **long-run franchise strategy** involves the development of new uses and new variations on a theme to help keep the product interesting to consumers for a long period of time.

◆ PRODUCT LIFE CYCLE MANAGEMENT

Entry strategies and the diffusion of innovation are two factors that influence the product life cycle. Because these factors have such an important influence on the product life cycle, the S-shaped diffusion curve tends to produce an S-shaped product life cycle curve. Both curves have an introduction stage, a growth stage, a maturity stage, and a decline stage (Urban & Hauser, 1993; Urban & Star, 1991). However, the dependent measures differ: The dependent measure for the diffusion curve is the percent of potential adopters, whereas the dependent measures for the product life cycle curve are sales and profits. (See Fig. 14-2.)

Product life cycles tend to be getting shorter because of intense competition, rapid advances in technology, and increasing complexity in the marketplace. Changes in consumer preferences and environmental changes (e.g., changes in the availability of supplies and raw materials, political and legal changes) also produce dramatic effects on the product life cycle. Different trial and repeat purchase rates can produce blips in the product life cycle curve that can be difficult to interpret. For example, automobiles and other consumer durables often have relatively lengthy repeat purchase cycles. Consequently, sales from initial trials (first-time purchases) often peak in an initial portion of the product life cycle curve, whereas sales from repeat purchases often peak in

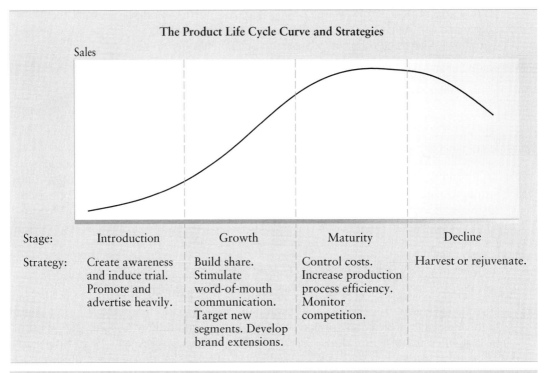

FIGURE 14-2

Dependent measures for the product life cycle curve are sales and profits.

a later portion. Hence, the peak observed from initial trials can be misinterpreted as an early maturity stage, in some instances. More generally, it is often difficult to determine when one stage ends and another begins, and this interpretative difficulty can reduce the usefulness of strategies built on product life cycle analysis.

Not surprisingly, when product life cycle curves are analyzed accurately, product life cycle analysis can serve as a very useful managerial tool. During the introduction stage, product managers must focus on building awareness and stimulating trial. Profits are usually not generated initially because of the up-front costs of new product production, promotion, and advertising. Losses may stimulate resistance from other divisions within a firm. However, managers should recognize that initial costs and lack of profitability are a natural part of the product life cycle. Moreover, new products are an important source of growth and opportunity for most consumer marketing firms.

During the growth stage of the product life cycle, the focus changes to holding and building market share. This is frequently achieved by improving the product ("New and improved!"), developing **brand extensions** (or variations on a theme, such as different shapes, sizes, flavors, colors) for different market segments, and lowering prices as production and marketing costs decrease because of the **experience curve** (or the tendency of managers to learn how to produce and market a product more efficiently over time as they gain knowledge and experience).

To maintain and stimulate growth of Herbal Essence shampoo, company marketers have offered a free trial of a new and improved product.
Source: © Dick Morton.

During the maturity stage, competition and segmentation increase, and the emphasis switches to budgeting, planning, and control. The individuals who serve as product managers are often different during the maturity stage than during the earlier stages. Marketing is the key during the introduction and growth stages, whereas production process and financial management become more important during the maturity stage.

Finally, during the decline stage, managers must decide whether to harvest or rejuvenate the product. **Harvesting,** or *milking,* involves minimizing costs (e.g., minimizing promotion, advertising, and other marketing costs) so that any sales that are generated through the past reputation of the product produce high profit levels. Of course, minimizing costs will cause sales to decrease faster, and this will bring about the decline of a product even if the product had some life left in it. That is, a **self-fulfilling prophecy,** or a prediction that changes behavior in a way that causes the prediction to become true, may occur. When managers predict that a product is finished, they minimize investment in the product, and when the product dies they say, "I told you so." However, the original prediction may have been wrong. Maybe the product would have survived if steps to rejuvenate the product had been taken.

EXTENDING THE PRODUCT LIFE CYCLE

Rejuvenation involves increasing investment costs by developing new uses, improvements, and strategies to keep consumers interested in the product, thereby increasing the length of the product life cycle. (See "Making the Decision: Baskin-Robbins Gets a Facelift.") For example, baking soda sales dropped as the percent of two-income families with no time for baking increased in the United States. Arm & Hammer developed new uses of the product to rejuvenate it. Now baking soda is used to deodorize refrigerators, freezers, sinks, and even carpets. Similarly, Dupont rejuvenated nylon by continually coming up with new uses for the product. Nylon was initially used in ropes and parachutes during World War II. Later, it was used in women's hosiery. Still later, it was used in other clothing fabrics, tires, and carpets.

Adding a Brand Name

Generic products can sometimes be rejuvenated by adding a brand name. Sunkist oranges are better than ordinary, generic oranges. Chiquita bananas are better than generic bananas. Perdue chicken is better than generic chicken. Advertising can also rejuvenate a product, under some circumstances. Condoms and hygiene-related products were at one time underadvertised because television advertising for these product

BASKIN-ROBBINS GETS A FACELIFT

For a half century, Baskin-Robbins stores have been scooping out its 31 flavors (never more, never less) all across the country to consumers who love eating their ice cream with pink plastic spoons. The stores were known for their pink-and-aqua-speckled walls, and the flavors were the same wherever you went: bubblegum, pralines and cream, peppermint stick. In an effort to update in recent years, the company added some new flavors such as French vanilla and mocha (not exactly radical) and even tried sprucing up the stores a bit, though not so much that consumers noticed.

But Baskin-Robbins's resistance to real change may have caused much of its market share to melt away. Inexplicably, the company completely missed out on the frozen yogurt trend, let the premium-ice-cream craze slide by (allowing firms like Ben & Jerry's to steal away customers), and even missed out on the resultant backlash in which consumers spooned more lowfat treats into their mouths. In short, the Baskin-Robbins brand slipped into decline.

Now the California-based division of Allied Domecq PLC (Baskin-Robbins's parent) is engaged in a fight for its life. "If we do not transform this brand quickly, the greater risk is that the Baskin-Robbins brand won't be fit to compete in the 21st century," predicts Michael Keller, the company's U.S. marketing director in charge of a huge rejuvenation.

Identifying new competitors like Starbucks and Jamba Juice (stores that sell specialty treats), Baskin-Robbins is giving itself a facelift. "We need to steal our market share back from specialty retailers," says Keller. "The franchisees say they are losing customers." Even stores that serve full meals (including desserts), such as Boston Market and McDonald's, are part of Baskin-Robbins's tar-

get, because they absorb consumer dollars. The company plans to go after "all the companies that have opened up in the last ten years that are competing for the same dollar," observes Glenn Yanow, who has been a Baskin-Robbins franchisee in Springfield, Illinois, since 1971.

Baskin-Robbins is campaigning to make over all its 2,700 stores nationwide, getting rid of the speckled walls, harsh fluorescent lighting, and dirty linoleum. Bright graphics, perky slogans, and new colors taken right from the ice cream barrels (like blackberry) will adorn the shops. The stores have already committed themselves to frozen coffee drinks and frozen-fruit smoothies, which now constitute up to 25 percent of their business, so the new shops will have a special beverage counter.

Franchisees have had mixed reactions to the makeover plans. Because they have to pay for most of the work, some are reluctant to follow along. But Baskin-Robbins is helping with financing, and some franchisees are already on the bandwagon. "The excitement is there," says Ken Madison, a franchisee who owns two stores in Georgia. "But the older people who have been around longer are resistant to change." Some franchisees are simply waiting to see results in other stores before signing on for remodeling. "Some of us are waiting to see what the store of the future really brings to the table," notes franchisee Yanow.

But John Schiro, a franchisee who plans to renovate his two California stores, hits the most important point. "I don't think it's a matter of what the franchisees or the company wants—it's what the customer wants." For those customers who want a few features of their favorite brand to remain familiar, two things won't change: Baskin-Robbins's low prices and the pink spoons.

Source: Stacy Kravetz, "Baskin-Robbins Scoops Up a New Look," *The Wall Street Journal,* September 4, 1997, pp. B1, B2.

categories was considered politically incorrect. Today, television advertising for these products is fairly common. Effective advertising can also sometimes turn disadvantages into advantages: "We're number two [Avis], we try harder"; "With a name like Smuckers it has to be good." Advertising can also be used to sell a product in a more effective way. Procter & Gamble's Pampers disposable diapers sold poorly when early advertising emphasized benefits to the mother (i.e., convenience). The product became a tremendous success when new advertising emphasized benefits to the baby (i.e., helps keep baby drier and healthier).

Identifying New Users

Identifying new users of a product can also be effective. Johnson & Johnson baby shampoo and milk are not just for babies anymore. Lipton tea is not just for little old ladies anymore. New target market segments represent important opportunities for market expansion. Cutting price can also be effective, as Datril did to successfully make inroads against Tylenol. Social trends should also be analyzed. Increasing concern about health, pollution, and the environment has increased the marketability of health foods, vitamins, and environmentally safe products.

Marketing Unused By-Products

Sometimes unused by-products can be marketed to enhance the profitability of a product in the decline stage. For example, kitty litter is made from disposable sawdust from lumberyards. Mesquite wood (for grilled meat and fish) comes from thorny mesquite bushes that Texas farmers once considered nuisance bushes; instead of burning mesquite bushes to get rid of them, Texas farmers now sell them. Similarly, cat food and dog food are made from unused by-products from people food.

Developing a New Channel of Distribution

Developing a new channel of distribution can also extend the longevity of a product. At one time, panty hose was distributed mainly in clothing stores. Developing a new channel of distribution for panty hose in food and drug stores was a great success for the Hanes Corporation. Hanes developed a distinctive egg-shaped package for L'eggs panty hose and a distinctive in-store display floor fixture that held many packages, took up little space, and could be placed in prime locations. Direct marketing is another distribution-based approach that has extended the life cycle of many different catalog products.

◆ BRAND EQUITY MANAGEMENT

A brand name is often one of the most important assets of a product (Aaker, 1991, 1996; Farquhar, 1989; Herr, Farquhar, & Fazio, 1996). A strong brand name or logo immediately triggers many important associations stored in the memories of consumers. Establishing a strong brand name and reputation, however, is difficult and costly. In many consumer industries, the costs associated with introducing a new brand name typically exceed $50 million. When a strong brand name is finally established, it should be protected and nurtured.

BRAND EQUITY

Brand equity refers to the value added to a product by a brand name. A strong brand name is a symbol and a promise of quality and consistency—quality because it conjures up images (such as images of the type of person who uses the product) and associations (attributes, benefits, uses) that differentiate the product from competitors' brands in ways important to consumers, consistency because a brand name tells consumers exactly what to expect. McDonald's restaurants offer the same menu and high standard of cleanliness and service from coast to coast. Sunkist oranges are bright and juicy, even though generic oranges vary greatly in appearance and quality. One bar of Ivory soap has the same appearance, properties, and characteristics as any other bar of Ivory soap. Quality and consistency enabled Ivory soap to hold the market leadership position for over 100 years (Aaker, 1991).

Perceived quality is the single most important predictor of profitability, as measured by return on investment (Jacobson & Aaker, 1987). Perceived quality is even more important than market share, R&D expenditures, and marketing expenditures for predicting profitability. Perceived quality is also more important than objective quality, because even a single poorly performing model in a product line can damage consumer perceptions of quality of other members of the product line even when these other models are objectively high in quality. This is exactly what happened to Audi

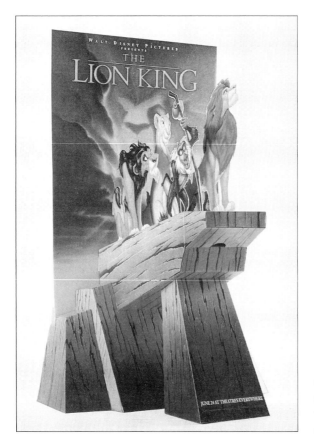

The Disney name added value to the movie *The Lion King,* which was a blockbuster.

Source: © Disney Enterprises, Inc.

BMW capitalizes on its brand
equity in the automobile market
to promote its high-end motor-
cycles.
Source: © Dick Morton.

automobiles (Sullivan, 1990). In November 1986, a CBS "60 Minutes" program reported interviews of several Audi 5000 owners claiming that the car accelerated suddenly and caused the deaths of loved ones. Not surprisingly, quality perceptions of the Audi 5000 plummeted. More important, quality perceptions of the Audi 4000 and the Audi Quattro also dropped even though these models were objectively high in quality and did not suffer from any sudden-acceleration problems. Hence, even one inconsistency (one poorly performing model) can damage the reputation of other objectively high-quality products.

Objective quality is only one factor that influences subjective or perceived quality; perceived quality is affected by many other factors as well. Consistency is tremendously important. The product must perform well consistently across owners and situations and over time. All products bearing the same brand name (e.g., Audi) must perform well. Even a single inconsistency can be quite damaging. A consistent brand image is also important. For example, Oldsmobile automobiles have traditionally been owned and operated by older consumers. Recently, Oldsmobile attempted to attract younger buyers with the "It's not your father's Oldsmobile" advertising campaign. This inconsistent advertising campaign created a great deal of confusion: Is the car for old people or for young people? Any inconsistency is potentially dangerous. (See "Making the Decision: Jamba Juice Stays Smooth.")

Complex brand strategies and alliances between firms can also reduce consistency. Many brand names that used to activate simple and singular brand images now trigger complex and multidimensional brand images. For example, Kraft used to stand for cheese and Oscar Mayer used to stand for wieners. Today, Kraft also stands for Kraft Free Singles and Kraft Miracle Whip, and Oscar Mayer also stands for Oscar Mayer Zappetites. There are also ingredient brands, such as Pillsbury Deluxe Chocolate Brownies with Hershey's chocolate syrup inside. There are also IBM, Compaq, Gateway, and Dell personal computers with Intel microprocessors inside (the Intel Inside campaign). All these brands have an "Intel Inside" logo in their ads, on their packages, and on their products. The Intel Inside program, budgeted at $100 million per year, has been tremendously successful for Intel (Aaker, 1996). However, it is unclear how competition among IBM, Compaq, Gateway, and Dell will play out.

JAMBA JUICE STAYS SMOOTH

When a brand-name product is successful, it can be very tempting to expand—offer more products, open new shops, franchise or license to others. But there are some pitfalls. Large organizations, which are capable of producing many similar products, run the risk of cannibalization. Smaller organizations, like Jamba Juice, run the risk of losing control of quality—and, ultimately, their customers.

Kirk Perron, founder of Jamba Juice Inc., found a formula that could turn fresh fruit into smoothie drinks that, his followers claim, are better than Mother Nature herself. So he started a juice bar that was so successful that within four years he had franchised his Juice Club to 16 entrepreneurs. He quickly realized that the "thousand little things" that consumers associate with a quality brand name—from the smoothie drinks themselves to store design and consistent quality—could quickly become diluted, doing damage to the fledgling brand name. Short of money, Perron hadn't been able to purchase or lease the stores for his franchisees, which left them on their own and Perron without control. Fortunately, Perron recognized the problem early. "I just could not see a future with, say, 100 stores," he explains. "It would have been total chaos." In the end, Juice Club would have destroyed itself.

In a stroke of luck, Perron received a phone call one day from a businessman who had seen the lines outside one of his stores and wanted to know what was up. One thing led to another, and Bob Kagle came aboard, with cash and the influence to procure more. "It was an early-stage technology," Kagle recalls, "but the customers were certainly responding to the offering."

So Jamba Juice got rolling with Kagle's initial $3 million, $19 million more from seven venture groups, and finally a whopping $44 million from a larger group of investors. Ironically, Perron is now opening more stores—his goal is 1,000 over the next five years—but with financial backing, this time he can keep the stores under his control. Store managers are compensated based on their performance, and every employee must receive 24 hours of training before serving at the bar. "There's too much upside potential in this business to give it away to franchisers," says Kagle.

In the meantime, Perron continues to improve on the Jamba Juice product. He freezes the best ingredients at the peak of the season, which, he explains, "level[s] out Mother Nature's uncontrolled inconsistencies." Perron believes in maintaining objective quality to back up the perceived quality of his product; it is the only way to fight off competitors. His product "does grow on trees, but we have some advantages." One major advantage is money: Now he has the cash to buy, if he wants to, the entire crop of a particularly delectable variety of Indian summer red peach. Recently, he did just that.

Source: Hal Plotkin, "Seeking Quality, Juicer Squeezes Out Franchisees," *Inc.*, July 1997, p. 25.

BRAND EXTENSIONS

Brand extensions, or new products sharing a brand name with a familiar established product, can either help or hurt an overall brand image. Consistent brand extensions, which are similar to the parent brand and share a consistent commitment to quality, can support and enhance an already strong brand image. Inconsistent brand extensions, which differ from the parent brand in important ways, can seriously damage the

Jockey, which originally made underwear for men, extended its brand to include underwear for women.

Source: JOCKEY, JOCKEY FOR HER, and Half JOCKEY FIGURE DESIGN are trademarks of and used with permission of Jockey International, Inc.

overall reputation and image of a brand (Loken & Roedder, 1993; Sullivan, 1990). Many different types of brand extensions are possible — including the same product in a different form (e.g., Cranberry Juice Cocktail, Dole frozen fruit bars), ingredient brands (e.g., Philadelphia Cream Cheese salad dressing, Arm & Hammer carpet deodorizer), companion brands (e.g., Mr. Coffee coffee beans, Colgate toothbrushes), ethnic-image brands (Pierre Cardin wallets, Benihana frozen entrees), expertise-sharing brands (e.g., Honda lawnmowers benefit from Honda's expertise in small motors; Bic razors benefit from Bic's expertise in disposable plastic products; Visa traveler's checks benefit from Visa's expertise in the personal finance industry; Gerber baby clothes benefit from Gerber's expertise in the baby product industry), and attribute/benefit-sharing brands (e.g., Ivory shampoo, Sunkist vitamin C tablets). A strong brand name can speed up and increase consumer acceptance of a new product and control costs by circumventing the need to create and build a new brand name (Tauber 1988). However, the brand-extension strategy is not without risk because products sharing the same brand name may seem consistent and coherent to managers but may seem inconsistent and incoherent to consumers. Managers and consumers do not always examine the same variables and do not always weigh different variables the same way.

MEASURING BRAND EQUITY

How should brand equity be measured? One simple and direct approach is to compare consumers' evaluations of a product with no brand name to consumers' evaluations of a product with a brand name attached (Kardes & Allen, 1991). This approach is especially useful in the early stages of market research, in which product concepts or ideas are examined for their feasibility. For example, one group of consumers could be asked

FIGURE 14-3

The Young & Rubicam Brand Asset Valuator

Differentiation	×	Relevance	=	Brand Strength
Disney		AT&T		A-1
Dr Pepper		Band-Aid		CNN
Ferrari		Campbell's		Disney
Grey Poupon		Hallmark		Dr Pepper
Jaguar		Heinz		Grey Poupon
Porsche		Kodak		Häagen-Dazs
Rolls-Royce		Kraft		Hallmark
Sharper Image		Reynold's Wrap		PBS
Snapple		U.S. Postal Service		"60 Minutes"
Victoria's Secret		United States		United States

Esteem	×	Knowledge	=	Brand Stature
Band-Aid		Campbell's		Campbell's
Campbell's		Coca-Cola		Coca-Cola
Hallmark		Heinz		Crest
Heinz		Hershey's		Hallmark
Hershey's		Jell-O		Heinz
Kodak		Kellogg's		Hershey's
Philadelphia Cream Cheese		Kodak		Jell-O
Reynold's Wrap		McDonald's		Kellogg's
Rubbermaid		Pepsi Cola		Kodak
United States		U.S. Postal Service		Kraft

Leading brands in each Young & Rubicam Brand Asset Valuator category.
Data Source: Aaker (1996).

to evaluate a series of new product ideas (e.g., garden-vegetable-flavored potato chips, Cajun-blackened steak frozen dinner, chunky peach cottage cheese, smoky-bacon-flavored hot dogs, Italian spice lunch meat, lemon mint soda). Another group could be asked to evaluate the same concepts with a brand name attached (e.g., Nabisco, Sealtest). If the same concepts are evaluated more favorably when a brand name is attached, the brand name adds value. Kardes and Allen (1991) found that the brand-extension strategy becomes more dangerous as the brand name becomes more variable and ambiguous. Moreover, consumers' attributions concerning why the parent company launched the brand extension are also important. Ideally, firms want customers to assume that the brand extension was developed because the product benefits from the unique skills of the manufacturer, not because the manufacturer is jumping on the bandwagon by adopting a "copycat" strategy in response to the activities of other firms.

The Young & Rubicam Brand Asset Valuator

At later stages of the market research process, the **Young & Rubicam Brand Asset Valuator** approach can be very useful (Aaker, 1996). (See Fig. 14-3.) This approach involves the use of a set of scales designed to measure differentiation (how distinctive is the brand compared with other products?), relevance (how relevant and useful is the brand to you personally?), esteem (is the brand considered the best or one of the best in its category?), and knowledge (does the brand have a clear and consistent image?).

Hallmark is a high-stature brand that has been around for many years. Its Web site (www.hallmark.com) is filled with information about the company, its cards and ornaments, and holiday television programming and information.

Source: Courtesy Hallmark Cards, Inc.

Brand strength (concrete brand-positioning effectiveness) is a function of differentiation multiplied by relevance. It is extremely difficult to have high scores on both dimensions because, in many product categories, as differentiation increases relevance decreases. Consequently, many brands that perform well on one dimension perform poorly on the other. A compromise approach is often most effective: moderately high differentiation and moderately high relevance. **Brand stature** (abstract brand-positioning effectiveness) is a function of esteem multiplied by knowledge. Whereas, in some cases, brand strength can be developed relatively quickly, brand stature usually requires many years to develop. High-stature brands, such as Campbell's, Coca-Cola, Hallmark, and Kodak, have been around for many decades and have a rich history and tradition that is familiar to most consumers.

According to Young & Rubicam, brand equity is a function of brand strength and brand stature. Brands that are high in brand strength and brand stature have the greatest amount of equity to protect and leverage. The Young & Rubicam Power Grid categorizes brands into one of four categories: high/high (high brand strength and high brand stature), high/low (high brand strength and low brand stature), low/high (low brand strength and high brand stature), and low/low (low brand strength and low brand stature). Brands that are high in brand strength and low in brand stature are usually strong niche brands that have an opportunity to grow by increasing their stature. Brands that are low in brand strength and high in brand stature are usually old,

FIGURE 14-4

The Young & Rubicam Power Grid

		Brand Stature (Knowledge and Esteem)	
		Low	High
Brand Strength (Differentiation and Relevance)	High	Dove Chocolates Teddy Grahams Snapple Swatch Molson Starbucks	Disney Sesame Street Doritos Sony Ocean Spray Kodak Mercedes-Benz Hallmark Coca-Cola
	Low	New dot-coms	Oldsmobile Bayer Wesson Ramada

The Young & Rubicam Power Grid tells marketing managers what they are doing right and where they need to improve.

Source: Adapted from Aaker (1996).

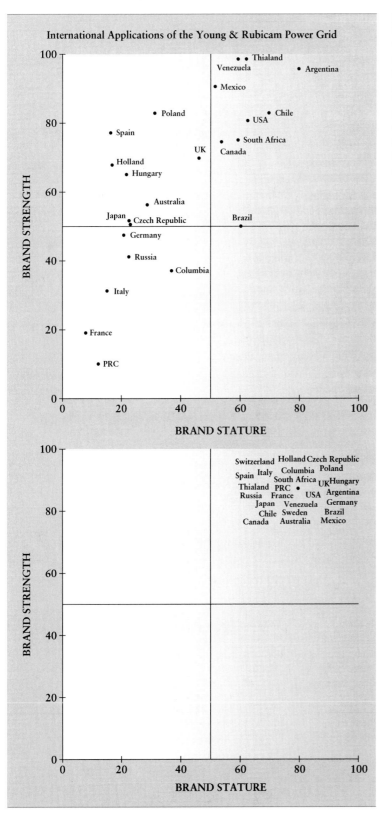

FIGURE 14-5

The top panel shows that Calvin Klein varies in brand strength and brand stature across the world. The bottom panel shows that Coca-Cola is consistently high in brand strength and brand stature across the world.

Source: Keller (1998).

International Applications of the Young & Rubicam Power Grid

Top panel (BRAND STRENGTH vs BRAND STATURE):

- Thialand
- Venezuela
- Argentina
- Mexico
- Poland
- Chile
- USA
- Spain
- South Africa
- UK
- Canada
- Holland
- Hungary
- Australia
- Japan
- Czech Republic
- Brazil
- Germany
- Russia
- Columbia
- Italy
- France
- PRC

Bottom panel (BRAND STRENGTH vs BRAND STATURE):

Switzerland Holland Czech Republic
Spain Italy Columbia Poland
South Africa UK Hungary
Thialand PRC
Russia France USA Argentina
Japan Venezuela Germany
Chile Sweden Brazil
Canada Australia Mexico

wornout brands that need to be rejuvenated. Brands in the low/low quadrant are usually new brands that need to move into the high brand strength/low brand stature category relatively quickly to be successful. The Young & Rubicam Power Grid is a useful diagnostic tool that tells managers what they are doing right and in what areas improvement is needed. (See Fig. 14-4 and Fig. 14-5).

◆ PRODUCT LINE MANAGEMENT

Many U.S. firms are increasing the emphasis on and the power of product line managers. Rather than assuming responsibility for a single product, product line managers must coordinate marketing and production activities across a line or a family of products. Presumably, having a single manager in charge of a series of products should result in synergistic opportunities that would not be available if a group of single-product managers was operating independently with no knowledge of the other product managers' activities. However, product line managers must face two key challenges: product line breadth and cannibalization. **Product line breadth** refers to the question of how many different products a firm should offer. Cannibalization refers to the question of how the firm should avoid one of its brands from competing with another of its own brands.

PRODUCT LINE BREADTH

Effective product line managers must learn how to coordinate activities not only across brands but also across the marketing and production functions. Marketing managers typically want to offer broader product lines because this enables a firm to meet consumer needs more closely by offering a wide range of products that appeal to a wide range of consumer segments. Production managers typically want to offer a narrower product line because breadth can increase overhead costs (Hayes & Wheelright, 1984) and manufacturing complexity (Bitran, 1988). Recent research on *KAISHA*, or Japanese corporations, shows that increasing the number of products offered also increases direct labor and material costs. Hence, breadth increases sales but also increases costs. In general, product line breadth should increase as consumer preference heterogeneity increases and as the availability of procedures for increasing breadth while controlling manufacturing and distribution costs increases.

Recent research on the effects of product line breadth on the competitiveness of U.S. Fortune 500 firms shows that total market share increases as product line breadth increases, as expected (Kekre & Srinivasan, 1990). Unexpectedly, however, product line breadth had no relation to total inventory costs, and product line breadth actually decreased manufacturing costs. Apparently, many U.S. Fortune 500 firms have learned how to increase the size of their product lines while controlling costs. This can be achieved through the use of just-in-time (JIT) computer-aided supply and product ordering procedures for controlling inventory costs (Hall, 1983). It can also be achieved through the use of flexible manufacturing technologies (Jaikumar, 1983) and manufacturing-cell-group-based technologies (Karmarkar, 1987). Manufacturing costs can also be reduced by offering a wide range of products that share a large number of common parts (Hayes, Wheelright, & Clark, 1988) and by adding noncommon parts at later stages of the manufacturing process (Kekre & Srinivasan, 1990).

CANNIBALIZATION

Even if manufacturing costs can be controlled effectively, increasing product line breadth may increase the likelihood of **cannibalization,** where one member of a product line takes market share away from another member of the same line. For example, Miller Lite takes share away from regular Miller beer. Coors Light takes share away from regular Coors beer. New Coke takes share away from Coke Classic. Cannibalization is an especially serious problem when the competitive market structure is brand-based rather than attribute-based (Urban, Johnson, & Hauser, 1984). A **brand-based market structure** exists when consumers first decide what brand they want and then decide what attributes they want. An **attribute-based market structure** exists when consumers first decide what attributes they want and then decide what brand they want. Generally, product line managers should decrease product line breadth when most consumers use a brand-based structure and should increase product line breadth when most consumers use an attribute-based structure.

Forced-Choice Switching Data

Consider the coffee market, for example. Do consumers first consider what brand they want (a brand-based structure) or do they first consider what attributes they want, such as ground or instant, caffeinated or decaffeinated (an attribute-based structure)? One way to address this question is to collect **forced-choice switching** data, where consumers are shown a set of products and asked to indicate their first choice (Urban et al., 1984). Then they are asked to assume that their first choice is not available and they must indicate their second choice. These data are then aggregated into overall choice probabilities and z-statistics are performed on these choice probabilities.

For example, suppose 100 consumers were asked to indicate their first and second choices among ground and instant coffees for Maxwell House, Taster's Choice, and Sanka brands. Table 14-1 shows their choices. Of the 100 consumers in the sample, 40 indicated Maxwell House ground coffee as their first choice. Of the 40 consumers who

TABLE 14-1   Hypothetical Forced-Choice Switching Matrix

		Second Choices					
		Ground Coffee			Instant Coffee		
	FIRST CHOICES	MAXWELL HOUSE	TASTER'S CHOICE	SANKA	MAXWELL HOUSE	TASTER'S CHOICE	SANKA
Ground Coffee							
Maxwell House	40	—	20	5	5	5	5
Taster's Choice	10	5	—	5	0	0	0
Sanka	10	5	5	—	0	0	0
Instant Coffee							
Maxwell House	20	2	2	1	—	10	5
Taster's Choice	10	0	0	0	5	—	5
Sanka	10	1	1	1	2	5	—

"—" represents the deleted brand.

preferred Maxwell House ground, 20 indicated Taster's Choice ground as their second choice, 5 indicated Sanka ground as their second choice, 5 indicated Maxwell House instant as their second choice, 5 indicated Taster's Choice instant as their second choice, and 5 indicated Sanka instant as their second choice. Using these data, we can now compute choice probabilities and z-statistics for determining whether these subjects used an attribute-based structure (e.g., ground versus instant matters), a brand-based structure (e.g., brand loyalty), or no structure. The formula for the z-statistic is

$$z = \frac{(P - P')}{\sqrt{[P'(1 - P')/N]}}$$

where P is the proportion of subjects who switched to another brand within the same submarket category [i.e., the proportion who switched to Taster's Choice ground and Sanka ground; $(20 + 5)/40 = .625$, which can be rounded to .63], P' is the predicted proportion of subjects who switched to another brand within the same submarket as determined by the Luce (1959) choice axiom, and N is the number of subjects (40 in the Maxwell House ground case).

   The Luce (1959) choice axiom states that the gain in share enjoyed by a target brand (or set of brands) when a different brand is deleted from the choice set is proportional to the target brand's (or set of brands') original market share. In our example, the original share for Taster's Choice ground is .10 (or 10/100) and the original share for Sanka ground is .10 (or 10/100). Deleting Maxwell House ground $(40/100 = .40)$ and forcing subjects to indicate their second choice results in a market share change that can be expressed as $1 - .40$. In this example, P' is $(.10 + .10)/(1 - .40)$, or .33.

   If subjects used an attribute-based structure, then P and P' should differ significantly. This difference is tested by the z-statistic, which is conceptually $(P - P')$ divided by an error term. In our Maxwell House ground example, $(P - P') = (.63 - .33) = .30$. The error term is

$$\sqrt{[P'(1 - P')]/N} = \sqrt{[.33(1 - .33)]/40} = .07$$

Therefore, $z = (.63 - .33)/.07 = 4.29$. Because the value of z is greater than 1.96, the consumers in our sample were more likely to switch from Maxwell House ground coffee to another brand of ground coffee than would be expected by chance alone (as defined by the Luce proportionality choice axiom). Therefore, the Maxwell House ground coffee drinkers appear to make a sharp distinction between the ground coffee submarket and the instant coffee submarket. Moreover, as Table 14-2 indicates, the value of z for the ground versus instant coffee submarket comparisons exceeds 1.96 for each brand. This pattern of results suggests that the consumers in our sample used an attribute-based structure and that ground coffee drinkers are unlikely to drink instant coffee, and vice versa.

   Table 14-2 also displays P, P', and z-values for brand-based tests in which each specific brand name was treated as a separate submarket. The z-statistic for the Maxwell House ground coffee brand-based submarket, for example, addresses the question: Do Maxwell House ground coffee drinkers switch to Maxwell House instant coffee when Maxwell House ground coffee is unavailable? That is, are consumers brand loyal? When one type of Maxwell House coffee is unavailable, do these consumers switch to another type of Maxwell House coffee? Note that the z-statistic is negative and greater

TABLE 14-2	Hypothetical Choice Probabilities and z-Statistics					
	Ground versus Instant Structure			*Brand-Based Structure*		
	P	*P'*	*z*	*P*	*P'*	*z*
Ground Coffee						
Maxwell House	.63	.33	4.29	.13	.33	−2.86
Taster's Choice	1.00	.56	2.75	.00	.11	−1.10
Sanka	1.00	.56	2.75	.00	.11	−1.10
Instant Coffee						
Maxwell House	.75	.25	5.00	.10	.50	−3.64
Taster's Choice	1.00	.33	4.47	.00	.11	−1.22
Sanka	.70	.33	2.47	.10	.11	−.10

than 1.96. This means that Maxwell House ground coffee drinkers are less likely to switch to Maxwell House instant coffee than would be expected by chance. The z-statistic is also negative and significant for Maxwell House instant coffee. This means that Maxwell House instant coffee drinkers are less likely to switch to Maxwell House ground coffee than would be expected by chance. Together, these results suggest that the Maxwell House product line manager can be highly confident that cannibalism is not a problem. Maxwell House instant coffee does not cannibalize sales of Maxwell House ground coffee, and vice versa.

The z-statistics for the remaining brands in the brand-based submarket analyses are less than 1.96 and are, therefore, nonsignificant. This means that the consumers in this sample are no more likely to switch to another type of product using the same brand name than would be expected by chance. In other words, the consumers in this sample are not using a brand-based structure. Therefore, cannibalism appears to be an unlikely problem for each brand name used in this example. The same procedure could be applied to other attribute-based comparisons, such as caffeinated versus decaffeinated coffees. As the number of attribute-based submarkets increases, the number of products that should be offered on a product line should also increase. The presence of brand-based submarkets, however, suggests that the product line might be too long and it might be advisable to decrease the size of the product line.

◆ MANAGING MARKET LEADERS

Strong brands that lead the market in market share are the easiest types of brands to manage. Strong brands are already successful, and success breeds success. (See Table 14-3.) Successful brands have the largest marketing, production, and R&D budgets. Moreover, successful brands already occupy a highly effective position in the perceptual map and in consumers' hearts and minds. Inertia, the status quo, and consumers' unwillingness to take a chance and try something new automatically benefit the strongest brands. Because change dethrones leaders, any type of change is potentially dangerous to a market leader. Hence, it behooves managers of market leaders to try to prevent change from occurring (Hoch & Deighton, 1989).

| Brand | Brand Rankings | | | | | |
	1990	1991	1992	1993	1994	1995
Kodak	1	3	3	2	2	3
Disney World	2	1	1	1	1	—
Mercedes	3	5	8	8	3	2
Disneyland	4	2	1	1	1	—
Hallmark	5	4	4	4	5	6
Fisher-Price	6	6	5	5	6	5

TABLE 14-3   Consistent Performance of Leading Brands

These leading brands have been around for many decades.

Data source: From Aaker (1996).

One way to prevent change from occurring is to tell consumers what they already know. "Stick with what works," "You get what you pay for," and "We're always there when you need us" are highly credible and effective arguments because consumers already believe that these claims are true. Emphasizing these claims in promotion and advertising produces little counterargumentation and reinforces the strength of these arguments in consumer memory. Moreover, these claims discourage consumers from experimenting by trying different brands.

INCREASING AMBIGUITY

Another way to prevent change from occurring is by increasing ambiguity in the marketplace. Ambiguity benefits market leaders because ambiguous information is often interpreted as consistent with a hypothesis or a belief (Ha & Hoch, 1989; Hoch & Ha, 1986). This is known as **confirmation bias.** It is generally easier to process information that supports (rather than fails to support) a given hypothesis. Consequently, people tend to continue believing what they already believe because support for their beliefs can be found everywhere. If consumers already believe that the market leader is the best, virtually any type of ambiguous evidence will be interpreted as consistent with this belief (Hoch & Deighton, 1989). Moreover, product information is frequently ambiguous. Perceived quality is a complex, multidimensional concept. Consumers often do not know what combination of features is the best combination, and they often passively accept the combination offered by the pioneering brand as the best combination (Carpenter & Nakamoto, 1989). Familiar combinations seem effective, and consumers are often unmotivated to go through the time and trouble to analyze other possible combinations of features. Furthermore, it is frequently difficult for consumers to imagine better alternatives to the products they are using now. How does one imagine unfamiliar alternatives?

Price Comparisons

Price comparisons across brands represent a particularly troublesome source of unambiguous information that could potentially disrupt the status quo (Hoch & Deighton, 1989). However, managers of strong brands can often increase ambiguity through the use of exclusive dealerships. For example, automobile manufacturers often require dealers to sell only their brands. Consequently, consumers cannot directly compare

BIRTHDAY BASHES: BOOM OR BUST?

Most people over the age of five don't like to sing the "How old are you now?" verse of "Happy Birthday." Companies, however, love to remind us how old they are. Disney World celebrated its 25th anniversary for an entire year with special events and products. Jell-O is wrapping its 100th birthday in new packaging and new flavors. Campbell's seems to be celebrating something every year, from the 125th anniversary of the company's founding to the 100th anniversary of condensed soup.

Why are marketers so intent on birthday celebrations for their brands? "It gets attention and people respond to the fact that something new is happening. It's not the same dreary item that they're used to," explains Richard Gerstman, president of branding consultancy Gerstman & Meyers. In addition, "It's saying that the company is tried and trusted and true. People like that."

But others would argue that this emphasis on an irrelevant attribute—age—is, well, irrelevant. "Buyers care last about how long you've been open for business," says Steve Lawrence, principal of corporate/brand identity consultancy Lippincott & Margulies. "Who cares that you've been doing something for 50 years?"

Vicki Freed, senior vice president of sales and marketing for Carnival Cruises, echoes Lawrence's sentiments. "I don't know if it's that meaningful. Do consumers really care? Is that going to motivate someone?" For its 25th anniversary, Carnival simply took out a one-page, one-day newspaper ad to thank its customers for their support. "It wasn't meant to promote bookings," explains Freed. "There's no 800 number [in the ad]."

For high-tech companies like Apple and auto companies like Oldsmobile, an anniversary can even be detrimental to a brand's image. "We did explore the possibility . . . of doing more with the [20th] anniversary, but we decided against it," says David Roman, Apple's vice president of brand marketing. In an industry where youth and cutting-edge technology mean everything, an anniversary isn't necessarily a positive reminder. The same thing goes for Oldsmobile, which for several years has been trying to remake its image by telling consumers that its new cars aren't their fathers' Oldsmobiles. The auto manufacturer had its golden age in the late 1960s and early 1970s, when big gas-guzzling cars were popular and Oldsmobile sold one million cars each year. Now Oldsmobile sells about one-third as many cars annually. So the company plans to mark its 100th year with dealers and employees but not necessarily consumers. "You want to celebrate it, for dealers and employees and some others," says Mike Sands, Oldsmobile's advertising director. "But it's not a great image perception for Olds. We do have deep roots, with our eyes set on the new millennium, but that's a difficult story to spin."

Who is right? Are birthdays good or bad for brand equity? "The anniversary in and of itself is not that interesting unless it can be made relevant to the product or company," says one expert. "The question that has to be answered is, 'Why is this important?' If that can't be answered in consumer-relevant terms, you should forget about promoting your age."

Jell-O and Campbell's think it is important. "We're looking for the 100th anniversary to provide a platform for us to tell consumers that the brand is alive and well," says Jell-O category business director Mary Beth Stone. "We're bigger and better than ever." Gary Fassak, marketing vice president for Campbell's, enthuses, "The idea is that we're one hundred years old and we're getting better. Our heritage is vibrant, yet we're linking it to the future by weaving it into a product launch." (Campbell's is doing a $15 million launch of soup in glass jars embossed with Joseph A. Campbell's signature.) Who knows? Maybe thousands of consumers are ready to sit down to a bowl of Campbell's vegetable soup for lunch right now. And maybe they'll have a Jell-O jiggler for dessert.

Source: Steve Gelsi and Pam Weisz, "You Say It's Your Birthday," *Brandweek,* April 7, 1997, pp. 33–40.

Chevrolets and Fords in the same dealership. Another way to increase ambiguity is to use different model numbers for virtually the same product. Automobiles, electronic products, and other consumer durables often have a string of numbers and letters appearing after the brand name. If the 505A is more expensive than the 502B or than a brand made by a different manufacturer, the salesperson can always argue that the 505A is not comparable because it has different features from the other brands.

Side-by-Side Comparisons

Retailers often share the strong-brand manufacturers' dislike of side-by-side comparisons. Consequently, retailers can often be encouraged to use different locations for different products, such as a separate display case for Frito-Lay potato chips. Moving Frito-Lay products away from the other snack foods makes brand comparison difficult. Moreover, some retailers are willing to use different brand names for the same product. For example, Whirlpools sold at Sears cannot be easily compared with Whirlpools sold at other stores because Whirlpools at Sears are called Kenmores.

Irrelevant Attributes

Another way to increase ambiguity is to differentiate strong brands on the basis of irrelevant attributes. (See "Taking Issue: Birthday Bashes: Boom or Bust?") Only Budweiser beer is "beechwood aged," and only Old Style beer is "fully kraeusened," and only Miller beer is "brewed the American way." These irrelevant attributes sound good, but they do not make the product taste any better. Folger's coffee being "mountain grown" and "Lay's potato chips: Bet you can't eat just one" are claims that are nonfalsifiable and therefore difficult to argue with. Easily visible attributes, such as blue specks in a laundry detergent, also tend to support or confirm the superiority of a strong brand because it is difficult for consumers to disprove the claim that the blue specks make white clothes whiter. Ambiguous information that supports the claim that the market leader is the best is remarkably easy to find and manufacture. Because supportive evidence is generally easier to process than unsupportive evidence, consumers are likely to continue believing what they already believe. Together, a lack of motivation or knowledge on the part of consumers and the presence of ambiguity in the marketplace work to the market leader's advantage.

◆ MANAGING MARKET UNDERDOGS

It is extremely difficult to overcome the incumbent brand advantage (Muthukrishnan, 1995). Ambiguity and confirmation bias favor strong brands and hurt weak brands. Weak brands have relatively small marketing, production, and R&D budgets; therefore, weak brands cannot confront strong brands directly. Unfortunately, most of you work for or will work for underdog brands. There can be only one market leader in a product category; therefore, statistically, it is unlikely that you will work for the market leader.

What should managers of underdog brands do? Basically, they must do the opposite of what managers of topdog brands try to do (Hoch & Deighton, 1989). Topdog product managers try to decrease consumer motivation to learn more about the various brands that are available in the marketplace and also try to increase ambiguity in the marketplace. Underdog product managers should try to increase consumer motivation to learn about different brands and should try to decrease ambiguity. One way

Our training for flight attendants is extremely rigorous. Maybe that's why our flights are so relaxing.

Simply to qualify for the Korean Air training program is an accomplishment. Of every thousand who apply, only a few possess just the right blend of grace and poise.

Then, nine hours a day, six days a week for a month or even more, their natural abilities are refined. They study world-class service. And hospitality. And a number of different languages.

By the time our flight attendants graduate, they're skilled in all the arts of comfort. Which leaves our passengers nothing to do but relax.

KOREAN AIR
Fly the spirit of dedication.™

In this ad, Korean Air, an underdog in the international airline industry, tries to persuade consumers that its flight attendants are among the most highly trained in air travel.

Source: Courtesy of Korean Air.

to increase motivation to learn is to encourage consumers to take a taste-test challenge or to directly compare an underdog brand with a market leader. Small free samples and a "try it, you'll like it" type of appeal can be effective for underdog brands.

Persuading consumers that their currently held beliefs may be incorrect can also be very effective (Hoch & Deighton, 1989; Kruglanski, Webster, & Klem, 1995). For example, a Stove Top Stuffing television commercial asked a housewife whether her family preferred potatoes or stuffing. The housewife confidently predicted that her family preferred potatoes. The narrator then asked the husband and the kids which product they would prefer. To the housewife's surprise, each member of the family registered an enthusiastic vote for stuffing. Surprises can encourage consumers to question their currently held beliefs and to reconsider the evidence.

HEARTLAND CANDLES ARE MADE WITH HEART

Being an underdog isn't necessarily a bad thing. You can take chances, do things in an unorthodox manner, gain attention, develop your brand. Michael and Lynette Richards, founders of Heartland Candleworks Inc., have learned this.

Although Heartland Candleworks is now located in Iowa—America's heartland—the company had its beginnings in New York City. Michael and Lynette Richards started the Candle Project with their savings; they bought beeswax and hired several homeless families to roll the wax into candles for sale. Hand-rolled candles are a low-tech, low-cost item; the Richardses didn't need a factory, and the families they hired didn't need much training to learn how to make the candles. But both sides benefited: The Richardses got a product to sell, and the families got work.

Lynette Richards was already employed at the Body Shop, which is known for its social activism and all-natural products. So getting permission to sell the handmade candles at the Body Shop was not difficult. Since the Body Shop has stores all over the country, the Richardses' candles soon had a wide distribution. Within a few years, however, the couple decided to move their operation back to their home state of Iowa, where commercial work space was more affordable than in New York. So Heartland Candleworks was born, in an Iowa barn leased for $125 a month (the barn had no electricity and no running water).

Today, roughly 100 homeless individuals, recovering substance abusers, and people with disabilities are employed at a more up-to-date, 10,000-square-foot manufacturing facility. "Our employees get self-esteem from working here," says Michael. "They feel like they're a part of something productive."

This year, Heartland Candleworks will bring in around $1.2 million in revenues. Workers craft about 250 different types of candles, totaling about 400,000 candles per year. The candles are sold in about 2,000 shops worldwide, including unorthodox channels like Ben & Jerry's gift shop in Vermont.

Still, Heartland Candleworks is far from a major player in the candle market. Procuring capital and supplies is a constant struggle. "It's challenging, but not unprecedented," notes Michael. "You have to convince the suppliers that if you grow, it will mean increased business for them. It's important to convey a mutual benefit."

But the Heartland brand has a lot going for it. First, the candles are of high quality—made of vegetable-wax derivatives, which appeals to consumers who want all-natural products. Second, consumers associate the Heartland name with social activism and feel good buying products that are made by individuals who might not otherwise be employed. Third, the handmade candles convey craftsmanship, which appeals to many consumers who like products with a "country" feel. Finally, handmade products make appealing gifts. After all, who doesn't like a gift from the heart, made by hand? Michael and Lynette Richards are hoping that everyone will.

Source: Jennifer Nathanson, "Waxing Profits, Rekindling Hope," *Success,* July/August 1997, pp. 30–31.

In addition to increasing consumer motivation to learn, managers of underdog brands should attempt to make consumer learning easier by reducing ambiguity in the marketplace. Store brands, for example, are often placed directly next to leading brands to encourage comparison and to bolster perceptions of store brands as being the same as leading brands but less expensive. To further enhance perceptions of similarity, store brands are often enclosed in packages with similar coloring or lettering to that of the packages of leading brands. Comparative advertising also tends to increase the perceived similarity of underdog and topdog brands (Gorn & Weinberg, 1984).

An unorthodox distribution channel, such as home parties (e.g., for Tupperware), can also increase attention to and learning about an underdog brand. Mary Kay cosmetic home parties and in-store cosmetic clinics can also increase consumer learning about an underdog brand. Similarly, underdog-brand-sponsored wine tasting classes and gourmet cooking classes can also put the spotlight on underdog brand foods and wines. Any tactic that disrupts the status quo has the potential to increase sales of an underdog brand. (See "Taking Issue: Heartland Candles Are Made with Heart.")

CHAPTER SUMMARY ■

Product management involves monitoring a product as it progresses through the product life cycle and developing different strategies at different stages. During the introduction stage, the manager must concentrate on increasing consumer awareness of a product and encouraging consumers to include the product in their consideration sets. The growth stage involves heavy promotion and advertising to encourage consumers to prefer your brand over competitors' brands. The maturity stage involves reducing production and marketing costs. The decline stage involves either drastically reducing costs in order to milk and retire the product or increasing costs in order to rejuvenate the product.

Many managers and researchers regard the reputation of a brand name as the most important asset of a product. Strong brand names help the product to get through difficult times and provide unique opportunities during good times. Attaching a familiar and well-regarded brand name to an unfamiliar new product is appropriate under some circumstances, whereas attaching different brand names to different products is appropriate under other circumstances. Both strategies should be entertained by managers who must organize and synchronize strategies for a line of products. The firm's resources, the risk of cannibalization, and consumers' perceptions of product heterogeneity are the key factors that determine which strategy is more likely to be effective.

Top-selling brands benefit from an unchanging marketplace, whereas underdog brands benefit from change. Because ambiguity and the status quo effect discourage change, managers of top-selling brands should increase ambiguity in the marketplace and encourage consumers to minimize regret. Managers of underdog brands should attempt to decrease ambiguity in the market and encourage consumers to try something new. Managers of both types of products need to be knowledgeable about and responsive to consumer judgment and choice processes.

KEY CONCEPTS ■

- Entry strategy
- Diffusion of innovation
- Rapid takeoff strategy
- Rapid acceleration strategy
- Maximum penetration strategy
- Long-run franchise strategy
- Brand extensions
- Experience curve

- Harvesting
- Self-fulfilling prophecy
- Rejuvenation
- Brand equity
- Young & Rubicam Brand Asset Valuator
- Brand strength
- Brand stature
- Product line breadth

- Cannibalization
- Brand-based market structure
- Attribute-based market structure
- Forced-choice switching
- Confirmation bias

DISCUSSION QUESTIONS ■

1. Name and describe briefly the four basic entry strategies that can influence the diffusion curve.
2. What type of entry strategy might be used over the next few years to promote digital television? Why?
3. How do the dependent measures of the product life cycle differ from those of the diffusion curve?
4. Think of a product brand from which you own several products, and jot down both the brand and the products. Once you bought the first product, what led you to buy the others?
5. What steps might marketers take to extend the longevity of a product that is in the decline stage of the product life cycle?
6. Choose one of the following brands and write down what you might expect when buying a product bearing this brand name: Burger King or Kentucky Fried Chicken; Panasonic electronic products; Saturn automobiles; Ben & Jerry's ice cream.
7. How does the Young & Rubicam Brand Asset Valuator help marketers?
8. What major factor may increase the likelihood of cannibalization?
9. How might marketers for a leading brand of coffee attempt to prevent changes from occurring that could knock their product down from the top position? Give some specific examples.
10. What steps might marketers for an underdog brand of cheese take to increase their product's success? Give some specific examples.

CHAPTER 15

Biases in Managerial Decision Making

◆ WIRELESS PHONE COMPANIES GO RETAIL

Buying a wireless phone isn't as simple as it used to be. You used to just pick one up at the same store where you bought your stereo and television. Now, traditional cellular carriers are opening up their own retail boutiques, and even start-up firms are getting into the act. So when you go to the mall, chances are you'll see a new "personal communications services" store—whether it is owned by AT&T, Verizon, or Let's Talk Cellular & Wireless Inc., a 100-store chain located in Miami.

The move into retail didn't just happen. Managers at various companies had to gather information, weigh it, and make the decision to enter the retail market. Whether they succeed may depend on the methods they used to make the decision. Competition was the basis of most decisions. All cellular phone companies want to reach consumers in the most effective way possible. "We need to make it easier for people to purchase phones, and that means having multiple points of presence," explains Karen Little, vice president of marketing for Dallas-based PrimeCo Personal Communications.

So marketers have decided to spend the money to build, stock, and staff retail stores in an effort to gain customers. Verizon Wireless claims that it costs about $185 to acquire a single customer through one of its new, company-owned stores, but it costs as much as $350 to win a customer through a third-party retail outlet like one of the big electronics stores. So the expenditure is worth it. Yet, because the company-owned stores are still relatively new, it is hard to tell whether enough of those $185 customers will walk through the doors to make the investment profitable. Marketers have to rely on their methods of predicting what will happen.

Often, marketing decisions are based on past experiences, which may or may not be relevant. The new wireless stores are opening in the shadow of the failed phone company stores of the past few years. AT&T lost so much money on its retail phone centers that the company finally shut them down. Does this mean that the cellular phone stores will fail, too?

So far, the carrier-owned stores have had some problems. Customers say the shops are crowded and service is poor. Carrier companies admit that they don't want to go overboard promoting their own stores at the expense of the relationships they already have with third-party electronics stores (despite the cost difference). As you read this chapter, observe how different biases affect marketers' decisions and how these decisions affect the success of their products and companies.

Source: Stephanie N. Mehta, "Rush to Retail: Wireless-Phone Firms Open Own Stores," *The Wall Street Journal,* September 16, 1997, p. B4.

◆ INTRODUCTION

Effective managerial decision making begins with a clear understanding of consumer judgment and decision processes. After developing a clear understanding of these processes, the manager should scrutinize his or her own judgment and decision processes. Although the typical manager is highly intelligent and highly educated, his or her decisions are nevertheless susceptible to many common judgment and decision errors (Bazerman, 1990; Russo & Schoemaker, 1989). Biases affect decisions, as in the case of the wireless phone companies. This chapter describes and analyzes these biases, and the following chapter discusses debiasing procedures for improving managerial judgment and decision making.

◆ BIASES RESULTING FROM ATTENTION- AND MEMORY-RELATED CONSTRAINTS

Just as consumers attend to only a few things at a time, so too are the attention spans of managers limited. Moreover, consumers and managers alike are willing to acknowledge limitations in attention and memory but are unwilling to acknowledge limitations in judgment and decision making. This is ironic because attention- and memory-related constraints have a strong impact on judgment and decision making. Because attention and memory influence decision making, unbiased decision making is impossible when attention and memory are biased.

SALIENCE AND VIVIDNESS EFFECTS

Because managers cannot attend to all available information relevant to a decision, they tend to focus on information that is interesting, attention-drawing, and easy to understand and process. Well-written and well-organized memos receive more attention than poorly written and poorly organized memos, regardless of the message content. At meetings, information that is presented in a colorful and interesting way receives more attention and weight than information presented in a dry or unappealing manner. Unfortunately, manner of presentation is unrelated to information relevance. If highly relevant information is presented in a dry manner, it tends to be neglected. In contrast, if less relevant information is presented in an interesting manner, it tends to have a greater impact on the final decision.

Salient information sticks out from a particular context or background (Nisbett & Ross, 1980). In the context of a sea of numbers, verbal information really sticks out. The same verbal information would not stick out, however, if the entire report or presentation was verbal in nature. In the context of a series of speakers wearing gray flannel suits, the presenter with the double-breasted aquamarine suit and multicolored tie really sticks out. The same flashy presenter, however, would not stick out if all presenters were equally flashy. Salient information sticks out in one particular setting but would not stick out in other possible settings.

Vivid information, on the other hand, always sticks out, regardless of the context or background in which it is perceived (Nisbett & Ross, 1980; Taylor & Thompson, 1982). Vivid information is emotionally interesting, concrete and image-provoking, and has immediate or direct implications for the decision maker (Nisbett & Ross, 1980). Our goals, hobbies, and interests determine what information is vivid to us personally. Of course, stimuli that are emotionally interesting to one individual may not be emotionally interesting to another. Hence, stimuli that are vivid to one individual may not be vivid to another.

Another factor that influences emotional impact and vividness is information concreteness. Concrete information pertains to only one specific object or issue, whereas abstract information is general and applies to a wide variety of objects or issues. A newspaper article about one poor victim's fight with cancer is much more disturbing than an article about millions who die from cancer. Specific, concrete information has a much greater emotional impact than general, abstract information. Concrete information is also much easier to think about. It is easier to imagine the plight of one individual with cancer than the plight of millions with cancer. Emotional information has a greater impact on our decisions than abstract information. This is unfortunate because abstract information and cold facts are often more relevant to a decision. For example, one influential study showed that American voters tend to vote for the candidate that makes them feel good, even when they recognize intellectually that this candidate would make a very poor president and that the other candidate has much more to say about the issues (Abelson, Kinder, Peters, & Fiske, 1982).

Information that has immediate and direct implications for the decision maker is more vivid and attention-drawing than information that has distant and indirect implications. For example, events occurring in one's own company, sales district, or market are much more vivid than events occurring in some other company, sales district, or market. Federal regulations, competitors' activities, and consumer preferences that

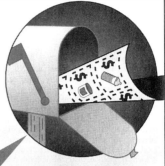

AT THE MANUFACTURER:
Brand managers select lifestyle and purchasing categories to pinpoint promotions. They can also target purchasers of competing brands. Vons then prepares monthly mailers with individually laser-printed coupons targeted to specific households.

MARKETING NUGGETS: THEY'RE IN THE CARDS
How the Vons card works for consumers and marketers

AT VONS HEADQUARTERS:
Customers are sorted into nearly 200 groups based on goods bought, ranging from antacids to wine, and into lifestyle groups—consumers of children's products, for instance.

AT THE CHECKOUT:
Customer swipes magnetic card and receives automatic deductions on selected items. Detailed purchase data is transmitted to a central computer.

Customers, marketers, and competitors of Vons would be most interested in this information about Von's electronic marketing system. Because it could directly affect their business, marketers would find the information vivid and attention-drawing.

Source: Courtesy of Laurel Daunis Allen.

affect your company's current operations are more vivid and attention-drawing than regulations, competitors' activities, and shifts in preferences that will affect your company some time in the future. Similarly, short-term profits are more vivid and attention-drawing than long-term profits; consequently, many managers tend to overemphasize short-term profits.

Finally, information obtained from firsthand experience is more vivid and compelling than secondhand information. We believe what we see and hear with our own eyes and ears more readily than we believe what others have seen or heard. This practice is often wise because other people often simplify what they have seen and heard to tell a more comprehensible and informative story (Gilovich, 1987). Moreover, they often exaggerate to tell a more entertaining story (Gilovich, 1987). It would be unwise to believe hearsay such as rumors that McDonald's uses worm meat in its hamburgers (Tybout, Calder, & Sternthal, 1981) or that playing video games causes brain damage (Gilovich, 1991). On the other hand, con artists and charlatans count on us to believe what we see and hear—their rigged demonstrations would be ineffective otherwise.

Regardless of whether information is salient or vivid, information that captures attention is likely to be stored in memory, retrieved, and have a disproportionate impact on subsequent judgments and decisions. Unfortunately, salience and vividness are poor criteria for information usage because the extent to which information captures attention is often unrelated to the relevance and usefulness of information. In other words, the most attention-drawing information is not always the most relevant information.

CONTEXT EFFECTS

Judgments pertaining to one piece of information, one object, or one issue are often influenced by other pieces of information, other objects, or other issues that happen to be present at the time of judgment. These other pieces of information, objects, and issues provide a context, or background, for judging a target. Unfortunately, these background factors often influence judgment even when they are irrelevant to the judgment task. For instance, judgments about the importance of an issue depend on other issues being considered. After deciding when to hold a firm's annual picnic, deciding which ad campaign is likely to be most successful for a new brand seems like a very important decision. However, after making a decision regarding the five-year strategic mission of a firm, the decision regarding which ad to use seems trivial. Hence, an issue can seem important or unimportant depending on the context in which it is judged.

The most common types of context effects are contrast, assimilation, and framing effects. A contrast effect is a shift in judgment away from a contextual reference point. Cold tap water seems warm after your hands have been exposed to the bitter cold of a midwinter's day. A $50 silk tie seems inexpensive after one buys a $500 wool suit. A decision pertaining to a single product offered by a firm seems less important than a decision pertaining to all product offerings of a firm. Whenever two very different objects or issues are compared, judgments of the target are displaced away from the reference point.

Conversely, when two similar objects or issues are compared, judgments of the target are displaced toward the reference point. This type of context effect is known as an *assimilation* effect. For example, managers who express opinions somewhat similar to yours seem to express opinions that are almost exactly the same as yours. Consequently, we tend to agree with similar others too readily because we tend to perceive their positions and our positions as being more similar than is actually the case. Perceived similarity tends to be greater than actual similarity, and this increases susceptibility to persuasion.

Framing effects are shifts in judgment that occur when managers focus on different possible reference points (Kahneman & Tversky, 1984; Tversky & Kahneman, 1981). For example, imagine that you are a hospital administrator preparing for an epidemic that is expected to kill 600 people. Your staff has developed two programs to combat the disease, and you can implement only one of these two programs. If program A is

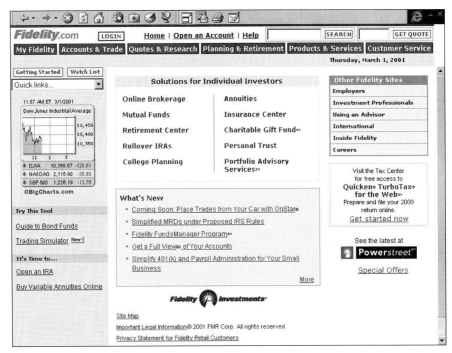

On its Web site (www.fidelity.com), Fidelity Investments puts retirement strategies in the context of a chess game. Both involve critical thinking and long-term planning for success.
Source: Courtesy of Fidelity Investments.

adopted, 200 people will be saved. If program B is adopted, there is a one-third probability that 600 people will be saved and a two-thirds probability that no one will be saved. When the decision problem is framed or presented this way, most managers prefer program A over program B. Now consider the very same problem with a slight variation in wording. If program A is adopted, 400 people will die. If program B is adopted, there is a one-third probability that no one will die and a two-thirds probability that 600 will die. When the decision problem is framed this way, most managers prefer program B over program A. This is inconsistent because the outcomes described by program A are identical in both problems, and the outcomes described by program B are also identical in both cases. The only difference is that in the former case outcomes are framed in term of lives saved, whereas in the latter case outcomes are framed in terms of lives lost.

Why does problem wording have such a large effect on managers' decisions? Several empirical studies have shown that when outcomes are framed in terms of gains—such as lives saved, sales gained, profits gained, and share gained—people are **risk-averse** (Linville & Fischer, 1991; Kahneman & Tversky, 1984; Puto, 1987; Qualls & Puto, 1989; Thaler, 1985; Tversky & Kahneman, 1981). That is, when people focus on gains and when two alternative courses of action yield similar outcomes in terms of expected utility, people prefer the sure thing over the risky option. (See Fig. 15-1.) If you can save 200 lives for sure, why take a chance and risk losing 600 lives? In contrast, when outcomes are framed in terms of losses—such as lives lost, sales lost, profits lost,

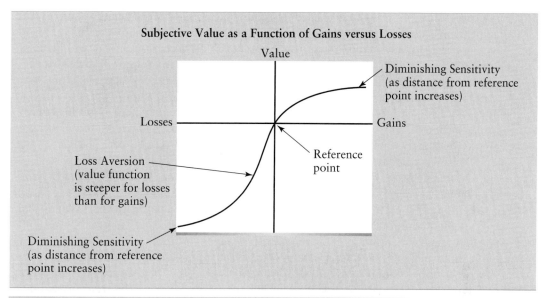

FIGURE 15-1

Subjective value as a function of gains versus losses.

and share lost—people are **risk-seeking.** Traditional economic theories suggest that the amount of pain experienced from losing $100 should be equivalent to the amount of pleasure experienced from winning $100. However, recent research has shown that the amount of displeasure associated with losing $100 is greater than the amount of pleasure associated with winning $100 (Linville & Fischer, 1991; Kahneman & Tversky, 1984; Puto, 1987; Qualls & Puto, 1989; Thaler, 1985; Tversky & Kahneman, 1981). That is, losses loom larger than gains (**loss aversion**). Furthermore, displeasure increases as losses increase, and pleasure increases as gains increase, but displeasure increases at a much faster rate than pleasure. Consequently, decision makers are risk-averse when outcomes are framed in terms of gains, and they are risk-seeking when outcomes are framed in terms of losses. Moreover, both gains and losses appear smaller as the distance between these relative outcomes and the reference point increases (**diminishing sensitivity**). For example, when zero serves as the reference point, the difference between $100 and $200 seems larger than the difference between $1,100 and $1,200. Similarly, the difference between −$100 and −$200 seems larger than the difference between −$1,100 and −$1,200.

BIASED ASSIMILATION

Our expectations frequently have a profound effect on the way we interpret events. When an event is ambiguous—that is, when there are many possible interpretations of an event—expectations guide interpretation. For example, imagine that you are participating in a board meeting in which you offered some suggestions about an upcoming promotional campaign. Immediately after you offered these suggestions, one of your fellow participants aggressively listed several problems with your ideas. How would you interpret the behavior of this aggressive board member? Several interpretations are possible. Perhaps he is an aggressive person by nature and always behaves aggressively at board meetings. Perhaps he had a bad day and is in a foul mood. Perhaps there really are serious problems with your suggestions and his concerns are valid. Other possibilities exist as well. However, if you have known this person for a long time, you are likely to have well-defined expectations based on prior experience and to use these expectations to interpret this person's behavior. For instance, if you expect this person to behave aggressively, you will interpret his behavior at this meeting simply as another typical, aggressive display and assume that there are no fundamental problems with your suggestions. This is **biased assimilation.**

Consider another scenario. In their classic example of biased assimilation, Lord and his colleagues presented "research evidence" bearing on the effectiveness of capital punishment to subjects who have strong prior opinions about the topic (Lord, Ross, & Lepper, 1979). Attitude strength was operationalized in terms of the extremity of ratings on standard attitude scales. Half the subjects strongly supported and half strongly opposed capital punishment. Both groups read descriptions of two studies, one supporting and one failing to support the deterrent efficacy of the death penalty. The descriptions contained detailed information about the procedures and the results of the studies. Although the results were held constant, two very different procedures were used, and these were counterbalanced across the two studies. That is, for half the subjects, procedure A was paired with study A and procedure B was paired with study B. In contrast, for the remaining subjects, procedure A was paired with study B and procedure B was paired with study A.

Though subjects were exposed to mixed evidence, one study supporting and one refuting the effectiveness of capital punishment, subjects were even more confident about the validity of their initial beliefs after reading about these studies. Regardless of whether procedure A or B was used in the study that supported their initial beliefs, subjects perceived the procedure as scientifically sound and viewed the study as providing important scientific evidence concerning the effectiveness of capital punishment. Conversely, regardless of whether procedure A or B was used in the study that contradicted their initial beliefs, subjects identified many fatal flaws in the procedure and the study was perceived to be so poorly conducted that the results were virtually ignored.

Similarly, Lee, Acito, and Day (1987) exposed M.B.A. students to two different ads and asked the students to indicate which ad they thought would be more effective. After making their predictions, they received marketing research data that indicated that the ad they preferred was ineffective and that the other ad was much more effective. Nevertheless, subjects persisted in believing that the ad they preferred would actually be more effective. Their beliefs and expectations colored how they interpreted the research evidence and led them to ignore research evidence that was inconsistent with their viewpoints.

PSEUDODIAGNOSTICITY

The appearance or illusion of **diagnosticity** (perceived relevance) is referred to as **pseudodiagnosticity** (Fischhoff & Beyth-Marom, 1983; Herr, Kardes, & Kim, 1991; Hoch & Deighton, 1989). Managers exhibit the pseudodiagnosticity effect any time they treat nondiagnostic (irrelevant) information as if it were diagnostic (relevant).

They are especially likely to do this when they focus on one possible hypothesis, one possible interpretation of ambiguous evidence, or one possible categorization of a novel object to the exclusion of others. Focusing on one possibility and ignoring other possibilities is known as **selective hypothesis testing** (Kardes & Cronley, 2000a; Sanbonmatsu, Posavac, Kardes, & Mantel, 1998). Selective or one-sided information search and interpretation often lead to the perception that there is strong support for a focal hypothesis or conclusion. This perception often leads to premature hypothesis confirmation: Managers often advertently or inadvertently come to the conclusion that they were right all along. Selective hypothesis testing causes weakly supportive evidence to appear strongly supportive, and this encourages managers to conclude that their preferred new product concept, ad, plan, or strategy is a good one.

Information diagnosticity or relevance depends on the extent to which information supports one hypothesis over others. Unfortunately, managers often entertain only one hypothesis rather than many hypotheses, and under these circumstances, the true diagnosticity or relevance of information cannot be established. Diagnosticity depends on the extent to which information implies one hypothesis or one category over other possible hypotheses or categories. For example, an executive for a prominent industrial firm was having lunch with a representative from a management consulting firm. The R&D division of the industrial firm had recently developed a new product, and the executive was looking for the right consulting firm to assist him in formulating an effective entry strategy. The consultant provided figures demonstrating that his firm enjoyed a 70 percent success rate with products similar to the one that the industrial firm had developed. The executive was so impressed that he hired the consultant.

Although it is true that a 70 percent success rate is an impressive rate of success for new product ventures, this figure becomes considerably less impressive if other consulting firms also enjoy a 70 percent success rate for this product category. It becomes even less impressive if the prominent industrial firm enjoyed a 70 percent success rate without the assistance of consultants. Thus, though the 70 percent figure seems to be diagnostic at first, it is not at all diagnostic if other possible courses of action produce the same outcome. (See Fig. 15-2.)

Obviously, the ability to separate relevant and irrelevant information is a very important managerial skill. Unfortunately, busy decision makers tend to focus on one hypothesis, one interpretation, one perspective, or one categorization much too intensely. Other possibilities are not very attention-drawing; consequently, other possibilities are easily overlooked. When this occurs, managers are susceptible to the pseudodiagnosticity effect.

GROUP DECISION MAKING

Managers often make decisions in groups or committees because they believe that many heads are better than one. Presumably, multiple decision makers bring different information and different perspectives to the table. In reality, however, most meetings are spent discussing information and issues already familiar to all present. Relatively little sharing of unique information takes place. This is known as the **common-knowledge effect** (Gigone & Hastie, 1993, 1997). In addition, group discussion often increases the extremity of the preferences shared by many individual group members.

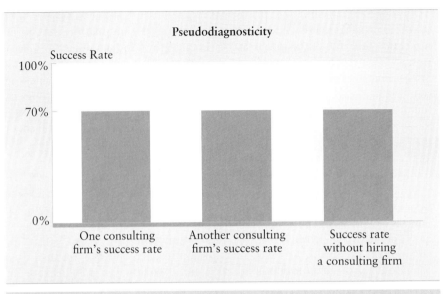

FIGURE 15-2

Managers who only examine one consulting firm's success rate are likely to conclude that this consulting firm is outstanding. Managers who use full information (one consulting firm's success rate, another consulting firm's success rate, the success rate without hiring a consulting firm) are more likely to realize that a consulting firm might not be able to improve the odds of success.

This is known as **group polarization** (Chandrashekaran, Walker, Ward, & Reingen, 1996; Vinokur & Burnstein, 1974; Ward & Reingen, 1990). Early research suggested that group discussion increases learning about new information favoring a specific option, and as the amount of information favoring the option increases, the collective preference for this option increases (Vinokur & Burnstein, 1974). However, recent research indicates that negative arguments toward unwanted options are much more persuasive than positive arguments toward favored options (Chandrashekaran et al., 1996). As evaluations of unwanted options become less favorable during group discussion, evaluations of favored options become even more favorable.

Groupthink, or excessive conformity due to an illusion of group invincibility, is another danger of group decision making (Janis, 1982). A powerful charismatic leader, insensitivity to information suggesting that the favored option might not be the best option, and extreme group polarization are common characteristics of groups suffering from groupthink. The best way to prevent groupthink is to frequently seek the opinions of impartial consultants who do not belong to the group and to encourage at least one group member to serve as a "devil's advocate," or a person who provides strong counterarguments to the group's arguments. In addition, the leader should attempt to remain impartial and should avoid revealing his or her preferences too early during the group discussion.

Selective hypothesis testing tends to be even more extreme in group decision making than in individual decision making (Schulz-Hardt, Frey, Luthgens, & Moscovici, 2000). When only one option is considered, or when the group has a single favorite option, group members strongly prefer information consistent rather than inconsistent with the decision to choose this option. Managers read a case study of an industrial firm that was considering investing $125 million in a developing country to relocate part of its production there. Equally strong arguments for and against investment were presented in the case. After forming individual decisions for or against investment, the managers participated in a 10-minute discussion of the case in three-person groups. After reaching a preliminary decision, the groups were given the opportunity to obtain additional information relevant to the decision. The additional information was in the form of articles written by expert economists. Five of the articles favored investment, and five were against investment. Although the groups were allowed to select all 10 articles, the groups selected more articles consistent as opposed to inconsistent with their preliminary decisions. This confirmation bias occurred in all groups but was more pronounced in unanimous groups. The reluctance to consider preference-inconsistent information increases group polarization and groupthink.

◆ BIASES RESULTING FROM UNDERPROCESSING

The previous section focused on judgmental biases resulting from limitations in our attentional and memory systems. We can attend to or recall only relatively small amounts of information at any one time. Unfortunately, we do not always attend to or recall the most diagnostic information. The previous section focused on what information is gathered or collected (because we cannot focus on all available information), and this section focuses on how information is used after it is gathered or collected. In particular, this section focuses on our overreliance on cognitive heuristics, or strategies designed to simplify judgment and decision making. Simplifying strategies reduce the amount of cognitive effort required to reach a judgment or decision, and this reduction is referred to as "underprocessing" (Gilbert & Krull, 1988).

Tversky and Kahneman (1974), two of the world's leading decision researchers, identified four key cognitive heuristics that people use to simplify judgment and decision making: the representativeness heuristic, the availability heuristic, the simulation heuristic, and the anchoring-and-adjustment heuristic. The following sections describe each of these heuristics in detail and illustrate how they can lead to poor decisions.

THE REPRESENTATIVENESS HEURISTIC

Many decisions are based on beliefs about the likelihood of uncertain outcomes, such as the likelihood of a successful new product launch, the likelihood that a particular advertising strategy will be successful, the likelihood of arranging a satisfactory deal with suppliers, the likelihood that competitors will choose one course of action over another, and so on. How do managers estimate the probabilities of uncertain events? This is a difficult question to answer because decision makers are often unable to articulate exactly how they arrived at a particular prediction. Often, they say that their prediction is based simply on an intuition, hunch, or educated guess. Nevertheless, Tversky and Kahneman were able to identify several key factors that influence intuitive prediction.

Judgments of Category Membership

What is the probability that object A belongs to category B? What is the probability that process X caused outcome Y? The **representativeness heuristic** involves assessing the likelihood that A belongs to B on the basis of the degree to which A is similar to B. If A and B are highly similar, it seems likely that A belongs to B. If A and B are dissimilar, it seems unlikely that A belongs to B. Also, if X and Y are highly similar, it seems likely that X caused Y. If X and Y are dissimilar, it seems unlikely that X caused Y. Hence, the representativeness heuristic involves judging probability on the basis of similarity.

For example, it is important to be able to predict whether consumers will categorize a new product either as a fad or as a new innovation that will replace the previous generation of products. If the new product is a fad, it will have a short life cycle (usually about one year) and it will be extremely difficult to attain a satisfactory return on investment. If the new product is really new, it will enjoy a lengthy product life cycle and a satisfactory return on investment. Hence, accurate prediction is extremely important. Using the representativeness heuristic, brand managers at Procter & Gamble categorized Pringles potato chips as a new innovation. Pringles appeared to be very similar to other successful new innovations: It looks new and different, it tastes good (it was preferred to other brands in blind taste tests), it has a long shelf life, it goes well with soft drinks and beer, and so on. After one year, however, it became clear that Pringles was just a fad, and P&G was never able to recoup its extremely high investment costs.

Causal Judgments

The representativeness heuristic influences causal judgments as well as judgments of category membership. It seems likely that process X caused outcome Y if X and Y are highly similar. It seems unlikely that process X caused outcome Y if X and Y are dissimilar. For instance, if process X is a large advertising campaign and outcome Y is a large profit, X and Y resemble each other in the sense that both involve large amounts of money. On the basis of the representativeness heuristic, large causes are expected to produce large effects and small causes are expected to produce small effects. Although the representativeness heuristic often leads to accurate and useful predictions, whenever one relies too heavily on a heuristic one runs the risk of overlooking something important. Imagine the difficulty Pasteur had convincing people that invisible germs (a very small cause) produce disease, death, and epidemics (very large effects)!

Underprocessing leads managers to overlook things. What are these things that are likely to be overlooked? One is the prior probability or the base rate of an outcome. A new product may have all the appearances of quality and success but still fail if the base rate or incidence of success in the product category is very low. Sample size is also neglected when people rely heavily on the representativeness heuristic. Extreme judgments are formed on the basis of a few casual observations, even though a large database is needed for accurate prediction. Misconceptions of chance are also likely when people rely heavily on the representativeness heuristic. After launching several new-product failures, a manager may believe that he is due for a success (the gambler's fallacy) because chance is expected to involve a mix of successes and failures (not all failures). Of course, this is true only in the very long run (i.e., when an infinitely large sample is examined).

Quality of Information

Managers also overlook the quality of the information they use as a basis for their decisions when they rely too heavily on the representativeness heuristic. Information quality is determined by two factors: reliability (or stability) and validity (or accuracy). If a competitor's prices for a given product offering remain fairly stable over time, and if you learn that the competitor's current price is $25.99, this information is reliable and useful. Conversely, if another competitor's prices fluctuate dramatically over time, and if you learn that this competitor's current price is $25.99, this information is unreliable and not very useful. Information validity refers to the extent to which the information refers to one and only one concept. For example, if you learn that a competitor's list price is $25.99, this information is valid and useful. On the other hand, if it is unclear whether $25.99 refers to a list price, a list price minus the manufacturer's discount, a list price minus the retailer's discount, or a manufacturer's suggested retail price, $25.99 is not very informative. It would be much more useful to know the exact breakdown of prices (i.e., the list price, the size of the manufacturer's discount, and the size of the retailer's discount).

Nonregressiveness

Finally, intuitive judgments based on the representativeness heuristic tend to be nonregressive. That is, when they rely too heavily on representativeness, managers overlook the fact that extreme events tend to shift toward the mean on subsequent occasions. For example, when one employee performs extremely well on one occasion, his supervisors tend to expect too much from him in the future. The employee's performance on the one occasion might have been artificially high because of many chance events. Perhaps he was in a good mood, had gotten a lot of sleep the night before, happened to stumble on information that turned out to be extremely useful, and so on. Subsequently, the employee will not perform as well because he is unlikely to have so many fortunate random events stacked up in his favor in the future. Conversely, when another employee performs extremely poorly on one occasion, the employee tends to perform more satisfactorily on subsequent occasions. Perhaps on the first occasion the employee was in a bad mood, had not gotten enough sleep, was unable to obtain the right information, and so on. Similarly, a product that breaks sales records in its first year (because of favorable economic or competitive conditions or because of other chance factors) performs less impressively in subsequent years. A product that performs poorly in its first year (because of unfavorable economic conditions or because of other chance factors) performs more satisfactorily in subsequent years (although often the product is taken off the market before regression to the mean can occur). Extremely good or extremely bad performances tend to be artificially high or low because of chance events or unusual circumstances.

It is extremely difficult to learn the true relationship between events when random events are confused with nonrandom events. For example, Tversky and Kahneman (1974) found that Israeli Air Force pilots observed that trainees frequently performed better following punishment and frequently performed worse after a reward was delivered. The officers concluded that punishment is effective whereas reward is ineffective. However, they overlooked the fact that extremely bad or good performances are likely to be influenced heavily by chance factors. All trainees have their bad days and their good days, and, in the long run, people typically perform at their mean level of performance (rather than at an extreme level). Consequently, an extremely poor performance is likely to be followed by a more typical performance, which is better than an extremely poor performance (regression to the mean). An outstanding performance is likely to be followed by a more typical performance, which is worse than an outstanding performance. Because poor performances are punished and outstanding performances are rewarded, regression to the mean creates the illusion that punishment is effective and reward is ineffective (in reality, both are effective in raising trainees' mean performance levels over time).

Similarly, Cox and Summers (1987) found that industrial buyers underestimate the influence of random factors on sales. Stores that experience extremely low sales in one sales period typically perform better in the next sales period. Stores that experience extremely high sales in one sales period typically perform worse in the next sales period. This is because extreme and atypical outcomes are likely to be followed by more moderate and typical outcomes. One of the main responsibilities of industrial buyers is to produce accurate sales forecasts to help store managers control inventory costs. When random fluctuations in sales are misinterpreted as meaningful fluctuations, extreme predictions, overordering for successful stores, and underordering for unsuccessful stores result.

THE AVAILABILITY HEURISTIC

Managers' predictive judgments are also influenced by the **availability heuristic.** This heuristic involves searching memory for relevant examples of the event one is trying to predict and basing one's prediction on the ease with which these examples come to mind. If examples come to mind quickly and easily (i.e., if examples are readily available from memory), the event one is trying to predict seems highly likely. Conversely, if examples do not come to mind readily, the event one is trying to predict seems highly unlikely. For instance, suppose an insurance salesman is trying to predict the likelihood that an earthquake will damage a client's home. If the salesman remembers many earthquakes, he will predict that future earthquakes are likely to occur. If he does not recall any earthquakes, he will predict that future earthquakes are unlikely. Of course, the cost of the insurance will be much higher if earthquakes are expected as opposed to unexpected. However, memory for earthquakes is influenced by many factors besides objective frequency. Earthquakes are highly publicized by the media; consequently, earthquakes are very memorable. This makes earthquakes seem more likely than is actually the case. Even in the Bay Area of California, homes are more likely to be damaged by fire than by earthquakes. However, outside California, people are more likely to see Bay Area earthquakes than Bay Area fires in the news. Moreover, events that occurred recently are much more memorable than events that occurred long ago. Events that occurred nearby are more memorable than events that occurred far away. Memory is influenced by many factors; consequently, basing predictions on memory can lead to highly erroneous predictions. It is better to base one's predictions on carefully recorded facts. This is why most insurance companies rely on actuarial data rather than on memory.

THE SIMULATION HEURISTIC

Just as a single event that is easy to retrieve in memory seems very likely to occur (the availability heuristic), a single event or sequence of events that is easy to imagine (or to simulate) also seems very likely to occur (the **simulation heuristic**). Simply imagining the occurrence of a hypothetical event increases the perceived likelihood of the event. Consumers who are asked to imagine using and enjoying cable television believe they are more likely to actually subscribe to cable television (Gregory, Cialdini, & Carpenter, 1982). Voters who are asked to imagine a particular political candidate winning an election believe that the candidate is actually more likely to win (Carroll, 1978). Sports fans who are asked to imagine one team winning believe that the team is actually more likely to win (Hirt & Sherman, 1985; Sherman, Zehner, Johnson, & Hirt, 1983). People who are asked to imagine contracting a disease believe that they are actually more likely to contract the disease (Sherman, Cialdini, Schwartzman, & Reynolds, 1985). Virtually any event seems more likely after one imagines its occurrence ("I can see that happening"). An event that is difficult to imagine, however, does not seem more likely after one attempts (and fails) to imagine its occurrence ("I can't see that happening"; Anderson, 1983; Anderson & Godfrey, 1987; Anderson, Lepper, & Ross, 1980; Sherman & Corty, 1984). Hence, imagining appears to make it so, even when our imaginations are not closely linked to reality.

Similarly, imagining the occurrence of a complex sequence of events makes this sequence of events seem more likely. An imagined sequence of events is a scenario. The finding that an imagined sequence of events seems more likely is known as the *scenario effect* (Dawes, 1988). If you ask managers how likely it is that a new product that sells very poorly in its first year will become the market leader by the end of its second year, most managers would respond that this scenario is very unlikely. Now imagine asking a manager how likely it is that a new product will sell poorly in its first year, be acquired by a larger firm with greater resources, be redesigned and marketed more effectively, and, finally, become the market leader by the end of its second year. The latter scenario seems much less unlikely even though it is actually more unlikely than the former scenario.

The reason for this is that the latter scenario is subsumed by the former scenario. The former scenario includes the latter scenario and many other possible scenarios for the turnaround of a failing product. The outcome "becomes the market leader by the end of its second year" includes the sequence "will be acquired by a larger and more successful firm that redesigns the product, markets it more effectively, and turns it into the market leader by the end of its second year" and many other possible sequences as well. One specific sequence cannot be more likely than any one of many possible different specified and unspecified sequences.

Even if each of the individual events described in the latter scenario are quite likely, the likelihood of their joint occurrence is surprisingly low. Suppose, for example, that the likelihood of each individual event in the sequence is 80 percent. That is, the probability of failure in the first year is .8, the probability of acquisition is .8, the probability of redesign is .8, the probability of developing a more effective marketing plan is .8, and the probability of becoming the market leader is .8. Subjectively, the likelihood of this particular scenario seems like it should be a little less than .8. Objectively, the likelihood of this particular scenario is $.8 \times .8 \times .8 \times .8 \times .8 = .33$. Just as our imaginations make it seem that a single event is more likely to occur, our imaginations also make it seem that a complex sequence of events is more likely to occur. We recognize that imagination allows us to depart from reality, but we fail to realize how far these departures really are. This leads to poor predictions when we attempt to predict by imagining the occurrence of a single event and even poorer predictions when we attempt to predict by imagining the occurrence of a complex sequence of events.

THE ANCHORING-AND-ADJUSTMENT HEURISTIC

Probability estimates or predictions can be based on many different types of information—such as the degree of similarity between a causal factor and the target event a manager is attempting to predict (the representativeness heuristic), the ease with which examples of the target event can be retrieved from memory (the availability heuristic), and the ease with which the target event can be imagined to occur (the simulation heuristic). Often, however, a situation is so ambiguous that the manager does not know where to begin when attempting to make a prediction. In these cases, even random anchors, or "starting points," can influence where the manager begins. This is the **anchoring-and-adjustment heuristic.**

For example, suppose a manager is interested in introducing a popular U.S. product to an international market. This particular manager is responsible for one specific international market, the African market. However, he or she recognizes that the product is inappropriate for all African nations, and he or she believes that the safest strategy is to introduce the product only to African nations belonging to the United Nations (UN), because these nations are likely to be better developed. Most managers do not know how many African nations belong to the UN. However, if they are given an anchor, or a "starting point," they can usually guess whether the actual number is greater or smaller than the starting point. Tversky and Kahneman (1974) presented subjects with a spinning wheel with numbers ranging from 1 to 100; the wheel was rigged to stop at either a high (65) or a low (10) number. Although subjects thought that the wheel was random, the high and low starting points had a profound effect on their estimates. In the high-starting-point (65) condition, subjects guessed that the actual percent was lower, and their average estimate was that 45 percent of African nations belong to the UN. In the low-starting-point (10) condition, subjects guessed that the actual percent was higher, and their average estimate was 25 percent. In both conditions, subjects' estimates were too close to the initial anchor. That is, their adjustments from the initial anchor were insufficient (underadjustment). Consequently, subjects in the high-starting-point condition overestimated the percent of African nations belonging to the UN, whereas subjects in the low-starting-point condition underestimated the percent of African nations belonging to the UN (the correct answer is 35 percent).

Even expert decision makers are heavily influenced by anchors, or initial estimates. In an important study, expert real estate agents were asked to estimate the value of a house. Even though the agents spent several hours examining the same house, their final estimates were remarkably close to the anchor list price that was provided to them by the experimenter: Those who randomly received a low list price seriously undervalued the house, whereas those who were given a high list price significantly overvalued the house (Northcraft & Neale, 1987).

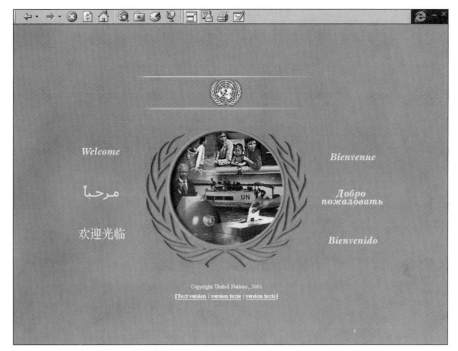

Managers now have a new resource available to assist with decision making. Instead of guessing how many African nations belong to the United Nations, they could access its Web site (www.un.org) and explore there.

Source: This Home Page is maintained by the UN Department of Public Information with the technical support of the Information Technology Services Division. © United Nations 1997.

Anchoring and adjustment is also involved in evaluating a risky decision, or a gamble. A gamble has two components: an outcome (e.g., the amount of money potentially available) and a probability (e.g., the likelihood of obtaining the outcome). For example, suppose Gamble A has an 11/36 probability of winning $16 and a 25/36 probability of losing $1.50, whereas Gamble B has a 35/36 probability of winning $4 and a 1/36 probability of losing $1 (the expected values of both gambles are about $3.85). When asked to indicate a "selling price" for each gamble (i.e., the amount of money they would charge others to play each gamble), most subjects focus on the outcomes and charge more for Gamble A because it has a greater outcome. However, when asked to indicate which gamble they themselves would prefer to play, most subjects anchor on the probabilities and choose Gamble B because the likelihood of winning is greater (Slovic & Lichtenstein, 1983; Tversky, Slovic, & Kahneman, 1990). This is known as a **preference reversal,** because subjects prefer one gamble when they anchor on outcomes but prefer the other gamble when they anchor on probabilities. (See Fig. 15-3.) This phenomenon is inconsistent with **subjective expected utility theory,** which suggests that preferences are stable and that people should always choose the gamble with the maximum expected utility (Slovic, 1995).

Although managers do not like to think of their alternative courses of action as gambles, an option is always linked to an outcome that can be achieved with some probability of success (this is the definition of a gamble). For example, product man-

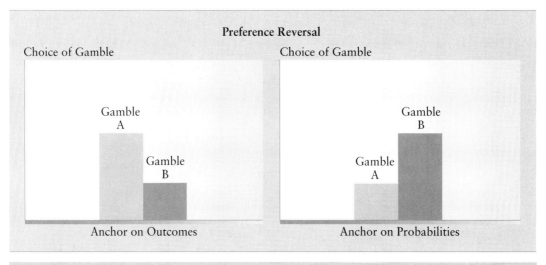

FIGURE 15-3

In preference reversal, subjects prefer one gamble when they anchor on outcomes and another when they anchor on probabilities.

agers must decide which new product concepts (or ideas) should be launched and which new product concepts should be abandoned. These decisions should be based on estimates of the probability of success for each new product concept and on estimates of profit potential if a particular new product concept is successful. In one study, subjects were asked to choose between pairs of new product concepts where one concept had a greater probability of success and the other concept had greater profit potential (Mowen & Gentry, 1980). When subjects were asked to indicate which option of each pair of options should be launched, they preferred the options with the greater probability of success. By contrast, when subjects were asked to assign dollar values to each option of each pair of options, they preferred the options with the greater profit potential. This pattern of results suggests that managers anchor on probabilities when deciding whether to launch or abandon a new product concept. However, managers anchor on profit potential when assessing the value of a new product concept. Focusing on different anchors in different situations leads to inconsistent preferences.

Did marketing managers who chose to enter the sports utility vehicle markets gamble?
Source: © Dick Morton.

How serious is the problem of preference reversal? Consider the decision faced regularly by oil company executives. Any given drilling site has some probability of success and some level of profit potential if oil is found. Kerr (1979) found that oil companies paid over $1 billion for the privilege of drilling in the Baltimore Canyon (in the Atlantic Ocean), even though leading oil geochemists determined that the probability of finding oil there was extremely low. Kerr (1979) suggested that oil company executives focused on the extremely large size of potential trapping structures in the Baltimore Canyon (profit potential) and neglected the probabilities provided by the geochemists. Ideally, of course, billion-dollar decisions should be based on both probabilities and potential.

◆ BIASES RESULTING FROM OVERPROCESSING

Busy decision makers are often unmotivated or unable to consider each and every piece of information that appears relevant to a particular judgment or decision. Under these circumstances, a relatively small sample of information is considered and cognitive heuristics are used to simplify judgment and decision making. Of course, "under-processing" leads to poor decisions when key pieces of information are overlooked or when the implications of information are not carefully considered. Ironically, "over-processing" can also lead to poor decisions. (See "Making the Decision: Deciding on Defense.") When decision makers are motivated and able to consider large amounts of information very carefully, they may read too much into irrelevant information. When irrelevant information is overinterpreted, it may seem relevant. Consequently, over-processing may result in overuse of irrelevant evidence.

CORRESPONDENCE BIAS

Managers are often unable to express their true opinions about a job-related topic because, in most firms, strong situational pressures exist that prevent managers from expressing them. Written and unwritten rules exert a powerful influence on managers while they perform their job-related functions. When situational constraints or norms (i.e., rules) require people to behave a certain way, norm-consistent behaviors provide little or no information about personal dispositions (personality characteristics and personal opinions). Nevertheless, managers tend to overinterpret the behavior of other individuals and, consequently, tend to draw strong inferences based on weak evidence. This phenomenon is known as the **correspondence bias** because observable behaviors are perceived to correspond with unobservable dispositions (personality traits, personal opinions) even when the behaviors are actually influenced by the situation (Jones & Davis, 1965; Gilbert & Jones, 1986; Gilbert, Jones, & Pelham, 1987; Gilbert & Krull, 1988; Gilbert & Malone, 1995).

Consider the job interview, for example. Job applicants are not free to behave as they typically behave. Instead, most job applicants form impressions of the type of traits and characteristics that are required to perform a particular job effectively (e.g., salespeople are supposed to be gregarious, market researchers are supposed to be brainy, brand managers are supposed to be confident, etc.). Consequently, during the job interview they tend to behave in a manner that implies that they possess these traits and characteristics. The interview situation imposes powerful constraints on the behavior of job applicants; consequently, normative behaviors are uninformative (of

DECIDING ON DEFENSE

If anything, most of us probably hope that decisions relating to national and world defense suffer from biases related to overprocessing rather than underprocessing. In the case of competition among defense contractors, overprocessing seems to be winning out.

The defense industry is complicated. Boeing is merging with McDonnell Douglas, giving the combined organization about $36 billion in revenues per year. Lockheed Martin boasts sales of $20 billion per year in its pure defense business (not including other segments of its business). Boeing and Lockheed have been quarreling over markets not only in the United States but in Europe and Asia as well. And that's just the beginning of the tangled story.

Anytime a decision is made in the defense industry, politics, finances, and technology all become part of the maneuvering. For instance, when the military wants a new plane—such as the Joint Strike Fighter—the contract is worth huge amounts of money, jobs, and prestige. The Joint Strike Fighter, ordered by the Air Force, Navy, and Marines, is worth $210 billion. Boeing and McDonnell Douglas both bid on the project, and Boeing won, but because of the merger, both win. Sort of. Correspondence bias—the necessity of making politically expedient decisions—plays heavily in the defense industry. The British government also wants the Joint Strike Fighter for its military. Politics dictate that British Aerospace be involved with the project, even though the company helped McDonnell Douglas with its initial losing bid. Recognizing an opportunity, Lockheed has also been wooing British Aerospace. If either American firm wins a partnership with British Aerospace, the alliance will help the American firm grow abroad. Although British Aerospace fits Boeing from a technological standpoint, British Aerospace also has a 20 percent stake in Airbus, which is a bitter rival of Boeing. So an alliance between Lockheed and British Aerospace might make more sense in terms of corporate politics.

Boeing and Lockheed have not confined their maneuvering to the United States and Western Europe. Boeing is taking a stake in the Czech firm Aero Vodochody after both firms examined the company, and the former is the prime contractor for the international space station (via its acquisition of Rockwell), the shuttle, and the Delta rocket (via its alliance with McDonnell Douglas). Lockheed builds Atlas and Titan rockets and will be building a replacement space shuttle. Lockheed and McDonnell Douglas have both been selected by the U.S. Air Force to compete for a new rocket.

Boeing and Lockheed have different strategies for making decisions in this incredibly complex market. Both have the same goal of being the leader in the effort to tie together all the parts of a complete weapons system. Boeing plans to stick to making complete aircraft rather than all the electronic components that go into the aircraft. Alan Mulally, president of Boeing's defense and space business, notes that "a vertically integrated company could take its eye off the ball and lose its ability to pick the best [technology]."

Lockheed Martin, on the other hand, has bought up a number of defense electronics companies, using the strategy that it can gain the most control by manufacturing everything. However, Norman Augustine, Lockheed's chairman, insists that each of Lockheed's separate divisions will stand on its own as a business unit. This strategy is intended to maintain a flexible company. Each of these strategies could suffer from the perseverance effect—that is, once the companies are committed to huge decisions involving billions of dollars, they are unlikely to change their beliefs about their strategies, whether or not they are successful. Ultimately, the marketplace—and world events—will determine which company's strategy will pay off.

Source: "Missile to Queen's Rook Four," *The Economist,* May 17, 1997, pp. 67–68. © 1997 The Economist Newspaper Group, Inc.

course, counternormative behaviors, such as showing up at the interview in jeans, are very informative). Nonetheless, most interviewers believe that they can learn a lot about the dispositions of most interviewees on the basis of situationally constrained behaviors.

Situational constraints force brand managers to emit an air of confidence. This is necessary, of course, because their assistants work much harder if they believe their brands are likely to be successful (if success is impossible, why work hard?). However, executives who observe the confident behaviors of their brand managers are likely to infer that the brand managers really believe their brands will succeed. This inference is incorrect because their confident behaviors were actually determined by their situation, not by their beliefs. However, if an executive infers that a brand manager really believes a brand will succeed and the brand fails, the executive may conclude that the brand manager exhibited poor judgment. This conclusion is likely to influence the executive's performance evaluation of the brand manager.

USING IRRELEVANT ANALOGIES

Often people we meet remind us of old acquaintances because their speech, clothing, or mannerisms are similar. When this happens, we often infer that two people who appear to be similar on some irrelevant dimension are also likely to possess similar traits and characteristics (Gilovich, 1981). For example, an interviewer may feel reluctant to hire a particular job candidate because the candidate is from the same hometown as a previous employee who was extremely unsuccessful. A brand manager may decide to launch a new product that performs poorly in pretest markets because it reminds him or her of another similarly packaged product that performed poorly in pretest markets but nevertheless turned out to be successful. An executive may decide to engage in a price war with an aggressive competitor because the competitor reminds him or her of a previous competitor with a similar corporate name that was driven out of business by a price war. Although focusing on similarities and reasoning by analogy can be a useful analytic strategy, reasoning based on irrelevant analogies can lead to poor decisions.

THE PERSEVERANCE EFFECT

Decision makers often continue to perceive a belief as true even when the basis for the belief is disproved. In the classic study on the perseverance effect, subjects received false feedback bearing on their performance on a judgment task (Ross, Lepper, & Hubbard, 1975). Half the subjects were told they performed extremely well on the task (success condition), and half were told they performed extremely poorly (failure condition). Subjects were randomly assigned to success or failure conditions; consequently, performance feedback was unrelated to actual performance. Later, subjects were told that the feedback was false and that they were randomly assigned to experimental conditions. The results indicated that even though subjects recognized that the feedback was false, those who were randomly assigned to the success condition continued to believe that they would perform well on this task in the future, and those who were randomly assigned to the failure condition continued to believe that they would perform poorly. Ross et al. (1975) suggest that random feedback is uninformative and should be ignored. Nevertheless, people tend to overinterpret uninformative feedback and attempt to generate explanations for the feedback (e.g., "I'm the type of person who would do well on this type of judgment task"). Subsequently, if the feedback is eliminated but the explanations for the feedback are not eliminated, the explanations continue to provide support for the original belief. As a result, the belief is remarkably persistent even when the basis for the belief is removed.

Unfortunately, the **perseverance effect** applies to any belief the decision maker may form, even erroneous beliefs. For example, a brand manager who worked with an ad agency to develop a novel advertising execution observed that sales increased dramatically after the ad was launched (success feedback). The brand manager concluded that this type of advertising execution is extremely effective. A good brand manager tries to understand why an ad is effective, and, consequently, the brand manager is likely to think of many reasons why the ad appeared to be so successful. Of course, many factors influence sales, and advertising is just one factor. In this particular case, the increase in sales was actually produced by a distribution difficulty affecting a major competitor at the time the ad was launched; the ad itself was completely ineffective. Nevertheless, the brand manager will continue to believe the ad execution is effective and will continue to use this execution in future ad campaigns, provided that he or she is not fired for running ineffective ads while media costs continue to skyrocket.

THE DILUTION EFFECT

The judgmental impact of diagnostic information is often diluted by the presence of nondiagnostic information (Nisbett, Zukier, & Lemley, 1981). This is known as the **dilution effect.** For example, subjects who were told that John has an extremely high grade point average (GPA) predicted that John would continue to earn extremely high grades in future courses. However, subjects who were told that John has an extremely high GPA, drives a Honda, wears plaid shirts, and used to work part-time as a draftsman, predicted that John would earn moderately high grades in future courses (Zukier, 1982). Hence, irrelevant information (e.g., drives a Honda, wears plaid shirts, used to work part-time as a draftsman) reduces the effect of relevant information (e.g., extremely high GPA), and less extreme inferences are formed when irrelevant information is present (versus absent). Moreover, the dilution effect is even more pronounced when subjects expect to justify their predictions to others (Tetlock & Boettger, 1989). Although irrelevant information should have no effect on judgment, managers tend to overinterpret, read too much between the lines, and weigh irrelevant information too heavily in judgment, especially when they are likely to overprocess all available information (including irrelevant information) because they expect to justify their judgments and decisions to superiors.

PREMATURE COGNITIVE COMMITMENT

Irrelevant information is also weighed too heavily in judgment when irrelevant information later becomes relevant (Chanowitz & Langer, 1981). For example, consumers are often exposed to ads for products that they would not consider purchasing. The information provided in these ads is likely to be accepted at face value, because consumers are unlikely to think extensively about irrelevant products. Consequently, even conclusions supported by weak arguments are likely to be encoded incidentally into long-term memory. Later, when consumers' attitudes, hobbies, or interests change, prior beliefs are likely to be weighed heavily in judgment even if these prior beliefs were based originally on weak evidence. For instance, children are exposed to many automobile ads. Although they are not old enough to purchase an automobile, much of the information presented in the ads is likely to be accepted uncritically with little or no counterargumentation. Years later, when children grow up and need to decide which brand of automobile they should purchase, they may be influenced unduly by prior beliefs formed on the basis of weak evidence that was accepted uncritically. Of course, **premature cognitive commitment** is not limited to children. Anyone who pursues a new hobby or a new interest is susceptible to the effects of prior beliefs that were formed on the basis of information that was accepted uncritically with little thought or elaboration.

When a manager accepts a new position in his or her own firm, or when a manager accepts a new position at another firm, his or her interests are likely to change. Unfortunately, interests change much more readily than prior beliefs. If prior beliefs were formed on the basis of information that was accepted uncritically, prior beliefs that should be ignored may continue to influence judgments and decisions. For example, if a manager heard that a particular product offered by another division or firm was positioned effectively, he or she may accept this conclusion without thinking carefully about its validity. Why think carefully about products that have no direct bearing on the products for which you are personally responsible? However, if circumstances change and you later become responsible for the "well-positioned" product, you may consider a change in pricing strategy rather than a change in positioning strategy because you believe (for the wrong reasons) that the product is positioned effectively.

OVERCORRECTION

The use of the anchoring-and-adjustment heuristic results in insufficient adjustment from an anchor or reference point. However, if a manager recognizes that an anchor can bias his or her judgments, he or she is likely to attempt to correct for the bias, and overadjustment, or **overcorrection,** can occur (Petty & Wegener, 1993; Wegener & Petty, 1995). For example, suppose an interviewer happens to be in an especially good mood one day. If the interviewer fails to recognize that this good mood could cause him or her to form favorable first impressions of job candidates, final evaluations of these candidates are likely to be adjusted insufficiently from the first impression anchor, and the candidates will be judged too favorably (an assimilation effect). However, if an interviewer recognizes and attempts to correct for the biasing effects of positive mood on judgment, the interviewer is likely to overcorrect, final evaluations are likely to be overadjusted, and the candidates will be judged too unfavorably (a contrast effect). Overcorrection occurs when managers overanalyze and overinterpret their decision-making processes.

CHAPTER SUMMARY ▪

Executives, managers, and decision makers are susceptible to a relatively lengthy list of judgmental biases. Some of these biases stem from attention and memory constraints. People are unable to attend to or remember all judgment-relevant information. Unfortunately, the risk of inaccurate judgment and suboptimal decision making exists whenever relevant information is overlooked or neglected. Underprocessing biases result when managers are unmotivated or unable to integrate judgment-relevant information in a systematic fashion. Under these circumstances, managers rely too heavily on cognitive heuristics, or shortcuts, that simplify judgment and decision making. By contrast, overprocessing biases result when managers overinterpret irrelevant information. Hence, judgmental accuracy is influenced jointly by the amount of processing effort a decision maker is likely to allocate to a judgment task and by the nature of the evidence available for judgment (e.g., the amount of relevant and irrelevant information that is present). Fortunately, decision researchers have achieved a deeper understanding of the psychological processes involved in judgment and decision making. One result of this deeper understanding is the development of debiasing procedures and decision aids that dramatically improve judgment and decision making. The following chapter turns to these debiasing techniques.

KEY CONCEPTS

- Risk-averse
- Risk-seeking
- Loss aversion
- Diminishing sensitivity
- Biased assimilation
- Diagnosticity
- Pseudodiagnosticity
- Selective hypothesis testing
- Group Decision Making

- Common-knowledge effect
- Group polarization
- Groupthink
- Representativeness heuristic
- Availability heuristic
- Simulation heuristic
- Anchoring-and-adjustment heuristic

- Preference reversal
- Subjective expected utility theory
- Correspondence bias
- Perseverance effect
- Dilution effect
- Premature cognitive commitment
- Overcorrection

DISCUSSION QUESTIONS

1. In what ways do salience and vividness affect managers' decisions? Are these good criteria for managerial decisions? Why or why not?
2. After a couple decides to get married, deciding where to eat dinner that night seems minor. What type of effect does this situation illustrate? Give three other examples illustrating this effect.
3. Imagine that your best friend is assigned an end-of-term project that includes a written report as well as an oral presentation. Without naming names, predict how you think your friend would handle the project. Would he or she begin early? Do a lot of research? Wait until the last minute to begin the project? Ask the instructor for an extension? Do as little work as possible? Try an innovative approach? Ask friends for help?

     On what information did you base your predictions? What type of bias effect does this exercise illustrate?
4. Name and describe briefly the four key cognitive heuristics that people use to simplify judgment making.
5. How might managers in industries like financial services, insurance, and health care use the availability heuristic to make decisions?

6. How might the simulation heuristic help or hinder or the success of a new product?
7. What do you think is the single most common reason that managers engage in underprocessing?
8. Why do personal interviews sometimes provide unreliable information?
9. Describe an instance in which you made a decision based on an irrelevant analogy.
10. How might premature cognitive commitment come into play when a person is promoted from a staff position to a managerial position?

CHAPTER

16

Strategies for Improving Managerial Decision Making

◆ Decision Frame Management
◆ Epistemic Unfreezing
◆ Increasing Predictive Accuracy
    What's the Base Rate?
    Assessing the Reliability and Validity of Information
    Distinguishing between Convergence and Redundancy
    Resisting Scenario Thinking
    Avoiding Overconfidence
◆ Judgment Updating and Revision

It's hard to imagine a world where there are no jeans—straight leg, boot cut, flared, stretch. Levi's have been with us for more than 100 years, when German-born dry-goods wholesaler Levi Strauss was approached by a Nevada tailor named Jacob Davis. Davis had an idea for work pants with pockets that were reinforced by metal rivets, but he needed $68 to file a patent for the idea. Strauss came up with the money, and together, the two produced the first pair of "waist-high overalls."

Since then, thousands of pairs of jeans have come and gone from the Levi's factory, amid thousands of managerial decisions. Some of those decisions have involved product development—for instance, the creation of entire product lines such as women's wear and Dockers. Some have involved social responsibility, as when Levi's discovered that two of its sewing contractors in Bangladesh were using child labor. (Levi's chose to remove the children from the factories but continued to pay their salaries as long as they attended school.) Some have involved the entire structure of the company, as was the case recently when top managers announced a program of sweeping change that included having employees resign and reapply for jobs.

Many of Levi's decisions have been a response to customer preferences and complaints. Prior to reengineering, Thomas M. Kasten, Levi's vice president and member of the company's U.S. Leadership Team, listened to customers tell him, "We trust many of your competitors implicitly. We sample their deliveries. We open all Levi's deliveries. Your lead times are the worst. If you weren't Levi's, you'd be gone." Clearly, change was necessary. The multibillion-dollar company was a leader in its field, but it had become overconfident. Well known for its attention to ethics, its humane treatment of workers, and its brand name, Levi's was failing terribly at satisfying its channel members.

So management embarked on an incredibly ambitious effort to reengineer the company—perhaps too ambitious. The cost of the program topped $850 million, employees were thrown into a state of chaos about what their jobs would be, and the time line for completion of changes grew much longer than intended by its planners. Goals for the change were unclear, yet the money flowed because the company had enjoyed such solid success for so long. Board member Warren Hellman recalls, "[We had the atmosphere of] 'Well, we've got a lot of cash, the business is doing wonderfully, we can spend our way through this thing.' We were too casual at the outset." Eventually, Thomas Kasten admitted, "It became clear to us that what we were trying to achieve was not doable."

The results were traumatic, including a leveraged buyout and a round of layoffs. But Levi's is still in business. Although competitors have gained ground, Levi's still rakes in $7.1 billion per year. And although layoffs at Levi's are unprecedented, they amount to just 2 percent of the company's employees. In addition, no one doubts that Levi's will find ways to take care of the employees it releases. Even fewer people doubt that Levi's will be around for another 100 years.

As you read this chapter, consider carefully the consequences that managers face when they try to make predictions about outcomes without using systematic strategies.

Sources: Stratford Sherman, "Levi's," *Fortune,* May 12, 1997, pp. 104–116; David Sheff, "Levi's Changes Everything," *The Greatest Hits,* Vol. 1, 1997, pp. 24–31.

◆ INTRODUCTION

As Chapter 15 emphasized, managers (and all people) are susceptible to a wide variety of judgment and decision-making biases and errors, as were Levi's managers. This final chapter discusses techniques for overcoming biases and for improving managerial judgment and decision making. Busy decision makers tend to consider a small amount of information and often fail to consider the quality of the information or the strength of the evidence that is readily available. Managers needing to meet tight deadlines tend to use heuristics that lead them to overlook important pieces of information (under-processing) in some circumstances. Conversely, managers allocating large amounts of time and effort to important business decisions tend to use too much information and to overinterpret and overweigh irrelevant or tangentially relevant information (over-processing). Fortunately, scientific research has increased our understanding of these problems and has led to the development of debiasing techniques that help managers to make better judgments and decisions.

◆ DECISION FRAME MANAGEMENT

The first step in decision making is to consider how a decision problem should be framed or interpreted, known as **decision frame management.** That is, what are the options, costs, and benefits associated with each option? Decision makers sometimes consider only one option and therefore run into trouble right at the start. Statistically, the more options that are considered, the greater the chance of finding the best option. Focusing narrowly on only one or two options often leads managers to overlook many important alternatives. Moreover, as research on the framing effect has shown, once the options have been identified, managers tend to focus mainly on costs (losses) or benefits (gains). Ideally, of course, managers should weigh costs and benefits equally because the asymmetric treatment of costs and benefits often leads to decisions that decision makers later regret. This occurs because focusing mainly on costs leads decision makers to be risk-seeking and to prefer options that offer a chance of avoiding a loss even if that chance is fairly slim. Conversely, focusing mainly on benefits leads decision makers to be risk-averse and to accept options that virtually guarantee a good outcome, even though riskier options may provide even better outcomes. If decision makers focus mainly on costs initially, they are likely to choose a risky option. If they later focus on benefits, they may wish they had chosen a less risky option and may regret their earlier decision. Preference reversals, however, are much less likely to occur when decision makers routinely treat costs and benefits as equally important.

A classic case of decision frame mismanagement occurred in the early 1970s when the U.S. automobile industry exhibited frame blindness while the Japanese automobile industry developed innovative new solutions to old production problems (Russo & Schoemaker, 1989). The U.S. automobile industry continued to use an operations research frame, or perspective, whereas the Japanese automobile industry was open to new frames and new perspectives. The operations research perspective suggests that the best way to control production costs is to produce many units of the same component (or set of components) before resetting the plant equipment to produce a different component. Frequently, thousands of units would be produced before the equipment would be changed to make a different type of component. This frame, however, makes sense only if it takes a long time (e.g., hours) to reset plant equipment to make different types of components. Instead of blindly accepting this assumption, the Japanese developed a way to reset plant equipment in a matter of minutes (rather than hours) and this innovation allowed the Japanese to offer a greater variety of models of automobiles while controlling costs and quality. This led to the downturn of the once seemingly invincible U.S. automobile industry.

Frames, perspectives, and assumptions should be questioned frequently, and decision makers should be willing to consider a wide range of frames, perspectives, and options. Moreover, managers should carefully consider the costs and the benefits of each decision option and avoid focusing too heavily on costs or benefits. Focusing too heavily on one or the other can lead to a decision that managers later regret when they consider the decision from a different perspective.

◆   EPISTEMIC UNFREEZING

Decision makers must frequently make a difficult trade-off between speed and accuracy. Some problems demand immediate action, and managers must make quick decisions. Other problems do not require immediate attention, which affords managers the opportunity to think about the problem more carefully for a longer period of time. Quick decisions run the risk of serving as mere "band-aids," or as temporary and partial solutions to a problem. Long periods of deliberation usually result in better decisions. How do managers make this difficult trade-off between speed and accuracy (or quality of a decision)? Recent research based on Kruglanski's (1989, 1990; Kruglanski & Webster, 1996) **theory of lay epistemology** (or theory of everyday knowledge formation and use) suggests that individuals differ in the degree to which they exhibit the **need for cognitive closure** and that situations differ in the extent to which they elicit this need. The need for cognitive closure is defined as a desire for definite knowledge—any knowledge rather than confusion or ambiguity. As the need for cognitive closure increases, people consider fewer alternatives, consider smaller amounts of information about each alternative, draw snap conclusions that have obvious and immediate implications for action, are insensitive to evidence inconsistent with these conclusions, and exhibit high levels of confidence in the appropriateness of their conclusions, decisions, and actions.

In short, the need for cognitive closure promotes **epistemic seizing** and **epistemic freezing.** *Seizing* refers to the tendency to attain closure quickly, even if this means oversimplifying an issue or failing to carefully consider all sides of an issue. *Freezing* refers to the tendency to maintain closure as long as possible, even if this means being closed-minded or unwilling to consider alternatives. People differ in their need for closure—some are strongly motivated to reach conclusions quickly at the risk of overlooking important qualifiers and limiting conditions; others are willing to deliberate carefully for a long period of time at the risk of appearing indecisive or unconfident. Situations also differ in the extent to which they increase or decrease the need for closure. Deadlines and time pressures increase the motivation to attain closure quickly. Concerns about accuracy and the long-term consequences of one's actions decrease the motivation to attain closure quickly.

Many firms try to hire decisive and confident people. Moreover, deadlines and severe time pressures are part of everyday life in the business environment. Some firms, like Procter & Gamble, have a rule stating that all memos must be limited to one page. This rule forces managers to oversimplify the issues, sweep complexities and ambiguities under a rug, and focus on a single clear course of action. It also forces managers to be "one-armed" psychologists and economists—only one possible scenario is offered, and managers are not allowed to waver by saying, "On the other hand. . . ." Of course, the dangers of oversimplifying and jumping to conclusions too readily include overlooking important information (including information inconsistent with a conclusion), overlooking important alternative courses of action (opportunity costs), and failing to develop contingency plans and safety measures to guard against potentially bad decisions.

Fortunately, many firms require their managers to justify and explain their judgments and decisions to a higher-ranking officer of the firm. Accountability pressures motivate managers to adopt the perspective of a senior executive when this perspective is known, or they motivate managers to think in more integratively complex ways about an issue when the senior officer's perspective is unknown (Kruglanski, 1989, 1990; Kruglanski & Webster, 1996; Tetlock, 1992). Simply adopting the perspective of the senior executive is potentially dangerous if this perspective is biased or limited in some way. A safer strategy is for the senior executive to hide his or her personal preferences and biases to force managers to think in more integratively complex ways. Integrative complexity means considering a wider range of options and considering the implications of greater amounts of information pertaining to each option. Ideally, managers should not consider just one positioning strategy; they should consider many (e.g., positioning by attributes/benefits, price, use, or user; repositioning). They should not consider just one segmentation strategy; they should consider many (e.g., segmenting by geography, demography, psychographics, or behaviors). Managers should consider many different new product concepts or ideas, many different pricing strategies, many different promotion and advertising strategies, and many different distribution strategies. Unseizing, unfreezing, and considering a wider range of possibilities generally improves managerial judgment and decision making.

◆ INCREASING PREDICTIVE ACCURACY

A critically important element of any decision is predicting what will happen if one option is selected instead of another. (See "Taking Issue: Are Price Wars Worth the Fight?") Unfortunately, extensive research shows that people are not very good at predicting the future (Kahneman, Slovic, & Tversky, 1982; Nisbett & Ross, 1980). Frequently, predictions are overly optimistic. For example, British Columbia agreed to join Canada in 1871 on the condition that the Canadian government would complete production of the transcontinental railroad by 1881 (Buehler, Griffin, & Ross, 1994); this project was not completed until 1885. In 1969, the mayor of Montreal predicted that the 1976 Olympics would feature a new state-of-the-art stadium with the first retractable roof. The mayor also predicted that the entire Olympic exhibition would cost $120 million and "can no more have a deficit than a man can have a baby" (Colombo, 1987, p. 269). The stadium was actually completed in 1989, 13 years following the Montreal Olympics, and the roof alone cost $120 million. More recently, it was predicted that the Eurotunnel, connecting Paris and London, would be completed in 1993 at a cost of about $7 billion; it was actually completed over a year later at a cost of over $15 billion. Yet another example of overoptimistic prediction is provided by the Sydney, Australia, Opera House, which was supposed to be completed in 1963 at a cost of $7 million; a scaled-down version was actually completed in 1973 at a cost of $102 million (Hall, 1980).

The overconfident belief that a project will proceed smoothly as planned is known as the **planning fallacy** (Buehler et al., 1994; Kahneman & Tversky, 1979). The planning fallacy has been shown to occur in major projects, such as those just mentioned, and in more mundane, everyday projects as well. How often have you taken books and schoolwork home over a weekend or a holiday expecting to get a lot of work done only to find that when the next working day rolls around you accomplished nothing at all?

ARE PRICE WARS WORTH THE FIGHT?

It's a knee-jerk reaction: Your competitor slashes prices, so you think you should, too. After all, won't your customers rush to pay your competitor's lower prices, leaving you with empty hands? Not necessarily. Before you decide to cut your prices, you had better do your homework.

"Pricing is a game," says Tom Nagle, a consultant with the Strategic Pricing Group of Boston. When one company takes a step, everyone else responds. The key to success, Nagle claims, is being able to predict how everyone else will respond. That means determining base rates, assessing the reliability and validity of information, and distinguishing between convergence and redundancy. But most managers fall prey to poor methods of decision making. Often, according to Nagle, companies measure their success by market share instead of by profitability. Michael Marn, a partner at McKinsey in charge of pricing practices, notes that companies get themselves into price wars by misreading or misunderstanding what their competitors are doing.

Slashing prices without thoroughly researching the situation can leave a company in much worse shape than it might be if it just rode out a wave of undercutting by competitors. Marn cites the case of one firm whose products clearly dominated the market. When a tiny, start-up competitor built a small factory in a remote area with no plans for expansion, the larger company immediately cut its prices nationwide between 15 percent and 20 percent. The result? The company "gave away profitability for two years," says Marn. If managers had engaged in clear strategies for decision making, they could have done a better job of predicting the outcome of their actions. Instead, they learned the hard way.

What steps do the experts recommend for avoiding price wars? Economists Adam Brandenberger of Harvard and Barry Nalebuff of Yale recommend finding ways to make it less attractive to compete on price. One example is the airline industry (which has been notorious for destructive price wars). If airlines faithfully maintain their frequent-flier programs and make them user-friendly, they won't have to lower prices to attract customers; people seem to value the free tickets more than lower prices. Another step, which may seem unusual, is to refrain from negotiating prices with customers whenever possible. Instead, remain firm. That way, customers concentrate on the value they are getting for their money instead of looking for ways to whittle the price down. Saturn automobile dealers use this approach, no-haggle pricing, and many consumers feel that this is a much more honest approach to selling cars.

In sum, price wars, like all other wars, rarely produce winners. Managers who use more reliable methods to make predictions about the outcomes of their decisions are much more apt to wind up ahead of the game, whatever their game may be.

Source: David R. Henderson, "What Are Price Wars Good For?" *Fortune,* May 12, 1997, p. 156.

Don't feel too bad. Professors do this, too. I completed the first draft of this textbook over a year past my deadline in a signed contract. Fortunately, my publisher is very familiar with the planning fallacy, and knew this would happen.

Why do people fall prey to the planning fallacy so easily? First, people tend to neglect base rates, or previous rates of occurrence (Buehler et al., 1994). The length of time and the costs of completing similar projects in the past provide useful guides for projecting completion times and costs of current projects. However, people often fail to consider base rates. Moreover, even when people do consider base rates they often discount them or treat them as irrelevant by inferring that unusual, unforeseen flukes caused previous plans to go awry. In addition, people tend to imagine themselves working hard on a project. They tend to overestimate the likelihood of an imagined sequence of events (scenario thinking). Scenarios tend to be optimistic generally and may be even more optimistic when the decision maker is trying to please a supervisor or a client. Together, neglecting base rates, discounting relevant past experiences, and scenario thinking can lead to unrealistic predictions that can result in planning disasters.

WHAT'S THE BASE RATE?

One of the most important pieces of information for accurate prediction is the **base rate,** or prior incidence of the to-be-predicted event. Events that have occurred frequently in the past are likely to occur again in the future. Events that have occurred infrequently in the past are less likely to recur. Sometimes, however, representativeness, or similarity, seems like a more appropriate cue for prediction. New products that are similar to other successful products seem likely to succeed, even when the base rate for new-product success is very low. New ads that are similar to other successful ads seem likely to succeed, even when the base rate of success for a particular advertising strategy is very low. Focusing on similarities and neglecting important base rates can lead to very poor predictions, especially when managers focus on salient but trivial similarities. Past success and failure rates are very important for predicting future successes and failures.

One reason people sometimes ignore or underuse base-rate information is because a base rate is a statistic (specifically, a percent) based on a distribution of scores. People not trained in statistics experience difficulty thinking in terms of distributions and find it much easier to approach each decision problem as a unique and isolated case (Kahneman & Lovallo, 1993). Treating each new problem as unique and isolated encourages people to ignore the past, even when the past is highly relevant. Fortunately, people do not always neglect base rates. They use base-rate information when this information is consistent with case-specific information (i.e., when both types of information imply the same conclusion; Lynch & Ofir, 1989). People also use base-rate information when the causal relevance of this information is apparent (Ajzen, 1977) and when they think about several different decision problems with differing base rates at the same time (Fischhoff, Slovic, & Lichtenstein, 1979). Nevertheless, decision makers can often improve their decisions by paying closer attention to base rates and thinking more carefully about the implications of base-rate information.

ASSESSING THE RELIABILITY AND VALIDITY OF INFORMATION

Managers sometimes try to use whatever information is available for solving a decision problem, even when the relevance or usefulness of this information is limited. Consequently, they tend to use differing types and amounts of information for different alternatives and to weigh or use this information inconsistently across alternatives and situations. Moreover, managers tend to be insensitive to the quality or usefulness of the available information. Usefulness is determined by the reliability or stability of the information and by its validity or specificity. **Unreliable information** varies because of poor measurement even when the target does not change (e.g., unreliable economic indicators shift even when the economy does not change). **Invalid information** confounds measures of the target with measures of nontargets (e.g., invalid economic indicators measure changes in the economy and other irrelevant changes). Managers do not routinely consider the reliability and validity of the information available to them. Instead, they tend to use whatever information is readily available, neglect important omissions (missing pieces of information) and limitations of evidence, and treat presented information as if it were complete and highly relevant (Sanbonmatsu, Kardes, & Herr, 1992; Sanbonmatsu, Kardes, & Sansone, 1991; Sanbonmatsu, Kardes, Posavac, & Houghton, 1997).

Unsystematic and inconsistent information use can lead to poor decisions. Ideally, decision options should be evaluated systematically on the same dimensions, and importance weights for each dimension should be held constant across alternatives and situations.

Linear Models

Fortunately, decision aids exist to help managers be more systematic and consistent when evaluating different decision options. One important decision aid is a **linear model** (Dawes, 1988, 1994; Russo & Schoemaker, 1989), which is an equation that contains a list of the most important attributes for evaluating and comparing decision options. Each option is evaluated on each attribute, and each attribute is rated for its importance. This evaluation and rating task forces managers to judge all options on all attributes, and the attribute importance weights do not vary across all alternatives. That is, a linear model forces managers to be systematic and consistent. Moreover, if a linear model is relatively complete (i.e., all important attributes are included in the model), it reduces the chances of overlooking important omissions (missing pieces of information) and increases sensitivity to limitations of evidence.

For example, suppose that a personnel director for a large firm needs to evaluate 100 job applicants to determine which candidates should be hired. The director could simply interview each candidate and hire the ones he or she likes best. This is a poor decision strategy, however, because interviews provide a very small and unrepresentative sample of a candidate's behavior. The sample is small because very little information can be conveyed in a one-hour interview. The sample is unrepresentative because people behave differently in interview situations than in normal, everyday workplace situations.

A better strategy would be to use a linear model. (See Table 16-1.) A file of information is collected for each candidate, including attributes such as the candidate's university degree (e.g., B.B.A. or M.B.A.), quality of the candidate's university (e.g., Stanford, MIT, and Ivy League schools would be rated very high; regional schools would be rated very low), quality of the candidate's letters of recommendation, quality of interviews with the candidate, the candidate's GPA, number of science and math courses completed, and number of years of work experience. Each candidate would be evaluated on each of these attributes, and each attribute would be weighted by importance ratings. Evaluations are made on a scale from 0 (very poor) to 100 (outstanding), and importance ratings are made by allocating 100 points across the attributes (more points indicate greater importance). Extremely important attributes, such as the quality of the candidate's university, would receive a large number of points; less important attributes, such as quality of interviews, would receive a much smaller number of points. This is a **subjective linear model,** because all inputs (evaluations and importance weights) are subjective judgments provided by the director or a committee. The model is systematic because all candidates are compared on all attributes; it is consistent because the attribute importance weights do not change across candidates. The model is used by multiplying the importance weight of an attribute by a candidate's rating for that attribute. This is done for each attribute and the products are added to yield a single overall score for each candidate. The candidates with the top 10 overall scores are hired. Hence, to use a subjective linear model, a decision maker needs to know only how to multiply and add.

TABLE 16-1   A Subjective Linear Model

(a) Summary Sheet of Applicant Information

Applicant	Personal Essay	Selectivity of Undergraduate Institution	Undergraduate Major
1	Poor	Highest	Science
2	Excellent	Above Average	Business
3	Average	Below Average	Other
.	.	.	.
.	.	.	.
.	.	.	.
117	Weak	Least	Business
118	Strong	Above Average	Other
119	Excellent	Highest	Science
120	Strong	Not Very	Business

(b) Rescaled Table for Subjective Linear Model

Applicant	Essay	Selectivity	Major	GPA
1	0	100	100	25
2	100	60	50	91
3	50	40	0	48
.	.	.	.	.
.	.	.	.	.
.	.	.	.	.
117	25	0	50	55
118	75	60	0	72
119	100	100	100	8
120	75	20	50	98
Weights Used	5%	20%	10%	25%

*The overall score was obtained by multiplying the weights shown in the last row with each attribute score and summing these product terms across attributes to arrive at a weighted average.

Data source: Russo & Schoemaker (1989).

Using a subjective linear model is also sometimes referred to as **bootstrapping,** because the model helps the decision maker to pick himself up by his own bootstraps. All inputs to the model are based on the decision maker's subjective judgments, and these inputs are integrated or combined mechanically (through multiplication and addition). (See Table 16-2.) In some situations, however, it is possible to use inputs based solely on objective data (rather than subjective judgments). Such models are known as **objective linear models** or **actuarial models.** Insurance firms, for example, base nearly all their decisions on actuarial data. They keep careful records of automobile theft and accident rates for different groups of potential automobile insurance clients; fire, theft, earthquake, and flood rates for different groups of potential home

TABLE 16-1 Continued

College Grade Point Average	Work Experience	GMAT Verbal	GMAT Quantitative
2.50	10	98%	60%
3.82	0	70%	80%
2.96	15	90%	80%
.	.	.	.
.	.	.	.
3.10	100	98%	99%
3.44	60	68%	67%
2.16	5	85%	25%
3.96	12	30%	58%

Work Experience	GMAT Verbal	GMAT Quantitative	Overall Score*
10	98	60	59.1
0	70	80	67.8
15	90	80	49.0
.	.	.	.
.	.	.	.
100	98	99	59.7
60	68	67	60.0
5	85	25	51.0
12	30	58	54.0
10%	10%	20%	

TABLE 16-2 **Linear Models Improve Prediction**

Types of Judgments Experts Had to Make	Degree of Correlation with the True Outcomes		
	Intuitive Prediction	*"Bootstrapped" Model*	*Objective Model*
Academic Performance of Graduate Students	.19	.25	.54
Life Expectancy of Cancer Patients	−.01	.13	.35
Changes in Stock Prices	.23	.29	.80
Mental Illness Using Personality Tests	.28	.31	.46
Grades and Attitudes in Psychology Course	.48	.56	.62
Business Failures Using Financial Ratios	.50	.53	.67
Student's Ratings of Teaching Effectiveness	.35	.56	.91
Performance of Life Insurance Salesman	.13	.14	.43
IQ Scores Using Rorschach Tests	.47	.51	.54
Mean (across many studies)	.33	.39	.64

Prediction is least accurate for intuition, more accurate with bootstrapping, and most accurate with objective linear models.

Data source: Russo & Schoemaker (1989).

insurance clients; and base rates for fatalities caused by different medical conditions for different groups of potential life insurance clients. Base rates for each relevant event are broken down for each segment to inform insurance salespersons how much to charge each prospective customer. Other types of companies also rely heavily on base rate or actuarial data. Banks, for example, use base rate data to determine credit limits for credit cards or loans to potential clients. (See Table 16-3.)

Linear models are useful any time a large number of alternatives (e.g., different job candidates, different ads, different product concepts, different potential clients) need to be compared on a large number of attributes. The models ensure that all alternatives are compared on all attributes and that the data are used consistently. Unfortunately, many managers are reluctant to use linear models because they think it dehumanizes the decision process or because they arrogantly think they can integrate large amounts of complex information in their heads and do so more effectively than a computer. This is a fallacy. The research evidence is unambiguous: Subjective linear models consistently outperform unaided human judgments, and objective linear models consistently outperform subjective linear models (Dawes, 1988, 1994; Russo & Schoemaker, 1989).

Busy decision makers need decision aids. Managers often think that they use large amounts of information and that they integrate complex configurations of information in ways that cannot be simulated with a computer. However, even when people think they are using large amounts of data and processing it in complex ways, they are usually using small amounts of information and they are usually processing it in a simple manner (Dawes, 1988, 1994; Russo & Schoemaker, 1989).

The Fault Tree

Other types of decision aids also help managers to use information more systematically and more consistently. A **fault tree** is a decision aid that consists of branches, or general categories, of common problems in a system. Each branch is broken down

TABLE 16-3	Credit Scoring System of Major Retail Chain

Zip Code

Zip Codes A	60
Zip Codes B	48
Zip Codes C	41
Zip Codes D	37
Not answered	53

Bank Reference

Checking only	0
Savings only	0
Checking and savings	15
Bank name or loan only	0
No bank reference	7
Not answered	7

Type of Housing

Owns/buying	44
Rents	35
All other	41
Not answered	39

Occupation

Clergy	46
Creative	41
Driver	33
Executive	62
Guard	46
Homemaker	50
Labor	33
Manager	46
Military enlisted	46
Military officer	62
Office staff	46
Outside	33
Production	41
Professional	62
Retired	62
Sales	46
Semiprofessional	50
Service	41
Student	46
Teacher	41

Unemployed	33
All other	46
Not answered	47

Time at Present Address

Less than 6 months	39
6 months–1 year 5 months	30
1 year 6 months–3 years 5 months	27
3 years 6 months–7 years 5 months	30
7 years 6 months–12 years 5 months	39
12 years 6 months or longer	50
Not answered	36

Time with Employer

Less than 6 months	31
6 months–5 years 5 months	24
5 years 6 months–8 years 5 months	26
8 years 6 months–15 years 5 months	31
15 years 6 months or longer	39
Homemakers	39
Retired	31
Unemployed	29
Not answered	29

Finance Company Reference

Yes	0
Other references only	25
No	25
Not answered	15

Other Department Store/Oil Card/Major Credit Card

Department store only	12
Oil card only	12
Major credit card only	17
Department store and oil card	17
Department store and credit card	31
Major credit card and oil card	31
All three	31
Other references only	0
No credit	0
Not answered	12

Data source: Russo & Schoemaker (1989).

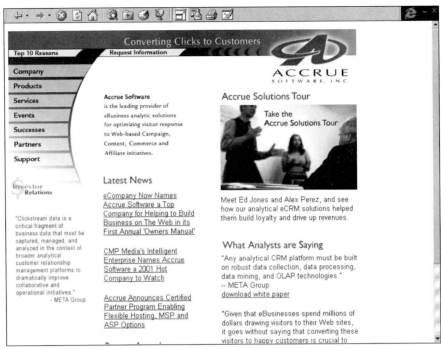

Accrue's data mining software helps managers deal with large amounts of information so they can avoid the decision biases discussed in this chapter and make better decisions.

further into specific examples of a general category of problems. (See Fig. 16-1.) Fault trees are used for troubleshooting or identifying causes of problems in many different industries—including restaurant management, hospital administration, nuclear power plant administration, and NASA space shuttle launch management (Dube-Rioux & Russo, 1988; Fischhoff, Slovic, & Lichtenstein, 1978; Hirt & Castellan, 1988; Russo & Kolzow, 1994). A well-designed fault tree helps managers to identify causes for problems in a system faster than would be possible if managers had to think of common causes on their own. For example, imagine that a manager is concerned about a restaurant suffering from declining profits. A restaurant fault tree suggests that this problem may stem primarily from one of two possibilities: decreasing revenues or increasing costs (Dube-Rioux & Russo, 1988). The decreasing revenues branch is broken down into two more branches: decreasing number of customers and decreasing average check sizes. These branches are broken down further into numerous examples of causes for each problem. This fault tree is quite comprehensive and provides lists of many common problems that a manager might otherwise overlook. Moreover, managers can usually identify the source of a problem more quickly when they have these lists of problems readily available at their fingertips.

DISTINGUISHING BETWEEN CONVERGENCE AND REDUNDANCY

To be useful, information (such as sales data, consumer preference data, consumer satisfaction data, etc.) must be measured reliably and validly. However, large data sets are likely to contain intercorrelated, or redundant, subsets of data. For example, suppose

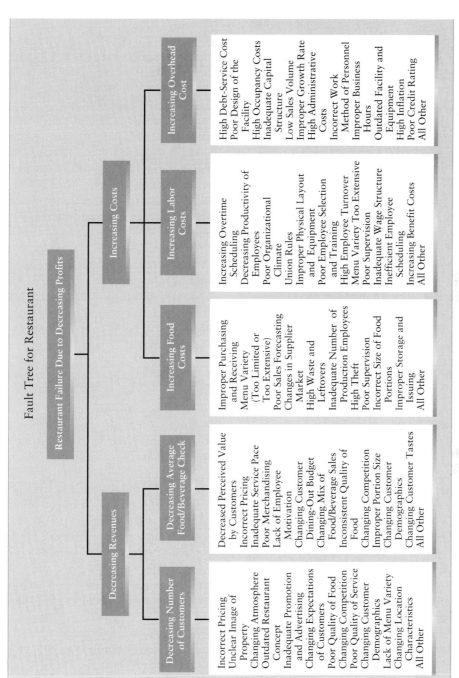

FIGURE 16-1

Fault trees can help managers identify the source of a problem quickly.

Source: Lurette Dube-Rioux and J. Edward Russo (1988). An availability bias in professional judgment, *Journal of Behavioral Decision Making,* 1, 224. Copyright John Wiley & Sons Limited. Reproduced with permission.

that market pretest data for a new product concept show that consumers have favorable beliefs about the new product, favorable attitudes about the new product, favorable preferences about the new product, and favorable intentions toward purchasing the new product. That is, several pieces of information point to the same conclusion: It is a good product. However, different pieces of information may point to the same conclusion for one of two different reasons: **convergence** and **redundancy.** Several independent or unrelated pieces of information converging on the same conclusion provide strong evidence for the conclusion. However, several correlated pieces of information suggesting the same conclusion provide relatively weak support for the conclusion. Unfortunately, a large amount of supporting evidence is often interpreted as strong support even when the individual pieces of information are highly correlated or redundant. Moreover, people are generally bad at estimating degree of correlation (Broniarczyk & Alba, 1994a, 1994b). Fortunately, degree of correlation between two or more variables can be estimated accurately and easily using statistical measures of association (e.g., the Pearson correlation coefficient, the Spearman rank-order test; the chi-square test for association), which are widely available on many different statistical software packages (e.g., SPSS, SAS). Managers should routinely examine correlation matrices to determine if a set of variables provides convergent or redundant support for a conclusion.

RESISTING SCENARIO THINKING

It is easier to think in terms of scenarios than in terms of probabilities and statistics. Moreover, a growing body of research evidence suggests that information is represented in memory in the form of scenarios, narratives, or stories and that people naturally and spontaneously think in terms of scenarios (Adaval & Wyer, 1998; Pennington & Hastie, 1986, 1988, 1993; Schank & Abelson, 1995). Unfortunately, scenario thinking can lead to erroneous likelihood judgments and poor predictions. A target event seems much more likely to occur when a story or sequence of events leading to the target event is presented rather than not presented. Of course, the presence or absence of a story does not influence that actual likelihood of the target event—the actual likelihood stays the same. However, a story makes an event easy to imagine, and easy-to-imagine events are perceived as likely. This is true even when many different scenarios can lead to the target event, which is usually the case. Statistically, the general likelihood of an event occurring through some unspecified sequence of events must be higher than the likelihood of the event occurring through just one specific sequence of events. Subjectively, however, the latter probability seems higher because of the operation of the simulation (or imagination) heuristic.

Some management consultants and managers are master storytellers. They can make an event seem inevitable. The best defense against good storytellers is to try to generate your own story or set of stories leading to very different conclusions. People are seduced too easily into focusing on only one possible story or outcome. Merely thinking about many different possible stories and outcomes helps managers to formulate more informed opinions and judgments.

AVOIDING OVERCONFIDENCE

Research on confidence suggests that people tend to be overconfident in many different settings (Lichtenstein, Fischhoff, & Phillips, 1982). Overconfidence is dangerous because confident managers believe that they do not need to develop contingency plans or safety measures to protect themselves against surprises; also, confidence influences how resources (e.g., budgets, time, effort) are allocated (Dunning, Griffin, Milojkovic, & Ross, 1990; Griffin, Dunning, & Ross, 1990; Vallone, Griffin, Lin, & Ross, 1990). For example, overconfidence on the part of the railroad industry in the 1920s led railway executives to ignore airplanes. Overconfidence on the part of U.S. automobile manufacturers in the early 1970s led them to ignore the Japanese. Shortly before the Challenger disaster, NASA officials stated that the odds of failure were 1 in 100,000 launches (or 1 in 300 years), and two months before the Chernobyl nuclear power plant disaster, Ukraine's minister of power and electrification stated that "the odds of a meltdown are one in 10,000 years" (Plous, 1993, p. 217).

What factors influence confidence? Set size or the amount of information available for judgment often influences confidence. Typically, people become more confident as the amount of information available for judgment increases, even when accuracy does not increase as the amount of information available increases (Fischhoff, Slovic, & Lichtenstein, 1977; Koriat, Lichtenstein, & Fischhoff, 1980; Oskamp, 1965).

Marketers can reduce overconfidence by thinking about many possibilities. One source for additional ideas is trade and professional journals. *Advertising Age* offers an online "e-zine" (www.adage.com), as well as its well-known print publication.

Source: Reprinted with permission of *Advertising Age.* Copyright, Crain Communications Inc., 1998.

Confidence also increases as insensitivity to omissions (missing information) increases (Sanbonmatsu et al., 1991, 1992). Confidence also increases as need for cognitive closure increases (Kruglanski, 1989; Kruglanski & Webster, 1996; Mayesless & Kruglanski, 1987). The pseudodiagnosticity effect also contributes to overconfidence, because people tend to focus on the extent to which the evidence supports the target conclusion and to neglect the extent to which the evidence supports other conclusions (Kruglanski & Mayesless, 1988; Sanbonmatsu et al., 1998; Tversky & Koehler, 1994). Moreover, confidence tends to be greatest when people are least sensitive to base-rate information and, therefore, least accurate (Dunning et al., 1990; Vallone et al., 1990).

How is the degree of overconfidence measured? **Calibration** refers to the degree to which confidence matches accuracy. Hence, when people are asked to provide an interval or range around their answers so that they are 90 percent confident that the correct answer lies within the interval, the correct answer should actually lie within the interval in 90 percent of the cases (e.g., in 9 out of 10 questions or 90 out of 100 questions). Instead, the typical finding is that people's confidence intervals are too small and the correct answer actually lies within the intervals in far fewer than 90 percent of the cases (Lichtenstein, Fischhoff, & Phillips, 1982). Calibration tends to decrease as accuracy decreases, and overconfidence tends to be greatest when people focus too heavily on one possibility (e.g., one alternative, one conclusion, one answer). The best way to reduce overconfidence is to think about many different possibilities (e.g., many different alternatives, many different conclusions, many different answers). Considering multiple possibilities not only decreases overconfidence, it also increases accuracy (Griffin et al., 1990; Hirt & Markman, 1995; Hoch, 1984, 1985; Lord, Lepper, & Preston, 1984; Sanbonmatsu et al., 1997).

◆ JUDGMENT UPDATING AND REVISION

Managerial judgment often involves forming an initial judgment, first impression, or anchor. Frequently, managers realize that their anchor is not quite right, so they adjust their judgment toward a more accurate position. Typically, however, the adjustment is insufficient (underadjustment). That is, the final judgment tends to be too close to the initial judgment (Tversky & Kahneman, 1974). So how much should people adjust their judgments?

Once again, probability and statistical theory provide the answer. According to **Bayes's theorem,** amount of adjustment depends on the diagnosticity (or relevance) of the information that is brought to bear after forming the initial opinion. More formally, Bayes's theorem states that

$$p(H \mid D) = \frac{p(D \mid H)}{p(D \mid H')} + \frac{p(H)}{p(H')}$$

That is, the probability of a hypothesis being correct given the data (this is a conditional probability rather than a simple probability) is equal to the probability of observing a particular pattern of data given that the hypothesis is correct (H) divided by the probability of the data given that the hypothesis is incorrect (H') plus the simple probability that the hypothesis is correct divided by the simple probability that the hypothesis is incorrect. The conditional probability of $p(D \mid H)$ divided by the conditional probability of $p(D \mid H')$ is known as the *likelihood ratio,* and this serves as a measure of diagnosticity, or relevance (i.e., the extent to which the data support one hypothesis H rather than other hypotheses [H']). The simple probability of $p(H)$ divided by $p(H')$ is the base rate, or prior (i.e., prior to the collection of new data) probability that the hypothesis is correct. The prior probability that the hypothesis, or conclusion, is correct can also be interpreted as the prior judgment, or anchor. As the likelihood ratio increases, adjustment should increase. If the likelihood ratio is equal to 1 (the numerator and the denominator are equal), no adjustment should be performed (the posterior probability equals the prior probability) because the data are uninformative. Basically, the more informative the data, the more a manager should adjust his or her initial judgment given the data.

Bayes's theorem can be rewritten as

$$p(H \mid D) = \frac{p(D \mid H)p(H)}{p(D \mid H)p(H) + p(D \mid H')p(H')}$$

That is, the posterior probability of the hypothesis being correct given the data is equal to the probability of observing the data given that the hypothesis is correct, multiplied by the simple probability that the hypothesis is correct divided by the probability of observing the data given that the hypothesis is true, multiplied by the simple probability that the hypothesis is correct plus the probability of observing the data given that the hypothesis is incorrect, multiplied by the simple probability that the hypothesis is incorrect.

Why is this important? Imagine that a manager of a leading pharmaceutical company must decide whether a new drug is safe enough to market. The drug was designed to reduce blood clots, but some doctors believe the drug may cause a rare form of cancer in some patients. The Food and Drug Administration requires clinical tests involving human subjects before a new drug is approved, so the drug is currently being tested on a small sample of patients. One patient develops a tumor, but the doctor running the study is initially unconcerned because the prior probability, or base rate, of this type of cancer is only 1 percent. To be safe, the doctor orders a test. The test comes back positive, so the doctor must adjust her judgment. Research has shown that the test is 80 percent reliable (i.e., there is an 80 percent chance of a positive test given cancer), and the test has a false positive rate of 10 percent (i.e., there is a 10 percent chance of a positive test given no cancer), so the doctor adjusts her estimate of the likelihood of cancer for this patient to 70 percent. Is this estimate appropriate?

Plugging the numbers into Bayes's formula yields

$$p(\text{cancer} \mid \text{positive test}) = \frac{(.80)(.01)}{(.80)(.01) + (.10)(.99)} = 0.75$$

That is, there is only a 7.5 percent chance that the patient has cancer given the positive test. This surprises most people (including most doctors) because they tend to focus on the 80 percent figure and adjust insufficiently from 80 percent. The actual answer (7.5 percent) is much lower because the base rate is very low (1 percent) and because the test is not perfect—there is an 80 percent chance of true positive tests and a 10 percent chance of false positive tests. Moreover, most people, including experts, tend to commit the **confusion of the inverse fallacy** (Dawes, 1988). That is, people tend to confuse $p(H \mid D)$ with $p(D \mid H)$. These two conditional probabilities are not at all equivalent.

In this example, $p(H \mid D) = .075$ and $p(D \mid H) = .80$. Moreover, in most cases $p(H \mid D)$ does not equal $p(D \mid H)$.

You probably found the logic underlying Bayes's theorem difficult to follow. This is because intuition does not follow the rules of Bayes's theorem. This is yet another example of how intuition can lead decision makers astray. This book is full of examples of how intuition can lead to poor decision making. The use of Bayes's theorem can improve decision making by (a) increasing attention to base rates, (b) reducing pseudodiagnostic thinking (i.e., the tendency to focus on hits and to ignore false alarms), (c) eliminating the confusion of the inverse fallacy, and (d) helping managers to adjust initial estimates appropriately in light of new information. Prediction should be based only on the base rate when no relevant information is available. Adjustment should increase as relevance increases. Relevance increases as the percentage of hits (i.e., correct predictions) increases and as the percentage of false alarms (i.e., predicted hits that turned out to be misses) decreases. Bayes's theorem integrates a large amount of information in an appropriate manner that usually cannot be duplicated by intuitive judgment, even by expert intuitive judgment (Dawes, 1988, 1993).

CHAPTER SUMMARY

Managers should not consider only one positioning strategy—they should consider many different alternatives (e.g., positioning by attributes/benefits, price, use, and user; repositioning). Similarly, managers should not consider only one segmentation strategy—they should consider many alternatives (e.g., segmenting by geography, demography, psychographics, or behavior). Managers should also consider many different new product concepts or ideas, many different pricing strategies, many different promotion and advertising strategies, and many different distribution strategies. Epistemic freezing, or focusing too heavily on one option or alternative, often leads to poor decisions. Even very busy and time-pressured individuals need to consider a wide range of options to reach good decisions. Managers should also use decision aids (such as linear models, fault trees, and Bayes's theorem) to improve their judgment and decision making by helping them to be more systematic, consistent, and careful in their thinking. Many managers prefer to base their decisions on feelings or hunches rather than models. However, relying too heavily on feelings, hunches, and stories (scenarios) causes managers to fall into the intuition trap.

I hope that this book will help you to be more scientific, systematic, and consistent in your thinking and reasoning. Being more analytic and less intuitive should help you to develop more effective and rewarding solutions to the difficult managerial judgment and decision-making challenges that lie ahead.

KEY CONCEPTS

- Decision frame management
- Theory of lay epistemology
- Need for cognitive closure
- Epistemic seizing
- Epistemic freezing
- Planning fallacy
- Base rate

- Unreliable information
- Invalid information
- Linear model
- Subjective linear model
- Bootstrapping
- Objective linear model
- Actuarial model
- Fault tree

- Convergence
- Redundancy
- Calibration
- Bayes's theorem
- Confusion of the inverse fallacy

DISCUSSION QUESTIONS ▪

1. Why do managers sometimes focus on only one frame in decision making? How can using multiple frames lead to better managerial decisions?
2. What five things begin to occur as the need for cognitive closure increases?
3. Some researchers believe that the need for closure may increase with age and experience. How might this hypothesis affect managerial decisions?
4. Describe a situation in which you engaged in planning fallacy. What was your thinking process? What was the outcome?
5. What is the difference between unreliable information and invalid information? Give an example of each.
6. How might a subjective linear model help a restaurant owner decide the best location for a new restaurant?
7. How might convergence and redundancy in data affect the success of a new product?
8. Describe an instance in which you either used scenario thinking to influence someone to make a decision in your favor or were influenced by scenario thinking to make a decision.
9. What factors influence confidence in one's decisions? Why is overconfidence dangerous for managers?
10. Why is Bayes's theorem a good tool for managers to use in adjusting original judgments?

# Glossary

accessibility-diagnosticity model Model that suggests that choice depends on the accessibility of an input, the accessibility of alternative inputs, and the diagnosticity of the inputs.

activation The transfer of information from inactive long-term memory to active short-term memory.

actuarial model A measurement using inputs based solely on objective data, rather than subjective judgments; also known as an *objective linear model.*

adaptation level A weighted geometric average of all stimuli that a person takes into account when making a judgment.

adaptation level theory A theory stating that all objects can be arranged in a meaningful order and can be ranked as bad/good, small/large, and so on and that all judgments have a psychological neutral point called the adaptation level.

additive-difference heuristic A heuristic that involves computing the difference between the values of each attribute of two brands, weighting the differences by attribute importance, and summing the weighted differences to obtain an overall score.

affective responses Feelings and emotions we experience when we read about, hear about, think about, use, or dispose of products.

affirmation of the consequent The erroneous belief that "if p, then q" implies "if q, then p."

aggregation A "one size fits all" strategy, opposite to segmentation, in which a single product is offered to an entire market.

anchoring and adjustment Heuristic that involves forming an initial judgment and then shifting this judgment upward or downward depending on the imagined possibilities.

arousal A state of wakefulness or alertness.

assimilation effect A shift in judgment toward a reference point.

association principle Rule of long-term memory that states that pieces of information stored in long-term memory are connected to other related pieces of information.

associations Links that connect ideas together in long-term memory.

associative interference Theory of forgetting due to retrieval failure.

associative network System of associations in long-term memory.

attention intensity The amount of information people can handle at a particular moment.

attitude function theory A theory that suggests that to be effective, a persuasion strategy must match the attitude function.

attitude heuristic A selection process in which consumers select a brand that they associate with the most favorable previously formed attitude.

attitude-based choice Choice that is based on a comparison of consumers' previously formed attitudes toward the considered alternatives.

attitude-based preferences Preferences formed on the basis of consumers' overall attitudes toward two or more products.

attitudes Evaluative judgments that consumers form of people, objects, and issues.

attraction effect Influencing consumers' choice of a product by introducing a similar but inferior product that acts as a decoy.

attribute-based choice Choice that is based on a comparison of specific attributes or features offered by the considered alternatives.

attribute-based market structure The market structure that exists when consumers first decide what attributes they want and then decide what brand they want.

attribute-based preferences Preferences formed on the basis of comparing one or more attributes of two or more brands.

attributional judgments Causal inferences, such as assumptions about why someone behaved as he or she did.

augmentation principle The idea that when there are strong situational forces that should prevent an event from occurring but the event occurs anyway, the cause of the event must be exceptionally powerful.

authority principle A principle that suggests that authority figures use titles, clothes, and expensive possessions that convey status to impress and influence others.

automaticity principle The cornerstone of all influencing techniques; this principle suggests that people sometimes use simple heuristics that enable them to make quick and easy decisions almost automatically.

availability The ease with which instances can be retrieved from memory.

base rate Prior incidence of a to-be-predicted event.

Bayes's theorem A principle stating that the amount of adjustment depends on the diagnosticity (or relevance) of the information that is brought to bear after forming the initial opinion.

because heuristic Cognitive shortcut whereby the use of the word *because* gives people a reason for complying with a request without taking the time to think about the reason.

behavioral responses Purchase decisions and consumption-related practices (i.e., actions involved in obtaining, using, and disposing of products or services).

behavioral segmentation A process that involves segmenting on the basis of usage situation (such as breakfast only, weekends only, or special occasions only) or usage frequency (such as nonusers, light users, medium users, or heavy users).

beliefs Nonevaluative judgments; the perceived relationship between two concepts held on a continuous scale; beliefs serve as building blocks for complex judgments, such as attitudes and preferences.

between-alternative processing Attribute-based heuristics in which many brands are compared one attribute at a time.

biased assimilation Perceiving information as more consistent with one's expectations than it really is.

blocking Learning about one conditioned stimulus prevents learning about another.

bootstrapping Using a subjective linear model, so called because the model helps the decision maker to pick himself up by his own bootstraps.

brand equity The value added to a product by a brand name.

brand extensions New products that share a brand name with a familiar, established product.

brand loyal A trait of consumers who tend to purchase one brand repeatedly and view competing brands as poor substitutes to their preferred brand.

brand stature Abstract brand positioning effectiveness; a function of esteem multiplied by knowledge.

brand strength Concrete brand positioning effectiveness; a function of differentiation multiplied by relevance.

brand-based market structure The market structure that exists when consumers first decide what brand they want and then decide what attributes they want.

calibration The degree to which confidence matches accuracy.

cannibalization A hidden cost that results when different brands on the same product line (e.g., Miller beer and Miller Lite) are so similar that they compete among themselves.

causal relationships Relationships in which there is a correlation between two variables and one variable influences the other, but not vice versa; in other words, the cause always precedes the effect.

central route to persuasion The idea that people focus on the most central, or important, information provided when forming an attitude or opinion about an advertised product.

classical conditioning The learning that occurs when a stimulus that elicits a response is paired with another stimulus that initially does not elicit a response on its own but will cause a similar response over time because of its association with the first stimulus.

coding Relating information stored in short-term memory to information stored in long-term memory.

cognitive capacity The amount of information people can attend to and think about at a particular moment.

cognitive dissonance theory A theory that asserts that people strive for consistency between a target behavior and a target attitude.

cognitive responses Beliefs, opinions, attitudes, and intentions pertaining to products and services.

combinatory principle Principle that suggests that personality is related to reception and yielding in opposite ways.

commitment and consistency principle The belief that people are expected to exhibit beliefs, attitudes, and behaviors that are coherent and that seem to go together.

commitment theory A theory that suggests that the purpose of commitment is to impart resistance to change and that commitment to a decision makes the decision less changeable.

comparison omission The practice of misleading consumers by omitting information in a claim.

compensatory strategies Attitude-based strategies that allow good attributes to compensate for bad attributes.

compromise effect Influencing consumers to choose an intermediate brand over a lower-level brand by adding a very high or very low level brand to the choices.

concreteness Specificity; concrete information is vivid and easy to visualize.

conditioned response The response produced by the conditioned stimulus alone when an association between the unconditioned stimulus and the conditioned stimulus is learned.

conditioned stimulus An unfamiliar object paired with an unconditioned stimulus to produce a response.

confirmation bias Bias that occurs as a result of ambiguous information being interpreted as consistent with a hypothesis or belief.

confusion of the inverse fallacy The tendency of people to confuse the probability of a hypothesis with its diagnosticity (or its relevance); that is, the conditional probability $p(H/D)$ is confused with $p(D/H)$; see also Bayes's theorem.

conjunctive heuristic A heuristic that involves setting a minimum acceptable cutoff level for each attribute and selecting the first alternative that meets the minimum standard for all attributes.

conscious awareness Information that is currently under active consideration.

consequences of attributes The features of a product that are of concern to consumers.

consideration set The group of products a consumer considers in making a purchase decision.

consistency principle A principle that states that people like consistency and dislike inconsistency; the focus of the major subtle motivational techniques.

consonance The consistency between a target behavior and a target attitude.

constant sum scale A preference measure in which 100 points are distributed across alternatives.

consumer behavior The study of human responses to products, services, and the marketing of products and services.

consumer choice Selecting one product from a set of possibilities.

consumer preference heterogeneity Variability in consumer preference.

consumer researchers Those who investigate a broad range of human responses, including affective, cognitive, and behavioral responses to products and services.

contextual variables Background variables.

continuous reinforcement A reward is given every time the response occurs.

contrast effect The effect that occurs when judgments of the target object shift away from the reference point.

convergence The condition that occurs when several independent or unrelated pieces of information point to the same conclusion.

core benefit proposition A single attribute/benefit that firms try to develop that differentiates their brand from competitors' offerings.

corrective advertising An action that requires companies to correct easily misconstrued information to the public.

correlational relationships Relationships in which an observed change in one variable is accompanied by a corresponding change in the other variable.

correspondence bias The overinterpretation of the behavior of individuals, which causes a person to draw strong inferences based on weak evidence.

counterarguments Reasons for not believing a message.

cued recall Memory measure using fill-in-the-blank questions.

curiosity statements Thoughts that are only tangentially related to the main points of a message.

decision frame management The first step in decision making: considering how a decision problem should be framed or interpreted.

demographic segmentation A process that involves segmenting on the basis of gender, age, education, occupation, income, marital status, household size, or ethnic background.

dependent variable The consequence, or effect, in a causal relationship.

descriptive beliefs Beliefs based on direct, first-hand experience with a product.

diagnosticity Perceived relevance.

diffusion of innovation The process by which a new product spreads throughout a population.

dilution effect Situation that results when the judgmental impact of diagnostic information is diluted by the presence of nondiagnostic information.

diminishing sensitivity The phenomenon that occurs when both gains and losses appear smaller as the distance between these relative outcomes and the reference point increases.

direction-of-comparison effect The order in which two products are compared has a strong influence on preference judgments.

discounting principle Expected information is viewed with skepticism because there are many reasons or causes for expected events to occur.

discrepancies Unexpected events, which often require our immediate attention.

disjunctive heuristic A heuristic that involves setting an acceptable standard for each attribute and choosing the first alternative that meets this standard on one attribute.

dissonance Behavior–attitude inconsistency.

dissonance arousal The unpleasant tension produced by dissonance.

dissonance effect A shift in attitude that increases behavior–attitude consistency.

diversification A strategy that involves developing new products for new markets.

door-in-the-face technique An influence technique that involves making a large request followed by a smaller request.

elaboration likelihood model A contingency theory that helps predict when celebrity spokespersons are likely to be effective versus ineffective, helps identify the conditions that favor the use of factual versus emotional appeals, and helps predict the reactions a consumer is likely to have to virtually any ad.

elimination-by-aspects heuristic A heuristic that involves comparing alternatives on an attribute selected on the basis of its importance and eliminating or rejecting alternatives that do not meet a minimum level.

emotion Intense affect, or affect plus arousal.

emotional appeals Appeals that encourage consumers to act on feelings rather than critical thinking.

encoding-specificity principle Rule of long-term memory that states that contextual or background cues present during learning and during retrieval influence memory performance.

entry strategy The strategy that involves how a product should be introduced to the marketplace.

epistemic freezing The tendency to maintain closure as long as possible even if this means being closed-minded or unwilling to consider alternatives.

epistemic seizing The tendency to attain closure quickly, even if this means oversimplifying an issue or failing to carefully consider all sides of an issue.

even-a-penny technique A way that salespeople can appear reasonable by making extremely small requests to influence customers to make a purchase or comply with a request.

excitation transfer Occurs when arousal combines and transfers from one stimulus to another.

expectancy disconfirmation model   Model suggesting that consumers form expectations about product performance before they purchase a product; their satisfaction depends on how the product's actual performance matches their expectancies.

experience curve   The tendency of managers to learn how to produce and market a product more efficiently over time as they gain knowledge and experience.

experiment   Systematically manipulating the independent variable to assess its impact on the dependent variable.

explicit memory   Memory that people are aware they are focusing on and consulting.

factor analysis   A statistical technique used to analyze attribute ratings; a correlation-based technique that reduces a large set of attributes to a smaller and more manageable number of underlying factors.

factorial design   A design in which all levels of each independent variable are crossed with or combined with all levels of the other independent variables.

factual appeals   Appeals that provide meaningful information about the specific features and uses of products.

fault tree   A decision aid consisting of branches, or general categories, of common problems in a system.

fear appeal   A type of emotional appeal that scares consumers into action.

figure-ground principle of perception   The process in which unique stimuli grab consumers' attention and everything else fades into the background.

foot-in-the-door technique   An influence technique that involves making a small request first, followed by a larger request.

forced-choice switching   A process by which consumers are shown a set of products and asked to indicate their first choice; then they are asked to assume that their first choice is not available and told that they must indicate their second choice.

framing effect   A phenomenon showing that how a product is framed, or described, influences how people think about the product.

free recall   Memory measure in which no cues are given.

frequency marketing   The process of targeting heavy users (i.e., the firm's best customers) and offering them special benefits and privileges.

frequency of good and bad features heuristic   An attitude-based strategy that involves forming a very simple attitude toward each considered alternative by counting the number of good features, counting the number of bad features, and choosing the brand with the largest number of good features and smallest number of bad features.

geographic segmentation   A process that involves segmenting on the basis of cultural differences among consumers living in different cities, states, regions, or countries.

harvesting   Minimizing costs so that any sales that are generated through the past reputation of the product produce high profit levels.

Heider's balance theory   A theory focused on perceived relationships among stimuli in a set of three; the three elements are p (the person who receives the persuasive message), o (another person known to p), and x (a stimulus such as a product or issue).

heuristics   Cognitive shortcuts.

higher-order conditioning   Involves pairing an unconditioned stimulus with a conditioned stimulus until an association is learned and then pairing the old conditioned stimulus with a new conditioned stimulus.

ideal vectors   Points on a perceptual map that show how important different combinations of attributes are to consumers; constructed through multiple regression.

implicit memory   Memory that people are unaware they are using; with such memory, people are also unaware that they are being influenced by prior experiences and memories.

impression management theory   A theory that suggests that people are motivated to give the appearance that their behaviors and attitudes are consistent.

independent variable   The antecedent, or causal, variable in a causal relationship.

indirect persuasion   The technique of purposely omitting portions of a message and subtly inducing consumers to draw inferences about this omitted information.

inference A conclusion derived from available information on the basis of a rule that associates the information to the conclusion in a subjectively logical fashion.

inferential beliefs Beliefs that go beyond the information given or the information that is available from firsthand or secondhand sources.

influence heuristics Cognitive shortcuts that influence behavior.

Information Integration Theory Theory that suggests beliefs are combined using an averaging rule to form attitudes.

informational beliefs Beliefs based on indirect, secondhand information.

involvement The perceived relevance or importance of an issue.

Kelley's attribution theory The theory that a change in one factor (the cause) should be accompanied by a change in the other factor (the effect).

Kelley's causal schemata The formation of attributions on the basis of prior knowledge and experience.

knowledge bias A situation in which the advertiser may not be aware of or knowledgeable about better brands.

knowledge function The function many attitudes serve by summarizing a large amount of complex or ambiguous information to provide people with an organized, meaningful, and stable view of the world.

latent inhibition Result occurring when a conditioned stimulus loses its effectiveness through prior presentation alone.

latitude of acceptance Believable claims fall in the consumer's latitude of acceptance.

latitude of noncommitment Neutral claims fall in the consumer's latitude of noncommitment.

latitude of rejection Unbelievable claims fall in the consumer's latitude of rejection.

lexicographic heuristic A process that involves choosing the best brand on the basis of the most important attribute.

lexicographic semiorder heuristic A similar choice strategy to the lexicographic heuristic except that close values are treated like ties.

liking principle Liking is power; the more people like you, the more power you have over them.

limits of attention The amount of information people can focus on is limited.

linear model An equation that contains a list of the most important attributes for evaluating and comparing decision options.

long-run franchise strategy A strategy that involves the development of new uses and new variations on a theme to help keep the product interesting to consumers for a long period of time.

long-term memory Memory system that has a very large storage capacity; information remains there permanently.

loss aversion A situation that occurs when losses loom larger than gains.

low-ball technique An influence technique that involves obtaining initial compliance and then changing the deal.

majority fallacy The action of focusing exclusively on the large "average" segment and neglecting smaller, less typical segments.

majority of confirming dimensions heuristic A heuristic in which the values of each attribute of two brands are compared, and the brand with the greatest number of superior attributes is chosen.

Mandler's theory of emotion A theory that states that discrepancies, or unexpected events, are arousal producing.

market development A strategy that involves introducing existing products to new markets.

market penetration A strategy that involves using heavy promotion and advertising to increase sales of existing products in existing markets.

market stimulus switchers Consumers who switch brands purposely because they tend to buy the least expensive brand, the brand for which they have a coupon, or the brand that is advertised the most heavily at the time of purchase.

maximum penetration strategy A strategy that involves attaining a long-term market leadership position through highly effective positioning, pricing, and protection from imitation.

McGuire's theory of personality and persuasion Theory that explains the effects of recipient factors on persuasion; it is composed of three key principles—the mediational principle, the combinatory principle, and the situational weighting principle—and focuses primarily on two stages: reception and yielding.

media clutter   Consumer exposure to large amounts of mass-media advertising.

memory-based choice   A choice situation in which none of the information that the consumer needs is directly available and comparisons between brands must be performed by retrieving relevant information from memory.

mere exposure effect   Repeated exposure to a neutral stimulus increases liking for that stimulus.

mere thought effect   The effect that occurs when we simply think about an object, making our opinion of the object more extreme.

message-learning approach   The approach developed by Yale University psychologists Hovland, Janis, and Kelley that suggested that effective persuasive communications are attention-drawing, comprehensible, convincing, and memorable; also known as the "who says what to whom" approach.

method of ordered alternatives   A method that involves constructing a series of statements ranging from very positive to very negative.

mixed choice   A choice situation in which some relevant information is directly observable and some information must be retrieved from memory.

MODE model   Theory that Motivation and Opportunity are key DEterminants of the manner in which attitudes guide behavior.

multiple regression   A correlation-based technique in which the relationships between specific attributes ratings and overall product evaluations are determined statistically; the stronger the correlation between an attribute and the overall evaluation, the more important the attribute.

multiple-deescalating-requests technique   An influence technique involving more than two requests to the consumer; if one request is rejected, the salesperson offers a smaller request, and so on.

need for cognitive closure   A desire for definite knowledge rather than confusion or ambiguity.

negative reinforcement   A process whereby the absence of punishment strengthens responses to stimuli.

node   Each concept, idea, or piece of information stored in long-term memory.

noncompensatory strategies   Strategies in which a high score on one attribute cannot compensate for a low score on another attribute.

norm theory   The theory that sets of stimuli serve as a norm or reference point in making judgments.

normal distribution   A bell-shaped curve.

norms   Rules that dictate what actions are appropriate or inappropriate.

objective linear model   A measurement using inputs based solely on objective data rather than subjective judgments; also known as an actuarial model.

one-sided message   A biased, lopsided message that contains only supporting arguments, or arguments consistent with the conclusion.

operant conditioning   The process through which attitudes can be influenced; very similar to classical conditioning except that the response precedes the stimulus.

organization   The process of grouping or chunking individual pieces of information into larger units on the basis of a specific relationship between the pieces.

organization principle   Rule of long-term memory that states that organization of information facilitates memory performance.

overcorrection   Overadjustment that is made in an attempt to correct biasing effects on judgment.

overjustification effect   The idea that many reasons undermine the perceived significance of a particular reason.

part-list cuing   Presenting the names of some brands when consumers are trying to recall as many brands as possible reduces the number of brands the consumers can recall.

partial reinforcement   The learning method in which a reward is given only some of the time the response occurs.

perceptual maps   Graphs constructed from the information gained from factor analysis and used to show patterns of competition.

peripheral route to persuasion   The idea that people form an opinion about an advertised product using relatively little thought or effort.

perseverance effect   Situation that results when the decision maker continues to believe a belief, with no basis.

person variables   Dimensions that are internal to a specific individual.

person-by-situation   interactions   Dynamics between consumers and the environment that require marketers to tailor advertising techniques for maximum effectiveness.

perspective theory   The theory that one's interpretation of the end points of a rating scale is another reference point that influences attitudinal judgments of objects and issues.

persuasion   An active attempt to change belief and attitude.

persuasion heuristics   Cognitive shortcuts that influence beliefs and attitudes.

phased strategies   Choice based on multiple heuristics and strategies.

phenomenon   An observable event.

pioneering advantage   The consumer preference advantage that first brands to enter a market enjoy over follower brands.

planning fallacy   The overconfident belief that a project will proceed smoothly as planned.

point of comparison   A person's judgment that is based on the context or background in which an object is judged; also known as a reference point, anchor, or standard of comparison.

positioning   Consumers' relative perceptions of a particular brand.

positioning strategies   The strategies firms develop based on consumer perceptions of a target brand relative to competing brands.

positive habituation   Familiarity and uncertainty reduction; with continued repetition, the effects of boredom may eventually overcome the effects of positive habituation.

positive reinforcement   A process whereby the presence of reward strengthens responses to stimuli.

pragmatic inferences   Everyday assumptions about claims that are literally true but figuratively false.

prediction heuristics   Cognitive shortcuts that influence likelihood judgments.

preference reversal   Preferring one object in one situation and another in a different situation.

preferences   Evaluative judgments of multiple objects.

premature cognitive commitment   Commitment based on information that was accepted uncritically with little thought or elaboration.

price-quality heuristic   Heuristic that applies when consumers assume that high price items are also high in quality.

priming effect   Information accessible from memory influences how we interpret, rate, and judge concepts and issues.

proactive associative interference   Principle by which information learned earlier interferes with remembering information learned later.

product development   A strategy that involves building on a firm's unique strengths and developing new products for existing markets.

product line breadth   The number of products that a firm should offer.

product trial   One way consumers learn about products and acquire product knowledge by trying or using the actual product.

protection motivation theory   Theory that suggests that three key variables jointly influence the effectiveness of fear appeals: likelihood of danger, coping effectiveness, and self-efficacy.

pseudodiagnosticity   Irrelevant information that seems relevant.

psychographic segmentation   A process that involves segmenting on the basis of personality characteristics, attitudes, beliefs, or lifestyles.

quality function deployment   Techniques for assessing the relationship between consumers' attribute ratings and engineering variables, which enable different business functions to work together more effectively.

random assignment   Assigning subjects to groups on the basis of a random number generation procedure, thereby ensuring that individual differences among subjects do not influence the results.

random switchers Consumers who seem to switch brands for no apparent reason.

rapid acceleration strategy A strategy that involves the heavy use of the mass media to influence early adopters and the early majority.

rapid takeoff strategy A strategy that involves identifying innovator consumers and concentrating all of one's marketing activities on these individuals.

rational appeals Appeals that contain factual details that are useful for generating an informed opinion.

reciprocal relationship Attitudes influence and are influenced by belief, affect, and behavior.

reciprocity principle The principle whereby when someone does a favor for a person, that person feels obliged to return the favor.

recognition Memory measure using multiple-choice questions.

rehearsal Repeating information over and over in one's head.

rejuvenation A process that involves increasing investment costs by developing new uses, improvements, and strategies to keep consumers interested in the product, thereby increasing the length of the product life cycle.

reporting bias A situation in which the advertiser may lie or not report what he or she really believes to trick consumers into buying the advertised brand.

representativeness heuristic The thought process that assesses the likelihood that A belongs to B on the basis of the degree to which A is similar to B.

response language effects Effects that refer to a shift in judgment due to the way consumers interpret the end points of a rating scale, which has an important influence on their ratings; also called *measurement effects*.

retroactive associative interference Principle by which information learned later interferes with remembering information learned earlier.

reward Expected profits or return on investment.

risk Uncertainty due to instability in the availability of supplies, rapidly changing consumer preferences, or changes in the legal environment.

risk averse What people are when they focus on gains; when two alternative courses of action yield similar outcomes in terms of expected utility, people prefer the sure thing over the risky option.

risk seeking What people are when outcomes are framed in terms of losses.

sales potential The potential size of a market in dollar sales.

sales–costs tradeoff Offering many different products increases sales but also increases costs.

salient beliefs Important, attention-drawing beliefs.

salient stimuli Novel or unexpected packaging or advertising used to draw consumers' attention involuntarily.

satisfaction A consumer judgment involving the comparison of a product's actual performance to its expected performance.

scale Cumulative sales volume.

scarcity principle A principle that suggests that since valuable objects are rare or scarce, scarce objects are assumed to be valuable.

schemas Prior knowledge structures.

science The process of knowledge development based on a set of formal rules and procedures.

scientific method A set of formal rules through which researchers achieve the goals of science.

segmentation A "divide and conquer" strategy that involves dividing a market into subcategories and pursuing different strategies for each subcategory.

self-fulfilling prophecy A prediction that changes behavior in a way that causes the prediction to become true.

self-perception theory A theory stating that people form inferences about their beliefs and attitudes on the basis of their behavior and the context in which the behavior occurs.

sensory proximity A measure of how close consumers are to product or service information; firsthand information is gained through consumers' own senses, and secondhand information is more distant, gained from others' experience.

set-size effect   The tendency to form more extreme and confident judgments as the amount of information available for judgment increases, even when the favorableness of the individual pieces of information is controlled.

shaping   A technique that reinforces successive approximations of the desired response.

short-term memory   Memory system that holds a small amount of information for a brief period of time.

simulation heuristic   The thought process whereby a single event or sequence of events that is easy to imagine also seems very likely to occur.

situational variables   External, environmental variables that provide the context in which behaviors are performed.

situational weighting principle   Principle that suggests that reception and yielding are not always equally important.

sleeper effect   A phenomenon occurring when a message becomes more persuasive over time as the result of a complex interaction among message factors, source factors, and time.

social judgment theory   A theory that explains contrast and assimilation effects using attitudes as a reference point.

social validation principle   A principle that suggests that the perceived validity of an idea increases as the number of people supporting the idea increases; also called the "proof in numbers" principle.

source amnesia   The condition in which we are unaware of where a feeling or belief comes from.

source derogations   A type of elaboration in which a consumer's dislike of the source delivering the persuasive message causes the consumer to think of reasons to not believe the source.

spatial proximity   Distance in space.

stimulus-based choice   A choice situation in which all relevant brand and attribute information is directly observable.

subjective expected utility theory   A theory that suggests that preferences are stable and

that people should always choose the option that maximizes value.

subjective linear model   An equation in which all inputs are subjective judgments provided by the director or a committee.

subliminal   Subconscious.

support arguments   Reasons for believing a message.

syllogistic inference rule   The idea that people will use syllogisms (if A implies B, and if B implies C, then A implies C) to infer conclusions.

temporal contiguity   A principle of classical conditioning that states that stronger associations are learned when events occur closer together in time as opposed to far apart in time.

temporal proximity   Distance in time.

that's-not-all technique   An influence technique that offers consumers free bonuses or a reduction in price before they have a chance to reject the initial offer.

Theory of Reasoned Action   Theory that suggests beliefs are combined additively to form attitudes; used to predict attitudes from beliefs and to diagnose problem attributes.

theory of lay epistemology   The theory of everyday knowledge formation and use.

tradeoff contrast effect   Influencing consumers' choice of a product by having consumers compare tradeoffs instead of single attributes between brands.

two-sided messages   Messages to consumers containing both pros and cons that enhance source credibility because some information goes against the source's vested interests.

unconditioned response   The affective response automatically produced when an unconditioned stimulus is presented.

unconditioned stimulus   A familiar and meaningful object that produces an affective response.

unconditioned stimulus pre-exposure effect   Effect caused when unconditioned stimuli are encountered alone without pairing, rendering the unconditioned stimuli ineffective.

VALS 2   Values and Life Styles—Version 2 psychographic technique.

variety seekers   Consumers who switch brands purposefully because they get tired of the same brand all the time and like to try many different brands.

vivid stimuli   Emotionally interesting, specific, and firsthand information.

wishful thinking   The belief that good things are likely to happen to us and bad things are not.

within-alternative processing   Attribute-based heuristics in which many attributes are examined one brand at a time.

Young & Rubicam Brand Asset Valuator   An approach involving the use of a set of scales designed to measure differentiation (the brand's distinction), relevance (the brand's usefulness), esteem (the brand's considered value), and knowledge (the brand's image).

Zanna and Rempel's (1988) Model   A model that states attitudes are formed on the basis of beliefs, affect, behaviors, or some combination of beliefs, affect, and behaviors.

Zillmann's theory of emotion   A theory that rests on four key principles of emotion: arousal is nonspecific with respect to emotion, people are insensitive to small changes in arousal, people often look for a single cause for their arousal, and physiological arousal dissipates at a slower rate than perceived arousal.

REFERENCES ▪▪

Aaker, D. A. (1991). *Managing brand equity.* New York: Free Press.

Aaker, D. A. (1996). *Building strong brands.* New York: Free Press.

Aaker, D. A., & Shansby, J. G. (1982). "Positioning your product." *Business Horizons, 36–62.*

Aaker, J. L. (2000). "Accessibility or diagnosticity? Disentangling the influence of culture on persuasion processes and attitudes." *Journal of Consumer Research, 26,* 340–357.

Aaker, J. L., & Maheswaran, D. (1997). "The effect of cultural orientation on persuasion." *Journal of Consumer Research, 24,* 315–328.

Abelson, R. P., Kinder, D. R., Peters, M. D., & Fiske, S. T. (1982). "Affective and semantic components in political person perception." *Journal of Personality and Social Psychology, 42,* 619–630.

Adaval, R., & Wyer, R. S. (1998). "The role of narratives in consumer information processing." *Journal of Consumer Psychology, 7,* 207–246.

Ajzen, I. (1977). "Intuitive theories of events and the effects of base-rate information on prediction." *Journal of Personality and Social Psychology, 35,* 303–314.

Ajzen, I., & Madden, T. J. (1986). "Prediction of goal-directed behavior: Attitudes, intentions, and perceived behavioral control." *Journal of Experimental Social Psychology, 22,* 453–474.

Alba, J. W., & Chattopadhyay, A. (1985). "Effects of context and part-category cues on recall of competing brands." *Journal of Marketing Research, 22,* 340–349.

Alba, J. W., & Chattopadhyay, A. (1986). "Salience effects in brand recall." *Journal of Marketing Research, 23,* 363–369.

Alba, J. W., & Hutchinson, J. W. (1987). "Dimensions of consumer expertise." *Journal of Consumer Research, 13,* 411–454.

Alba, J. W., Hutchinson, J. W., & Lynch, J. G. (1991). "Memory and decision making." In T. S. Robertson & H. H. Kassarjian (Eds.), *Handbook of consumer behavior* (pp. 1–49). Englewood Cliffs, NJ: Prentice-Hall.

Alba, J., Lynch, J., Weitz, B., Janiszewski, C., Lutz, R., Sawyer, A., & Wood, S. (1997). "Interactive home shopping: Consumer, retail, and manufacturer incentives to participate in electronic marketplaces." *Journal of Marketing, 61,* 38–53.

Alba, J. W., Marmorstein, H. (1987). "The effects of frequency knowledge on consumer decision making." *Journal of Consumer Research, 14,* 14–25.

Alba, J. W., Marmorstein, H., & Chattopadhyay, A. (1992). "Transitions in preference over time: The effects of memory on message persuasiveness." *Journal of Marketing Research, 29,* 406–416.

Altheide, D. L., & Johnson, J. M. (1977). "Counting souls: A study of counseling at evangelical crusades." *Pacific Sociological Review, 20,* 323–348.

Anderson, C. A. (1983). "Abstract and concrete data in the perseverance of social theories: When weak data lead to unshakable beliefs." *Journal of Experimental Social Psychology, 19,* 93–108.

Anderson, C. A., & Godfrey, S. S. (1987). "Thoughts about actions: The effects of specificity and availability of imagined behavioral scripts on expectations about oneself and others." *Social Cognition, 5,* 238–258.

Anderson, C. A., Lepper, M. R., & Ross, L. (1980). "Perseverance of social theories: The role of explanation in the persistence of discredited information." *Journal of Personality and Social Psychology, 39,* 1037–1049.

Anderson, J. R. (1983). *The architecture of cognition.* Cambridge, MA: Harvard University Press.

Anderson, J. R. (1993). *Rules of the mind.* Hillsdale, NJ: Lawrence Erlbaum Associates.

Anderson, N. H. (1981). *Foundations of information integration theory.* New York: Academic Press.

Anderson, N. H. (1982). *Methods of information integration theory.* New York: Academic Press.

Anderson, N. H., & Shanteau, J. C. (1970). "Information integration in risky decision making." *Journal of Experimental Psychology, 84,* 441–451.

Andreaoli, V., & Worchel, S. (1978). "Effects of media, communicator, and position of message on attitude change." *Public Opinion Quarterly, 42,* 59–70.

Ansoff, H. I. (1957). "Strategies for diversification." *Harvard Business Review, 35,* 113–124.

Armstrong, G. M., Gurol, M. N., & Russ, F. A. (1979). "Detecting and correcting deceptive advertising." *Journal of Consumer Research, 6,* 237–246.

Aronson, E., Ellsworth, P. C., Carlsmith, J. M., & Gonzales, M. H. (1990). *Methods of research in social psychology.* New York: McGraw-Hill.

Asch, S. (1948). "The doctrine of suggestion, prestige, and imitation in social psychology." *Psychological Review, 55,* 250–276.

Assmus, G., Farley, J. U., & Lehmann, D. R. (1984). "How advertising affects sales: Meta-analysis of econometric results." *Journal of Marketing Research, 21,* 65–74.

Atkinson, R. C., & Shiffrin, R. M. (1968). "Human memory: A proposed system and its control processes." In K. W. Spence & J. T. Spence (Eds.), *Advances in the psychology of learning and motivation research and theory* (Vol. 2). New York: Academic Press.

Axsom, D., Yates, S. M., & Chaiken, S. (1987). "Audience response as a heuristic cue in persuasion." *Journal of Personality and Social Psychology, 53,* 30–40.

Bacheldor, B. (2000). "Amazon.com." *Informationweek, 773,* 50.

Baddeley, A. D. (1966a). "The influence of acoustic and semantic similarity on long-term memory for work sequences." *Quarterly Journal of Experimental Psychology, 18,* 302–309.

Baddeley, A. D. (1966b). "Short-term memory for word sequences as a function of acoustic, semantic, and formal similarity." *Quarterly Journal of Experimental Psychology, 18,* 362–365.

Bagozzi, R. P., Baumgartner, H., & Yi, Y. (1992). "State versus action orientation and the theory of reasoned action: An application to coupon usage." *Journal of Consumer Research, 18,* 505–518.

Bagozzi, R. P., & Silk, A. J. (1983). "Recall, recognition, and the measurement of memory for print advertisements." *Marketing Science, 2,* 95–134.

Bagozzi, R. P., & Warshaw, P. R. (1990). "Trying to consume." *Journal of Consumer Research, 17,* 127–140.

Bagozzi, R. P., Wong, N., Abe, S., & Bergami, M. (2000). "Cultural and situational contingencies and the theory of reasoned action: Application to fast food restaurant consumption." *Journal of Consumer Psychology, 9,* 97–106.

Bahrick, H. P., Bahrick, L. E., Bahrick, A. S., & Bahrick, P. E. (1993). "Maintenance of foreign language and the spacing effect." *Psychological Science, 4,* 316–321.

Bahrick, H. P., Bahrick, P. O., & Wittinger, R. P. (1975). "Fifty years of memory for names and faces: A cross-sectional approach." *Journal of Experimental Psychology: General, 104,* 54–75.

Bahrick, H. P., & Hall, L. K. (1991). "Lifetime maintenance of high school mathematics content." *Journal of Experimental Psychology: General, 120,* 20–33.

Bahrick, H. P., Hall, L. K., & Berger, S. A. (1996). "Accuracy and distortion in memory for high school grades." *Psychological Science, 7,* 265–271.

Bandura, A., Grusec, J. E., & Menlove, F. L. (1967). "Vicarious extinction of avoidance behavior." *Journal of Personality and Social Psychology, 5,* 16–23

Bandura, A., & Menlove, F. L. (1968). "Factors determining vicarious extinction of avoidance behavior through symbolic modeling." *Journal of Personality and Social Psychology, 8,* 99–108.

Batra, R., & Ray, M. L. (1986). "Affective responses mediating acceptance of advertising." *Journal of Consumer Research, 13,* 234–249.

Batra, R., & Stayman, D. M. (1990). "The role of mood in advertising effectiveness." *Journal of Consumer Research, 17,* 203–214.

Baumgardner, M. H., Leippe, M. R., Ronis, D. L., & Greenwald, A. G. (1983). "In search of reliable persuasion effects: II. Associative interference and persistence of persuasion in a message-dense environment." *Journal of Personality and Social Psychology, 45,* 524–537.

Bazerman, M. H. (1990). *Judgment in managerial decision making.* New York: Wiley.

Bearden, W. O., & Etzel, M. J. (1982). "Reference group influence on product and brand purchase decisions." *Journal of Consumer Research, 9,* 183–194.

Bearden, W. O., & Rose, R. L. (1990). "Attention to social comparison information: An individual difference factor affecting consumer conformity." *Journal of Consumer Research, 16,* 461–471.

Bearden, W. O., Netemeyer, R. G., & Teel, J. E. (1989)." Measurement of consumer susceptibility to interpersonal influence." *Journal of Consumer Research, 15,* 472–480.

Beatty, S., & Smith, S. (1987). "External search effort: An investigation across several product categories." *Journal of Consumer Research, 14,* 83–95.

Becherer, R. C., & Richard, L. M. (1978). "Self-monitoring as a moderating variable in consumer behavior." *Journal of Consumer Research, 5,* 159–162.

Beckwith, N. E., & Lehmann, D. R. (1975). "The importance of halo effects in multi-attribute attitude models." *Journal of Marketing Research, 12,* 265–275.

Bem, D. J. (1965). "An experimental analysis of self-persuasion." *Journal of Experimental Social Psychology, 1,* 199–218.

Bem, D. J. (1972). "Self-perception theory." In L. Berkowitz (Ed.), *Advances in experimental social psychology* (Vol. 6, pp. 1–62). New York: Academic Press.

Berger, I. E., & Mitchell, A. A. (1989). "The effect of advertising on attitude accessibillity, attitude confidence, and the attitude-behavior relationship." *Journal of Consumer Research, 16,* 269–279.

Berlyne, D. E. (1970). "Novelty, complexity, and hedonic value." *Perception and Psychophysics, 8,* 279–286.

Berlyne, D. E. (1971). *Aesthetics and psychobiology.* New York: Appleton-Century-Crofts.

Bettman, J. R. (1979). *An information processing theory of consumer choice.* Reading, MA: Addison-Wesley.

Biehal, G. J., & Chakravarti, D. (1982). "Information presentation format and learning goals as determinants of consumers' memory retrieval and choice processes." *Journal of Consumer Research, 8,* 431–441.

Biehal, G. J., & Chakravarti, D. (1983). "Information accessibility as a moderator of consumer choice." *Journal of Consumer Research, 10,* 1–14.

Biehal, G. J., & Chakravarti, D. (1986). "Consumers' use of memory and external information in choice: Macro and micro processing perspectives." *Journal of Consumer Research, 12,* 382–405.

Bierley, C., McSweeney, F. K., & Vannieuwkerk, R. (1985). "Classical conditioning of preferences for stimuli." *Journal of Consumer Research, 12,* 316–323.

Bitran, G. R. (1988). "How the new math of productivity adds up." *Business Week,* June 6.

Bochner, S., & Insko, C. A. (1966). "Communicator discrepancy, source credibility, and opinion change." *Journal of Personality and Social Psychology, 4,* 614–621.

Bounds, W. (1999). "Online: Here comes the bride, clicking a mouse." *Wall Street Journal,* January 14, B1.

Bower, G. H., Clark, M. C., Lesgold, A. M., & Winzenz, D. (1969). "Hierarchical retrieval schemes in recall of categorical word lists." *Journal of Verbal Learning and Verbal Behavior, 8,* 323–343.

Bornstein, R. F. (1989). "Exposure and affect: Overview and meta-analysis of research, 1968–1987." *Psychological Bulletin, 106,* 265–289.

Bransford, J. D., & Johnson, M. K. (1972). "Contextual prerequisites for understanding: Some investigations of comprehension and recall." *Journal of Verbal Learning and Verbal Behavior, 11,* 717–726.

Brehm, J. W. (1956). "Postdecision changes in the desirability of alternatives." *Journal of Abnormal and Social Psychology, 52,* 384–389.

Brehm, J. W. (1966). *A theory of psychological reactance.* New York: Academic Press.

Brickman, P., Coates, D., & Janoff-Bulman, R. (1978). "Lottery winners and accident victims: Is happiness relative?" *Journal of Personality and Social Psychology, 36,* 917–927.

Britt, S. H., Adams, S. C., & Miller, A. S. (1972). "How many advertising exposures per day?" *Journal of Advertising Research, 12,* 3–9.

Brockner, J., Guzzi, B., Kane, J., Levine, E., & Shaplen, K. (1984). "Organizational fundraising: Further evidence on the effect of legitimizing small donations." *Journal of Consumer Research, 11,* 611–614.

Broniarczyk, S. M., & Alba, J. W. (1994a). "The role of consumers' intuitions in inference making." *Journal of Consumer Research, 18,* 325–345.

Broniarczyk, S. M., & Alba, J. W. (1994b). "Theory versis data in prediction and correlation tasks." *Organizational Behavior and Human Decision Processes, 57,* 117–139.

Brown, C. L., & Carpenter, G. S. (2000). "'Why is the trivial important?' A reasons-based account for the effects of trivial attributes on choice." *Journal of Consumer Research, 26,* 372–385.

Brown, S. P., Homer, P. M., & Inman, J. J. (1998). "A meta-analysis of relationships between ad-evoked feelings and advertising response." *Journal of Marketing Research, 35,* 114–126.

Buehler, R., Griffin, D., & Ross, M. (1994). "Exploring the 'planning fallacy': Why people underestimate their completion times." *Journal of Personality and Social Psychology, 67,* 366–381.

Burger, J. M. (1986). "Increasing compliance by improving the deal: The that's-not-all technique." *Journal of Personality and Social Psychology, 51,* 277–283.

Burke, R. R., & Srull, T. K. (1988). "Competitive interference and consumer memory for advertising." *Journal of Consumer Research, 15,* 55–68.

Byrne, D. (1971). *The attraction paradigm.* New York: Academic Press.

Cacioppo, J. T., Marshall-Goodell, B. S., Tassinary, L. G., & Petty, R. E. (1992). "Rudimentary determinants of attitudes: Classical conditioning is more effective when prior knowledge about the attitude stimulus is low than high." *Journal of Experimental Social Psychology, 28,* 207–233.

Cacioppo, J. T., & Petty, R. E. (1982). "The need for cognition." *Journal of Personality and Social Psychology, 42,* 116–131.

Cacioppo, J. T., & Petty, R. E. (1985). "Central and peripheral routes to persuasion: The role of message repetition." In L. F. Alwitt & A. A. Mitchell (Eds.), *Psychological processes and advertising effects: Theory, research, and application* (pp. 91–111). Hillsdale, NJ: Lawrence Erlbaum Associates.

Cacioppo, J. T., Petty, R. E., & Kao, C. F. (1984). "The efficient assessment of need for cognition." *Journal of Personality Assessment, 48,* 306–307.

Calder, B. J., & Sternthal, B. (1980). "Television commercial wearout: An information processing view." *Journal of Marketing Research, 17,* 173–186.

Cann, A., Sherman, S. J., & Elkes, R. (1975). "Effects of initial request size and timing of a second request on compliance: The foot-in-the-door and door-in-the-face." *Journal of Personality and Social Psychology, 32,* 774–782.

Cantor, J. R., Bryant, J., & Zillmann, D. (1974). "Enhancement of humor appreciation by transferred excitation." *Journal of Personality and Social Psychology, 30,* 812–821.

Carpenter, G. S., Glazer, R., & Nakamoto, K. (1994). "Meaningful brands from meaningless differentiation: The dependence on irrelevant attributes." *Journal of Marketing Research, 31,* 339–350.

Carpenter, G. S., & Nakamoto, K. (1989). "Consumer preference formation and pioneering advantage." *Journal of Marketing Research, 26,* 285–298.

Carroll, J. S. (1978). "The effect of imagining an event on expectations for the event: An interpretation in terms of the availability heuristic." *Journal of Experimental Social Psychology, 14,* 88–96.

Celsi, R. L., & Olson, J. C. (1988). "The role of involvement in attention and comprehension processes." *Journal of Consumer Research, 15,* 210–224.

Chaiken, S. (1980). "Heuristic versus systematic information processing and the use of source versus message cues in persuasion." *Journal of Personality and Social Psychology, 39,* 752–766.

Chaiken, S., & Eagly, A. H. (1976). "Communication modality as a determinant of message persuasiveness and message comprehensibility." *Journal of Personality and Social Psychology, 34,* 605–614.

Chaiken, S., & Eagly, A. H. (1983). "Communication modality as a determinant of persuasion: The role of communicator salience." *Journal of Personality and Social Psychology, 45,* 241–256.

Chaiken, S., Liberman, A., & Eagly, A. H. (1989). "Heuristic and systematic information processing within and beyond the persuasion context." In J. S. Uleman & J. A. Bargh (Eds.), *Unintended thought* (pp. 212–252). New York: Guilford.

Chaiken, S., & Yates, S. M. (1985). "Affective-cognitive consistency and thought-induced attitude polarization." *Journal of Personality and Social Psychology, 49,* 1470–1481.

Chandrashekaran, M., Walker, B. A., Ward, J. C., & Reingen, P. H. (1996). "Modeling individual preference evolution and choice in a dynamic group setting." *Journal of Marketing Research, 33,* 211–223.

Chanowitz, B., & Langer, E. J. (1981). "Premature cognitive commitment." *Journal of Personality and Social Psychology, 41,* 1051–1063.

Childers, T. L., & Houston, M. J. (1984). "Conditions for a picture-superiority effect on consumer memory." *Journal of Consumer Research, 15,* 643–654.

Cialdini, R. B. (1993). *Influence: Science and practice.* New York: HarperCollins.

Cialdini, R. B., Borden, R. J., Thorne, A., Walker, M. R., Freeman, S., & Sloan, L. R. (1976). "Basking in reflected glory: Three (football) field studies." *Journal of Personality and Social Psychology, 34,* 366–375.

Cialdini, R. B., Cacioppo, J. T., Bassett, R., & Miller, J. A. (1978). "Low-ball procedure for producing compliance: Commitment then cost." *Journal of Personality and Social Psychology, 36,* 463–476.

Cialdini, R. B., & Shroeder, D. A. (1976). "Increasing compliance by legitimizing paltry contributions: When even a penny helps." *Journal of Personality and Social Psychology, 34,* 599–604.

Cialdini, R. B., Vincent, J. E., Lewis, S. K., Catalan, J., Wheeler, D., & Darby, B. L. (1975). "Reciprocal concessions procedure for inducing compliance: The door-in-the-face technique." *Journal of Personality and Social Psychology, 31,* 206–215.

Cialdini, R. B., Wosinska, W., Barrett, D. W., Butner, J., & Gornik-Durose, M. (1999). "Compliance with a request in two cultures: The differential influence of social proof and commitment/consistency on collectivists and individualists." *Personality and Social Psychology Bulletin, 25,* 1242–1253.

Clee, M. A., & Wicklund, R. A. (1980). "Consumer behavior and psychological reactance." *Journal of Consumer Research, 6,* 389–405.

Collins, A. M., & Loftus, E. F. (1975). "A spreading-activation theory of semantic processing." *Psychological Review, 82,* 407–428.

Collins, A. M., & Quillian, M. R. (1969). "Retrieval time from semantic memory." *Journal of Verbal Learning and Verbal Behavior, 8,* 240–247.

Colombo, J. R. (1987). *New Canadian quotations.* Edmonton, Alberta: Hurtig.

Comer, J. M., Kardes, F. R., & Sullivan, A. K. (1992). "Multiple deescalating requests, statistical information, and compliance: A field experiment." *Journal of Applied Social Psychology, 22,* 1199–1207.

Cook, T. D., Gruder, C. L., Hennigan, K. M., & Flay, B. R. (1979). "History of the sleeper effect: Some logical pitfalls in accepting the null hypothesis." *Psychological Bulletin, 86,* 662–679.

Cooper, J., & Fazio, R. H. (1984). "A new look at dissonance theory." In L. Berkowitz (Ed.), *Advances in experimental social psychology* (Vol. 17, pp. 229–266). New York: Academic Press.

Corteen, R. S., & Wood, B. (1972). "Autonomic responses to shock-associated words in an unattended channel." *Journal of Experimental Psychology, 94,* 308–313.

Cox, A. D., & Summers, J. O. (1987). "Heuristics and biases in the intuitive projection of retail sales." *Journal of Marketing Research, 24,* 290–297.

Csikszentmihalyi, M. (1990). *Flow: The psychology of optimal experience.* New York: Harper & Row.

Dalrymple, D. J., & Parsons, L. J. (1990). *Marketing management.* New York: Wiley.

Darby, M. R., & Karni, E. (1973). "Free competition and the optimal amount of fraud." *Journal of Law and Economics, 16,* 66–86.

Davis, B. P., & Knowles, E. S. (1999). "A disrupt-then-reframe technique of social influence." *Journal of Personality and Social Psychology, 76,* 192–199.

Dawes, R. M. (1988). *Rational choice in an uncertain world.* San Diego: Harcourt Brace Jovanovich.

Dawes, R. M. (1994). *House of cards: Psychology and psychotherapy built on myth.* New York: Free Press.

DeBono, K. G., & Harnish, R. J. (1988). "Source expertise, source attractiveness, and the processing of persuasive information: A functional approach." *Journal of Personality and Social Psychology, 52,* 279–287.

DeJong, W. (1979). "An examination of self-perception mediation of the foot-in-the-door effect." *Journal of Personality and Social Psychology, 37,* 2221–2239.

Deutsch, M., & Gerard, H. B. (1955). "A study of normative and informational social influences upon individual judgment." *Journal of Abnormal and Social Psychology, 51,* 629–636.

Dickson, P. R., & Sawyer, A. G. (1990). "The price knowledge and search of supermarket shoppers." *Journal of Marketing, 54,* 42–53.

Dodson, J. A., Tybout, A. M., & Sternthal, B. (1978). "Impact of deals and deal retraction on brand switching." *Journal of Marketing Research, 15,* 72–81.

Dube-Rioux, L., & Russo, J. E. (1988). "An availability bias in professional judgment." *Journal of Behavioral Decision Making, 1,* 223–237.

Dunning, D., Griffin, D. W., Milojkovic, J. D., & Ross, L. (1990). "The overconfidence effect in social prediction." *Journal of Personality and Social Psychology, 58,* 568–581.

Dutton, D. G., & Aron, A. P. (1974). "Some evidence for heightened sexual attraction under conditions of high anxiety." *Journal of Personality and Social Psychology, 30,* 510–517.

Dwyer, P., Landler, M., Melcher, R., & Weber, J. (1994). "The trouble with Saatchi." *Business Week, 3368,* 102–103.

Eagly, A. H. (1974). "Comprehensibility of persuasive arguments as a determinant of opinion change." *Journal of Personality and Social Psychology, 29,* 758–773.

Eagly, A. H., Ashmore, R. D., Makhijani, M. G., & Longo, L. C. (1990). "What is beautiful if good, but . . . : A meta-analytic review of research on the physical attractiveness stereotype." *Psychological Bulletin, 110,* 109–128.

Eagly, A. H., & Chaiken, S. (1993). *The psychology of attitudes.* Fort Worth, TX: Harcourt Brace.

Eagly, A. H., & Warren, R. (1976). "Intelligence, comprehension, and opinion change." *Journal of Personality, 44,* 226–242.

Eich, J. E. (1980). "The cue-dependent nature of state-dependent retention." *Memory and Cognition, 8,* 157–173.

Eich, J. E. (1989). "Theoretical issues in state-dependent memory." In H. L. Roediger & F. I. M. Craik (Eds.), *Varieties of memory and consciousness* (pp. 331–354). Hillsdale, NJ: Lawrence Erlbaum Associates.

Einhorn, H. J. (1970). "The use of nonlinear, noncompensatory models in decision making." *Psychological Bulletin, 73,* 221–230.

Etgar, M., & Goodwin, S. M. (1982). "One-sided versus two-sided comparative message appeals for new brand introductions." *Journal of Consumer Research, 8,* 460–465.

Faison, E. W. (1961). "Effectiveness of one-sided and two-sided mass communications and advertising." *Public Opinion Quarterly, 25,* 468–469.

Farquhar, P. H. (1989). "Managing brand equity." *Marketing Research, 1,* 24–33.

Fazio, R. H. (1986). "How do attitudes guide behavior?" In R. M. Sorrentino & E. T. Higgins (Eds.), *The handbook of motivation and cognition: Foundations of social behavior* (pp. 204–243). New York: Guilford.

Fazio, R. H. (1989). "On the power and functionality of attitudes: The role of attitude accessibility." In A. R. Pratkanis, S. J. Breckler, & A. G. Greenwald (Eds.), *Attitude structure and function* (pp. 153–179). Hillsdale, NJ: Lawrence Erlbaum Associates.

Fazio, R. H. (1990). "Multiple processes by which attitudes guide behavior: The MODE model as an integrative framework." In M. P. Zanna (Ed.), *Advances in experimental social psychology* (pp. 75–109). New York: Academic Press.

Fazio, R. H. (1995). "Attitudes as object-evaluation associations: Determinants, consequences, and correlates of attitude accessibility." In R. E. Petty & J. A. Krosnick (Eds.), *Attitude strength: Antecedents and consequences* (pp. 247–282). Hillsdale, NJ: Lawrence Erlbaum Associates.

Fazio, R. H., Powell, M. C., & Herr, P. M. (1983). "Toward a process model of the attitude-behavior relation: Accessing one's attitude upon mere observation of the attitude object." *Journal of Personality and Social Psychology, 44,* 723–735.

Fazio, R. H., Powell, M. C., & Williams, C. J. (1989). "The role of attitude accessibility in the attitude-to-behavior process." *Journal of Consumer Research, 16,* 280–288.

Fazio, R. H., Sanbonmatsu, D. M., Powell, M. C., & Kardes, F. R. (1986). "On the automatic activation of attitudes." *Journal of Personality and Social Psychology, 50,* 229–238.

Fazio, R. H., Zanna, M. P., & Cooper, J. (1977). "Dissonance and self-perception: An integrative view of each theory's proper domain of application." *Journal of Experimental Social Psychology, 13,* 464–479.

Feinberg, R. A. (1986). "Credit cards as spending facilitating stimuli." *Journal of Consumer Research, 13,* 348–356.

Feldman, J. M., & Lynch, J. G. (1988). "Self-generated validity and other effects of measurement on belief, attitude, intention, and behavior." *Journal of Applied Psychology, 73,* 421–435.

Festinger, L. (1954). "A theory of social comparison processes." *Human Relations, 7,* 117–140.

Festinger, L. (1957). *A theory of cognitive dissonance.* Evanston, IL: Row and Peterson.

Festinger, L., & Carlsmith, J. M. (1959). "Cognitive consequences of forced compliance." *Journal of Abnormal and Social Psychology, 58,* 203–210.

Fine, B. J. (1957). "Conclusion-drawing, communicator credibility, and anxiety as factors in opinion change." *Journal of Abnormal and Social Psychology, 54,* 369–374.

Fischhoff, B., & Beyth-Marom, R. (1983). "Hypothesis evaluation from a Bayesian perspective." *Psychological Review, 90,* 239–260.

Fischhoff, B., Slovic, P., Derby, S. L., & Keeney, R. L. (1981). *Acceptable risk.* Cambridge, UK: Cambridge University Press.

Fischhoff, B., Slovic, P., & Lichtenstein, S. (1977). "Knowing with certainty: The appropriateness of extreme confidence." *Journal of Experimental Psychology: Human Perception and Performance, 3,* 552–564.

Fischhoff, B., Slovic, P., & Lichtenstein, S. (1978). "Fault trees: Sensitivity of estimated failure probabilities to problem representation." *Journal of Experimental Psychology: Human Perception and Performance, 4,* 330–344.

Fischhoff, B., Slovic, P., & Lichtenstein, S. (1979). "Subjective sensitivity analysis." *Organizational Behavior and Human Decision Processes, 23,* 339–359.

Fishbein, M., & Ajzen, I. (1975). *Belief, attitude, intention, and behavior: An introduction to theory and research.* Reading, MA: Addison-Wesley.

Fisk, R. P., Grove, S. J., & John, J. (2000). *Interactive services marketing.* Boston: Houghton-Mifflin.

Fiske, S. T., & Taylor, S. E. (1991). *Social cognition.* New York: McGraw-Hill.

Folkes, V. S. (1984). "Consumer reactions to product failure: An attributional approach." *Journal of Consumer Research, 10,* 398–409.

Folkes, V. S. (1985). "Mindlessness or mindfulness: A partial replication and extension of Langer, Blank, & Chanowitz." *Journal of Personality and Social Psychology, 48,* 600–604.

Folkes, V. S. (1988). "Recent attribution research in consumer behavior: A review and new directions." *Journal of Consumer Research, 14,* 548–565.

Folkes, V. S., & Kotsos, B. (1986). "Buyers' and sellers' explanations for product failure: Who done it." *Journal of Marketing, 50,* 74–80.

Fong, G. T., Krantz, D. H., & Nisbett, R. E. (1986). "The effects of statistical training on thinking about everyday problems." *Cognitive Psychology, 18,* 253–292.

Fong, G. T., & Nisbett, R. E. (1991). "Immediate and delayed transfer of training effects in statistical reasoning." *Journal of Experimental Psychology: General, 120,* 34–45.

Ford, G. T., & Smith, R. A. (1987). "Inferential beliefs in consumer evaluations: An assessment of alternative processing strategies." *Journal of Consumer Research, 14,* 363–371.

Freedman, J., & Fraser, S. (1966). "Compliance without pressure: The foot-in-the-door technique." *Journal of Personality and Social Psychology, 4,* 195–202.

Friestad, M., & Wright, P. (1994). "The persuasion knowledge model: How people cope with persuasion attempts." *Journal of Consumer Research, 21,* 1–31.

Friestad, M., & Wright, P. (1995). "Persuasion knowledge: Lay people's and researchers' beliefs about the psychology of persuasion." *Journal of Consumer Research, 22,* 62–74.

Gaes, G. G., Kalle, R. J., & Tedeschi, J. T. (1978). "Impression management in the forced compliance situation." *Journal of Experimental Social Psychology, 14,* 493–510.

Gavanski, I., & Roskos-Ewoldson, D. R. (1991). "Representativeness and conjoint probability." *Journal of Personality and Social Psychology, 61,* 181–194.

Gigone, D., & Hastie, R. (1993). "The common knowledge effect: Information sharing and group judgment." *Journal of Personality and Social Psychology, 65,* 959–974.

Gigone, D., & Hastie, R. (1997). "Proper analysis of the accuracy of group judgments." *Psychological Bulletin, 121,* 149–167.

Gilbert, D. T. (1991). "How mental systems believe." *American Psychologist, 46,* 107–119.

Gilbert, D. T., & Jones, E. E. (1986). "Perceiver-induced constraint: Interpretations of self-generated reality." *Journal of Personality and Social Psychology, 50,* 269–280.

Gilbert, D. T., Jones, E. E., & Pelham, B. W. (1987). "Influence and inference: What the active perceiver overlooks. *Journal of Personality and Social Psychology, 52,* 861–870.

Gilbert, D. T., & Krull, D. S. (1988). "Seeing less and knowing more: The benefits of perceptual ignorance." *Journal of Personality and Social Psychology, 54,* 193–202.

Gilbert, D. T., Krull, D. S., & Malone, P. S. (1990). "Unbelieving the unbelievable: Some problems in the rejection of false information." *Journal of Personality and Social Psychology, 59,* 601–613.

Gilbert, D. T., & Malone, P. S. (1995). "The correspondence bias." *Psychological Bulletin, 117,* 21–38.

Gilbert, D. T., Tafarodi, R. W., & Malone, P. S. (1993). "You can't not believe everything you read." *Journal of Personality and Social Psychology, 65,* 221–233.

Gilovich, T. (1981). "Seeing the past in the present: The effect of associations to familiar events on judgments and decisions." *Journal of Personality and Social Psychology, 40,* 797–808.

Gilovich, T. (1987). "Secondhand information and social judgment." *Journal of Experimental Social Psychology, 23,* 59–74.

Gilovich, T. (1991). *How we know what isn't so: The fallibility of human reason in everyday life.* New York: Free Press.

Gilovich, T., Vallone, R., & Tversky, A. (1985). "The hot hand in basketball: On the misperception of random sequences. " *Cognitive Psychology, 17,* 295–314.

Glanzer, M., & Cunitz, A. R. (1966). "Two storage mechanisms in free recall. " *Journal of Verbal Learning and Verbal Behavior, 5,* 351–360.

Godden, D. R., & Baddeley, A. D. (1975). "Context-dependent memory in two natural environments: On land and underwater. " *British Journal of Psychology, 66,* 325–332.

Goldberg, M. E., & Hartwick, J. (1990). "The effects of advertiser reputation and extremity of advertising claim on advertising effectiveness. " *Journal of Consumer Research, 17,* 172–179.

Golder, P. N., & Tellis, G. J. (1993). "Pioneer advantage: Marketing logic or marketing legend?" *Journal of Marketing Research, 30,* 158–170.

Goldman, K. (1995). "Fresh alarm is sent over interactive age." *Wall Street Journal,* February 2, B6.

Gorn, G. J. (1982). "The effects of music in advertising on choice behavior: A classical conditioning approach." *Journal of Marketing, 46,* 94–101.

Gorn, G. J., Chattopadhyay, A., Yi, T., & Dahl, D. W. (1997). "Effects of color as an executional cue in advertising: They're in the shade." *Management Science, 43,* 1387–1400.

Gorn, G. J., & Weinberg, C. B. (1984). "The impact of comparative advertising on perception and attitude: Some positive findings." *Journal of Consumer Research, 11,* 719–727.

Gouldner, A. W. (1960). "The norm of reciprocity: A preliminary statement." *American Sociological Review, 25,* 161–178.

Granberg, D., & Brent, E. E. (1974). "Dove-hawk placements in the 1968 election: Application of social judgment and balance theories." *Journal of Personality and Social Psychology, 29,* 687–695.

Greenwald, A. G., & Leavitt, C. (1984). "Audience involvement in advertising: Four levels." *Journal of Consumer Research, 11,* 581–592.

Gregory, W. L., Cialdini, R. B., & Carpenter, K. M. (1982). "Self-relevant scenarios as mediators of likelihood estimates and compliance: Does imagining make it so?" *Journal of Personality and Social Psychology, 43,* 89–99.

Griffin, D. W., Dunning, D., & Ross, L. (1990). "The role of construal processes in overconfident predictions about the self and others." *Journal of Personality and Social Psychology, 59,* 1128–1139.

Gurumurthy, K., & Urban, G. (1992). "Dynamic effects of the order of entry on market share, trial penetration, and repeat purchases for frequently purchased consumer goods." *Marketing Science, 11,* 235–250.

Ha, Y., & Hoch, S. J. (1989). "Ambiguity, processing strategy, and advertising-evidence interactions." *Journal of Consumer Research, 16,* 354–360.

Hall, P. (1980). *Great planning disasters.* London: Weidenfeld & Nicolson.

Hall, R. W. (1983). *Zero inventories.* Homewood, IL: Irwin.

Han, S., & Shavitt, S. (1994). "Persuasion and culture: Advertising appeals in individualistic and collectivistic societies." *Journal of Experimental Social Psychology, 30,* 326–350.

Hannah, D., & Sternthal, B. (1984). "Detecting and explaining the sleeper effect." *Journal of Consumer Research, 11,* 632–642.

Harris, R. J. (1977). "Comprehension of pragmatic implications in advertising." *Journal of Applied Psychology, 62,* 603–608.

Harris, R. J., & Monaco, G. E. (1978). "Psychology of pragmatic implications in advertising: Information processing between the lines." *Journal of Experimental Psychology: General, 107,* 1–22.

Hastie, R. (1983). "Social inference." *Annual Review of Psychology, 34,* 511–542.

Hastie, R. (1984). "Causes and effects of causal attribution." *Journal of Personality and Social Psychology, 46,* 44–56.

Haubl, G., & Trifts, V. (2000). "Consumer decision making in online shopping environments: The effects of interactive decision aids." *Marketing Science, 19,* 4–21.

Haugtvedt, C. P., & Petty, R. E. (1992). "Personality and persuasion: Need for cognition moderates the persistence and resistance of attitude changes." *Journal of Personality and Social Psychology, 63,* 308–319.

Haugtvedt, C. P., Schumann, D. W., Schneier, W. L., & Warren, W. L. (1994). "Advertising repetition and variation strategies: Implications for understanding attitude strength." *Journal of Consumer Research, 21,* 176–189.

Haugtvedt, C. P., & Wegener, D. T. (1994). "Message order effects in persuasion: An attitude strength perspective." *Journal of Consumer Research, 21,* 205–218.

Hawkins, S. A., & Hoch, S. J. (1992). "Low-involvement learning: Memory without evaluation." *Journal of Consumer Research, 19,* 212–225.

Hayes, R., & Wheelright, S. (1984). *Restoring our competitive edge.* New York: Wiley.

Hayes, R., Wheelright, S., & Clark, K. B. (1988). *Dynamic manufacturing.* New York: Free Press.

Heider, F. (1958). *The psychology of interpersonal relations.* New York: Wiley.

Heine, S. J., & Lehman, D. R. (1995). "Cultural variation in unrealistic optimism: Does the West feel more vulnerable than the East?" *Journal of Personality and Social Psychology, 68,* 595–607.

Heine, S. J., & Lehman, D. R. (1997). "The cultural construction of self-enhancement: An examination of group-serving biases." *Journal of Personality and Social Psychology, 72,* 1268–1283.

Helson, H. (1959). "Adaptation level theory." In S. Koch (Ed.), *Psychology: A study of a science* (Vol. 1). New York: McGraw-Hill.

Hemsley, G. D., & Doob, A. M. (1978). "The effect of looking behavior on perceptions of a communicator's credibility." *Journal of Applied Social Psychology, 8,* 136–144.

Herr, P. M. (1986). "Consequences of priming: Judgment and behavior." *Journal of Personality and Social Psychology, 44,* 1106–1115.

Herr, P. M. (1989). "Priming price: Prior knowledge and context effects." *Journal of Consumer Research, 16,* 67–75.

Herr, P. M., Farquhar, P. H., & Fazio, R. H. (1996). "Impact of dominance and relatedness on brand extensions." *Journal of Consumer Psychology, 5,* 135–160.

Herr, P. M., Kardes, F. R., & Kim, J. (1991). "Effects of word-of-mouth and product-attribute information on persuasion: An accessibility-diagnosticity perspective." *Journal of Consumer Research, 17,* 454–462.

Herr, P. M., Sherman, S. J., & Fazio, R. H. (1983). "On the consequences of priming: Assimilation and contrast effects." *Journal of Experimental Social Psychology, 19,* 323–340.

Higgins, E. T. (1996). "Knowlege activation: Accessibility, applicability, and salience." In E. T. Higgins and A. W. Kruglanski (Eds.), *Social psychology: Handbook of basic principles* (pp. 133–168). New York: Guilford.

Higgins, E. T., & King, G. (1981). "Accessibility of social constructs: Information processing consequences of individual and contextual variability." In N. Cantor & J. Kihlstrom (Eds.), *Personality, cognition and social interaction* (pp. 69–122). Hillsdale, NJ: Lawrence Erlbaum Associates.

Hirt, E. R., & Castellan, N. J. (1988). "Probability and category redefinition in the fault tree paradigm." *Journal of Experimental Psychology: Human Perception and Performance, 14,* 122–131.

Hirt, E. R., & Markman, K. D. (1995). "Multiple explanation: A consider-an-alternative strategy for debiasing judgments." *Journal of Personality and Social Psychology, 69,* 1069–1086.

Hirt, E. R., & Sherman, S. J. (1985). "The role of prior knowledge in explaining hypothetical events." *Journal of Experimental Social Psychology, 21,* 519–543.

Hirt, E. R., Zillmann, D., Erickson, G. A., & Kennedy, C. (1992). "Costs and benefits of allegiance: Changes in fans' self-ascribed competencies after team victory versus defeat." *Journal of Personality and Social Psychology, 63,* 724–738.

Hoch, S. J. (1984). "Availability and interference in predictive judgment." *Journal of Experimental Psychology: Learning, Memory, and Cognition, 10,* 649–662.

Hoch, S. J. (1985). "Counterfactual reasoning and accuracy in predicting personal events." *Journal of Experimental Psychology: Learning, Memory, and Cognition, 11,* 719–731.

Hoch, S. J., & Deighton, J. (1989). "Managing what consumers learn from experience." *Journal of Marketing, 53,* 1–20.

Hoch, S. J., & Ha, Y. (1986). "Consumer learning: Advertising and the ambiguity of product experience." *Journal of Consumer Research, 13,* 221–233.

Hof, R. D., Green, H. & Brady, D. (2000). "Suddenly, Amazon's books look better: The e-tailer is raking in a bundle—from other merchants." *Business Week,* Feb. 21, 78–84.

Hoffman, D. L., & Novak, T. P. (1996). "Marketing in hypermedia computer-mediated environments: Conceptual foundations." *Journal of Marketing, 60,* 50–68.

Hong, S., & Wyer, R. S. (1989). "Effects of country-of-origin and product-attribute information on product evaluation: An information processing perspective." *Journal of Consumer Research, 16,* 175–187.

Hong, S., & Wyer, R. S. (1990). "Determinants of product evaluation: Effects of the time interval between knowledge of a product's country of origin and information about its specific attributes." *Journal of Consumer Research, 17,* 277–288.

Houghton, D. C., & Kardes, F. R. (1998). "Market share overestimation and the noncomplementarity effect." *Marketing Letters, 9,* 313–320.

Houston, D. A., Sherman, S. J., & Baker, S. M. (1991). "Feature matching, unique features, and the dynamics of the choice process: Predecision conflict and postdecision satisfaction." *Journal of Experimental Social Psychology, 27,* 411–430.

Houston, M. J., Childers, T. L., & Heckler, S. E. (1987). "Picture-word consistency and the elaborative processing of advertisements." *Journal of Marketing Research, 24,* 359–370.

Hovland, C. I., Janis I. L., & Kelley, H. H. (1953). *Communication and persuasion.* New Haven, CT: Yale University Press.

Hovland, C. I., Lumsdaine, A. A., & Sheffield, F. D. (1949). *Experiments on mass communication.* Princeton, NJ: Princeton University Press.

Hovland, C. I., & Mandell, W. (1952). "An experimental comparison of conclusion-drawing by the communicator and by the audience." *Journal of Abnormal and Social Psychology, 47,* 581–588.

Hovland, C. I., & Weiss, W. (1951). "The influence of source credibility on communication effectiveness." *Public Opinion Quarterly, 15,* 635–650.

Howard, D. J. (1990). "The influence of verbal responses to common greetings on compliance behavior: The foot-in-the-mouth effect." *Journal of Applied Social Psychology, 20,* 1185–1196.

Howard, D. J., Gengler, C., & Jain, A. (1995). "What's in a name? A complimentary means of persuasion." *Journal of Consumer Research, 22,* 200–211.

Huber, J., & McCann, J. W. (1982). "The impact of inferential beliefs on product evaluations." *Journal of Marketing Research, 19,* 324–333.

Huber, J., Payne, J. W., & Puto, C. (1982). "Adding asymmetrically dominated alternatives: Violations of regularity and the similarity hypothesis." *Journal of Consumer Research, 9,* 90–98.

Huber, J., & Puto, C. (1983). "Market boundaries and product choice: Illustrating attraction and substitution effects." *Journal of Consumer Research, 10,* 31–44.

Insko, C. A. (1965). "Verbal reinforcement of attitude." *Journal of Personality and Social Psychology, 2,* 621–623.

Insko, C. A. (1981). "Balance theory and phenomenology." In R. E. Petty, T. M. Ostrom, & T. C. Brock (Eds.), *Cognitive responses in persuasion* (pp. 309–338). Hillsdale, NJ: Lawrence Erlbaum Associates.

Insko, C. A. (1984). "Balance theory, the Jordan paradigm, and the Wiest tetrahedron." In L. Berkowitz (Ed.), *Advances in experimental social psychology* (Vol. 18, pp. 89–140). New York: Academic Press.

Insko, C. A., & Butzine, K. W. (1967). "Rapport, awareness, and verbal reinforcement of attitude." *Journal of Personality and Social Psychology, 6,* 225–228.

Insko, C. A., & Cialdini, R. B. (1969). "A test of three interpretations of attitudinal reinforcement." *Journal of Personality and Social Psychology, 12,* 331–341.

Isen, A. M. (1984). "Toward understanding the role of affect in cognition." In R. S. Wyer & T. K. Srull (Eds.), *Handbook of social cognition* (Vol. 3, pp. 179–236). Hillsdale, NJ: Lawrence Erlbaum Associates.

Isen, A. M. (1987). "Positive affect, cognitive processes, and social behavior." In L. Berkowitz (Ed.), *Advances in experimental social psychology* (Vol. 20, pp. 203–253). New York: Academic Press.

Isen, A. M., Aspinwall, L. G., O'Brien, T. C., & Fadem, T. J. (2000). *Integrating basic research on consumer motivation with new business development: New ways to consider consumers.* Unpublished manuscript.

Isen, A. M., Daubman, K. A., & Nowicki, G. P. (1987). "Positive affect facilitates creative problem solving." *Journal of Personality and Social Psychology, 52,* 1122–1131.

Jacoby, L. L. (1991). "A process dissociation framework: Separating automatic from intentional uses of memory." *Journal of Memory and Language, 30,* 513–541.

Jacoby, L. L., Kelley, C. M., & Dywan, J. (1989). "Memory attributions." In H. L. roediger & F. I. M. Craik (Eds.), *Varieties of memory and consciousness: Essays in honor of Endel Tulving* (pp. 391–422). Hillsdale, NJ: Lawrence Erlbaum Associates.

Jacoby, L. L., woloshyn, V., & Kelley, C. M. (1989). "Becoming famous without being recognized: Unconscious influences of memory produced by dividing attention." *Journal of Experimental Psychology: General, 118,* 115–125.

Jaikumar, R. (1986). " Post industrial manufacturing." *Harvard Business Review, 64,* 69–76.

Janis, I. L. (1982). *Groupthink.* Boston: Houghton Mifflin.

Janis, I. L., & King, B. T. (1954). "The influence of role-playing on opinion change." *Journal of Abnormal and Social Psychology, 49,* 211–218.

Jenkins, J. G., & Dallenbach, K. M. (1924). "Oblivescence during sleep and waking." *American Journal of Psychology, 35,* 605–612.

Johnson, E. J., & Russo, J. E. (1984). "Product familiarity and learning new information." *Journal of Consumer Research, 11,* 542–550.

Johnson, R. D., & Levin, I. P. (1985). "More than meets the eye: The effect of missing information on purchase evaluations." *Journal of Consumer Research, 12,* 169–177.

Jones, E. E., & Davis, K. (1965). "From acts to dispositions: The attribution process in person perception." In L. Berkowitz (Ed.), *Advances in experimental social psychology* (Vol. 2, pp. 219–266). New York: Academic Press.

Jones, E. E., & Goethals, G. R. (1971). "Order effects in impression formation: Attribution context and the nature of the entity." In E. E. Jones, D. E. Kanouse, H. H. Kelley, R. E. Nisbett, S. Valins, & B. Weiner (Eds.), *Attribution: Perceiving the causes of behavior* (pp. 95–120). Morristown, NJ: General Learning Press.

Jones, E. E., & Sigall, H. (1971). "The bogus pipeline: A new paradigm for measuring affect and attitude." *Psychological Bulletin, 76,* 349–364.

Jones, E. E., & Wortman, C. (1973). *Ingratiation: An attributional approach.* Morristown, NJ: General Learning Press.

Judd, C. M., & Lusk, C. M. (1984). "Knowledge structures and evaluative judgments: Effects of structural variables on judgmental extremity." *Journal of Personality and Social Psychology, 46,* 1193–1207.

Kahle, L. R., Beatty, S. E., & Homer, P. (1986). "Alternative measurement approaches to consumer values: The list of values (LOV) and values and life style (VALS)." *Journal of Consumer Research, 13,* 405–409.

Kahn, B. E., & Isen, A. M. (1993). "The influence of positive affect on variety seeking among safe, enjoyable products." *Journal of Consumer Research, 20,* 257–270.

Kahneman, D. (1973). *Attention and effort.* Englewood Cliffs, NJ: Prentice-Hall.

Kahneman, D., & Lovallo, D. (1993). "Timid choices and bold forecasts: A cognitive perspective on risk taking." *Management Science, 39,* 17–31.

Kahneman, D., & Miller, D. T. (1986). "Norm theory: Comparing reality to its alternatives." *Psychological Review, 93,* 136–153.

Kahneman, D., Slovic, P., & Tversky, A. (Eds.) (1982). *Judgment under uncertainty: Heuristics and biases.* Cambridge, UK: Cambridge University Press.

Kahneman, D., & Tversky, A. (1979). "Intuitive prediction: Biases and corrective procedures." *TIMS Studies in Management Science, 12,* 313–327.

Kahneman, D., & Tversky, A. (1984). "Choice, values, and frames." *American Psychologist, 39,* 341–350.

Kardes, F. R. (1986). "Effects of initial product judgments on subsequent memory-based judgments." *Journal of Consumer Research, 13,* 1–11.

Kardes, F. R. (1988). "Spontaneous inference processes in advertising: The effects of conclusion omission and involvement on persuasion." *Journal of Consumer Research, 15,* 225–233.

Kardes, F. R. (1993). "Consumer inference: Determinants, consequences, and implications for advertising." In A. A. Mitchell (Ed.), *Advertising exposure, memory and choice.* Hillsdale, NJ: Lawrence Erlbaum Associates.

Kardes, F. R., & Allen, C. T. (1991). "Perceived variability and inferences about brand extensions." *Advances in Consumer Research, 18,* 392–398.

Kardes, F. R., & Cronley, M. L. (2000a). "Managerial decision making." In S. B. Dahiya, (Ed.), *The Current State of Business Disciplines* (Vol. 6, pp. 2921–2934). Rohtak, India: Spellbound Publications.

Kardes, F. R., & Cronley, M. L. (2000b). "The role of approach/avoidance asymmetries in motivated belief formation and change." In S. Ratneshwar, D. G. Mick, & C. Huffman (Eds.), *The why of consumption: Contemporary perspectives on consumer motives, goals, and desires* (pp. 81–97). London, England: Routledge.

Kardes, F. R., Cronley, M. L., Pontes, M. C., & Houghton, D. C. (in press). "Down the garden path: The role of conditional inference processes in self-persuasion." *Journal of Consumer Psychology.*

Kardes, F. R., & Gurumurthy, K. (1992). "Order-of-entry effects on consumer memory and judgment: An information integration perspective." *Journal of Marketing Research, 29,* 343–357.

Kardes, F. R., Gurumurthy, K., Chandrashekaran, M., & Dornoff, R. J. (1993). "Brand retrieval, consideration set composition, consumer choice, and the pioneering advantage." *Journal of Consumer Research, 20,* 62–75.

Kardes, F. R., & Herr, P. M. (1990). "Order effects in consumer judgment, choice, and memory: The role of initial processing goals." *Advances in Consumer Research, 17,* 541–546.

Kardes, F. R., Kim, J., & Lim, J. (1994). "Moderating effects of prior knowledge on the perceived diagnosticity of beliefs derived from implicit versus explicit product claims." *Journal of Business Research, 29,* 219–224.

Kardes, F. R., & Kimble, C. E. (1984). "Strategic self-presentation as a function of message valence and the prospect of future interaction." *Representative Research in Social Psychology, 14,* 2–11.

Kardes, F. R., & Sanbonmatsu, D. M. (1993). "Direction of comparison, expected feature correlation, and the set-size effect in preference judgment." *Journal of Consumer Psychology, 2,* 39–54.

Karmarkar, U. S. (1987). "Lotsizing, manufacturing lead times and utilization." *Management Science, 13,* 11.

Katz, D. (1960). "The functional approach to the study of attitudes." *Public Opinion Quarterly, 24,* 163–204.

Kekre, S., & Srinivasan, K. (1990). "Broader product line: A necessity to achieve success?" *Management Science, 36,* 1216–1231.

Keller, K. L. (1987). "Memory in advertising: The effect of advertising memory cues on brand evaluations." *Journal of Consumer Research, 14,* 316–333.

Keller, K. L. (1998). *Strategic brand management: Building, measuring, and managing brand equity.* Upper Saddle River, NJ: Prentice Hall.

Kelley, H. H. (1967). "Attribution theory in social psychology." In D. Levine (Ed.), *Nebraska symposium on motivation* (Vol. 15, pp. 192–238). Lincoln, NE: University of Nebraska Press.

Kelley, H. H. (1971). "Attribution in social interaction." In E. E. Jones, D. E. Kanouse, H. H. Kelley, R. E. Nisbett, S. Valins, & B. Weiner (Eds.), *Attribution: Perceiving the causes of behavior* (pp. 95–120). Morristown, NJ: General Learning Press.

Kelley, H. H. (1973). "The processes of causal attribution." *American Psychologist, 28,* 107–128.

Kelman, H. C. (1961). "Processes of opinion change." *Public Opinion Quarterly, 25,* 57–78.

Kelman, H. C., & Hovland, C. I. (1953). " 'Reinstatement' of the communicator in delayed measurement opinion change." *Journal of Abnormal and Social Psychology, 48,* 327–335.

Kenrick, D. T., & Gutierres, S. E. (1980). "Contrast effects and judgments of physical attractiveness: When beauty becomes a social problem." *Journal of Personality and Social Psychology, 38,* 131–140.

Kerr, R. A. (1979). "Petroleum exploration: Discouragement about the Atlantic outer continental shelf deepens." *Science,* 1069–1072.

Kiesler, C. A. (1971). *The psychology of commitment.* New York: Academic Press.

Kim, J., Allen, C. T., & Kardes, F. R. (1996). "An investigation of the mediational mechanisms underlying attitudinal conditioning." *Journal of Marketing Research, 33,* 318–328.

King, B. T., & Janis, I. L. (1956). "Comparison of the effectiveness of improvised versus noimprovised role-playing in producing opinion change." *Human Relations, 9,* 177–186.

Kisielius, J., & Sternthal, B. (1984). "Detecting and explaining vividness effects in attitudinal judgments." *Journal of Marketing Research, 21,* 54–64.

Kisielius, J., & Sternthal, B. (1986). "Examining the vividness controversy: An availability-valence interpretation." *Journal of Consumer Research, 12,* 418–431.

Knox, R. E., & Inkster, J. A. (1968). "Postdecision dissonance at post time." *Journal of Personality and Social Psychology, 8,* 310–323.

Koriat, A., Lichtenstein, S., & Fischhoff, B. (1980). "Reasons for confidence." *Journal of Experimental Psychology: Human Learning and Memory, 6,* 107–118.

Krishnan, H. S., & Smith, R. E. (1998). "The relative endurance of attitudes, confidence, and attitude-behavior consistency: The role of information source and delay." *Journal of Consumer Psychology, 7,* 273–298.

Krosnick, J. A., & Alwin, D. F. (1989). "Aging and susceptibility to attitude change." *Journal of Personality and Social Psychology, 57,* 416–425.

Krosnick, J. A., Betz, A. L., Jussim, L. J., & Lynn, A. R. (1992). "Subliminal conditioning of attitudes." *Personality and Social Psychology Bulletin, 18,* 152–162.

Kruglanski, A. W. (1989). *Lay epistemics and human knowledge: Cognitive and motivational bases.* New York: Plenum Press.

Kruglanski, A. W. (1990). "Lay epistemic theory in social cognitive psychology." *Psychological Inquiry, 1,* 181–197.

Kruglanski, A. W., & Freund, T. (1983). "The freezing and unfreezing of lay inferences: Effects on impressional primacy, ethnic stereotyping, and numerical anchoring." *Journal of Experimental Social Psychology, 19,* 448–468.

Kruglanski, A. W., & Mayesless, O. (1987). "Motivational effects in the social comparison of opinions." *Journal of Personality and Social Psychology, 53,* 834–842.

Kruglanski, A. W., & Mayesless, O. (1990). "Classic and current social comparison research: Expanding the perspective." *Psychological Bulletin, 108,* 195–208.

Kruglanski, A. W., & Webster, D. M. (1996). "Motivated closing of the mind: 'Seizing' and 'freezing.' " *Psychological Review, 103,* 263–283.

Kruglanski, A. W., Webster, D. M., & Klem, A. (1993). "Motivated resistance and openness to persuasion in the presence or absence of prior information." *Journal of Personality and Social Psychology, 65,* 861–876.

Kunst-Wilson, W. R., & Zajonc, R. B. (1980). "Affective discrimination of stimuli that cannot be recognized." *Science, 207,* 557–558.

LaFrance, M. (1985). "Postural mirroring and intergroup relations". *Personality and Social Psychology Bulletin, 11,* 207–217.

Landner, M. (1994). "Steve Dworin tries to reach out and save Ayer." *Business Week, 3371,* 60.

Langer, E. J. (1975). "The illusion of control." *Journal of Personality and Social Psychology, 32,* 311–328.

Langer, E. J. (1978). "Rethinking the role of thought in social interaction." In J. H. Harvey, W. I. Ickes, & R. F. Kidd (Eds.), *New directions in attribution research* (Vol. 2, pp. 35–58). Hillsdale, NJ: Lawrence Erlbaum Associates.

Langer, E. J. (1989). *Mindfulness.* Reading, MA: Addison Wesley.

Langer, E. J., Blank, A., & Chanowitz, B. (1978). "The mindlessness of ostensibly thoughtful action: The role of 'placebic' information in interpersonal interaction." *Journal of Personality and Social Psychology, 36,* 635–642.

Langer, E. J., Blank, A., & Chanowitz, B. (1985). "Mindlessness–mindfulness in perspective: A reply to Valerie Folkes." *Journal of Personality and Social Psychology, 48,* 605–607.

Larrick, R. P., Morgan, J. N., & Nisbett, R. E. (1990). "Teaching the use of cost-benefit reasoning in everyday life." *Psychological Science, 1,* 362–370.

Larrick, R. P., Nisbett, R. E., & Morgan, J. N. (1993). "Who uses the cost–benefit rules of choice? Implications for the normative status of microeconomic theory." *Organizational Behavior and Human Decision Processes, 56,* 331–347.

Latane, B., & Darley, J. M. (1968). "Group inhibition of bystander intervention in emergencies." *Journal of Personality and Social Psychology, 10,* 215–221.

Latane, B., & Rodin, J. (1969). "A lady in distress: Inhibiting effects of friends and strangers on bystander intervention." *Journal of Experimental Social Psychology, 5,* 189–202.

Lavinsky, D. (1993). "When novelty wears off soft drinks clearly will fail." *Marketing News,* March 15, Vol. 27, No. 6, 4.

Lee, H., Acito, F., & Day, R. L. (1987). "Evaluation and use of marketing research by decision makers: A behavioral simulation." *Journal of Marketing Research, 24,* 187–196.

Lee, H., Herr, P. M., Kardes, F. R., & Kim, C. (1999). "Motivated search: Effects of choice accountability, issue involvement, and prior knowledge on information acquisition and use." *Journal of Business Research, 45,* 75–88.

Lehman, D. R., Lempert, R. O., & Nisbett, R. E. (1988). "The effects of graduate training on reasoning: Formal discipline and thinking about everyday life events." *American Psychologist, 43,* 431–443.

Lehman, D. R., & Nisbett, R. E. (1990). "A longitudinal study of the effects of undergraduate education on reasoning." *Developmental Psychology, 26,* 952–960.

Lehmann, D. R., & Pan, Y. (1994). "Context effects, new brand entry, and consideration sets." *Journal of Marketing Research, 31,* 364–374.

Lepper, M. R., Greene, D., & Nisbett, R. E. (1973). "Undermining children's intrinsic interest with extrinsic reward: A test of the 'overjustification' hypothesis." *Journal of Personality and Social Psychology, 28,* 129–137.

Levin, I. P., & Gaeth, G. J. (1988). "How consumers are affected by the framing of attribute information before and after consuming the product." *Journal of Consumer Research, 15,* 374–378.

Levin, I. P., Johnson, R. D., & Chapman, D. P. (1988). "Confidence in judgments based on incomplete information: An investigation using both hypothetical and real gambles." *Journal of Behavioral Decision Making, 1,* 29–41.

Lichtenstein, D. R., & Burton, S. (1989). "The relationship between perceived and objective price-quality." *Journal of Marketing Research, 26,* 429–443.

Lichtenstein, M., & Srull, T. K. (1985). "Conceptual and methodological issues in examining the relationship between consumer memory and judgment." In L. F. Alwitt & A. A. Mitchell (Eds.), *Psychological processes and advertising effects: Theory, research, and application* (pp. 113–128). Hillsdale, NJ: Lawrence Erlbaum Associates.

Lichtenstein, S., Fischhoff, B., & Phillips, L. D. (1982). "Calibration of probabilities: The state of the art to 1980." In D. Kahneman, P. Slovic, & A. Tversky (Eds.), *Judgment under uncertainty: Heuristics and biases.* Cambridge, UK: Cambridge University Press.

Lind, E. A., & O'Barr, W. M. (1979). "The social significance of speech in the courtroom." In H. Giles & R. St. Clair (Eds.), *Language and social psychology.* Oxford, UK: Blackwells.

Lingle, J. H., & Ostrom, T. M. (1981). "Principles of memory and cognition in attitude formation." In R. E. Petty, T. M. Ostrom, & T. C. Brock (Eds.), *Cognitive responses in persuasion* (pp. 399–420). Hillsdale, NJ: Lawrence Erlbaum Associates.

Linville, P. W., & Fisher, G. W. (1991). "Preferences for separating or combining events." *Journal of Personality and Social Psychology, 60,* 5–23.

Locke, K. S., & Horowitz, L. M. (1990). "Satisfaction in interpersonal interactions as a function of similarity in level of dysphoria." *Journal of Personality and Social Psychology, 58,* 823–831.

Lord, C. G., Lepper, M. R., & Preston, E. (1984). "Considering the opposite: A corrective strategy for social judgment." *Journal of Personality and Social Psychology, 47,* 1231–1243.

Lord, C. G., Ross, L., & Lepper, M. R. (1979). "Biased assimilation and attitude polarization: The effects of prior theories on subsequently considered evidence." *Journal of Personality and Social Psychology, 37,* 2098–2109.

Lumsdaine, A. A., & Janis, I. L. (1953). "Resistance to 'counterpropaganda' produced by one-sided and two-sided 'propaganda' presentations." *Public Opinion Quarterly, 17,* 311–318.

Lynch, J. G. (1985). "Uniqueness issues in the decompositional modeling of multiattribute overall evaluations: An information integration perspective." *Journal of Marketing Research, 22,* 1–19.

Lynch, J. G., & Ariely, D. (2000). "Wine online: Search costs affect competition on price, quality, and distribution." *Marketing Science, 19,* 83–103.

Lynch, J. G., Chakravarti, D., & Mitra, A. (1991). "Contrast effects in consumer judgments: Changes in mental representations or in the anchoring of rating scales?" *Journal of Consumer Research, 18,* 284–297.

Lynch, J. G., Marmorstein, H., & Weigold, M. F. (1988). "Choices from sets including remembered brands: Use of recalled attributes and prior overall evaluations." *Journal of Consumer Research, 15,* 169–184.

Lynch, J. G., & Ofir, C. (1989). "Effects of cue consistency and value on base-rate utilization." *Journal of Personality and Social Psychology, 56,* 170–181.

Lynch, J. G., & Srull, T. K. (1982). "Memory and attentional factors in consumer choice: Concepts and research methods." *Journal of Consumer Research, 9,* 18–37.

MacInnis, D. J., & Park, C. W. (1991). "The differential role of characteristics of music on high- and low-involvement consumers' processing of ads." *Journal of Consumer Research, 18,* 161–173.

MacKenzie, S. B. (1986). "The role of attention in mediating the effect of advertising on attribute importance." *Journal of Consumer Research, 13,* 174–195.

MacKenzie, S. B., Lutz, R. J., & Belch, G. E. (1986). "The role of attitude toward the ad as a mediator of advertising effectiveness: A test of competing explanations." *Journal of Marketing Research, 23,* 130–143.

Mackintosh, N. J. (1974). *The psychology of animal learning.* London: Academic Press.

Maddux, J. E., & Rogers, R. W. (1983). "Protection motivation and self-efficacy: A revised theory of fear appeals and attitude change." *Journal of Experimental Social Psychology, 19,* 469–479.

Maheswaran, D., Mackie, D. M., & Chaiken, S. (1992). "Brand name as a heuristic cue: The effects of task importance and expectancy confirmation on consumer judgments." *Journal of Consumer Psychology, 1,* 317–336.

Mandler, G. (1982). "The structure of value: Accounting for taste." In M. S. Clark & S. T. Fiske (Eds.), *Affect and cognition: The 17th Annual Carnegie Symposium on cognition* (pp. 3–36). Hillsdale, NJ: Lawrence Erlbaum Associates.

Mandler, G. (1984). *Mind and body: Psychology of emotion and stress.* New York: Norton.

Mantel, S. P., & Kardes, F. R. (1998). "The role of direction of comparison, attribute-based processing, and attitude-based processing in consumer preference." *Journal of Consumer Research, 25,* 335–352.

Markus, H. R., & Kitayama, S. (1991). "Culture and the self: Implications for cognition, emotion, and motivation." *Psychological Review, 98,* 224–253.

Mazis, M. B., & Adkinson, J. E. (1976). "An experimental evaluation of a proposed corrective advertising remedy." *Journal of Marketing Research, 13,* 178–183.

Mazursky, D., & Schul, Y. (1988). "The effects of advertisement encoding on the failure to discount information: Implications for the sleeper effect." *Journal of Consumer Research, 15,* 24–36.

McGuire, W. J. (1968). "Personality and susceptibility to social influence." In E. F. Borgatta & W. W. Lambert (Eds.), *Handbook of personality theory and research* (pp. 1130–1187). Chicago: Rand McNally.

McGuire, W. J. (1972). "Attitude change: The information-processing paradigm." In C. G. McClintock (Ed.), *Experimental social psychology* (pp. 108–141). New York: Holt, Rinehart & Winston.

McGuire, W. J. (1976). "Some internal psychological factors influencing consumer choice." *Journal of Consumer Research, 2,* 302–319.

McSweeney, F. K., & Bierley, C. (1984). "Recent developments in classical conditioning." *Journal of Consumer Research, 11,* 619–631.

Meeus, W. H. J., & Raaijmakers, Q. A. W. (1986). "Administrative obedience: Carrying out orders to use psychological-administrative violence." *European Journal of Social Psychology, 16,* 311–324.

Meyer, D. E., & Schvaneveldt, R. W. (1971). "Facilitation in recognizing pairs of words: Evidence of a dependence between retrieval operations." *Journal of Experimental Psychology, 90,* 227–234.

Meyer, R. J. (1981). "A model of multiattribute judgments under attribute uncertainty and information constraints." *Journal of Marketing Research, 18,* 428–441.

Meyers, Levy, J., & Peracchio, L. A. (1992). "Getting an angle in advertising: The effects of camera angle on product evaluations." *Journal of Marketing Research, 29,* 454–461.

Meyers-Levy, J., & Tybout, A. M. (1989). "Schema congruity as a basis for product evaluation." *Journal of Consumer Research, 16,* 39–54.

Milgram, S. (1963). "Behavioral study of obedience." *Journal of Abnormal and Social Psychology, 67,* 371–378.

Millar, M. G., & Tesser, A. (1986). "Thought-induced attitude change: The effects of schema structure and commitment." *Journal of Personality and Social Psychology, 51,* 259–269.

Miller, G. A. (1956). "The magical number seven, plus or minus two: Some limits on our capacity for processing information." *Psychological Review, 63,* 81–97.

Miller, N., & Campbell, D. T. (1959). "Recency and primacy in persuasion as a function of the timing of speeches and measurements." *Journal of Abnormal Social Psychology, 59,* 1–9.

Miller, N., Maruyama, G., Beaber, R. J., & Valone, K. (1976). "Speed of speech and persuasion."*Journal of Personality and Social Psychology, 34,* 615–625.

Miniard, P. W., Sirdeshmukh, D., & Innis, D. E. (1992). "Peripheral persuasion and brand choice." *Journal of Consumer Research, 19,* 226–239.

Mitchell, A. A. (1986). "The effects of verbal and visual components of advertisements on brand attitudes and attitude toward the advertisement." *Journal of Consumer Research, 13,* 12–24.

Mitchell, A. A., & Olson, J. C. (1981). "Are product attribute beliefs the only mediator of advertising effects on brand attitudes?" *Journal of Marketing Research, 18,* 318–322.

Mitra, A., & Lynch, J. G. (1995). "Toward a reconciliation of market power and information theories of advertising effects on price elasticity." *Journal of Consumer Research, 21,* 644–659.

Mitra, A., & Lynch, J. G. (1996). "Advertising effects on consumer welfare: Prices paid and liking for brands selected." *Marketing Letters, 7,* 19–29.

Mizerski, R. W., Golden, L. L., & Kernan, J. B. (1979). "The attribution process in consumer decision making." *Journal of Consumer Research, 6,* 123–140.

Moore, D. J., Reardon, R., & Durso, F. T. (1986). "The generation effect in advertising appeals." *Advances in consumer research, 13,* 117–120.

Moore, D. L., Hausknecht, D., & Thamodaran, K. (1986). "Time compression, response opportunity, and persuasion." *Journal of Consumer Research, 13,* 85–99.

Moore, T. E. (1982). "Subliminal advertising: What you see is what you get." *Journal of Marketing, 46,* 38–47.

Morwitz, V. G., Johnson, E., & Schmittlein, D. (1993). "Does measuring intent change behavior?" *Journal of Consumer Research, 20,* 46–61.

Mowen, J. C., & Gentry, J. W. (1980). "Investigation of the preference-reversal phenomenon in a new product introduction task." *Journal of Applied Psychology, 65,* 715–722.

Muthukrishnan, A. V. (1995). "Decision ambiguity and incumbent brand advantage." *Journal of Consumer Research, 22,* 98–109.

Nedungadi, P. (1990). "Recall and consumer consideration sets: Influencing choice without altering brand evaluations." *Journal of Consumer Research, 17,* 263–276.

Nelson, T. O. (1971). "Savings and forgetting from long-term memory." *Journal of Verbal Learning and Verbal Behavior, 10,* 568–576.

Nelson, T. O. (1978). "Detecting small amounts of information in memory: Savings for nonrecognized items." *Journal of Experimental Psychology: Human Learning and Memory, 4,* 453–468.

Newell, A., & Simon, H. A. (1972). *Human problem solving.* Englewood Cliffs, NJ: Prentice-Hall.

Nisbett, R. E., & Gordon, A. (1967). "Self-esteem and susceptibility to social influence." *Journal of Personality and Social Psychology, 5,* 268–276.

Nisbett, R. E., & Ross, L. (1980). *Human inference: Strategies and shortcomings of social judgment.* Englewood Cliffs, NJ: Prentice-Hall.

Nisbett, R. E., Zukier, H., & Lemley, R. E. (1981). "The dilution effect: Nondiagnostic information weakens the implications of diagnostic information." *Cognitive Psychology, 13,* 248–277.

Norman, R. (1976). "When what is said is important: A comparison of expert and attractive sources." *Journal of Experimental Social Psychology, 12,* 294–300.

Northcraft, G. B., & Neale, M. A. (1987). "Experts, amateurs, and real estate: An anchoring and adjustment perspective on property pricing decisions." *Organizational Behavior and Human Decision Processes, 39,* 84–97.

Nosanchuk, T. A., & Lightstone, J. (1974). "Canned laughter and public and private conformity." *Journal of Personality and Social Psychology, 29,* 153–156.

Novak, T. P., Hoffman, D. L., & Yung, Y. (2000). "Measuring the customer experience in online environments: A structural modeling approach." *Marketing Science, 19,* 22–42.

Nussbaum, B. (1993). "Hot products." *Business Week, 3322,* 54.

Oliver, R. L. (1980). "A cognitive model of the antecedents and consequences of satisfaction decisions." *Journal of Marketing Research, 17,* 460–469.

Oliver, R. L. (1981). "Measurement and evaluation of satisfaction processes in retail settings." *Journal of Retailing, 57,* 25–48.

Oliver, R. L., & DeSarbo, W. S. (1988). "Response determinants in satisfaction judgments." *Journal of Consumer Research, 14,* 495–507.

Ono, Y. (1995). "Think thin? Not at Kraft, home of Velveeta." *Wall Street Journal,* January 25, B1.

Ortega, B. (1993)." Jewelers bet honest image, price cuts and gimmicks will make sales glitter." *Wall Street Journal*, December 6, B1, B10.

Orvis, B. R., Cunningham, J. D., & Kelley, H. H. (1975). "A closer examination of causal inference: The roles of consensus, distinctiveness, and consistency information." *Journal of Personality and Social Psychology*, *32*, 605–616.

Oskamp, S. (1965). "Overconfidence in case-study judgments." *Journal of Consulting Psychology, 29*, 261–265.

Ostrom, T. M., & Upshaw, H. S. (1968). "Psychological perspective and attitude change."In A. G. Greenwald, T. C. Brock, & T. M. Ostrom (Eds.), *Psychological foundations of attitudes* (pp. 217–242). New York: Academic Press.

Pallak, S. R. (1983). "Salience of a communicator's physical attractiveness and persuasion: A heuristic versus systematic processing interpretation." *Social Cognition, 2*, 158–170.

Pallak, S. R., Murroni, E., & Koch, J. (1983). "Communicator attractiveness and expertise, emotional versus rational appeals, and persuasion: A heuristic versus systematic processing interpretation." *Social Cognition, 2*, 122–141.

Pan, Y., & Lehmann, D. R. (1993). "The influence of new brand entry on subjective brand judgments." *Journal of Consumer Research, 20*, 76–86.

Pavelchak, M. A., Antil, J. H., & Munch, J. M. (1988). "The Super Bowl: An investigation into the relationship among program context, emotional experience, and ad recall." *Journal of Consumer Research, 15*, 360–367.

Payne, J. W. (1976). "Task complexity and contingent processing in decision making: An information search and protocol analysis." *Organizational Behavior and Human Decision Processes, 16*, 366–387.

Payne, J. W., Bettman, J. R., & Johnson, E. J. (1992). "Behavioral decision research: A constructive processing perspective." *Annual Review of Psychology, 43*, 87–131.

Payne, J. W., Bettman, J. R., & Johnson, E. J. (1993). *The adaptive decision maker.* Cambridge, UK: Cambridge University Press.

Pechmann, C. (1992). "Predicting when two-sided ads will be more effective than one-sided ads: The rold of correlational and correspondent inferences." *Journal of Marketing Research, 29*, 441–453.

Pechmann, C., & Ratneshwar, S. (1991). "The use of comparative advertising for brand positioning: Association vs. differentiation." *Journal of Consumer Research, 18*, 145–160.

Pechmann, C., & Stewart, D. W. (1990). "The effects of comparative advertising on attention, memory, and purchase intention." *Journal of Consumer Research, 17*, 180–191.

Pechmann, C., & Stewart, D. W. (1991). "How direct comparative ads and market share affect brand choice." *Journal of Advertising Research*, 47–55.

Penfield, W. (1959). "The interpretive cortex." *Science, 129*, 1719–1725.

Pennington, N., & Hastie, R. (1986). "Evidence evaluation in complex decision making." *Journal of Personality and Social Psychology, 51*, 242–258.

Pennington, N., & Hastie, R. (1988). "Explanation-based decision making: Effects of memory structure on judgment." *Journal Experimental Psychology: Learning, Memory, and Cognition, 14*, 521–533.

Pennington, N., & Hastie, R. (1993). "Reasoning in explanation-based decision making." *Cognition, 49*, 123–163.

Percy, L., & Rossiter, J. R. (1992). "A model of brand awareness and brand attitude advertising strategies." *Psychology & Marketing, 9*, 263–274.

Peter, J. P., & Tarpey, L. X. (1975). "Comparative analysis of three consumer decision strategies." *Journal of Consumer Research, 2*, 29–37.

Petty, R. E., & Cacioppo, J. T. (1981). *Attitudes and persuasion: Classic and contemporary approaches.* Dubuque, IA: William C. Brown.

Petty, R. E., & Cacioppo, J. T. (1986). "The elaboration likelihood model of persuasion." In L. Berkowitz (Ed.), *Advances in experimental social psychology* (Vol. 19, pp. 123–205). New York: Academic Press.

Petty, R. E., Cacioppo, J. T., & Schumann, D. (1983). "Central and peripheral routes to advertising effectiveness: The moderating role of involvement." *Journal of Consumer Research, 10*, 135–146.

Petty, R. E., & Krosnick, J. A. (Eds.) (1995). *Attitude strength: Antecedents and consequences* (pp. 247–282). Hillsdale, NJ: Lawrence Erlbaum Associates.

Petty, R. E., & Wegener, D. T. (1993). "Flexible correction processes in social judgment: Correcting for context-induced contrast." *Journal of Experimental Social Psychology, 29*, 137–165.

Petty, R. E. Wells, G. L., & Brock, T. C. (1976). "Distraction can enhance or reduce yielding to propaganda:

Thought disruption versus effort justification." *Journal of Personality and Social Psychology, 34,* 874–884.

Pollock, C. L., Smith, S. D., Knowles, E. S., & Bruce, H. J. (1998). "Mindfulness limits compliance with the that's-not-all technique." *Personality and Social Psychology Bulletin, 24,* 1153–1157.

Popkowski-Leszczyc, P. T. L., & Rao, R. C. (1990). "An empirical analysis of national and local advertising effect on price elascticity." *Marketing Letters, 1,* 149–160.

Power, C., Kerwin, K., Groover, R.,& Alexander, K.(1993). "Flops." *Business Week, 3332,*76.

Pratkanis, A. R., & Aronson, E. (1992). *Age of propaganda: Everyday use and abuse of persuasion.* New York: Freeman.

Pratkanis, A. R., & Greenwald, A. G. (1989). "A sociocognitive model of attitude structure and function." In L. Berkowitz (Ed.), *Advances in experimental social psychology* (Vol. 22, pp. 245–285). New York: Academic Press.

Pratkanis, A. R., Greenwald, A. G., Leippe, M. R., & Baumgardner, M. H. (1988). "In search of reliable persuasion effects: III. The sleeper effect is dead. Long live the sleeper effect." *Journal of Personality and Social Psychology, 54,* 203–218.

Preston, I. L.(1977). "The FTC's handling of puffery and other selling claims made 'by implication.' " *Journal of Business Research, 5,* 155–181.

Puto, C. (1987). "The framing of buying decisions." *Journal of Consumer Research, 3,* 301–315.

Qualls, W. J., & Puto, C. (1989). "Organizational climate and decision framing: An integrated approach to analyzing industrial buying decisions." *Journal of Marketing Research, 26,* 179–192.

Quigley-Fernandez, B., & Tedeschi, J. T. (1978). "The bogus pipeline as lie detector: Two validity studies." *Journal of Personality and Social Psychology, 36,* 247–256.

Rangan, V. K., & Bell, M. (1998). "Case study: Dell online." *Journal of Interactive Marketing, 12,* 63–86.

Ratneshwar, S., & Chaiken, S. (1991). "Comprehension's role in persuasion: The case of its moderating effect on the persuasive impact of source cues." *Journal of Consumer Research, 18,* 52–62.

Reingen, P. H. (1978). "On inducing compliance with requests." *Journal of Consumer Research, 5,* 96–102.

Reingen, P. H. (1982). "Test of a list procedure for inducing compliance with a request to donate money." *Journal of Applied Psychology, 67,* 110–118.

Reingen, P. H., & Kernan, J. B. (1977). "Compliance with an interview request: A foot-in-the-door, self-perception interpretation." *Journal of Marketing Research, 14,* 365–369.

Reingen, P. H., & Kernan, J. b. (1979). "More evidence on interpersonal yielding." *Journal of Marketing Research, 16,* 588–593.

Reitman, V. (1992). "Buoyant sales of Lever2000 soap bring sinking sensation to Procter & Gamble." *Wall Street Journal,* March 19, B1, B3.

Rhodes, N., & Wood, W. (1992). "Self-esteem and intelligence affect influenceability: The mediating role of message reception." *Psychological Bulletin, 111,* 156–171.

Riche, M. F. (1989). "Psychographics for the 1990s." *American Demographics,* 24–26ff.

Ries, A., & Trout, J. (1981). *Positioning: The battle for your mind."* New York: McGraw-Hill.

Robinson, W. T., & Fornell, C. (1985). "Sources of market pioneering advantages in consumer goods industries." *Journal of Marketing Research, 22,* 305–318.

Rogers, E. M. (1983). *Diffusion of innovations.* New York: Free Press.

Rose, R. L., Bearden, W. O., & Teel, J. E. (1992). "An attributional analysis of resistance to group pressure regarding illicit drug and alcohol consumption." *Journal of Consumer Research, 19,* 1–13.

Rosenbaum, M. E. (1986). "The repulsion hypothesis: On the nondevelopment of relationships." *Journal of Personality and Social Psychology, 51,* 1156–1166.

Rosenthal, A. M. (1964). *Thirty-eight witnesses.* New York: McGraw-Hill.

Ross, L., Lepper, M. R., & Hubbard, M. (1975). "Perseverance in self-perception and social perception: Biased attribution processes in the debriefing paradigm." *Journal of Personality and Social Psychology, 35,* 485–494.

Ross, W. T., & Creyer, E. H. (1992). "Making inferences about missing information: The effects of existing information." *Journal of Consumer Research, 19,* 14–25.

Rossiter, John R., Percy, L., & Donovan, R. J. (1991). "A better advertising planning grid." *Journal of Advertising Research, 31,* 11–21.

Rotter, J. B. (1966). "Generalized expectancies for internal versus external control of reinforcement." *Psychological Monographs, 80* (1, Whole No. 609).

Rundus, D. (1971). "Analysis of rehearsal processes in free recall." *Journal of Experimental Psychology, 89,* 63–77.

Rundus, D. (1973). "Negative effects of using list items as recall cues." *Journal of Verbal Learning and Verbal Behavior, 12,* 43–50.

Russo, J. E. (1977). "The value of unit price information." *Journal of Marketing Research, 14,* 193–201.

Russo, J. E., & Dosher, B. A. (1983). "Strategies for multiattribute binary choice." *Journal of Experimental Psychology: Learning, Memory, and Cognition, 9,* 676–696.

Russo, J. E., & Kolzow, K. J. (1994). "Where is the fault in fault trees?" *Journal of Experimental Psychology: Human Perception and Performance, 20,* 17–32.

Russo, J. E., & Schoemaker, P. J. H. (1989). *Decision traps: The ten barriers to brilliant decision-making and how to overcome them.* New York: Simon & Schuster.

Russo, J. E., Staelin, R., Nolan, C. A., Russell, G. J., & Metcalf, B. L. (1986). "Nutrition information in the supermarket." *Journal of Consumer Research, 13,* 48–70.

Ryan, R. M., & Deci, E. L. (2000). "Self-determination theory and the facilitation of intrinsic motivation, social development, and well-being." *American Psychologist, 55,* 68–78.

Saegert, S. C., Swap, W. C., & Zajonc, R. B. (1973). "Exposure, context, and interpersonal attraction." *Journal of Personality and Social Psychology, 25,* 234–242.

Sanbonmatsu, D. M., & Fazio, R. H. (1990). "The role of attitudes in memory-based decision making." *Journal of Personality and Social Psychology, 59,* 614–622.

Sanbonmatsu, D. M., & Kardes, F. R. (1988). "The effects of physiological arousal on information processing and persuasion." *Journal of Consumer Research, 15,* 379–385.

Sanbonmatsu, D. M., Kardes, F. R., & Gibson, B. D. (1991). "The role of attribute knowledge and overall evaluations in comparative judgment." *Organizational Behavior and Human Decision Processes, 48,* 131–146.

Sanbonmatsu, D. M., Kardes, F. R., & Herr, P. M. (1992). "The role of prior knowledge and missing information in multiattribute evaluation." *Organizational Behavior and Human Decision Processes, 51,* 76–91.

Sanbonmatsu, D. M., Kardes, F. R., & Sansone, C. (1991). "Remembering less and inferring more: The effects of the timing of judgment on inferences about unknown attributes." *Journal of Personality and Social Psychology, 61,* 546–554.

Sanbonmatsu, D. M., Posavac, S. S., Kardes, F. R., & Mantel, S. P. (1998). "Selective hypothesis testing." *Psychonomic Bulletin & Review, 5,* 197–220.

Sanbonmatsu, D. M., Posavac, S. S. & Stasney, R. (1997). "The subjective beliefs underlying probability overestimation." *Journal of Experimental Social Psychology, 33,* 276–295.

Sawyer, A. G. (1988). "Can there be effective advertising without explicit conclusions? Decide for yourself." In S. Hecker & D. W. Stewart (Eds.), *Nonverbal communications in advertising* (pp. 159–184). Lexington, MA: Lexington.

Sawyer, A. G., & Howard, D. J. (1991). "Effects of omitting conclusions in advertisements to involved and uninvolved audiences." *Journal of Marketing Research, 28,* 467–474.

Schacter, S., & Singer, J. E. (1962). "Cognitive, social, and physiological determinants of emotional state." *Psychological Review, 69,* 379–399.

Schank, R. C., & Abelson, R. P. (1995). "Knowledge and memory: The real story." In R. S. Wyer (Ed.), *Advances in social cognition* (Vol. 8, pp. 1–86). Hillsdale, NJ: Lawrence Erlbaum Associates.

Schneider, W., & Shiffrin, R. M. (1977). "Controlled and automatic human information processing: I. Detection, search, and attention." *Psychological Review, 84,* 1–66.

Schofield, J. W. (1975). "Effects of norms, public disclosure, and need for approval on volunteering behavior consistent with attitudes." *Journal of Personality and Social Psychology, 31,* 1126–1133.

Schul, Y., & Mazursky, D. (1990). "Conditions facilitating successful discounting in consumer decision making." *Journal of Consumer Research, 16,* 442–451.

Schulz-Hardt, S., Frey, D., Luthgens, C., & Moscovici, S. (2000). "Biased information search in group decision making." *Journal of Personality and Social Psychology, 78,* 655–669.

Schuman, H., & Presser, S. (1981). *Questions and answers in attitude surveys: Experiments on question form, wording, and context.* New York: Academic Press.

Schumann, D. W., Petty, R. E., & Clemons, D. S. (1990). "Predicting the effectiveness of different strategies of advertising variation: A test of the repetition-variation hypotheses." *Journal of Consumer Research, 17,* 192–202.

Scott, C. A., & Yalch, R. F. (1978). "A test of the self-perception explanation of the effects of rewards on intrinsic interest." *Journal of Experimental Social Psychology, 14*, 180–192.

Semenik, R. J., & Bamossy, G. J. (1993). *Principles of marketing: A global perspective,* Cincinnati, OH: South-Western.

Shanteau, J. C., & Anderson, N. H. (1969). "Test of a conflict model for preference judgment." *Journal of Mathematical Psychology, 6*, 312–325.

Shavitt, S. (1990). "The role of attitude objects in attitude functions." *Journal of Experimental Social Psychology, 26*, 124–148.

Sheppard, B. H., Hartwick, J., & Warshaw, P. R. (1988). "The theory of reasoned action: A meta-analysis of past research with recommendations for modifications and future research." *Journal of Consumer Research, 15*, 325–343.

Sherif, C. W., Sherif, M., & Nebergall, R. E. (1965). *Attitude and attitude change: The social judgment–involvement approach.* Philadelphia: W. B. Saunders.

Sherif, M., & Hovland, C. I. (1961). *Social judgment: Assimilation and contrast effects in communication and attitude change.* New Haven, CT: Yale University Press.

Sherman, S. J. (1973). "Internal-external control and its relationship to attitude change under different social influence techniques." *Journal of Personality and Social Psychology, 26*, 23–29.

Sherman, S. J. (1980). "On the self-erasing nature of errors of prediction." *Journal of Personality and Social Psychology, 39*, 211–221.

Sherman, S. J., Cialdini, R. B., Schwartzman, D. F., & Reynolds, K. D. (1985). "Imagining can heighten or lower the perceived likelihood of contracting a disease: The mediating effect of ease of imagery." *Personality and Social Psychology Bulletin, 11*, 118–127.

Sherman, S. J., & Corty, E. (1984). "Cognitive heuristics." In R. S. Wyer & T. K. Srull (Eds.), *Handbook of social cognition* (Vol. 2, pp. 189–286). Hillsdale, NJ: Lawrence Erlbaum Associates.

Sherman, S. J., Zehner, K. S., Johnson, J., & Hirt, E. R. (1983). "Social explanation: The role of timing, set, and recall on subjective likelihood estimates." *Journal of Personality and Social Psychology, 44*, 1127–1143.

Shiffrin, R. M., & Schneider, W. (1977). "Controlled and automatic human information processing: II. Perceptual learning, automatic attending, and general theory." *Psychological Review, 84*, 127–190.

Shimp, T. A., Stuart, E. W., & Engle, R. W. (1991). "A program of classical conditioning experiments testing variations in the conditioned stimulus and contents." *Journal of Consumer Research, 18*, 1–12.

Simonson, I. (1989). "Choice based on reasons: The case of attraction and compromise effects." *Journal of Consumer Research, 16*, 158–174.

Simonson, I. (1992). "The influence of anticipating regret and responsibility on purchase decisions." *Journal of Consumer Research, 19*, 105–118.

Simonson, I. (1993). "Get closer to your customers by understanding how they make choices." *California Management Review, 35*, 68–74.

Simonson, I., Carmon, Z., & O'Curry, S. (1994). "Experimental evidence on the negative effect of product features and sales promotions on brand choice." *Marketing Science, 13*, 23–40.

Simonson, I., Huber, J., & Payne, J. W. (1988). "The relationship between prior brand knowledge and information acquisition order." *Journal of Consumer Research, 14*, 566–578.

Simonson, I., Nowlis, S. M., & Simonson, Y. (1993). "The effect of irrelevant preference arguments on consumer choice." *Journal of Consumer Psychology, 2*, 287–306.

Simonson, I., & Tversky, A. (1992). "Choice in context: Tradeoff contrast and extremeness aversion." *Journal of Marketing Research, 29*, 281–295.

Sinclair, R. C., Hoffman, C., Mark, M. M., Martin, L. L., & Pickering, T. L. (1994). "Construct accessibility and the misattribution of arousal: Schacter and Singer revisited." *Psychological Science, 5*, 15–19.

Sinha, I. (2000). "Cost transparency: The net's real threat to prices and brands." *Harvard Business Review*, 43–50.

Slovic, P. (1995). "The construction of preference." *American Psychologist, 50*, 364–371.

Slovic, P., & Lichtenstein, S. (1983). Preference reversals: A broader perspective." *American Economic Review, 73*, 596–605.

Smith, G. H., & Engel, R. (1968). "Influence of a female model on perceived characteristics of an automobile." *Proceedings of the 76th annual convention of the American Psychological Association, 3*, 681–682.

Smith, M. B., Bruner, J. S., & White, R. W. (1956). *Opinions and personality.* New York: Wiley.

Smith, R. E., & Hunt, S. D. (1978). "Attributional processes and effects in promotional situations." *Journal of Consumer Research, 5,* 149–158.

Smith, R. E., & Swinyard, W. R. (1983). "Attitude-behavior consistency: The impact of product trial versus advertising." *Journal of Marketing Research, 20,* 257–267.

Snyder, M. (1974). "Self-monitoring of expressive behavior." *Journal of Personality and Social Psychology, 30,* 526–537.

Snyder, M. (1979). "Self-monitoring processes." In L. Berkowitz (Ed.), *Advances in experimental social psychology* (Vol. 12, pp. 86–131). New York: Academic Press.

Snyder, M. (1982). "When believing means doing: Creating links between attitudes and behavior." In M. P. Zanna, E. T. Higgins, & C. P. Herman (Eds.), *Consistency in social behavior: The Ontario symposium* (pp. 105–130). Hillsdale, NJ: Lawrence Erlbaum Associates.

Snyder, M., & DeBono, K. G. (1985). "Appeals to images and claims about quality: Understanding the psychology of advertising." *Journal of Personality and Social Psychology, 49,* 586–597.

Sparkman, R. M., & Locander, W. B. (1980). "Attribution theory and advertising effectiveness." *Journal of Consumer Research, 7,* 219–224.

Srivastava, R. K., Alpert, M. I., & Shocker, A. D. (1984). "A customer-oriented approach for determining market structures." *Journal of Marketing, 48,* 32–45.

Staats, C. K., Staats, A. W., & Crawford, H. L. (1962). "First-order conditioning of meaning and the parallel conditioning of a GSR." *Journal of General Psychology, 67,* 159–167.

Stayman, D. M., Alden, D. L., & Smith, K. H. (1992). "Some effects of schematic processing on consumer expectations and disconfirmation judgments." *Journal of Consumer Research, 19,* 240–255.

Stayman, D. M., & Kardes, F. R. (1992). "Spontaneous inference processes in advertising: Effects of need for cognition and self-monitoring on inference generation and utilization." *Journal of Consumer Psychology, 1,* 125–142.

Sternthal, B., & Craig, C. S. (1982). *Consumer behavior: An information processing perspective.* Englewood Cliffs, NJ: Prentice-Hall.

Stuart, E. W., Shimp, T. A., & Engle, R. W. (1987). "Classical conditioning of consumer attitudes: Four experiments in an advertising context." *Journal of Consumer Research, 14,* 334–349.

Swinyard, W. R. (1981). "The interaction between comparative advertising and copy claim variation." *Journal of Marketing Research, 18,* 175–186.

Taylor, S. E., & Thompson, S. C. (1982). "Stalking the elusive 'vividness' effect." *Psychological Review, 89,* 155–181.

Tedeschi, J. T., Schlenker, B. R., & Bonoma, T. V. (1971). "Cognitive dissonance: Private ratiocination or public spectacle?" *American Psychologist, 26,* 685–695.

Tesser, A. (1978). "Self-generated attitude change." In L. Berkowitz (Ed.), *Advances in experimental social psychology* (Vol. 11, pp. 289–338). New York: Academic Press.

Tesser, A., & Rosen, S. (1975). "The reluctance to transmit bad news." In L. Berkowitz (Ed.), *Advances in experimental social psychology* (Vol. 8, pp. 193–232). New York: Academic Press.

Tesser, A., & Leone, C. (1977). "Cognitive schemas and thought as determinants of attitude change." *Journal of Experimental Social Psychology, 13,* 340–356.

Tetlock, P. E. (1992). "The impact of accountability on judgment and choice: Toward a social contingency model." In M. P. Zanna (Ed.), *Advances in experimental social psychology* (pp. 331–376). New York: Academic Press.

Tetlock, P. E., & Boettger, R. (1989). "Accountability: A social magnifier of the dilution effect." *Journal of Personality and Social Psychology, 57,* 388–398.

Thaler, R. (1980). "Toward a positive theory of consumer choice." *Journal of Economic Behavior and Organization, 1,* 39–60.

Thaler, R. (1985). "Mental accounting and consumer choice." *Marketing Science, 4,* 199–214.

Troutman, C. M., & Shanteau, J. (1976). "Do consumers evaluate products by adding or averaging attribute information?" *Journal of Consumer Research, 3,* 101–106.

Tversky, A. (1969). "Intransitivity of preferences." *Psychological Review, 76,* 31–48.

Tversky, A. (1972). "Elimination by aspects: A theory of choice." *Psychological Review, 79,* 281–299.

Tversky, A. (1977). "Features of similarity." *Psychological Review, 84,* 327–353.

Tversky, A., & Kahneman, D. (1974). "Judgment under uncertainty: Heuristics and biases." *Science, 185,* 1124–1131.

Tversky, A., & Kahneman, D. (1981). "The framing of decisions and the psychology of choice." *Science, 211,* 453–458.

Tversky, A., & Kahneman, D. (1986). "Rational choice and the framing of decisions." *Journal of Business, 59,* S251–S278.

Tversky, A., & Koehler, D. J. (1994). "Support theory: A nonextensional representation of subjective probability." *Psychological Review, 101,* 547–567.

Tversky, A., Slovic, P., & Kahneman, D. (1990). "The determinants of preference reversal." *American Economic Review, 80,* 204–217.

Tybout, A. M., Calder, B. J., & Sternthal, B. (1981). "Using information processing theory to design marketing strategies." *Journal of Marketing Research, 18,* 73–79.

Tybout, A. M., & Scott, C. A. (1983). "Availability of well-defined internal knowledge and the attitude formation process: Information aggregation versus self-perception." *Journal of Personality and Social Psychology, 44,* 474–491.

Tyler, S. W., Hertel, P. T., McCallum, M. C., & Ellis, H. C. (1979). "Cognitive effort and memory." *Journal of Experimental Psychology: Human Learning and Memory, 5,* 607–617.

Unnava, R. H., & Burnkrant, R. E. (1991). "An imagery-processing view of the role of pictures in print advertisements." *Journal of Marketing Research, 28,* 226–231.

Upshaw, H. S. (1978). "Social influence on attitudes and on anchoring of congeneric attitude scales." *Journal of Experimental Social Psychology, 14,* 327–339.

Urban, G. L., Carter, T., Gaskin, S., & Mucha, Z. (1986). "Market share rewards to pioneering brands: An empirical analysis and strategic implications." *Management Science, 32,* 645–659.

Urban, G. L., & Hauser, J. R. (1992). *Design and marketing of new products.* Englewood Cliffs, NJ: Prentice Hall.

Urban, G. L., Johnson, P. L., & Hauser, J. R. (1984). "Testing competitive market structures." *Marketing Science, 3,* 83–112.

Urban, G. L., & Star, S. H. (1991). *Advanced marketing strategy: Phenomena, analysis, and decisions.* Englewood Cliffs, NJ: Prentice Hall.

Urbany, J. E., Dickson, P. R., & Wilkie, W. L. (1989). "Buyer uncertainty and information search." *Journal of Consumer Research, 16,* 208–215.

Vallone, R. P., Griffin, D. W., Lin, S., & Ross, L. (1990). "Overconfident prediction of future actions and outcomes by self and others." *Journal of Personality and Social Psychology, 58,* 582–592.

Venkatraman, M. P., Marlino, D., Kardes, F. R., & Sklar, K. B. (1990). "The interactive effects of message appeal and individual differences on information processing and persuasion." *Psychology & Marketing, 7,* 85–96.

Vinokur, A., & Burnstein, E. (1974). "Effects of partially shared persuasive arguments on group-induced shifts: A group-problem-solving approach." *Journal of Personality and Social Psychology, 29,* 305–315.

Walster, E., Aronson, E., & Abrahams, D. (1966). "On increasing the persuasiveness of a low prestige communicator." *Journal of Experimental Social Psychology, 2,* 325–342.

Ward, J. C., & Reingen, P. R. (1990). "Sociocognitive analysis of group decision making among consumers." *Journal of Consumer Research, 17,* 245–262.

Watkins, M. J., & Tulving, E. (1975). "Episodic memory: When recognition fails." *Journal of Experimental Psychology: General, 104,* 5–29.

Watts, W. A. (1967). "Relative persistence of opinion change induced by active compared to passive participation." *Journal of Personality and Social Psychology, 5,* 4–15.

Webb, P. H. (1979). "Consumer initial processing in a difficult media environment." *Journal of Consumer Research, 6,* 225–236.

Webb, P. H., & Ray, M. L. (1979). "Effects of TV clutter." *Journal of Advertising Research, 19,* 7–12.

Wegener, D. T., & Petty, R. E. (1995). "Flexible correction processes in social judgment: The role of naive theories in corrections for perceived bias." *Journal of Personality and Social Psychology, 68,* 36–51.

Weiner, B., Frieze, I., Kukla, A., Reed, L., Rest, S., & Rosenbaum, R. M. (1971). "Perceiving the causes of success and failure." In E. E. Jones, D. E. Kanouse, H. H. Kelley, R. E. Nisbett, S. Valins, & B. Weiner (Eds.), *Attribution: Perceiving the causes of behavior* (pp. 95–120). Morristown, NJ: General Learning Press.

Weir, W. (1984). "Another look at subliminal 'facts.'" *Advertising Age,* October 15, p. 46.

Wicker, A. W. (1969). Attitude versus actions: The relationship of verbal and overt behavioral responses to attitude objects." *Journal of Social Issues, 25,* 41–78.

Wilkie, W., McNeill, D., & Mazis, M. (1984). "Marketing's 'scarlet letter': The theory and practice of corrective advertising." *Journal of Marketing, 48,* 11–31.

Wilson, T. D., & Brekke, N. C. (1994). "Mental contamination and mental correction: Unwanted influences on judgments and evaluations." *Psychological Bulletin, 116,* 117–142.

Wilson, T. D., Gilbert, D. T., & Wheatley, T. P. (1998). "Protecting our minds: The role of lay beliefs." In V. Y. Yzerbyt, G. Lories, & B. Dardenne (Eds.), *Metacognition: Cognitive and social dimensions* (pp. 171–201). Thousand Oaks, CA: Sage.

Wind, J., Mahajan, V., and Bayless, J. L. (1990). *The role of new product models in supporting and improving the new product development process: Some preliminary results.* Cambridge, MA: The Marketing Science Institute.

Wood, W., & Eagly, A. H. (1981). "Stages in the analysis of persuasive messages: The role of causal attributions and message comprehension." *Journal of Personality and Social Psychology, 40,* 246–259.

Woodside, A. G., & Davenport, J. W. (1974). "Effects of salesman similarity and expertise on consumer purchasing behavior." *Journal of Marketing Research, 11,* 198–202.

Worchel, S., & Arnold, S. E. (1973). "The effects of censorship and the attractiveness of the censor on attitude change. *Journal of Experimental Social Psychology, 9,* 365–377.

Worchel, S., Arnold, S. E., & Baker, M. (1975). "The effect of censorship on attitude change: The influence of censor and communicator characteristics." *Journal of Applied Social Psychology, 5,* 222–239.

Worchel, S., Lee, J., & Adewole, A. (1975). "Effects of supply and demand on ratings of object value." *Journal of Personality and Social Psychology, 32,* 906–914.

Wright, A., & Lynch, J. G. (1995). "Communication effects of advertising versus direct experience when both search and experience attributes are present." *Journal of Consumer Research, 21,* 708–718.

Wright, P. (1975). "Consumer choice strategies: Simplifying vs. optimizing." *Journal of Marketing Research, 12,* 60–67.

Wyer, R. S. (1974). *Cognitive organization and change: An information processing approach.* Hillsdale, NJ: Lawrence Erlbaum Associates.

Wyer, R. S. (1976). "An investigation of the relations among probability estimates." *Organizational Behavior and Human Decision Processes, 15,* 1–18.

Wyer, R. S., & Carlston, D. E. (1979). *Social cognition, inference and attribution.* Hillsdale, NJ: Lawrence Erlbaum Associates.

Wyer, R. S., & Srull, T. K. (1989). *Memory and cognition in its social context.* Hillsdale, NJ: Lawrence Erlbaum Associates.

Yalch, R. F., & Elmore-Yalch, R. (1984). "The effect of numbers on the route to persuasion." *Journal of Consumer Research, 11,* 522–527.

Yi, Y. (1990). "The effects of contextual priming in print advertisements." *Journal of Consumer Research, 17,* 215–222.

Younger, J. C., Walker, L., & Arrowood, A. J. (1977). "Postdecision dissonance at the fair." *Personality and Social Psychology Bulletin, 3,* 284–287.

Zaichowsky, J. (1985). "Measuring the involvement construct." *Journal of Consumer Research, 12,* 341–352.

Zajonc, R. B. (1968). "Attitudinal effects of mere exposure." *Journal of Personality and Social Psychology, 9* (No. 2, Pt. 2).

Zajonc, R. B. (1980). "Feeling and thinking: Preferences need no inferences." *American Psychologist, 35,* 151–175.

Zajonc, R. B., Crandall, R., Kail, R. B., & Swap, W. (1974). "Effect of extreme exposure frequencies on different affective ratings of stimuli." *Perceptual and Motor Skills, 38,* 667–678.

Zajonc, R. B., & Markus, H. (1982). "Affective and cognitive factors in preferences." *Journal of Consumer Research, 9,* 123–131.

Zajonc, R. B., & Markus, H. (1985). "Must all affect be mediated by cognition?" *Journal of Consumer Research, 12,* 363–364.

Zajonc, R. B., Markus, H., & Wilson, W. R. (1974). Exposure effects and associative learning." *Journal of Personality and Social Psychology, 10,* 248–263.

Zanna, M. P., & Cooper, J. (1974). "Dissonance and the pill: An attribution approach to studying the arousal properties of dissonance." *Journal of Personality and Social Psychology, 29,* 703–709.

Zanna, M. P., Higgins, E. T., & Herman, C. P. (Eds.) (1982). *Consistency in social behavior: The Ontario symposium.* Hillsdale, NJ: Lawrence Erlbaum Associates.

Zanna, M. P., Kiesler, C. A., & Pilkonis, P. A. (1970). "Positive and negative attitudinal affect established by classical conditioning." *Journal of Personality and Social Psychology, 14,* 321–328.

Zanna, M. P., & Rempel, J. K. (1988). "Attitudes: A new look at an old concept." In D. Bar-Tal & A. W. Kruglanski (Eds.), *The social psychology of knowledge* (pp. 315–334). Cambridge, UK: Cambridge University Press.

Zellner, M. (1970). "Self-esteem, reception, and influenceability." *Journal of Personality and Social Psychology, 15,* 87–93.

Zillmann, D. (1971). "Excitation transfer in communication-mediated aggressive behavior." *Journal of Experimental Social Psychology, 7,* 419–434.

Zillmann, D. (1978). "Attribution and misattribution of excitatory reactions." In J. H. Harvey, W. Ickes, & R. F. Kidd (Eds.), *New directions in attribution research* (Vol. 2, pp. 335–368). Hillsdale, NJ: Lawrence Erlbaum Associates.

Zimbardo, P. G., Ebbesen, E. B., & Maslach, C. (1977). *Influencing attitudes and changing behavior.* Reading, MA: Addison-Wesley.

Zinn, L. (1991). "This BUD's for you. No, not you—her." *Business Week, 3238,* 86.

Zukier, H. (1982). "The role of the correlation and the dispersion of predictor variables in the use of nondiagnostic information." *Journal of Personality and Social Psychology, 43,* 1163–1175.

Name Index

Subject Index